Peter Norton's®
Complete Guide
to Windows® 2000
Professional

Peter Norton, John Mueller, and Richard Mansfield

SAMS

A Division of Macmillan USA
201 West 103rd Street, Indianapolis, Indiana 46290 USA

Peter Norton's Complete Guide to Windows 2000 Professional

Copyright © 2000 by Peter Norton

International Standard Book Number: 0-672-31778-8

Library of Congress Catalog Card Number: 99-64729

Printed in the United States of America

First Printing: February 2000

02   01   00   4   3   2   1

Trademarks

Warning and Disclaimer

Associate Publisher
Michael Stephens

Acquisitions Editor
Angela C. Kozlowski

Development Editor
Mark L. Kozlowski

Managing Editor
Charlotte Clapp

Senior Editor
Karen A. Walsh

Copy Editor
Bart Reed

Indexer
Diane Brenner

Proofreaders
Candice Hightower
Wendy Ott
Tony Reitz
Matt Wynalda

Technical Editors
John Cronan
Dallas Releford
Rob Tidrow
Jason Wright

Team Coordinator
Pamalee Nelson

Interior Design
Gary Adair

Cover Design
Aren Howell

Copywriter
Eric Borgert

Production
Stacey Richwine-DeRome
Ayanna Lacey
Heather Hiatt Miller

Overview

Contents

Dedications

John Mueller dedicates this book to Sneakers the Wonder Cat (1981 to 1999).

Richard Mansfield dedicates this book to Jim Coward.

Acknowledgments

John Mueller thanks his wife, Rebecca, for working with him to get this book completed. I really don't know what I would have done without her help in proofreading my rough draft. Both Rebecca and Micah Schlobohm deserve thanks for helping to research, compile, and edit some of the information that appears in this book. Micah worked especially hard in helping me set up the various lab environments required to test Windows 2000 features.

Richard Mansfield thanks his friends Jim Coward, Larry O'Connor, and David Roach for their enduring support. Jim Coward passed away during the writing of this book. He was an intelligent, gentle, extraordinary man. He will be greatly missed by me, as well as by all who were privileged to know him.

Dallas Releford, John Cronan, Rob Tidrow, and Jason Wright deserve thanks for their technical edit of this book. They greatly added to the accuracy and depth of the material you see here.

We would like to thank Scott Clark for his help and direction. His input was instrumental in helping this book achieve the depth of information it required.

Matt Wagner, our agent, deserves credit for helping us get the contract in the first place and taking care of all the details that most authors don't really think about.

The technical support staff at Microsoft (especially those on the Internet beta newsgroups) deserve credit for answering the questions that helped fill in the blanks and made the Windows 2000 learning experience go faster.

Finally, we would like to thank Angela Kozlowski, Mark Kozlowski, and Karen Walsh of Sams Publishing for their assistance in bringing this book to print. We especially appreciated their willingness to work with us under a very demanding schedule.

About the Authors

Computer software entrepreneur and writer **Peter Norton** established his technical expertise and accessible style from the earliest days of the PC. His Norton Utilities was the first product of its kind, giving early computer owners control over their hardware and protection against myriad problems. His flagship titles, *Peter Norton's DOS Guide* and *Peter Norton's Inside the PC* (Sams Publishing), have provided the same insight and education to computer users worldwide for nearly two decades. Peter's books, like his many software products, are among the best selling and most respected in the history of personal computing.

Peter Norton's former column in *PC Week* was among the highest regarded in that magazine's history. His expanding series of computer books continues to bring superior education to users, always in Peter's trademark style, which is never condescending nor pedantic. From their earliest days, changing the "black box" into a "glass box," Peter's books, like his software, remain among the most powerful tools available to beginners and experienced users, alike.

In 1990, Peter sold his software development business to Symantec Corporation, allowing him to devote more time to his family, civic affairs, philanthropy, and art collecting. He lives with his wife, Eileen, and two children in Santa Monica, California.

John Mueller is a freelance author and technical editor. He has writing in his blood, having produced 43 books and almost 200 articles to date. The topics range from networking to artificial intelligence and from database management to heads-down programming. Some of his current books include a COM+ programmers guide and a Windows NT Web server handbook. His technical editing skills have helped over 23 authors refine the content of their manuscripts, some of which are certification related. In addition to book projects, John has provided technical editing services to both *Data Based Advisor* and *Coast Compute* magazines. A recognized authority on computer industry certifications, he's also contributed certification-related articles to magazines such as *Certified Professional Magazine*.

When John isn't working at the computer, you can find him in his workshop. He's an avid woodworker and candle maker. On any given afternoon you can find him working at a lathe or putting the finishing touches on a bookcase. One of his newest craft projects is glycerine soap making, which comes in pretty handy for gift baskets. You can reach John on the Internet at JMueller@mwt.net. John is also setting up a new Web site at http://www.mwt.net/~jmueller/. Feel free to take a look and make suggestions on how he can improve it.

Richard Mansfield has written 23 computer books, four of which became bestsellers: *Machine Language for Beginners, The Second Book of Machine Language, The Visual Guide to Visual Basic,* and *The Visual Basic Power Toolkit* (with Evangelos Petroutsos). He used to write two columns and frequent articles in computer magazines, but for the past 10 years he has focused full time on writing books. Overall, his books have sold more than 500,000 copies worldwide and have been translated into nine languages. He lives with several friends in a breathtakingly lovely area in North Carolina.

Tell Us What You Think!

As the reader of this book, *you* are our most important critic and commentator. We value your opinion and want to know what we're doing right, what we could do better, what areas you'd like to see us publish in, and any other words of wisdom you're willing to pass our way.

As an Associate Publisher for Sams, I welcome your comments. You can fax, email, or write me directly to let me know what you did or didn't like about this book—as well as what we can do to make our books stronger.

Please note that I cannot help you with technical problems related to the topic of this book, and that due to the high volume of mail I receive, I might not be able to reply to every message.

When you write, please be sure to include this book's title and author as well as your name and phone or fax number. I will carefully review your comments and share them with the authors and editors who worked on the book.

Fax: 317-581-4770

Email: michael.stephens@macmillanusa.com

Mail: Michael Stephens
              Sams Publishing
              201 West 103rd Street
              Indianapolis, IN 46290 USA

Introduction

This book has been completely revised to reflect the many changes that have occurred since it was first published. The primary change, of course, is the concussive blowout of information generated by the Internet.

Only a few years ago, computers primarily looked inward for information, to their hard drives and a new storage device, the CD-ROM. Now computers have turned outward to the unimaginably massive universe of information available on servers the world over. This major shift has impacted operating systems along with all other elements of computing, not to mention such disparate human activities as commerce, research, and purchasing pharmaceuticals.

One benefit of the Internet involves the more or less constant flow of bug fixes made available. As you have probably realized, software is never perfect and never finished. Complex software, like an operating system, is more or less reluctantly "released" to the public at some point in its life. However, patches, updates, new features, bug fixes, and other modifications are made available to the public relatively frequently thereafter. Windows NT 4 benefited from two major upgrades since its initial release: an Option Pack and Service Pack 3. Doubtless, Windows 2000's release will be followed by a Service Pack or two as well.

Microsoft calls this process of constantly improving the quality of software *continuous reinvention*, and the Internet has greatly simplified the process of getting fixes and new features to customers. Any upgrades are downloadable anytime, by anyone.

Among the major features covered in this book is the coalescence of the Explorers: Windows Explorer and Internet Explorer. The underlying principle of this blending of what used to be two entirely different utilities is that, in theory, you should experience no real distinction between your hard drive and the Internet.

You should be able to easily manage and retrieve information either locally or worldwide, without having to use different tools or techniques. Of course, at current Internet speeds, you'll generally get data off your drive faster than it comes over the Internet. However, Windows 2000 includes features such as Explorer's Search facility (formerly called *Find*) that operate seamlessly in both realms and help blur the distinction. Chapter 6, "There's Really Only One Explorer," covers the blending of the Explorers in depth. That chapter asks whether you can tell the difference between Windows Explorer and Internet Explorer. The chapter then answers that question (and the answer is no).

Of course, there have been many other improvements since NT 4, both on the visible user interface and below decks in the engine room. This book covers them all.

As you read this book, you'll learn about all the new features Windows 2000 offers. I'll also spend some time telling you about the features that haven't changed, those that need a bit more work, and some of the unexpected ways you can use the new features. In this book you'll find, in addition to the step-by-step instructions and in-depth tutorials, hundreds of shortcuts, tips, and techniques to make your computing more efficient and more fun.

Who Should Read This Book

The intended audience for this book is the intermediate to advanced Windows 2000 user who wants to maximize the computing power of his or her machine. This isn't a book filled with abstractions and obscure technical notes, understandable only to network administrators and gurus. It's for the intelligent Windows 2000 Professional user. I'll provide you with tips and techniques that make Windows 2000 easier to use, enhance overall system performance, and improve system stability. Of course, every Windows 2000 user will have something to gain from this book, even if it only means that you'll gain a better understanding of how Windows 2000 works.

We'll also spend some time looking at the internal workings of Windows 2000. Not only will you learn about where Windows 2000 is today, but I'll help you understand how Windows 2000 differs from its predecessors, NT 4 and Windows 95/98, and how these differences will help you become more productive. If you want the most detailed description of Windows 2000 available, this is the book for you.

What You Will Learn

Here are some of the more important topics I cover in this book:

- Getting the most from the Internet
- Customizing your working (and playing) environment
- Exploring all the new features
- Installation tips everyone can use
- Migrating from Windows 95, 98, NT 4 or other operating systems to Windows 2000
- Turning your machine into a speed demon
- How to make Outlook Express your Internet (or intranet) communications hub
- Examining architectural details—how things work under Windows 2000's hood
- Exploiting the new utilities Windows 2000 provides
- Making dozens of useful changes to the Registry
- Understanding and fully exploiting the power of "docucentricity"

- Understanding the purpose of the more salient files in the \SYSTEM32 folder
- Moving Windows 2000 onto your laptop (it's easier than you think)
- Creating effective Web pages with FrontPage Express
- Using Windows 2000 fonts and making them simpler to use
- Creating your own setup script files
- Navigating both Explorer interfaces
- Examining the object-oriented approach to using resources on your machine
- Looking at compatibility tips about what works and what doesn't under Windows 2000
- Using the objects on context menus and modifying those menus to meet your needs
- Customizing system setup to fully meet your needs
- How to use the best troubleshooting utilities, if something goes wrong
- Looking at workarounds for potential Windows 2000 problems

I spend considerable time talking about the Windows 2000 architecture in some of the chapters. There are two reasons for this extensive coverage of what might at first seem merely theoretical background information. First, as a user, you really do need to know how the operating system works—or at least get an overview—so that you can best exploit its features. Second, you need to know what Windows 2000 provides that Windows 95 and 98 don't. Exploring the architecture is one of the best ways to achieve this goal.

New and technical terms are explained as soon as they're introduced. If you've forgotten the meaning of a term when you come across it later, you'll usually find a concise, yet thorough, definition in the comprehensive Glossary in the back of the book.

How This Book Is Organized

This book divides Windows 2000 into functional and task-oriented areas. These parts of the book explore each piece of Windows 2000 to see how it ticks and how you can best use it. Of course, many chapters help you understand what's going on under the hood, too. Without this information, it would be difficult, at best, to make full use of all the features Windows 2000 offers.

One of the things I'd like to point out now is that this book is fine-tuned for Windows 2000 Professional—the version of the operating system most people will use on their PCs. However, I haven't taken an exclusively (or even primarily) corporate view in many areas. Although Microsoft's strategy used to point to a corporate orientation for this product, today's affordable computer systems have plenty of power to host Windows 2000, and this extends the Windows 2000 audience to home and small-business users as well as corporate installations (even portables).

What's more, Windows 98 and Windows 2000 are clearly merging into a single, all-purpose, future operating system. Also, projections show that more and more average users are choosing Windows 2000 as their OS of choice. Windows 2000 offers stability, security, and power to spare. What's more, the fact that many games are now written for both the Windows 95/98 and NT 4/Windows 2000 operating systems speaks volumes about the increasingly broad popularity of Windows 2000.

I'd like to offer one final piece of advice. Windows 2000 is a very user- and data-oriented operating system. Unlike Windows 95/98, it won't sacrifice security for the sake of making your favorite game run. The game makers have to follow Windows 2000's rules if they want to sell into that swelling audience. From a business-use point of view, Windows 2000 is quite a bit ahead of Windows 95/98. Windows 2000 is doubtless the most business-user-friendly product available right now for the PC. This means neither that Windows 2000 is perfect, nor that everything is as it seems. Sometimes, you'll find something so difficult to use that you'll wonder why Microsoft did it that way. At first, I found the Registry really difficult to work with, for example, until I discovered all the tools Microsoft (and shareware and freeware) provides to make that job easier (see the Peter's Principle at the end of Chapter 10, "Understanding the Windows 2000 Registry").

You should take the time to really explore Windows 2000 and figure out which techniques work best for you. Windows 2000 offers more than one way to accomplish virtually every task. You need to find the one that's best for you.

Part I: Getting Started with Windows 2000

This first section explores the blending of the familiar traditional Windows-style operating system features with the latest Internet tools. You'll find that the distinction between being online and offline is increasingly blurred as computers turn outward from classic hard drive–oriented data processing to the Internet, that rich and measureless database.

Chapter 1, "Choosing Windows 2000," explains why you ought to congratulate yourself for having selected Windows 2000 for your operating system. Chapter 2, "Windows to the Internet," plunges you into the details about the origin and impact of the Internet. The third chapter, "What's New in Windows 2000," summarizes all the things that have changed since NT 4. The fourth chapter, "Installing Windows 2000 Professional: A Setup Primer," steps you through the process of installing Windows 2000, including coverage of all the optional setup alternatives. You'll also find out what you need to know if you're moving to Windows 2000 from a different operating system. Chapters 5, "Exploring the Interface," and 6, "There's Really Only One Explorer," focus on the all-important user interface: what you can do with the "two" Explorers—Windows Explorer and Internet Explorer. After you finish Part I, you'll be working with your computer in ways you never thought possible.

Part II: Power to Spare

There are two chapters in this section. The first chapter, "Performance Power," deals with tuning tips. Getting the best performance and highest reliability is the concern of everyone who's just starting to use a new operating system. Windows 2000 offers many ways to tune your system. It would seem that all these controls could help you get a tuned system with a very minimal amount of effort. Actually, the exact opposite is true. Many of these controls interact, and you have to take these interactions into account as you change settings. Optimizing one area can mean "detuning" another area by an equal amount.

The second chapter in this section, "Customizing Windows 2000 for Maximum Productivity," covers important topics such as shortcut key combinations, various ways to launch applications efficiently and automatically, the new single-click Internet-style mouse control, and making the most of Windows 2000's docucentricity features.

One thing is certain: Windows 2000 offers more in the way of reliability and performance than other Microsoft operating system. Your job now is to decide how to use Windows 2000's performance features to your benefit. Getting that high-performance system together is the first goal you'll want to achieve under Windows 2000. After that, the docucentric approach to managing your system should make operating it a breeze.

Part III: A Look Under the Hood

Learning to use an operating system often means learning a bit about how it works inside. For some people, a quick overview of Windows 2000's internals will be enough, especially if you only plan to use Windows 2000 in a single-user mode and really don't need to get every ounce of power from your machine. The first chapter in this section, "An Architectural Overview," offers an overview of what I'll describe in detail throughout the five chapters that constitute the rest of Part III. If you only want to know the basics, you'll be able to look at this overview and get everything you need.

But if you do have to manage a network of machines or want to really get inside and learn how things actually work, you'll appreciate the detailed information in this section of the book. I don't go into highly technical bits-and-bytes descriptions for the most part, but this section blows the lid off all the architectural aspects of Windows 2000. We'll examine every major component of Windows 2000, from the file system to the API. You'll also find Chapter 10, "Understanding the Windows 2000 Registry," enlightening. Most of the questions I've seen pop up on the various Internet sites that I monitor revolve around the issue of configuration and performance. Learning about the Registry is the most important step you can take to resolve issues of this type. That chapter also contains many useful and creative techniques only possible by directly modifying the Registry.

Part IV: Advanced User's Guide to Windows 2000

Some people learn to use a computer but never learn to use it well. The problem, in many cases, is that they lack knowledge of some of the hidden features a product provides. In other cases, a lack of system optimization is to blame. Still other people have problems understanding the documentation that comes with the product.

This section of the book is filled with tips and techniques that are often missing from the vendor documentation. There's a big difference between the way things should work and the way they really do. Use this section of the book to gain the real-world information you'll need to really use Windows 2000 to its full potential.

The five chapters in this section take a look at the user topics I consider essential to using Windows 2000 to its full potential: OLE, ActiveX, DCOM, software optimization, hardware optimization, printing, and multimedia. I'm not going to tell you about every intricate feature of Windows 2000—the Microsoft documentation already does that to a certain degree, and you can always get the Windows 2000 Resource Kit if you need truly particular information. What I am going to do is show you how to make the best use of those features to perform everyday tasks—something the Microsoft documentation doesn't really tell you very much about.

Part V: A Look Outside

The trade press is just packed with stories about the Internet. Companies are paying serious attention to the resources the Internet can make available to their workers. Retail companies are jumping like fleas onto the Internet as a hot new method for marketing their wares. Some companies are also switching from WANs to intranets.

No matter why your company is looking at the Internet or other online services, you need to know how to make connections. After you establish a connection, you need to know how to access the service from within your applications. That's what this section of the book is all about. We'll take a look at what you have to do to get connected in today's worldwide communications environment. Chapter 20, "Windows 2000 Connections," looks at hardware connections for peripherals such as your modem, software connections for communication, and the messaging and telephony APIs (MAPI) and (TAPI). That chapter also covers communications protocols and RAS, the Remote Access Server, which lets you manage users and connections to make it easier for people to get into Windows 2000 at the main office while at home or on the road (without, of course, compromising security).

Chapter 21, "Outlook Express," covers Outlook Express in depth. After reading this chapter, you'll know how to get the most out of Microsoft's powerful email and newsgroup utility. Chapter 22, "Mobile Computing," is all about Windows 2000 on laptops. Surprised? You shouldn't be. A while back, during the days of 66MHz, 8MB notebooks, you would have been right to expect that Windows 2000 was overkill on the road. But today's portables are far more powerful and are fully capable of accommodating Windows 2000 without slowing to a crawl under its weight. What's more, there are obvious security advantages to using Windows 2000 rather than Windows 95/98. Beyond that, having the same operating system on your notebook as you do on your desktop machine makes life that much simpler.

Part VI: Networking with Windows 2000

The primary original reason for creating Windows 2000 was to provide a stable, bullet-proof environment for networks. The fact that Microsoft has split Windows 2000 into two products—one for the server and one for the workstation—doesn't change that first design orientation. That's why an entire section on the topic of networks is so important.

I cover networking from several viewpoints in this section. First of all, in Chapter 23, "Network Basics," I look at the basics of networking. After reading that chapter, you'll have a firm foundation for understanding the current complexity of networking due to the various models, vendors, protocols, network operating systems, servers, and other components available. Those of you in a smaller company or who work within a workgroup will appreciate the peer-to-peer networking coverage in Chapter 24, "Peer-to-Peer Networking," as well. Chapter 25 explores FrontPage Express (FPE), a surprisingly useful and full-featured Internet page designer.

We'll also take a look at the big network scene. You'll find out all about Microsoft's powerful Internet Information Services. Also, I'll show you what you need to know about the client/server network model.

Security is an obvious source of problems, no matter what kind of network you use. We'll spend some time looking at the ways in which Windows 2000 protects your data and grants various levels of permission to users. I'll demonstrate how the Windows 2000 method of managing security is far superior to that provided by Windows 95/98. (Anyone who has written 32-bit applications knows all about the lack of security API support in Windows 95/98.)

Part VII: Troubleshooting

Have you ever installed something and gotten it to work right the first time? That's what I thought. I usually have some problems, too. Unlike the original Macintosh, the PC is made up of parts that come from myriad vendors. All these parts are supposed to work together, but sometimes they don't.

A lot of hardware and software installation-related problems have nothing to do with hidden agendas or vendor ineptitude. Some problems occur because of a poorly written specification. One vendor interprets a specification one way, and another uses a very different interpretation. The result is hardware and software that really don't work together. Each one follows the "standard," yet each follows it differently.

Other times, a user will be the source of the problem. How many times have you thought you did something according to the instructions, only to find out that you really didn't? It happens to everyone. Even a bad keystroke can kill an installation. Take the Windows Registry: It's all too easy to misstep when editing it and end up with an operating system that won't boot (see Chapter 10, "Understanding the Windows 2000 Registry," for ways to create safety backups of your Registry and what to do if even that safety backup won't work).

Even if you do manage to get a fully functional system the first time through and you keep from shooting yourself in the foot, what are the chances that the installation will stay stable forever? Pretty unlikely. Your system configuration changes on a daily basis as you optimize applications, adjust the position of desktop icons, customize your OS, and perform various tasks. That's why you always see that message when you shut Windows 2000 down: Please wait while the system writes unsaved data to the disk.

As you can see, the typical computer has a lot of potential failure points, so it's no wonder that things fall apart from time to time. This section of the book will help you quickly diagnose and fix most of the major problems you'll run into with Windows 2000. We'll even look at a few undocumented ways to determine what's going on and how to interpret the information you get. Finally, I'll give you plenty of preventative medicine as well.

Part VIII: Appendixes

Appendix A, "Using the Scripting Host with Windows 2000 Professional," shows you, step by step, how to make Windows 2000 dance to your tune. The topic is the Windows Scripting Host (WSH), a utility that allows you to write programs that access and control the objects in the Windows object model. That's right. You heard it correctly. You can get down and grab hold of things in the operating system itself. You'll see how to use the scripting host with several sample scripts. There's also an extensive list—with examples for you to try out—of various methods and properties that work within WSH scripts. I also explain where and how scripts of this kind can be employed (as if you can't imagine ways to use this cool tool yourself).

Conventions Used in This Book

I've used the following conventions in this book:

File, Open	Menus and the selections on them are separated with a comma. For example, "File, Open" means "Access the File menu and choose Open."
`monospace`	It's important to differentiate the text that you'll use in a macro or type into a DOS window command line from the text that explains it. I've used monospace type to make this differentiation. Every time you see monospace text, you'll know that the information you see will appear in a macro, within a system file such as `CONFIG.SYS` or `AUTOEXEC.BAT`, or as something you'll type at the command line. You'll even see the switches used with Windows commands in boldface monospace text.

italic monospace	At times, you'll need to supply a value for a command. When you use the DIR command, for example, you might need to supply a filename. When I want you to substitute your own word for one printed in this book, I'll use *italic* or *italic monospace*. For example, you can locate many of your drivers in \WINNT\PROFILES*YourLogonName*. In this example, you're supposed to replace the term *YourLogonName* with the actual name you use to log onto Windows 2000.
[<Filename>]	When you see square brackets around a value, switch, or command, it means that this is an optional component. You don't have to include it as part of the command line or dialog box field unless you want the additional functionality the value, switch, or command provides.
italic	I use italic text wherever the actual value of something is unknown. I also use italic text when more than one value might be correct. You might see FILE*xxxx* in text, for example. This means that the value could be anywhere between FILE0000 and FILE9999. Italic text is also used to introduce new terms.
ALL CAPS	Commands use all capital letters. Some Registry entries also use all caps, even though they aren't commands. Normally, you'll type a command at the DOS prompt, within a PIF file field, or within the Run dialog box field. If you see all caps somewhere else, it's safe to assume that the item is a case-sensitive Registry entry or some other value. Filenames also appear in all caps.

Special Information

Several types of special information are highlighted in boxes or the margins to help you quickly identify important points. The following paragraphs describe the purpose of each special section.

> **Note:** Notes tell you about interesting facts that don't necessarily affect your capability to use the other types of information in the book. I use note boxes to give you bits of information that I've picked up while using Windows 2000. Think of notes as subordinate to the primary text, although not as highly specialized and ignorable as traditional footnotes.

Technical Note: Technical notes come closer to the purpose of traditional footnotes: They include background of such detail and specificity that their value is more theoretical than practical. You can skip this information if you're only looking for an overview of a Windows 2000 process or feature. If you're an advanced computer user, though, such technical information can be of considerable interest. They often provide you with clues as to where you can look for additional information.

Tip: Everyone likes tips because they tell you new ways of doing things that you might not have thought about before. Tip boxes also provide an alternative way of doing something that you might prefer to the first approach I provided. I recommend that you pause to try them out at least once before you lose yourself in all the other exciting discoveries that await you in this book.

Caution: This means watch out! Cautions almost always tell you about some kind of system or data damage that will occur if you perform (or fail to perform) a certain action. Make sure that you understand a caution thoroughly before you follow any instructions that come after it.

Peter's Principle: I usually include a Peter's Principle to tell you how to manage your Windows environment more efficiently. They may be smart workarounds, insights into the tradeoffs in making a decision, or simply productivity techniques. These recommendations are not hard-and-fast rules. They are, however, invariably based on my personal experience with different ways of doing the same thing. Peter's Principle boxes might also include ideas on where to find additional information. You'll find the names of shareware and freeware utility programs here, too.

LOOKING AHEAD

It's always good to know what you'll find along the road. Whenever you see a Looking Ahead icon, I'm providing a road sign that tells you where we're headed. It also serves to reassure you that a fuller discussion of the current topic has been merely postponed. Impatient readers can easily jump ahead and then return to where they left off. This way, you can follow the path of a particular subject as I provide more detailed information throughout the book.

ARCHITECTURE

Knowing how something works inside is important to some people and not important to others. Whenever you see the Architecture icon, I'm talking about Windows 2000's internal workings. Knowing just how Windows 2000 performs its job can help you determine why things sometimes don't work as they should, and it also helps you discover features you didn't even know existed. You'll particularly appreciate these insights when you get to Part VII, "Troubleshooting." Beyond that, the insides of Windows 2000 are often just plain interesting.

COMPATABILITY

Whenever you change something as important as your operating system, there will be problems with older devices and applications that were designed for the previous OS. You might also wonder how Windows features and issues common to all current Microsoft operating systems translate between the Windows 95/98 environment and Windows 2000. Or perhaps you're confused about how Windows 2000 Professional works best within, say, a Novell NetWare network environment. The Compatibility icon clues you in to tips, techniques, and notes that can help you achieve compatibility.

NETWORKING

Even some home users need to consider networking issues these days. It's no surprise, then, that this book provides a wealth of networking tips and techniques that everyone can use. Expect to find one of these tidbits of knowledge wherever you see the Networking icon.

PERFORMANCE

I use the Performance icon to designate a performance-related tip. These tips cover a variety of monitoring and optimization techniques. You'll want to read them carefully and decide which of them suits your situation and how best to apply them. Not every performance tip is for everyone (there are often tradeoffs, which I'll mention in the tip).

TROUBLESHOOTING

Everyone encounters problems now and then. It doesn't matter if the problem is hardware or software related if it's keeping you from getting your work done. Every time you see the Troubleshooting icon, I'm providing you with a tool you'll need to locate and fix a problem. (You'll find such diagnostic insights scattered throughout the book, not just in Part VII, "Troubleshooting.")

SECURITY

Everyone's concerned with safeguarding their private data these days—from personal credit card numbers to business plans. Windows 2000 excels in security, and when you see this icon, you'll find a description of one of the ways that Windows 2000 ensures what's for your eyes only remains confidential.

STANDARDS

Square pegs that had to fit in round holes—that's what some products were in the past. In the past few years, standardization efforts have helped reduce the number of square pegs on the market. I think it's important to know what those standards are so that you can make the best buying decisions possible. Getting a cheap square peg isn't cost effective if you have to spend hours trying to make it round. Every time you see the Standards icon, you'll know that I'm talking about some standard that defines a product that will fit into your system with relative ease.

PART I

Getting Started with Windows 2000

Choosing Windows 2000

You made a wise choice when you decided to go with Windows 2000. I believe that Microsoft would like nothing more than to have everyone choose Windows 2000 as his or her operating system; then Microsoft could quietly retire the mixed-code, all-too-pliable, built-on-DOS, but still wildly popular Windows 95/98 systems.

Windows and NT have been converging now for several years—now even the name *NT* has been dropped. And on the surface, they're functionally identical now. Take a look at a computer running Windows 98 and compare it to a machine running Windows 2000. You would be hard pressed to tell them apart. The Windows and NT technologies have merged already, if you limit your comparison to their user interfaces, their desktops, the browser they share, and many, many other features.

Windows 2000 is more expensive than Windows 98 and it's a bit bulkier, and generally a bit slower (compare how quickly you see the Start menu after clicking the Start button, for instance). Some games won't run on Windows 2000, and some peripherals don't have good Windows 2000 drivers. Windows 2000 requires marginally better hardware. But if you want stability (who doesn't?) and need strong security features, there's no comparison: You'll definitely want to go with Windows 2000.

Windows 2000 also boasts various efficiencies you won't find in Windows 98, such as NTFS (the Windows 2000 File System) and pure 32-bit code. In any case, eventually the various Windows will coalesce, leaving Windows 2000, possibly by some other name, the sole Microsoft operating system. My guess is that the name Windows 2000 will evaporate in favor of a more accurate name; perhaps it will be called, simply, *The Browser*. After all, even Help files are now being written in HTML. And, if you stop to think about it, the old distinction between information on your hard drive and hard drives all over the world on the Internet is becoming a little blurred.

This chapter is an overview of Windows 2000 Professional and what you can expect it to do for you. The purpose of this chapter is to help you see the big picture. Future chapters take a detailed look at each of Windows 2000's features. For now, we'll take a brief tour of the origins of Windows 2000 to get a sense of its place in the world of operating systems, and then we'll compare it specifically to Windows 98.

Windows 2000: A Brief History

The first version of Windows NT (Windows 2000 was called Windows NT until this latest version) was Microsoft's third attempt at a new operating system. (The first two
operating systems were DOS and OS/2.) I've always maintained that the first few
versions of Windows NT were an operating environment akin to DESQview—not a
full-fledged operating system. In Windows NT, however, users got a full-fledged GUI
operating system.

By the way, Windows NT was originally a text-based operating system! The primary
Windows NT developer, Dave Cutler, was actually pretty upset about having to add a
graphical interface. What's more, that GUI was originally going to be the OS/2 interface
but ended up being a modified Windows for Workgroups interface. Later still, of course,
it was modeled on the Windows 95 interface.

Regardless of the tortured history of the Windows NT GUI, the main question remains:
Why should anyone even consider buying a hardware-intensive operating system like
Windows 2000 when the Windows 95/98 product is so successful and so relatively cheap?

The quick answer: mission-critical and heavy-duty applications. You're not going to host
a Web site with Windows 98 or use it as a database server, for example. What if the
server went down in the middle of a transaction? The results could be devastating, even
in a workgroup setting.

Windows NT/2000 solves this kind of problem by getting rid of DOS altogether. It provides a pure environment that looks like the other operating system interfaces but nevertheless runs completely in protected mode. Windows 2000 provides many other features
as well. For one thing, it isn't restricted to the Intel family of processors. The initial version of Windows NT came out with support for the Hewlett-Packard Alpha processor as
well. Later versions added support for the MIPS R4x00 and PowerPC processors (note,
however, that Microsoft is now phasing out support for MIPS and PowerPC, eventually
leaving only Alpha and Intel as the supported processor lines).

The original version of Windows NT, this new and improved Windows, came with a big
price tag. Microsoft first designed Windows NT as a server operating system. Some users
complained that the high hardware price tag required to host Windows NT just wasn't
worth the additional security Windows NT provides. Corporate America, on the other
hand, moved rapidly to embrace Windows NT. Microsoft, itself, pointed corporations
toward NT Workstation rather than toward Windows 98. This strategy is working, in spite
of the hoopla surrounding the release of Windows 98. What's more, Europe in general
went directly to NT rather than Windows 95 because it saw NT as more secure and stable.

Microsoft finally came out with a Workstation version of Windows NT that required a bit
less hardware power. But these days, even notebook computers have the hardware capacity to host Windows 2000.

Windows 95 and 98

Undaunted by originally slow Windows NT sales, and still wanting to give users an alternative, Microsoft developed Windows 95. It appeared in August 1995, but just barely. The OS was delayed so often that many beta testers jokingly renamed it Windows 96. Deadlines caused a lot of problems in the development of the first version of this operating system. I was surprised at the number of times Microsoft cut the feature set—cuts that made it possible to release the operating system on time but probably killed it as a contender in the corporate environment. (Microsoft included many of the cut features in an add-on package called the Plus Pack.)

The delays Microsoft experienced also forced it to make some concessions that really were not in the best interest of the user. A lot of 16-bit code is still included with Windows 95, for example, and this OS was supposed to get rid of most, if not all, of that old code. Fortunately, most of the important subsystems are 32 bit, and that has greatly improved Windows reliability and performance. The 32-bit interface also enables the user to load 32-bit applications—a big plus from a reliability and performance standpoint.

Even Windows 98—although closer to Windows NT than Windows 95—is still riddled with aging 16-bit code. Although the Windows 98 and Windows NT/2000 Registry structures and API sets are quite similar, DOS compatibility is still an issue in Windows 98, and that holds it back. From here on, for convenience, I'll refer to them collectively as Windows 95/98. (I *won't* refer to Windows NT/2000 very often, though.)

Despite the long development time and the jettisoned features, Windows 95/98 does have many positive qualities. For one thing, it doesn't rely on DOS when running Windows applications—at least not on a newer machine. All the Windows DLLs and supporting code run in protected mode. Windows 95/98 does rely on a copy of DOS running on a virtual machine to run DOS applications, to provide some low-level BIOS support on non-Plug and Play machines, and to support antiquated devices that use real-mode drivers. This level of DOS activity is far less than what previous versions of Windows required, however. Windows 95/98 also uses a subset of the Windows NT 32-bit programming interface and runs completely in protected mode (except for real-mode drivers).

Those qualities and the interface aren't the only things that Windows 95/98 users have to boast about; other valuable features are also offered for the user. Windows 95 was the first version of Windows to include Plug and Play as an integral part of the operating system, for example (Windows 2000 also boasts Plug and Play). It also provided support for the Messaging Application Programming Interface (MAPI) and the Telephony Application Programming Interface (TAPI). The peer-to-peer network was greatly enhanced, and system configuration was a snap compared to earlier operating systems. All these features really set Windows 95 apart from its predecessors.

Windows 98 or Windows 2000?

The alternative to Windows 2000 is Windows 98. Should you switch to Windows 98, combine Windows 98 machines with Windows 2000 Professional machines on a network, or stick strictly with Windows 2000? Let's examine the main features that distinguish Windows 98 from Windows 2000, and then you can decide whether you want to make a switch, mix and match, or even wait for Windows 2001 (or whatever it will be called). Windows 2000's user interface is basically indistinguishable from the GUI of Windows 98 (see Figure 1.1). They both permit you to use Web view in Explorer—a highly customizable version of the traditional Windows Explorer. They both enable you to place resizable Internet site windows on your desktop and have them refresh at certain intervals. You can also add ActiveX components or Java applets to your "wallpaper."

But the key difference is the three Ss: stability, scalability, and security. Windows 2000 is designed for heavy-duty Internet and intranet office use. Windows 98 is mainly for stand-alone home systems or small businesses.

FIGURE 1.1

Is it Windows 2000 or Windows 98? It's hard to tell from the user interface.

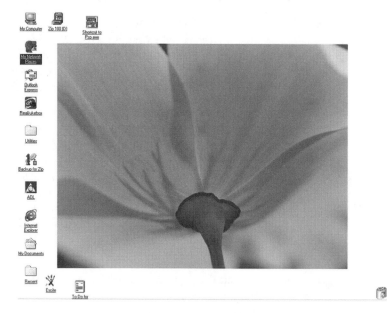

Continuous Reinvention

As you have doubtless realized, software is never perfect and never finished, like people. Complex software such as an operating system is "released"; after that, patches, updates, new features, bug fixes, and other modifications are made available to the public relatively frequently. Windows NT 4 benefited from an Option Pack and several Service Packs. (The latest is Pack 6.) Most of these offerings were major upgrades following

NT 4's original release. Microsoft calls this process of persistently improving the quality of the software *continuous reinvention*, and the Internet has greatly simplified this process of getting fixes and new features to customers.

Windows 98 and Windows 2000 take things one step further by formalizing it and building it into the operating system itself. A feature called Windows Update simplifies the process of upgrading Windows 98 and Windows 2000. A central Web site devoted to Windows can be contacted on regular intervals, checking to see whether that new driver or bug fix is available that hasn't yet been downloaded into your system. Try choosing Tools, Windows Update in Internet Explorer 5.

One improvement offered by Windows 98 over Windows 95 (an improvement that Windows 2000 doesn't require) is the conversion of the FAT16 to the FAT32 file system. Initially during setup, Windows 98 requires about 70MB more hard drive space than Windows 95, but in the long run, you actually get more free hard drive space because FAT32 is a more efficient file system than its 16-bit predecessor. Note that NTFS cannot be read by Windows 98. See Chapter 12, "The Windows 2000 File Systems: FAT and NTFS," for all the details on the various file systems. Another improvement in Windows 98 is enhanced system stability. System files are checked and, if necessary, replaced automatically. The Registry Checker attempts to keep the Registry clean and coherent. Memory management has been improved as well. All these changes, however, still don't bring Windows 98 anywhere near the stability offered by Windows 2000.

Microsoft markets Windows 98 to home computer users and small businesses—it requires less in the way of hardware and administration, it can run legacy hardware and software better, it has more diversified driver support, it's more geared to multimedia and games, and it displays menus and windows a bit faster on average. Windows 2000, by contrast, boasts heavy-duty security and strong networking features, and it's highly stable.

The Benefits of Using Windows 2000

Now that you have a sense of where Windows 2000 came from and how it differs from Windows 98, let's consider in detail the qualities that make Windows 2000 the operating system of choice for power users and businesses.

LOOKING AHEAD

Chapter 9, "An Architectural Overview," provides an overview of the Windows 2000 architecture. It will help you understand why Windows 2000 is more robust than both Windows 95 and 98. Read Chapter 9 if you want to find out more about the specific features Microsoft has included to beef up Windows 2000 reliability. If you want to know more about the Windows 2000 File System, read Chapter 12, "The Windows 2000 File Systems: FAT and NTFS," which compares the various forms of disk access used by previous versions. Other architectural chapters include Chapter 10, "Understanding the Windows 2000 Registry," Chapter 11, "Memory Management," Chapter 13, "Graphics Windows 2000 Style," and Chapter 14, "Printing Under Windows 2000." Also read

Part VI, "Networking with Windows 2000," for a complete description of the Windows 2000 networking architecture. All these elements work together to make Windows 2000 a superior operating system for both the server and workstation.

Both Windows 2000 and Windows 95/98 come with dual network protocol support built right in. Windows 2000 provides an enhanced network configuration interface originally developed for Windows 95, making Windows 2000 not only more robust but also just as easy to configure as its Windows 98 counterpart. Theoretically, all you need to do is select both networks in the Network Configuration dialog box. After performing a few additional setup steps, you should have a local peer-to-peer network that also connects to your company's main network on the file server.

LOOKING AHEAD

Networking under Windows 2000 is more complex than the Windows 95/98 environment for several reasons. First, it works with more platforms than Windows 95/98 does. Second, you'll often find Windows 2000 on a corporate desktop—one that might need to connect to a wide variety of sources—rather than the home or small-business machine with one or two sources. Part VI of this book, "Networking with Windows 2000," covers the wide variety of Windows 2000 networking situations in detail.

Windows 95/98 Versus Windows 2000

So far, I've spent a lot of time talking about Windows 95/98 and Windows 2000 in tandem. The reason is simple: We are no longer dealing with a simple computing environment. There were no corporate-versus-small-business-user issues to resolve when Windows first arrived on the scene. All that has changed. PC users now work in more specialized computing environments. "One size fits all" just doesn't cut it anymore.

Windows 2000 Professional is designed for a machine that has a lot to do. Sure, it can require more in the way of hardware than Windows 95/98, but the multitasking and security performance edge is noticeable. You can't help but see that Windows 2000 is capable of running more tasks more efficiently. The big culprit, of course, is all that 16-bit baggage that Windows 95/98 still carries around. The main operating system components use 32-bit code, but many of the subsystems don't. Those subsystems rob a workstation of performance in small but noticeable (and cumulative) ways.

Will a home user notice that it takes two or three seconds less to load an application such as Word in Windows 2000? Probably not. A corporate user might not use just one or two applications at a time, however. I'm currently running four applications on my machine besides the standard utility programs, such as Windows Explorer and Outlook Express. I'm also running a word processor, Internet Explorer, and my graphics program. Of these, only the graphics program is actually sitting idle.

Am I representative of a typical corporate user? Probably not, but I assume that most of you are running at least two applications simultaneously. Is Windows 98 up to the task? Maybe, but corporate America can't accept "maybe" as an appropriate response.

Maybe you only run one application at a time and perhaps leave an email application running. Windows 98 can certainly handle that load, but you need to look at other problem areas. A security hole in Windows 95/98 results from the inclusion of MS-DOS mode as part of the operating system. Even without that loophole, Windows 95/98 can't provide the same level of security as Windows 2000 and still maintain the same degree of compatibility. Windows 2000 gives up some compatibility with older applications and hardware so that it can provide the brawny security businesses often demand. Think about it this way: How would you feel if someone read reports about your finances, all because of a hole in Windows security? Businesses get into lawsuits and other kinds of problems, such as industrial espionage, when security issues are not addressed. Suffice it to say that security is a very big business issue—one that Windows 95/98 is not equipped to handle.

One final area where Windows 95/98 just can't handle the corporate environment is reliability. A single inaccurate transaction entry in a database could cost some businesses millions of dollars. I'm not talking about a simple inconvenience here; I'm talking b ankruptcy. A business needs to know beyond a shadow of a doubt that its data is secure. An operating system that fails to protect its data, even in the smallest way, won't meet the needs of a large business. The issue is compatibility versus reliability when you look at Windows 95/98 versus Windows 2000. Windows 95/98 has to stretch the rules a bit to broaden its compatibility, but Windows 2000 provides no such luxury.

Multithreading and Multitasking

There's a technical difference between Windows 95/98 and Windows 2000 that you should also consider. *Multitasking* is one of those nebulous words everyone uses but no one takes the time to define. The first thing you need to do before you can understand multitasking is to define the word *task*. A task is essentially an application that's running. When you start Windows, you might think that nothing is running, but several applications are already getting work done on your machine. Right-click the taskbar in Windows 2000 and then click the Task Manager button. Click Processes to see all the support running under Windows 2000. Explorer is considered a task, for example. Any network connections or print spoolers are considered tasks. A screen saver is yet another task. There are numerous system-related tasks as well. The Windows kernel is considered a task. The industry uses two terms to refer to a running application or thread: process and task. I prefer *task* because it's a little less hazy. You'll probably see both terms used in documentation you read, however.

Some 32-bit applications use a technique called *multithreading*, which enables them to perform more than one task at a time. You can recalculate your spreadsheet and print a document at the same time if the application supports multithreading, for example. The spreadsheet starts another job (called a *thread*) to take care of printing. It might even start a second thread to do the recalculation so that you can continue to enter data. A thread can also be considered a subtask under the application that's running. Keep this distinction in mind: A *task* is a relatively large job, and a *thread* is a little bit of code performing some relatively minute job. It's like the difference between an entire application and one of the options in that application's menus.

Now that you understand what a task is, it's time to look at the definition of *multitasking*. Everyone assumes that multitasking is just that—several tasks (or processes) running simultaneously on one machine. This is a good start for a definition, but it doesn't end there. An important consideration is how the operating system allocates time between tasks. With Windows operating systems, it becomes important to actually define the method used to manage tasks and differentiate between different kinds of multitasking. Windows 2000 supports two kinds of multitasking: cooperative and preemptive.

This is how cooperative multitasking is supposed to work: Application A runs for a little while—just long enough to get one component of its task finished. It then gives control of the system back to Windows so that Windows can take care of any housekeeping chores (keypresses, for instance) and allow application B to run for a while. This cycle continues in a round-robin fashion between all the tasks running at any given time.

What really happens is that some applications follow the rules, but others, the time hogs, don't. Under *cooperative multitasking*, the operating system gives up too much control; an application can grab all the system resources if it wants to. Some applications do just that, and the result is that cooperative multitasking doesn't really work very well. It makes the piglet application look good and efficient and makes everything else, including the OS, look sluggish and awkward. Most of the time the user spends looking at the hourglass symbol is really time in which Windows has temporarily lost control of the system to an application that doesn't want to share with anything else.

Any legacy applications that run under Windows 2000—any 16-bit applications—still have to run in a cooperative multitasking mode. That's why Windows 2000 bothers with that mode at all. Windows 2000 minimizes the impact of these applications, however, by running each one in its own address space. (Contrast this with Windows 95/98, in which all the 16-bit applications share one address space.) Windows 2000 preemptively (a term that I define in the next few paragraphs) multitasks each 16-bit address space with all the 32-bit applications on the system. (Under Windows 95/98, you'll see the one shared address space preemptively multitasked with the 32-bit applications—a significant difference for a number of reasons that I cover in Part III, "A Look Under the Hood.") Unlike in Windows 95/98, 16-bit applications don't compete with each other or affect any 32-bit applications running on a Windows 2000 machine. This includes Explorer and any other OS tools. (Of course, you'll upgrade most of your commonly used 16-bit applications, such as your word processor and spreadsheet, to Windows 95/98 or Windows 2000 32-bit versions.)

When Microsoft designed Windows 2000, it wanted something better than cooperative multitasking, so it designed an operating system that uses preemptive multitasking. Windows 2000 currently supports preemptive multitasking for any 32-bit application you run. Think of it this way: Preemptive multitasking works like a traffic light. Traffic goes one way for a while, but then the light changes and traffic goes the other way. The actual amount of time each task gets is weighed by the user and the operating system to meet certain criteria, but this access is supposed to be fair. Every application is supposed to get its fair share of processor time, and preemptive multitasking enforces this principle. Windows 2000 monitors each application and interrupts it when its time is up. It doesn't matter whether the application wants to give up control over the system; Windows 2000 doesn't give it a choice.

> **Technical Note:** The term *multitasking*, although frequently and popularly applied to Windows 95 and Windows 98, isn't technically accurate in the case of those two operating systems. They are not multitasking operating systems. All they do is enable you to open multiple applications simultaneously. The naked truth is this: No operating system can do more than one thing at a time (true *multitasking*, properly so-called) unless it supports more than one CPU chip. A CPU can only perform one action at a time. If you have two CPUs, you can perform two actions at a time. It's the same with you: Unless you have a friend next to you when you're cooking dinner, you can only do one thing at a time— although you might rapidly switch between the things you're doing. That's not the same as *simultaneously* doing two things. Windows 2000, in fact, does this, but the others do not. Technically, what Windows 95 does is more properly called *task switching*. It may be able to run a lot of code very fast, but it's still only doing one thing at a time. But even in those situations, Windows 2000 is faster at switching tasks and servicing requests. Task switching gives the illusion of multitasking, just as sliding still pictures rapidly past a projector gives the impression of motion pictures. We'll stick with the popular terminology in this book, however, but you should remember that, strictly speaking, multitasking requires multiprocessing.

Preemptive multitasking can claim another, more important difference from cooperative multitasking in the way the system reacts. Under earlier versions of Windows, an hourglass means that the system is tied up. You can't do anything else until the hourglass goes away. On the other hand, an hourglass under Windows 2000 means only that the current task is tied up. You can always start another task or switch to a different, currently running task. If that task isn't busy, you can perform some work with it while you wait for the initial task to complete its work. You know when the original application has finished because the hourglass goes away when you place your cursor over the task's window. Have you noticed that your mouse pointer can change to the hourglass symbol when you merely move it onto a particular window and then change back to the usual pointer when you move it to a different window or onto the desktop? Preemptive multitasking is the reason.

The bottom line? Preemptive multitasking means that you do not have to wait for the system as often. (Both Windows 95/98 and Windows 2000 actually provide two hourglass cursors. The first cursor is a simple hourglass that means the system is performing a task that you can't interrupt; the second is a pointer-cursor-with-hourglass combination that means you can move to another task.)

Technical Note: On the lower levels of the OS, preemptive multitasking actually works exclusively with *threads*, not individual applications. Threads are running on the processor. A thread can be bumped off of the processor for one of three reasons: Its little time slice (or quantum) is over; it has become I/O bound and is waiting for hardware to respond; it's kicked off (preempted) by a thread of higher priority. The upshot? Any task of higher priority, such as Kernel mode operations, will kick a thread off the processor that is, say, performing an Excel calculation.

Note: Windows 2000 actually enforces preemptive multitasking better than Windows 95/98 because of the security features Windows 2000 provides. The same security API that Windows 95/98 ignores in the name of flexibility also reduces its capability to force errant applications to give up the processor. The result is that you'll still see an occasional hourglass under Windows 95/98—something you'll never (or almost never) see under Windows 2000 in similar circumstances. In addition, the fact that Windows 95/98 uses one shared address space for 16-bit applications affects its capability to multitask. Placing each 16-bit application in its own environment might consume a bit more memory and place a larger burden on the operating system, but it also enhances the smooth flow of resource sharing among various threads and reduces the chance that any one thread will freeze the system.

Finally, cooperative multitasking has a very serious additional flaw. When Windows loses control because an application takes over, there's no way to shut down that application if the machine freezes. Because Windows 2000 maintains constant control of the machine, however, you no longer need to worry about the machine freezing in the middle of a task. Even if one application does hang, you only need to end that task—you don't have to reboot the entire machine. Pressing Ctrl+Alt+Del doesn't automatically reboot a Windows 2000 machine—instead, it provides an option menu. The Task Manager in Windows 2000 displays a list of applications, and you get to choose which one to terminate (see Figure 1.2).

You might wonder why Microsoft (or any other vendor) would use cooperative multitasking if preemptive multitasking is so much better. There are a few good reasons. First, DOS is nonreentrant. This means you have to allow DOS to complete one task before you give it another one. If you disturb DOS in the middle of a task, the entire system will freeze. The second problem with preemptive multitasking is really a two-part scenario. Both aspects relate to how easy it is to design the operating system. When an operating system provides preemptive multitasking, it also has to include some kind of method for monitoring devices. What if two applications decide they need to use the COM port at the same time? With cooperative multitasking, the application that started to use the COM port gains control of it and locks out the other application. But in a preemptive multitasking environment, the first application can get halfway through the allocation process and get stopped; then the second application can start the allocation process. What happens if the first application is reactivated by the system? You have two applications that think they have access to one device. In reality, both applications have access, and you have a mess. Windows 2000 handles this problem by using a programming construct called a *critical section*. (I discuss this feature more in a moment.)

FIGURE 1.2

Windows 2000 lets you decide which running task should be shut down during a hang.

Preemptive multitasking also needs some way to prioritize to ensure that critical tasks get a larger share of the processor's time than noncritical tasks. Remember that a task can no longer dictate how long it needs system resources; that's all in the hands of the operating system. Theoretically, you should be able to tell the operating system how you want your applications prioritized and then allow the operating system to take care of the rest. What really happens is that a low-priority task can run into a fault situation and need system resources immediately to resolve it. A static priority system can't handle that situation. In addition, that low-priority task can end up getting few or no system resources when a group of high-priority tasks starts to run.

The priority system Windows 2000 uses provides a dynamic means of changing a task's priority description. When a high-priority task runs, Windows 2000 lowers its priority. When a low-priority task is passed over in favor of a high-priority task, Windows 2000 increases its priority. This clever dynamic priority system enforces the idea that some tasks should get more system resources than others, yet ensures that every task gets at least some system resources.

Preemptive multitasking involves one final consideration. Even if you use the best dynamic priority system in the world and every piece of the operating system works just the way it should, you'll still run into situations when a task has to complete a sequence of events without being disturbed. The application might need to make certain that a database transaction is written to disk before it hands control of the system back to the operating system, for example. If another task tries to do something related to that transaction before the first task completes, you can end up with invalid or damaged data in the database. Can we trust the application to define its needs? Or will the time-hog effect reappear?

Programmers call a piece of code that performs the job of handling a necessary, crucial job a *critical section*. A critical section usually occurs with system-related tasks, such as memory allocation, but it also can happen with intra-application tasks, such as writing information to a file. Cooperative multitasking systems don't have to worry as much about critical sections because the task decides when the operating system regains control of the system. On the other hand, a preemptive multitasking system needs some way for a task to communicate the need to complete a critical section of code. Under Windows 2000, a task tells the operating system that it needs to perform a critical section of code by "waving" a semaphore (a flag). If a hardware interrupt or some other application asks to perform a task that doesn't interfere with any part of the critical section, Windows 2000 can allow it to proceed. All a critical section guarantees is that the task and its environment will remain undisturbed until the task completes its work.

Multiplatform Support

One of the reasons the corporate environment selects Windows 2000 rather than Windows 95/98 (besides reliability, of course) is the fact that Windows 2000 can be used on more than one platform. To understand the full meaning of the word *platform*, you have to begin with the operating system. Every operating system provides something called a *service*. Essentially, a service is the capability to communicate with a device or perform some kind of task, such as reconfiguring the system. Think about that for a second. Even the task of writing data to a hard disk is a form of communication.

A *platform* is a machine that uses one type of processor (or a processor family) and a similar hardware architecture. For example, every IBM family computer uses the same Intel family of processor: the 80x86. You'll also find that the buses used in the various computers follow specific guidelines and that the peripheral boards that plug into the buses have to maintain a certain level of compatibility. You get the idea—a platform is one type of computer.

How does the idea of a platform affect operating services such as writing to the disk? Providing a service in DOS terms means talking directly to the hardware. When you write to a file, the data you want to write passes through DOS, to the ROM BIOS routines, and finally to the hard disk itself. Windows 95/98 follows a similar procedure. The big difference is that Windows 95/98 provides a protected-mode substitute for the ROM BIOS in the form of drivers, allowing it to maintain better control of the Windows environment and preventing direct communication between software and peripherals.

Windows 2000 includes the idea of a Hardware Abstraction Layer (HAL). A write to the hard drive means that you send the data first to Windows 2000, which in turn passes it along to the protected-mode hard disk driver (the ROM BIOS substitute) and then through the HAL to the actual hard disk. The HAL enables you to move the entire operating system to another machine—a MIPS 2000 processor, for example—without rewriting anything but the HAL. As far as Windows 2000 is concerned, you're still sitting on an Intel-based machine (actually, HAL makes it possible to deal with virtual machines). Obviously, this added capability doesn't come without a cost—you pay for it with reduced performance in some operations, such as writing to the hard disk. Fortunately, Microsoft has tuned the routines to a point where most users would have to actually time the performance of Windows 95/98 and Windows 2000 to see any difference.

Windows 2000's Disadvantages

Perhaps I am prejudiced, but this section is short. Windows 2000 doesn't really have many disadvantages: It's strong, stable, efficient, and secure. But no one should ever confuse Windows 2000 with a low-end workstation operating system. It requires a reasonable level of hardware power. Can you justify a relatively fast Pentium machine with a minimum of 64MB of RAM just to start the operating system as a word processing workstation? Probably. These days a system like that is far, far less expensive than it was only a year or two ago.

Windows 2000 does need this level of hardware to perform well—there's no way around it. If you want to use Windows 2000 as an operating system, you had better be prepared to buy the hardware it needs to get the job done—and that means more than the minimal requirements Microsoft puts on the Windows 2000 package.

Using Windows 2000 as a low-end workstation can cause other problems as well. For one thing, anyone who has ever tried to run certain older DOS applications (and even some misbehaving Windows 95 applications), such as games, has been disappointed with Windows 2000. The reason is simple: Windows 2000 is designed to be inflexible with errant programming. The only thing it knows is that a rogue application just violated system integrity. As a result, the application gets squashed. Microsoft wrote this operating system to run as reliably as possible, which means that it can't bend to the needs of an application that thinks it needs to run alone or needs to directly modify the video or otherwise violate the well-known rules of the road.

Windows 95/98 as well as any other future versions of the "home" operating system will never be as stable as Windows 2000. It will bend as much as possible to allow that old or rogue application to run. Because of this added flexibility, Windows 95/98 will run most (if not all) your DOS and rogue applications with just a little tinkering. Microsoft even provided a special startup mode (called MS-DOS mode) for applications that don't run well in either a full-screen or windowed DOS session under Windows 95/98. Each MS-DOS mode can have its own CONFIG.SYS and AUTOEXEC.BAT settings; you won't find that in Windows 2000. With all this additional assistance, you might even find that these old applications run better under Windows 95/98 than they used to from the DOS prompt. The tradeoff is that you don't get the same level of reliability. Do you have a lot of this kind of old software that you still want to use?

LOOKING AHEAD

Finally—and there isn't any way to get around this issue—Windows 2000 is a bit more difficult to install than Windows 95/98, if for no other reason than all the advanced capabilities Windows 2000 includes. I hope, however, and expect that Chapter 4, "Installing Windows 2000 Professional: A Setup Primer," will make the process entirely painless for you.

On Your Own

Consider running some familiar applications on both a Windows 2000 Professional and a Windows 98 machine. See whether you can find any differences in performance. Try running several applications simultaneously under both operating systems. Can you detect any differences in the smoothness of their multitasking?

If you're considering a purchase, take your "essential" software programs, including games and especially any irreplaceable old DOS applications, and try them out on a Windows 2000 system. See whether you can get them working or should consider upgrading to Windows 2000–compatible versions of these important applications. Also, ensure that you have drivers for any peripherals that you'll want to use with a new Windows 2000 system.

If you simply cannot give up some of your favorite games but also want the stability and security offered by Windows 2000 for your serious work, consider creating a dual-boot system (see Chapter 4, "Installing Windows 2000 Professional: A Setup Primer"). That way, your computer can host both Windows 98 and Windows 2000, and you can choose which OS to use each session during startup.

Windows to the Internet

The Internet explosion shows no signs of deceleration. What's more, the media certainly has done nothing to discourage this phenomenon; if anything, it has fanned the flames by giving the Internet massive publicity, including displaying the names and URLs of Internet sites virtually everywhere. Just look at any newspaper ad or the ads and shows on your television set. During one evening, a friend and I watched as several of the new television shows, not to mention the commercials, included Internet addresses. Many news shows close by telling you that you can get additional information on their Web sites. Of course, traditional media isn't the only industry making using of the Internet. Many games and other products now include Internet capabilities of one sort or another as standard fare, not to mention your tax accountant, who has probably printed his Web site's URL on his office stationery.

A Little History

Some people are laboring under the misconception that the Internet is a new phenomenon. It's not; it's older than the personal computer. Let's take a brief tour, just to understand how this largely unregulated, self-modifying, essentially adventitious volcanic eruption of information got started and then grew so big.

The first rumblings of the Internet started in the 1960s, when computer scientists saw the need to connect their computers together to exchange information. They weren't the only ones to see a need, however. The U.S. government found that enabling researchers to communicate through a computer network assisted in the efficient completion of projects. The Department of Defense (DOD) was the first group on the bandwagon, with an Internet predecessor known as the U.S. Advanced Research Projects Agency Network (ARPAnet) . Then educators saw a need to exchange information as well. A nationwide computer hookup helped academics keep up-to-date with current information. Something known as the National Science Foundation Network (NSFnet) was born.

LOOKING AHEAD

How do you create what will eventually become an international network? Well, the first thing you've got to do is figure out a way to get the various mainframe computers talking to each other. That's where the Transmission Control Protocol/Internet Protocol (TCP/IP) comes into play. This is still the common language of the Internet today. TCP/IP allows computers to talk with one another even if their architectures are totally different. The TCP portion tells the computers how to talk to each other, and the IP portion can be compared to an envelope used to transfer messages from one computer to the other. Two computers establish communication and then exchange data. The only requirement for the data itself is that it appear in an IP envelope. If you think about it in the form of an envelope, the idea of the IP protocol is a lot easier to understand. I go into more detail about the exact workings of TCP/IP in the "Understanding the Open Systems Interconnection (OSI) Model" section of Chapter 24, "Peer-to-Peer Networking."

The First Utilities

After computers had a standardized method of communication, it became possible to start allowing user access to data. The mainframe interfaces of the time were less than user friendly, however. To give users something they could interact with, the developers of ARPAnet started putting together some of the services we take for granted today. The very first Internet services included File Transfer Protocol (FTP) , electronic mail (email), and Telnet (remote logon). These services worked together to provide a *front end*—a user interface. Although these utilities are still around today, they have changed a great deal over time. Suffice it to say that today's interface is both friendlier and easier to use, not to mention graphical.

Now that we have a standardized language and a method of accessing the data a server contains, you might think we have everything needed to allow the Internet to bloom. A wide area network such as the Internet can't function without one additional feature, however. You need a method for adding and removing computers from the network in a way that doesn't disrupt existing communications. That was one of the main goals of the U.S. Advanced Research Projects Agency. It combined TCP/IP, the user interface, and the modularity to allow computers to connect and disconnect from the network with ease into what was called *ARPAnet*. That was the first name for the Internet as we know it today. (Ethernet also contributed to the development of these features.)

By the early 1980s, ARPAnet was less than a large single network. Instead, it closely resembled what we now call a *backbone*. A backbone on a network is the connection between major network sites—it's like the relationship between a freeway and city streets. Now, there were a lot of local area networks (the city streets) connected to one major network (the freeway). Something else happened during this time as well. The last of the computer systems on the network converted to full TCP/IP support in 1983. After this last piece of the puzzle dropped into place, the Internet was born. Many computer networks were now connected to a single backbone called ARPAnet—essentially the same structure we use today. However, another decade passed before the Internet detonated into the worldwide phenomenon we know today.

Who Administers the Internet, Anyway?

Eventually, the Internet (as it's now officially called) grew too large for the NSF to administer. In April 1993, a consortium of companies formed a group called the Internet Network Information Center (InterNIC). This group was assigned to manage the daily running of the Internet. However, recent legislation has been enacted that now permits other companies to register domain names as well.

If you want to build a server and add it to the Internet, for example, you have to contact InterNIC or some other registration company to get an IP address and register a domain name. Why is this management needed? Think about it this way: The IP address is equivalent to your mailing address. If your mailing address weren't unique, the postal department would have a difficult time delivering your mail. The domain name has to be unique as well. A domain name is the first step in finding a particular resource on the Internet using a browser (more on this topic later).

Letting Anyone In

In the early 1990s, it was proposed that the Internet be made public so that everyone could participate. At first, the NSF was reluctant to make something designed for educational use available to the public at large. (The National Science Foundation coordinated the original connections between research institutions that later grew into the Internet as we know it today.) There must have been reasons. After a lot of conversation, however, it was agreed that a commercial concern could access the Internet if it agreed to pay network usage fees. These fees would provide funds for NSF-sponsored projects and the upkeep of the network itself.

And that's how you get access today. Your Internet service provider pays fees to access the Internet, and you pay the service provider for your share of that access. One odd fact: Most people vastly increase their telephone usage after they get a taste of the Internet but pay no extra telephone costs because the service provider is usually just a local call away. How long this free phone time will last is anyone's guess, but it's likely that the several new high-speed Internet hookup schemes currently coming on board will be far from free. These initiatives include cable TV/Internet hookup, satellite, high-speed telephone, and even wireless hookups.

Of course, the Internet today is immense, and such a large network needs *some* kind of management. Here's where two other groups come into play. The Internet Architecture Board (IAB) is the head honcho of network management. It approves new network standards and protocols. Essentially, the IAB is a consortium of all the service providers on the Internet. Under the IAB are several committees. The most important committee from a user perspective is the Internet Engineering Task Force (IETF). It's composed of scientists and engineers who design new Internet technology. I describe this group in more detail as this chapter progresses.

URLs Defined

The history of the Internet, interesting as it is, gives you only a part of the picture—it only tells you why some things are the way they are. Now, it's time to look at the Internet today—what you can expect to see when you log on. I cannot cover in just a couple chapters all the specifics that some authors take an entire book to cover. What we'll look at instead is targeted to what you, the user, need to know.

I begin with a discussion of one very important Internet topic: uniform resource locators (URLs). You can't get anywhere on the Internet without knowing something of this topic, yet very few texts really tell you much about them. I'm going to give you an overview of URLs from the layman's point of view: How they are put together and what you need to know to use them.

Another important topic is protocols. If you read through the history section of this chapter, you saw that the Internet was founded on different protocols, such as TCP/IP and FTP. Today's computing is more complex, and the protocols you'll use of necessity provide more in the way of flexibility than earlier protocols.

The URL is the basis for moving around the Internet, so it's worth understanding how it works. Let's begin by looking at the default Internet Explorer home page address—that's where Microsoft would like you to check in before exploring the rest of the Internet (you can change your home page in Internet Explorer by choosing Tools, Internet Options, General):

```
http://www.msn.com/
```

At first, you might think that it's all gibberish, but there are some very definite standards for putting these site location addresses together.

Actually, this is a typical URL that identifies a particular server and clues you in about its capabilities. Let's begin with the http:// portion of the URL. This tells you what kind of data-exchange protocol you use to access the server. In this case, you use Hypertext Transfer Protocol. I describe the two major data-transfer protocols (HTTP and FTP) in the next section. There are other data-transfer protocols as well, such as Gopher and Archie, but by far the most popular are HTTP and FTP. Knowing the data-transfer protocol tells you a lot about what to expect from the server. An FTP site, for example, doesn't provide much in the way of user-friendly graphics. FTP is mainly used to transfer large files.

The next section contains the domain name system (DNS) address for the site you want to visit (in this case, www.msn.com). Every DNS address has three sections. (A fourth section in some DNS addresses contains the computer name, but you won't see it very often.) The first section of the DNS address tells you about the service (or, as some call it, the *subdomain*). We're going to visit the World Wide Web (WWW) in this case.

WWW sites almost always provide some type of graphics in addition to text. They also include familiar input/output controls such as command buttons, text boxes, and so on. These controls are familiar to every Windows user.

The second section of the DNS address contains the domain name itself. In this case, it's MSN (for Microsoft Network). You'll find that most domain names are acronyms for the organization, some of which can get quite convoluted. A new Internet site must register the domain name with InterNIC or one of the other domain registering companies. The domain name is the unique identifier you use in place of an IP address. Imagine having to try to remember a 32-bit number rather than a convenient name for each site you want to visit.

The third section of the DNS address is the domain identifier. Table 2.1 shows the basis for this part of the DNS address. InterNIC and other companies just pick the one that fits the organization best. Currently new identifiers are popping up all over the place as the old *.com* becomes filled up with all possible permutations. For example, the country of Tonga uses *.to*, so somebody is then able to purchase amazon.to and hope for the best.

Table 2.1   Common Internet Domain Identifiers

Identifier	Description
.com	Any kind of commercial company such as Microsoft or CompuServe. Most online service Internet access providers will have a .com domain identifier. In fact, .com is so common that it's the default extension. You can leave it off when you type in an address in Internet Explorer.
.edu	Educational institutions use this domain identifier as long as they represent a not-for-profit site.
.gov	All government agencies use this domain identifier. If you see it, you know you're dealing with someone from the U.S. government.
.mil	The U.S. military uses this special domain identifier to keep it separated from the rest of the government.
.net	Normally, this is reserved for Internet access providers using this domain identifier. The exception to the rule is if the access provider is a commercial concern. In that case, it normally uses the .com domain identifier. Some ISPs, however, employ both .com and .net.
.org	Sites outside of these other designations. They use the .org domain identifier. In theory, the .org extension is supposed to be reserved for not-for-profit entities.

Shorthand Addressing

Tip: You don't have to type in `http://` or even `www` in Internet Explorer 4 and later. Nor do you need to add the `.com` extension. All these terms are the defaults for site addressing in Internet Explorer. In the Address bar in Internet Explorer, you can just type in `msn` and press the Enter key and you'll be taken to the Microsoft Network. Internet Explorer extends your shorthand "msn" to something like this:

`http://www.msn.com/welcome/default.asp.`

Likewise, you can get to Microsoft's home page by merely typing `microsoft` or to Netscape by typing `netscape`. You'll also find that the Internet Explorer Address bar automatically completes the URLs of sites that you have previously visited, even if they're highly specific (such as a particular page buried deep within a site). The autocompletion feature watches as you type each character and makes educated guesses about possible matches, displaying them as you type. If I just type the letter b, for example, Internet Explorer instantly displays `bible.gospelcom.net/` because that's the site beginning with *b* that I most recently visited. If I continue by typing **a**, however, Internet Explorer replaces the Bible site with `backoffice.microsoft.com/`. It will continue guessing until it runs out of ideas. If Internet Explorer hasn't correctly anticipated your wishes, just keep typing and the guessed URLs disappear.

Okay, that's all there is to a basic URL. Some URLs are a lot longer than the one I showed, however. What does the rest of the information mean? It's similar to the increasing specificity you find as you read through a disk file's path—for example, `C:\DOCS\LETTERS\JANUARY\DENTIST.DOC`. Let's look at an example. In this case, we'll look at a page for the National Science Teachers Association (NSTA):

`http://www.gsh.org/NSTA_SSandC/nses_home.htm`

In this case, we're looking at an organization that has rented space on someone else's server. The NSTA SSC (Scope, Sequence, and Coordination Project) actually exists within a subdirectory on the `gsh` server. Think of those forward slashes in the same way you would think of the backslashes that indicate subdirectories in a hard drive path.

We're in a particular area of the NSTA SSC site—in this case, the `/nses_home` page that contains National Science Education Standards information. The extension `.htm` stands for Hypertext Markup Language (HTML). I describe it more in the next section. For now, all you need to know is that when you see this extension, you're looking at a page that has been graphically formatted by your browser. These days, however, HTML is so pervasive that it, like `http` and `www`, is an understood default and you'll very rarely see `.htm` appended to an URL any more.

Understanding Email Addresses

I want to talk about one other form of URL, email addresses. Understanding how these work is really easy now that you understand the basic URL format. You normally see something like this: `richard@worldnet.att.net` or `Richardm@msn.com`. The first part of the address is the person you want to contact (in this case, `richard` or `Richardm`). The `@` (at) sign separates the person's name from the DNS address of the server that handles the email. Because we've already covered how to decipher the DNS address, I won't cover that again.

A Quick View of Internet Standards

Because the Internet consists of diverse types of computers communicating with one another, the Internet has spawned several standards. You can use the Internet effectively without knowing much about the ins and outs of the various standards, but it helps to be able to recognize them when you see them. Table 2.2 shows some of the newer (and older) standards you'll run into while surfing the Net.

Table 2.2   Common Internet standards.

Acronym	Full Name	Description
HTML	Hypertext Markup Language	This page description language is used as the basis of all Internet pages. As a computer language, HTML is limited; it primarily describes the size, position, and color of text and graphics, but does no actual computation (you can't add 2+2 in HTML). To provide computation, script languages such as VBScript and JavaScript are embedded into HTML. Also, objects such as ActiveX components and Java applets can be inserted into HTML source code.
CGI	Common Gateway Interface	This is a special method for accessing an application from a Web page. When a vendor asks you to enter information on a form, for example, you're using CGI. The most common use for CGI is database applications. This is the only Web-server-to-background-application standard currently supported by the IETF. (I talk about them shortly.) Two other proposed methods are ISAPI and NSAPI.

continues

Table 2.2   Continued.

Acronym	Full Name	Description
DCOM	Distributed Component Object Model	You might be more familiar with this acronym as *ActiveX*. (They aren't precisely the same thing, but that doesn't matter much for this discussion.) This is Microsoft's latest experiment in distributed mini applications (applets). You can use OLE over the Internet in a new way. The applets provide all the features covered in Chapter 15, "OLE, ActiveX and DCOM." The big difference is that you can use these features over the Internet. ActiveX applications require Internet Explorer 3.0 or later.
FTP	File Transfer Protocol	This represents one of the earliest forms of communication that the Internet recognized. There aren't any graphics to speak of at an FTP site—just files to download. This is the only file-download protocol currently supported by the IETF. The limitations of this particular protocol have prompted other standards such as CORBA and DCOM.
HTTP	Hypertext Transfer Protocol	Whenever you go to a Web site that begins with `http:`, you're using this protocol. It's the technology that enables you to download an HTML document—the kind that includes fancy graphics and buttons. Essentially, HTTP allows you to download an HTML script—a document containing commands rather than actual graphics. Your browser reads these script commands and displays buttons, text, graphics, or other objects accordingly. That's why the capabilities of your browser are so important (and also the reason you need a new browser if you want to use any of the new protocols I mentioned in this table). Some vendors are already complaining, however, that the IETF standard versions of both HTTP and HTML are old and less than optimal for tomorrow's needs. That's why there's such a proliferation of other protocol standards and associated HTML script commands on the Internet today; people are looking for better ways of making information accessible.

Acronym	Full Name	Description
INFS	Internet Network File System	Think of this protocol as you do the file system on your own computer. Whether you use NTFS, HPFS, or VFAT, they all represent a way to organize the information on your drive and provide fast access to it. This file system does essentially the same thing for Internet files. However, it has to have a connection to the data. That's done with TCP/IP— the networking standard I talk about elsewhere in this chapter.
ISAPI	Internet Server Application Programming Interface	This is another Microsoft protocol. I've talked about other types of application programming interfaces elsewhere. ISAPI does the same thing for an Internet server; it enables you to access the features that the server has to offer. In this case, a programmer uses ISAPI to enable you to access a host application through an Internet server. You'll probably see ISAPI restricted to database and email applications at first, but other application types are on the horizon. You might see it used as part of a turn-based game or even an online word processor, for example.
NSAPI	Netscape Application Programming Interface	Not to be outdone by Microsoft (see ISAPI), Netscape has come up with its own API for connecting Web servers to background applications. As with ISAPI, NSAPI enables you to write a data-entry or other application for the Internet by using advanced HTML scripting commands and allows it to interact with applications on your network. As with Microsoft's offering, the major application that I see for this API right now is some type of data-entry or email system.

It's probably better to look at Table 2.2 as a sampling of some of the more interesting technologies you'll use. The problem with all these new technologies is that they aren't standardized. As I mentioned earlier, the Internet has its own standards committee called the Internet Engineering Task Force (IETF). It's responsible for providing a standard set of HTML script commands. The problem with all these new protocols is that they introduce new scripting commands that could cause problems in the future. How can a browser handle a proprietary script command? In most cases, it ignores the command, but you can't be sure. Even if the browser does ignore the foreign command, you'll be stuck without access to some of the features on a given Web page. There are other problems with the current trend as well. What if a vendor just modifies an existing script command? A browser won't know to ignore it in this case, and you could end up with a frozen machine as a result. Standards are useful.

The problem is more severe than you might think. New Internet technologies are cropping up that don't have any old standards to follow. Just about every vendor out there has its own form of Virtual Reality Modeling Language (VRML), for example. Without a standard way to access this feature, you might find support for your browser spotty at best.

And don't even ask about the push to "enhance" or, some argue, even replace, HTML with XML. That's a real nest of snakes. Find out more about XML at the following address:

http://www.w3.org/XML

Added to these potential woes for programmers and Internet surfers is the fact that even HTML is implemented differently on different browsers. Not to mention Microsoft's worthwhile extension DHTML (Dynamic HTML), which you should restrict to intranet use because it requires Internet Explorer and, therefore, will exclude Internet visitors to your site who use Netscape.

It's frustrating to think that the muddying of protocols and language may affect your capability to surf the Net in the future. However, I think the problem is going to be a short-term one. I'm often reminded of the problems with graphics adapters when IBM decided to introduce the 8514 adapter instead of upgrading VGA. Sure, we'll probably go through several years of trying to figure out what standards are best; in the long run, though, some technologies will win out and we'll eventually end up with a standard. The trick for right now is to figure out which technologies are going to gain market share and stick with them.

What Are Intranets?

Let's briefly consider the idea of local "internets." An intranet is a local area network, or LAN, that might or might not be actually connected to the Internet. An intranet, though, does behave somewhat similarly to the Internet, though on a much smaller scale, of course. Usually an intranet is a network confined to a single company, but it employs HTML and browsers such as Internet Explorer, just as people using the Internet would. Intranets are a significant tool for many companies. They include everything from a company Web site to database access to discussion groups and training. Obviously, most of these companies plan to use their intranets for more than one purpose.

One significant benefit of intranets is the efficiency of upgrading company-wide software. For example, you can store objects (ActiveX components, for instance) in a Web page on a server. Each time one of the employees loads that page and the component in it, the browser checks the user's version of the component. If it's an older component than the one on the server, the component is downloaded to the employee's workstation. Clearly, if you're replacing a utility or other application used by 50 people, its easier to distribute it in this fashion than having to replace it on each of their hard drives.

Let's take a quick step back before we look at why this is important to you. PC interconnections started with LANs (local area networks). Essentially, LANs provided the means to connect a group of people in the same physical location together so that they could share resources such as printers and files (a LAN is still the backbone of an intranet). Next came WANs (wide area networks). This "wide" version of the network allowed companies to connect people in different physical locations—workers in other branches, workers on the road, and telecommuters. With a WAN, the need to share physical resources was not the most compelling reason; instead, the goal was to just share information. A WAN typically enables its users to share a variety of files, with databases and email topping the list.

It might seem at first that everyone's needs would be met by either a LAN or a WAN (or some combination thereof), but they aren't. A LAN is fairly low cost, but it won't enable people in different areas—say, in two different countries—to talk to each other. On the other hand, a WAN can be very expensive. The problem is getting all the required connections together. Each company has to define a separate set of connections. Every time you want to expand the WAN, you have to define yet another set of connections. Intranets simplify all this because they merely rely on the connections already established for the Internet. All you have to do to expand is to add a new computer with a modem and provide an Internet account. In comparison to the very inflexible solution of a WAN, intranets add much needed suppleness, without too much additional work.

It doesn't take too long to realize that WANs suffer from another problem as well. Consider the cost of temporarily adding a connection for someone outside the company or of providing service to someone on the road. Dial-up networks take care of part of this need, but now you're looking at long-distance expenses and a loss of security. An intranet can provide very low-cost connectivity to a company network today. Vendors are working on solutions that will make security as airtight as possible, although you won't see those solutions right away. Best of all, a user with high-speed communications needs can access the Internet through something other than a standard telephone line. T1, DSL and ISDN are viable solutions for permanent sites today, and cable, wireless, and other high-speed solutions are coming down the pike.

The bottom line? Intranets won't solve every need. You'll still experience some problems—the greatest of which are security and speed. Of the two, security is the most pressing problem. Will WANs and LANs go away completely? I don't think so. Each of these network structures serve specific needs. Of the two, however, WANs appear to be most vulnerable to the intranet incursion.

Tip: You don't necessarily need an Internet connection to implement an intranet. A company could use an Internet server and browser on a closed local network to act as an office bulletin board or the front end to a database, for example. It could also put an HTML copy of a users' manual where everyone can use it. This also offers a degree of platform independence because there are servers and browsers for most software platforms.

All About Internet Explorer

Now it's time to turn to Internet Explorer, an excellent and powerful collection of Internet applications, utilities, and tools. There are other browsers on the market—I'm not saying that Internet Explorer 5.0 is the browser you must use. It's a matter of personal preference, and my choice is Internet Explorer. What's more, it just happens to be the one supplied with Windows 2000, and I appreciate a number of its features. If you don't have the latest version (5.0), this chapter will likely convince you to download it from

```
http://microsoft.com/windows/ie/default.htm
```

Tip: You can always ensure that you're using the latest versions of Microsoft software (including new features and bug fixes) by choosing Tools, Windows Update in Internet Explorer 5. Your system is analyzed to see what products you're using (but don't be a paranoiac—no data is sent back to Microsoft). Then you're offered a list of applicable updates. You can choose to have them downloaded and your software automatically updated, if you wish. Updates are described and categorized (critical, fun, and for advanced users).

Of course, as we all know, there's Netscape, the primary alternative browser to IE. Netscape was there first; it's a browser that's still the choice of those who dislike Microsoft, who like Netscape's features, or who are just used to it and don't want to conduct a head-to-head test of Netscape against IE. Most software reviews have given the kudos to IE, and its market share continues to increase; however, if you suspect you might like Netscape, by all means give it a go. Aficionados claim that although it's not faster, it does behave differently. Previous versions of Netscape didn't autocomplete URLs, for example. Of course, the latest version of Netscape's browser does. See which you prefer.

LOOKING AHEAD   Microsoft offers two primary tools for accessing the Internet: Internet Explorer and Outlook Express. Outlook Express is a newsgroup and email application, and it's covered in Chapter 21, "Outlook Express." This chapter focuses on the Internet and Internet Explorer.

LOOKING AHEAD

Microsoft Internet Explorer is, first and foremost, a Web browser—that is, a viewer designed to access and display Web pages and other HTML documents. As such, it's a direct competitor to Web browsers such as Netscape Navigator. As Internet Explorer has evolved, however, it has become much more than just a Web browser. The current version, Internet Explorer 5, is integrated into your Windows 2000 operating system. Internet Explorer 5 even includes an application to help you create your own Web pages (FrontPage Express, *see* Chapter 25 "Using FrontPage Express and Peer Web Services," for more information).

There's so much in Internet Explorer that I decided to cover various aspects of it in several different chapters. This chapter concentrates on setting up Internet Explorer 5 to use your Internet connection, using it as a traditional Web browser, and customizing the browser program. You'll even find out how to customize Internet Explorer's context menus to add your own utilities to it.

> **Tip:** You might not want Internet Explorer's icon on your desktop. Can you remove it? Yes. Right-click its icon and choose Delete. It won't go to the Recycle Bin. It will really be gone. You can always create a Ctrl+Alt+*key* shortcut to it or use the Internet Explorer icon on the QuickLaunch toolbar on the Windows Taskbar. Also, you can toggle the IE icon on the desktop from IE's Tools | Internet Options | Advanced tab | Show Internet Explorer on the desktop.

Without further ado, it's time to discover how to set up Internet Explorer for some Web browsing. I assume that you have installed it already. For details on NT setup, *see* Chapter 4, "Installing Windows 2000 Professional: A Setup Primer."

Starting and Setting Up Internet Explorer

After you get Internet Explorer installed, you want to set it up for use. There are two routes to go here, but they're both essentially the same. What you need to do is specify some type of ISP (Internet service provider). Microsoft provides full support for MSN, but there are AOL, ATT Worldnet, and hundreds of others happy to get your monthly payment. An update for this support is available at `https://signup.msn.com/signup/signup.hts?`. You can also choose to use any other ISP at this point; the only requirement is that you have the proper support (a Dial-Up Networking connection) installed for contacting them. I used PBI (Pacific Bell Internet) in this case because of its low cost and level of support. Note that most corporate users won't need a dial-up account, as they will connect through their LAN.

Here's a handy tip: The first time you run Internet Explorer, you use the Internet
Connection Wizard to install support for it. You can always rerun this program using the
Connection Wizard (Start, Programs, Accessories, Communications, Internet Connection
Wizard). Always run this wizard whenever you change your ISP or make some other
major change to your Internet Explorer setup. Here are the steps to follow:

1. Double-click the Internet Explorer icon on the desktop if this is the first time
   you're running it. Otherwise, select the Internet Connection Wizard option from
   the Internet Explorer folder (or use the Start button menus described in the preceding paragraph) to start the wizard. (First-time users can double-click "Connect to
   the Internet" on the desktop. This feature disappears from the desktop after making its connection.)

2. Click Next. Figure 2.1 shows the first setup options dialog box. You need to decide
   how you want to connect to the Internet. As you can see, there are three ways to
   do so. The first option is for someone who has no Internet access arrangements in
   place. The Internet Connection Wizard supplies a list of ISPs that service your
   area (if any are participants in the Microsoft Internet Referral Service) and lets
   you select one and sign up for an account. Then it takes you through the steps to
   set up a connection to your new ISP. During the setup process, the wizard might
   prompt you for your Windows 2000 CD-ROM to copy files to your system and
   might require you to restart your computer. However, if no ISP in your area is a
   member of the Microsoft Internet Referral Service, you're told to click Finish and
   then restart the Internet Connection Wizard. If this happens, you want to select the
   second option shown in Figure 2.1.

   The second option says that you want to transfer your existing account to your
   computer. This option behaves as the first option does (dialing the Microsoft
   Referral Service), but in this case, if it fails to find any local ISPs on that service,
   it walks you through the process of setting up a new Internet connection. The third
   option is the one to use if you already have an Internet connection set up through
   your LAN or modem connected to a phone. If you choose the "modem" option,
   you then follow the same steps as the second option.

3. Click the first option if you want to try to locate an ISP in your area that's a member of the Microsoft Referral Service. Otherwise, click the third option. (If you
   choose the second option, and no local ISP is found in your area after the 888
   number is dialed, you're asked if you want to now manually "restore" your
   Internet settings. Agree to that and click Next.)

   If you choose the third option on the first page of this wizard, click Next and then
   choose the "modem" option. (If you choose the LAN connection rather than the
   phone-line connection in the preceding step, the wizard presents a couple of dialog
   boxes asking whether your LAN goes through a proxy server; if it does, the wizard asks you to supply the proxy server name.) Click Next.

FIGURE 2.1

In the first setup options dialog box, you can choose the method of creating an Internet connection.

4. You fill in the phone number and optional advanced data about your connection, as shown in Figure 2.2.

FIGURE 2.2

On this page, you fill in your ISP's phone number and also specify whether it's necessary to dial an area code and country code in addition to the ISP's number.

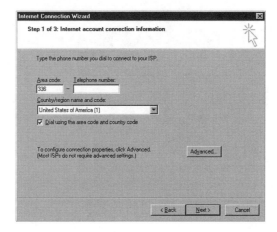

5. Click Next.

6. Fill in your name and password, as shown in Figure 2.3.

7. Click Next. On the next page you give your new connection a name. You can have multiple connections for different purposes, different line speeds, and so on (see Figure 2.4).

8. Click Next. You're now asked whether you want to set up an email account, as you can see in Figure 2.5. If you choose *No* and *don't* have any existing email accounts, after clicking *Next* you are not shown the page of settings, but go directly to the final page instead.

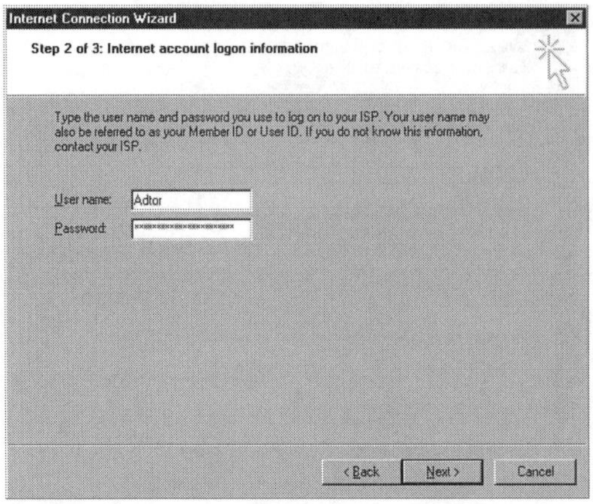

FIGURE 2.3

*Type in the user-
name and pass-
word required by
your ISP. (This is
not the same as
your Windows
2000 password or
username.)*

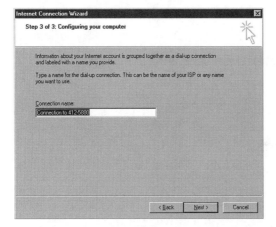

FIGURE 2.4

*In this text box
you can give your
connection a
meaningful name.
Perhaps you want
to call it
Connection to
Internet or some-
thing similar.*

FIGURE 2.5

*You can take the
time to set up an
email account at
this point, if you
wish.*

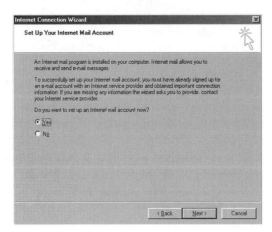

Note that your ISP is likely to be your email provider as well as your Internet connection. You can get information from the ISP telling you the name of your mail host and news host, as well as any other information required by Outlook Express to handle your mail. You're probably anxious to get on the Net and do some Web browsing, so you can just click No and skip the email account setup for now. Later, in Chapter 21, "Outlook Express," I show you how to set up your email account in Outlook Express.

9. Click Next.

10. If you chose No in step 8, you're shown any existing email accounts and asked if you want to establish a new one. At this point you're almost done. If you already have an email account, select it in this page so you don't have to fill in all the specifications a second time.

11. Finally, when you've finished filling in the various text boxes, check boxes, and option buttons in this wizard, you're shown all the settings and given a chance to change any of them, as shown in Figure 2.6.

FIGURE 2.6

This is your chance to correct any errors in your connection.

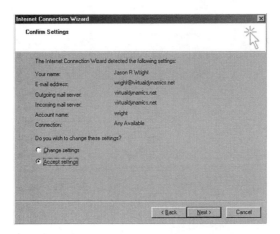

12. The final page lets you choose whether to connect immediately to the Internet. Click Finish. The wizard closes. You're now connected to the Internet (if you left the appropriate check box checked).

Navigating the World Wide Web

By this time, you're probably wondering what else you have to do to get online. Actually, the setup and configuration are finished. All you need to do now is double-click the Internet Explorer icon on your desktop or single-click its icon on your taskbar. You can also click Start, Programs, Internet Explorer. If you're connected to the Internet via your LAN, IE5 opens immediately. If you connect to the Internet via a Dial-Up Connection, you see a Connect To dialog box offering you multiple dial-up accounts. Enter your user-name and password (if necessary) and click Connect to get started. You'll then see the progress report of the dialing in a box at the bottom of the Connect To dialog box.

At this point, a number of things could happen, depending on how you created your Internet connection. (You can also change the configuration of Internet Explorer to get a variety of results.) You'll likely see the home page of your ISP. If you've elected to use the Microsoft Network, the first time you start Internet Explorer you'll see something similar to the Web page shown in Figure 2.7.

FIGURE 2.7

You can start each Internet session at the MSN Start home page, if you wish. Like most "portal" sites— such as Excite, Yahoo, and all the rest—MSN is cus-tomizable.

Customizing Your Start Page

If you don't see the Microsoft customizable home page, type msn in the Internet Explorer Address bar and press Enter. Internet Explorer will automatically expand *msn* into http://www.msn.com for you. You can, of course, set any Web page as your start page. I like to use Microsoft's version as well as another nice customizable start page from Excite (http://www.excite.com/). It's easy to switch between home pages. To change your home page, choose Internet Options from the Internet Explorer Tools menu. Click the General tab and you can specify your Home Page option.

You can use Internet Explorer's scrollbars to view different portions of a Web page. From there, the details of how to navigate various Web pages and sites can vary, depending on the design of the sites you're viewing. However, the basics remain fairly consistent. Most pages are composed of a combination of graphics and text, and they include hyperlinks to enable you to jump from the page you're viewing to another related page. Hyperlinks in text are usually highlighted in color (typically blue) and underlined. Hyperlinked graphics often look like buttons, icons, or symbols so that their intended use is easy to understand. Hyperlink graphics are often accompanied by a label that's highlighted and underlined to cue you that the graphic is, in fact, a link. Here's another cue: When you point to a hyperlink, the normal mouse pointer changes to a pointing hand to designate the presence of a hyperlink. Click it and Internet Explorer loads and displays the Web page referenced in the hyperlink (or it goes elsewhere within the currently displayed page sometimes). In this way, you maneuver from page to page and site to site throughout the World Wide Web, thereby surfing the Net.

Using Internet Explorer Toolbars

Now that you're online and have viewed a Web page, start taking a look at some of Internet Explorer's controls in more detail. Everything you need is on the toolbar. I rarely use the menu system in Internet Explorer except to select a favorite site or modify Internet Explorer's configuration settings.

In addition to the toolbars that have become a standard feature of Web browsers (and other programs as well), Internet Explorer also features Explorer bars. An *Explorer bar* is a panel on the left side of the browser pane that acts like an expanded toolbar. The contents of the Explorer bar remain visible, while the contents of the main Web page viewing pane on the right change as you surf. The Search bar, shown in Figure 2.8, is just one example of an Explorer bar. There are also Explorer bars for Favorites, History, and Folders. Favorites is where you store Web pages you want to visit again. History contains sites you've visited in the past three weeks (handy if you wish you could remember a particular site and know you visited it recently). Think of the History bar as a kind of super Back key. The Folders bar transforms the left side of Internet Explorer into the tree diagram of your system that you see on the left side of *Windows* Explorer. This is one additional feature that helps break down the distinction between Internet Explorer and Windows Explorer (see Chapter 5, "Exploring the Interface," for more information).

> **Tip:** Unlike the other bars, Folders doesn't have an icon on the IE toolbar by default. However, you can add one for it: Right-click the toolbar at the top of Internet Explorer and then choose Customize from the context menu.

> **Tip:** If you're interested in seeing a tip about using Internet Explorer displayed each time you run IE, choose View, Explorer Bar, Tip of the Day. A pane will open on the bottom with a different tip each time IE starts up, until it runs out of tips and starts over.

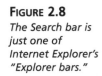

FIGURE 2.8

The Search bar is just one of Internet Explorer's "Explorer bars."

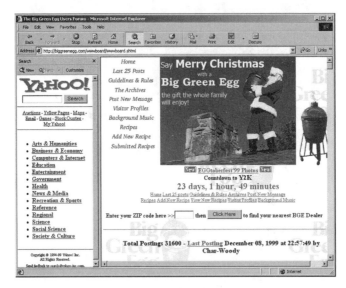

The following list gives you a quick overview of the various controls on the toolbars. I cover some of these controls in more detail as the chapter progresses:

- *Back/Forward.* You'll find that these two buttons come in handy when you want to move quickly among several areas that you've already visited. I use the Back button most often to move from the current page back up to a previously viewed page in a Web site. A special feature of these buttons is that each has a small arrow button on its right side. When you click the down arrow, Internet Explorer displays a drop-down list of recently visited Web pages (visited during this session—it's not as complete as the History feature described previously). You can go directly to any page on the list by clicking it in the list. This enables you to jump backward or forward several pages without having to repeatedly click the Back or Forward button.

> **Tip:** You can also go back a page by pressing the Backspace key.

- *Stop.* Some Internet sites seem to provide more than the usual number of graphics. You could wait for them to all download, but I usually click this button instead. It tells the browser to stop downloading the page. The disadvantage is that you don't see all the graphics and buttons the Web page designer placed on the page. The advantage is that you can get back to work faster. Another reason to click this button is when you've already clicked the Back button or a hyperlink—but, whoa!—you notice something on the current page that you have to see. If you want to halt the transfer and you want the current page to remain onscreen, just click Stop and you're okay.

- *Refresh*. Explorer, like most browsers, uses a cache to store images. Sometimes the Internet page changes without your knowledge because your browser is looking at the cached page rather than the live page on the Internet. Use this button to reload the current page and update its contents.

- *Home*. Some browsers use the term *start page* for the place you always start surfing the Internet; Internet Explorer uses the term *home page*. In my case, the home page is excite.com. Clicking this button always takes you to your home page. (You can redefine which page Internet Explorer loads when you click the Home button. I show you how later in this chapter.)

- *Search*. The Search button is the first of three buttons that activate Explorer bars. Click it once to add the Search Explorer bar to your Internet Explorer window. The button looks "depressed" when it's active. Click the depressed button to toggle the Search Explorer bar off. I cover this button (and other search-related procedures) in the section titled "Searching," later in this chapter. The short version is that this button opens an Internet page that you can use to search for items and topics. Normally you use some form of keyword search to accomplish the task.

- *Favorites*. Internet Explorer enables you to maintain a list of favorite places. You can access the Favorites list from the Favorites menu. You can also click this button to display a list of your favorite places in an Explorer bar. I cover using Favorites in more detail in a separate section of this chapter titled "Favorite Sites."

> **Tip:** In Internet Explorer version 4 there was a television metaphor—an Explorer bar named *channels* and you were to "subscribe" to them (subscribing involved offline viewing). This amounted to background updating of pages you could work with offline or see on your desktop. This metaphor, and the channels bar, are gone in Windows 2000. You can still view cached pages offline in Windows 2000, but the metaphor is no longer in use. If you were among those who did use channels in your previous version of Internet Explorer, you can find the channels in a folder named Channels in your Favorites list.

> **Tip:** You can trigger a limited, but sometimes interesting, variation on the usual search by choosing Tools, Show Related Links. This feature displays a list of Web sites similar to the one you're currently viewing in IE. A Search bar appears on the left pane of IE with a brief list that the specialized search engine (named Alexa) considers the closest sites to the one you're now viewing.

- *History*. The History button activates the History Explorer bar, which lists the Web sites you've visited over the last couple of weeks. The sites are listed by day or week and the individual pages are subgrouped into folders by site. To revisit a site, just click its listing in the History Explorer bar. It's a handy way to locate and return to that cool site you remember visiting a few days ago. On the other hand, it's also a way that someone (your boss perhaps) can track the sites you've been surfing. (I show you how to adjust the length of time Internet Explorer keeps track of your browsing history and how to clear the history listing in the section titled "Customizing Internet Explorer," later in this chapter.)

- *Fullscreen.* If you right-click the toolbar at the top of Internet Explorer and then choose Customize from the context menu, you'll see various additional buttons you can add to the toolbar. One of them I sometimes find useful is *Fullscreen.* Some Web pages are just too full of information to fit comfortably within the confines of the normal Internet Explorer browser window. Even if you maximize the Internet Explorer window, the title bar, menus, toolbars, and other accoutrements of the application window conspire to eat up a lot of screen space, leaving a limited amount of space for viewing the Web site itself. To relieve the crowding, Internet Explorer offers you the option of viewing Web pages in Fullscreen mode. When you click the Fullscreen button, Internet Explorer does more than just maximize its window; it also does away with the window border, menus, and nearly everything else. The entire screen is devoted to displaying the Web page. The only exception is a small toolbar at the top of the screen, as shown in Figure 2.9. To return to the Normal view, click the Fullscreen button in that toolbar.

> **Tip:** To quickly toggle between Fullscreen and Normal view in IE, press F11.

FIGURE 2.9

In Fullscreen view, your entire screen is devoted to displaying a Web page.

- *Mail*. Clicking this button drops a menu containing five options: Read Mail, New Message, Send a Link, Send Page, and Read News. The Read Mail option displays Outlook Express or another mail reader, such as Windows Messaging (depending on which application you choose as your mail reader). Internet Explorer requests any new mail from your ISP's mail server and displays it in the window. The New Message option brings up a new message dialog box, using the capabilities of either Outlook Express or Windows Messaging. I cover the messaging capabilities of Outlook Express further in Chapter 21, "Outlook Express." The Send a Link option works much like creating a new message. In this case, however, the message includes a link to the Web site you're currently viewing in Internet Explorer. This enables you to have a discussion with someone else concerning the particulars of an Internet site. The Send Page option is similar to Send a Link, except that Internet Explorer attaches a copy of the Web page to the message instead of just sending a link to the page's URL. Finally, the Read News option brings up the Outlook Express program in its Internet News Reader mode. As with the other Outlook Express features, I discuss it in Chapter 21 as well.

- *Size*. Generally, you'll find that Internet sites use an easy-to-read font. At times, however, you might need to see larger or smaller text. Use this button to change the font size. A menu will appear with options relative to the current size: larger, smallest and so on.

- *Print*. Use this option to send the current page content to the printer.

- *Edit*. Clicking this button imports the current Web page into an editor. Internet Explorer defaults to sending the Web page to FrontPage or FrontPage Express, if you have one of them installed.

- *Address*. The Address bar is easy to spot; it's the big text box that occupies a toolbar of its very own. When you want to visit a Web site, you can type its URL (or a part of the URL) and press Enter. Internet Explorer loads and displays the Web page (or other resource, such as your hard drive) you specified. What isn't as obvious is that the Address bar is also a drop-down list box that contains the last several URLs you entered. If you want to return to any of the sites on the list, you can select the URL from the Address list and save yourself some typing. There's a new Go button next to the Address bar that, when clicked, tries to locate the site described in the Address bar. In NT4, you would instead type the word *go* as the first word in the Address bar, then type the URL, then press Enter to have Internet Explorer change to a different view. Note that you need not click the Go button; merely pressing the Enter key has the same effect.

- *Links*. The Links toolbar is composed of buttons, each linked to a Web page. Clicking a button takes you to that Web page. Initially, you see three buttons: Customize Links, Free Hotmail, and Windows. They are links to popular pages on the Microsoft Web site. You can redefine the Links buttons, however, by changing the contents of the Links folder in your Favorites list. Put shortcuts to your most-used Web pages in the Links folder and you have easy one-click access to those sites, right on a toolbar.

> **Tip:** To remove a link icon, right-click it and then choose Delete. To define a Ctrl+Alt shortcut key combination for the link's Web site, right-click it and then choose Properties. To add a new link to the Links toolbar, visit the Web site and then drag its URL from the Address bar onto the Links toolbar.

> **Tip:** You can find the latest Internet Explorer tips and tricks concerning the Links toolbar at this site:
>
> `http://www.microsoft.com/windows98/usingwindows/internet/tips/advanced/`
> `CustomizeLinksBar.asp`
>
> If you're replacing your operating system or want to transfer your Favorites list or existing cookies to a disk for backup—you're in luck. Internet Explorer 5 includes a wizard (choose File, Import and Export) that does just that. Cookies are little collections of data on your hard drive that make Web surfing more convenient—they store information such as your username and password for sites that require them, and that way you don't have to type them in each time you visit such sites. Cookies also store customization information, if you have, for example, requested a particular TV guide listing for your area or arranged the order in which you want a new site's topics to appear onscreen. Your collection of favorites and those cookies took perhaps months to build. You do want to keep a backup of them, somewhere off your hard drive, just to be sure. Same advice applies to saving a backup of your Inbox messages and your Address Book in Outlook Express (see Chapter 21, "Outlook Express.").

Keyboard Shortcuts

As a respectable, full-fledged Microsoft application, Internet Explorer has its own set of built-in keyboard shortcuts. I've already mentioned the Backspace key as a substitute for clicking the Back icon, but Table 2.3 specifies the rest of the shortcuts.

Table 2.3 IE Keyboard Shortcuts

Action	Shortcut Key(s)
Back	Backspace or Alt+left arrow
Forward	Alt+right arrow
Move to hyperlink target	Enter
Move to next hyperlink	Tab
Move to preceding hyperlink	Shift+Tab
Scroll down	Down Arrow
Scroll up	Up Arrow
Scroll down a page (approximately)	Page Down

Action	Shortcut Key(s)
Scroll up a page (approximately)	Page Up
Go to top of document	Home
Go to bottom of document	End
Refresh	F5
Refresh from site (not disk cache)	Ctrl+F5
Stop downloading	Esc
Toggle Fullscreen/Normal	F11

You're aware that there's a collection of Windows keyboard shortcuts as well. They can be defined in the Properties page of any program and can consist of the key combination Ctrl+Alt+*whateverkey*. For example, you might have assigned Ctrl+Alt+D to a DOS session or Ctrl+Alt+N to Notepad. These Windows-wide shortcuts are triggered whether you're on the desktop, within Explorer (either Explorer), or even working in an application. Now here's the question: Can you create Windows-wide keyboard shortcuts for your favorite Internet sites? Yes. Here's one way. Run Internet Explorer and choose the Organize Favorites option from the Favorites menu. Locate the site you want and then right-click it. Choose Properties and click the Shortcut Key box and press whatever key you want to use (perhaps *P* for your favorite pictures site). Click OK. Now, whenever you press Ctrl+Alt+P, off you go to your favorite pictures site. A similar technique can be used to define shortcut keys for sites on the Links bar (see the tip a few paragraphs ago in which the links are described).

Peter's Principle: From Static to Dynamic Web Pages

In the early days of the Web, almost all Web pages were static—the content and formatting remained fixed until the Webmaster changed it. All the visitors to a site would see the same Web pages in much the same way. Now, Webmasters are using tools such as Java, ActiveX, Cascading Style Sheets, and Dynamic HTML to create truly animated and dynamic Web sites—Web sites filled with pages that evolve, adapt, and change in response to input from the viewer, the time of day, and many other factors. The Web page you view might be generated on the fly by the server just seconds before you see it. The server uses information you supply to select bits and pieces from its database to build a Web page custom tailored to you. The result is a more engaging Web-browsing experience. In the case of DHTML, processing occurs within your machine. For example, one DHTML effect is that one image dissolves into another. This dissolve is accomplished by your computer.

continues

As a Web surfer, you don't really need to be concerned about the new techniques and technologies that make Dynamic HTML possible. All the hard work falls on the shoulders of the software developers and the Web site designers. They're the ones who must make the dynamic Web sites work. You just need a Web browser capable of displaying the pages they produce. Internet Explorer 3 can display some of these effects, but Internet Explorer 4 supports most, and IE 5 support all the latest features, such as Cascading Style Sheets. You need that capability to be able to display the latest dynamic Web sites. If you're still using Internet Explorer 3 or some other browser that cannot handle DHTML, the idea of missing the benefits of dynamic Web sites is, for many of us, probably sufficient justification for upgrading or switching your browser software.

Favorite Sites

As I mentioned, Internet Explorer enables you to maintain a list of favorite places—a collection of shortcuts containing the URLs of Web sites you want to revisit in the future. (Other Web browsers have a similar feature called *bookmarks*.) You might want to maintain a list of favorite Internet research sites or create a listing of sites related to a current project, for example. Internet Explorer's Favorites menu and the Favorites Explorer bar display a list of your favorite places. There are also commands that enable you to add new Web sites to your Favorites list or organize your favorite places into a hierarchy of folders. As a result of the increasing blending of the Internet into the Windows 2000 operating system, the Favorites menu is now a fixture in Windows Explorer in addition to Internet Explorer. You can find the Favorites menu in windows for My Computer and even Control Panel.

If you want Favorites (in other words, a list made up mostly of Internet Web sites) to always appear on your *Windows* Explorer—just right-click the Windows Explorer toolbar and then choose Customize. Then double-click the Favorites icon in the left pane of the Available Toolbar Buttons list in the dialog box. Note, though, that you can add paths *on your hard drive* to favorites, if you wish (it need not simply be a list of locations on the Web). If you have a folder that you frequently want to open, even from within Internet Explorer, you can add it to Favorites by selecting it in the right pane (of Windows Explorer) and then clicking the Add icon at the top of the Favorites Explorer bar. Also, there's another way to add *documents* to Favorites. If you have documents on your local hard drive or a network drive that you need to access frequently, you can create shortcuts to them and add the shortcut in the Favorites list. Just open the Windows\Favorites folder, right-click a blank area in the folder, choose New, Shortcut from the context menu, and then enter the full filename and a display name in the Create Shortcut Wizard. When you finish with the wizard, you have a shortcut to your document on your Favorites list. Now you can use the Favorites list to open your document just as you use it to open Web pages. (Note that if you've installed Windows 2000 from scratch rather than upgrading over a previous NT4, you'll find the Favorites folder in this path: \Documents and Settings*username*\\Favorites.)

Click the Favorites button in the toolbar and Internet Explorer displays the Favorites Explorer bar, as shown in Figure 2.10. The Explorer bar is like having a Favorites menu that stays open and available rather than disappearing after you make each selection. It's great for moving quickly through a series of favorite sites.

FIGURE 2.10

Click the Favorites button in the toolbar, and Internet Explorer displays the Favorites Explorer bar.

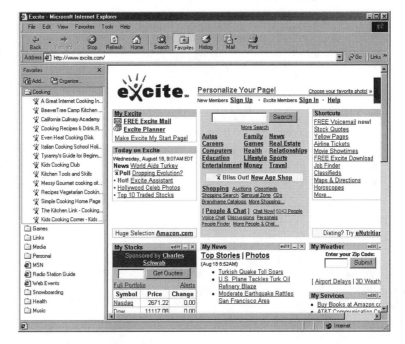

Whether you use the Favorites menu in Internet Explorer, the Favorites menu in another Explorer window, or the Favorites Explorer bar in Internet Explorer, the technique for opening a favorite site is basically the same. You open the menu or Explorer bar, click a subfolder in the list (if necessary) to display a list of sites in that folder, and then click the desired favorite site in that list. Internet Explorer loads and displays the selected Web page. If you're not already connected to the Internet, Internet Explorer initiates a connection to load the Web page. If you elect to work offline, Internet Explorer attempts to load the page from the cache on your hard drive (see Chapter 6, "There's Really Only One Explorer," for more information).

> **Tip:** What does the Work Offline option on Internet Explorer's File menu do? It disconnects Internet Explorer from your ISP (although if you have another Internet application running in your standalone computer, it might not disconnect your machine from the ISP). Internet Explorer becomes local, however, and must look to your hard drive's cache of Web pages that you've recently visited. If you try to link to a page not in the cache, you'll get an error message from Internet Explorer and will politely be asked whether you want to go back online.

Adding a Page to Your Favorites

For the Favorites list to be truly useful, it needs to contain Web sites that really are your favorites—sites that you return to time and time again. That means you need to be able to add your own Web sites to the Favorites list. Fortunately, it's easy to do just that.

First, go to the site you want to add to the Favorites list. Make sure you're viewing the proper page because Internet Explorer uses the URL of the current Web page for the favorite place entry. When the page you want to add is visible in the Internet Explorer window, choose Favorites, Add to Favorites from the Internet Explorer menu. (You can also click the Add icon at the top of the Favorites Explorer bar.) Internet Explorer opens the Add Favorite dialog box, as shown in Figure 2.11 (this is the expanded view of this dialog box). To just add the Web page to your list of favorite places, just click OK. The dialog box closes and the Web site is added to the root list in Favorites, not in a folder. If you want to put this URL in an existing Favorites folder, select that folder in the list box. You can also use this opportunity to create a new folder if you wish. Finally, if you want to give this item a different name than the one you see in the text box, just edit the text box before clicking OK. The Make Available Offline option gives you an opportunity to include this page in the cache, or not, as you choose.

FIGURE 2.11

Just click OK if you want to add this page to the root of your Favorites list.

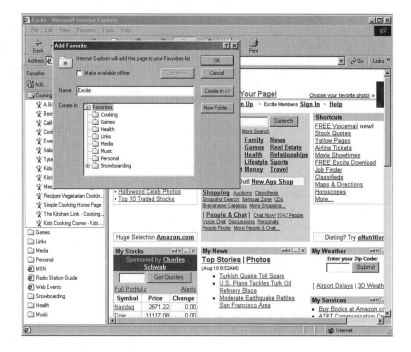

Tip: Don't forget the easiest way to add a Web site to Favorites is just to drag its URL from the Address bar and drop it into the Favorites bar.

Organizing Favorites

After you begin to build a collection of favorite places, you need to organize your list; otherwise, it will get too long to display conveniently. The Organize Favorites option displays a dialog box that you can use to move your favorite places around and create folders (subdirectories) in which to store them.

To begin maintenance work on your Favorites list, choose Favorites, Organize Favorites from the Internet Explorer menu (or click the Organize icon at the top of the Favorites bar). Internet Explorer opens the Organize Favorites dialog box, as shown in Figure 2.12. Using this dialog box is pretty straightforward. You can click the Create New Folder button at the top of the dialog box to create a new subfolder that appears as a submenu in the Favorites list. You can select a favorite place item and then click one of the buttons at the bottom to move, rename, or delete the selected item. To move a favorite place shortcut to a subfolder the easy way, just drag and drop it onto the folder. That's all there is to it. After you finish rearranging items in the Favorites list, click Close to close the dialog box.

FIGURE 2.12

The Organize Favorites dialog box differs somewhat from the Add Favorite dialog box shown in Figure 2.11.

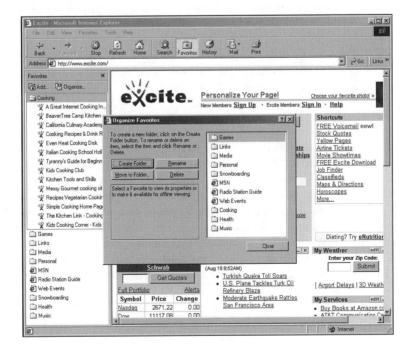

Note: The Favorites list is really just a collection of shortcuts stored in the Favorites subfolder of your Windows 2000 directory. (It's usually C:\WINNT\Profiles*Yourname*\, or C:\Documents and Settings*Yourname*\ for a fresh Windows 2000 instalation, where *Yourname* is whatever your sign-on name is. Or you may find it in a /Documents and Settings folder.) You can use Windows Explorer to create folders and move most Favorites shortcuts around in the Favorites folder, just like moving objects in any other folder.

When the Favorites bar is open, you can easily move URLs around or put them in folders by dragging and dropping them. Likewise, you can rearrange your Favorites folders by dragging and dropping them.

Browsing Offline

As you may be aware, when you connect to a site, the information you view is cached locally to speed up future visits to the site (the cache size can be set in Tools, Internet Options, General, Temporary Internet Files, Settings). It's actually possible to view the Web using only the cache when you're not connected. This can be useful if it costs you money to stay online, or if it ties up a server. For instance, when you're traveling, each minute online in a hotel room can sometimes be quite expensive. The solution is to visit some sites, but then disconnect and actually read the pages offline. Obviously, however, you can only view sites stored in the cache. To work offline, follow these steps:

1. Start Internet Explorer.
2. From the File menu (of either IE or Outlook Express), choose Work Offline.
3. You can enter URLs and links as normal, but you'll receive an error if you attempt to link to a site that's not cached.
4. To stop working offline, just deselect Work Offline.

If you want to ensure that a page on your Favorites list be available for offline viewing (and current), right-click the Web page you want to work with, then choose Make Available Offline from the context menu. The new Offline Favorite Wizard dialog box appears and you can specify various ways that this page should be cached. You can request that any additional pages linked within this page also be cached. Clearly, this could easily get out of hand and eat up considerable memory, so there's also a provision for defining how many links deep from the page you want stored. Then you can define how frequently you want the page refreshed, specifying a schedule when the browser should download that page again and replace the older, cached version. Finally, you can enter a name and password if the site requires it—to automate the process of refreshing the cache.

Searching

If you do a lot of research on the Internet, as I do, you realize the benefit of finding what you need quickly. Internet Explorer and its links to the Microsoft Web site provide you with some really handy tools in this regard.

Of course, numerous search engines and directories are available on the Web. To use any one of them, you can just type the search engine's URL (or usually, just its name, such as Yahoo) into Internet Explorer's Address bar to go to that Web site and begin your search. Internet Explorer actually makes use of these same engines for its searching tools. The difference is that Internet Explorer includes some features that make the popular search engines and directories a little more accessible and easier to use.

Starting a Search from the Toolbar

Take a look at the most basic tool first. Just click the Search button on the IE toolbar, and you see a display similar to the one shown in Figure 2.13. (You see a different search page if you don't use MSN as your search engine.) Click the Customize icon at the top of the Search bar, shown in Figure 2.13, and you can select other search engines or make one your default engine. You can also define how IE behaves when you use the Address bar to do your searching, by typing in a shorthand version of a URL into the Address bar and then clicking the Go button next to it or pressing Enter. To do this, click the Autosearch Settings button at the bottom of the Customize dialog box. I use the MSN and Go to most likely site as my settings for the Autosearch feature. I find that it works quite well.

FIGURE 2.13
Searching can be highly specific, if you wish.

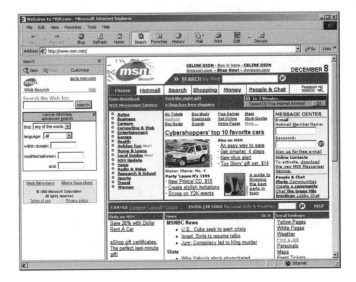

If you want to conduct a search using the Search bar, enter a keyword in the text box and click the button that starts the search. (The button is labeled Search in Figure 2.13, but some search engines use different names for this button.) Internet Explorer enters your search request at the selected search engine's Web site and then displays the results of your search (see Figure 2.14). If you have not specified a search engine, one is chosen for you based on MSN's best fit for the data you're after.

Of course, you don't have to use the search engine that's preselected when you arrive at the Search the Web page. After all, that's the point of a page like this—to give you easy access to any of several search resources. If you prefer to use one of the other search resources listed on the Search the Web page, just select it by clicking its name on the page. After a few seconds, the data-entry form for that search resource replaces the default selection and you can proceed with your search.

FIGURE 2.14
After a search is finished, you see a list of hits; it can be a very, very large list.

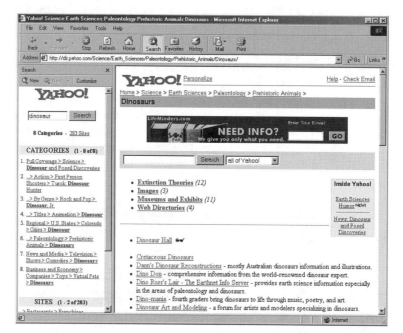

Normally, when you click an ordinary hyperlink, Internet Explorer locates the target of that link and displays the Web page in the main viewing window, replacing the current page. That works fine on normal Web pages, but it's not always great when you're following multiple links from a page of search engine hits. The problem is that a lot of search engine hits turn out to be dead ends, so you wind up clicking the Back button to return to the page displaying the search results links to try another hit. You can spend a lot of time waiting while Internet Explorer reloads that results links page of search engine results again and again.

The Search bar cures this problem. When you click a hyperlink for a hit in the Search bar, Internet Explorer loads the target Web page and displays it in the main viewing window to the right of the Search bar, as shown in Figure 2.15. Notice that the Search bar remains onscreen. If you want to check out another hit from your search, you don't have to click the Back button and wait for Internet Explorer to return to the search results page; you can just click the hyperlink for the next hit in the Search bar.

FIGURE 2.15

Click a hit in the Search bar and view the target Web page in the main viewing panel to the right of the Search bar.

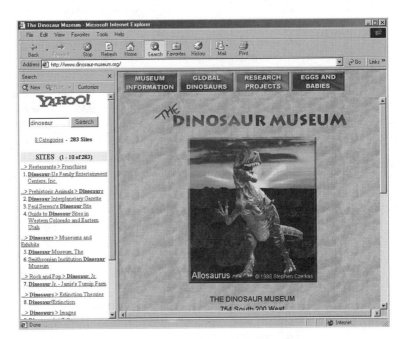

Using Autosearch

Autosearch is another handy built-in search Internet Explorer feature. There are no buttons to click or commands to select when you use Autosearch; all the action takes place in the Address bar. To initiate an autosearch, you just type a partial URL, usually the name of something, such as Microsoft, or an acronym, such as CNN. When you press Enter, or click the Go button next to the Address bar, Internet Explorer automatically submits the keyword to the search engine. Which engine is used depends on you: Click the Customize button on the Search pane (or choose Search | Customize). The Customize Search Settings dialog box opens and you can select your favorite engine from a list.

Search Engines Compared

Here's a summary of the qualities of several of the most popular search engines, listed alphabetically.

- *Alta Vista* (http://www.altavista.digital.com/). One of the benefits of using this search engine is that you won't suffer from information overload. It returns only the amount of information you want about each hit. The service tends to focus on Web pages containing articles, meaning that you get some pretty narrow hits when using it. Alta Vista uses excerpts from the articles or other sources of information that it accesses. This service uses a somewhat esoteric Boolean search engine, making it difficult to narrow your search criteria in any simple way.

- *AOL NetFind* (http://netfind.aol.com/). Beneath the surface, this is really the Excite search engine in disguise and, predictably, the results of a keyword search are essentially the same as you get using the Excite service directly. The reason for selecting AOL NetFind rather than Excite is for the Time Savers features, such as Car Corner and Manage Your Investments, which provide quick access to pages of information and links related to those topics. The particular features change rather frequently.

- *Deja News* (http://www.dejanews.com/). I have used this particular search engine when I needed to find a lot of information fast. You'll notice a Power Search option on the Deja News home page. "Power search" might be something of an understatement; you literally have to test it to see all that you can do. Although it is quite flexible, it is also well-designed. Therefore, it's one of the easier sites to use. It uses a lot of graphics, including radio buttons and other familiar controls. The only problem with this particular engine is that you might find yourself doing a search more than once to get everything it provides. There are so many search options that you'll find yourself thinking of new ways to search for a particularly tough-to-find bit of information. You can get two levels of detail—neither of which tell you much. All you can count on getting for each hit is an article title. This service doesn't provide excerpts or summaries, but it does provide a broad base of information, meaning that you'll find just about anything you search for; you'll just spend some time weeding out the entries that really don't fit. Note, however, that Deja News is from Usenet and that it's good at answering questions. When you're researching a problem, Deja News can be an excellent place to see whether others have had the same problem and, if so, what their solutions to it were.

- *Excite* (http://www.excite.com/). Excite tends to focus on Web sites rather than pages on a particular site. In other words, you get to a general area of interest and then Excite leaves it to you to find the specific information you're looking for. I find that this is an advantage when I'm not really sure about the specifics of a search. A wide view, in this case, helps me see everything that's available, and then I can make some refinements. Excite also provides a summary of what you'll find at a particular site. It tends to concentrate on discussion groups and vendor-specific information.

- *Google* (http://www.google.com/). Using an interesting approach, this engine tests its hits based on how often the URLs are accessed or linked to by other pages. According to Google's self-description, "Google uses a complicated mathematical analysis, calculated on more than a billion hyperlinks on the Web, to return high-quality search results so you don't have to sift through junk. This analysis allows Google to estimate the quality, or importance, of every Web page it returns. The importance of a Web page is entirely independent of any query."

- *HotBot* (http://www.hotbot.com/). Many people consider this to be the premier search engine on the Web today, and with good reason. The searches are fast and comprehensive, and HotBot gives you access to some power-searching tools for customizing your searches that most of the other search engines reserve for advanced users only. On the other hand, you'll probably need to take the time to learn about and use those extra searching tools to refine your HotBot searches; otherwise, the results you get may be overwhelming. When I searched for ActiveX on HotBot, for example, I got more than 130,000 hits.

- *Infoseek* (http://www.infoseek.com/). This service provides just the facts. It uses excerpts from the articles or other sources of information from which it draws excerpts. The hits are a lot narrower than some search engines provide because Infoseek concentrates on Web pages rather than sites. The only problem with this particular service is that your ability to narrow the search criteria is severely limited.

- *Lycos* (http://www.lycos.com/). Of all the search engines I have used, Lycos tends to provide the most diverse information. It catalogs both Web sites and pages but concentrates on pages whenever possible. Lycos provides a combination of summaries and excerpts to describe the content of a particular hit. Its capability to narrow your search is superior to most of the search engines available right now. One of the downsides to using this particular search engine is that there's almost too much detail. You'll quickly find yourself searching false leads and ending up with totally unusable information if you aren't sure what you're looking for.

- *Magellan* (http://www.mckinley.com/). You'll tend to find esoteric sources of information with this search engine. It doesn't appear to provide a broad base of information, but it usually provides interesting facts about what you're searching for. Magellan concentrates on Web sites rather than pages, so the view you get is rather general. You'll also find that it provides few methods for narrowing the search criteria. This search engine relies on summaries rather than extracts to convey the content of a particular hit.

- *MetaCrawler* (http://www.metacrawler.com/). Instead of using various search engines individually, the MetaCrawler search engine enables you to query multiple search engines simultaneously. That way, you won't have to check the same query with different search engines such as Yahoo! and Excite.

- *Open Text* (`http://search.opentext.com/`). *Extremely comprehensive* and *flexible* are the words to describe this engine. I find that this is one of the easier engines to use, and it provides a moderately broad base of information from which to choose. It relies on extremely short excerpts, in most cases. It concentrates on Web pages rather than sites, meaning that you get a fairly narrow result. This site tilts its features toward business users.

- *Web Crawler* (`http://www.webcrawler.com/`). You'll find that this search engine requires a bit more work to use than most because it doesn't provide much in the way of excerpts or summaries. On the other hand, it provides a full Boolean search engine and an extremely broad base of information. The only search engine that provides a broader base in this list is Lycos.

- *Yahoo!* (`http://www.yahoo.com/`). Many people's favorite as well as one of my favorites (my default, in fact), Yahoo! is highly structured, providing the best organization of all the engines. It categorizes every hit in a variety of ways, greatly improving your chances of finding the information you're after. Sites are categorized very clearly. This service does not provide the broad range of information that you can find with some other search engines, however. It also relies on short summaries to tell you the content of a particular hit. I sometimes rely on Yahoo! as a first-look engine—it generally gives me a quick, useful result from a single keyword.

Searching for Text on a Page

Before I leave the subject of searches, there's one more kind of search to consider: finding text on a Web page. To start a search for some text, first display the Web page you want to search and then choose Edit, Find (on this page) or press Ctrl+F. Internet Explorer displays a Find dialog box like the one you use to find text in a word processor or similar application. Enter the text you want to search for in the Find What text box, check the appropriate options, and select whether you want to search up or down from the current cursor position. When you click the Find Next button (or just press Enter), Internet Explorer searches the current Web page and highlights the first match it finds. Note that you can repeatedly press the Enter key to continue to locate additional instances of your target throughout the page.

Customizing Internet Explorer

Internet Explorer is a highly customizable program. I already covered how you can customize your list of favorite places, display Explorer bars, and view Web pages in Fullscreen mode. In addition, you can use a lot of options and settings to change the appearance of the Internet Explorer window and the Web pages it displays as well as to change many of Internet Explorer's default actions and configuration.

LOOKING AHEAD I cover most of the Internet Explorer configuration options in this chapter, but I leave the settings related to Internet security until Chapter 28, "Security Issues."

Rearranging Toolbars

One of the simplest changes you can make in the appearance of the Internet Explorer window is to rearrange the toolbars. Actually, there's not one toolbar; there are four. The Standard Buttons toolbar contains the navigation buttons (Back, Forward, Stop, Refresh, and Home) along with the Explorer bar buttons (Search, Favorites, and History), and optional buttons for other features such as Fullscreen and Print.

The Address bar is where you type URLs. You can also click its down-arrow button to see a list of recently visited sites you can navigate to. The Links toolbar contains a series of buttons you can use to access individual Web sites. Finally, the Radio toolbar (new in IE5) allows you to listen to world radio stations broadcast over the Internet. This toolbar is available in Internet Explorer only if you install Windows Media Player. You can define a custom list of favorite stations, adjust the volume, and mute the sound. If you want to see the Radio toolbar, right-click any other toolbar and choose Radio from the context menu.

You can choose to display or hide any or all the toolbars. If the Standard Buttons toolbar is visible, for example, you can choose View, Toolbars, Standard Buttons (or just right-click any toolbar) to remove the toolbar from the Internet Explorer window. Repeat the same steps to display it again. There are similar commands for the other toolbars. Choosing View, Toolbars, Customize (or right-click, then Customize) enables you to toggle the text labels that appear on the standard buttons on and off, use only selected (Microsoft-selected) labels to the right of some icons, or adjust the size of the icons. You can also right-click any of the toolbars to toggle them on and off. Using the Customize dialog box, you can also add optional buttons such as Fullscreen or Folders.

At first you will probably need the text labels to identify the buttons on the toolbar. After you get used to using the program, however, you might find that the text labels are superfluous; the icons on each button sufficiently identify their purpose. Without the text labels display, the buttons of the Standard Buttons bar take up only about half as much space onscreen.

You can do more than just decide whether you want to see each of the toolbars. You can also change their positions. Although you can't move the toolbars just anywhere in the Internet Explorer window—they must remain in a horizontal band immediately below the menu bar—you can change the horizontal size of each toolbar and its relative position. To move or resize a toolbar, click its handle (the small vertical bar at the left end of the toolbar) and then drag.

Configuring the Internet Options

The rest of the configuration options I address in this section of the chapter are all contained in the Internet Options dialog box. To open it, choose Tools, Internet Options. Internet Explorer displays the dialog box shown in Figure 2.16. You can also access the same set of options by opening the Control Panel and double-clicking the Internet icon. The dialog box that appears has a slightly different title (Internet Properties), but all the tabs and options are identical to those found in the Internet Options dialog box.

Take a look at the options available in the Internet Options dialog box, beginning with those found on the General tab (refer to Figure 2.16).

FIGURE 2.16

The General tab of the Internet Options dialog box presents an assortment of options.

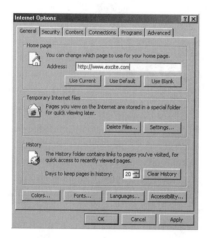

Changing Your Home Page

The first option available on the General tab of the Internet Options dialog box is to define your home page. This is the Web page that loads automatically when you start Internet Explorer or when you click the Home button in the standard toolbar. See the section titled "Customizing Your Start Page," earlier in this chapter, for more about this option.

> **Note:** Note that if you click the Use Blank button, Internet Explorer displays a blank page when you first run IE. If you use a dial-up connection to the Internet, selecting this option has the interesting side effect of preventing Internet Explorer from attempting to establish an Internet connection when you first start the program. Basically, it means that Internet Explorer automatically starts in offline mode. I use this setting on my laptop computer for just that reason.

Temporary Storage

Internet Explorer creates a lot of temporary files. Most of the Web pages and graphics that you view are downloaded and stored in a cache on your hard drive, and Internet Explorer accesses them from there. The files remain in the cache even after you move on to another Web page (or go offline) so that Internet Explorer can retrieve the Web pages quickly when you return to a previously viewed site. The size of the cache is limited, and the oldest temporary files are automatically removed from the cache to make room for newer files.

The buttons in the Temporary Internet files area enable you to control the size and location of the folder Internet Explorer uses for its temporary files and flush out the cache when that becomes necessary. Click the Settings button to open the dialog box shown in Figure 2.17. The four options at the top of the dialog box enable you to specify how often Internet Explorer should check for the existence of a newer version of a given page before loading it from the cache. I prefer to use the artificial intelligence built into the Automatically option under Check for Newer Versions of Stored Pages. It's similar to the Every Visit to the Page option but is more, well, intelligent. It only checks the cache if a page was viewed on a previous day or previous session with IE. Furthermore, if a page is found to be infrequently changed (by the content provider at its Web site), IE will load it more often from the cache. If you *do* want to have IE reload a page that appears to be behind the times, just press F5 to force a refresh of the current page (for example, if a page containing world news displays 1 p.m. and it's now 6 p.m., press F5).

The current location of your temporary Internet files is displayed in the center of the dialog box. The slider enables you to specify the maximum amount of hard drive space Internet Explorer can use for its temporary files. Drag the slider left or right to decrease or increase the space allocation. Click the Move Folder button to open a browse box where you can select another folder to use as the cache for temporary Internet files. Because the cache files can gobble up a lot of disk space, you might want to move the folder off of your c: drive and on to another drive. This can open some much needed hard drive space for Windows and your various applications. If you do decide to move the Temporary Internet Files folder, note that the change won't take effect until you reboot your machine. Click the View Files button to open an Explorer window where you can view the files currently in the cache. Clicking the View Objects button also opens an Explorer window, but this one shows the contents of the Downloaded Programs folder where the ActiveX controls are stored. These are stored permanently so they only need to be downloaded once.

When you want to clean out the cache and get rid of all the temporary files (not controls) Internet Explorer has stored there, click the Delete Files button in the middle of the General tab of the Internet Options dialog box. The Delete Files dialog box appears so that you can confirm your action. The dialog box has one option—a check box that enables you to delete all the subscription content stored on your local hard drive, along with the rest of the temporary Internet files. Generally, you want to delete the temporary files from the cache periodically but keep the subscription content intact.

FIGURE 2.17
*You can define
how much space
on your hard drive
will be devoted to
Internet Explorer's
temporary files.*

History

As I mentioned earlier, Internet Explorer maintains a list of links to the Web sites you've visited recently. The History Explorer bar displays a list of those sites so that you can locate and return to them easily. The History area of the General tab is where you can determine just how long links to the recently viewed sites should remain available. Set the appropriate number of days in the number box. If you want to flush out your History list and start over, click the Clear History button and then click Yes to confirm. Internet Explorer erases all the links in the History folder. Use this option any time the History list starts to get large and cumbersome—or any time you want to erase your tracks so that no one can tell which Web sites you've been visiting. However, IE also leaves several other "traces" that reveal where you've been, such as temporary files, cookies, and so on. So simply cleaning out your History doesn't really erase all your tracks if someone is determined to find out about your surfing.

Text, Background, and Hyperlink Colors

If you feel the need to do some redecorating, click the Colors button at the bottom of the General tab. This opens a Colors dialog box, where you can adjust the default colors for Web page elements. You can adjust the text and background colors in the Colors area on the left. Clicking either button in the Colors area opens a standard Windows Color dialog box where you can click a sample color and then click OK to select that color. Although you can select the text and background colors individually, you'll normally want to check the Use Windows Colors option to instruct Internet Explorer to use the same colors you selected for other Windows 2000 applications.

In the Links area of the Colors dialog box, you can specify separate colors for hypertext links that you've visited and those that you haven't clicked yet. If you check the Use Other Color option, you can specify a third color that IE will use to display a hypertext link when your mouse pointer moves over it.

Fonts

If you want to change the fonts Internet Explorer uses when it displays Web pages, click the Fonts button at the bottom of the General tab to open an unusual Fonts dialog box (it's not the standard Windows 2000 dialog box; see Figure 2.18). First, you can select a language script from the list at the top of the dialog box. Then you can specify separate proportional and fixed-width fonts for that character set by making selections from the corresponding list boxes. Note that the category of "Latin based" fonts include English and Western European languages.

> **Note:** I'm skipping the settings on the Security and Content tabs of the Internet Options dialog box for now, but I'm not ignoring them. I cover those settings in Chapter 28, "Security Issues."

FIGURE 2.18

If you're tired of the same old fonts, you can choose some new ones in this dialog box.

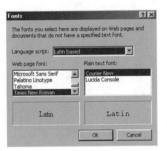

Making a Connection

Click the Connections tab of the Internet Options dialog box to display the settings shown in Figure 2.19. This is where you specify how Internet Explorer should make its connection to the Internet.

Clicking the Setup button reruns the Internet Connection Wizard that you probably saw when you first started Internet Explorer (it's described earlier in this chapter). Generally, you need to run the wizard only once, but it's there if you need it.

Perhaps the most important setting on the Connection tab is the choice between connecting to the Internet using a modem or using a local area network. If you use a proxy server (a network server that controls access to and from the Internet, sometimes called a *firewall*) on your network, you need to check that option in the Proxy Server area and supply the appropriate address and port information. If, on the other hand, you connect to the Internet using a modem, be sure to click the Settings button to open the Dial-Up Settings dialog box. This dialog box contains a number of important settings, such as the Dial-Up Networking connection that Internet Explorer should use when making connections to the Internet. The Properties button enables you to edit the properties of an existing connection if necessary. Most of the other settings are self-explanatory. You can set the number of times Internet Explorer should attempt to make a connection and how long it should wait between each attempt (click Settings, Advanced); you can specify the username, password, and domain to be used to log on; and you can instruct Internet Explorer to disconnect the modem if the connection isn't used for a number of minutes. In order to see the Proxy server area you need to click LAN Settings.

FIGURE 2.19

Here's where you specify how Internet Explorer and Outlook Express should connect to your ISP.

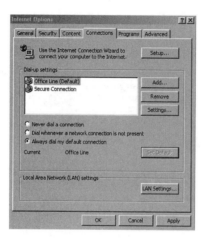

Links to Other Programs

Unlike some other browsers, Internet Explorer doesn't require a whole set of helper applications to display most Web site content. However, Internet Explorer does need to call other programs for major tasks such as handling email. The Programs tab of the Internet Options dialog box, shown in Figure 2.20, is where you identify the programs you want to use to edit HTML source code and process mail, news, Internet calls, Internet calendar appointments, and your contact list. To choose a program for a category, select it from the corresponding drop-down list box. These are the programs Internet Explorer calls when you choose commands such as Mail and News from the Tools menu. You can also call the mail program by clicking the Mail button in the toolbar. Internet Explorer uses the same program to generate and send an email message when you click a mailto: link on a Web page. If you check the option at the bottom of the page, IE5 checks whether it's the default application for viewing Web pages. If not, you see a dialog box when you start the program, giving you the opportunity to make IE5 the default Web viewer. Normally, this is a good thing because it enables you to quickly repair changes that may have been made by some program that you recently installed or ran. If you have Netscape Navigator installed and a similar option enabled in that program, however, the two browsers end up trying to change the default Web page viewer setting back and forth every time you start the programs.

FIGURE 2.20

These are the programs Internet Explorer calls on to handle tasks such as sending email messages.

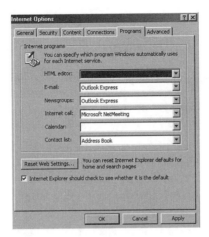

Multimedia and Other Advanced Settings

The Advanced tab of the Internet Options dialog box, shown in Figure 2.21, is misnamed. Despite the large number of options contained in its list box, most of the settings are not particularly advanced. In fact, it's easy to understand what most of the options do, and enabling or disabling an option is as simple as clicking a check box or option button. (Option buttons are radio buttons—choose one of them in a set and the others will be deselected. By contrast, you can select as many check boxes in a group as you want.)

FIGURE 2.21

Despite the large number of options contained in this list box, most of the settings are not particularly advanced.

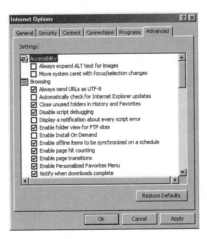

If you're not sure what a particular option does, click the question mark (?) button in the title bar of the dialog box and then click the feature that you're wondering about; a pop-up description of the feature appears.

The options on the Advanced tab are grouped under several broad headings. Because most of the individual options are self-explanatory, seldom used, or both, I don't attempt to describe all of them. Instead, I just describe what kind of options you can expect to find under each heading and mention a few of the ones you're likely to want to change:

- *Browsing*. This is really a catch-all heading for anything remotely related to the process of Web browsing and the user interface of the Internet Explorer browser. Do leave Enable Page Transitions checked so that you can view the cool special effects coming soon to a Web site near you courtesy of the new Dynamic HTML technology.

- *Multimedia*. The options under this heading enable you to select whether Internet Explorer displays graphics and plays animations, videos, and sounds. You want to enable all these options to get the full Web experience, but you might need to disable some of them to speed up browsing over a slow connection.

- *Security*. The default settings for the options under the Security heading are appropriate for most people. The setting you want to pay attention to here is the Cookies option (click Custom Level, then locate the Cookies entry in the list). You can choose one of these options: Permit cookies to be stored on your hard drive or merely permit per-session cookies. Either option permits you to request a prompt prior to permitting any kind of cookie. I address the cookie issue in detail in Chapter 26, "Working with Internet Information Server (IIS)." For now, just note that this is where you set the Cookies option. Cookies are information that is stored by a Web page on your machine. The purpose is generally to save a password so you don't have to type it each time you visit—or to store other custom preferences. Perhaps you modified the Web page and your preference should be stored. Cookies are generally considered harmless.

- *Microsoft VM*. There are three options under the *Microsoft* VM (virtual machine) heading, but the only one you need to concern yourself with is the third (it's checked by default). The second option causes Internet Explorer to keep a log of all Java activities so that you can look at it later if you're having problems related to the Java engine. Unless you're a Java programmer, you probably don't need the Logging option enabled. The third option enables Internet Explorer's built-in Java compiler. You do want that option checked unless you have some special reason for shutting down Java programming.

- *Printing*. The sole option under the Printing header determines whether Internet Explorer includes background colors and images when you print a Web page.

- *Search from the Address bar*. These options determine how Internet Explorer handles searching for the domain name in an URL it failed to find.

Understanding Browser Compatibility Problems

The browser wars certainly haven't done much for compatibility among the products offered by various vendors. The browser marketplace is constantly changing, and the next version of Netscape Navigator might add native support for DTHML, and then again it might not. Only time will tell. Microsoft has included built-in support for JavaScript and Java applets in Internet Explorer, however. But, for now, if you're a Web developer, you've got to confine your programming of the sometimes highly useful DHTML technology to *intranets*, because a percentage of people on the Internet use Netscape, and it cannot deal with DHTML.

DHTML has just one problem area: The browsers even differ in the way they handle certain HTML tags, which are the very foundation of Web pages. Navigator, for example, implements plug-in support using a tag that Internet Explorer doesn't recognize. On the other hand, Internet Explorer supports specialty tags such as the background sound tag that Navigator ignores. Suffice it to say that testing every Web page using both browsers and then figuring out why one page won't work with a certain browser is a major expenditure of time for Webmasters. Do the problems end there? No, that's really only the beginning. There are differences in the browsers' implementations of scripting languages, such as JavaScript, and more. There are even differences between versions of the same browser for different languages and platforms.

Given the politically charged environment of software development, you can almost understand some of the differences in implementation between browsers. It's the differences in product strategy that have helped or hindered software developers from day one.

The very nature of the Internet supposes that everyone can use the information that a Web site provides—not just a fortunate few. Although it might not be possible (or even reasonable) to expect complete access to every site by every individual, it's important to make the effort. Unfortunately, browser incompatibilities make this nearly impossible.

Some Webmasters have handled this situation by adding alternate text to their sites. If your browser doesn't support graphics for whatever reason, for example, you might see some text that says you would be seeing a picture of a house if your browser could display it. This is a reasonable attempt to make the site more accessible to everyone, but let's face it: Seeing some text that tells you about the house isn't the same as actually seeing it. The HTML element that displays graphics includes an optional `ALT="This is a picture of Maria Richardson holding a peach"` attribute that enables a Web programmer to include a narrative for those who can't see the graphic, which includes blind people who must rely on such text descriptions (blind people can use a special text-to-speech utility to "hear" the text on their computer screen).

Another form of browser incompatibility repair by Webmasters is the "Best when viewed by" icons that they're using. This little icon tells the person visiting a site that the site works best with a certain browser. It's kind of frustrating to view a site designed for Internet Explorer when you have Netscape Navigator (or vice versa), but at least knowing that there isn't a problem with your software is a bit of a comfort.

By now you're perhaps wondering what all this has to do with you as a user. It means that you're going to be limited by browser incompatibilities of all kinds until browser vendors start to adhere to standards. You might even need to keep two or more browsers installed on your machine if you spend a lot of time on the Internet. At times I need the information that a site will provide, and if that means using a different browser, that's the price to pay for the information. There's no magic bullet that transforms a single browser machine into something that can access every site on the Internet—at least not as of this writing. However, it does seem that Internet Explorer displays what you need to see virtually all the time.

Will this multiple browser situation last forever? I don't think so. Right now the Internet is in a state of growth. The various standards bodies are working to create new standards that address the needs people have expressed for content. Eventually, there will be a standard for VRML. You'll also eventually see a standard for ActiveX (provided that Microsoft keeps its promise and releases ActiveX to a standards body). Netscape is planning on loosening its hold on JavaScript as well. If it does so before too many versions get released on the market, we'll also probably end up with a standardized scripting language. Unfortunately, all this standardization takes time. And, by that time, we'll probably be into the next big thing. Perhaps quantum computing (just kidding).

On Your Own

Configure Internet Explorer 5 and then go online and look around. Specifying a default home page is usually a good place to start, but don't limit your choices.

Build a list of favorite Web sites. Don't forget to include Internet search sites such as Lycos.

Install several browsers on your machine to see how they work on various Internet sites. As a minimum, try both Netscape Navigator and Internet Explorer. You can download a free trial copy of Netscape Navigator at `http://www.netscape.com/computing/download/index.html?cp=hom07tdow`.

Note: The latest version of Netscape Communicator (4.7) includes Navigator. You cannot purchase Navigator as a separate application like you could with earlier versions.

Make sure you try out some of the add-ons such as the sound-enhancing Real Audio Player (`http://www.realaudio.com/`) for both browsers. Although Navigator does make heavier use of plug-ins than Internet Explorer does, both products benefit from third-party add-ons. If you're curious, give them both a run for your money. See which user interface is superior and which is more customizable. Do you like Netscape's email utility as much as Outlook Express?

Try several different kinds of Internet searches, progressing from simple to advanced. Learn the difference between searching for precise phrases and using a loose search for the words you specify (they can be in any order). See what happens when you put quotes around a phrase you're searching for. What happens when you omit the quotes? Compare the results of the same search using different engines. Some engines, such as Google, now even claim to make highly intelligent distinctions to assist you in narrowing down the number of hits.

Create a logical hierarchy in your Favorites list (or as Netscape calls it, the *Bookmarks list*). Create folders and even use duplicate entries if that's useful.

What's New in Windows 2000

Windows 2000 is, by definition, Microsoft's most advanced operating system to come to the public to date. Sure, there might be (and, in fact, likely *are*) more futuristic operating systems being tested in the Advanced Systems Labs or whatever they call it in Redmond. The pure theorists at Microsoft doubtless take systems to great distances in the testing labs—interplanetary distances.

But what people here on earth want, and business needs, are computers they can count on day in and day out—reliable, scalable, and secure. Windows 2000 has been more widely tested, by more beta testers for a longer period of time, than any software product in history. You hold the results in your hands.

Major improvements over previous versions of Windows (NT and others) include automatic DNS configuration, COM+ integration (although this is primarily a server technology), terminal services integration, improved security, setup and upgrade enhancements, larger disk volumes, Active Directory, USB (Universal Serial Bus) support, Plug and Play, user interface improvements, Zip drive support, DVD support, ActiveX version 7, dynamic disk partition resizing, DLL version checking, support for physical memory greater than 4GB (up to 64GB in some configurations), easier overall management, and many security enhancements.

This book covers all that's new in Windows 2000 in depth; chapter by chapter, you'll see what you need to know to take this operating system to its full potential. Nevertheless, if you're interested in an overview of the advances and special features of Windows 2000, this chapter is for you. Let's start with what most of us notice first and use most often—the user interface.

Improvements to the Interface

First, a brief history of Windows (two paragraphs). Moving from DOS to Windows remains the single biggest leap in computer user-interface history: from black and white to color, from text based to graphics, from keyboard to keyboard plus mouse. It was a giant leap for computer users. Yet, early versions of Windows were, to put it politely, lame. They were slow, clumsy, inconsistent, not all that attractive, one-dimensional, and inclined to crash for no good reason. Windows 3.1 was probably the first good, usable version.

The transition from Windows 3.1 to Windows 95 was another major leap forward: It had better graphics, more stability, and usability testing ironed out many of its kinks. Windows NT was a significant departure in itself, bifurcating off from the "consumer" versions (Windows 3.1 and 95), it offered rather poor game facilities (most of them didn't run), and it was relatively slow—at least in displaying menus, directories, and the like. However, it could handle larger jobs (more data and more people), support relatively robust networking, was less likely to crash (it's version of a general collapse was the dreaded *blue screen*, where you saw a data dump on a simple, deceptively calming blue background—fortunately blue screen incidents are rare nowadays), and was more secure. Now with Windows 2000, you get all the attractive and efficient user-interface features of Windows 95/98, plus the strength and steadiness of the NT system. Security, stability, strength—businesses need these features more than they need pretty user interfaces. With Windows 2000, though, you can have the best of both worlds. (Well, the list of files in a directory takes longer to display than in Windows 95/98, but there must be *some* tradeoffs.)

Move To, Copy To

What's new in the Windows 2000 user interface? My favorite feature is that when you look at the Explorer toolbar, you don't see Cut and Copy buttons anymore. Instead, they've been replaced with the more usable Move To and Copy To buttons. Why? Because when you use a Cut feature, what you're really trying to do is *move* something (otherwise, you'd use Delete). So, instead of the two, wasteful steps of Cut and Paste, you now have Move To. What's more, when you do click Move To, you immediately see a file browser dialog box so you can locate where you want to move the file to (you can even create a new folder), as shown in Figure 3.1.

FIGURE 3.1

This unique Browse For Folder dialog box pops up when you click the new Move To button.

The Copy To feature is similar, except after you move the copy of the file to a new location, the original remains as well. Again, though, that same useful Browse For Folder dialog box appears, making the job of finding a target location for the file easy while not messing up your current location in Explorer.

Autocomplete

Microsoft had promised that NT's user interfaces will become increasingly *adaptive* and "auto everything." One thing Microsoft might mean by that is the new Autocomplete File/Folder Selection feature. Here's how this works: After you use Windows 2000 six times, it starts to display folders and files that you use most often. It doesn't display the entire Start, Programs list—instead, you see a little symbol of two arrows pointing downward (a double chevron), indicating that some of the programs and folders have been hidden from you. You must then click the down arrows to see the rest of the items, or if you wait three seconds, the currently selected folder will automatically expand. As you can see in Figure 3.2, these little double down-arrow symbols can appear in more than one menu and can also appear on the Favorites menu.

Figure 3.2

Some people might like the new autocomplete menu system, which shows you only a part of your Start button's file/folder contents or only one or two of your Favorites. Notice the helpful little cartoon balloon explanation, lest you panic.

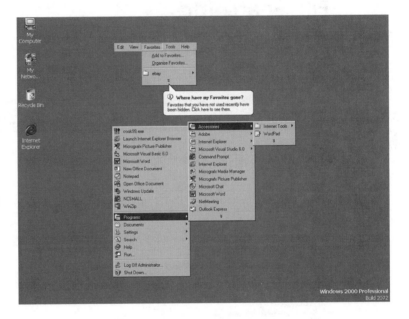

The idea behind autocomplete is that Windows 2000 can keep track of your most frequently accessed files and folders (or most recently accessed Favorites) and therefore know what you probably need to see. That's why it takes six sessions before going into effect; it's learning your preferences. Not all people like this feature. To turn it off, right-click on the bottom menu bar and select Properties. In the dialog box, uncheck the box Use Personalized Menus. I'm one of those users who leaves the Explorer's view set to Details because I like to see everything at once.

Tip: There is a Use Autocomplete option in the Registry, but it's for the feature in Internet Explorer 5 that completes URLs and other data you've previously typed in. For example, if you type Mic in the Address bar, you'll see a drop-down list box that includes all previous URLs you've typed in that begin with those three letters.

The menu options change over time as your file and folder usage changes. The claim is that this feature makes it easier for users to quickly locate frequently used objects, without having to search through lengthy menus and submenus.

File Searching

The search utility has been changed to take on the new Explorer-type interface. Click Start, Search, For Files or Folders and you'll see the redesigned Find utility shown in Figure 3.3.

FIGURE 3.3
The search utility has a new face.

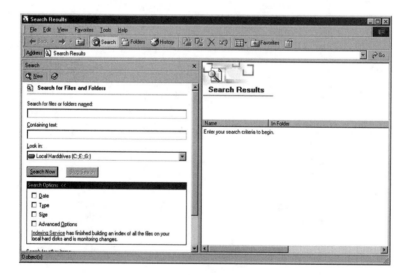

When you're searching for a particular document that contains, say, *Aunt Audrey* in its text, but you can't remember the filename, this utility is just the ticket. When you want to see all versions of the JanuaryCash*.DOC file, this is where you search for them.

One difference is that there is no Browse button in the new utility. Although this may present a hitch in the user interface, this utility is meant to be a general search of your computer. This is actually just an extension of your new Explorer window. If you were attempting to find a file in a specific directory, you now just browse there and click on the Search button on your menu bar. Or for other users you can just type the path in which you wish to search.

Pictures Everywhere

People who work with graphics will appreciate several new features. You can display thumbnails (choose View, Thumbnails in Explorer) for each supported graphics file (including .HTM Internet pages) in any folder. Also, if you enable Web content (Tools, Folder Options), you'll see preview images on the left side of the folder. You can display a large thumbnail of the selected file in a folder by right-clicking the folder and choosing Customize This Folder from the context menu. Use the wizard to choose HTML Template and the Image Preview template. You can view and edit graphics in the Imaging for Windows accessory (Start, Programs, Accessories, Imaging).

Also, in addition to the My Documents folder, there's now a My Pictures folder for graphics files (it's inside My Documents). It automatically provides a nice large preview—including the ability to zoom it or see it full screen—of any image you store in this folder (see Figure 3.4). Try clicking the Zoom button and then clicking somewhere within the preview of the graphic. These features mean you don't have to load a graphic into your image-editing application just to see it. Also, if you're using the NTFS file system, you can type in a text description of the graphic.

FIGURE 3.4

Locating or organizing graphics files is easy with the new high-resolution preview you get of any selected file.

The number of type of data files you can view using thumbnails is partly dependent on the applications you use. Not all file types are recognized by the thumbnail viewer, and the way your images are saved many produce different results in how the images are viewed.

Language Advances

Windows 2000 boasts improved support for languages other than English (although 85% of current computing on the Internet is English, and English, like Latin before it, seems likely to become the default mode of communication of the connected classes). Windows 2000's primary novelty in the languages area is an international character set that permits users to view and edit documents in 64 different languages. Administrators, however, must specifically add third-party add-on utilities and set up localized versions of Windows to serve international clients.

Application Compatibility

The big news in application compatibility is that Microsoft has made every effort to improve the overall stability of the Windows 2000 system. There's an improved application installation engine. Worried about your existing applications not working if you migrate to Windows 2000? Don't. All my applications, with one exception, worked perfectly. And I expect that exception to be working by the time Windows 2000 ships commercially. The new installation engine does improve things, but it also requires that some applications be modified. Microsoft has stated that Windows 2000 must be the most reliable version of Windows ever sold. To make that possible, applications must toe the line.

There are now standardized installation APIs (application programming interfaces) in the operating system, and with them, Windows 2000 can, itself, effectively govern the way applications are installed and uninstalled. Naturally, this is possible only with newly installed applications. However, it's nice to have all setup and removal under one protocol. In addition, the new APIs include an installation-on-demand capability. This feature means that when someone sends you a document file (but you don't have its application installed on your machine), if the setup for that application is available on the network, the application can be automatically installed on your local computer. Also, optional additional elements of the application (such as tutorials and templates) can be automatically downloaded from the server as requested.

Hardware Compatibility

Reports are that the hardware requirements for Windows 2000 Professional are roughly double those of Windows 95: at least 64MB of memory and a 233MHz Pentium, minimum. However, as usual, Microsoft's official minimum hardware power specs are somewhat lower: 166MHz Pentium with 32MB of RAM.

To ensure maximum peripheral compatibility, Microsoft and hardware vendors have been working overtime to certify device drivers in the little-known Windows Hardware Quality Lab. Also, Windows 2000 drivers can now be signed digitally and, therefore, automatically loaded by the system over the Internet. (Presumably if you give permission first for this automation. I wouldn't!)

Of course, the really big news in hardware compatibility is Plug and Play. This feature notices when you install a new device (and power on) and, usually successfully, gets the right driver for it, assigns it to the right port, assigns IRQs correctly, and avoids conflicts with your other peripherals. In my experience, Plug and Play is working surprisingly well at this stage in the development of Windows 2000. In addition, the Plug and Play Manager now tries to work out conflicts—assigning and reallocating resources such as I/O ports, IRQs, and memory as necessary. Plus, the new Computer Management consolidates what used to be a variety of utilities located in a variety of places. (Take a look at Start, Settings, Control Panel, Administrative Tools, Computer Management). This new snap-in console is where you can observe and configure all hardware and software, including network options. Also, device management can now be administered using a single tool. You can detect a problem (such as an IRQ conflict or a SCSI ID problem) and repair it within the same utility. Accomplishing this in NT 4 required the navigation of several menus and several interfaces.

Setup and Migration

I found that upgrading my NT 4 machine to Windows 2000 was essentially automatic. All I had to do was put in the Windows 2000 CD, answer a couple of questions, and walk away. It *did* take over an hour, but I didn't have to intervene at all. Also, all my applications, settings, and everything else were preserved perfectly—down to the most recent changes to my Inbox and Address Book. A few things were different, though. The Links bar on Internet Explorer had been overwritten, but I think that's by design. Now the question is, if it's all that automatic, why Chapter 4, "Installing Windows 2000 Professional: A Setup Primer"? Because things don't always go that easy for everyone, so you need to know what to do if something does go wrong. Also, I explain how to perform a clean installation—from a reformatted hard drive.

Things might not go as smoothly for you as they did for me (it *was* wonderful for me!). Installation efficiency depends quite a bit on the kind of system that you have. The better the computer, the more contemporary the peripherals and the less software that is already installed, the better the installation will go.

In any case, Microsoft has said its goal was to make Windows 2000 setup the best, most trouble-free operating system installation ever. I think Microsoft has done it. The migration path is rather wide, including systems running FAT32 on Windows 95 or 98, NT 3.51, NT Workstation 4 (of course), and also Windows 3.*x* systems. (However, because Windows 3.*x* machines do not support domains, network settings must be configured manually during installation for this leap between operating systems). The only possible oddball is NT 3.1. You first have to move from it up to NT 4 (or 3.51) before you can make the final trip to Windows 2000.

Upgrading from a previous OS is faster than a clean install, just as upgrading from a CD is faster than from disk. Is Windows 2000 fat? Yes, it's bigger than any previous OS, and more files are copied to your hard drive. However, if it's your job to migrate a whole office of workstations to Windows 2000, consider automating the process even further using the scripting capabilities (Host) available in Windows 2000 (see Appendix A, "Using the Scripting Host with Windows 2000 Professional").

Multimedia

Windows 2000 will include DirectX 7.0, making it every bit the multimedia player that its other Windows cousins have been for some time. Games particularly benefit from the various ways DirectX permits *direct* contact with hardware—for added speed and flexibility. For an in-depth discussion of DirectX 7, see Chapter 19, "Windows 2000 Multimedia."

This, along with the OpenGL 1.1 API, promises great graphics. OpenGL encapsulates geometric data and can handle multiple textures dynamically. If you want to develop high-performance, high-resolution graphics applications (modeling, animation, CAD/CAM, simulations, and so on), OpenGL assists you in reaching your goals.

The new version of OpenGL boasts a beefy rendering pipeline that's two to four times faster than the previous OpenGL standard. Among other things, this provides improved frame rates when using texture objects.

Mobile Computing

Windows 2000 supports both Plug and Play and power management—features that laptop users want but were not part of the original NT 4 offerings. Plug and Play is valuable because you can swap cards as well as hot-dock your portable into your desktop when you get back from a trip. Lots of travelers spend part of their time on the local area network (in house or via modem) and the rest of their time working offline. Naturally, this behavior creates a version problem—users want the latest versions of files they work on, no matter *where* they work on them. Windows 95 offered a Briefcase utility to help synchronize desktop and laptop files.

Replacing Briefcase is the more powerful and effective Synchronization Manager in Windows 2000. Choose Tools, Synchronize in Explorer (you can choose either Explorer, Windows, or Internet). You see the Synchronization Manager in Figure 3.5.

You can choose to automate the synchronization or do it manually. In either case, you can specify files or folders you want to maintain the latest versions of and then let Windows 2000 worry about which file or folder is the newer version. You govern when your offline files are synchronized with files on the network. Here are your choices:

- Every time you log on or off your computer (or both)
- At specific times
- At specific intervals

FIGURE 3.5

The new Synchronization Manager replaces the less-capable Briefcase utility as a way of dealing with the version problem.

How does it work? The Synchronization Manager compares files or folders stored on the network with any files or folders you updated (or even merely opened) while working offline. The Manager then removes any older versions, leaving the most recent version available on both your laptop as well as on the network. You can also choose to synchronize offline Web pages.

If you're concerned about security—strangers in strange buildings peeping at your data while you're in a meeting or something—you can either remember to keep your laptop with you at all times or take advantage of Windows 2000's Encrypted File System (EFS) feature. You can specify that particular files or folders be encrypted, and they can only be decrypted via the proper public key. Don't be fooled by the word *public.* The idea of *public key encryption* is that, in theory, someone can know the key but still cannot decrypt the message. This level of security should suffice, unless you're highly placed in the government.

As for power, Windows 2000 supports both Advanced Power Management (APM) and also the Advanced Configuration and Power Interface (ACPI)—a new set of specifications supported by some of the latest machines. ACPI provides previously unheard of control over a computer's power management features. However, not many existing laptops feature ACPI, so to use the new power management facilities of Windows 2000, users will want to upgrade their laptops' BIOSes.

Tip: BIOS-related power management problems aren't limited to laptops. My desktop computer required a BIOS upgrade before I was able to get some of these Windows 2000 features to work. And before the BIOS upgrade, I was having some pretty weird problems that didn't appear to be related to power management.

Accessories

Windows has always offered a generous suite of free applications and utilities. Here's the list of what are sometimes called *accessories* that come bundled with Windows 2000:

- Address Book—Your Outlook Express list of contacts.

- Backup—The Windows 2000 backup, restore, and emergency repair utilities.

- Calculator—A virtual adding machine, plus other math functions.

- CD Player—Play music from your computer.

- Certificates—A way to "ensure" (if that's ever possible) the security of communication when data is sent across non-secure lines, like the Internet.

- Character Map—A window where you can select from a grid of special characters to insert into your documents (like the circumflex).

- Computer Management—This utility includes many Windows 2000 administrative tools in a single utility. It's available from within the Control Panel (double-click the Administrative Tools icon), not on the Start submenus. Many utilities found elsewhere in Windows NT 4 have been gathered into this single, all-encompassing, rather broad collection.

- Device Manager—This one resolves port conflicts and does many other things. It is one of the utilities now in the Computer Management collection. See the previous item.

- Disk Cleanup—This one helps you delete unneeded files to get more free space on your hard drive. It searches your hard drive for .TMP and other temporary files that you can get rid of without any problems. You get to this on the Start submenus (Start, Programs, Accessories, System Tools).

- Disk Defragmenter—Similar to Disk Cleanup (same path), but this one reconnects files that are broken into pieces. It makes them again contiguous. They load faster that way, and can take up less space as well.

- Dr. Watson—This creates a .LOG file (drwatson.log) that contains information about a program that caused problems with the operating system (it closed, but in a bad way such as creating a memory leak.)

- DVD Player—Plays the newest storage medium.

- Event Viewer—Find this in Administrative Tools. It keeps logs about security, application, and system events. You can use these logs to try to solve hardware or software problems, or check on security issues.

- Fax Service Management—Use this utility to specify security permissions, set fax priorities, and other properties such as how many times the phone rings before answering.

- FreeCell—A game. I don't care for it myself.

- Group Policy—This is an administrator's main utility to give or refuse permissions to users who belong to domains, organizational units or sites. See Chapter 28.

- HyperTerminal—HyperTerminal is a way to connect to various locations (BBSs or Internet sites) via modem, or to connect two computers together via a null modem cable.
- Imaging—A utility from Kodak for working with photographs. It works with both normal and thumbnail views; allows you to annotate photos; and can perform basic visual manipulations on graphics files or fax documents. It accepts input from scanners and digital cameras, too.
- Indexing Service—A nice new utility that creates a very rapidly searched database of any of your folders. Give it a try.
- Internet Explorer—The premier Internet browser, independent critics agree.
- IP Security Policy Management—See Chapter 28. This snap-in (Internet Protocol) is an important component of Windows 2000 security—designed to encrypt data sent over networks or the Internet, and thereby guard against hackers.
- Local Users and Groups—With this utility you can modify groups: adding or removing users; disabling accounts and other security moves. See Chapter 28.
- Magnifier—A utility that magnifies the part of the screen under the mouse pointer, or under the component that currently has the focus. For visually challenged users.
- Minesweeper—Remember this game from school?
- NetMeeting—A way to "conference call" over the Internet.
- Notepad—The old standby for quick notes and quick viewing of text files. Still useful after all these years.
- Outlook Express—The premier mail and news browser, many agree.
- Paint—If you don't have any other graphics application, use this to view, and edit, graphics files.
- Phone Dialer—Place a call semiautomatically.
- Pinball—The game.
- Private Character Editor—This is a new one. Use it to design logos or other custom characters to add to your font library. To run it, choose Start, Run, then type eudcedit.
- Removable Storage—Manages tape, optical disk, and other backup media.
- Security Configuration and Analysis—This tool takes a cold look at your security setup. It scans your tactics and recommends improvements.
- Services—Another MMC snap-in. Use it to specify recovery behavior for failed services, and add descriptions and modify the names of services.
- Shared Folders—A security feature. Administrators or Power Users can give or deny users on other machines access to specified folders.
- Solitaire—Do you need a description?
- Sound Recorder—A utility that lets you set specifications for recording, or edit, mix, and play sounds.

- Synchronization Manager—Use this to ensure that you're avoiding the version problem—more than one copy of the same file on your portable or workstation and the network. Which is the latest and which should be deleted? The Manager can be set to automatically synchronize at intervals you specify.

- System Information—A list of specifications that describe your system. Hardware resources, drivers, and such are all described. Useful for tracking down problems.

- Telnet—This is a utility to assist you in using Telnet, a protocol used to connect to TCP/IP networks and other remote computers.

- Windows Media Player—Plays video and audio.

- Windows Task Manager—Shows currently running applications and their status. Can be used to shut down a frozen application. Press Ctrl+Alt+Del, and then click the Task Manager button.

- Windows Update—A feature whose time has come. Microsoft calls its ongoing process of fixing bugs and improving its products *continuous reinvention*. To you, the user, that means that a better driver might now be available for your Microsoft Word spell-checker, or a feature of Windows 2000 might now run faster. Windows Update connects to an Internet site, scans your computer for out-of-date drivers and other old software, and then asks if you want them automatically updated with the latest and greatest versions. Use this.

- WordPad—More features than Notepad, fewer than Word. An in-between word processor. Used mostly when you want a quick view of a text file that's too large to fit into Notepad.

Many of these appear on the Start, Programs, Accessories menu, but others (such as Windows Update on the Internet Explorer Tools menu) only appear in special locations (the Control Panel, for example).

Disk Management and Printer Services

Windows 2000 boasts the new Windows NT File System (NTFS) version 5.0. Among the major improvements are the ability to specify disk quotas for each user and also to locate files by owner. You can employ a user's security ID (SID) to see all his or her documents and use the bulk Access Control List (ACL) to find out which files the user has permission to access. As an administrator, you can specify limits to what each user can do with each file or folder. (In NT 4, administrators could only set permissions on folders, not individual files.) Likewise, administrators can now limit the disk space allowed each user in which to store files.

Several new Microsoft Management Console (MMC) snap-ins improve disk drive management. There's the Dynamic Volume Management feature with which you can enlarge an existing volume dynamically—users need not log off because no reformatting is necessary, nor does the server need to be restarted. You can also configure and observe the drives and volumes on remote servers from within the MMC. Data protection is improved with the Hierarchical Storage Management (HSM) feature—use it to back up or offload rarely used files to tape or some other backup medium. HSM works only with two tiers or two devices. It has drivers for DAT, DLT, and autoloaders.

Advances on the network printer front have also been achieved. There's a new feature called Point and Print (AutoPublish) that can install a printer driver automatically on a client PC from any application. If a user chooses File, Print in Access, for instance, and then browses the network for a particular printer, Windows 2000 will automatically install the appropriate driver on that user's workstation.

Improved Security Protocols

Moving from the proprietary security system in NT 4, Windows 2000's security is based on Kerberos, a protocol developed at MIT. Kerberos boasts the important safeguard that when a user authenticates himself or herself, it's no longer necessary for the user's password to be sent through the network or even stored on a local machine. Rather, the user is given a unique key at logon from the KDC (Key Distribution Center), a central security authority on the domain controller. Each time thereafter when that user asks for a network service (such as to open a file located on the server), Kerberos uses the unique key to contact the KDC. If the KDC authenticates the key, it then sends a "ticket" to the user that permits a connection to the requested service. This ticket is stored locally on the user's computer and can be used repeatedly if needed to connect to the particular service that the ticket was created for. Reuse of the ticket does not require the intervention of the KDC. Keys have a time limit (normally eight hours).

A secondary advantage of using Kerberos is that it gives outsiders access to your network in ways you can trust and therefore permit. For instance, the Kerberos system has been employed on UNIX installations for several years. Therefore, UNIX Kerberos users can be authenticated and allowed into the Windows system. Another secure portal for outsiders: They can use digital certificates and get into your network (with your permission) through Virtual Private Networks (VPNs). With certificates and improving standards such as IPSec (IP Security Protocol, an encrypted version of IP), Windows 2000 opens safe doors into your local network for outsiders to access. With these precautions in place, you can even send encrypted files over the Internet, without (much) fear. If you're not quite ready to go the certificate route, you can retain a current PPTP (Point-to-Point Tunneling Protocol) or upgrade to Layer 2 Tunneling Protocol (L2TP) or IPSec—both of which are included in Windows 2000.

The Active Directory: Brave, New Architectures

One of the most widely anticipated and widely discussed elements of Windows 2000 is the Active Directory and the related IntelliMirror technology. Both servers and workstations must be upgraded to Windows 2000 for these features to work, so administrators will likely want to get rid of any legacy workstations. The Registries in Windows 95/98 and Windows 2000 are different enough that it's not easy to create a common policy management system that will work on both platforms. Likewise, applications, too, must be made compliant with the IntelliMirror technology for that technology to do everything it's capable of doing (read on). With those caveats in mind, the Active Directory does promise to eventually solve several problems for both users and network administrators.

The idea of Active Directory is to create a distributed directory system that can help large organizations better manage their networking—better structure, maintenance, and access. Technically, the Active Directory is a hierarchical, object-based directory service. Its primary goal is the efficient management of users, groups, and other network resources.

Active Directory offers a single repository for management information for a complete corporate network. In this way, it's similar to Novell's Novell Directory Services. The Active Directory includes a specialized feature named IntelliMirror that permits users to roam from machine to machine but still retain all the customization information about their particular desktop settings, applications, and documents. It frees users from being bound to a single physical machine. A user can now log on to any Windows 2000 computer and see everything right away as if the new machine were their own workstation. A side benefit of storing desktop/application configurations on the server is that an administrator will have a far easier time restoring people's personal settings after they lose a laptop, a systemic crash occurs, or some other event damages or destroys a user's Registry and applications.

Another benefit of IntelliMirror is that the group policy-editing tool permits an administrator to forbid users from changing configuration settings on a desktop and then rebooting. An application distribution utility creates a connection between users and the applications they use frequently. When a user logs on, IntelliMirror looks up the user profile and sends those applications to the workstation where the user just logged in. Of course, an administrator can prevent as well as permit this downloading of applications.

Domains remain the primary organizational concept in Active Directory. Domains continue to be used as the defining boundaries for replication, security, and general administration. Domains are now more advanced, though, in Windows 2000: They can be thought of as hierarchical trees with many branches. The Windows 2000 domains can be much larger than previously; nevertheless, even a large network installation should probably define multiple domains. This reduces replication between domain controllers (every controller must maintain a copy of the entire domain directory). Traffic is generated by replication updates between domain replicas.

Administrators will appreciate the new Active Directory Manager when managing users and groups and working with other services such as printers. Backup domain controllers (BDCs) have been replaced by Active Directory replicas, which keep in sync with each other using update sequence numbers (USNs). Any problems are worked out by merely using whatever update has the latest timestamp.

On Your Own

Take a look at the user interface. Are its elements familiar to you? If they're not, turn to Chapter 5, "Exploring the Interface" to get acclimated.

Run the Search utility (Start, Search, For Files or Folders). See if you think the utility works as you would like it to. Also try clicking the Advanced tab to get a taste of the new Indexing Service.

Try displaying thumbnails (choose View, Thumbnails in Explorer) to see previews of graphics files (including .HTM Internet pages) in any folder.

Make a list of the items you see on the Windows 2000 user interface that you don't understand. Then turn to the index to find out what they can do for you.

Installing Windows 2000 Professional: A Setup Primer

This chapter focuses on installing Windows 2000 Professional. Because this is an entirely new version of the operating system, we'll assume that most of you are performing either a new installation or an upgrade from an older version of the Windows operating system, such as Windows NT 4 or Windows 95/98. However, even if you've installed Windows 2000 Professional in the past, you can rerun Windows 2000 setup any time you want. You can use a reinstallation to repair a suspect or wobbling Windows 2000 operating system.

And just because the operating system is operating doesn't mean that you might not want to modify it in some way. If your original installation was done at the factory where your computer was assembled, or if an administrator installed it, for example, you might want to add (or remove) some features that were originally specified. Perhaps you want to add the Briefcase or WordPad utilities. Beyond that, you might find that a complete reinstallation or a Registry cleaning will improve how quickly Windows 2000 does its various jobs (see the section titled "Reinstalling or Scouring the Registry?" at the end of this chapter).

> **Tip:** To find out which optional Windows 2000 components aren't installed on your machine, click Start, Settings, Control Panel, Add/Remove Programs. Then, when the dialog box appears, click Add/Remove Windows Components. This starts the Windows Components Wizard. Click Next, and you'll see a scrollable list of the major categories of Windows 2000 components. If a check box is checked and white, that means all the components in that category are installed. If a check box is unchecked, none of those components are installed. If a check box is checked but gray, some of those components are installed. Also see the section titled "Special Utility Installation," later in this chapter.

If you're about to install Windows 2000, these next few sections are for you. I'm often surprised at just how little emphasis some people put on the installation of their software. Many people—including me—got the idea somewhere along the way that the installation of Windows 2000 was essentially automatic: You'd stick a CD into the drive, type a command (or double-click an icon, or just wait for the Windows 2000 Autorun feature to kick in and display a menu), and then forget about anything other than merely waiting for the process to finish. This is the way software installation *should* work, for the most part, but it doesn't.

The reality is somewhat different from the theory. I recently spent half an hour configuring a piece of software for installation and another 15 minutes installing it from the CD-ROM. Software now comes with so many different configuration options because some people want bells and whistles, and others don't.

But there's a dark side to this profusion of features. Suppose that you're a network administrator (perhaps you don't need to try supposing too hard, because you are one). How many weeks would you spend installing some feature-rich software on the company network of about 100 machines if each installation takes an hour and 15 minutes (assuming, of course, that the installation on each machine went perfectly and that you worked eight hours a day)? You're looking at a minimum of three weeks—just for one application! Now, suppose that you must install all the applications required by each machine, in addition to a copy of Windows 2000. This is one of the major reasons that the move from Windows 3.x to Windows 95/98 or Windows NT hasn't been faster than it was. To its credit, Windows 2000 does provide some methods to automate the installation process, but the transition still takes a lot of time for most network administrators.

My previous installation experiences were still fresh in my mind as I tore open my copy of Windows 2000. I was relieved to find that although Windows 2000 still isn't as easy to install as Windows 95 or 98, Microsoft has taken large strides in making the installation experience at least a bit more tolerable. One of the major new features of Windows 2000 that makes it a lot easier to use than Windows NT is that it supports Plug and Play. This means that you'll spend a lot less time telling Windows 2000 what hardware you have on your machine (provided that Windows 2000 has the required support in the form for drivers and INF files, which are explained later in the chapter). Partially offsetting the new speed advantages of Plug and Play, though, is the wealth of new product features you'll have to wade through. For example, you now must decide whether you want to install Microsoft Message Queue (MSMQ) support for things such as disconnected applications (those used on the road without a connection to the server), among other things.

Caution: Windows 2000 is an entirely new operating system, in many respects. It provides support for both Plug and Play and the Windows Driver Model (WDM) . In addition, there's a myriad of new low-level features, such as Windows NT File System Version 5 (NTFS 5) , to worry about. What this means to you is that you can't use old Windows NT drivers to get Windows 2000 to recognize a piece of hardware. If the Windows 2000 package doesn't provide the support you need, you'll need to check with the vendor for updated drivers. Unfortunately, while Windows 2000 gives you a few ambiguous warnings about using those old Windows NT drivers, it doesn't really check what you're doing. The end result is that you can potentially install those old drivers without hearing much from Windows 2000. When you reboot your machine, there's a chance (a very slight one) that the operating system won't start because of the "foreign" driver. In short, it's probably better to get rid of those old Windows NT drivers rather than take a chance that someone will use them by mistake.

Before you go much further, let's get a few important items out of the way. If you're installing the upgrade version of Windows 2000 to your system, you need to install one of the following operating systems first. (Fortunately, the standalone version doesn't require any kind of preinstalled software.) The upgrade version of Windows 2000 looks for these operating systems as a prerequisite to starting the installation process:

- Windows 95/98
- Windows NT 3.51/4 (or above)

You also need to do a quick check of your hardware. Microsoft has a list of minimum hardware specifications, but I don't think you'll want to use them. The problem is that the "minimum" system description is really low; it's too minimal to get any reasonable kind of performance. If you want a system that really works with Windows 2000, use the following parameters:

- **Pentium or higher processor**—Don't even try anything less than a 350MHz processor; otherwise, you'll be very disappointed with the results you get. For the most part, if you're running business applications, you'll want a Pentium II/III processor under the hood before you install Windows 2000.

- **128MB memory minimum**—Really think about increasing your memory to 256MB (or even 512MB, which is what I use) as soon as possible. However, even a 64MB system will get the job done (albeit very, very slowly).

- **5GB of free hard disk space**—Actually, this is just a rough estimate for a machine that's used for basic business computing at the time of this writing. You'll definitely need to include a hefty amount of space for Windows 2000 and its associated applications, such as Internet Explorer (Microsoft recommends setting aside a minimum of 650MB for the operating system and operating system-specific features). Office 2000 consumes even more space than its predecessor does, and most businesses have one or two custom applications today. In addition, you still must consider the storage requirements for your data. In short, you may very well need more than 5GB if you plan to install a lot of applications on your system.

- **High-density 3 1/2-inch floppy disk**—Everyone who installs Windows 2000 will want to create an emergency boot disk. You need a high-density floppy disk on which to store the emergency files; alternate storage devices such as ZIP drives won't work because the repair program looks only for a floppy during a repair. Windows 2000 can automatically create this disk for you during installation. You can also create or update the disk later by going to Programs, Accessories, System Tools, Backup.

- **SVGA (800×600) or higher display adapter**— You can get by using a VGA display with Windows 2000, but it doesn't really provide enough space to get much work done. The Explorer interface does clear a lot more room than you had under Windows 3.x, but let's face it: Was a VGA display really adequate? In addition, some standard Windows 2000 dialogs such as the Display Properties dialog box take up more space than a 640×480 display area can hold. In short, you need the additional space provided by an 800×600 display to see some of the essential dialog boxes for the system.

- **Mouse**— Someone will try to tell you that you can work efficiently in Windows 2000 using the keyboard. You can get around, there's no doubt about it. But a mouse makes Windows 2000 so much more efficient that I can't understand why anyone would want to go without one.

- **CD-ROM or DVD-ROM drive**—You must have a CD-ROM drive to install Windows 2000 at all. I strongly recommend a minimum of a 32X CD-ROM drive if you plan to do anything worthwhile with your machine. In fact, faster is better as far as CD-ROM drives go, with 50X being state-of-the-art at the time of this writing. DVD-ROM drive owners find that they have a lot more flexibility when it comes to media. Standard DVD-ROM drives run at 3X or 5X, but you can easily find 7X drives as of this writing. The speed rating on the box normally refers to the DVD-ROM read speed—many DVD-ROM drives can read CD-ROMs at the same 32X to 50X speed of their CD-only counterparts. Be sure to check the vendor-supplied manuals to learn what CD-ROM read speed your DVD-ROM drive will support.

- **Optional devices**—You can also install any number of optional peripheral devices. I strongly recommend that you install a modem as a minimum. Windows 2000 provides much better multimedia capabilities as well: You'll probably want to install a soundboard somewhere along the way, and now is as good a time as any. In addition, if your data is important to you, then now is also a good time to install a tape drive and an uninterruptible power supply (UPS) setup.

Windows 2000 automatically detects the majority of your hardware, as long as that hardware is on the hardware compatibility list (HCL). We'll discuss this list and what it means in the "Checking the Hardware Compatibility List (HCL)" section of the chapter. All you need to know now is that Windows 2000 does a great job with supported plug-and-play hardware. If it doesn't recognize a device on your machine as being plug-and-play-compatible, Windows 2000 does an adequate job of detecting your hardware using the INF files provided by Microsoft.

I installed the product on a variety of machines using all the methods mentioned here. I met with a variety of successes when it came to hardware detection, but at least Windows 2000 provides a starting point for future efforts. I also like the way the software led me by the hand in getting things configured. Again, there were choices to make, but the way they were laid out made it a lot easier to figure out what I wanted to do. In addition, unlike previous versions of Windows, the online help for this installation routine actually told me a little bit about what I was installing.

Tip: By default, the .INF (information) extension is not displayed in Explorer; neither are any other known file extensions (such as .TXT, .DOC, .EXE, and so on). "Known" here means that the extension is listed in the File Types tab of the dialog box displayed when you choose Folder Options from Explorer's Tools menu. To force Explorer to display all file extensions—I find them quite useful to identify a file's type of data or whether it's executable—click the View tab in the Folder Options dialog box. Then deselect the Hide File Extensions for Known File Types option.

Is the new installation for Windows 2000 perfect? In a word, no. I saw some truly weird problems during installation, from hardware that was detected fine during one installation but not during another, to utility programs that installed even when I asked Windows 2000 not to install them (more about that later). Some of the worst failings of the installation routine in one way were the highlights in another. During one installation, for example, I found it nearly impossible to get through the installation procedure and end up with the correct sound card installed in my machine. Admittedly, this was a non-plug-and-play sound card; Windows 2000 does a remarkable job with plug-and-play-compatible hardware that appears on the HCL. (I finally figured out a surefire method for getting an accurate detection from Windows 2000. I explain it later in this chapter.)

Preparing for Installation

You might want to spend a little time preparing for your Windows 2000 installation, especially if you're the ill-fated network administrator who will spend the next few weeks getting it installed on all 100 network workstations. Of course, the first aspect of preparation is to make a complete backup of each system before you start the installation. Trying to back out of a failed installation can prove to be quite a problem in some situations. In fact, if you have the upgrade version of Windows 2000, you might find recovering from a failed installation quite impossible without reinstalling your old software first.

Getting all the required equipment together to perform the installation is only the first step; you need to do other things before you actually perform the installation. The following sections give you the inside scoop on all the preinstallation steps you should take. I cover the four installation techniques you can use with Windows 2000 later in the chapter that include upgrade, GUI start, character mode start, and network.

Checking Your Hardware

Windows 2000 automatically detects most items of hardware. The detection capabilities Windows 2000 currently provides are less than perfect, however, so you'll want to spend a little time checking your system hardware for potential problems.

Obviously, the best way to avoid problems is to get plug-and-play hardware that appears on Microsoft's HCL. However, if you can't get plug-and-play hardware that meets your needs, then you'll have to look for alternatives. Microsoft uses INF (information) files to implement all the Windows 2000 autodetection capabilities for non-plug-and-play hardware. This means that Windows 2000 checks the characteristics of your hardware against a list of characteristics stored in its INF files. If a piece of hardware matches those characteristics perfectly, Windows 2000 recognizes it.

I can almost guarantee that you'll run into problems with certain types of hardware under Windows 2000. If you have hardware with the following characteristics, you might want to take a second look at it before you install Windows 2000. Of course, you can always try to install it, but I've run into more than my share of problems with these hardware types:

- **Machines that use a clone BIOS**—Some older machines use what I call a clone BIOS. These are machines that boot with some strange logo from a company you've never heard of before. A machine containing a BIOS from one of the mainstream companies, such as AMI or Phoenix, is almost always a better bet than a clone BIOS machine. Of course, machines containing a BIOS from IBM or some other major hardware vendor are the safest bet. You might be able to replace the BIOS on a motherboard containing a clone BIOS, but replacing that dinosaur is probably the easiest way to fix the problem.

- **Machines with an old BIOS**—Most reputable motherboard vendors today provide regular updates to their BIOS code. For example, the ASUS motherboard in my machine had a problem allowing Windows 2000 to detect the actual status of the attached serial ports. A BIOS patch fixed the problem. Make sure that you have the latest BIOS patches for all your hardware before you begin installation.

- **Nonstandard peripheral devices**—Developers who latch on to new technology early in the game are often applauded by everyone when they first introduce an item. Later, the same people who applauded these developers wonder why they would ever buy such a nonstandard piece of equipment. Standards evolve as users and companies gain knowledge about a particular area of technology. Unfortunate as it might seem, some of the hardware that appeared before the standard was introduced just isn't compatible with it. Without a standard way to access the hardware, it's very difficult to talk to it and determine what capabilities it provides. Windows 2000 easily detects standard devices, but it might have problems with older peripherals that don't adhere to the standards.

- **Revision-level hardware**—I have three soundboards installed in three different machines. (You might notice how problematical soundboards are, given the number of references to them and their uncertainties in this chapter.) They're all the same soundboard, but they have different revision levels. One soundboard is revision level C, and the other two are revision level D. One of the revision level D boards has an interim-level fix for a problem with that board, and the other doesn't. What I have, in effect, are three different soundboards with the same exact name. Windows 2000 recognized the two level D boards without a problem; the level C board caused problems that rendered it silent within Windows 2000. You'll find that more than a few vendors use revision levels to fix problems and then don't bother to tell anyone about them. The result is that the Windows 2000 INF files may assume something that's true at one revision level of the board, but not at another. In addition, this is one place that the HCL won't help you because Microsoft doesn't check for revision-level problems very often.

- **Peripherals that almost emulate something else**—IBM and other vendors are to blame for this problem because they started placing their company name in the BIOS of some types of hardware. When someone would try to use some piece of generic software developed by these companies, the first thing the software would do is check the BIOS for the correct company name. Clone makers aren't stupid, so they started putting the IBM (or other) company name where it was needed in their BIOS chips, too. That isn't a problem as long as the device in question completely emulates the hardware it replaces. The problems begin when the clone vendor adds some additional "features" that render this emulation incompatible with the original. Because Windows 2000 has no way to recognize the clone from the real McCoy, you could end up installing the wrong kind of support during installation.

There's also some marginal hardware out there that you can fix after the initial installation is over. A soundboard is one big item that falls into this category. Windows 2000 does a pretty good job of detecting soundboards, considering that one soundboard is designed to emulate the qualities of another. Just about every soundboard claims some sort of SoundBlaster emulation mode. Trying to detect this hardware is a nightmare. In some cases, you just have to manually install the hardware later. You'll see the procedure for performing a manual installation later in this chapter.

A final difficult-to-install hardware category is the older stuff that depends on a real-mode driver for support. I had an old Hitachi 1503S CD-ROM drive that fell into this category. Believe it or not, it worked just fine under Windows 95, even though I had to use real-mode drivers. This same device won't work under Windows 2000 at all. If you have old hardware and you plan to run Windows 2000, take the plunge and get something that will work. Trying to install an advanced operating system on old hardware just doesn't make sense. (On the other hand, if the boss absolutely won't spring for that new piece of hardware, consider using Windows 95/98 instead of Windows 2000.)

After you figure out whether or not you have any potential problems with your hardware, you should create an inventory of what you have. Some hardware, such as the newer soundboards (again!), use a real-mode driver that accepts configuration parameters as part of the device driver command line. Record these parameters just as you would any jumper settings; they're required to make the board work. If you plan to move your current CONFIG.SYS and AUTOEXEC.BAT to Windows 2000, you'll want to remove all driver references from them. Just REM them out for right now; you don't want to destroy a potential source of documentation if you don't need to. Obviously, you'll want to keep these files intact if you plan to create a dual-boot setup.

Some hardware still uses jumpers for configuration purposes. The one big item that just about everyone must consider is a network interface card (NIC) . NICs usually have one or more address settings and an IRQ setting. You need to write down the settings of any boards that use jumpers before you start your Windows 2000 installation. This list will come in handy later as you try to resolve any IRQ or address conflicts that arise during installation. Changing a soft setting is easy, but changing jumpers is a lot more difficult.

When you get to this point, you have just about every piece of hardware information you need. It doesn't seem like such a big deal to take care of this step prior to installation if you're doing it on your personal machine. Gathering all this information before you leave the office to work on a remote machine is essential if you want to do it with any level of efficiency.

> **Tip:** If you own a bootable CD-ROM drive, simply place the Windows 2000 CD-ROM into the drive, and it should be capable of booting right into the Windows 2000 Setup program without a lot of extra work on your part. Using a bootable CD-ROM drive saves you a lot of time because you don't have to worry about a lot of things, such as the current state of the AUTOEXEC.BAT and CONFIG.SYS files on the installation machine. In addition, you'll avoid problems that can crop up with CD-ROM drivers and other "additions" required to make DOS work.

You should check for one final piece of information for machines that use file compression: Windows 2000 won't work with any disk-compression software that requires a CONFIG.SYS entry. This means that you're probably out of luck unless you use Microsoft's DriveSpace or DoubleSpace drive compression. You'll definitely be out of luck with other drive-compression schemes until you install that vendor's Windows 2000–specific software. Obviously, this also means that your boot drive can't use any form of compression.

A few people I've talked with say they had problems getting Windows 2000 to work properly with their disk-compression software—even the Microsoft variety. This is one reason, along with the fact that hard drive size has vastly increased in the past few years, why hardly anyone uses disk-compression schemes any more. In most cases, it turned out to be some kind of interaction between the compression software, the drive controller, and Windows 2000. If you want to make absolutely certain that there aren't any problems, decompress the drive prior to installation, and then never recompress it. Get one of those ultra-cheap EIDE hard drives instead of trying to solve, via software, what's really best dealt with by replacing hardware.

Checking the Hardware Compatibility List (HCL)

I can't emphasize one particular point too often: If you have a choice about the hardware you're going to use with Windows 2000, then check it against the HCL before you buy anything. While the hardware on the HCL doesn't always work with every other combination of hardware out there, you'll at least be able to get support from Microsoft in finding the problem and be assured that there are Windows 2000–specific drivers for the hardware.

So, where do you find the latest version of the HCL? Look at http://www.microsoft.com/hcl/default.asp, and you'll see display similar to the one shown in Figure 4.1. All you need to do is type Windows 2000 in the Search for the Following field, and select a product category in the In the Following Types field. Click Go, and you'll see a list of hardware that matches your requirements.

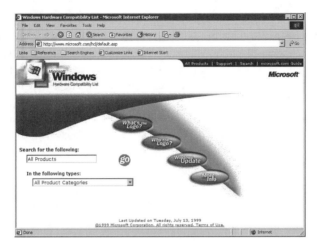

FIGURE 4.1

The HCL allows you to quickly find a piece of hardware that fits your needs and that's compatible with Windows 2000.

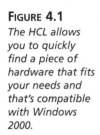

Four buttons also are present on the Web page shown in Figure 4.1. These buttons provide you with additional compatibility information. The two logo-specific buttons tell you about Microsoft's logo program. These Web pages help you understand what a product meeting the logo requirements and displaying the Microsoft logo has to offer. The Windows Update button takes you to the Windows Update Web site, where you can check your machine for the latest Microsoft support in the form of applications and drivers. This is a good place to go after you use your Windows 2000 setup for a while. Finally, the More Info button takes you to Microsoft's Hardware Developer Web site. Most of the information on this Web site is provided for developers who want to create drivers, rather than for people who use them. In most cases, you really don't need to spend any time at this Web site unless you want a better understanding of how things work under Windows 2000.

Getting Ready to Install

At this point in the chapter, you should have inventoried your hardware. You should also have decided whether you plan to retain your AUTOEXEC.BAT and CONFIG.SYS (for a dual-boot setup) or to modify these files for use under Windows 2000. Before you begin the setup process, you might want to make a few additional changes to these two files if you plan to move them. It might seem like a pain to have to first set up your machine to provide the best possible environment for an operating system installation, but you really will get better results this way.

> **Note:** You can skip the vast majority of the preparations in this section if you have a bootable CD-ROM drive. The drive can be used to boot a copy of Windows 2000 that's right on the CD. This means that you won't really need to worry about anything other than SET commands within the AUTOEXEC.BAT file. If you think you have a bootable CD-ROM drive and the Windows 2000 CD won't boot, then check your BIOS settings to ensure that the CD-ROM drive is the first place that your machine checks for an operating system. (Your BIOS will display a message during the boot process, in most cases, that tells how to access the CMOS setup. For example, my machine uses the Delete key to provide this access.)

The first thing you want to do is REM out any unneeded legacy information in your AUTOEXEC.BAT file. ("REM out" means to type the letters REM at the start of any line that you want ignored during Windows 2000's boot process.) Don't worry about little utility programs, such as DOSKey or other TSRs. Windows 2000 ignores the data in AUTOEXEC.BAT and the CONFIG.SYS files when it boots up, except for the PATH, PROMPT, and SET commands. The other commands are just disregarded, including the commands to run other programs and TSRs. Even if you run a DOS program, the Windows 2000 versions (AUTOEXEC.NT and CONFIG.NT) are run, not the original BAT files. Therefore, the only thing to really worry about in AUTOEXEC.BAT and CONFIG.SYS are the SET commands that you should REM out.

After you complete these final modifications, reboot your system. You should now have a completely clean environment in which to install Windows 2000. One last check using the MEM /C command (from within DOS) to verify that memory is as clean as possible is always a good idea.

Now let's look at some of the WINNT and WINNT32 command-line switches. WINNT is the DOS-executable installation program, and WINNT32 is the GUI version. These will help you get around any problems that you might experience while installing Windows 2000. Table 4.1 is a complete list of these switches. You'll find that WINNT supports a superset of the WINNT32 switches, so the list specifically mentions any switches that WINNT32 supports. WINNT supports all the switches in the list.

> **Note:** There's one thing you need to know about the way I present this information. When you see a term in italic between angle brackets, it means that you must supply a value of some kind. The description tells you what to provide. Don't type the square brackets when you type the switch.

Table 4.1   WINNT and WINNT32 Command-Line Switches

Command	Results
/?	Displays a list of currently documented command-line switches. You also can use undocumented switches, but these aren't guaranteed to work.
/A	Enables the Accessibility Options so that you can use the accessibility features during installation.
/B	Performs a floppyless installation of Windows 2000. You use this option if you want to install Windows 2000 on a diskless workstation. You must use the /S switch with this switch to tell Windows 2000 where to find the files it needs. Both WINNT and WINNT32 support this switch. You'll also want to use the /B switch if you're going to install over the network, or any time you don't want to be bothered to create the three floppy disks during the install process.

Command	Results
/C	Tells the installation program to skip the free space check for the boot floppy disks.
/E	Allows you to execute a command at the end of the GUI-mode setup.
/F	Tells the installation program to copy the files to the floppy disk without verifying them afterward. You can save a little time during the installation process by using this switch. Of course, the downside to using this switch is that you have no way of knowing whether the floppy disks were created successfully.
/I[:<*INF filename*>]	Creates a new INF file and provides its name. Normally, the installation program uses DOSNET.INF to provide a list of installation file locations. The default file assumes that you'll install Windows 2000 from a local drive and use the three boot floppy disks. Obviously, that won't work over a network. Use a copy of DOSNET.INF as a template for your INF file. Both WINNT and WINNT32 support this switch.
/L	Creates a log file named $WINNT.LOG that lists any problems that Setup encounters while installing the operating system.
/O	Creates a set of boot floppy disks, but doesn't actually install Windows 2000. Both WINNT and WINNT32 support this switch.
/OX	Forces the installation program to create the boot floppy disks automatically. Unlike the /O switch, this switch does start the installation process. Both WINNT and WINNT32 support this switch.
/R:<*directory*>	Installs an optional directory from the Windows 2000 CD-ROM. You can use this feature to install one of the other platforms on your server, for example.
/RX:<*directory*>	Copies an optional directory from the Windows 2000 CD-ROM. You can use this feature to copy one of the optional directories, such as Internet server, from your CD-ROM or the network to your machine's hard drive.
/S[:<*source path*>]	Tells Windows 2000 to use a specific source path for its installation files. That source path can include a local drive or the universal naming convention (UNC) network drive (such as //SERVER/SOURCE). The installation program assumes that you want to use the current

continues

Table 4.1   Continued.

Command	Results
	directory if you don't specify this parameter. Both WINNT and WINNT32 support this switch.
/T[:<temporary directory>]	Tells Windows 2000 which drive to use as a temporary directory. It normally tries to use the drive you're using for installation. If the drive you choose is a little short on space, you can use this switch to redirect installation-specific items to another drive. Both WINNT and WINNT32 support this switch.
/U[:<script file>]	Performs an unattended installation using a script file. You must use the /S switch with this option.
/UDF:<ID> [, <UDF name>]	Allows you to override the basic installation question answers provided in a script file using the /U switch. You'll need to supply an ID that tells which answers in a Uniqueness Database File you want to use to override the basic script. In short, you can create a generic script file that works with all installations and specify it using the /U switch; then provide specific answers for this particular installation using the /UDF switch.
/X	Starts a standard installation that uses floppy disks but doesn't actually create them. You'd use this switch in cases where you had already created the boot floppy disks during a previous installation. Both WINNT and WINNT32 support this switch.
/tempdrive:drive_letter	Directs Setup to place temporary files on the specified partition and to install Windows 2000 on that partition.
/unattend	Upgrades your previous version of Windows 2000 in unattended Setup mode. All user settings are taken from the previous installation, so no user intervention is required during Setup. Using the /unattend switch to automate Setup affirms that you've read and accepted the End User License Agreement (EULA) for Windows 2000. Before using this switch to install Windows 2000 on behalf of an organization other than your own, you must confirm that the end user (whether an individual or a single entity) has received, read, and accepted the terms of the Windows 2000 EULA. OEMs may not specify this key on machines sold to end users.
/unattend[num]: [answer_file]	Performs a fresh installation in unattended Setup mode. The answer file provides Setup with your custom specifications. "Num" represents the number of seconds between the time that Setup finishes copying the files

Command	Results
	and the time it restarts your computer. You can use num on any computer running Windows NT or Windows 2000. "Answer_file" is the name of the answer file.
/copydir:folder_name	Creates an additional folder within the folder in which the Windows 2000 files are installed. For example, if the source folder contains a folder called Private_drivers that has modifications just for your site, you can type /copy-dir:Private_drivers to have Setup copy that folder to your installed Windows 2000 folder. Then the new folder location would be C:\Winnt\Private_drivers. You can use /copydir to create as many additional folders as you want.
/copysource:folder_name	Creates a temporary additional folder within the folder in which the Windows 2000 files are installed. For example, if the source folder contains a folder called Private_dri-vers that has modifications just for your site, you can type /copysource:Private_drivers to have Setup copy that folder to your installed Windows 2000 folder and use its files during Setup. Then the temporary folder location would be C:\Winnt\Private_drivers. Unlike the folders /copydir creates, /copysource folders are deleted after Setup completes.
/cmd:command_line	Instructs Setup to carry out a specific command before the final phase of Setup. This would occur after your computer has restarted twice and after Setup has collect-ed the necessary configuration information, but before Setup is complete.
/debug[level]:[filename]	Creates a debug log at the level specified, for example, /debug4:C:\Win2000.log. The default log file is C:\%Windir%\Winnt32.log, with the debug level set to 2. The log levels are as follows: 0—severe errors, 1—errors, 2—warnings, 3—information, and 4—detailed information for debugging. Each level includes the levels below it.
/syspart:drive_letter	Specifies that you can copy Setup startup files to a hard disk, mark the disk as active, and then install the disk into another computer. When you start that computer, it automatically starts with the next phase of the Setup. You must always use the /tempdrive parameter with the /syspart parameter. The /syspart switch for Winnt32.exe runs only from a computer that already has

continues

Table 4.1   Continued.

Command	Results
	Windows NT 3.51, Windows NT 4.0, or Windows 2000 installed on it. It can't be run from Windows 9x.
/checkupgradeonly	Checks your computer for upgrade compatibility with Windows 2000. For Windows 95 or Windows 98 upgrades, Setup creates a report named Upgrade.txt in the Windows installation folder. For Windows NT 3.51 or 4.0 upgrades, it saves the report to the Winnt32.log in the installation folder.
/cmdcons	Adds to the operating system selection screen a Recovery Console option for repairing a failed installation. It's used only post-Setup.
/m:folder_name	Specifies that Setup copy replacement files from an alternate location. Instructs Setup to look in the alternate location first; if files are present, it uses them instead of the files from the default location.
/makelocalsource	Instructs Setup to copy all installation source files to your local hard disk. Use /makelocalsource when installing from a CD to provide installation files when the CD isn't available later in the installation.
/noreboot	Instructs Setup to not restart the computer after the file copy phase of WINNT32 is completed so that you can execute another command.
/tempdrive:drive_letter	Directs Setup to place temporary files on the specified partition and to install Windows 2000 on that partition.
/unattend	Upgrades your previous version of Windows 2000 in unattended Setup mode. All user settings are taken from the previous installation, so no user intervention is required during Setup.
	Using the /unattend switch to automate Setup affirms that you've read and accepted the End User License Agreement (EULA) for Windows 2000. Before using this switch to install Windows 2000 on behalf of an organization other than your own, you must confirm that the end user (whether an individual or a single entity) has received, read, and accepted the terms of the Windows 2000 EULA. OEMs may not specify this key on machines sold to end users.
/unattend[num]: [answer_file]	Performs a fresh installation in unattended Setup mode. The answer file provides Setup with your custom specifications.

Command	Results
	"Num" represents the number of seconds between the time that Setup finishes copying the files and the time it restarts your computer. You can use num on any computer running Windows NT or Windows 2000.
	"Answer_file" is the name of the answer file.
/copydir:folder_name	Creates an additional folder within the folder in which the Windows 2000 files are installed. For example, if the source folder contains a folder called Private_drivers that has modifications just for your site, you can type /copydir:Private_drivers to have Setup copy that folder to your installed Windows 2000 folder. Then the new folder location would be C:\Winnt\Private_drivers. You can use /copydir to create as many additional folders as you want.
/copysource:folder_name	Creates a temporary additional folder within the folder in which the Windows 2000 files are installed. For example, if the source folder contains a folder called Private_drivers that has modifications just for your site, you can type /copysource:Private_drivers to have Setup copy that folder to your installed Windows 2000 folder and use its files during Setup. Then the temporary folder location would be C:\Winnt\Private_drivers. Unlike the folders /copydir creates, /copysource folders are deleted after Setup completes.
/cmd:command_line	Instructs Setup to carry out a specific command before the final phase of Setup. This would occur after your computer has restarted twice and after Setup has collected the necessary configuration information, but before Setup is complete.
/debug[level]:[filename]	Creates a debug log at the level specified, for example, /debug4:C:\Win2000.log. The default log file is C:\. %Windir%\Winnt32.log, with the debug level set to 2. The log levels are as follows: 0—severe errors, 1—errors, 2—warnings, 3—information, and 4—detailed information for debugging. Each level includes the levels below it.
/syspart:drive_letter	Specifies that you can copy Setup startup files to a hard disk, mark the disk as active, and then install the disk into another computer. When you start that computer, it

continues

Table 4.1 Continued.

Command	Results
	automatically starts with the next phase of the Setup. You must always use the /tempdrive parameter with the /syspart parameter.
	The /syspart switch for Winnt32.exe only runs from a computer that already has Windows NT 3.51, Windows NT 4.0, or Windows 2000 installed on it. It can't be run from Windows 9x.
/checkupgradeonly	Checks your computer for upgrade compatibility with Windows 2000. For Windows 95 or Windows 98 upgrades, Setup creates a report named Upgrade.txt in the Windows installation folder. For Windows NT 3.51 or 4.0 upgrades, it saves the report to the Winnt32.log in the installation folder.
/cmdcons	Adds to the operating system selection screen a Recovery Console option for repairing a failed installation. It's used only post-Setup.
/m:folder_name	Specifies that Setup copy replacement files from an alternate location. Instructs Setup to look in the alternate location first; if files are present, it uses them instead of the files from the default location.
/makelocalsource	Instructs Setup to copy all installation source files to your local hard disk. Use /makelocalsource when installing from a CD to provide installation files when the CD isn't available later in the installation.
/noreboot	Instructs Setup to not restart the computer after the file copy phase of WINNT32 is completed so that you can execute another command.

Performing an Upgrade Installation

The process for upgrading from Windows 95/98 or Windows NT 3.51/4 is relatively easy: Just stick the CD in your drive. If you have the Autoplay feature enabled, Setup will automatically start and detect your current operating system. You can always double-click the Setup icon in Windows Explorer or use the Run dialog box to start Setup manually. When Setup detects that it can automatically update your current operating system, it displays a dialog box such as the one shown in Figure 4.2.

All you need to do, at this point, is click Yes, and the upgrade process begins. The next dialog box you see is the Windows 2000 Setup dialog box, where you choose between an upgrade install (automatically selected) and a clean install. Choose the upgrade installation, and then click Next. You'll see a licensing dialog box. Read through the licensing agreement, choose I Accept This Agreement, and then click Next. After you get past the licensing dialog box, Setup takes care of just about everything for you automatically, including rebooting the machine as needed. I tried this setup on a Windows NT 4 machine and didn't have much to do during the entire setup process.

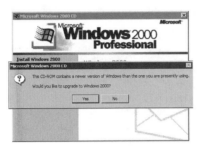

FIGURE 4.2
The Windows 2000 CD automatically detects your current operating system and offers you a chance to upgrade it.

The only caveat to using this approach is that Microsoft makes certain assumptions for you. For example, very few of the new Windows 2000 features will get installed: Microsoft assumes that you want to retain your current Windows feature set. Notable exceptions to this rule include Internet Explorer, which always gets upgraded. Of course, you can always install these features later.

Another potential problem is that an upgrade install keeps all your current application settings and files. Normally, this would be an advantage because you won't have to reinstall and configure your applications. However, if you've installed quite a few applications, uninstalled others, and performed some application updates, too, the registry can get quite messy. An operating system update often represents the best time to get a clean start with the application environment.

Finally, an upgrade install can cause problems when it comes to device detection and driver installation. While I didn't personally run into any problems, I've heard reports of other people who did, especially with new devices that aren't supported by Windows 2000. Obviously, you always want to keep a backup of your data and application configuration files available because you could end up performing a clean install after a failed upgrade attempt. Your backup should include the entire Documents and Settings folder because this folder contains the individual application data settings for the Start menu and Internet Explorer (among other things).

Performing a Character Mode Installation

Character mode installations are usually used on new machines without an operating system or those with only DOS installed. Microsoft suggests that if you're migrating, you install Windows 2000 from an existing copy of Windows rather than DOS—and it's true that this approach provides you with a better initial interface. The next section of the chapter describes the GUI mode installation that you'll use when starting the installation from within Windows.

The following paragraphs walk you through the character mode installation procedure. I'll be using the bootable CD-ROM approach for this section, so be aware that there may be very small differences in the way the installation is presented if you go another route. For example, you may need to click Continue rather than press Enter to continue.

> **Note:** Be aware that there are actually two installation programs provided with Windows 2000: WINNT and WINNT32. The WINNT file is designed for DOS users. Windows 95/98 and Windows NT users should use the 32-bit WINNT32.EXE program. Throughout this procedure, I refer to the installation program as Setup because that's the term that Microsoft uses for this utility. It's also the name of the program that you'll see at the top of various dialog boxes during the installation process.

1. Insert your Windows 2000 installation CD-ROM into the CD drive and reboot your machine. If you have a bootable CD-ROM drive, you should select the option during the boot process for booting from the CD-ROM drive (your machine may automatically boot from the CD-ROM drive for you). Another alternative is to boot your machine using the boot floppies provided with the Windows 2000 package. If your machine doesn't include a bootable CD-ROM drive and you don't have the bootable floppies at your disposal, boot your machine using DOS. At the command prompt, type the following:

   ```
   <CD Drive Letter>:\<Platform>\WINNT
   ```

   Then press Enter. The installation program checks the amount of free space on the drives on your workstation. If there's enough space, you'll see a dialog box containing any required setup notifications.

2. Press Enter. You'll see a Welcome to Setup dialog box. This is where you can choose to repair an existing installation rather than start a new one.

3. Press Enter to continue. You'll see a Windows 2000 Licensing Agreement dialog box. Make sure you take the time to read through the agreement because the terms for licensing software change constantly.

4. Press F8. Setup asks you to choose a place to install the operating system on the hard drive. If this is a clean installation on a new machine, you should see the entire hard drive as unpartitioned space. Dual boot users will likely see part of the hard drive used by another operating system and another part as unpartitioned space. An update installation will likely show an existing partition that you can use for the operating system.

5. Choose a partition on which to install Windows 2000, and then press Enter to install. Setup asks how you want to format the partition.

Note: Windows 2000 supports several disk formats, but you get a limited selection of these formats during installation. At the time of this writing, you have two choices: NTFS or FAT. These options are a tad deceiving. First of all, you need to know that NTFS always refers to the NTFS5 version provided with Windows 2000, not the NTFS4 version used with Windows NT 4. Second, the FAT selection defaults to FAT16 for drives less than 1GB, while drives over that limit automatically use FAT32 to gain the space-saving features that it provides.

6. Choose a formatting method, and then press Enter. Setup creates a new partition and formats it for you. When the formatting process is complete, Setup performs a check of the hard drive for errors and then copies the initial setup files to the hard drive. Your system then reboots, and Setup continues. At this point, Setup automatically detects the devices attached to your machine. Be patient during the hardware detection process because it can appear that Setup has quit working. Eventually you'll see a Regional Settings dialog box. This dialog box contains two Customize buttons. The first allows you to change your regional settings, such as how monetary values are displayed onscreen; the second allows you to change your keyboard settings.

7. Choose any Locale configuration settings, and then click Next. You'll see a Personalize Your Software dialog box that allows you to enter your name and the name of your company.

8. Type your name and the name of your company in the fields provided. Click Next. You'll see a Computer Name and Administrator Password dialog box. Setup automatically chooses a name for your computer (which you don't have to keep).

9. Type a name for your computer, and then type the administrator password twice (once for verification purposes). Click Next. You'll see a Date and Time Settings dialog box.

10. Configure the date and time settings. Make sure you check the Time Zone field. Click Next. You'll see a Networking Settings dialog box. Setup will automatically begin installing networking components if it detects a network. When the automatic installation is complete, the dialog box changes to show two different configuration options: Typical Settings and Custom Settings. The Typical Settings option automatically installs TCP/IP, file and printer sharing, and support for the Microsoft Networks client. If you require additional support, then you must choose the Custom Settings option. This procedure assumes that you'll go the custom route.

11. Choose Custom Settings, and then click Next. You'll see a Networking Components dialog box. This is where you can install, uninstall, or configure networking components.

12. Install, uninstall, or configure networking components as required, and then click Next. You'll see a Workgroup or Computer Domain dialog box. If your network includes a Windows NT/2000 server, then you'll probably want to join a domain. Otherwise, you'll join a workgroup.

13. Choose between a workgroup or a domain. Type a workgroup or domain name in the Workgroup or Computer domain field, and then click Next. Setup may ask for your login name and password on the domain. Provide this information, and then click OK. After Setup has logged you in to either the workgroup or domain, you'll see an Installing Components dialog box. Setup automatically installs some components for you. Eventually you'll see a Windows 2000 Setup Wizard completion dialog box.

14. Click Finish. Your system then reboots again, and you're ready to use Windows 2000 Professional.

Performing a GUI Installation

Most people who have Windows already installed on their machine will perform either an update installation or a clean installation using the GUI mode installation method. We've already discussed an upgrade installation in this chapter. This section assumes that you want to perform a clean installation using Setup's GUI. The following steps will get you started.

1. Insert the Windows 2000 installation CD in your CD-ROM or DVD-ROM drive. Start the installation program by double-clicking the Setup icon in Explorer. (The Windows 2000 CD has an AUTOPLAY.INF file, so simply inserting the CD into the drive may be sufficient.) You'll see a Microsoft Windows 2000 CD dialog box.

2. Click Install Windows 2000. You'll see a Welcome to the Windows 2000 Setup Wizard dialog box like the one shown in Figure 4.3. This dialog box allows you to upgrade an existing installation or install a new copy of Windows 2000.

FIGURE 4.3
This dialog box allows you to choose between an update and a clean installation.

3. Choose the Install a New Copy of Windows 2000 (Clean Install) option, and then click Next. You'll see a License Agreement dialog box. Make sure that you read through the licensing agreement because the licensing conditions for software changes on a continual basis.

4. Choose the I Accept This Agreement option, and then click Next. You'll see a Select Special Options dialog box like the one shown in Figure 4.4. Here you can choose the language and accessibility options used for setup purposes. (The accessibility options include the Magnifier and the Narrator, but not any of the other features.) This dialog box also includes an Advanced Options dialog box that allows you to choose the source and destination directories, gives you the ability to copy all setup files from the Setup CD to the hard drive, and offers you the option to choose an installation partition. In most cases, you'll want to choose the installation partition as a minimum (this procedure assumes that you will).

FIGURE 4.4

The Select Special Options dialog box allows you to choose special setup settings.

5. Use the buttons on the Select Special Options dialog box to choose one or more special installation features. This procedure assumes that you'll check the I Want to Choose the Installation Partition During Setup option as a minimum. Click Next, and you'll see the Upgrading to the Windows 2000 NTFS File System dialog box. From here you can upgrade your drive from FAT, FAT32, or NTFS4 to NTFS5, the native file system for Windows 2000. In most cases, you'll want to perform the update so that you can get the maximum benefit from Windows 2000. However, if you're working in a mixed operating system environment, the update might make it difficult for you to maintain the system.

6. Choose an update option, and then click Next. Setup copies the installation files and then restarts your machine. When your machine restarts, you'll be in character mode. You begin with a dialog box that contains any setup notification information.

7. Press Enter. You'll see a Welcome to Setup dialog box. This is where you can choose to repair an existing installation rather than start a new one.

8. Press Enter to continue. If you're performing a clean install on a machine that already has Windows NT/2000 installed on it, Setup will detect the installation and display it for you. At this point, you have another chance to repair the existing

installation. Since we're performing a clean install, you must press Escape to get past this informational dialog. Setup asks you to choose a place to install the operating system on the hard drive. In most cases, you'll see at least one existing partition that you can use for installation purposes. If your intent is to create a clean installation, then it's normally a good idea to delete the exiting partition and allow Setup to create a new one for you. Dual boot users will likely see part of the hard drive used by another operating system and another part as unpartitioned space. You'll want to install Windows 2000 in the unpartitioned space.

9. Choose a partition on which to install Windows 2000, and then press Enter to install. Setup asks how you want to format the partition.

10. Choose a formatting method, and then press Enter. Setup creates a new partition and formats it for you. When the formatting process is complete, Setup performs a check of the hard drive for errors and then copies the initial setup files to the hard drive. Your system then reboots, and Setup continues. At this point, Setup automatically detects the devices attached to your machine. Be patient during the hardware detection process because it can appear that Setup has quit working. Eventually you'll see a Regional Settings dialog box. This dialog box contains two Customize buttons. The first allows you to change your regional settings, such as how monetary values are displayed onscreen; the second allows you to change your keyboard settings.

11. Choose any Locale configuration settings, and then click Next. You'll see a Personalize Your Software dialog box in which you enter your name and the name of your company.

12. Type your name and the name of your company in the fields provided. Click Next. You'll see a Computer Name and Administrator Password dialog box. Setup automatically chooses a name for your computer (which you don't have to keep).

13. Type a name for your computer, and then type the administrator password twice (once for verification purposes). Click Next. You'll see a Date and Time Settings dialog box.

14. Configure the date and time settings. Make sure you check the Time Zone field. Click Next. You'll see a Networking Settings dialog box. Setup automatically begins installing networking components if it detects a network. When the automatic installation is complete, the dialog box changes to show two different configuration options: Typical Settings and Custom Settings. The Typical Settings option automatically installs TCP/IP, file and printer sharing, and support for the Microsoft Networks client. If you require additional support, then you must choose the Custom Settings option. This procedure assumes that you'll go the custom route.

15. Choose Custom Settings, and then click Next. You'll see a Networking Components dialog box. This is where you can install, uninstall, or configure networking components.

16. Install, uninstall, or configure networking components as required, and then click Next. You'll see a Workgroup or Computer Domain dialog box. If your network includes a Windows NT/2000 server, you'll probably want to join a domain. Otherwise, you'll join a workgroup.

17. Choose between a workgroup or a domain. Type a workgroup or domain name in the Workgroup or Computer domain field, and then click Next. Setup may ask for your login name and password on the domain. Provide this information, and then click OK. After Setup has logged you in to either the workgroup or domain, you'll see an Installing Components dialog box. Setup automatically installs some components for you. Eventually you'll see a Windows 2000 Setup Wizard completion dialog box.

18. Click Finish. Your system reboots again, and you're be ready to use Windows 2000 Professional.

Installing from a Network

A server installation differs from the floppy disk or bootable CD-ROM version in only a few ways. Whether you install Windows 2000 from a server or a CD-ROM, the same sequence of events must take place. The only factor is how you choose to smooth the way for the users on the system.

What do you need to do to create a server setup? About the only thing you need to worry about is copying the contents of the folder for the processor you want to support to a drive on the server. If you plan to support Intel processors, for example, just use the XCOPY command to copy the I386 folder from the CD to your network drive (or select the entire I386 folder in Explorer and drag it over).

Obviously, the users need to have read access to the directory. I also suggest creating a batch file of some kind. I covered the batch file switches for both WINNT and WINNT32 in the section titled "Getting Ready to Install" earlier in this chapter. Just decide which installation program you want to use, and create a batch file that calls it using the switches you need. Adding the commands required to log the user into the system and change directories to the installation directory will make things a bit easier.

Understanding Special Network Considerations

Depending on the size of your company, installing Windows 2000 on every workstation in your company can be a small or a large chore. In most cases, you can make this chore a little easier to deal with if you can automate part of the setup process and install Windows 2000 over the network. As with any operating system installed over a network, Windows 2000 requires that you perform specific pre-setup tasks. The following steps give you an overview of the various tasks that you'll need to perform.

1. You must have the network setup and tested. This means that you'll want to install any special network features as well. A network installation requires a server that's fully functional and configured.

2. Copy Windows 2000 to a directory on the network. Obviously, you could tune this copy for your specific needs, but in most cases, it's a lot better to make a full copy of the operating system to ensure that a network installation doesn't fail. In addition to the Windows 2000-specific files, you also need to copy any device drivers that a client workstation may require for full functionality.

> **Tip:** Having a full copy of all the device drivers needed by every machine attached to the network in one place doesn't just help with installation—it also helps with various types of operating system failures. Sometimes a device driver gets corrupted, is overwritten by an incompatible version, or is deleted by the user. Having the right device driver to fix the problem at your fingertips is a big plus because it can greatly reduce the time required for fixing a problem.

3. It's important to set up any required security so that user-assisted installations don't result in network security breaches. Obviously, making the installation as automatic as possible reduces the amount of user interaction time, but you still must act as if the user has full control of the interface during the entire installation.

4. Any workstation that you want to boot from the network requires boot instructions, normally included in the form of an additional chip added to the NIC. Make sure that all the client hardware is configured properly, especially when it comes to the NIC.

These are the four basic steps that you'll need to follow to prepare for any network-oriented installation. You also could perform a lot of other tasks, depending on your company and client needs. For example, most clients require some sort of application setup. You could perform this task automatically by using /E switch with either of the Setup programs.

Installing Windows 2000 to a New Hard Drive

If you decide to upgrade to a new, larger hard drive, and if Windows 2000 is already installed on your existing hard drive, you can easily move Windows 2000 to the new hard drive. The following procedure shows you how.

1. Click Start, Run and type Rdisk. This utility enables you to make a repair disk, should you need one.

2. Save your Registry to a disk (see Chapter 10, "Understanding the Windows 2000 Registry," for instructions).

3. Back up your entire Windows 2000 disk to tape or another storage medium sufficiently large to hold it.

4. Locate the four original disks that you used to install Windows 2000 onto the old hard drive. If you can't find them, run WINNT32 with the /OX switch. After you've installed the new hard drive, use the disks to install Windows 2000 on the new drive, but install the program into a folder you create named WINNEW. Don't use the default WINNT folder name.

5. When the WINNEW installation is finished, restore the backup version you saved to tape (or wherever). (It'll probably go into the WINNT folder, unless for some reason you originally installed into a folder with a different name.) The idea is that your new install shouldn't be overwritten by the restore.

6. Reboot your machine. If the operating system boots, at this point, you're ready to go. On the other hand, if you notice any problems at this point, turn off the power and then insert the Windows 2000 Installation disk.

7. Choose Repair when the option presents itself during Setup initialization.

8. Deselect Check System Files, but select all other options displayed. You'll be asked for the emergency repair disk that you created earlier when the repair process starts.

9. Insert the emergency repair disk, and wait for Setup to complete the repair process.

10. Reboot the machine again. At this point, everything should work as anticipated.

The last task you'll want to perform is removing the WINNEW folder that you created during the initial installation. Theoretically, Setup should perform any other required cleanup for you automatically. All you should have when you finish is your Windows 2000 setup on a new hard drive.

Dual-Booting: Working with Multiple Operating Systems

For the most part, you'll find that the Windows 2000 Setup program guides you through a multiboot setup, just as it did in the section titled "Performing a GUI Installation." The big difference is that you'll have two operating systems on your machine rather than one. You'll find that you need to do a little additional setup after the process is finished, however. Microsoft assumes that Windows 2000 is going to be your primary operating system, for example. This might be a valid assumption, in most cases, but there are certainly situations in which it isn't.

You can choose a default operating system by right-clicking the My Computer icon, choosing Properties from the context menu, and selecting the Advanced page of the System Properties dialog box, and then clicking on the Startup/Recovery button. The default operating system appears in the System Startup group in the Startup field. This same group enables you to select how long Windows 2000 displays the boot menu before starting the default operating system. Obviously, you must have more than one operating system installed on your machine to use this feature. The operating system you choose is selected automatically if you don't make a selection within the time specified in the Show List Box field.

There are other installation gotchas as well. The one that gives most people problems is that Windows 2000 changes the active partition during installation. This usually isn't a problem because you'll use Windows 2000 as your primary operating system. Unfortunately, if you plan to use Windows 2000 and OS/2 on the same machine, you must reset the active partition. Use the OS/2 FDISK utility to reset the active (or boot) partition to the Boot Manager partition. You'll be able to select the Windows 2000 partition from the menu Boot Manager displays. Obviously, you'll have to configure Boot Manager to select a default operating system.

Getting Everything to Work

I'm a great fan of automation that works. Anything that makes my job easier or faster is a good idea, in my book. Using INF files to automatically install the hardware Windows 2000 recognizes is one example of that kind of automation. It makes sense that a computer could figure out a set of port and interrupt settings faster and with greater accuracy than the average human. One of the reasons this is possible under Windows 2000 is that the computer usually has all the statistics it needs to do the job. The majority of this information is contained in the INF files Windows 2000 uses to communicate with the rest of the machine. (Some of the information appears in the peripheral devices' BIOS and within Windows 2000 itself.)

So, where's all this configuration information stored? If you look in the \WINNT\INF directory, you'll see some of these files (all have an .INF extension). Besides storing the required configuration information on disk, Windows 2000 gives older hardware first choice of ports and interrupts. This allows older hardware to work most of the time.

So, now that you have some idea of what the problem is, let's take a quick look at ways you can fix it. This list isn't exhaustive, but it'll help you with the majority of the problems that you're likely to run into:

- Avoid interrupt and port address conflicts whenever possible. This is probably the number one reason that Windows 2000 fails to recognize the board. If two devices use the same address, there's no way that Windows 2000 can test for the presence of the second board.

- Plug all your older boards into the slots next to the power supply whenever possible. The BIOS checks the slots in order during POST. Placing these older boards first, followed by the software-configurable boards, ensures that the BIOS sees the older ones first.

- Try different board configurations to see whether Windows 2000 recognizes one of them. In some situations, the INF files that Windows 2000 uses to check for your hardware contain only the default board settings. A good rule of thumb is to try the best setting first and then the default setting, if that doesn't work.

- Check the INF files to see whether they contain all the settings for your boards. There's an INF directory directly below the main Windows 2000 directory. It contains ASCII text files that Windows 2000 uses to search for the hardware on your machine. Modifying these files is a tricky proposition, but it can help Windows 2000 find the peripherals in your machine.

Adding Your Own Devices

Now that you have Windows 2000 installed, let's take some of the magic out of the new Windows 2000 detection capability. If you take a look in your \WINNT\INF directory, you'll see a special type of file there. The INF file is part of the database of information Windows 2000 uses to recognize hardware that isn't Plug and Play-compatible. These files are enhanced versions of the OEMSETUP.INF files that used to appear on the vendor-supplied installation disks under Windows 3.x. They contain a description of the hardware—the same type of information the Plug and Play BIOS would normally provide when Windows 2000 scanned it.

> **Caution:** Avoid using INF files written for other versions of Windows, even Windows NT 4, with Windows 2000. These older INF files contain outdated information and may rely on drivers that won't work with Windows 2000.

As good as the new INF files are, sometimes you may want to modify them. For example, you might have a piece of hardware that provides interrupt and port address settings in addition to those found in the INF file. Modifying the INF file to reflect these additional capabilities could help you install a piece of hardware in some cases.

General INF File Characteristics

Let's look at some of the general characteristics every INF file has. You might find all or only some of these sections in the file; it really depends on what kind of hardware the INF file is trying to define. An INF file needs to contain only the information required to fully define the characteristics of the hardware. A display adapter needs to define the resolutions it supports, for example. A multiscanning monitor, such as the NEC MultiSync series, needs to define the precise frequency ranges it supports. This includes the refresh rate, an important specification for the new ergonomic display adapters. Table 4.2 shows these generic sections and tells you what they mean. You might even want to open one of the INF files to see whether you can identify each section. (Just make certain that you don't save the file or change its contents in any way.)

Table 4.2   INF File Generic Sections

Heading	Description
Version	This section provides version-specific information, such as the operating system, the vendor name, and the device class supported by the INF file. It also provides the name of the general setup file. The general setup file contains the definitions common to all the devices of that type. You might see some additional entries in this section. One special entry enables the vendor to link a new INF file into the list of files for a specific device type. Never change the contents of this section.
Manufacturer	This section contains a list of all the manufacturers for devices of this class. Not every INF file contains this section. For example, this section appears in the MONITOR.INF file, but not in the MSPORTS.INF file. The only time you need to change this section is if you want to add a new vendor. The list might seem incomplete if more than one INF file is required to describe a specific class of device. Four monitor files exist, and each one contains only the vendors that appear in that particular file. You need to check all the INF files for a particular device class before you resort to adding a new vendor. Make sure that you add the new vendor in alphabetical order to the correct INF file. (You'll see an example later in this chapter.) A subsection after this one provides specifics about each device supported by that vendor. If the vendor already appears in the manufacturer list, adding a new device consists of adding an entry here, in the Install section, and in the Strings section.
Detect	This section tells you how Windows 2000 will detect the device. In most cases, it contains a simple set of instructions. To detect a display adapter, for example, you attempt to load its miniport and display drivers. If the load fails, Windows 2000 hasn't found the right driver. In a few cases, you'll see a device name pointer to a detailed Detect section in the file. All you need to do is find a section with that name. Section names are always contained within brackets—[Section]—so they're easy to find.
Install	This is the most important section of the file. It describes all the characteristics of the hardware and the device drivers needed to activate it. It also contains macro commands that perform the actual installation of support in the Registry. Follow the example of other entries in this section when adding a new device. Only change physical characteristics, such as port address and interrupt, when modifying an existing entry.

Heading	Description
Miscellaneous Control	A vendor can use this section to describe how a device works with the Windows 2000 interface. If you see this section, you need to use other entries as an example for creating your own entries. Most INF files don't contain this section.
Strings	You'll see how to add a new device to Windows 2000 using the Add New Hardware dialog box, discussed later in this chapter. When you use this dialog box, you'll see some descriptive strings that tell you about the hardware. This is the section that contains those user-friendly strings; it identifies the device in human-readable form.

New Device Support for an INF File

It's fairly easy to add support for a new device to an INF file. The big word of warning here is that you don't want to modify your original INF file without making a safety copy of it first. You must modify the original, or Windows 2000 won't know what to do with your new entry; therefore, making the copy is absolutely essential. Let's go through this exercise to make the process of adding a new device a little clearer. Before we begin, however, here's an outline of a few guidelines I used during the modification process:

- Always print a hard copy of the original INF file as well as making a disk copy. This way, you can read through the listing quickly as you make a new entry. Some entries depend on the contents of other entries in the file. A mistyped or misinterpreted entry will make the INF file useless.

- Use the other entries in the file as a guideline for your new entries. Windows 2000 performs a very strict interpretation of the contents of the INF file. Adding your own "enhancements" to what seems like an inadequate entry will make the INF file unusable. Remember that some of the INF file entries appear in one or more generic files that appear in the Version section of the file.

- Double-check punctuation marks, spelling, and capitalization carefully when making a new entry. Windows 2000 is extremely sensitive when it comes to how you format the entries in an INF file. There's absolutely no artificial intelligence operating during this process.

- Never change the Version section of the file. Yes, it's very tempting to fiddle with what looks like an interesting file section, but don't do it in this case.

- Make your entries to an existing file. You might be tempted to create your own unique INF file—don't do it! Always add new devices to existing files. That way, you can be absolutely sure that your entries look like the other entries in the file.

Now that you have a better idea of what an INF file contains, let's go through the procedure for modifying one. You can use the same set of steps to modify any of the files in the INF folder. The only thing that changes from file to file is the precise format of the entries themselves and the sections the file supports. To modify an INF file, follow these steps:

1. Use Notepad or WordPad to open MONITOR2.INF. You must change several sections in the INF file; Table 4.1 discussed these sections. The first section to modify contains the manufacturer information. Because I wanted to add an entry for a Sony Multiscan 17sf II monitor, I used Notepad's FIND command to see whether I could find the vendor name. Sony is already in the vendor list as SONY, so I didn't need to add it. If you decide to add a new vendor, however, all you need to do is follow the format of the other vendor entries in the first [Manufacturer] section. In the case of monitors, all the [Manufacturer] section entries contain a single line, like this: %SONY%=SONY. All this says is to look for the Sony information in the [SONY] section of the INF file.

2. After I found the vendor name entry, I searched for the device subsection that would contain the list of devices from that vendor that Windows 2000 supports. I added the following text to this section (shown in bold) so that Windows 2000 would know to add a new device:

```
[SONY]
%CPD-1302%=CPD-1302, MonID_CPD-1302
%CPD-1304%=CPD-1304, MonID_CPD-1304
%CPD-1304S%=CPD-1304S, MonID_CPD-1304S
%CPD-1430%=CPD-1430, MonID_CPD-1430
%CPD-1604S%=CPD-1604S, MonID_CPD-1604S
%CPD-1730%=CPD-1730, MonID_CPD-1730
%GVM-1310%=GVM-1310, MonID_CPD-1310
%GVM-2020%=GVM-2020, MonID_CPD-2020
%GDM-1936%=GDM-1936, MonID_CPD-1936
%GDM-2038%=GDM-2038, MonID_CPD-2038
%GDM-17SE1%=GDM-17SE1, MonID_GDM-17SE1
%MS-15SF%=MS-15SF, MonID_MS-15SF
%MS-17SF%=MS-17SF, MonID_MS-17SF
%MS-17SFII%=MS-17SF-II, MonID_MS-17SFII
%MS-20SE%=MS-20SE, MonID_MS-20SE
```

3. As you can see, I formatted my entry to look exactly like the existing entry. This is a very important part of the process for adding an unsupported device to Windows 2000. This entry tells Windows 2000 that Sony produces an MS-17SFII model of monitor and that it can find further details about that monitor in the [MS-17SFII] section of the INF file.

4. Use the FIND command to locate the [MS-17SF] section of the INF file. This is the section directly before the new [MS-17SFII] section that we'll add. This next section tells Windows 2000 what needs to be installed for this particular monitor. Other devices are automatically detected by Windows 2000; these devices use a detect section instead of an install section, as in this case. For example, display adapters are automatically detected. You can usually tell when a device uses a detect section instead of an install section because Windows offers to detect the device for you automatically. In this case, we're going to add four registry entries. The first tells Windows what installation commands to perform, the second contains the maximum display resolution of the monitor, the third says that this

monitor has multiscanning capabilities, and the fourth says that we want to use the ICM13 color matching settings. These are the entries (in bold) that you'll need to add right after the [MS-17SF] section, as shown.

```
[MS-17SF]
DelReg=DCR
AddReg=MS-17SF.Add, 1280, DPMS, ICM13

[MS-17SFII]
DelReg=DCR
AddReg=MS-17SFII.Add, 1280, DPMS, ICM13

[MS-20SE]
DelReg=DCR
AddReg=MS-20SE.Add, 1600, DPMS, ICM13
```

5. Use the FIND command to find the [MS-17SF.Add] entry in the next section of the file. I added the following bold text to tell Windows 2000 how to modify the Registry to support this new monitor. We're still in the Install section of the file.

```
[MS-17SF.Add]
HKR,"MODES\1280,1024",Mode1,,"31.0-64.0,50.0-120.0,+,+"

[MS-17SFII.Add]
HKR,"MODES\1280,1024",Mode1,,"31.0-65.0,50.0-120.0,+,+"

[MS-20SE.Add]
HKR,"MODES\1600,1200",Mode1,,"31.5-85,50-150,+,+"
```

The Registry entry section of any .INF file requires some detective work on your part. I always look at the Registry itself as a starting point. Knowing how the existing device modified the Registry can help you to determine how to add support for a new device. You should also check the specification sheet that comes with the device for "common" characteristics. Any change you make to an .INF file will ultimately require this type of detective work. In this case, the first important component is "MODES\1280,1024". This describes the operational resolution for that monitor mode. The second component, Mode1, tells Windows 2000 that this is the first mode supported by the monitor.

Looking at other entries in this .INF file shows that some monitors support multiple modes. The final component, "31.0-65.0,50-120,+,+", looks a bit mysterious until you check a monitor manual. The first set of numbers, 31.0-65.0, is the horizontal scanning frequency range. You could supply a numeric range here as well. The second numeric range, 50.0-120.0, is the vertical scanning frequency. The two plus signs tell you that this is a multiscanning monitor. I figured this out by checking the other entries in the file. After looking at a few monitor models that I recognized, it was pretty evident that the ones with multiscanning capabilities used plus signs. If you're adding a fixed scan monitor, you use minus signs in place of the plus signs.

6. Let's get to the final section of the INF file: the Strings section. This is where you describe the monitor in terms that the user can understand. To do this, use the FIND command to search for the last occurrence of the MS-17SF string. We'll need to insert a string for the Sony Multiscan 17sf II monitor, as shown in bold type.

```
MS-17SF="SONY Multiscan 17sf"
MS-17SFII="SONY Multiscan 17sf II"
MS-20SE="SONY Multiscan 20se"
```

That's all there is to it. When you get the hang of it, you can add support for just about any unsupported device to Windows 2000. Of course, that won't solve some problems, such as the incompatibilities you'll experience with some older devices. But it will make it easier to install an older device. If you want to see how the new entry looks, save the MONITOR2.INF file and close Notepad (or WordPad, if you were using it). Right-click on the desktop, and choose Properties from the context menu to display the Display Properties dialog box, shown in Figure 4.5. You can use this quick procedure to show the display adapter entries:

FIGURE 4.5

The Display Properties dialog box is the first stop for testing the new display adapter.

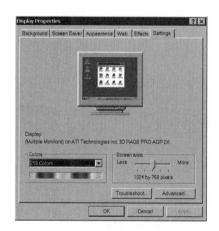

1. Click the Settings tab, as shown in Figure 4.5.

2. Click Advanced, and then choose the Monitor tab to display the dialog box shown in Figure 4.6.

3. Highlight your standard monitor entry; then click Properties and the Driver tab to display the Monitor Properties dialog box shown in Figure 4.7.

4. Click Update Driver to start the Upgrade Device Driver Wizard.

5. Click Next. You'll see two update options: The first allows Windows to search for a new device driver for you. This is normally a good idea, but in this case, you'll want to use the second option, which allows you to choose a device driver manually.

FIGURE 4.6

You'll need to use this dialog box to change the monitor that you're using.

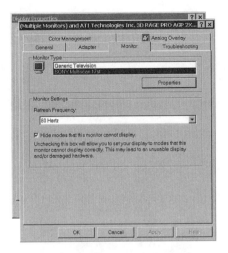

FIGURE 4.7

The Driver tab of the Monitor Properties dialog box allows you to change the current monitor driver.

6. Choose the Display a List of the Known Drivers for This Device So That I Can Choose a Specific Driver option, and then click Next. Choose the Show All Hardware of This Device Class option. You'll see a Select a Device Driver dialog box, like the one shown in Figure 4.8.

7. Scroll through the list of vendors until you find SONY. You should see the new monitor selection, as shown in Figure 4.8.

8. Click Cancel four times to cancel the installation process without adding a new device. As you can see, adding a new device to an INF file can be time-consuming and even frustrating at times. The benefits in reduced maintenance time, however, are well worth the effort.

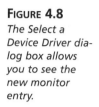

FIGURE 4.8

The Select a Device Driver dialog box allows you to see the new monitor entry.

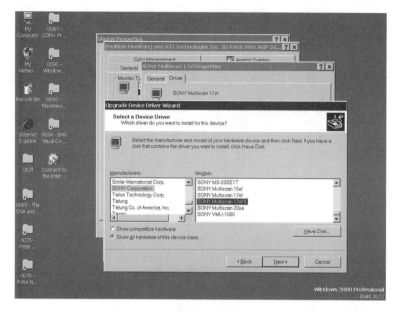

This is a quick tour showing you how to add new devices to Windows 2000. You might find that some devices are so complex that you'll end up downloading the full INF file specification (see the tip earlier in this chapter) to really understand how to make the change. The worst thing you can do is to try to tackle a complex device addition as your first project. Look for something fairly easy, such as a display adapter, as your first project so that you can get a better idea of what the modification will require. Leave the notorious soundboard job for a day when you're calm and patient.

Dealing with Nonstandard Devices

For as long as PCs have been around, there have been nonstandard devices to cause problems. At one time, what qualified as a nonstandard device was truly astounding and included everything from printers to display adapters. Today, however, the realm of the nonstandard device is much smaller and easier to deal with. You'll find that Windows 2000 can work with most display adapter types, and printers usually aren't much of a problem. To sum it all up, most of the devices you need to start the computer and get the operating system installed will work just fine.

When you start looking at devices such as digital cameras, scanners, and the recordable aspect of CDR devices, however, you run into trouble in most cases. Obviously, your first line of defense is to check the HCL to make sure that Windows 2000 supports the device. Failing that, you should verify that the vendor will provide a Windows 2000–specific driver. Make sure that the vendor isn't offering you a Windows NT driver and calling it Windows 2000–compatible; you must get a driver that's specifically designed for Windows 2000 use.

Obviously, in some situations you'll already have the hardware you're going to use before you install Windows 2000. In some cases, it's actually better to wait to upgrade your system until the vendor provides the required drivers. You can still use Windows NT 4 or another operating system for which you have a driver. Then when the vendor delivers the required driver, you can perform the system upgrade without any loss of capability.

In other cases, you may want to retire the hardware and get something that will work with Windows 2000. For example, even though my soundboard did everything I needed it to do, I retired it and got a newer soundboard when I upgraded to Windows 2000. The new soundboard uses fewer system resources and provides better sound. While I don't use all the capabilities of my new soundboard, they're available for future needs, and I get better sound quality out of my speakers in the mean time. The old soundboard found a home in a system that I use for compatibility testing.

A third possibility is to upgrade your system to Windows 2000 immediately and leave the device turned off (or disabled) until the vendor provides a Windows 2000-specific driver. Unless you're a professional photographer, the loss of a digital camera for a few weeks may be a minor problem, while the increased capability provided by Windows 2000 may be a major productivity boost. You need to weigh the productivity gains you'll get from Windows 2000 against the loss of a device for some time frame. Make sure the vendor actually has a driver in testing, and get a firm commitment for a delivery date; otherwise, you may find that access to a device may be lost for good.

Dealing with Nondetected Devices

What do you do when a device doesn't get detected during the initial installation process, especially if that device is on the HCL? In most cases, you must find the reason for the lack of detection. When you find the source of the detection problem, Windows 2000 will automatically install support for it. For example, one of the most common causes of detection problems is resource conflict. Even a Plug and Play-compatible device may fail to operate if the resources it needs aren't available. Use the following list as a starting point for helping Windows 2000 detect devices that defy detection.

- **Shuffle resources**—The Resource tab of a Device Properties dialog box can be your best friend when you know that another device is out there waiting to be detected. Normally, you don't want to define odd settings yourself, but most devices do provide more than one basic configuration setting. Try alternative settings for the devices in your machine to see if you can free up the resources required by a nondetected device.

- **Temporarily remove cards**—I have a DVD decoder card in my system that Windows 2000 misses on some occasions. There's a conflict between this card and my soundboard. Removing the soundboard and allowing Windows 2000 to detect the DVD decoder first usually solves my problem.

- **Remove cards permanently**—You'd think that the hardware and software vendors would have figured out a way around IRQ and I/O address problems by now, but they haven't. In some situations, you still can't stuff every card you'll ever need into your machine and get it to work. In some cases, you just have to make the hard decision of getting rid of one device so that another will work.

- **Update the system BIOS**—My machine is connected to a network, so I don't need the parallel port. Disabling the port to free up resources seemed like a good idea—in fact, it was mandatory if I wanted to get another device to work. Unfortunately, Windows 2000 insisted that the parallel port was still active even after I disabled it in the CMOS setup for my computer. In this case, the problem turned out to be the BIOS. An upgrade of the BIOS told Windows 2000 that the port was no longer in use and freed up the resources required for that other device.

- **Update the peripheral BIOS**—One of my peripherals has no less than 10 different BIOS versions available for it, and only two of these work with Windows 2000. In many situations, updating your system BIOS won't be enough to make your machine work. You may also need to check the status of any peripherals in your machine. In short, keep your system up-to-date when it comes to hardware, firmware, and software.

- **Do a forced install**—Some devices aren't detected very well by Windows 2000 because Microsoft depends on the user to install the device. Monitors fall into this category. As we saw in the "Adding New Device Support to an INF File" section of the chapter, the INF file for a monitor contains an install section rather than a detect section. Microsoft is counting on the user to manually install this device rather than wait for Windows 2000 to detect it. Fortunately, this is an exception rather than the rule.

- **Do an INF file repair or update**—Windows 2000 can detect only the devices that its INF files are designed to detect. File corruption or lack of INF file support renders a device invisible, even if the device is both functional and accessible. With this in mind, you'll want to get the latest updates from Microsoft to ensure that your system can actually detect that new device you want to install.

Configuring Windows 2000 Applets

One topic we haven't covered yet is the process of installing and removing applets on your system. Part of the installation process always involves configuring an applet before you use it. When you install Dial-Up Networking, for example, Windows 2000 automatically asks you for information regarding your computer setup. You can't network without a telephone number, so it makes sense that Windows 2000 would ask about this information before it completes the installation process. The same reasoning holds true the first time you start Backup. Although Windows 2000 automatically takes care of the configuration, it displays a dialog box telling you that it got the job done (in this case, creating a set of backup files for you). You can use the sample file as the basis for your own configuration sets. That's one of the reasons why Backup creates it for you. The other is that you can't perform a backup without at least some idea of what to do. This sample file can help you learn how Backup works. The following sections outline four methods of installing applets on your system:

- The standard method I cover initially is the one you're probably most familiar with. It enables you to install or remove standard Windows 2000 features.

- The section titled "Special Utility Installation" tells you how to install some of the extra utilities Windows 2000 provides. You'll use this procedure to install the Policy Editor and other utilities the standard user probably shouldn't know about, for example. Make sure that you read any text files provided with these utilities, because it's unlikely that you'll find sufficient documentation elsewhere.

- Windows 2000 also provides printer utilities that help you manage this resource better when using certain types of printers. I tell you how to install them in the section titled "Special Printer Installation."

- Finally, you'll find that Windows 2000 provides a wealth of network-management tools. You'll find the installation procedure for them in the section titled "Special Network Installation." A few of the applets you can install are so specialized that Microsoft provides a special installation method for them. I was a little surprised when I finally figured out how this works. Although I can understand Microsoft's willingness to figuratively bury nonstandard utilities from a user who might not know how to use them properly, it seems to me that there's got to be a better way.

Part of the reasoning behind this four-layered approach to installation is the nature of the applets themselves: They aren't all necessarily applets in the full sense of the word. You can't really execute them and expect something useful to happen. Some of them are halfway between a driver and an applet. Other types of applets work almost as TSRs, helping Windows 2000 to monitor specific items of information in the background.

Standard Installation and Removal

You start the standard installation in the Control Panel. Just double-click the Add/Remove Programs applet, and select the Windows Components page. If you look through the list of applications you can install, you'll see all the familiar utility programs Windows provides. You'll notice one thing: This list has no network-administration tools. We take care of that deficiency a little later.

Completing this particular installation process is easy. Just check the items you want to install, and click OK. The Add/Remove Programs applet takes care of the rest. You might need to supply a disk or two if you aren't using the CD-ROM installation. Otherwise, the rest of the process should be fairly automated.

Most of the Windows 2000 applets wait until you run them the first time to automatically detect the required configuration information or to ask you to supply it. Some of them, however, ask for this information immediately if they provide a system service. Installing modem support requires an immediate answer, however, because the system never knows when it'll need that information.

Special Printer Installation

Windows 2000 provides some special printer support. It would seem that you should use the standard installation methods to install these applets, but Microsoft decided to take a different path. The printer applet installation looks almost the same as a printer installation, with a few important differences.

To begin the installation process, open the Printers folder and double-click the Add Printer icon. You should see the Add Print Wizard opening display. Click Next to get past the opening display. Select Local Printer, and click Next to get to the next screen. When working with a plug-and-play compatible local printer you have the option of allowing Windows 2000 to detect it automatically. Select a port for the printer, and click Next to get to the next screen. Note that you can create special port types, like a TCP/IP port, on this dialog. You'll now see a list of standard printers that Windows 2000 supports.

> **Tip:** Microsoft is constantly updating the drivers for existing printers and adding new ones to the list. Clicking the Windows Update button when you see the list of supported printers will allow your machine to connect to the Windows Update Web site on the Internet. This site may contain additional print drivers that you can use when setting up a new printer.

Click the Have Disk button to display the Install From Disk dialog box. Click the Browse button, and use the Open dialog box to find the applet's INF file. Double-click this file to add its name to the Copy Manufacturer's Files From field of the Install From Disk dialog box. Click OK to complete the selection process. Windows 2000 displays a dialog box. Use the Add Printer Wizard dialog box to select the applets you want to install. Notice that the method of listing the potential resource has changed.

Windows 2000 copies some files to disk and then asks some additional questions based on the type of resource you want to install. Following the prompts is fairly easy and should resemble the process of adding a printer.

Special Network Installation

Some special network administration tools exist on your CD-ROM as well. As with the printer-specific resources, you don't use the standard installation routine to add these applets to your system. The following procedure will help you perform a special network installation:

1. Right-click My Network Places, then choose Properties from the context menu. You'll see a Network and Dial-Up Connections dialog box.

2. Right-click the Local Area Connection icon, and then choose Properties from the context menu. You'll see a Local Area Connection Properties dialog box.

3. Click Install. Highlight the type of network component you want to install (Service in most cases), then click Add. If you've chosen to install a Service, you'll see a Select Network Service dialog box.

4. Click the Have Disk button to display the Install From Disk dialog box. Click the Browse, button and use the Open dialog box to find the applet's INF file. Double-click this file to add its name to the Copy Manufacturer's Files From field of the Install From Disk dialog box. Click OK to complete the selection process. Use the Select Network Service dialog box to select the applets you want to install. Notice that the method of listing the potential resource has changed.

5. Click OK. Windows 2000 copies some files to disk and then displays the Network dialog box with a new entry added.

Uninstalling Windows 2000

You can install Windows 2000 on your system, but you won't get it back off very easily—that is, unless you took my advice earlier in this chapter. It wasn't too difficult to figure out that there wasn't going to be an easy way to get rid of Windows 2000 after I installed it (as an upgrade) if it overwrote all my system files and changed quite a few others. Even if I did manage to get my old operating system to boot, I would have to spend a lot of time reinstalling applications.

There's an easier way. The following procedure assumes that you have three things. First, it assumes that you have a DOS or other operating system disk that you can use to boot the machine outside of the normal Windows 2000 boot processes. (Many people create a special boot disk containing DOS and the drivers required to activate items such as their CD-ROM drives.) Second, it assumes that you made a copy of your DOS directory. Finally, it assumes that you installed Windows 2000 to a clean directory. If you didn't follow one of these three steps, you won't have the resources to put your system back together. Follow these steps:

1. The first step in this process is to get DOS to boot again. Use your boot disk to reboot your machine from the floppy disk. (Make sure that you shut down Windows 2000 properly first.)

2. Use the SYS command to restore the system files. Then copy COMMAND.COM and an original copy of AUTOEXEC.BAT and CONFIG.SYS from your floppy disk to the hard drive.

3. Copy the contents of the DOS directory backup that you made to the DOS directory.

4. Take the floppy disk out of the drive, and reboot your system. You should now get to a DOS prompt.

5. Carefully erase all the Windows 2000-specific files. Make absolutely certain that you look for all the hidden files that Microsoft thoughtfully stored in your root directory. You can find these by using the DOS DIR /AH /S command. The /AH switch displays every file that has a hidden attribute. The /S switch tells DIR to look in any subdirectories as well as the root directory. Don't erase any DOS-specific files such as IO.SYS and MSDOS.SYS. The date stamp on the file should give you a clue about which files belong to DOS and which ones belong to Windows 2000. If in doubt, leave the file in place rather than removing it and taking the risk that your system will become nonoperational. It's going to take a little effort to find all the entries; in fact, this is where a good disk editor comes into play.

6. Reboot your machine again to make sure that everything works correctly.

That's it. This isn't the fanciest uninstall method in the world, but it works. You'll probably find bits and pieces of Windows 2000 lying around on your system for a few weeks. If you were careful when you installed it, the pieces should appear in the root directory of all your drives. Of course, the first directory you'll erase is the \WINNT directory. Make sure that you get all the Recycle Bin directories (there's one on each drive) and the program directory that accessory applications.

Reinstalling or Scouring the Registry?

If you've been using computers for a while, you've no doubt observed that there's nothing as slick and efficient as a fresh, untouched operating system. When an OS is first installed, it's as zippy as it'll ever be. Like so many things in life—cars, people—an OS becomes increasingly sluggish over time. For people, the rejuvenation process varies as fads come and go. In my lifetime, suggestions have ranged from immersions, various irrigations, aromatherapy, and even monkey glands. For cars, it's a tune-up. For Windows 2000, your best approach is to scour the Registry. The Registry grows every time you install new applications, and even when you just make small custom changes such as creating a new shortcut icon. And Windows 2000 slows down over time partly because it has to look things up in the Registry—that's where configuration and customization options are kept, among other things. Chapter 10 discusses the Registry in much greater detail; for now, be aware that cleaning your Registry will speed up Windows 2000.

In the old days, I used to always advise people to look at Windows 3.x's WIN.INI and SYSTEM.INI files to see whether they could remove things such as unneeded fonts. Aficionados of Corel and other graphics packages offering 45,000 fonts often didn't realize that you don't have to install all 45,000 or didn't understand what damage that does to the speed of your OS in general. Now, my advice is to take a look at the uninstallation process when you rid yourself of unwanted applications.

Of course, reinstalling Windows 2000 from scratch is the best solution—that's like a major irrigation. All outdated, no-longer-needed drivers and configurations for deleted applications will be gone. But reinstallation is usually too drastic a step; it takes too long to reinstall and reconfigure all the applications you do still use, not to mention customizing Windows 2000 itself. The solution is to do what you can to clean your Registry by hand from time to time.

You can do some preventative maintenance by avoiding installing every application on your main Windows 2000 computer. If you have two computers, install software you're merely trying out—perhaps shareware or demos—on your second, backup computer. That way your main Registry won't become bloated with refuse entries no longer used. Also be sure to uninstall software, if possible, using the Add/Remove Programs utility in the Control Panel. Although software developers might be angry that you've decided to uninstall their product, if they're responsible, they'll have provided a way for all their support files and other clutter to be removed. Don't just erase the folder containing an application you no longer want; use the Control Panel Uninstall utility instead (if the application is listed in that utility).

But in this imperfect world, you'll find that some developers' applications don't completely uninstall even if they have used the Add/Remove Programs utility and enable you to remove them that way. (Punishing you, are they?) And other manufacturers don't participate at all in the Uninstall utility. In those cases, erasing folders is your primary way to delete them. And then, you should try to see what you can do about the Registry.

Run Regedit by pressing Start, Run and typing Regedit. Look for the application in HKEY_LOCAL_MACHINE\SOFTWARE. You'll certainly see an entry for Microsoft, and you'll see other software manufacturers. Like Microsoft, many software developers store all their Registry information using their name as the primary key. Click the main key to drop down the subkeys and see whether you find the application you've deleted. Note that you shouldn't delete a software manufacturer's entire main key unless you want to delete all the subkeys (which might contain applications you do want to continue using). In other words, always expand all subkeys fully to make sure they apply only to the application you're trying to clean out of the Registry. To delete a subkey, right-click its name and choose Delete.

Applications sometimes also store your customizations (options you've chosen) in HKEY_CURRENT_USER\SOFTWARE, so look there as well. And, again, fully expand all subkeys before deleting anything.

Don't assume, however, that an application's developer hasn't also sprinkled debris elsewhere in the Registry. After all, these kinds of developers are, by definition, unkind; otherwise, they would have provided a clean uninstallation in the first place. You can try using Regedit's search feature (press Ctrl+F) to see whether you can track down any additional references to the product.

On Your Own

Create your own boot disk that contains the drivers required to bring your machine up to a minimal level of performance. This boot disk could use any operating system, but most people use DOS because it is a small operating system that provides the minimal functionality required to start most installation programs. Make sure that you test the boot disk before you install Windows 2000. You'll also want to create a Windows 2000–specific startup disk during installation. Label both disks, and keep them until you're certain that your Windows 2000 installation is stable.

Make a list of all the equipment you think you might have problems with. Include all the items that Windows 2000 doesn't provide entries for in the existing INF files. Do you see any entries that you can fix using the procedures provided in this chapter? Are there any ways to eliminate some of the 16-bit drivers you might need to use to keep older equipment running? Develop a comprehensive strategy for handling any problem areas before you begin the installation process.

Exploring the Interface

If you're moving from Windows 95—or especially Windows 98 or NT 4—to Windows 2000, you'll find the user interface quite familiar (although there *are* some interesting new features: Try right-clicking a DOC filename in Windows Explorer and then choose Properties, Summary).

If you're jumping from the Macintosh or an earlier version of Windows or Windows NT (versions 3 and earlier), however, you can expect to make some major adjustments in the way you interact with your desktop.

Most people find the changes, once learned, quite beneficial. After all, Microsoft spent countless years studying how people interact with its graphical user interface (GUI). All that analysis has culminated in the latest incarnation: Windows 2000. It's a window into your computer's hard drive, but also a window into the world of the Internet.

If you're familiar with the Windows 95/98 or Windows NT 4 desktop, you might want to just read the tips sprinkled throughout this chapter (you'll doubtless discover some that can make your work more efficient and pleasant). If you're new to the Explorer desktop metaphor, however, this chapter is for you.

This chapter gives you a bird's-eye view of what you can expect from Windows 2000. This includes the utilities and applications, called *accessories*, as well as a quick look at the internal workings of Windows 2000. Of course, we'll cover more specific details of some of these items in later chapters. Right now, just sit back and enjoy the view of this popular operating system.

Explorer Borrowed from Windows 95

The first thing every new Windows 2000 user will notice is the interface—it actually started with Windows 95 and has been undergoing subtle (and sometimes not-so-subtle) modifications ever since. Windows 2000 boasts a clean, well-designed look that most every user will come to enjoy using. In fact, it's amusing to recall just how cumbersome earlier versions of Windows were (remember Program Manager and File Manager?). Explorer offers something for everyone and does its job in a way that makes it simultaneously powerful and easy to use.

It's Your Choice

Explorer is far more flexible than previous ways of viewing and organizing a hard drive, or for that matter, your Internet surfing. One of the subtle but powerful shifts in Windows in the past couple years is the blending of inner space (hard drive) and world computing (the millions of hard drives and connections exposed by the Internet). Many people don't realize it, but switching between Internet Explorer and Windows Explorer is as easy as a click of the mouse (see Chapter 6, which is appropriately titled "There's Really Only One Explorer"). Are you in Windows Explorer? Select a site on the Favorites menu and see what happens to "Windows" Explorer.

For now, though, the focus is strictly on your hard drive and its portal, Windows Explorer. To begin, Windows Explorer is highly customizable—it offers a choice of two basic ways to view your data: single pane or double pane, as you can see in Figure 5.1.

FIGURE 5.1

Explorer offers two basic views of your data: a one-pane and a two-pane interface. Take your choice.

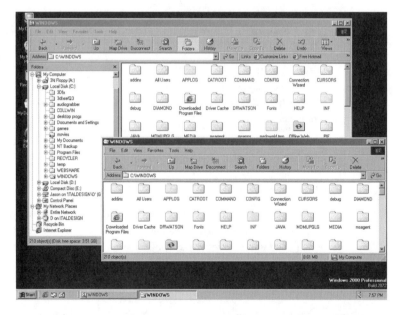

Tip: To launch Explorer, you can click the Start button and then select Programs, Accessories, Windows Explorer. This is a rather cumbersome way to launch such an important tool. A much better alternative is to click the My Computer icon or any folder icon that you've placed on your desktop. However, the best way to launch Explorer works even when your screen is filled with your word processor or from anywhere else in Windows: If you have a keyboard with the special Windows key on it, just press Windows+E.

Viewing information is only the tip of the Explorer iceberg. To really use an interface, you need to get inside and work with it. Your data has to be accessible at all times without getting in the way.

> **Note:** It is possible that the folder names and filenames are underlined. This is to remind you that you're using what I call the *Web view* option (technically it's not called *Web view*, it's just another folder option). The items in the Explorer are illustrated like links in a Web browser (hyperlinks are usually underlined in Web pages): When you single-click, you launch or open underlined files. I have more to say about Web view in Chapter 6, "There's Really Only One Explorer," which is all about the melding of the Windows and Internet Explorers.

Figure 5.2

The Explorer's features are easier to understand when you look at them individually.

Let's begin our tour of Explorer by examining how it's organized. Figure 5.2 shows the two-pane configuration of Explorer and the Large Icons view. On the left side of the display is the directory tree. You need to make note of several features of this directory tree for future reference. The first thing you'll notice is that the tree doesn't represent a single drive or even the contents of all the drives; it's really a machine tree. This machine tree is divided into the following three elements:

- *The drive section*. This is the area where the contents of all your data drives are displayed. This includes any network drives you're connected to.

- *The configuration section*. This area contains only one icon in the sample display in Figure 5.2. (You might see other icons here as well on your system.) The Control Panel provides access to every machine configuration component that

Windows 2000 offers. It includes both hardware and software configuration. We'll take a much more detailed look at this particular component later in the book. (NT 4 included a printer icon in this section, but it's missing in Windows 2000. The printer icon is still available in the Control Panel, though.)

- *The ancillary section.* This section can contain any number of icons. Figure 5.2 contains several icons, including the Recycle Bin icon. The Recycle Bin is where any documents you erase end up when you use the Delete key in Explorer to remove a file or folder (or even other items, such as shortcut icons). We cover the Recycle Bin feature in greater detail later. The Recycle Bin, the Desktop, and My Computer are the only icons that always appear. If you right-click any of these three icons, you won't see a Delete option on the context menu. To me it's odd that the Recycle Bin cannot be removed—after all, many people don't use its icon to drop items into it (they just press the Delete key). I suppose that someone thought the notion was conceptually impossible—like trying to use a garbage disposal to grind itself up. The My Network Places icon appears when you have a network installed on your machine. This icon enables you to attach to network resources and view network data. The My Network Places is a very handy way to discover what types of information you have at your fingertips. Also notice that Internet Explorer appears in the ancillary section (though it can be deleted), as well as any folders that you've created on your desktop.

LOOKING AHEAD

We'll look at other aspects of Explorer in future chapters. Read Chapter 8, "Customizing Windows 2000 for Maximum Productivity," if you want some additional tips on using Explorer to optimize your work environment.

Now that you have some idea of what the left pane contains, let's look at the right pane. Clicking any of the objects in the left pane displays its contents in the right pane. If you click a drive icon, you see the folders and files the drive contains in the right pane. Click My Network Places and you'll get a view of all the machines attached to the network. You can also use the icons in the right pane to open a file or folder. Double-click a folder to see what it contains. Double-click a file to perform the default action associated with that file. (If you've turned on the special Web view option, as I call it, you only need to single-click. Choose Tools, Folder Options in Windows Explorer.)

LOOKING AHEAD

Double-clicking is optional. You can switch to Internet hyperlink-style clicking if you prefer. To jump to a link, you merely single-click rather than double-click. If you would prefer to open files and folders as well as launch applications by just single-clicking their icons, you can select this option from the Folder Options dialog box, as shown in Figure 5.3. Choose Tools|Folder Options in Windows Explorer. I'll have more to say about these options in Chapter 6, "There's Really Only One Explorer."

You can use Explorer in a number of ways to organize your data. Each tool provides a different method of viewing and working with your data. Let's begin with one of the first tools you'll want to master in Windows 2000: the context menu. The following sections look at the various ways you can use Explorer to enhance your productivity by organizing your data.

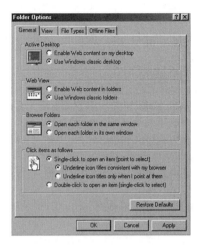

FIGURE 5.3
Here's where you can choose to switch from the classic Windows double-click to the Web-style single-click.

Objects and the Context Menu

Every object you use in Windows 2000 displays its context menu when you right-click it. If you want to customize the object, a simple right-click will offer you various options. Figure 5.4 shows a typical context menu. Don't let its simplicity fool you. There's a lot more here than meets the eye.

FIGURE 5.4
The context menu provides one way to discover exactly what you can do with an object.

Every context menu for a file or folder contains five or six major sections. Each section tells you something about the object associated with that menu. The following list outlines each section and its purpose (seven sections are actually listed, but you won't find any context menus that use them all):

- *Actions.* The first section of the context menu tells you what kinds of actions you can perform with the object. The default action—normally Open—appears in boldface. Chapter 8, "Customizing Windows 2000 for Maximum Productivity," shows you how to change the default action to meet your needs. Besides the Open action, you'll sometimes see a Print action. And, if you have WinZip installed, the menu will offer two options: general zipping and quick zip, based on the name of the object.

  You'll see one other type of entry in the context menu. If the file extension doesn't appear in the Registry, Windows 2000 won't know what to do with it. In this case, you'll see an Open With... entry. If you right-click a folder icon (as opposed to a file icon), you'll normally see an Explore and a Search action listed along with Open.

- *Compression.* You'll only see these two entries on NTFS-formatted drives. One enables you to compress the file; the other enables you to decompress it. This is a handy feature for files you don't use on a constant basis. You can still access the file—it just may take a few additional seconds to do so (although on a Pentium over 300MHz, you'll likely see a file instantly). However, incompatibilities, the speed penalty, and other drawbacks of compression usually make it something many people choose to avoid—particularly these days, when 8GB drives and larger are common. Therefore, unless you're managing immense databases or are a graphics artist and work frequently with huge high-resolution, disk space–grabbing files, you might want to avoid disk compression altogether.

Technical Note: that a compressed file or folder can still be shared and used by users on the network, even if they're not Windows 2000 Professional/Server users. People are sometimes confused by this.

Windows 2000 takes a different approach from Windows 95/98 to displaying the results of file compression. Windows 95/98 retains the uncompressed size of the file, but increases the size of the drive to compensate for any space savings realized during compression. In other words, the file looks the same as it did before, but the drive looks bigger. Windows 2000 shows the compressed file size but doesn't adjust the size of the hard drive. This method gives you a more accurate representation of the file-compression process because you can determine exactly how much of a space savings you get.

- *Network*. This is an optional section that normally contains a single entry: Sharing. Some objects support sharing and others don't. It all depends on how you have your network set up. Normally, peer-to-peer networks enable this option only for folders. Larger networks, such as those from Novell, provide this entry for both files and folders.

- *Send To*. Use this special entry if you want to send the folder or file to a floppy drive or other location. You can modify the destinations listed in this entry to include just about any target where you commonly store things. Windows 2000 comes installed to support any floppy disks connected to your system, Desktop (creates a shortcut), Mail Recipient, My Documents and the Briefcase as destinations. You can add destinations to this handy feature by adding shortcuts to them in the Send To folder found in WINNT\Profiles*YourName*\Send To if you upgraded from NT 4. If your Windows 2000 system was installed fresh on a formatted drive, the \Profiles folder will be replaced by a \Documents and Settings folder.

- *Editing*. Believe it or not, you can edit an object. For the purposes of this discussion, the term *object* includes essentially everything on the desktop or within Explorer. This section of the context menu contains entries for Cut, Copy, and, if there's something in the Clipboard, Paste. You can place a copy of the object on the Clipboard and then paste as many copies as needed onto other objects. These are full-fledged copies, not the shortcuts (object links) we'll examine in the next section. If you cut an object, Windows 2000 doesn't remove the icon from the display. It grays out the icon and waits until you paste the object somewhere else before removing it permanently. This prevents you from accidentally erasing objects. Cutting a new object before you paste the first one leaves the first object intact; Windows 2000 thoughtfully waits to remove the first file until you find a new location for it.

Tip: Always remember that you can cut, copy, and paste objects using the keyboard shortcuts you use to perform those same operations in documents to move pieces of text. After an object is highlighted in, say, Explorer (in other words, it's selected when you click it), use Ctrl+C for Copy, Ctrl+V for Paste, and Ctrl+X for Cut. There are additional, optional, redundant key combinations as well, such as Shift+Del for Cut.

- *Manipulation*. This section usually contains three entries, but it can contain more. The Create Shortcut option enables you to place a link to a file or folder somewhere else. Chapter 8, "Customizing Windows 2000 for Maximum Productivity," shows you how to use this feature to make your desktop a friendlier place. The Delete option sends the file to the Recycle Bin. You can still recover it later if necessary. The Rename option enables you to change the name of the object.

Tip: You can also rename an object by *slowly* double-clicking the filename in Explorer; just wait a second between clicks. Then you can just type the new name underneath the icon. This presupposes that you've chosen to use the classic Windows clicking mode. (If you're using Web-style single-click, you must right-click to drop down the context menu before renaming.) However, you can also press F2 to trigger the Renaming mode, or you can right-click and choose Rename from the Properties context menu.

You don't have to send objects to the Recycle Bin if you don't want to. Just select the object you want to delete and then press Shift+Del to erase it permanently (as far as Windows is concerned). Even if an object is erased by accident, you can usually unerase it using The Norton Utilities for some length of time after you "permanently" erase it. (The time interval varies by the amount of empty space on your drive and the amount of use that drive gets.) Because the Recycle Bin's space is limited, you'll probably want to reserve it for objects you might need later. Also, you'll probably want to right-click the Recycle Bin icon and choose Empty Recycle Bin fairly often.

Caution: If you're deleting from an NTFS partition, after you erase it, it's gone for good! There's no recovery if it doesn't go to the Recycle Bin. This is a security precaution. Also, note that in NT 4 if you deleted something that exceeded the size of the available space in the Recycle Bin, it was not sent to the Recycle Bin; it was simply deleted entirely. However, in Windows 2000, the Recycle Bin deletes older contents as new content comes in when it is pushing its limit.

- *Properties*. Nearly every object—it doesn't matter what—contains a Properties entry on its context menu. You'll even find Properties within applications. Try right-clicking an object, such as a graphics file, embedded within a Word 97 document. The Properties entry always displays a dialog box that enables you to view and configure the properties of that particular object. Figure 5.5 shows the Properties dialog box for a file. As you can see, this dialog box shows the full filename, any attributes associated with the file, and some statistical information. Folders usually contain about the same information as files but provide some additional statistics as well. Disks, on the other hand, contain a wealth of information about the drive as a whole. The Disk Properties dialog box even provides access to the three maintenance tools Windows 2000 provides to manage disk drives. You'll find that the Properties dialog boxes for other objects, such as the Desktop, contain a wealth of information, too. The Desktop Properties dialog box enables you to change the system colors and display resolution, for example. You can even use it to change your wallpaper.

Some objects in your system have very specialized context menu entries. Recall that if you right-click the Recycle Bin, for example, you'll see an option to empty it. Right-clicking the desktop provides a New option that you can use to create new files. (You'll see the same menu option if you right-click a blank area of Explorer.)

FIGURE 5.5

All objects have Properties dialog boxes—just right-click the object.

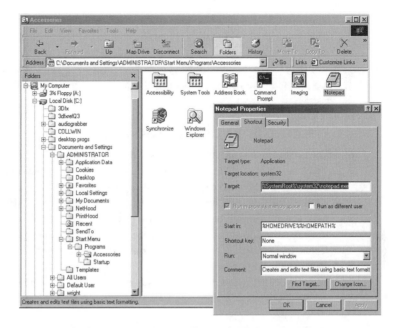

If you click the Advanced button on the General tab, you can specify that the file should be archived (if your backup program supports this option). You can also add this file to the new Indexing service (see details on this later in the chapter), compress the file (if supported), and encrypt the contents. If you click the Shortcut tab on the Properties dialog box (EXE files have this tab; HTM and other document files don't), you can add comments to this file, define a shortcut key to it, and specify the window size and startup default location. The Security tab allows those with permission to adjust this object's security settings.

Peter's Principle: Learning by Doing: An Enjoyable Way to Increase Your Windows 2000 Knowledge

Get used to right-clicking objects. Even links within Web pages and other unlikely locations can surprise you with a valuable context menu and, often, properties you can customize. You'll want to spend some time right-clicking various objects on your system to see their context menu options. It also pays to spend a little time looking at the Properties dialog boxes for various objects, even if you don't use certain objects very much. Windows 2000 provides a variety of methods to access each of the configuration dialog boxes on your system, and most of them appear in these context menus or within the Properties dialog box. If you think, as I do, that changing common configuration items using the Control Panel is a waste of time, Windows 2000 often provides a faster method for doing so via the context menus.

Remember these two things when you're experimenting with your system: First, always click Cancel rather than OK when backing out of a Properties dialog box to avoid making inadvertent changes to your system. Second, how do you close a context menu without using Cancel or OK? Clicking outside of a context menu closes it without performing any action. In most cases, the safest place to click is the desktop. You can also click the Esc key.

Using the Explorer Toolbars

The context menu isn't the only tool Windows 2000 provides an intrepid computerist. You'll also enjoy the capabilities provided by Explorer's various other features. The toolbars, shown in Figure 5.6, are used quite a bit. With a single click, they enable you to change your view, turn Windows Explorer into Internet Explorer, listen to an Internet radio station, see your current hard drive path, click a quick link to a pet Web site, search for you name it, switch between two-pane and one-pane views, use the new Move To feature (a combination of cut, browse, and paste), see your Internet Favorites channel bar (replaces the Folders bar on the split view), switch from icons to text (and vice versa), and get your hair washed. Well, maybe not that last one, not yet anyway. However, you get the idea—lots of stuff is only a click away.

FIGURE 5.6
Explorer Toolbars
*The Windows
2000 Explorer's
toolbars are func-
tionally identical
to the Internet
Explorer version 5
toolbars.*

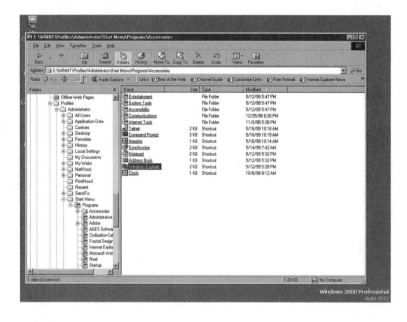

The following list describes the various toolbar features:

- *Address list box.* Contains a list of drives, Internet Explorer, and other upper-level objects. Try dropping the list by clicking the down-arrow icon on the right. It also contains the tree used to access the current folder (the left pane in Explorer).

You can use this list box to quickly move from one area of your machine to another. It's useful for those who prefer the single-pane Explorer option. This way, you can drop down the contents of the left pane when you want to move globally to a different drive or other major location on your system, or out through Internet Explorer into the Internet. Type in an Internet address, such as MSN, and hit Enter to see what happens. If Internet Explorer is not currently running, it will be started—giving you two explorers running: both Windows and Internet. However, if IE is already running, your Windows Explorer will transform itself into Internet Explorer when you hit Enter.

- *Back and Forward*. These icons are the equivalent of the same icons found on Internet Explorer and other browsers. Clicking them moves you through the history of your surfing. You can go back to see the past few Explorer views you've chosen. And, after you've gone back, the Forward icon becomes active, enabling you to return by climbing back up your history tree during this session with Explorer. Also, notice the two black arrows next to these icons. Click one of those arrows and a list drops down in which your history is listed; you can jump anywhere within it by clicking.

- *Up One Level*. Moves up one level in the directory tree. This tool isn't quite as handy in this view of Explorer as it is in others. The Up One Level tool is especially helpful when you're moving between levels in the single-pane view of Explorer.

- *Map Network Drive*. Explorer displays this tool only if you're connected to a network, and then only if you add it to the toolbar by hand. It's not a default button on the toolbar. (Right-click any toolbar and then choose Customize.) It displays a dialog box that enables you to map one of your drives to a network drive. Of course, you can still access the drive using My Network Places, even if you don't map it. Notice that this dialog box provides an expanded view that you can use to find a particular drive selection. It uses a hierarchical structure similar to My Network Places.

- *Disconnect Network Drive*. This tool becomes active only when you install a network and map some network drives to your local drives. Clicking this tool displays a dialog box that you can use to disconnect from any network drive. Of course, the drives remain accessible using My Network Places even after you disconnect. You have to add Disconnect Network Drive "by hand" as well as Map Network Drive.

- *Move To*. Displays a file browser where you click the target folder or drive. After that destination is specified, the selected object is cut from its current location and moved to the new one. This is much better than the multiple-step project that moving an object used to be.

- *Copy To*. Same as Move To, but it doesn't delete the original. (Better than Copy.)

- *Delete*. Same as pressing the Delete key.

- *Undo*. Reverses your previous action. Restores the original name if you renamed a file and brings it back from the Recycle Bin if you deleted it. The Undo tool doesn't work for some types of actions. You can't undo a permanent erase (Shift+Del), for example.

  The Cut, Copy, and Paste icons from previous versions of Windows have been removed from the Windows 2000 Explorer. However, you can still accomplish these jobs by pressing shortcut keys, or by selecting them from the Edit menu.

- *Properties*. Displays the Properties dialog box for the currently selected object. Nothing happens if you don't select an object. This one can be useful, but it's not a default icon. You must add it by right-clicking the toolbar and then choosing Customize.

- *Views*. This drop-down list lets you switch quickly between the five elemental Explorer views. A new one is *Thumbnails*, which quickly shows you a quite large thumbnail of any graphics files, as shown in Figure 5.7.

FIGURE 5.7

This new Thumbnail view is quite handy if you do any work with graphics or photography.

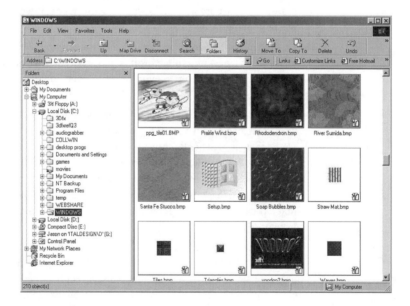

The classic Explorer views include Large Icons, which displays the objects in the right pane using the Large Icon format, Small Icons, which displays the objects in the right pane using the Small Icon format, List, which uses the List format to display objects in the right pane (it doesn't include any details about the objects), and Details, which displays the objects in a list format but also includes all the details about those objects, including file size, type, and date last modified.

Explorer also permits you to fiddle with the look of its right pane, turning it into a Web view—a style that features a large icon, individual backgrounds for each folder, Web content (HTML) and other customizations. This topic is covered in Chapter 6, "There's Really Only One Explorer," in the section "The Classic View Versus the Web View."

Explorer Fields-O-Plenty!

You can see many, many fields in the right pane in Windows Explorer. If you're used to the traditional Name, Size, Type, and Modified fields, you can have a *field day* (forgive me) by adding lots of new fields if you like. To see what you can do, right-click the column header bar in Explorer (the bar that contains Name, Size, Type, and Modified) and then click More in the context menu. (Note that you must select View|Details in Explorer to see column headers.) You'll see a list of 28 fields you can add to your Explorer's right pane. To modify these fields for an individual file, right-click the filename and then click Properties and the Summary tab. Only certain file types permit you to add these additional fields, including graphics, ZIP (archive), DOC (word processor) and MDB (database) files.

I started this section by saying that Explorer contains three distinct sections: drive, configuration, and ancillary. I didn't go into much detail about these sections at the time because I wanted to talk about some of the tools Explorer provides. It's important to know that the sections exist, but it's even more important to know how to use them to build an information center.

What do I mean by an *information center*? Think of it this way: Explorer can provide access to everything you, as a user, need to work with Windows. Unlike the 3.x previous versions of Windows, separate utilities aren't hanging around waiting for you to find them. I like the Explorer approach because between it and the Start button, all the tools you need are always present. The following sections tell you all about using Explorer as an information center—your one stop for everything related to your computer from a user's perspective.

The Control Panel

As is often the case in Windows 2000 and recent versions of Windows, you can access the Control Panel and its components in many different ways. Even Explorer provides a method of access, as shown in Figure 5.8.

The number and types of icons you find in Control Panel will vary with the applications and equipment you install. Items such as the Printers folder always appear in your Control Panel. On the other hand, you won't always see an ODBC folder or some of the other specialty items the Control Panel provides. We'll take a detailed look at the Control Panel's features later in the chapter.

FIGURE 5.8

There are several ways to get to Control Panel. In Explorer's Folders pane, just click the Control Panel's Folder's icon.

The Printers icon, which used to be on the outer level of the Explorer left pane, is now a subfolder within the Control Panel folder (see Figure 5.9).

FIGURE 5.9

Activate and organize your printers in this folder.

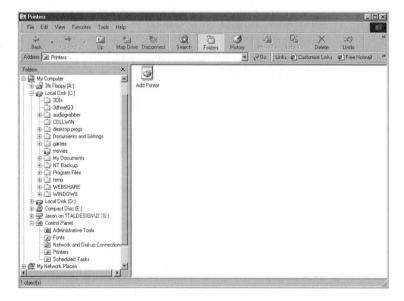

Looking Ahead Chapter 18, "Fonts and Printing," covers all the details of managing your printers. It also looks at the process of adding a new printer to your system. The second half of that chapter looks at the details of using fonts to dress up your output.

My Network Places

Think of My Network Places as a dynamic extension of Explorer for a network. Figure 5.10 shows a typical My Network Places folder. As you can see, the Entire Network icon includes more than your local machine. No longer are you looking at a local machine but at all the resources you can access on the network as a whole.

FIGURE 5.10

Use the My Network Places feature to navigate your network and reorganize the "places."

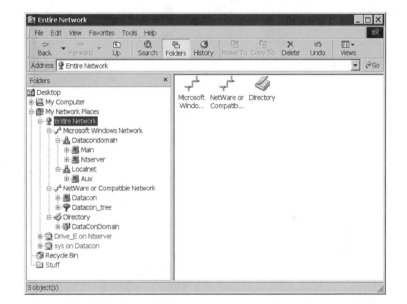

You might also see other entries at the same level as the Entire Network. These are machines you can access on peer-to-peer or client/server networks. You can always access your own resources, so you'll always see your machine listed here (unless your network administrator has prevented you; administrators can hide even your computer or hard drive from you if they wish). In this case, two workstations and one file server are on the network. Notice that you can see only the shared drives for the machines, not any drive that's local. I also found it interesting that not every shared resource appears on the tree. You have to actually select the drive to see any resources beyond the drive. Figure 5.11 shows a printer resource on the Main machine in addition to the four shared drives that show up in the tree listing.

You need to know a few interesting things about My Network Places that make it different from the rest of Explorer. First, you can't access the properties for the Entire

Network. Unfortunately, this means that you can't disable the War and Poverty settings. All joking aside, Entire Network is just a placeholder for My Network Places; it doesn't exist as a concrete object.

FIGURE 5.11
Always check the machine in question if you want to see all the resources; the directory tree shows only shared drives.

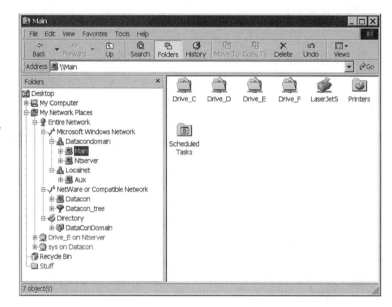

Below Entire Network are entries for each network you're currently connected to. In most cases, you'll see the actual workgroup or domain name rather than the name of the network vendor or product. This list changes as your connections change. You can look here to see whether a problem is application or network related. An application error, such as the inability to open a file, might look like a network error for a variety of reasons. If you look in the Entire Network folder and see the connection, however, it's very unlikely that the connection is the problem. Chapter 31, "Solving Hardware Problems," contains tips that help you locate and fix other problems with the hardware and software on your machine.

If you attach to a peer-to-peer network, the machine names appear before each network entry in the My Network Places hierarchy. Below the machine entries, a list of the drives you can access appears. The method for listing other types of network machine names and their resources differs according to the network. Figure 5.11 shows a NetWare network using NetWare Directory Services (NDS) rather than bindery emulation. The tree icon shows the NDS part of the network. I cover client/server networks such as NetWare in more detail in Chapter 27, "Client/Server Networking."

My Network Places works the same as the rest of Explorer from a user perspective. Of course, you can't change the properties of network resources in most cases. If you right-click the My Network Places icon, a new, single-pane Explorer window displays your connections as well as any dial-up connections you've defined.

Recycle Bin

The Recycle Bin works the same in Explorer as it does on the desktop. You can drop things into it, examine its contents, empty it, and restore a file to its original (or another) location. The Explorer copy of the Recycle Bin comes in handy if you see a file you want to erase and the desktop Recycle Bin is covered by another application. Figure 5.12 shows the Recycle Bin. As you can see, it looks just like any other folder in Windows 2000.

FIGURE 5.12

Items tanked into the Recycle Bin look just the same as their still-healthy cousins elsewhere on the hard drive.

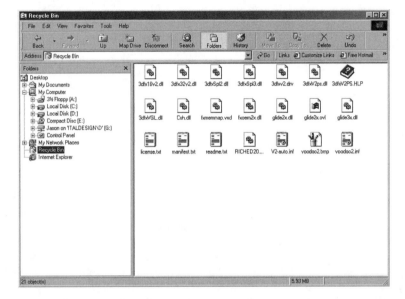

> **Tip:** Files in the Recycle Bin continue to take up space on the drive. Windows 2000 moves deleted files to the Recycle Bin—a special folder—until you erase them for good. Any short (old DOS) filenames are changed to allow multiple files of the same name to coexist peacefully in the Recycle Bin. If you find that you're short on hard drive space, you might want to see whether you can get rid of anything in the Recycle Bin.

Sometimes, your Recycle Bin won't contain anything. Files in the Recycle Bin look just like files anywhere else. You can move objects in the Recycle Bin to other areas of Explorer to unerase them. Until you do unerase them, the Properties dialog box won't tell you much except the filename and the date you deleted it.

The context menu for objects in the Recycle Bin looks a little different, as shown in Figure 5.13. One of the really handy items on this list is Restore. You can select one or more files and then restore them by choosing this entry. Another handy option is Delete. This enables you to select just one or two Recycle Bin entries and delete them for good without disturbing the rest of the items in the Recycle Bin.

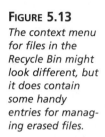

FIGURE 5.13

The context menu for files in the Recycle Bin might look different, but it does contain some handy entries for managing erased files.

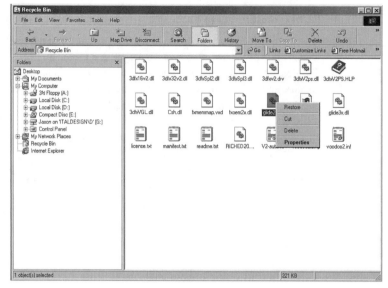

Peter's Principle: Making Explorer Both a Local and a Worldwide Gateway

Explorer is your portal to all the main components of your system, enabling you to easily customize your machine, print documents, discard or update files, and reach out in any direction to manage or access information. I say "in any direction" because it's important to realize that Explorer quite easily turns from a gateway to your local hard drive(s) into a gateway to the hard drives on servers worldwide (in other words, the Internet).

How simple is it to turn Explorer's attention to the Internet? As Chapter 6, "There's Really Only One Explorer," shows in detail, Windows Explorer can morph into Internet Explorer in a flash. Try one of these approaches while Explorer is displaying your hard drive's contents: Drop down the Address box and click Internet Explorer (if the Address box isn't showing, choose Toolbars from the View menu and activate it). Boom! Explorer's right pane transforms into your home page on the Internet. Want to go right back to viewing your hard drive? Click the Back button. You're back in local view. (If you're using Explorer in the dual-pane view, you can get back to your hard drive by just clicking one of the folders or drives displayed in the left pane.) Many people don't realize they can display their local systems in the left pane while displaying Internet sites in the right pane, all within Explorer.

The simplest way of all to get back to your hard drive after moving on to the Internet is to just press the Backspace key. (Of course, the Backspace key moves you back by one view. If you've done any surfing, you'll have to press Backspace repeatedly to get back to Windows Explorer hard drive view.)

Want another way to toggle between the micro and macro world views in Explorer? Click the View, Go To menu. A list of the most recently viewed targets appears. (In NT 4, this list used to be on the File menu.) Hard drive locations will be mixed in with Internet sites if you've been using Explorer to go in both directions (as you can see in Figure 5.14). Click whatever you want to return to, or, if you've just returned to the hard drive from Internet surfing, just click the Forward button.

FIGURE 5.14

You can have a Folders (hard drive) pane on the left side and an Internet page on the right side of Explorer.

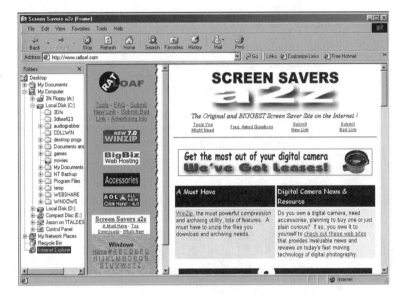

As you might expect, there are yet other ways to transform a "hard drive" view to an Internet view in Explorer. Try choosing Explorer Bar from the View menu to activate various Internet access tools, such as Search, Favorites, and History. Of course, the Favorites menu (or Favorites button on the toolbar) is likely crammed with Internet sites you've enjoyed and saved in Favorites for future visits. (You might be surprised to learn you can add folders on your system's local hard drive to the Favorites list. When a file or folder is selected—it has reversed colors or is underlined because you clicked it—just choose Add to Favorites from Explorer's Favorites menu.)

One final tip: Just in case you don't know whether you're viewing your hard drive or someone's Web page, you can look at the status bar at the bottom of the Explorer window. It will read *My Computer* when you're local, Local intranet if you're viewing a shared drive, and *Internet* when you're out on the Web.

The Startup Folder

The Startup folder replaces the ancient WIN.INI file, with its LOAD= and RUN= entries that eventually become a confused, tangled mess. Instead, you use the Startup folder to maintain a certain level of order. (Of course, some applications still insist on using the antiquated INI method of automatically starting an application, so Windows 2000 has to support it. You'll find good old WIN.INI in your WINNT folder.) Think of the Startup folder as a sort of auto–launch pad for your Windows applications. Windows automatically looks in this folder during the boot process and launches anything it finds there.

In earlier versions of Windows, some types of files didn't work very well. I found it difficult to automatically open any kind of data file, for example, even when it was associated with an application. Under Windows 2000, you can stick just about anything in the Startup folder and expect it to open like a flower.

Like most everything else in Windows 2000, you'll find the Startup folder in Explorer. Unfortunately, it's deep in the directory tree. If you look in the folder

```
\WINNT\profiles\<your name>\Start Menu\Programs
```

```
(Recall that if your Windows 2000 system was intalled fresh on a formatted drive,
rather than upgraded from NT4, the \Profiles folder will be replaced by
\Documents and Settings folder.)
```

you'll see the Startup folder, as shown in Figure 5.15. Another, faster way to access the folder is to right-click Start then choose the Explore option. This displays a two-pane version of Explorer that you can use to get to the Startup folder more quickly.

FIGURE 5.15
The Startup folder is buried deep in the directory tree under the Start menu.

An Accessory Overview

Windows 2000 has a lot more to offer than just Explorer. A whole group of utility programs is available to make your life easier. In the past, some of these applications were previously available only from third parties, but today you can get them as part of the operating system package. The following sections look at some of the new accessories provided with Windows 2000.

LOOKING AHEAD

This overview includes only accessory applications. I discuss security-related programs and features in Chapter 28, "Security Issues." Most of the standard communications application information appears in Chapter 20, "Windows 2000 Connections." You'll also want to spend some time checking out the Internet Explorer coverage in Chapter 2, "Windows to the Internet."

Accessories

Windows 2000 doesn't add very much when it comes to accessory applications. The multimedia offerings (now called *Entertainment* rather than the previous *Multimedia*) are much the same as they have been for years, with one exception. The CD player has gone from dull, old gunmetal gray to a sleek new retro look (see Figure 5.16). The Entertainment accessories group consists of the CD player, Sound Recorder, and Volume Control, which is actually a more complex control than a single volume bar. The Volume Control used to be called the *Mixer*, but that was not an accurate name (see Figure 5.17).

Note that you can now download, from the Internet, CD descriptions (play list information) on the artist and tracks of many CDs. Just click the Internet Button shown in Figure 5.16.

> **Tip:** Click the Advanced tab in the Volume Control dialog box to adjust tone (treble and bass) and also add a 3D stereo enhancement. Precisely what you can do in this dialog box depends on your sound card, but the "enhancements" most often used include playing around with small delays and fiddling with phase in order to smear the stereo field "beyond" the two speakers. Some people even claim to hear sounds coming from above or behind them. Try clicking the 3D check box on and off while listening to a MID file or a favorite CD—see if you notice a difference and, moreover, if you *like* that difference. I generally do, although you'll probably have to adjust the overall balance after choosing 3D. (If you don't see an Advanced tab, try clicking the Options menu, changing to Record from Playback, clicking the Advanced Controls option on the Options menu (which is now available), then clicking the Advanced button.) This feature appears to be sound card dependent.

FIGURE 5.16

Not much is new in the Entertainment division, except the CD Player utility has gone sleek and retro.

FIGURE 5.17

The Volume Control manages various sources and also controls stereo balance.

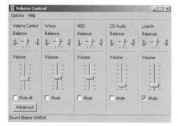

Windows 2000 also includes some of the other familiar utilities from previous versions of Windows, including Calculator and the ever-reliable Notepad.

The Control Panel in Depth

Few people ever get comfortable with the Control Panel. You access it to change a major hardware or software configuration item; then you leave, and you don't come back to it until your system needs adjustment again. In other words, you don't visit the Control Panel on a daily basis.

> **Tip:** You can now "expand" the Start | Settings | Control Panel option so you can pick an applet instead of opening the full window. It's a new Start menu option.

The reason I bring up this point is simple: This lack of contact with the Control Panel is probably the reason why some people seem to forget it's there. I've spent hours trying to figure out how to change certain settings in Control Panel. It's not just that the Control Panel is difficult to use or illogically laid out but rather that too few people have experience with it.

Figure 5.18 shows a typical Control Panel folder. No two Control Panels are alike, however. The Control Panel usually contains a set of default icons and a bunch of icons related to your particular system configuration.

FIGURE **5.18**

The Control Panel is a deep, dark secret to some people, and none too familiar to everyone else.

Now might be a good time to check out some of the applets in the Control Panel. Some of them will seem familiar because we've already talked about them elsewhere in the book. Others will be new because we haven't really covered them yet. The following list provides an overview of the Control Panel's primary contents:

- *Accessibility Options.* We'll visit the shortcuts for this particular applet in Chapter 8, "Customizing Windows 2000 for Maximum Productivity." These options enable you to change some Windows 2000 features to make them easier to operate for people challenged in various ways. This applet enables you to enable the StickyKeys option for the keyboard, for example.

- *Add/Remove Programs.* Adding and removing software is relatively simple in Windows 2000, but probably not as easy as it could be. We looked at some of the difficulties of using this particular applet in Chapter 4, "Installing Windows 2000 Professional: A Setup Primer."

- *Administrative Tools.* This is a folder, not just a single utility. It's now the repository of other utilities that in some cases (ODBC, for example) used to be in the main Control Panel folder. Most of these utilities are covered elsewhere in this book. Component Services manages COM+ applications. This, and other administrative tools are part of the new MMC (Microsoft Management Console) snap-ins set. MMC hosts administrative tools for managing individual computers, networks, and other system components. The Computer Management utility embraces many, somewhat unrelated utilities. It includes disk drive management (such as defragmentation) but also includes a variety of disparate utilities such as the new Indexing Service, IIS (Internet Information Service), Hardware Resources, Components, and others. Many of these same utilities can be reached via other paths—press Windows+F, choose Indexing Service, and then click the Advanced button to start the Indexing Service, for instance. The ODBC utility is described later in the list. The Internet Services Manager allows you to host Internet/intranet sites—and also to test Web pages on your own machine without having to involve

a server (see Chapter 25, "Using FrontPage Express"). The Local Security Policy
(IP Security refers to Internet Protocol) utility can be used (depending on your
level of permissions) as a way to protect against both Internet-based intruders as
well as people in your own organization who might want to intercept data as it
moves around your network. See Chapter 28, "Security Issues," for more on various security issues. The Performance utility includes both the Performance
Monitor (displaying graphs of your system's behavior) and also the Performance
Log feature. The Personal Web Manager (PWM) is a useful utility if you work
with Web sites—see Chapter 25. The Server Extensions Administrator manages the
FrontPage Server Extensions, three utilities that are useful with FrontPage-extend-
ed Webs (see Chapter 25). Finally, the Services utility allows you to stop, pause, or
start various services (Event Log, Indexing, Fax, and many others) on your local
machine or a remote machine. You can also use it to specify what should happen if
a service fails (restart the machine or restart the service). Some of the above services are not installed by default—you have to add them yourself using the
Add/Remove Programs applet.

- *Date/Time*. Keeping the date and time current on your machine will become more
  important as your machine makes more connections to other resources. Older
  installations worry about the date and time only when it comes to timestamping
  files. New users rely on the clock to schedule automated tasks, to keep track of
  appointments, to schedule automatic downloads from the Internet, and to carry out
  a variety of other responsibilities.

- *Display*. I use this applet the most. Not only does it enable me to change my display resolution and colors with ease, but I can use it to enlarge the display fonts
  and change the wallpaper on the desktop. All these features add up to an incredibly flexible and easy-to-modify display system. The big surprise is that you don't
  even have to reboot your machine to see the effect of a change. You can also
  access this applet from the desktop by right-clicking and then choosing Properties.

- *Fax*. Open this applet and you see a Properties dialog box. You can use it to specify the information you want on your cover pages, organize a collection of cover
  pages, define the behavior of the Fax utility's status indicators, or open the Fax
  Service Management Console to set up fax devices, define options for archiving
  and phone dialing retries, or add a printer to the fax feature.

- *Folder Options*. This feature displays the same Properties dialog box that you see
  when you choose Tools|Folder Options in Windows Explorer. These various
  important options—defining just how Windows Explorer looks and acts—are
  explained in Chapter 6.

- *Fonts*. When I started out computing with PCs, the only font available was the one
  that came in the character ROM of the printer or display adapter. Now you can
  quickly overwhelm—and slow down—your system with fonts you'll never use.
  One drawing package I purchased recently included more than 500 fonts. It's no
  wonder people need an applet like this to manage their font libraries. However,
  you should try to install only those fonts you'll use often.

- *Game Controllers*. This relatively simple utility lets you test and configure joysticks and similar input devices.

- *Internet Options*. Click this icon and you see the same properties dialog box you get when you choose Tools|Options in Internet Explorer. These features are covered in depth in Chapter 2.

- *Keyboard*. If you've ever had to write entire sentences using the Character Map utility under Windows 3.*x*, you'll really appreciate the keyboard support in Windows 2000. Now you can have more than one language available, as needed. A simple click of the International icon on the taskbar enables you to choose from any of the installed keyboard layouts. This applet not only installs support for these languages, but it also provides other forms of keyboard support, such as repeat-rate adjustment.

- *Mouse*. In some respects, I miss the old purple Logitech Mouse setting in my Control Panel. Not only did the Logitech applet enable me to do a few things that even the Windows 2000 applet won't, but it looked kind of neat, too. The purpose of the Windows 2000 Mouse applet is to help you configure the mouse. This doesn't mean just the double-click speed and other mouse-specific features; it also includes the actual pointers the mouse uses and whether Windows 2000 displays mouse trails. I find the use of pointers in Windows 2000 a welcome feature. The animated icons might prove bothersome on some displays, but they show up very well on the LCDs I've checked out.

- *Network and Dial-Up Connections*. We'll spend a lot of time with this particular applet in Chapter 24, "Peer-to-Peer Networking," and Chapter 27 "Client/Server Networking." This applet enables you to install new network components or get rid of old ones. It's also where you set how the network controls access to your resources, as well as where you see dial-up connections. TCP/IP users will use this applet to configure the various addresses needed to make their network functional. Overall, this is the one place you need to go to get the overall picture of your network's current setup.

- *ODBC*. This used to be on the main Control Panel folder but now is located within the Administrative Tools folder. Anyone who deals with database management systems for very long will understand the importance of this applet. It enables you to create new table connections and modify old ones. You can also see which drivers your system has available. Note that there might also be a separate ODBC32 applet. If so, you'll want to check both applets to locate a particular driver—the 32-bit applications are not necessarily correctly put into the ODBC32 applet.

- *Power Options*. This utility helps conserve power. You have several choices of power-saving schemes: Home/Office Desk, Portable/Laptop, Presentation, Always On, Minimal Power Management, Max Battery. The various suggested settings determine how long a period of inactivity before the screen and/or hard drive are turned off. In the Advanced tab, you can add an icon for the Power Options utility to your taskbar. The Hibernate feature is similar to the "sleep" feature found on some portables—it stores the current contents of RAM to your hard drive and then shuts down. When you restart the machine, the saved contents are dumped back into RAM, thus restoring you to where you were (as if you'd never turned off power in the first place). The APM (Advanced Power Management) feature enables the Hibernate feature and also offers battery status information.

- *Phone and Modem*. This properties dialog box is where you can add or edit "locations" (places from which you dial). Choose Edit and you then specify any special numbers that get you an outside local or long distance line. You can also defeat call-waiting. Provisions are also available to describe how to work with area codes and charge to calling cards. The Modems tab is where you can add, remove, or change the properties of modems attached to your system. The Advance tab allows you to manage telephony providers.

- *Printers*. A printer is the one item no one can do without. If you don't have a printer connected directly to your machine, there's a good chance you maintain a network connection to one. The Printers applet enables you to configure existing printers or add new ones. It also enables you to maintain control over any print jobs the printer is processing.

- *Regional Options*. This applet manages all the text-formatting information required to make the output of an application correct. It includes the actual time zone. You also use this applet to change the numeric, currency, time, date, and regional settings.

- *Scanners and Cameras*. Click this icon to add or troubleshoot those devices.

- *Schedules Tasks*. You can tell Windows 2000 to run applications or utilities at scheduled times, automatically. Click the Add Scheduled Task button and the Scheduled Task Wizard opens up, guiding you through the process of choosing a program and then telling Windows 2000 how often, or when, to run it.

- *Sounds and Multimedia*. This applet controls everything relating to the sound and video features supported by Windows 2000. It not only controls the actual drivers and their settings, it helps you configure the interface as well. This applet is the one you want to check out when you have a sound or video problem. This is one of my favorite applets. It enables you to add a sound to just about any Windows event. I really like the fact that Windows 2000 isn't limited in the number of events it can monitor. The list of events will definitely change as you install and remove applications from your system.

- *System*. This applet enables you to maintain your computer as a whole. It enables you to select hardware profiles and configure the system environment. You'll also use it to select some shutdown features and determine which operating system appears as the default on the boot menu. This applet also displays a list of things you can do to enhance system performance. And, as Chapter 31, "Hardware Problems," shows, it can also prove useful when troubleshooting hardware problems.

- *UPS*. You can adjust your uninterruptible power supply options here if you have one.

Your Control Panel might have more or fewer applets than mine, but this list should give you a good idea of what the common applets do. If you have a few additional icons, the vendor documentation should tell you what types of configuration tasks you can use them for.

- *Users and Passwords*. With this applet you can make yourself a mini-administrator. You can require that people who use your workstation must enter a password. You can also see to it, in the Advanced tab, that users must press Ctrl+Alt+Del to log on; manage local users and groups; and, if you've added a certification service to your system, you can create new certificates to attach to email so others can feel more secure when getting files from you.

Warning: Some applications insist on installing a custom applet in the Control Panel. In most cases, Windows 2000 ignores any incompatible applets that it doesn't need to work with the hardware or software you installed. If you do get into a situation where the old driver gets loaded and affects system stability, call the vendor to see whether there's an easy way to remove the applet. In most cases, you can eliminate the problem by deleting a few lines of text from SYSTEM.INI. However, if possible, you should use the Add/Remove Programs utility in Control Panel to delete the applet. If that isn't possible (the applet isn't listed in Add/Remove's selection of uninstallable programs), try deleting the CPL file for the applet, which is typically located in the C:\WINNT directory.

What other kinds of applets can you expect to see in the Control Panel? The only limitation is the types of applications and hardware you install. A few less common examples include a digitizer pad, CAS-compliant fax, and data-capture boards. You'll probably see special applets for certain types of network connections. Most mail packages require an entry here. It's surprising to note that applications such as Lotus 1-2-3 might place an applet here to manage its data connections. (Most applications use ODBC now, so you'll see more options in the ODBC applet rather than more applets.)

Customizing Icon Displays

Some people fail to realize that the Control Panel is just yet another incarnation of Explorer, albeit in a somewhat specialized form. You saw how to access the Control Panel from Explorer earlier in this chapter. The display even looks the same as the other displays. There's nothing strange about Explorer's capability to interact with the Control Panel.

That earlier section really showed you all the similarities. There are a few differences between a standard Explorer interface and the Control Panel, too. I think the most obvious difference is that you can't manipulate Control Panel objectsthe same way you can other objects. The context menu shown in Figure 5.19 reveals this fact. Notice that just about the only thing you can do with a Control Panel object is open it or create a shortcut. Even the Properties option is missing—and it's nearly always available when you're working with objects.

FIGURE 5.19

Objects in the Control Panel don't provide much flexibility through their context menus.

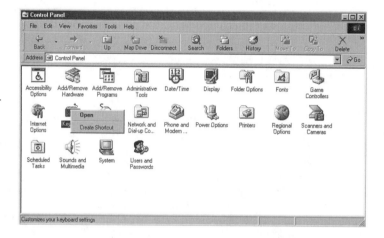

There are other display differences, too. A standard Explorer display provides five methods of displaying objects (the new Thumbnails view); the Control Panel provides four methods. When it comes to arranging these objects, however, you have only two choices: by name and by comment (a new field displayed if you're in the Details view). In actuality, you'll probably never even rearrange these icons. There are so few to look at, most people leave them just the way they are.

If you open a context menu in Control Panel itself (right-click the background of Control Panel instead of one of its applet icons), you'll notice a Refresh option. Every time you add a new application or piece of hardware and want to see whether it added a new Control Panel icon, you can use this command to refresh the display. Unlike with Explorer, closing Control Panel might not force it to display any new icons you add. Using this command ensures that you get an accurate picture.

Tip: You can always refresh Control Panel (or Explorer, Outlook Express, and Internet Explorer, for that matter) by pressing F5.

If you just leave the Control Panel alone, you might never see some of the nice features it provides. Use the View, Details command (on the context menu) to change the way Control Panel icons are displayed. Normally, you see a list of files, the date of last modification, the size, and so on. However, Figure 5.20 shows a completely different picture. As you can see, the Control Panel displays a comments field for each of the applets instead of just showing statistics. This is a very handy feature if you ever see an applet you can't figure out.

FIGURE 5.20

A comment about each applet is probably the last thing you'd expect to see in Details view.

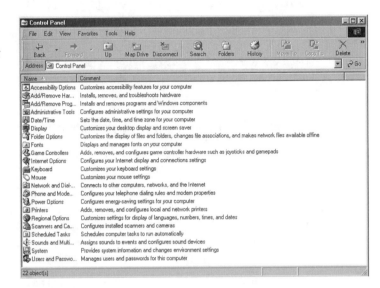

I never thought I would use the Control Panel's shortcut option, but I did. After reading the last few pages, you've probably figured out that there's no fast method to access all the applets in the Control Panel. You can right-click the desktop and change your display settings, and right-clicking the My Computer icon grabs the System applet for you. But what if you want to change your system sounds? You have to go to the Start menu or use some other method to bring up the Control Panel and then the appropriate applet.

Placing a shortcut to the applet on the desktop is one of the best ways to optimize your setup. Just think: Any time you want to change your system sounds (or any other configuration item), you can just click the icon on the desktop. The problem, then, is how to create the shortcut. If you use the context menu entry (right-click an applet's icon in Control Panel and then choose Create Shortcut), Windows either ignores you or displays an error message saying that it can't create the shortcut in the present location (within Control Panel). However, it does offer to create one on the desktop.

You can also right-click the applet's icon and drag it to wherever you want the shortcut to appear. After you release the mouse button, Windows displays a brief context menu. All you need to do is choose the Create Shortcut(s) Here option.

> **Tip:** Don't get icon happy. Crowding your desktop with unneeded icons is one sure way to decrease efficiency. Instead of spending your time working, you'll spend time looking for the icon you need. Try to keep the number of icons on your desktop to 10 or fewer. Any more than that and you'll start making a mockery of the term *shortcut*. What I have done on my systems at work and at home is to create a folder named "Control Panel" on the Start menu. Then I just dragged the entire contents of the Control Panel into this new folder. This automatically populates it with shortcuts to all the applets and also keeps them separate from everything else. What's more, it's fast when you want to get to Control Panel without having to navigate submenus.

Customizing Your Desktop

You probably don't have a "formal" desk at work. In fact, I'll bet that it's customized to meet most every need you have. It's a sure thing that your desk reflects the way you work. After all, no one forced you to place the stapler in the upper-right corner.

Windows 2000 doesn't force you to do things its way either. The Explorer interface is so flexible that I doubt any two people ever have the same desktop. The desktop, just in case you haven't figured it out yet, is the area where everything else in Windows sits. The Windows 2000 desktop is an object, just like everything else.

The Windows 2000 desktop has some features that you might not think about right away. Remember earlier in this chapter when I told you to try right-clicking on everything? You can even right-click the desktop. It has a context menu, shown in Figure 5.21, just like everything else in Windows 2000. I won't go into detail about the contents of the context menu right now; all that information appears later. Suffice it to say that there are plenty of nice surprises when it comes to arranging things under Windows 2000.

FIGURE 5.21

The desktop is an object itself, just like most everything else. It even has its own context menu.

I would like to briefly mention two entries on the desktop context menu: Arrange Icons and Line Up Icons. Arrange Icons enables you to rearrange your desktop in a specific order. It works just like the same entry in Explorer's Views button. (See how everything seems to have a bit of Explorer in it?) You can rearrange your icons by name, type, size, or date. I find ordering the lists by type and name the most convenient, but sometimes you'll want to find out the size (when you're trying to free up space on your hard drive, for example) or the date (when you're trying to reconcile several versions of the same document to see which is the most recent).

Some people detest all the standard arrangements, so they just stick the icons in whatever order they want them. If you're not one of these people, you might find that the Line Up Icons option is custom tailored for you. It keeps the icons in the order you want them but arranges them in neat rows and columns. This option provides a sort of "grid" effect that enables you to keep your desktop neat but arranged in the order that you want to see it. (Remember that if you've selected the Auto Arrange option, you can't place your icons willy-nilly. They will snap to.)

The following sections look at the desktop as a whole. They're meant as a guide for making your desktop more usable, but I probably won't stop there. Think of this section as the most common tricks people use to optimize their Windows 2000 environments. This is the "must do" checklist you should look at when trying to get the most out of your setup.

Taskbar

A major feature of Windows 2000 is the taskbar. This is the gray bar shown at the bottom of Figure 5.22. The taskbar is the central control area for most of the things you'll do under Windows 2000. It contains four major elements: a Start Menu button, the taskbar buttons, the toolbars, and a system tray.

FIGURE 5.22

This is a typical taskbar, but don't be fooled—it can contain additional toolbars.

Like the other objects under Windows 2000, the taskbar also provides a Properties dialog box (just right-click the taskbar and choose the Properties option to display it). This dialog box has two tabs. One controls the Start menu setup, and the other controls the taskbar itself. The five settings on the General tab enable you to change how the taskbar and Start menus react. You can remove the taskbar from view by removing the check mark from the Always On Top check box, for example. The Show Clock check box enables you to clear more space for applications on the taskbar by removing the clock from view. My favorite is the Auto Hide check box: When you select this option, the taskbar appears as a thin gray line at the bottom of the display. The second the mouse cursor approaches it, the taskbar resumes its normal size. This enables you to get rid of the taskbar to make space for application windows, yet keep it handy for when you need it. A new option in Windows 2000 is called Use Personalized Menus and it toggles whether or not you see *every* program listed on the Start | Programs menu, or whether Windows 2000 keeps track of your usage of the programs, and only displays the most frequently used few. To see all of them, you click a down arrow on the bottom of the menu.

The Advanced menu offers various new Start menu settings. Click it and you can add or remove shortcuts; sort the shortcuts; decide whether or not to see Tools, Favorites, Log Off on the Start menu. You can also "expand" Control Panel, Printers, My Documents, or Network and Dial-up Connections. *Expand* in this context means to add a submenu that can be displayed if the user selects the usual right-arrow symbol that signals a submenu is available. There's an additional option to Scroll Programs Menu, but I cannot figure out what it does.

Right-clicking the taskbar displays a few other object-specific options as well. All of them affect the way Windows 2000 organizes the applications currently displayed on the taskbar (desktop):

- *Cascade Windows*. When you select this option, all the application windows are resized to the same size. Windows 2000 arranges them diagonally, much like the display you would normally see in a spreadsheet when opening more than one file. You can select any application from the entire list by clicking its title bar (the area at the top of the application window that contains the application's name).

- *Tile Windows Horizontally or Tile Windows Vertically*. Use either of these options if you want to see the window areas of all your applications simultaneously. Windows 2000 uses every available inch of desktop space to place the applications side by side or one on top of the other. Each application receives about the same amount of space.

- *Task Manager*. Select this if you want to view the Task Manager utility. It's particularly useful if one of your programs is hung (not responding). You can close it down (without having to reboot the machine).

- *Minimize All Windows*. If you ever get to the point where your screen is so cluttered that you can't tell what's open and what's not, use this option to clean up the mess. This option minimizes every application you have running on the desktop.

- *Adjust Date/Time*. This brings up the same dialog box you see if you double-click the clock on the far right of the taskbar.

You can also add some Internet Explorer–inspired toolbars to the taskbar if you wish. Right-click the taskbar and then choose Toolbars and select Address (shows the current hard drive file path or URL), Links (a set of Internet sites), or Desktop (the icons you see on your desktop).

The Taskbar also includes the Quick Launch toolbar—a set of small icons that when clicked launch such applications as Internet Explorer or can display the desktop (the same effect ask clicking Windows+M). You can drag this toolbar to reposition it on the Taskbar, or you can hide it by right-clicking the Taskbar, then choosing Toolbars on the context menu and deselecting it.

> **Tip:** If you want to define a set of icons in a custom toolbar of your own devising, just right-click the taskbar and then choose Toolbars, New Toolbar. You can select any folder or subfolder on your desktop, and all its contents will appear as icons on the new toolbar.

The Start Menu

The Start menu appears on the far-left side of the taskbar. It contains a complete listing of all your applications, access to some system settings, and a few other things thrown in for good measure. Figure 5.23 shows how the Start menu looks.

FIGURE 5.23

The Start menu lists your applications, gives you access to some system settings, and more.

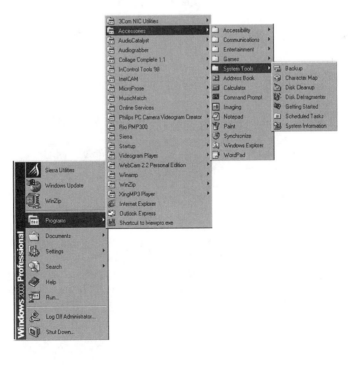

Tip: Press the Windows key to pop up the Start menu.

The following list describes the major features of the Start Menu in detail:

- *Programs*. This is the list of applications installed on your machine. The Explorer interface enables you to place folders within folders (programmers call this *nesting*). As Figure 5.23 shows, you can place applications several levels deep within the menu tree.

- *Documents*. Use this option to select a document you recently opened or saved. The list can contain up to 15 document names, and it also contains the My Documents folder.

- *Settings*. Windows 2000 provides you with a number of ways to change your environment. The Settings menu is just one centralized location for this information. It provides access to the Control Panel, the Printers Configuration dialog box, networking and dial-up connections, and the Taskbar/Start Menu Configuration dialog box.

- *Search*. This option enables you to find any file on your hard drive or on a network drive using a variety of search criteria; you can also locate people and Web sites. Not only can you select a file by name and location but by modification date as well. The Advanced option in this utility's window even enables you to look for a file based on its contents or size, or other specifications such as author. I find this utility quite useful for locating a file when I don't know the filename, but I do remember that it was a letter I wrote to my Uncle Ned and I know I mentioned my cat, Crankshaft. All you have to do to find a document is fire up the Search utility, and then in the Containing Text field type the most unique word or phrase you suspect is going to distinguish this file from all others. In my example, I would use the name *Crankshaft*.

Note: that you can also launch the Search Results window by pressing Windows+F if you're currently on the Windows 2000 desktop. If you click the taskbar to give it the focus, pressing F3 will also pop up the Search Results window. Remember that for many applications, F3 is the key that brings up a text search feature.

Peter's Principle: The Indexing Service

The Indexing Service, available from the Search utility, is new in Windows 2000 and can be, by far, the fastest way to locate files based on a piece of text in them. Try it by clicking it—you'll see the dialog box shown in Figure 5.24.

You can use the Indexing Service to create a kind of indexed database of your documents' contents and their parameters (properties such as date of creation). It even features a query language to allow you to retrieve recordsets of some sophistication and precision. The Indexing Service can index data from these sources: HTML, plain text, Microsoft Office 95 and later documents, Internet mail and news, or any other document for which a document filter is available. The Indexing Service works in the background, and each time a new document is encountered, it does it's indexing.

Figure 5.25 illustrates the main indexing dialog box. You get to it by clicking the Advanced button, shown previously in Figure 5.24 (oddly enough).

To actually conduct a search, double-click the System entry or another catalog of your choice. (The default Web entry is not the Internet; it's your IIS directory.) Then double-click Query the Catalog in the next dialog box displayed. You'll see the Indexing Service search window, as shown in Figure 5.26.

FIGURE 5.24

This new Indexing Service works in the background, organizing your document files into indexes that make later searches lightning fast.

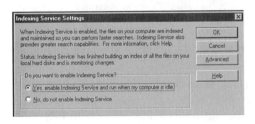

FIGURE 5.25

Click the Advanced button in the Indexing Service Settings dialog box shown in Figure 5.24 to get here.

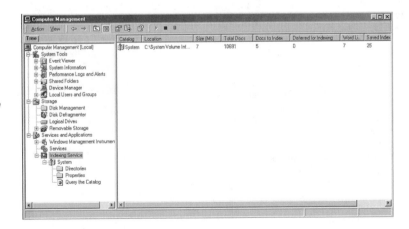

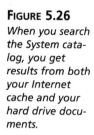

FIGURE 5.26

When you search the System catalog, you get results from both your Internet cache and your hard drive documents.

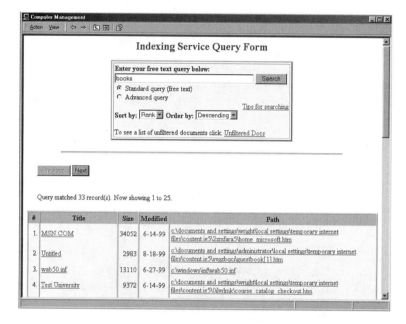

- *Help*. The Help option opens the main Windows 2000 Help file. You can use this file to search for just about any information you need to run Windows 2000. Microsoft has gone a long way in improving its Help files over the years. Instead of providing you with dry facts, these files actually provide procedures you can use to get the job done. As if that weren't enough, some of the Help screens provide angled arrows or hyperlinks, as shown in Figure 5.27. When you click an angled arrow, Windows 2000 starts the utility relating to the Help topic or transfers you elsewhere in Help. The browser-style Help window is new to Windows 98 and Windows 2000.

FIGURE 5.27

Help now includes small arrows and hyperlinks that launch utilities and accessories or take you elsewhere in Help.

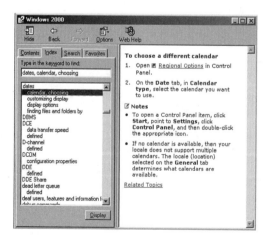

- *Run.* The Run menu option opens a dialog box that enables you to start an application by typing its path and name. You can also include any appropriate parameters. (You can also launch the Run dialog box by pressing Windows+R.) Notice too the down-arrow that shows previously triggered programs.

- *Shut Down.* Windows 2000 is more complex than other operating systems, including Windows 95/98. This option enables you to perform an orderly shutdown of Windows 2000. This includes making sure that all the data is written to disk and that the Registry information is saved. It can take a bit of time. You have to be patient when you see the message Please Wait While the System Saves Unsaved Data to the Disk. The Registry is large. You can also press Alt+F4 when the desktop has the focus (click it) as an alternative way to enter the shutdown procedure.

Peter's Principle: Start Menu Secrets

The Start button offers more than a set of menus containing frequently needed applications and utilities. It took me several years with Windows before I caught on to some of the following tips. To save you that delay, I have collected them here. First, like many of Windows 2000's primary features (Favorites, Send To), the Start menu is a folder. Therefore, you can easily put items into that folder using Explorer—just as you would with any other folder. You can drag and drop other folders or files; you can also copy and paste. However, there's a faster way. Open an Explorer window and then drag a file, folder, or shortcut from Explorer and drop it onto the Start button at the bottom of your screen. Instantly, a copy of the object joins whatever else is on the primary Start menu (primary meaning the *root* menu, the one that first appears when you click Start or press the Windows key). For a visual reminder of what the Start menu looks like, refer to Figure 5.23. You can go in the other direction, too—drag something off the Start menu onto the desktop or into Explorer. (Note that when you drag an item onto Start, the item is copied, but when you drag an item off of Start, the item is moved; that is, it no longer resides on Start.) You can also right-click items on the Start menu and then choose from the options on their context menu, including deleting them or seeing their properties (where you can define a Ctrl+Alt+*key* shortcut key).

Remember that some items on the Start menu (those below the separator bar) behave a little differently from those above the bar (the ones you add to the menu): There's no context menu for those below.

After you drag items onto the Start button, the items will be listed on the Start menu in alphabetic order. If you want to reorder the items, it used to be too bad for you. Now, though, Windows 2000 lets you drag items and drop them into a different order on the Start menu. (The Explorer's Favorites list used to force alphabetization, too, but that's also been fixed now.)

Don't forget about working with the Start button itself. Try right-clicking the Start button. The Start button's context menu contains several useful choices. The Open option displays the Start folder in a single-pane window. The Explore option displays the Start folder in the standard Explorer window. The Search option displays the Windows Search utility described earlier in this chapter. The Open All Users option shows you a single-pane window containing the general users' Start menu items. These are the basic Start menu items for this computer. Along with these basic files and folders, you see the Start items you've added for your personal use. In other words, anyone who logs on to this machine will see the All Users items on the Start menu, but in addition to these items, each user has a different personal set of items. Explore All Users displays those same basic items but in the standard Explorer window.

The Taskbar Buttons

The taskbar proper contains one icon for each application currently running on the machine. In addition to using the Alt+Tab key combination to switch between running applications, you can now switch to an application much as you would select a television station using a remote control. All you need to do is click the appropriate button.

You should be aware of a few features. For one thing, the buttons shrink in size horizontally as needed to accommodate all the running applications. You can increase the size of the taskbar to hold two, three, or even more rows of buttons (if you so desire). Dragging the edge of the taskbar produces the same double arrow you use to resize other objects under Windows 2000. Of course, the buttons will get only so big and then they'll stop growing.

The System Tray

The area on the far right of the taskbar is known as the *system tray*, because it looks like a tray for holding icons (why it's not called the *taskbar tray* is a mystery to me). The system tray usually contains two or more icons. Each icon can serve multiple purposes, depending on what piece of hardware it's supposed to control. The two most common entries in this area are the Clock and Volume icons. In the preceding section, I explained how each of these controls reacts when you position the mouse cursor over their respective icons.

The Volume icon does a couple of things, depending on the action you take. A single click produces a master volume slider. You can use this to adjust the volume of all sounds produced by the sound board. Double-clicking the same icon displays the Volume Control dialog box, which provides detailed control of each input to your sound board. It also includes a master volume slider. Right-clicking the icon displays the context menu. In this case, it displays only two entries. The first takes you to the Volume Control dialog box; the second displays the Audio Properties dialog box. We take a closer look at the Volume controls later in this book.

The Clock icon provides similar functionality. A double-click displays the Date/Time Properties dialog box. A right-click shows the context menu. Detailed information about the clock appears later in this chapter.

You can obtain more information about an item in the tray (such as the clock) by just holding the mouse cursor over its icon for a time. After a few seconds, Windows 2000 displays additional data. Holding the mouse cursor over the time indicator, for example, shows today's date. In some cases, the information you receive from a button is less than awe inspiring. For example, the Volume icon displays a single word: Volume.

Desktop Settings

Everyone looks at desktop settings in one way—as improving the appearance of his or her computer. For the most part, that's right. Just changing the color of something under Windows won't make it work better—at least most of the time. Configuring your desktop for a pleasing appearance might not provide much in the way of a direct efficiency increase, but a new piece of wallpaper or a change of color can greatly affect the way you view your machine. Any positive change in attitude usually translates into improved efficiency. I find that changing my wallpaper and my display colors from time to time gives my computer that "new" feel everyone needs occasionally.

There are other reasons for a change of configuration. In Chapter 7, "Performance Power," you'll learn that wallpaper, although attractive to the eye, chews up valuable memory. You might run into a situation where memory is at a premium. Giving up your wallpaper is one way to get the memory you need to complete a specific task or have enough room to simultaneously run multiple applications without forcing the disk drive to grind away, trying to swap data in and out of memory.

Eye strain is also a common problem among computer users. Let's face it: Sitting eight hours in front of what amounts to a television (albeit with higher resolution and a more stable refresh) at close range won't do anyone's eyes much good. If you're like me, however, you probably spend more than eight hours a day staring at that screen. Somewhere along the way, you may want to make your icons and text bigger to reduce eye fatigue. Changing your desktop settings to improve readability is a very practical use of this feature.

Selecting Wallpaper

Wallpaper is one of those personal items every computer user wants to customize. Windows 2000 makes changing your wallpaper easy. All you need to do is right-click the desktop and choose Properties. You should see the dialog box shown in Figure 5.28.

This dialog box has two major sections. The first section contains a monitor. Changing any of the wallpaper or pattern settings immediately affects the contents of this display. The monitor gives you a thumbnail sketch of how your background will appear.

> **Tip:** Patterns are a memory-efficient way to dress up a system. Because a pattern uses only two colors, it's a lot faster to draw and doesn't consume many system resources. If your system is short on memory, but you would still like an interesting background, consider using patterns rather than wallpaper.

FIGURE 5.28

Several brand-new wallpaper graphics and photos are included in Windows 2000.

To change a pattern, click the Pattern button, then select a pattern. Click Edit Pattern. Windows 2000 will display a bitmap editor similar in function to those used by most paint programs.

The Wallpaper list box defaults to the files found in your main Windows folder. Of course, you don't have to use these files. Click the Browse button if you want to look in other folders on your drive. There are two ways to display wallpaper. You can center it on the background (the best choice for pictures) or tile it (the best choice for patterns).

Screen Saver

A very healthy third-party market exists for one particular item: screen savers. Some Windows users buy screen savers in bulk. You can find them in stores and at many Internet sites devoted to shareware/software. Unless you own an older system, using a screen saver probably isn't necessary—it's just fun. I own a Star Trek screen saver for the fun of it.

Windows 2000 provides a screen saver feature. Some of the built-in screen savers are every bit as gorgeous and interesting as commercial versions. You'll find them on the Screen Saver tab of the Display Properties dialog box, shown in Figure 5.29.

Just like the Wallpaper selection, this dialog box contains a miniature view of your monitor. You can use it as a thumbnail sketch of what the display will look like when you configure the screen saver. The Screen Saver drop-down list box enables you to choose from one of the screen savers (they're stored in your SYSTEM32 folder). If you decide to use a third-party screen saver that uses the Windows format, you need to place the file in the same directory as the others; otherwise, Windows won't see it.

After you select a screen saver, you can use the Settings button to change its settings. In most cases, the settings affect how Windows 2000 displays the screen saver. It might change the number of lines you see, the resolution, the size, or the number of colors, for example.

FIGURE 5.29

Use this dialog box to select a screen saver and adjust its properties.

The Wait field enables you to change the number of minutes Windows 2000 waits before it activates the screen saver. To turn off the screen saver, just move the mouse cursor or press a key.

You can also password-protect your screen saver. This enables you to leave the room without any fear that someone will use your machine while you're gone, because that person will have to type a password to turn the screen saver off after it comes on. I like the third-party screen savers that automatically restore their current condition even if you turn off the machine and reboot. Unfortunately, the Windows 2000 screen saver doesn't provide this feature, so you can circumvent password protection by rebooting the machine. Of course, this does have the advantage of resetting the display so that no one knows what you were working on before the machine was rebooted. Rebooting the machine also means that whoever wants access to your machine will need a password for it, because Windows 2000 always displays a password screen.

The final button, Preview, enables you to see what the display will look like when Windows 2000 turns on the screen saver. I've used this as a quick way to hide my display when someone walks into my office and I don't want him or her to see what's on my display. It's a quick solution to a potential problem. Of course, you'll want to be very careful around the mouse and keyboard if you use this method. Unless you enable the Password Protected check box, your display will clear if you bump the mouse or tap a key on the keyboard.

Warning If you have control over the settings for a machine acting as a server on a network, avoid screen savers like the plague! Set Screen Saver to the None option. Screen savers are CPU cycle hogs. This doesn't matter if you're away from your workstation and the computer has nothing else to do, but chewing up CPU cycles does matter a lot on a server.

Palette

The Appearance page of the Display Properties dialog box, shown in Figure 5.30, enables you to change the actual appearance of your displays, not just the desktop. All you need to do is click the picture of the display to select an item.

Windows 2000 enables you to change the font used to display text in this dialog box, and it gives you a lot of flexibility. I have several configurations with "tired eyed" text settings. You can change the size of the menu and title bar text individually. Everything that has text also has a setting for the font and type size here.

FIGURE 5.30

Change the colors and font sizes (with side effects changing the way windows look) in this dialog box.

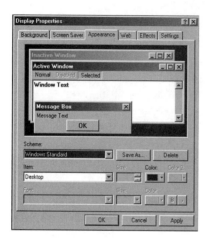

Changing an entry consists of making list box selections. The first three selections affect the contents of the item, itself, and include the item name, size, and color. The size, in this case, is the size of the window or another display element. You can change the width of a menu bar using this option, for example. The second three selections control the text used within that display element. These settings include font style, size, and color. You may select any installed font as your display font, but most people find that the MS Serif and MS Sans Serif fonts work best on displays. They were specially designed for this purpose. I occasionally use Arial and find that it works pretty well. It's all up to you.

This dialog box also contains a list box for selecting from existing color schemes, a Delete button for removing the schemes you no longer want, and a Save As button for adding new schemes.

The Web

A feature called *Active Desktop* was introduced in NT 4. It allows you to add Internet content to your desktop, such as scrolling stock tickers, your home page, and your Internet Channels (a folder in your Favorites list). This feature never caught on with most people, though. Seems that stock tickers scrolling across your monitor are, for many people, distracting at best and hideously annoying at worst. I deal with this topic and other efforts to integrate browser effects into Windows in Chapter 6, "There's Really Only One Explorer."

Adding Pizzazz!

You'll likely want to customize the Effects tab on the Display Properties dialog box, shown in Figure 5.31. (It used to be the Plus! tab in previous versions of Windows.)

FIGURE 5.31

You'll find several cool effects to try out in this page.

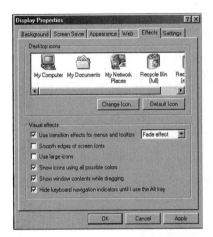

The Effects page is divided into several functional areas. The top area enables you to change the appearance of the My Computer, My Documents, My Network Places, and Recycle Bin icons. One button enables you to change the icon; a second enables you to return the icons to their default settings. Unfortunately, this page of the Display Properties dialog box still won't enable you to change the names of the various items; you still must resort to other methods to get the job done in some cases.

Look at the next section. It contains six check boxes designed to improve the appearance of your display. The first tells Windows 2000 to animate the appearance and disappearance of menus and tooltips. You can select a fade or scroll—both are nice. The second option tells Windows 2000 to use shading to smooth onscreen fonts. Some people find this feature helps prevent eye fatigue and leave it on as a general rule. You'll need to experiment to see whether it actually helps on your display. Option three specifies that Windows 2000 use large icons. Generally, this option makes the icons about twice the size they normally are. I find that this is a helpful option if you use large icons in Explorer and need a little extra help at the end of the day. The fourth option tells Windows 2000 to display icons using all the colors it can for very high-resolution displays. Normally, Windows 2000 displays icons using 16 colors.

The fifth option displays the contents of a window as you drag it. If you have enough graphics power, you should use this option—it makes items look like they do in the real world. Otherwise, when you drag a window around on your desktop, only an animated frame moves, not the entire contents of the window. Finally, you can tell Windows 2000 that you want it to suppress the underlining of Alt+*key* shortcuts in menus and elsewhere as well as selection indicators (dotted rectangles around the object with the focus). These indicators appear only when you press the Alt key, Tab key, or arrow keys. I cannot imagine why you would want to hide these useful visual cues.

Resolution

The Settings page of the Display Properties dialog box, shown in Figure 5.32, enables you to change your display resolution and the number of colors. Unlike Windows 95, some Windows 2000 systems require a reboot after you change the settings on this page.

Figure 5.32

On the Settings page, you can adjust your display and color resolution settings.

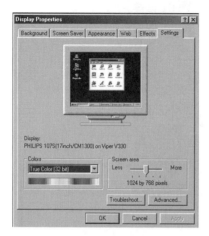

Tip: The number of colors you choose defines an important aspect of the quality of the graphics you'll see. It doesn't matter with text, but if you want to see images that are photorealistic in their crispness and have rich, smooth color gradations and shading, go for the True Color setting.

If you're ever in doubt as to the capabilities of your display, you can always click the Advanced button. You can then work with a full properties sheet to define your monitor and video card, test them, and specify font sizes. You'll also see how the screen size (area) affects the number of objects that can appear onscreen at the same time.

Tip: Refresh Frequency option (in the Advanced tab) determines how often your video is redrawn. This is similar to the number of "frames" in an animation—that is, the frame rate. Just as a movie looks better with more frames per second, a higher TV refresh produces a more stable image with less flicker. Also, note that the higher refresh rates may limit the available screen size and color attributes. This is sometimes confusing. If you change your refresh rate to, say, 75MHz, the colors might drop to only 16, or the resolution might fall from 1024∞720 to 800∞600. This isn't a bug in Windows 2000. Lower the requested refresh rate and your previous color or resolution options will be restored. All this depends on the video system you've installed on your machine.

The Clock

We took a quick look at the clock earlier when talking about the taskbar. The clock utility actually affects the way the system reacts. You can use it to change the CMOS clock setting and, therefore, the timestamp on all your files. Of course, it will also affect any events you might schedule and anything else that relies on the clock.

The clock properties consist of a single check box on the Taskbar and Start Menu Properties dialog box named Show Clock. The only thing this entry does is display or hide the clock on the taskbar. In most cases, you'll want to keep the clock displayed because there's nothing to be gained from shutting it off.

Double-clicking the clock icon displays the dialog box shown in Figure 5.33. It contains a calendar and a clock. You use these items to change the system settings.

The second page of this dialog box, Time Zone, enables you to change the time zone setting for the current area of the world you're in (see Figure 5.33). It's the same dialog box you saw when you completed the installation of Windows 2000. Setting this dialog box is self-explanatory. The Daylight Saving Time check box allows the computer to automatically adjust the time for you.

FIGURE 5.33

The Time Zone page of the Date/Time Properties dialog box enables you to change the world-locale designation.

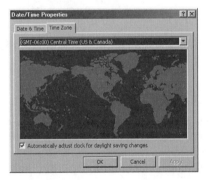

Working with Desktop Objects

Making your desktop efficient is very easy under Windows 2000. The first thing you need to do, however, is throw away any outdated application-centric behavior you may be laboring under. You need to learn to work with *data* instead—the way we should have learned to work with computers in the first place. After all, what's more important: the tool that creates an object or the object itself? The end result is the most important goal in working with Windows (or working with anything else, for that matter).

The following sections give you some ideas on how to arrange your desktop to make maximum use of the data-centric approach. This is by no means the only way to make this adjustment, but it's the way that many people now work. Try this approach and then modify it to meet your needs.

We'll start by looking at the methods of moving data around. Remember that Windows 2000 uses *objects*. Nearly everything is an object of some sort. Objects are easy to copy, cut, and paste. You can move them around like an object in the physical world. After we look at data-movement techniques, we'll take a quick look at the methods you can use to organize that data on your desktop.

Making Copies

Many people use cutting and pasting to move data around. You cut the data from the place where you no longer need it and then paste it to a new location. Windows 2000 supports cut and paste for objects as well. All you need to do to move a file from one location to another is cut it and then paste it. The beauty of this approach is that the copy of the file resides temporarily on the Clipboard. This means that you can make as many copies of it as you want. Of course, anything you can cut, you can also copy. Copying the object means that you leave the original in place and create copies where needed. Notice the Copy, Cut, and Paste entries on most context menus. (The Paste option won't appear on the context menu until you first select Copy or Cut.)

Obviously, you can't paste a file into another file or into itself. You can paste a copy of a file on the desktop or into a folder, however. If you take a logical, real-world approach to moving objects under Windows 2000, you'll never run into problems getting objects to work. Also, recall the new Copy To and Move To buttons on the main Windows Explorer toolbar, described earlier in this chapter.

And don't neglect using drag and drop with the Ctrl/Shift keys to cut, copy, and paste.

Creating New Objects

Everywhere you can paste an existing object, you can also create a new object. The desktop, Explorer, and most Windows 2000 folders have a New option on their context menus. This menu option displays a list of file types Windows 2000 can produce automatically. Notice that one of the entries here is a folder. You can always place a folder within another object that's normally used for storage—even another folder. Using folders helps you organize your data into more efficient units. You'll see later how to combine these elements to make your desktop an efficient place to work.

Using a Template

One of the problems with the New submenu on context menus is that it always creates objects of a default type. Take Microsoft Word, for example. If you create a new Word for Windows object using the selection on the context menu, that new object will use the Normal style sheet. What you really want is the Accounts style sheet, but there isn't a fast way to create a document using the current system.

I got around this problem by placing a folder named Templates on my desktop. Inside are copies of each of the sample files I use to create new documents. If you write a lot of letters that use the same format, for example, you might want to use your word processor to create a document that contains everything that normally appears in a letter. Now all you need to do is place a copy of the Letter template in your Templates folder. Every time you need to write another letter, right-click the template for it in your Templates folder and drag the template to a new destination, such as a project folder. After the context menu appears, choose Copy to create a copy of your template. This template approach to creating new documents can greatly reduce the time you need to start a task. You can create enough copies of a template to satisfy project needs in a few seconds. Using the template also means that all your settings will be correct when you enter the document for the first time.

You can use a template document in several ways. You can right-click and choose Copy and then right-click your project folder and choose Paste from the context menu. Another method is to drag the template while pressing the mouse key. When Windows asks what you would like to do, choose Copy from the menu.

Creating Work Areas

Now that you have some idea of how to move and copy data, let's look at a more efficient way to work with it. I've started using a method of organizing information because of the way Windows 2000 works. You can follow these easy steps to get any project started:

1. Create a main project folder on the desktop.

2. Open the folder and place one folder inside for each type of data you plan to work with. When writing this chapter, for example, I created one folder for the word processor document, another for the electronic research information, and a third for the graphics files.

3. Open the first data folder. Create a copy of your template and then create as many copies as you'll need of that template within the data folder.

4. Rename the data files to match what they'll contain.

5. Close this data folder and repeat steps 3 and 4 for each of your other data folders.

6. Complete your project by filling each data folder.

Of course, this is still only one approach to managing your data. The trick is to find the method that works best for you, one that reflects the way you get your work done.

By now, you're wondering why you should go this route. After all, your old familiar methods of managing your data seem to provide just about the same results as the method I've outlined. Consider this: The new data-centered techniques offer several advantages that you just can't get using an application-centered approach:

- *Data transmittal*. Giving someone else access to a group project means sending him or her a folder, not a bunch of individual files. How often have you thought you had all the files for a project together, only to find that you didn't send an important one? This method of organizing data prevents such problems. It encapsulates data into a logical container.

- *Application independence*. It doesn't matter which application you need to use to modify a file. If everyone in your office uses the same applications, modifying a file means double-clicking it and nothing else. You no longer need to worry about which application to open or where that application is located. All that matters is the data.

- *Location*. Where is your data? Do you ever find yourself searching to find that small file you thought was located somewhere on your hard drive but now is missing? This method enables you to place all the data relating to a project in one place. Its physical location no longer matters after you get the pieces together. Of course, you still need to know where the data is when you organize the project folder. However, would you rather look for a file once or 100 times? Using desktop folders means that you find the data once and never worry about it again.

- *Ease of storage*. After I get done with a project under Windows 2000, I don't worry about getting all the bits and pieces together. I send one folder to storage. When I need to work on the project again, I know that all I'll need to do is load that one folder back onto my local drive.

Tip: Also consider making use of the new My Documents folder (by default located on your desktop). It's icon shows a folder with a sheet of paper inside. Some Windows accessories and Microsoft application files (WordPad, Paint, photos taken by a digital camera, Visual Studio, files saved from Internet Explorer) are automatically saved to this folder by default unless you specify otherwise.

Peter's Principle: The User Interface and the Windows Facelift

This chapter, Chapter 6, "There's Really Only One Explorer," and Chapter 8, "Customizing Windows 2000 for Maximum Productivity," endeavor to show you all the techniques you need if you want to be a power user of the visual Windows 2000 interface and all its utilities and features. This chapter, however, concentrates on the bedrock of classic Windows techniques: working with shortcuts, Explorer, and the Start button. These elements have been part of Windows since their introduction in 1995. However, there's been a transformation in the past year, a paradigm shift. Instead of a traditional operating system that processes data situated on a local system hard drive, we're now getting most of our data from sources distributed throughout the world. In other words, your user interface must now not only look inward to find information stored on your private hard drive but also be capable of looking outward to find information stored anywhere on the Internet.

For this reason, the classic concept of an operating system has been transformed. Instead of just presiding over your local system, the OS now must also handle information streaming in from the outside where new, significant issues of bandwidth (speed of data transfer) and security become concerns. Microsoft realized that the *browser*, not the classic window, represented the future of the user interface. To this end, Microsoft is currently blurring the distinction between the Windows Explorer and the Internet Explorer. In fact, as the next chapter demonstrates, there now remains no practical distinction between the two tools whatsoever.

On Your Own

Spend some time getting used to the Explorer interface and trying out the various display modes. Click the column headings in the Details view to see how Explorer rearranges the filenames.

Context menus are also an important part of Windows 2000. Try right-clicking all the objects you see. See how the context menus vary from object to object. Don't forget that even the desktop is an object with a context menu. Make sure you click the desktop to close its context menu without selecting anything.

Go ahead and add items to your Send To menu on the context menu. Then reorganize those items by adding "1.", "2.", and so on to put them in order of the most frequently used.

Open Explorer and check out each of the special sections we talked about in this chapter. Try to identify each section and its purpose without referring back to the discussion. Also, look at some of the unique capabilities provided by your machine. See whether any special applets are in the Control Panel, for example. You'll also want to check out your machine's network capabilities.

Try adding items, both folders and files, to your Start menu. Also, delete items that you don't use that often.

6

There's Really Only One Explorer

If you're like most of us, you still tend to think in terms of Windows Explorer as the tool you use with data on your hard drive, and you think of Internet Explorer as a separate tool you use with the Internet. Underneath our noses, though, the two Explorers have been melding into a single, unified utility that's equally at home on your hard drive or the hard drives holding Web sites all around the world.

This chapter focuses on Microsoft's ongoing Explorer merge and the ways you can customize Windows 2000 to access information from your local storage as well as from hard drives around the world.

Anything Goes, Anywhere

The underlying principle of the new fusion is that, in theory, you should experience no real distinction between your hard drive and the Internet. You should be able to easily manage or retrieve information locally and worldwide, without having to switch between different tools or techniques. Of course, at current Internet speeds, you'll generally get data off your drive faster than it comes over the Internet. However, features such as Favorites and Search should operate seamlessly in both realms.

Many New Ways to Search

If you look at the Search utility on the Start menu, for example, you'll see that it lists the classic options: Files and Folders. However, now there are two new options:

- *On the Internet*. Launches Internet Explorer with its Search bar in the left pane.
- *For People*. A search engine that accesses your email Address Book, Yahoo!'s People Search, the Active Directory, Bigfoot, InfoSpace, Verisign, and other people-locating utilities.

Peter's Principle: The Latest, Greatest Search Engines

Yahoo! is my favorite search engine, probably because I'm used to it, but also because it works well. However, there are some new search engines that might be just what you're looking for. I use them from time to time because they provide specialized services. First, try the Mother of All Engines: Metacrawler (http://www.go2net.com/). When you start a search in this "meta" engine, it formats your query correctly for six of the most popular search engines: Alta Vista, Infoseek, Excite, Lycos, Yahoo!, and WebCrawler. This way, you don't have to try each one individually (and remember their individual search phrase syntax requirements). Just ask Metacrawler.

Google (Google.com) is an interesting engine—it tests the popularity of pages as a way of finding the most useful ones.

And, finally, no list of hot engines is complete without a mention of HotBot, a searcher that has among the widest reaches of all the engines. If you're looking for something highly specific, be assured that HotBot will likely conduct the most exhaustive search. Check out http://www.hotbot.com.

Take a look at "Search Engines Compared" in Chapter 2 for more information.

Adding Desktop Links

Another manifestation of the collapse of the old barrier between local and global information is the Active Desktop concept that first appeared in NT 4—although it never became very popular. Right-click your desktop, choose Properties, and then click the Web tab. You can put an automatically updateable version of your browser's Home Page on your desktop.

You can also put Internet links on your desktop along with the traditional hard drive shortcuts to your local applications and data. You already know that you can put folders and application icons on your desktop—but try this: Open Internet Explorer 5 (IE5) as a normal window, not maximized. Then hold down the left mouse button and drag the URL of whatever Web page you're viewing from the Internet Explorer's Address bar onto your desktop, as shown in Figure 6.1. (To do this, just drag the *e* icon at the left of the URL address.) Now you have a shortcut to this Web site.

Tip: If you don't see the Address bar on IE5's toolbar, choose Toolbars from IE's View menu and then click Address Bar.

Now try something even better. This will show you why the desktop is called *active*. This time, hold down the right mouse button while you drag the URL's *e* icon from the Internet Explorer Address bar and drop it onto your desktop. You'll now see a context menu. Choose Create Active Desktop Item(s) Here and then simply follow the Wizard's requests. Now you've put this Web site on your desktop. It's not merely a shortcut—it's an actual window into the site, like a mini browser. What's more, this Active Desktop item will be updated any time you press F5 to refresh your Active Desktop. You can also schedule refreshes. Unfortunately, because of a combination of performance hits and the annoyance at having one's desktop *too* active—and therefore distracting—the idea of the Active Desktop has never gained much popularity.

FIGURE 6.1

Adding a favorite Internet site link to your desktop is as simple as dragging it from Internet Explorer's Address bar.

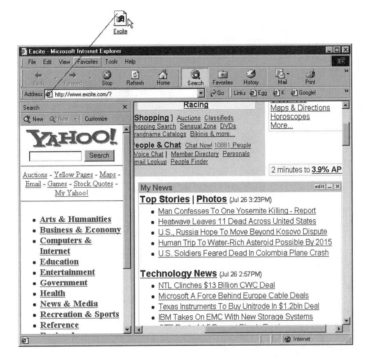

Modifying the IE Quick Launch Taskbar

You can do some interesting things with the taskbar. To add a new link to the Quick Launch toolbar, drag one from your desktop, from the IE Address bar, or from the IE Favorites bar; then drop it onto the Quick Links toolbar. To move a link within the Quick Links toolbar, drag it and drop it in a new location. To delete a link, right-click it to reveal its context menu and then click Delete. You can also switch to a different icon for the link by right-clicking the link and choosing Properties, selecting the Internet Shortcut tab, and then clicking the Change Icon button.

Creating Your Own Toolbars

This technique is mentioned in Chapter 5, "Exploring the Interface," (at the end of the section titled "Customizing Your Desktop") but it's worth repeating. If none of the standard Windows taskbar's toolbars meet your needs, you can create a custom toolbar. Just as you can use the Desktop toolbar to display the contents of your Desktop folder as buttons in a toolbar, you can add any folder to your taskbar as a custom toolbar. Windows then displays the contents of the folder as buttons in a toolbar, and clicking those buttons has the same effect as selecting and opening the objects in the folder.

You can use any folder or Internet address as the basis of a custom toolbar. You might want to create a toolbar from a project folder you're working in, for example. That way, the documents in the folder are available from the taskbar, without your searching through Explorer windows.

> **Tip:** A quick way to create a custom toolbar and add it to your taskbar is to just drag a folder icon from an Explorer window and drop it on the taskbar.

After you identify a folder that you want to use as a toolbar, adding the toolbar to your taskbar is easy. Just right-click the taskbar and choose Toolbars, New Toolbar to open the New Toolbar dialog box, shown in Figure 6.2. Select a folder from the list or type an Internet address into the text box and then click OK. Windows creates a toolbar with buttons for each object in the folder and adds it to your taskbar.

Figure 6.2

Just select a folder (or type in a URL) and Windows makes a toolbar out of it for you.

> **Tip:** The only problem with creating a toolbar from a project folder is that there are likely to be files and documents in the folder that you don't need or want to appear as buttons in the toolbar. Scrolling through a lot of superfluous buttons to find the one you need can negate the speed advantage of having the buttons available on the taskbar in the first place. As a result, when I need a custom toolbar, I usually create a special folder to use for the toolbar and populate it with selected shortcut icons. This gives me control over the buttons in the toolbar.

Getting Rid of a Toolbar You Don't Need

Sooner or later, you'll need to get rid of a toolbar that you no longer need on your taskbar. You can remove any of the standard toolbars as well as any custom toolbars you've added. Perhaps the most obvious technique for removing toolbars is to repeat the same process you used to add standard toolbars: Right-click the taskbar, choose Toolbars from the context menu, and then click the toolbar you want to add/remove from the list of toolbars on the context menu. The technique I prefer is to right-click the toolbar I want to remove and choose Close from the context menu. The first time you use this technique, you have to confirm the action in the Confirm Toolbar Close dialog box; however, a check box appears in the dialog box that enables you to skip the confirmation dialog box in the future, which makes the Close command a little faster.

> **Tip:** One advantage to adding a link to your taskbar is that you can create a shortcut key that will launch the link very quickly (just press Ctrl+Alt+*key* and you're on your way to the site). You do this the same way you create a shortcut key for any item on your desktop or in the Start menu: right-click the link, choose Properties, and then define your shortcut key.

There's Really Only One Explorer

It should be no surprise—just based on their names—that Internet Explorer and Windows Explorer have been morphing into a single, all-purpose entity. They're not quite entirely fused yet, but with IE5 and Windows 2000, they're almost one. I've already mentioned that Windows 2000 includes Internet/intranet searches on its Search menu. That's one clue that everything is intended to work in multiple realms. Of course, at this point, choosing to find something on the Internet does launch IE5 as a seemingly separate application. However, that, too, will eventually pass. IE5 and Windows Explorer now share so many toolbar icons, the Address bar, and other features that once you learn how to use IE, you know how to use Windows Explorer—and vice versa.

The goal is clear: You're interested in information. You want to navigate, search, store, retrieve, and otherwise manage information. With the blurring of the distinction between Windows Explorer and your Internet browser, you now only need to learn how to use a single tool. For instance, recall that when you customize the Quick Launch toolbar in IE, the Quick Launch toolbar in Windows Explorer simultaneously changes as well. Same for the Favorites list.

Eventually, given the constant implosion of applications into a single, all-purpose implementation, we can expect that Outlook Express will become just another aspect of Internet Explorer. You can already launch Outlook Express from the Mail button on a standard IE toolbar. What's more, clicking a link within an email message, on your desktop, within a Word document, and in many other places launches IE.

You gain several valuable benefits when you combine your file managers, browsers, search utilities, email organizers, and other information/communication applications. After all, you don't have one car that you use to drive to the dentist and a separate car you use to pick up groceries. Here are some of the benefits you'll see:

- The browser becomes an all-purpose quick-view tool. It's fast—at least when displaying information stored locally—and it's rich (that is, text and graphics mix freely). Even animation and eventually high-definition TV will comfortably appear within the same all-embracing viewer.

- Toolbars can distinguish between inner and outer space. Whether you type the path to a file on your hard drive or a URL, the taskbar's Address bar knows the difference.

> **Tip:** When using the Address bar on the taskbar, you must be clear about whether you're looking for a filename or an Internet address. Typing `result.txt` will launch a search for a URL (`http://result.txt/`) on the Internet rather than a search for a file on your hard drive, as you intended. Instead, to locate a file on your hard drive, type the path, like this: `C:\result.txt`. Here's another trick: Try using the word *go*. Type, for example, `go farm` in the Address box; Internet Explorer will launch itself and run the Microsoft search engine to find all hits for the word *farm* on the Internet. Or you can omit the word *go* and merely click the Go button to the right of the Address bar.

- Favorites, links, toolbars, toolbar buttons, and shortcuts are universal. When you put icons on your desktop or add items to your Favorites list or toolbar, they can be links to either files on your system's hard drive or Internet addresses that bring up Web sites.

- The Web view changes the appearance of Windows Explorer's right pane (see the next section for more details).

The Classic View Versus the Web View

Windows Explorer offers what is called a *Web view*—it's a style, a layout, and a set of features. You can switch back and forth between Explorer's classic view and the new Web view easily. Just choose Tools, Folder Options and then choose Enable Web Contents in Folders, as shown in Figure 6.3.

In Web view, when you select a file, folder, or other object, a brief description appears within the right pane. You can see the description of the E: drive in Figure 6.4 (compare this with the traditional Explorer view shown in Figure 6.5).

When you're in the traditional Explorer view, the status bar at the bottom of the Explorer window displays some information about a selected item—the size of a file or drive or perhaps a bit of information about objects in the Control Panel, but no information about folders at all. By contrast, the Web view tells you the date a folder was modified as well as quite a lot of information about specialized folders such as Printers, Dial-Up Networking, and Control Panel. In fact, when you're in the Control Panel, the Web view displays a hyperlink to Microsoft's home page and its technical support site.

FIGURE 6.3

Here's where you can jazz up Windows Explorer's right pane.

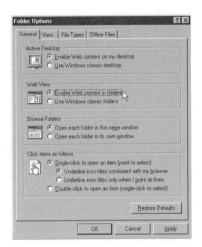

FIGURE 6.4

This is the Web view style in Windows Explorer.

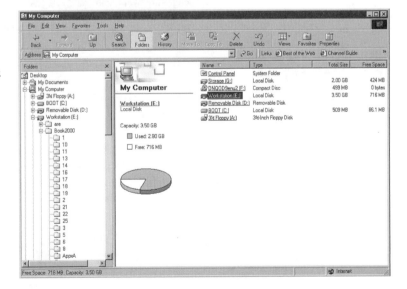

FIGURE 6.5

Here's the same location as shown in Figure 6.4, but in the classic Explorer style.

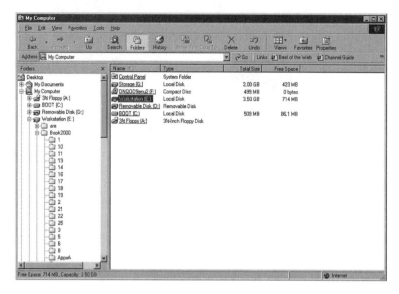

Wallpaper for Your Folders

You may have asked yourself this question: I can specify wallpaper for my desktop, but is it possible to use wallpaper within Explorer itself? Yes. You can use the Customize This Folder Wizard to create your own Web views—even within the classic Explorer view. Follow these steps to change the "wallpaper" within a folder:

1. Select the folder you want to customize by clicking it in Explorer's left pane. Be in the Web view to see the effect.

2. Right-click the background (not an icon) in the right pane and then choose Customize This Folder.

3. You'll now see the Customize This Folder Wizard. Click Next. You can choose an HTML template, add a comment, or specify a color or graphics file for your folder's background.

4. To change the wallpaper on your folder's background, click the Modify Background Picture and Filename Appearance check box, and then click Next. Either select the graphic from the displayed list or use the Browse option. You can also specify a text color and a background for the text (the title of the file or folder).

> **Tip:** The list of available graphics files includes both any such files (like .BMP) residing in the folder, as well as some new Windows 2000 graphics. The files are listed alphabetically, so you'll find your folder's files mixed in with the Windows files.

At the very least, adding a background to some of your folders provides a visual clue of the contents, thus distinguishing one folder from another. In addition, textures and even some unobtrusive (pale) high-resolution graphics, look better than a plain white background (see Figure 6.6).

FIGURE 6.6
Add custom backgrounds to indicate the contents of special folders.

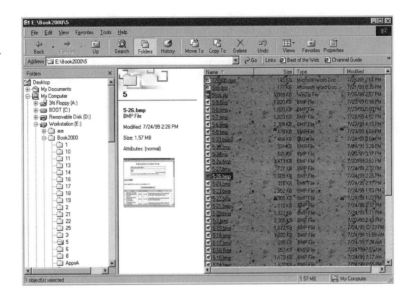

Web Page Backgrounds

You can also opt to add any kind of HTML page as the background for your Explorer's folders (you can also specify an HTML document as your desktop wallpaper).

If you want to use an HTML page as a background, start the Customize This Folder Wizard, as described in the preceding steps, but choose the Choose or Edit an HTML Template check box and then click Next. You'll see four templates from which you can choose, and you can edit the selected template, too, if you leave the check box checked. Don't use Save As; use the Save option from your editor's File menu to preserve the same filename and path. Also note that if you do want to edit the template, check the *I want to edit this template* check box.

Click Next again. A file named Folder.HTT will appear within Notepad (unless you've specified a different editor). The .HTT extension stands for *hypertext template*.

> **Tip:** If you prefer to use a more dedicated Web page editor than Notepad, click the Start button and then click Settings, Control Panel. Next, double-click the Folder Options icon. Click the File Types tab and then choose .HTT (Hypertext Template) from the list. Click the Advanced button and then click New. Type Open in the Action box and locate the editor you want to use instead of Notepad (C:\Program Files\Microsoft FrontPage\bin\fpeditor.exe, for example, if you want to use FrontPage).

In any case, after you're in the editor, you can modify the existing HTML code, create your own HTML page entirely from scratch, or just copy and paste the source code from an existing HTML Web page you're fond of (perhaps it has a list of links you frequently use or a nice DHTML animation).

The Image Preview template—which is great for folders holding graphics—produces a display similar to the one shown in Figure 6.7.

FIGURE 6.7
This Image Preview template works great with folders that contain graphics files. Try the various buttons on the toolbar above the image for some useful shortcuts.

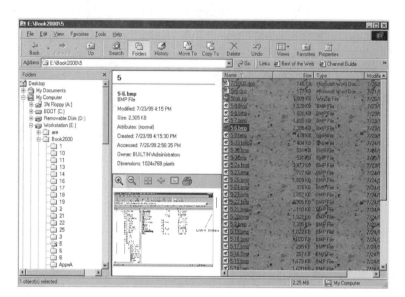

Windows Explorer and Internet Explorer: Is There Any Difference Anymore?

The simple answer is *not really*. They're quite alike now—you use them in very similar ways, and they both have Address bars in which you can type or paste file paths or Internet addresses. They both have Go To options on their View menus, with various targets on them, and both have Favorites menus (you can put files and folders on your disk drive in the Favorites list). Above all, you can transform Windows Explorer into Internet Explorer (and vice versa) with a click of your mouse. Here's how.

Open Windows Explorer. Select Explorer Bar from the View menu and then choose Favorites. As you can see in Figure 6.8, the left pane transforms itself from the usual directory tree to the IE Favorites bar.

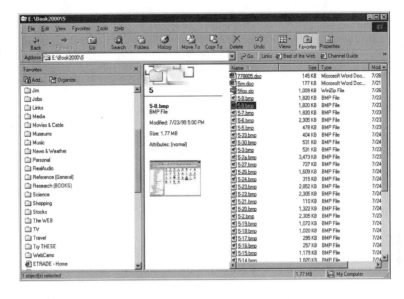

FIGURE 6.8

Windows Explorer or Internet Explorer? You be the judge.

Figure 6.8 shows the Internet in the left pane and a local hard drive in the right pane. Note that the standard toolbar options (Move To, Copy To, and so on) remain. Therefore, you're probably correct to think of this as a little bit more Windows than Internet Explorer at this stage.

The Transformation into a Browser

Now select one of the Web sites listed in your Favorites menu. The transformation into IE is now complete, as shown in Figure 6.9.

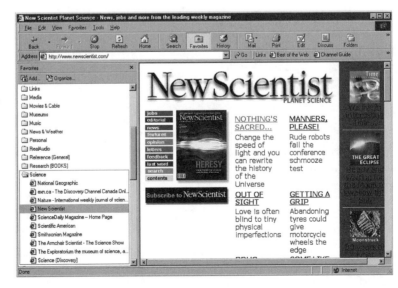

FIGURE 6.9

Morphing into IE. Notice the Mail and Print buttons have replaced Move To and Copy To, and other features have adjusted to the full Internet Explorer experience.

The standard toolbar at the top has transformed into a toolbar with Internet Explorer's buttons (Refresh, Home, and so on). Also, you might notice differences in your settings for the buttons, the Address bar, and the links between the two Explorers.

Notice that when you're looking at folders and files on your hard drive, Windows Explorer lists My Computer (or whatever other top-level zone you're in) on the status bar in its lower-right corner. Whenever you switch to Internet view, the status bar indicates Internet.

The Transformation Back to Windows Explorer

Going back from the Internet Explorer state to the original Windows Explorer is simple. Just choose Explorer Bar from the View menu and then select Folders. Click the Folders icon in the Standard Buttons toolbar or select a filename or folder in the Favorites menu or the Favorites Explorer bar.

As easy as it is to change Windows Explorer into Internet Explorer, and then back again, it used to be hard to metamorphose Internet Explorer into Windows Explorer (in NT 4). However, now you can find a Folders option in Internet Explorer's View menu, and you can add the optional Folders button to the standard IE toolbar.

On Your Own

Here are some things to try on your own:

- See whether you prefer to open each folder in a new Windows Explorer window (use the Tools, Folder Options feature).
- Try the various kinds of backgrounds, text colors, and other effects you can create by using the Customize This Folder feature.
- Add and modify HTML templates to your Windows Explorer.

PART II

Power to Spare

Performance Power

Tuning or optimizing a machine for optimum performance is one of the first things many people think about when they install a new operating system. After they get all their applications set up and check out some of the new utilities, they want to see just how much they can get out of their new toy.

The first thing you need to consider when reading this chapter is what "tuning" means. Getting every last ounce of power out of a system to make it perform a specific task optimally is one type of tuning. Allowing a system to boost the performance of a variety of specific tasks simultaneously (multitasking) is another. General tuning to provide the best performance in a variety of situations is yet another. I could go on. The fact of the matter is that there's no default configuration and no standard machine. All users have different needs and different hardware they need to use to get the job done. Any meaningful optimization will take your specific needs into account.

I won't tell you how to tune your specific machine in this chapter. There's no way I can provide step-by-step tuning instructions for anyone without knowing his or her situation. Instead, I'll provide you with guidelines and tips you can use to create your own solutions. You'll need to decide which tips you should implement and which you should ignore. I'll provide tips for a variety of machine configurations, and your machine will appear somewhere in the list.

So, do you start reading right this second and hope to find the tips you need the first time through? You probably won't. It takes a bit of time and patience to really tune a system for optimum performance. To get some idea of what I'm talking about, consider race car drivers. A race car is tuned to fit its particular "personality." The mechanic and driver work together to come up with the best configuration for that particular car. In addition, the car is tuned to fit the track it will race on and even for the weather conditions. Tuning the car is probably the easy part of the process; planning how to tune it requires a bit more effort.

You won't need to worry about the weather when tuning your system, but many other principles do apply. Planning how you need to tune your system is always a good idea. As with any other worthwhile endeavor, tuning your system requires that you create a few goals and take a few potholes into account. Your machine contains hardware from a variety of sources, and it probably contains a combination of components unique within your company. You need to consider how that hardware will react. Your applications are unique. Even if your job isn't unique, your way of doing that job probably is. That means that a system perfectly tuned for the way I work probably won't do a lot for you.

Keeping these personal needs in mind, let's look at some of the things you should consider before you start tuning up for the big race. The following list describes criteria you must consider before you begin to tune your system. Of course, the time and effort you expend on this effort is directly proportional to the amount of performance you can expect to receive.

Microsoft states that minimum system requirements for Windows 2000 Professional are as follows: a 166MHz Pentium processor, 32MB of RAM (64MB recommended), and 280MB of free hard disk space (in addition to the space required by the operating system). However, these specifications are extremely minimal. You'll want much more memory and a much larger hard drive. (We look at the minimum requirements for a functional Windows 2000 system in Chapter 4.) The following list talks about the kinds of requirements you should look at for a well designed Windows 2000 system.

- **Memory**—The amount of real memory your system contains is a big factor in how well Windows 2000 will operate. You shouldn't consider starting to tune until you have a minimum of 128MB of RAM. You need to tailor this number to meet the demands of the applications you plan to run. A spreadsheet requires a lot of memory, for example, and a database requires even more, but a word processor is relatively light when it comes to memory consumption. You might find that a graphics application requires a major amount of memory and also takes a heavy toll on both the processor and the graphics adapter. The number of simultaneous applications you plan to run also affects the point at which you should start to tune your system. I equipped my system with 512MB of RAM because I often run a word processor, a graphics application, and Internet Explorer simultaneously. Virtual memory helps take up the slack between real memory and what you need, but you can't count on it to assume the full burden. You don't want to sit there waiting while the disk drive grinds away trying to swap memory contents when you switch from one program to another.

- **Hard disk size**—Windows 2000 runs best, however, when you do give it a large pagefile to work with. In addition, you need space for each application and additional space for data files that support that application. The one factor many people underestimate is the size of data files. Just as applications have grown enormously over the years, so have embedded codes, styles, macros, and other support information within the data files themselves. This is partly the result of object-oriented programming. The current theory of programming is that you should include bits of executable programming right there within data. So, in addition to words in your .DOC file, you might expect to also find embedded behaviors that actually do something to those words (such as format them). It's an interesting experiment to save a Word 2000 .DOC file that contains no other visible content than the single word "hello." Theoretically, this file requires only 10 bytes on your hard drive because the current character codes require 2 bytes per character (that way, complex alphabets such as Chinese can be accommodated). It should be safe to assume that the 10 bytes in your .DOC file could easily fit within a 1024-byte sector on the hard drive. However, on my system, the hello .DOC file takes up 19456 bytes! The general rule of thumb I use for figuring out the amount of hard disk space I need is to add up the space required for installed configurations of my applications and then triple it. This is a very coarse calculation, but it works for me.

> **Note:** The memory storage zone that Windows 2000 creates on the hard drive has also been called the swap file in the past because it allows the operating system to swap the contents of memory from RAM to the hard drive. However, recently people have been referring to this as the pagefile, after its filename pagefile.sys, and also because moving the data into and out of that file is called paging. A page of memory is a predefined piece of a specific size, just as the pages in a book are all a specific size. The operating system can place some pages of the book of memory used by your application on the hard drive, while other pages reside in memory. We use the newest term, pagefile, in this chapter.

- **Hard disk speed**—Older operating systems were a lot less disk-intensive than Windows 2000 is. Not only do you have the pagefile that Windows 2000 creates, but applications also make greater use of the hard drive today for temporary storage. To see what I mean, open just about any application and check for the number of .TMP files on your drive (probably located in your C:\TEMP or C:\WINDOWS\TEMP folder). You might be surprised by what you see. All this disk access means just one thing: You must have a fast drive to make Windows 2000 jump through the hoops you want it to. Drive speed isn't the cure-all for every problem, but in the past few years, it has become a much bigger part of the overall picture than it used to be.

- **Processor speed**—Your processor speed affects the way your computer runs. No other factor so greatly affects your system after you meet the basic storage requirements. Herein lies the rub: Many people opt for a high-speed processor and then choke it with limited memory, a slow system bus, and inadequate hard drive space. Remember that the processor makes a big impact on system throughput, but only if you meet the basic storage requirements first. A thrashing hard drive can eat up every bit of extra speed you add to a system. The L2 cache is also an important contributor to the overall responsiveness of your system. See Chapter 11, "Memory Management," for details on this and the L1 cache.

- **Peripheral devices**—I/O has always been a bottleneck in the PC. That was true yesterday, and it's even truer today. The two peripherals you need to concentrate on the most are your disk controller and display adapter. Think about the way Windows is designed for a second, and you'll understand why. Windows is a GUI;

it consumes huge amounts of time just drawing all those pretty images you see on the display. A display adapter that uses processor cycles efficiently (or even that unloads some processing tasks) can greatly affect the perceived speed of your system. The less time Windows spends drawing icons and other graphics, the more time it has to service your application. Likewise, a slow controller will make even a fast hard disk look slow. The controller becomes the bottleneck with many systems today. The short take on peripherals? Always get, at a minimum, 32-bit peripherals, and make certain that they're fully compatible with Windows 2000. (Because Windows 2000 doesn't support real-mode drivers, you don't have any easy way of getting around problem devices.)

- **Bus speed**—You might not think very much about the little connectors you stick cards into, but the system does. The system bus has been a source of major concern for a great number of years, and I don't see this changing anytime soon. What good is a fast peripheral if you can't access it at full speed? The most common bus today is the PCI bus, although a lot of alternatives are on the horizon. A standard machine today contains Accelerated Graphics Port (AGP) , PCI, and ISA connectors, each of which is designed to work with a different type of peripheral. If you have an older motherboard that uses an older bus such as VL, MCA, or EISA, you should really consider buying a new motherboard, which will also mean buying a faster processor.

- **Network interface card (NIC)**—If you spend a lot of time working on the network, you'll most certainly want a high-capacity NIC. The cost of a 16-bit card compared to 32-bit card makes me suggest that anything less than a PCI 32-bit card is a silly purchase. However, note that the 32-bit path benefits only the communication from processor/system to network interface. Those 10Mbps LANs are still the bottleneck, even with the 16-bit card, so if you get a 32-bit card you may also want to look at updating your network to use 100Mbps cards. Anything less than 32 bits is a waste of perfectly good network bandwidth. People who share graphics or other large files across the system should consider getting 32-bit NICs for their machines.

After you get your hardware configuration out of the way, it's time to consider your software configuration. Windows 2000 does a much better job of managing resources than previous versions.

In previous versions of Windows, you could start to run out of resources after loading your word processor, spreadsheet, communications program, and one or two small utility programs such as a screen saver or Notepad. I usually consider closing an application or two when I get to the 35% system resources level, which is about where I was with this configuration. Windows 2000, however, still has around 78% of its resources free when using the same configuration. This means that I can usually open two or three more applications on top of my usual configuration.

Of course, system resources are only one memory factor; there's the actual level of RAM to take into consideration as well. Prior to Windows 2000, you'd start to notice a fairly large performance penalty when you got to the point where the pagefile was as large as real memory. Under Windows 2000, this doesn't seem to be as much of a problem, but it's still very noticeable. The bottom line is that if your pagefile starts approaching the size of your installed memory, it's time for an upgrade.

You need to take into consideration the combination of system resources and system memory when thinking about your software situation. A memory-constrained system always lacks enough memory to perform the job you need it to. It's a subjective type of measurement based on how you actually use your system. You should load the Resource Monitor and, over a few days, track both the size of your pagefile and the number of resources you have available. If you start to see a pattern of low memory, read the next section. You might even find that the problem isn't the amount of installed memory on your machine, but the way you use that memory.

Windows 2000 users have a plethora of other concerns that Windows 95/98 users don't share. For one thing, the platform you choose can make a great deal of difference. Even if you choose an Intel platform, you need to consider some of the advanced capabilities Windows 2000 provides. You can get over part of the performance hurdle, for example, by using a multiprocessor machine. There's also the availability of multiple hard disk formats to consider. An NTFS partition may reduce flexibility (because you can access it only from within Windows 2000), but it also enhances performance. (Having an NTFS only system also prevents you from creating a multi-boot system, should you need to create one later.)

By now, you can see what all this preliminary checking is leading to. A mechanic would never consider tuning a car before checking it over for the first time. Likewise, you should never consider tuning your system before you know what type of system you have and how you use it. It's not enough to say that you have 128MB of RAM installed. The way you use that RAM determines whether it's sufficient. A 20GB hard drive might sound impressive, unless you're trying to create a lot of multimedia presentations with it. Then a hard drive this size sounds like—and in practice is—a rather paltry amount.

Performance Tips for a Minimal Setup

Memory would seem to be the biggest problem most people face on a system, but it really shouldn't be. Memory prices have crashed in the past three years, and $60 now gets you 64MB, on average (using mid-1999 prices). Although memory isn't free, it's certainly reasonable, and few new items can provide as much potential for a noticeable increase in system performance as adding memory. Remember that applications and data files continue to balloon, so today 128MB isn't an unreasonable amount to ask for when you're upgrading to a new computer.

Microsoft will try to tell you that you can get by with as little as 32MB of RAM when running Windows 2000 Professional. As I mentioned, you really want more than that. The absolute minimum I recommend is 64MB, and that's if you intend to run only two or perhaps three applications at a time. Just think about these numbers for a second. How many of you can honestly say that you run a single application at a time? Think about how many applications you do run. At the very least, you'll probably find four or five applications running on your machine. Even with 64MB of RAM, you'll find that your system is constrained at times.

When working with previous versions of Windows, the opposite extreme exists as well. Few people I've talked to report any noticeable improvement in system performance after they exceed 128MB when using these older products. Windows 2000 is very much improved when it comes to memory usage. My system steadily improved in performance as I built it up to 512MB, and I see no reason why I shouldn't expect continued performance improvements well beyond that limit. However, there's a practical limit of 4GB when using Windows 2000, only 2GB of which can be used for applications (unless they're specially programmed to take advantage of a new 3GB limit on application size).

Suppose, for the moment, that your boss absolutely won't buy any additional memory for your museum piece machine, and you're stuck at that 32MB level. What can you do to improve the situation? How can you stretch your 32MB of RAM enough to make your single-tasking system (from a memory perspective) work as a multitasking system? The following sections provide you with tuning tips that will at least reduce the time you wait between tasks.

General Tuning Tips for Windows

I recommend that you start with a few quick and easy methods. The techniques we talk about in this section work with any version of Windows, not just Windows 2000. I've also looked for simple fixes that anyone can use, but these methods always involve some level of compromise you might not be willing to make. The following list shows my quick fixes to memory problems:

- **Wallpaper**—Did you know that it costs you a little memory and some processing time to keep wallpaper on your system? If you have a memory-constrained system and can do without some bells and whistles, here's one item to get rid of. Don't think you'll save much by using smaller wallpaper or restricting yourself to patterns—both items chew up some memory.

- **Colors**—The number of colors you use for your display directly affects the amount of memory it uses. A 16-color display uses roughly half the memory of a 256-color display. Although a 16-color display doesn't look as appealing as its 256-color or the True Color counterpart, using one does help you save memory. You probably won't notice much of a difference in appearance if the programs on your machine are word processing and spreadsheets. (In practice, however, you should really just spend that $60 and get at least 64MB.)

- **Screen resolution**—The resolution at which you set your display affects processing speed and, to a much smaller degree, memory. Of course, the problem with changing your display resolution is fairly simple to figure out. You can probably get by with fewer colors, but fewer pixels are a whole different matter. You'll probably want to save changing the screen resolution as a last-ditch effort to get that last bit of needed performance.

- **Doodads**—I put a whole realm of utility programs into the "doodad" category. If you run one of the fancier screen savers rather than the built-in Windows counterpart, for example, you're wasting memory. Some people also keep a small game program such as Solitaire running. These small applications might provide a few minutes of pleasure here and there, but you really don't need to keep them active all the time. If you insist on using that screen saver, run it right before you leave the room for a while, and then exit it when you return. The same holds true with a game program; keep it open when you play it, and then close it before you get back to work. To determine whether you have extra programs running, look for program icons on the System Tray (which appears on the taskbar).

- **Icons and other graphics**—Every icon displayed on your desktop consumes memory. The same holds true for any other form of graphics image or window. At least Windows 2000 doesn't penalize you for opening a folder, as previous versions of Windows NT did. You can actually recover the memory by closing the folder. The simple way of looking at this is to organize your data into folders and open only the folders that you need at any given time.

- **Leaky applications**—Some programs leak memory. They allocate memory— telling Windows 2000 that they need so much space—but never give it back, even after they terminate. After a while, you might find that you don't have enough memory to run programs, even though you should. This problem was severe under Windows 3.x, although it's less so under Windows 95/98 and Windows NT. It's almost nonexistent in Windows 2000 because this latest version of the operating system does a much better job of looking for errant programs that don't release memory when they're done. However, the data-centric interface provided by Explorer in the latest versions of Windows (including Windows 2000) tends to accelerate the rate at which memory dissipates if you open and close an application for each data file. You can alleviate this situation by keeping leaky applications open until you know that you won't need them again. You can identify a leaky application by checking system resources and memory before you open it, opening and closing the application and associated documents a few times, and then checking the amount of free memory and resources again after the last time you close it. If you find that you have less memory or fewer resources—I mean a measurable amount, not a few bytes—the application is leaky.

- **Extra drivers**—Windows 2000 does a fairly good job of cleaning old drivers out of the Registry. Even so, you want to take the time to see whether all the drivers got removed from the system after you remove an application. This isn't such a big deal for newer applications that are specifically designed for Windows 95/98 or Windows NT/2000. All these newer operating systems provide a special installation utility that removes newer applications from the system, including the files they stick in the SYSTEM directory and any references to them in the system files. Unfortunately, in most cases, old Windows 3.x applications don't remove anything.

> **Tip:** Always look for applications that bear the Windows logo. This logo assures you that Microsoft has tested the application and that it should perform reasonably well on your machine. The Windows 2000 logo requires the most stringent support of Windows features and is the logo that you should look for first on an application.

- **DOS applications**—Nothing grabs memory and holds it like a DOS application under Windows. Unlike other applications, Windows normally can't move the memory used by a DOS application around to free space. This means that you might have a lot of memory on your system, but Windows won't be capable of using it because it's all too fragmented. If your system is so constricted on memory that it can't tolerate even the smallest amount of memory fragmentation, you'll probably want to avoid using DOS applications.

Windows 2000–Specific Tuning Tips

Now that we've gotten past the generic tips, let's look at a few Windows 2000–specific ways to enhance overall system performance and the amount of memory you have available. All these tips are Windows NT/2000–specific; don't try using them with earlier versions of the product because you won't get the desired results.

- **Use Pentium II/III processors, if possible**—Before Windows NT/2000 and 95/98, the operating system didn't even care about the processor you used—only the processing speed was important. The facts are plain: Old 16-bit code runs equally well on any 386 or above processor. But there's a big difference in performance when using different processor types under Windows 2000 because it uses 32-bit code. A 486 processor is better optimized to take advantage of 32-bit code, and the Pentium or Pentium II with MMX is better still. Theoretically, you should notice a fairly substantial improvement in processing capability between a machine equipped with a Pentium II and a Pentium machine of the same processor speed. In reality, the difference is noticeable, but not that noticeable. You'll want to get the extra performance if possible, but don't worry about it until you take care of other problems, such as upgrading your memory.

Note: It's hard to tell just what kind of performance boost you'll get when moving from a Pentium II processor to a Pentium III processor. You'll definitely get the boost provided by any close speed difference; but, in many cases, that's about all you'll see. An application must be written to take advantage of the new features that the Pentium III provides before you'll see a noticeable performance boost with this processor. To you, as a user, this means making careful purchasing decisions: It might actually be better to stick with a Pentium II processor for the moment and spend any extra money on additional memory or a faster hard drive.

- **Increase the number of processors**—One of the most common ways to add more performance to a Windows 2000 system is to add more than one processor. Some machines are designed to move from one to two or four processors. I saw one file server system that accepted 16 processors, but now we're getting out of the realm of possibility for a workstation. Don't think, however, that you'll get double the performance by adding another processor to a single processor machine. Some amount of overhead is involved in keeping the two processors working together. I've typically seen about one and three-fourths processors' worth of work come out of a two-processor system. Obviously, your results will vary depending on how you use your system and the way in which the hardware is designed.

Caution: Windows 2000 handles multiprocessor machines differently than Windows NT did, in part because of the new Plug and Play features that it provides. In some situations Windows 2000 may not recognize that your machine has more than one processor due to BIOS or configuration problems. Make absolutely certain that your multiprocessor machine is on the HCL before you buy it. If you have an existing machine and find that Windows 2000 can't see the multiple processors it contains, then start with a BIOS upgrade to see if that fixes the problem. In most cases, you should also contact the motherboard manufacturer to determine if you need to make other Windows 2000 changes.

- **Use an efficient hard drive format**—Hard drive format affects system performance in several ways. The most obvious is direct file access; you'll get the best level of performance using an NTFS partition. (However, you'll give up some flexibility to get this speed boost.) The second area is a little less obvious. Placing your pagefile on an NTFS partition can actually improve performance because NTFS is an optimized disk-formatting technology. I wouldn't count on a large speed improvement; however, moving your pagefile is more in the line of an incremental improvement.

- **Eliminate 16-bit drivers and DLLs**—Windows 2000 is a 32-bit operating system with some 16-bit compatibility components and a few items left over from Windows 3.x. It runs every 32-bit application in a separate session. Doing this allows Windows 2000 to perform some very intense memory management on the resources needed by that application. The 16-bit applications also run in separate sessions (unlike Windows 95/98, where they run in a single session) but share resources. The amount of management Windows 2000 can perform on these shared resources is a lot less than what it can do for the individual 32-bit sessions because it can't make certain assumptions about how that memory is being used. In addition, the 32-bit memory space is flat, reducing the number of clock cycles required to make a function call or look at something in memory. On the other hand, the segmented address space used by 16-bit components requires two to three times the number of clock cycles to process.

- **Theoretically, the single-pane folder window is more streamlined and more efficient than the two-pane Explorer window**—In fact, I used to advise using folder windows, but I was wrong. This might seem like a contradiction in terms because folders use the Explorer interface. However, a folder displays just the interface, not the full Explorer. Opening a copy of Explorer eats up a lot more system resources than opening a folder. The idea is that you place all your data in folders and then place a shortcut to those folders on the desktop. You can still get to all your important files without opening a copy of Explorer. The actual memory savings you get by using this tip are generally small, however, so you should organize your work the way you find easiest. Take a look at Task Manager's Performance display (press Ctrl+Alt+Del, and then choose Task Manager). Click the Performance tab, and watch what happens to memory usage (on the very bottom status bar: Mem Usage) when you open Explorer instead of merely opening a folder. On my system, opening explorer extracts a memory penalty of only 176 bytes, and opening a folder costs 368 bytes. Neither approach has much impact on memory at all.

- **Use context menus in place of the Control Panel**—I find that I occasionally need to adjust the properties of various system elements during a session. Note that you don't have to open the Control Panel to make these adjustments. Old habits die hard. It took me a while to adjust to the Windows 2000 way of dealing with this situation. Chapter 5, "Exploring the Interface," looks in detail at the context menu that's attached to nearly every object (right-click an object to see the menu). Using that context menu isn't only an efficient way to access information about the object, but it uses less memory as well. This is something to consider if you need to keep an object's Properties dialog box open for any length of time.

- **Reset your printer for RAW printing**—Windows 2000 automatically installs support for Enhanced Metafile Format (EMF) printing on systems that it thinks will support it. This feature allows Windows 2000 to print faster by translating the output to generic commands in the foreground and then creating printer-specific output in the background. Creating generic commands requires a lot less processing time than writing printer-specific output. Changing the setting of the Default Datatype field in the Print Processor dialog box to RAW forces Windows 2000 to create a printer-specific output in the first pass. (You can access this dialog box by selecting the Advanced tab of the Printer Properties dialog box and clicking the Print Processor button.) Using the RAW setting means that less operating system code is maintained in memory during the print process. Some memory-constrained systems receive a large benefit by using this print mode. Of course, the trade-off is longer foreground print times.

- **Keep your disk defragmented**—Earlier versions of Windows enable you to create a permanent pagefile. Using a permanent pagefile improves performance by reducing hard disk head movement to read pagefile data. It doesn't matter how fragmented your drive gets after you set up the swap file, because the swap file always resides in the same contiguous disk sectors. Windows 2000 doesn't provide the permanent swap file option; it always uses a temporary file. Microsoft has improved the access algorithms and has reduced the penalty for using a temporary swap file, however. Of course, the system doesn't work perfectly. You can still get a highly fragmented drive that reduces system performance as Windows moves from area to area in an attempt to read the swap file. Defragmenting your drive reduces the possibility that the swap file will become too fragmented. Most people find that a monthly maintenance session takes care of this requirement.

Tip: There's a method for simulating a permanent pagefile under Windows 2000. Simply set the minimum and maximum pagefile sizes to the same value. In addition, you can incrementally enhance the performance of your system if you have a two-disk system. Simply move the pagefile to the first drive while you completely defragment the second. After you've defragmented the second drive, move the pagefile from the first drive to the second drive. In short, you'll create a simulated permanent drive that resides in one contiguous section of the hard drive, which will improve system performance.

- **Place your pagefile on the fastest drive**—Windows 2000 usually chooses the NTFS-formatted drive with the largest amount of available space for the pagefile. (On other occasions the exact criteria Windows used to select a swap file location eludes me; it seems to use hit-and-miss tactics from time to time.) In most cases, the drive it chooses doesn't make that big of a difference. If you have a system with one large, slow drive and a second small, fast drive, however, you'll probably want to change the virtual memory settings. (Right-click My Computer, choose Properties from the context menu, click the Advanced tab of the System Properties dialog box, click Performance Options, and finally click Change in the Performance Options dialog box).

• **Get rid of nonessentials**—You'll find that some parts of Windows 2000 make your system slightly more efficient, but at a fairly large cost in memory. Enabling the International Settings feature (described in Chapter 5) makes your system more efficient if you work with several languages, for example, but that enhancement costs you some memory. Unfortunately, after you activate this feature, you can't deactivate it until you reboot the machine; the memory is gone for good. The same holds true for the Resource Monitor and many of the other icons that appear on the taskbar near the clock. All these features are nice to have but aren't essential. For example, the Accessibility options are a nice enhancement, but you might want to get rid of them on a memory-constrained system unless you actually use them. Even though this feature doesn't display an icon on the taskbar, installing it consumes some memory every time you start Windows 2000.

Finding Unneeded Hidden Drivers

At times, Windows 2000 does a less-than-perfect job of setting up your machine. Earlier, I mentioned that you should remove any unneeded drivers. What would happen if you had some hidden drivers you really didn't need installed on your system? Figure 7.1 shows a dialog box that illustrates this point perfectly. I installed Windows 2000 on a network with both a Windows 2000 Server and a Novell NetWare file server. Notice that it installed both NetBIOS and IPX/SPX support. In fact, because this is a NetWare 5 system, I don't need either protocol—running TCP/IP is enough. Unchecking these two protocol options won't remove them from your My Network Places (which means that the files are still on disk), but it does prevent them from starting, which saves memory and processing cycles.

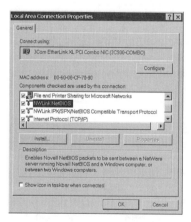

FIGURE 7.1
Sometimes Windows 2000 will install drivers you don't need.

Obviously, not every driver will be this easy to spot, but with patience, you can find most of the extra drivers on your system. If you find yourself in this particular situation, follow these three steps:

1. Eliminate additional network support. You need to install support for only one network if you're using a peer-to-peer setup. In most cases, this means that you'll retain the Microsoft network and discard NetWare support. Likewise, if you don't plan to set up a peer-to-peer network, remove the Microsoft network support in a NetWare environment.

2. Reduce the number of protocols you have installed. I typically maintain NetBEUI (or TCP/IP, if I'm using the Internet) support for a peer-to-peer setup, if at all possible (see Chapter 24, "Peer-to-Peer Networking," for much more detail). Of course, the protocol you choose must reflect the capabilities of the network you install. (You'll find a list of installed protocols in the Connection Properties dialog box, such as the one shown in Figure 7.1, for a local area connection.) Note, however, that in almost all other situations NetBEUI is neither needed nor recommended. Often users confuse NetBEUI with NetBIOS, which are two, quite different things. Your application may say that NetBIOS-supported protocol is required, however. You might erroneously think that the NetBEUI protocol is a requirement, but IPX and TCP/IP as implemented by MS are also NetBIOS-supported protocols. Keep that in mind.

3. Install the fewest possible network services. Installing sharing support for a floppy drive is a waste of memory because it's unlikely that someone will need it. If someone does need it, you can always add the support later. Try starting out with the lowest level of support possible. You'll also want to think about which workstation printers you really want to share. If a workstation has an older printer attached, you probably won't want to install print sharing support for it.

DOS Application Performance Tips

I'd love to say that Windows 2000 will run every DOS application you ever owned without any major configuration problems, but that wouldn't be very accurate. In fact, if you're going to run a lot of DOS applications, Windows 2000 isn't even the best operating system you could choose. Even Microsoft has admitted this recently by providing continued updates to the Windows 9x operating system instead of moving everyone to Windows 2000. The bottom line is that Windows 95/98 runs these older applications far better than Windows 2000. If you plan to run only a few well-behaved DOS applications, however, Windows 2000 can still get the job done. It's best to remember that you'll encounter problems when running certain DOS applications, and you need to tune your system to avoid them.

Note: Windows 2000 does do a much better job of running DOS applications than Windows NT does, yet at an even higher level of security. This means that Windows 2000 is becoming a better choice for the home game enthusiast, but it probably isn't the best choice yet. If you're running well-behaved Windows game software, then Windows 2000 is about as good a choice as Windows 98, but games are seldom well-behaved and not all of them run in Windows yet.

The good news is that you can make all the required changes using the application's Properties dialog box. Windows 2000 supports all the old configuration features and adds quite a few of its own. This means that you can make the required changes by right-clicking the object and choosing Properties from the context menu. The first thing you'll see is an Application Properties dialog box, similar to the one shown in Figure 7.2. Everything you need to run DOS applications efficiently under Windows 2000 appears in this dialog box; it replaces the PIF Editor used in some previous versions of Windows.

FIGURE 7.2

The General tab of the Application Properties dialog box tells you the size, location, and attributes of the application.

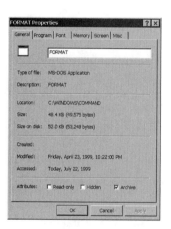

Many similarities exist between the entries you'll find in the Properties dialog box and those in the PIF files of some previous versions of Windows. Don't be fooled. Windows 2000 provides much the same functionality as those previous versions; it just makes it a bit easier to change the settings. Fortunately, the Properties dialog box does add some much-needed fields and a new mode or two.

Several tabs directly affect the way a DOS application behaves under Windows 2000. The first one we look at appears in Figure 7.3. The Program tab contains some fields that tell Windows 2000 what application to run and where to run it. This includes the application name and its working directory. The area of concern for this chapter is the Windows NT button, near the bottom of the dialog box. Clicking that button displays the Windows PIF Settings dialog box, shown in Figure 7.4, which contains some of the DOS-specific settings that affect how Windows 2000 will react.

You get only a few tools to run DOS applications under Windows 2000. The fact that you can choose a special AUTOEXEC.BAT and CONFIG.SYS file to run a troublesome application certainly helps. You place the name and location of those files in this dialog box, and this particular feature helps you run two categories of DOS applications.

The first category is game programs. Using special AUTOEXEC.BAT and CONFIG.SYS files can make a big difference. Even this advantage won't enable you to run an ill-behaved DOS application, however. Notice the Compatible Timer Hardware Emulation check box. I usually select this option for games as well because many games use timing loops rather than interrupt-driven programming techniques to keep game components in sync. Unfortunately, checking this box also involves a penalty. Running an application that has this box checked usually wastes processor cycles because Windows 2000 must spend additional time running "do nothing" application loops used for timing purposes.

FIGURE 7.3

The Program tab of the Application Properties dialog box allows you to adjust the Windows-specific information for the application.

FIGURE 7.4

The Windows PIF Settings dialog box allows you to change the name of the CONFIG.SYS and AUTOEXEC.BAT files used to run an application.

The other category, strangely enough, is older graphics applications. Using tuned AUTOEXEC.BAT and CONFIG.SYS files can help these applications use system memory more efficiently and run better, in most cases. For example, the old copy of Harvard Graphics I had lying around performed almost twice as fast using hand-tuned files as it did using the default files shown in Figure 7.4. After a bit of research, I concluded that this was due to a combination of factors, such as direct-screen writing and other rule-breaking behaviors that create problems for these applications. I'd still say that this is the exception to the rule, though. The best idea is to check out an application using the default files first; creating hand-tuned files is a very time-consuming and resource-wasting endeavor. Better yet, replace the application with a Windows 2000-specific product, if at all possible.

The Memory tab, shown in Figure 7.5, can also help you obtain the best possible setup for your application. In most cases, you'll want to stick to the Auto setting. However, I have several applications that require more environment space than the Auto setting provides. All you need to do is adjust the setting of the drop-down list box as required. The same thing holds true for any other memory settings you might need to adjust.

FIGURE 7.5

The Memory tab
allows you to cus-
tomize the DOS
application's
memory settings.

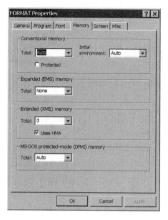

FIGURE 7.5

*The Memory tab
allows you to cus-
tomize the DOS
application's
memory settings.*

You should always keep one thing in mind with this tab: Setting any memory entries you don't need to None saves system memory and allows Windows 2000 to provide better services to the rest of the applications on your machine. Windows 2000 always assumes a worst-case scenario with DOS applications; setting the various memory options gives it a little more information to work with.

The Protected check box in the Conventional Memory group is a two-edged sword. Setting it allows some applications to run. It also prevents Windows 2000 from moving applications around in memory. Some applications that access memory directly need this kind of protection. The downside of checking this box is that a fixed session in memory always increases memory fragmentation and the chance that you'll artificially run out of memory.

The last tab we look at from a performance perspective is the Screen tab, shown in Figure 7.6. We talk about only two check boxes in this chapter; the rest are covered in Chapter 16, "Exploiting Your Software." Not surprisingly, both check boxes appear in the Performance group.

FIGURE 7.6

*The Screen tab
provides two per-
formance-
oriented settings.*

The Dynamic Memory Allocation check box is the important one here. As with the Protected check box on the Memory tab, this check box determines whether Windows 2000 can move memory around. Here's the problem: Many graphics applications resort to using direct screen writes to get the performance they need. Those same graphics applications won't work under Windows 2000 if you keep this box checked because Windows might move the "virtual" screen to which the application is actually writing somewhere else. The warning sign you need to look for on a graphics application is some type of distortion. Most applications display vertical bars or some type of striation. You might see part of the display shift, or you might see what appears to be cursor trails onscreen. These types of distortions tell you that you need to uncheck the Dynamic Memory Allocation check box.

The Fast ROM Emulation check box determines how the application gains access to display instructions normally held in the computer's ROM chip. Accessing the ROM chip directly is slow because ROM takes longer to read than RAM and because Windows needs to make a processor mode transition to read it. Windows can place a copy of the ROM instructions in RAM so that the application can access them faster. So, for the most part, you want to keep this box checked to get the best possible performance from your application. The only clue you'll get that an application actually needs this Fast ROM Emulation feature disabled is that the application will refuse to work at all. About the only time you'll run into this problem is with very old games and a very few poorly designed graphics applications.

Multitasking System Performance Tips

Getting more than one application to run on a system at the same time usually involves making some compromises. You can tune a single-tasking system to provide the best performance for that one application. You can tune your system in such a way that a disk-intensive application gets everything it needs to get the job done quickly, for example. But what happens if you run one application that's disk-intensive and another that's CPU-intensive? Do you starve the resources of one to get better performance from the other?

We've already looked at most of the generic ways to provide additional memory. This is one area you need to concentrate on if you plan to multitask. Running more than one application simultaneously always consumes a lot of memory. What you might not realize is that your performance levels might become artificially low because of the way in which Windows 2000 handles memory management.

Disk swapping, the same feature that provides so much virtual memory for your applications, can also wreak havoc in a multitasking environment. Two big clues tell you when disk swapping has become a problem, not a cure. First, you'll notice a dramatic increase in your system's disk activity. This isn't always a bad thing under Windows 2000, but it can be an indicator. Windows 2000 uses a very aggressive disk-writing algorithm to make the most of system idle time. You might see what seems like a lot of disk activity, when all Windows 2000 is doing is writing some of the data from memory to disk.

The second clue will tell you just how bad the memory situation is. Look at the size of your swap file. If your swap file is about the same size as your real memory, your system is memory starved, and you really can't run the number of applications you're trying to run. Windows 2000 will try its best to provide a satisfactory level of performance, but the truth is that you just won't see it.

Far more scientific ways exist to precisely measure system performance, and we look at them in the next section. The two clues we just discussed provide you with a very quick idea of what your system performance is like right this minute without wasting a lot of your time trying to define it completely. Of course, using System Monitor to display your actual system performance for your boss could get you the memory upgrade you've been wanting.

You want to also take into account the needs of the LAN as a whole if your system doubles as a file server. A peer-to-peer network depends on the resources of one or more workstations to act as file and print servers. This doubling of tasks is really another form of multitasking. You might run only one or two tasks on your machine, but it will run very slowly if you don't take into account the needs of other people who are using your system. In this case, however, a simple look at the swap file and disk activity probably won't provide you with enough information. You'll have to monitor the network statistics using the System Monitor program.

Windows 2000 also provides another method for viewing network statistics that comes in handy here. The Shared Folders/Sessions folder of the Computer Management Microsoft Management Console (MMC) snap-in provides information about who's logged on and what type of resources are being used. (This feature was provided by the Server applet in Windows NT Workstation.) You can combine this information with that obtained from System Monitor to create a clear picture of how your machine is being used in the network environment. Figure 7.7 shows a typical example of the type of information you can expect. Making a correlation between who's using which resource and what the level of activity is might seem like a difficult task, but after a while you'll notice certain patterns emerging. You can use those patterns as basis for tuning your system.

Note: You'll find most of the predefined MMC snap-ins provided by Windows 2000 in the Administrative Tools folder found in the Control Panel. Open the Control Panel using the Start | Settings | Control Panel command, and then double-click Administrative Tools to display a list of the tools that we'll discuss in this chapter.

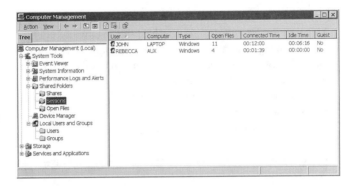

FIGURE 7.7

The Computer Management MMC snap-in provides information about who's using resources on your machine.

Load balancing was a term I thought I'd never have to apply to a PC, but here it is: You can get better performance out of your system if you balance the types of tasks it performs. Scheduling all your disk-intensive tasks to run at the same time is one sure way to bring your system to its knees. Likewise, scheduling all your CPU-intensive tasks at the same time will garner the same result, only faster. If you're working on a spreadsheet in the foreground, that might be a good time to compile an application or perform some database-related task in the background. Of course, the opposite is true as well. You can always perform that really intense spreadsheet recalculation in the background while performing data entry in the foreground.

You need to think about one final consideration when you want to get the most out of your multitasking environment. Using 16-bit applications under Windows 2000 also means that you must suffer the consequences of cooperative multitasking. In essence, a program can be a bad sport and grab the system for a long period of time. (Fortunately, Windows 2000 maintains positive control of the system so that it can reduce the impact of this system-hogging behavior.) But 32-bit applications don't get this kind of treatment. Ready or not, they have to turn control of the system back over to Windows 2000 at specific intervals. The difference between multitasking 16-bit and 32-bit applications will absolutely amaze you. If multitasking is the name of the game, 32-bit applications are what you need to make it work smoothly.

Checking for Interactions with Event Viewer

Windows 2000 is a complex operating system; there's no doubt about it. A change that looks fine when you make it might cause unexpected results later. You might remove a device driver that you think is no longer in use, for example, only to find that it really is being used by some part of the system. Windows 2000 does a good job of keeping you out of trouble for the most part, but it's not perfect.

A certain tool can help you out, however. You can use the Event Viewer MMC snap-in to keep track of the workstation as a whole (see Figure 7.8). Any events logged in here tell you something about your computer. Separate logs exist for application, directory service, file replication, security, and system events. (The actual number of logs you see will depend on how you have your system set up.) If these logs won't do the job, you can always create additional logs for special purposes. I want to concentrate on those events found in the System log that affect your performance-tuning efforts in this section. We look at other event types as the book progresses.

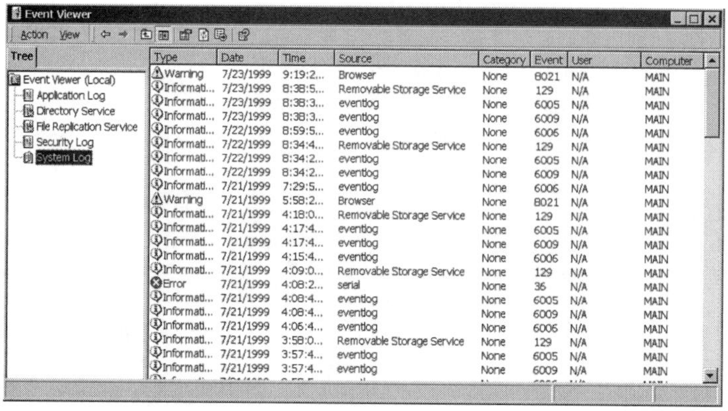

FIGURE 7.8

You can use the Event Viewer to keep track of system events and monitor your system for any negative results from performance tuning.

You want to make sure that you're looking at the System log. Just select the appropriate folder in the Event Viewer MMC snap-in. Now that you have the right log selected, look for any red circle with an X sign (Error) icons. Those are the icons that tell you that something is wrong in the system. Figure 7.8 shows several of these icons. In this case, I forced them to appear to show you what they look like. You'll notice two other icons here as well. The blue information icon just tells you about a noncritical system event. For the most part, you can ignore these icons unless you want to track some specific system event. The warning icons (the yellow exclamation points) tell about a special event. You'll want to check out the warning icons, but they're usually noncritical as well. Event Viewer also supports two other icons—Success Audit and Failure Audit—but we won't see them here.

Obviously, the short descriptions shown in the Event Viewer window don't tell you enough to fix a problem. Select any of the lines, and press Enter to see the Event Detail dialog box shown in Figure 7.9. Notice that it tells you exact details about what caused a particular event to happen. You can use this information to troubleshoot the problem. This dialog box doesn't tell you about the interactions that take place between system components, however. In other words, you might remove a much-needed driver, but some other component will fail as a result. You might see the failed component in the Event Viewer and have to work your way back to the missing driver.

FIGURE 7.9

The Event Viewer provides detailed information about the cause of a particular problem entered in the log.

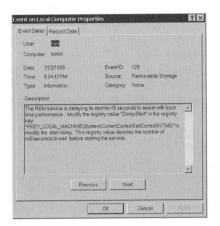

FIGURE 7.9

The Event Viewer provides detailed information about the cause of a particular problem entered in the log.

Monitoring the Results of Performance Enhancements

I use three methods to monitor the results of any optimization changes I make. The first is to look at the Resource Monitor. Checking how much system resource memory you have left after an optimization is one way to see whether the change was effective. I also monitor the size of the swap file. Even though this isn't a precise measure of the state of system memory, it does provide an overall indicator of system memory. Windows 2000 increases the size of the swap file as it needs more memory, so checking the size of the swap file is one way to see how much memory Windows 2000 needs over the physical memory available on the system.

The third method is using an actual monitoring tool. The System Monitor MMC snap-in is installed by default with Windows 2000, and it's a very worthwhile tool because it enables you to track a variety of system statistics, including CPU usage and actual memory allocation. Monitoring these statistics tells you whether a certain optimization strategy was successful. System Monitor also provides a means of detecting performance-robbing hardware and software errors on the system. Figure 7.10 shows a typical System Monitor display.

Understanding the Views

When you start System Monitor for the very first time, you get a blank screen. Before you can do anything, you need to select some events to monitor. I decided to monitor CPU usage statistics for the machine I was testing (the percentage of time spent performing user-related tasks in this case). Figure 7.10 shows one way to display this information.

Five buttons on the toolbar change the way you track information: View Current Activity, View Log File Data, View Chart, View Histogram, and View Report. The first two view options determine whether you view current system activity or the contents of a log that you've created over a period of time. Some types of system configuration changes will require the log file approach because you'll need to see how the change affects system performance over an entire day, or even longer. We'll look at logs in more detail in the "Creating and Using Logs" section of this chapter.

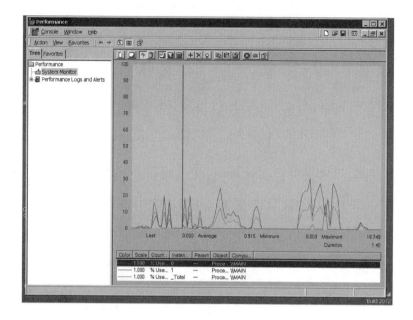

The other three buttons affect the actual presentation of information onscreen. I find that the View Chart presentation, shown in Figure 7.10, is the most helpful when I need to monitor system performance over a long interval. This view also helps me to see the interaction of various statistics.

The View Histogram option, shown in Figure 7.11, provides the best method for performing instantaneous comparisons of system data. I can use this view to make quick comparisons of two statistics when I'm adjusting a configuration option that makes a fairly large change in system performance.

The third button, View Report, is very useful when you need to compare large quantities of data or save the information to an application that normally requires text input, such as a spreadsheet. Figure 7.12 shows an example of this view. Note that you can change the presentation of the data; this figure shows the default view that you'll normally see when you first select this view.

System Monitor uses a default-monitoring period of one second, which is great if you're troubleshooting a bad NIC or want instant feedback on a configuration change. However, this might be too fast in certain situations. For example, if you're performing long-term monitoring, you might want to set the monitoring period to a high value. Click the Properties button within any of the views to change this setting. Figure 7.13 shows the dialog box that changes the interval for the chart presentation.

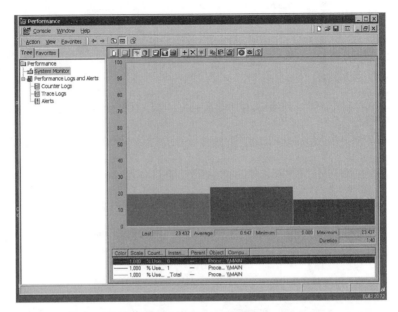

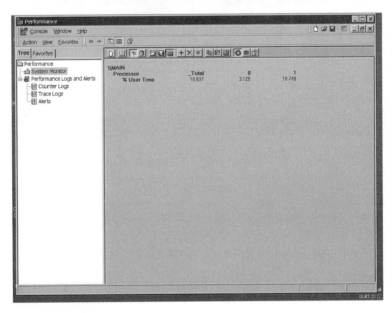

FIGURE 7.13

Use the System Monitor Properties dialog box to change the various view options for System Monitor.

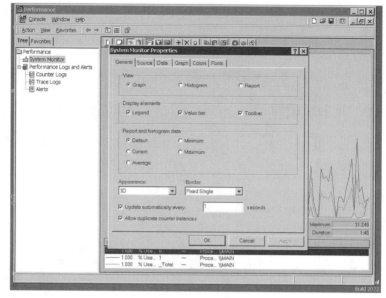

This is also the dialog box that you'll use to embellish the default System Monitor views. For example, you can add both a horizontal and a vertical grid to either the chart or histogram views. Options also enable you to change the chart colors, font, and other display features. Using the Source tab, you can choose between current system data or logged data. This tab also allows you to select a source of logged data.

Adding and Removing Counters

Next to the view buttons that we talked about in the previous section are three buttons that affect the "counters" used to display information for System Monitor. A counter is a special kind of program that keeps track of a system statistic for a specified time and then passes the count (the amount of that statistic) to System Monitor for display. These three buttons enable you to change and highlight the items that System Monitor displays.

Use the Add button to add new items to the list. Figure 7.14 shows a typical Add Counters dialog box. You select an object, such as the processor to monitor, and then select an instance of that object. In the case of a processor, you may have only one instance, but disk drives usually provide several instances. After you select an instance of an object, you can select one of the counters (the items that System Monitor will track). Notice that there are special radio buttons for adding all counters for a specific object, or all instances of a specific counter to the display. You can also monitor statistics from more than one computer by selecting another in the Select Counters from Computer field.

> **Tip:** Clicking the Explain button in the Add Counters dialog box provides a full description of the selected counter. This makes it easier for you to determine which counters to monitor.

FIGURE 7.14

Use the Add Counters dialog box to add new counters to your System Monitor display.

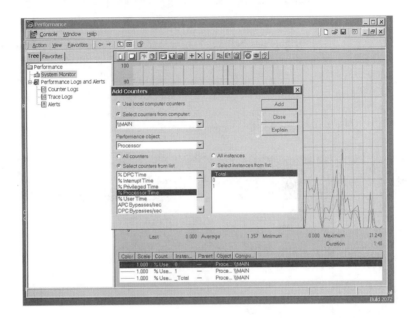

Use the Delete button to remove an item from the monitoring list. Remember that the more items you display onscreen, the less screen area each item receives. This, in turn, limits the accuracy of the readings you'll take. Make sure that you monitor only the essentials. For that matter, you might want to break the items into groups and monitor a single group at a time.

Finally, the Highlight button will allow you to highlight a specific item found in the monitoring list. This particular feature is available only in chart view, where highlighting a line will help you see it better. The highlighted line defaults to an extra-wide white line that you can see with relative ease when compared to the other lines on a chart.

What types of things will System Monitor track for you? You can track everything from the number of bytes the disk writes per second to the number of times someone tries to access your machine from the network. System Monitor tracks many more items than I have room to talk about here, and Microsoft keeps adding more items with every version of Windows 2000. In addition, there's no limit to the ways in which you can arrange the items you want to track. It's also important to note that you can track each resource (called an *instance* of an object) individually. This means that you can display the same statistic for each disk drive on your machine.

Creating and Using Logs

As mentioned earlier, you can create log files of counters that you plan to monitor over a long period of time. Obviously, the first thing you need to do is create the log before you can view the results. The following steps show you how to create a new log:

1. Open the Performance Logs and Alerts\Counter Logs folder.

2. Right-click in the right pane, and then choose New Log Settings from the context menu. You'll see the New Log Settings dialog box.

3. Type a name for the new log setting (the example uses Temp). You'll see a Log Settings dialog box like the one shown in Figure 7.15. This is where you'll add counters and perform any required setups for the log. The one requirement for every log is selecting one or more counters to track.

FIGURE 7.15

This dialog box allows you to define what Windows will record in the log file for you.

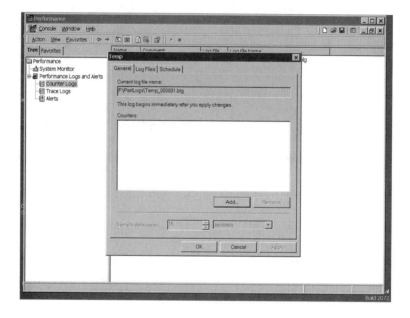

4. Click Add. You'll see a Select Counters dialog box that looks very similar to the Add Counters dialog box in Figure 7.14.

5. Select one or more counters to track. (Highlight the counter and instance information that you want, and then click Add.) Click Close in the Add Counters dialog box when you've finished adding new counters. At this point, your counters are ready to go, but you haven't decided when to record the log.

6. Click the Schedule tab, and you'll see a dialog box like the one shown in Figure 7.16. Notice that you can start the log at a specific time, or you can manually start it using a shortcut menu command. Likewise, stopping the log can be automatic or manual. Special considerations also come into play when stopping the log. For example, you can stop the current log at the end of a specific time interval and automatically begin a new one.

FIGURE **7.16**

The Schedule tab allows you to determine when the log will start and stop.

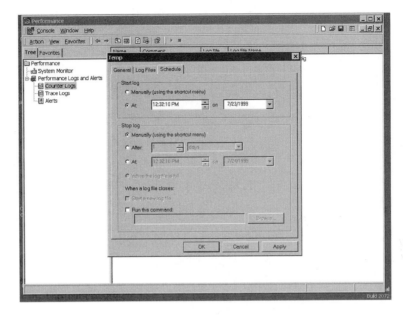

7. Choose the starting and ending time for your log, and then click OK. The log settings are now ready to use.

Depending on how you've set up your log, Windows may start recording it automatically. You can also right-click the log entry in the Counter Logs folder and choose Start from the context menu. Stopping the log recording process is just as easy: Just select Stop from the context menu when you right-click the log settings icon. Log file icons are red when stopped and green when started, making it easy to see what Windows is currently logging for you.

Okay, so you've recorded a log and want to view the results in System Monitor. All you need to do is click the View Data Log File button on the toolbar, select a filename in the Select Log File dialog box, and then click Open. System Monitor opens the log file and shows you any of the counters that you select using the Add Counter dialog box. Note that when you open the Add Counters dialog box, instead of seeing all the available counters, you'll see only those that are recorded in the log.

Now that your recorded counters are displayed, let's look at another important feature of System Monitor. If you're recording data for days or even weeks, you won't want to look at all the data in one big lump. Wouldn't it be nice if you could look at just a small piece of it? System Monitor enables you to do just that. Right-click the chart and choose Properties from the context menu. Click the Source tab, and you'll see a dialog box similar to the one shown in Figure 7.17.

Notice the Total Range bar at the bottom of the dialog box. On the upper-left side is the starting time for the log, while the upper-right side shows the stopping time. On the bottom-left side is the starting view time, and the bottom-right side shows the stopping view time. You can move the two thumbs on this bar to change the starting and stopping view times, which will then affect the display you see in the chart.

FIGURE 7.17

The Source tab of the System Monitor Properties dialog box allows you to select log file options.

On Your Own

Spend some time learning to use the Event Viewer. What kinds of events does your system appear to monitor as a default? Do you see any events that require your immediate attention? How do the Event Viewer entries help you diagnose problems?

Learn to use the System Monitor as both a diagnostic aid and a tuning tool. What type of setup helps you most when it comes time to tune your system? Make sure that you try various setups to perform specific kinds of tuning. You'll want to monitor disk statistics when tuning your hard drive, for example, and network statistics when monitoring your connection efficiency. Likewise, what setup works best for various types of diagnostic situations?

Customizing Windows 2000 for Maximum Productivity

I have found that some computer users coming to Windows 2000 have developed some terrible habits over the years. Do you automatically assume that the machine is going to be tied up every time you use the modem, for example? As an experiment, I tried performing a background download with one additional task running: my word processor. The download completed in the background at 31.1bps without a single missed character while I worked in the foreground. The next day I decided to add another task. This time, I compiled a program in one background session, downloaded a few files in another, and typed away in a third. Everything went perfectly. I tried a third task and then a fourth; Windows 2000 handled everything without a hitch.

Of course, you're going to run into a wall somewhere along the way; no machine in the world can keep adding tasks without eventually running out of resources to handle them. I did try this same experiment with Windows 95 loaded on the same machine, keeping everything but the operating system the same as before. Everything bombed after I added the third task. Windows 95 might be more flexible, but research shows that Windows 2000 will handle more tasks on the same machine, given its superior architecture.

What's the moral of this story? I don't think any operating system will ever be capable of performing every task there is to perform and simultaneously communicate in the background. You need to have the required resources if you want to get the job done. In my case, three or four tasks in addition to the background download are about all my machine can handle.

I did learn something important, however. Using Windows 2000 enabled me to get three times the amount of work done that I would have accomplished doing one task at a time. I want to emphasize this point because if you haven't exploited the power of Windows 2000, it, too, can be very inefficient.

This chapter looks at some of the ways you can make yourself a little more efficient so that you can get the full benefits of using Windows 2000 as an operating system. This means everything from the way you start your applications to the way you arrange your desktop. Windows 2000 provides many tools that you can use to make each step a little faster.

The Windows 2000 Shortcut and ActiveX

Let's look at one unique way that Windows 2000 promotes docucentricity. (Docucentricity means you focus on the task rather than the application. The most dramatic example of docucentricity is double-clicking a .DOC file and not worrying about running your word processor—Windows starts it for you and loads the document you double-clicked.)

Every shortcut you create is a form of ActiveX integration. It's an actual link to another object on your machine. Windows 2000 provides some special handling for these objects.

Unlike an application (a word processor can store linking information to embedded objects, such as graphics, right in its .DOC file), Windows 2000 must store that information someplace on the drive. After all, the drive is the container Windows 2000 uses to store information. The LNK file is Windows 2000's answer to this problem. It contains all the linking information needed to keep the shortcuts on your desktop current with the real object.

You can easily test this by creating a shortcut to a folder on your desktop. Every change you make (such as adding a new file) to the real folder will appear in the linked copy. Likewise, every change you make in the linked copy will appear in the real thing.

Faster Startups

Starting an application might not seem like a big deal, but Windows 2000 provides more than just one or two ways to start your applications:

- Right-click the application's icon while in Explorer, and then choose Open from the context menu.
- Double-click the application's icon while in Explorer or File Manager. (File Manager is a legacy program from Windows 3.x. It's only available on a machine where you upgraded from a previous version of NT. I suggest you avoid it. It's old, outdated, and clumsy.)
- Double-click a data file associated with the application while in Explorer. (This requires you to create a file association or to instruct the application to create it for you.)
- Choose Start | Run, and then type the application's path and filename. Click OK to start the application.
- Choose Start | Run, and then drag and drop the application's icon into the Run dialog box. Click OK to start the application.
- Choose the application's entry from the Start menu.
- Create a shortcut icon on the desktop. You can start the application by right-clicking or double-clicking the icon. You can also drag and drop a shortcut to the Quick Launch toolbar.

- Assign a shortcut key to the application, and then start it using the keyboard short-cut. (You must create a LNK file to do this. You'll look at this process later.)

- Use the Windows 3.x Program Manager (located in the \WINNT\SYSTEM32 directo-ry) to run the application. This application, like File Manager, isn't part of a new installation of Windows 2000; to see it, you must have upgraded over a previous version of NT. Same suggestion: Forget this utility.

- Place the application's icon or associated data file in the Startup folder in the Start menu to run it automatically the next time you start Windows. Placing a data file in the Startup folder automatically opens it for you.

- Use the Search Results dialog box to find your application, and then right-click or double-click it.

- Embed or link the application's data in an OLE compound document. The user can start the application by double-clicking the object embedded in the document. (The application must support OLE for this to work.)

> **Tip:** Many of the techniques described in this chapter involve ways to use the keyboard rather than having to move your hand over to the mouse, click, and then move your hand back to the keyboard. When typing text—and when prac-tical—good typists prefer to keep their hands in the correct position on the keys; this means that they don't have to switch gears all the time, going back and forth to the mouse. (This is a primary reason that most mouse activity can be replicated with keypresses.)
>
> Did you know that you can use context menus from the keyboard? You can right-click from the keyboard by pressing Shift+F10. The context menu pops up, and you can continue using the keyboard to make your selection from the menu. Just use the arrow keys to locate the feature you want, and then press Enter to activate it. Here's another context menu tip: One option on many con-text menus is in boldface (it's usually the Open option). This is the default, the option that will be triggered if the object is double-clicked. Some Windows key-boards also have a context menu key (between the Windows and Ctrl keys on the bottom right row).

Because I grew up using DOS, and because I do a lot of writing, I really hated using the mouse just to start an application, so I didn't. Windows 2000 provides shortcut keys for those of us who like to keep our hands mainly on the keyboard. Let's take a look at how you can maximize your use of the keyboard—although you really do need to use the mouse, if for no other reason than the fact that your hand is resting on it at that particular moment. Like many people, I spend my share of time mousing around. Drawing programs come in handy for some of the work I do, and moving files around within Explorer is cer-tainly easier with the mouse. And the mouse is nothing new, for most people.

Windows 2000 provides a lot of neat ways to use the mouse with your applications. You will find that you can do a lot of things you might not have thought of with a simple mouse click. We'll examine some of these mouse techniques in this section.

Startups from the Keyboard

Nothing beats the keyboard, if you're a writer. Some shortcut keys come installed with Windows 2000. I find that many of them are attached to the Accessibility options, but you can change all that with a just a little effort. (We'll examine how later in this section.) Table 8.1 provides a list of keystrokes and the actions they perform. You're probably familiar with many of them, but if you're not, you might find them invaluable.

Peter's Principle: Many Ways of Doing the Same Thing: A Happy Redundancy

Windows 2000 provides a way to drop a Control menu using just the keyboard: Just press Alt+Spacebar. Although few people use it, this Control menu is available if you like it. You can also access it by clicking the icon in the upper-left corner of most applications' windows. Control menus contain features that you can generally use more easily without dropping down these menus: moving the window, minimizing or maximizing it, closing it, and so on. One of the intelligent design decisions of good software providers—including Microsoft—is to provide *redundancy*.

Redundancy in computer interface design comes in handy because some people just work differently than other people. If your hands are on the keyboard at the time, you might prefer a keyboard shortcut. If your hands are on the mouse, you might prefer to click on a button.

In the computer world, redundancy is usually not a bad word because it proves useful in keeping multiple backup files, being able to italicize using either the keyboard or the mouse, and so on. You will find that Microsoft even extends this concept into its applications, often providing three levels of sophistication. For example, there's Notepad, WordPad and Word, in order of increasing sophistication. Likewise, Visual Basic is sold in Standard, Professional, and Enterprise editions. In turn, Windows 2000 is offered in Professional, Server, Enterprise, and Datacenter versions.

The Control menu icons in the upper-left corner of most windows are miniature versions of the program's own icon. The things you see when you click on them—to close the application, for example—are more easily accomplished by pressing Alt+F4 or by double-clicking either that corner icon itself or the X icon in the opposite corner. But, in the true spirit of "let them do it their way," single-clicking the Document Control icon (as it's called) drops down a menu for those who prefer menu maneuvers. Besides, using Alt+Spacebar is the *only* way to move or size a window, if for some reason you can't use the mouse.

Table 8.1   Windows 2000 Shortcut Keys

Key or Key Combination	Purpose
Alt+F4	This is arguably the second most useful shortcut combination: It shuts down the current application. You can also use this key combination to turn off Windows itself if you're at the desktop.
F4	Used by itself, F4 drops down a list, such as the Address field in Explorer and Internet Explorer. Then you can use the arrow keys to locate the item you want; finally, you press Enter to activate that item.
Alt+Shift+Tab	This combination switches to the preceding window.
Alt+Tab	I would vote for this as the single most useful of all shortcut combinations: It switches among all currently running applications. Note that if you have several applications open, you can still toggle between two applications. Alt+Tab always moves first to the most recently accessed application. So pressing Alt+Tab once and then releasing the keys, takes you to the last application you used. Holding down Alt and repeatedly pressing Tab, by contrast, cycles you through all running applications.
	You can also cycle backward. If you have several programs running, you might Tab one past the program you're after. Instead of going through the whole row again, go backward by holding down the Shift key (while also holding down Alt and pressing Tab). During the cycling, if you decide that you don't want to switch to another application, keep holding down the Alt key, but press Esc. (Actually, you can press almost any key to abort your cycling. But don't release Alt until you have escaped; otherwise, the selected application will appear and Esc will have no effect.)
Ctrl+Tab	Some applications feature internal windows, also called child windows. Use Ctrl+Tab to cycle among child windows, such as the document windows in Word. In fact, Ctrl+Tab cycles among child windows even if they're maximized within the application. Some applications don't support Ctrl+Tab and use Ctrl+F6 for this purpose instead.
Alt+Hyphen	This combination drops the Control menu of the currently active child window. Child windows often have specialized Control menus, which offer options appropriate to the purpose of the child window (but options that differ from the right-click context menu).

continues

Table 8.1   Continued

Key or Key Combination	Purpose
Delete	This key places the selected shortcut, file, or other item in the Recycle Bin.
Shift+Delete	This combination deletes the selected item *without* putting it in the Recycle Bin.
Ctrl+Esc	This combination opens the Start menu. You can then use the arrow keys to select an application. Pressing Enter starts the application you selected. If you have the Windows key, just press it to open the Start menu.
Esc	This key cancels the last action, in most cases. You can't back out of some actions, however.
F1	You can display online help with this key.
F2	Pressing this key while an icon or filename is highlighted in Explorer enables you to rename the file. This feature is particularly useful if you have turned on the Web Style option in Explorer's View|Folder Options menu.
F3	Unless your application uses this key for something else, you can press it to access the Find dialog box (or Find Next, in some applications). Alternatively, you can often get the same result by pressing Ctrl+F. Pressing F3 while on the desktop brings up the Search For Files and Folders Explorer utility. You can also use this key at the taskbar and the Start menu.
Left Alt+Left Shift+Num Lock	Holding down these three keys turns on the MouseKeys feature of the Accessibility options.
Left Alt+Left Shift+Print Screen	Holding down these three keys turns on the High Contrast feature of the Accessibility options.
F5	This key refreshes the currently opened window (reloads the currently viewed page in Internet Explorer, for example, or does a fresh download of any new email in Outlook Express).
Num Lock (for 5 seconds)	Holding down the Num Lock key for 5 seconds turns on the ToggleKeys feature of the Accessibility options.
Right Shift (for 8 seconds)	Holding down the Right Shift key for 8 seconds turns on the FilterKeys feature of the Accessibility options.
Shift (five times)	Pressing the Shift key five times turns on the StickyKeys feature of the Accessibility options.
Windows+U	This combination opens the Utility Manager, where you can turn on the magnifier and the narrator disability features.

Key or Key Combination	Purpose
Shift+F1	This combination displays context-sensitive help if the current application supports it.
Shift+F10	This displays the context menu. Considering the number of options on the context menu, this key combination enables you to do almost anything with the object. Here's redundancy again: This combination also displays the desktop's context menu.
Alt+letter	This shortcut opens a menu, triggers a menu item, or activates an option in a dialog box. In most applications, for example, Alt+F opens the File menu, at which point you could press S to save your work. You don't need to hold down the Alt key during this operation (so that you are simultaneously pressing Alt and some other key). Instead, you can press Alt and then release it.
	Applications differ, however, in their behavior if you press the Alt key and then release it. You might notice that the first menu title (usually File), is selected, indicating that the menus now have the focus. After pressing Alt, you can use the arrow keys to move among the menu titles, and then press Enter to open whatever menu is currently highlighted. When a menu is opened, press the up or down arrow keys to select among the menu entries, and make your choice by pressing Enter. (Windows trivia: The F10 key does the same thing as Alt. Press it once to move to the menu bar.)
	Alternatively, you can press Alt along with the character for the menu you want (Alt+E for Edit, Alt+T for Tools, or whatever menu items are available at the time). Each menu item in Windows has an underlined letter: File, Edit, View, Insert, and so on. After pressing Alt, you can then press the underlined character to select that menu and drop it, revealing its contents. Many dialog boxes and property sheets also contain underlined characters in labels that quickly identify the corresponding keyboard combination. For example, a button labeled Screen Saver tells you that you can press that button from your keyboard by typing Alt+S.
Ctrl+Home	In most browsers, word processors, and other document-processing applications, pressing Ctrl+Home moves you to the first line at the top of the document. Likewise, pressing Ctrl+End moves you to the bottom. The Home key by itself moves you to the start of the current line; the End key by itself moves you to the end of the current line.

continues

Table 8.1   Continued

Key or Key Combination	Purpose
Alt+Left arrow and Alt+Right arrow	Use Alt with the right and left arrow keys to trigger the Back and Forward buttons in Internet Explorer.
Alt+Enter	This toggles a DOS screen between full screen (Text mode) and windowed. Note that this effect isn't the same as maximizing a window to make it fill the screen. To maximize the current Windows application window using the keyboard, press Alt+Spacebar, X (and use Alt+Spacebar, N to minimize). You can minimize all open windows if you have the Windows key+M. This has the same effect as right-clicking any empty part of the taskbar with the mouse and choosing Minimize All Windows. Use Shift+Windows key+M to restore all windows.
Alt+Enter	This combination displays the properties of the selected item.
PrtScr	When you press the PrtScr key, you capture your entire monitor screen in the Clipboard, as if it has been photographed. When it's in the Clipboard, it then can be pasted into almost any application. The PrtScr key can also still be used to print the screen of a DOS program if it's running in full screen Text mode (press Alt+Enter to switch between windowed and fullscreen Text mode). If the DOS program is running in a window, PrtScr will still copy the entire screen. Alt+PrtScr works like PrtScr, but it copies only the currently active window (sometimes called the client area), not the entire screen.
Spacebar	When a dialog box, such as the Desktop Properties window, becomes visible, you can toggle (turn on or off) the currently selected option button or check box by just pressing the Spacebar. This is an alternative to clicking the mouse pointer on an option button. You can also trigger a command button (such as OK or Cancel) by pressing Tab to move to the button and then pressing the Spacebar to trigger it. (Recall that Tab will cycle you through all the options in a dialog box, including any buttons.)
Ctrl+Shift+ PageUp	In many word processors, you can use this key combination to select the text from the current cursor position to the top of the page. Ctrl+Shift+PageDn selects from the current position to the bottom of the page.
Ctrl (while dragging an item)	This key copies the selected item.

Key or Key Combination	Purpose
Ctrl+Shift (while dragging an item)	This combination creates a shortcut for the dragged item.
Insert	Pressing the Insert key toggles between Insert and Overstrike mode. When you type in Insert mode, existing text is pushed ahead, making room for the words you're typing. In Overstrike mode, text is overwritten by what you type. Most professional writers remain in Insert mode all the time.
Alt+Backspace	Generally, this shortcut triggers an Undo, reversing the previous action. If you just deleted a word, Alt+Backspace restores that word. Usually, several levels of Undo are available to you, so you can repeatedly press Alt+Backspace to see the effects of several of your recent actions.
Ctrl+Backspace	This triggers a Redo, the opposite of Undo. In other words, if you have just deleted a word and pressed Alt+Backspace to undo it (restoring the word), pressing Ctrl+Backspace would again delete that word. Repeatedly pressing Ctrl+Backspace deletes a word to the left of the cursor.
Ctrl+Z	This is usually the same as using Alt+Backspace.
Ctrl+Y	This is usually the same as using Ctrl+Backspace.
Tab	You can use this key while at the desktop to switch among the desktop, taskbar, and Start menu. Unless you're in a text-only context such as a word processor, Tab moves you through the various controls (buttons, text entry boxes, and so on) within an application or dialog box.
	Within applications, repeatedly pressing Tab generally cycles you among controls (text boxes, command buttons, and so on). This can be especially useful when several text boxes must be filled in, such as with a structured database entry window. Pressing the Enter key doesn't usually move you to the next text box in Windows applications (although I think it should if the text boxes are single lines). Knowing that the Tab key moves you to the next input zone in a document can be a great time-saver; you fill in one box and then press Tab to move to the next one. To cycle in the opposite direction, press Shift+Tab.
Windows key	Many of us use a keyboard with the Windows key (actually there are two of them, on each side of the Spacebar, just like the dual Ctrl and Alt keys. Don't ignore the Windows key; it can be of considerable value. Here are its shortcuts:

continues

Table 8.1   Continued

Key or Key Combination	Purpose
Windows key	This displays the Start menu,
Windows+Break	This brings up the System Properties dialog box. You don't have to navigate the deep menu: Start|Settings|Control Panel|System.
Windows+D	This minimizes (or restores) all windows (see Windows+M),
Windows+E	This launches Explorer (My Computer view).
Windows+F	This launches the Search For Files or Folders utility, or Find, in an application.
Ctrl+Windows+F	This launches Search for Computers.
Windows+F1	This combination launches Windows 2000 Help.
Windows+M	Use this combination to minimize all windows. (Shift+Windows+M reverses this action.) (See Windows+D.)
Windows+R	This launches the Run dialog box.
Windows+Tab	Use this to switch between open items. (This combination merely shows the taskbar icons of running applications; it does not actually switch between them. Use Alt+Tab instead).
Windows+U	This opens the Utility Manager, where you can turn on the magnifier and the narrator disability features.
Ctrl+O	This opens the selected item.
Ctrl+A	Use this to select all.
Ctrl+Alt+Del	This combination is the bomb. This key combination is purposely complex, and the keys are spread wide apart on the keyboard. The idea is similar to requiring that two soldiers with two keys on opposite sides of the silo must simultaneously trigger a nuclear missile. It is quite impossible to accidentally press Ctrl+Alt+Del while typing.
	This key combination was originally designed to trigger a warm boot. In Windows 2000, however, a dialog box appears; if you have the permissions, it enables you to do any of the following six things: change your password, lock the workstation, log off, display the Task Manager, shut down the machine, or cancel the dialog box and return to Windows 2000.

The Task Manager shows you a list of currently running applications. You can then choose to close down any one of the applications by clicking the task name and then clicking the End Task button.

Ctrl+Alt+Del is useful if one of your applications stops responding. Windows 2000 is so well designed that unless the OS itself is hanging, you can usually just shut down the misbehaving application and return to a solid, stable Windows 2000. You rarely have to reboot. (Note: You can also bring up Task Manager by right-clicking the taskbar.)

Other useful shortcuts include Ctrl+C, Ctrl+V, and Ctrl+X. Ctrl+C copies whatever is currently selected (text, graphic, object, whatever). Ctrl+V pastes whatever was previously copied. Ctrl+X deletes whatever is currently selected.

Combining the various keystrokes makes them much more powerful. What if you have a lot of applications open and need to quickly get to the desktop, for example? Press Ctrl+Esc to display the Start menu, Esc to close the menu itself, Tab to get to the taskbar, and Shift+F10 to display the context menu. All you need to do now is select Minimize All Windows and press Enter. Pressing Tab one more time takes you to the desktop. Of course, if you're lucky enough to have a keyboard with the special Windows key, just press Windows key+M to close all windows.

> **Tip:** If you can get to an opened window using Alt+Tab, try Alt+Esc. Unlike Alt+Tab, Alt+Esc also cycles through any hidden dialog boxes and windows; it displays *everything* running. Alt+Esc will not, however, display any applications that have been minimized and that, although still running, are now merely icons on the taskbar (you will notice this effect when you press the Esc key repeatedly and nothing happens—you're hitting the minimized programs). Alt+Esc imitates the old Windows 3.0 behavior, in which Alt+Tab was used to visit every currently open window. However, with Windows 2000, most dialog boxes in general (as in Windows 3.0) do get displayed with Alt+Tab.

Peter's Principle: Legacy Keys: Scroll Lock and SysRq

It's a bit surprising that a couple of redundant, functionally useless keys reside on your keyboard. Like the utterly puzzling human appendix—that 4-inch-long blind tube that leads nowhere and does nothing except sometimes get infected—these two keys sit, taking up valuable space, sometimes getting stuck. How can we explain the existence of the Scroll Lock key (with its own light on the keyboard!) and the SysRq key?

In the early 80s, Scroll Lock was used by a very few DOS file-viewing utilities and primitive word processors. Scroll Lock is an evolutionary remnant. Its existence on every computer keyboard reminds us that it must have been thought useful in some way at one time, but it's sure hard to explain now.

In theory, when you press Scroll Lock, the cursor should then freeze in the center of the screen. When you use the up and down arrow keys to scroll through a document, Scroll Lock keeps the cursor on the 12th line while the document scrolls up or down. So the cursor is "locked" during scroll. But this was such a bizarre technique that it died out well over a decade ago.

continues

Scroll Lock is one of those keys that can be toggled on and off, so some few contemporary applications use it. And because it turns on a light on the keyboard, it would be used as a state or mode indicator. Its light could indicate that italics are on or that the Insert mode is in effect, for instance. In practice, however, it's rarely used for anything.

The other suspect key, SysRq (System Request), is also widely ignored. It was added by IBM when the company expanded the personal computer keyboard to 101 keys only because there was a SysRq key on some of the commercial terminal keyboards. It means "System Request," but because applications don't use it, it's actually used to capture the screen (or current window). In other words, in its unshifted state, it nonetheless triggers a PrtScr (the shifted part of this key). To capture the entire screen, press SysRq. To capture the current window, press Alt+SysRq. Yet a third key could also be considered a legacy in the Windows 2000 world: The Pause/Break key doesn't have any effect in Windows 2000 unless you are running a DOS application or an application such as Visual Basic, which uses Ctrl+Break to stop a running program. The Windows+Break shortcut brings up the System Properties dialog box.

Shortcut Keys

After you spend some time with Windows 2000, you will discover that it is well designed and, for the most part, quite user-friendly. That still doesn't make me happy about moving my hand from the keyboard to the mouse to start a new application, however.

Remember the first section of this chapter, in which I talked about the desktop and documentricity? This is one of those times when that fact comes into play. If you want to add a shortcut key combination to launch one of your applications, you first must create a shortcut to that application. It doesn't matter where the shortcut is located, but it must be a shortcut.

Tip: *Every* entry on the Start menu is a shortcut, except for the first five items. If your application appears on the Start menu, you already have a shortcut to use. If it doesn't appear on the Start menu, add it there or to the desktop. The first five items (Run, Help, Search, Settings, Documents) don't behave like ordinary shortcuts—right-click does not bring up a Properties dialog box.

Find a shortcut on your desktop or the Start menu. Right-click it, and choose Properties in its context menu. Click the Shortcut tab on the dialog box. Click the Shortcut Key field to select it, and then press a key that will be memorable (N for Notepad, W for Word, and so on). Windows 2000 will add the Ctrl+Alt+ to your chosen key. To save the new shortcut key, just close the dialog box by clicking OK. The next time you press that key combination, Windows 2000 will open the application for you.

Startups from the Desktop

Windows 2000 comes installed with several icons already on the desktop. NT 4 had more of these default icons, though. To make the desktop neater and simpler, Microsoft removed four NT 4 icons (Administrative Tools, Scheduled Tasks, and Network and Dial-Up Connections) and put them in the Control Panel in Windows 2000.

The big question is why you would even consider adding an application shortcut to the desktop. The big reason is convenience: It's faster to grab an application on the desktop than to burrow through several layers of Start menus to find it. Of course, your desktop has only so much space, so placing all your applications here would very quickly lead to a cluttered environment.

Using the desktop to hold icons for only one or two applications you use regularly could mean an increase in efficiency. Just think about how nice it would be if your word processor or communications program were a double-click (or, if you're using the new Web-style Explorer option, a single-click) away. You could open the applications as needed and close them immediately after you finished using them.

Placing a shortcut to your application on the desktop might provide an increase in efficiency, but double-clicking isn't the only way to open an application. The next few sections describe other ways you can access your applications faster by placing shortcuts to them on the desktop.

Click Starts

Previous chapters took a quick look at the context menu. It's such an important concept, however, that I want to take a special look at right-clicking for applications. To start an application with the context menu, all you need to do is choose the Open option after right-clicking the icon. This has the same effect as double-clicking, and it might be more convenient if you have slower fingers. Some people really do have a hard time getting the double-click action to work. This method of starting an application has the advantage of requiring only a single click. Recall that you can also start applications with a single-click if you have them on the Quick Launch toolbar (on your taskbar).

Auto Starts and Advanced Power Management

Windows 2000 provides a Startup folder that automatically runs (when you first boot Windows 2000) any applications located in that folder. You might want to start a copy of Windows Explorer this way so that you're ready to roll the instant Windows completes the boot process. Some people like to put Internet Explorer or Outlook Express in this folder as well.

Try this, too, and see whether it works for you: Some people drag the .DOC or other data files they're going to be working on for the next few days into their Startup folder. The reason is simple: Not only does this automatically start the application associated with that data file, but it also automatically loads the file itself. This makes morning startups extremely efficient. When they get back to Windows after starting it, their machine is completely set up for use. Every application they need is already loaded with the files they want to edit. Of course, personal preferences matter in these situations. Perhaps you have little use for the Startup folder simply because you leave your machine on all the time.

Windows 2000 does offer new power-down options. For example, I normally don't shut my machine down at all at night. I just set it up to go into hibernate mode after a while. When I turn the machine on the next morning, the document that I was editing the previous night is still available for editing.

I do find that I have to clean the machine more often because the fan runs a lot more (dragging any dust in the air right into the computer).

If your computer manufacturer has provided hibernate capabilities, and you're logged on as Administrator, you can specify automatic hibernation by following these steps:

1. Double-click the Power Options icon in the Control Panel.

2. Click the Hibernate tab.

3. Click the Enable Hibernate support check box, and then click the Apply button.

4. Click the APM tab, and then select Enable Advanced Power Management support. Again click the Apply button.

5. Click the Power Schemes tab and choose a time interval after which the system hibernates. (There's a listbox at the bottom of the page.)

> **Tip:** If you want to manually force hibernation, set it up first following the previous instructions, and then choose Start | Shut Down. Choose Hibernate from the dropdown list under the heading *What do you want the computer to do?*

Peter's Principle: Becoming Too Efficient for Your Own Good

Have you ever seen the ransom note effect produced by someone who has just discovered the joy of using multiple fonts in a document? To that person, it looks like the most incredible document he has ever produced—and creating it was such fun! The rest of us think the document is pretty incredible, too, but not for the same reason.

You can get into a similar difficulty with Windows 2000 and its advanced features. Consider the Startup folder: It would be easy for people to load every document they think they would use for the entire week so that the documents would be ready when they booted the machine the next morning.

The best way to use this feature is to think about what you plan to do first thing the next morning. Don't open more than two or three documents unless they all use the same application. Someone who works on the same document, such as a writer, can really benefit from this feature. People who create presentations or who work on other documents for long periods of time can also benefit. If you work a little bit on one document and then a little bit on another one, however, you might be better off just starting the main application you use and letting it go at that.

How do you add entries to the Startup folder? You can just copy them. The procedure is the same as it is for any other folder. The following steps show you an alternative quick way to do it using some of new features Windows 2000 provides:

1. Right-click the taskbar to display the context menu. Choose the Properties option. The Taskbar Properties dialog box appears. Click the Advanced tab.

2. Click the Add button. You should see the Create Shortcut dialog box.

3. Click the Browse button to look for the file you want to add. As an alternative, you can type the full path and filename right into the Type the Location of the Item field of this dialog box. Then click Next. You should see the Select Program Folder dialog box at this point. This dialog box enables you to select the location of the shortcut in the Start menu. In this case, you should select the Startup folder (it's near the bottom of the list), but you could just as easily select something else. Notice that you can add a new folder as well.

4. Scroll through the list of folders, and highlight the Startup folder. Click Next. You should see the Select a Title for the Program dialog box, which is the final dialog box of the process. From here you can change the name of the shortcut. Using a name you can remember is the best idea. Changing the name here won't change the name of the file, only the shortcut.

5. Type the name you want associated with this file. This is the entry that will appear in the Startup folder. It won't affect the actual name of the file.

6. Click Finish to complete the task, and then click OK to close the Taskbar Properties dialog box.

After you complete this task, the application or data file you added to the Startup folder will load automatically each time you start Windows 2000. Setting up your system efficiently means that you can do a little extra reading or perform some other task while you wait for everything to load. Of course, adding a file to the load sequence won't make it load faster, but it will give you a bigger block of time.

Tip: If you prefer to copy an application or .DOC (or other data) file directly, use Explorer to locate the item you want to put into the Startup folder. Right-click it, and select Copy from the context menu. Right-click the Start Button, and choose Open All Users. Double-click the Programs icon, and then double-click the Startup folder. Finally, choose Edit I Paste.

Controlled Starts

I won't spend a lot of time on this category of starting your application because you are already familiar with most of what you can do here. Everyone is familiar with double-clicking an application to start it. The fact that Windows 2000 provides so many places to double-click doesn't really change the mechanics one iota. It might be useful, however, to take a quick look at the several ways you can double-click to start an application. The following list does just that:

- **Explorer**. You can double-click an application or its associated data file.

- **Search**. The Search For Files or Folders dialog box comes in very handy. You can look for a data file and then double-click it to bring up the application associated with it.

- **Desktop**. Any data file or application sitting on the desktop follows the same rules as items in Explorer.

- **My Network Places**. If you have permission from the owner of the file, you can double-click any application or file sitting on someone else's machine.

That's the long and short of double-clicking. Hopefully, this section provided some food for thought on other—and perhaps better—ways of using the Windows 2000 interface.

Peter's Principle: Try the New Web-Style Single-Clicking

Don't forget the new replacement for double- and single-clicking. If you prefer—and I do—you can make your life easier (after you get used to it) by using the "Web-style" clicking with Explorer and other elements of Windows 2000. In Web-style, single-clicking replaces the older style of double-clicking (it launches applications, opens folders, and so on). Just pointing with the mouse pointer to an object or filename *selects* that object. In other words, if you pause a moment with your mouse pointer on top of a file or icon, that object is selected (just as if you had singled-clicked it in the older, classic clicking technique).

Similarly, if you pause your pointer to select one filename and then hold down the Shift key and pause over another filename somewhere else in the list of filenames, the entire range is highlighted and can then be deleted, moved, cut, or copied as a unit. Holding the Ctrl key while pausing on filenames or icons toggles them between being selected and deselected. Believe me, you get used to this after a while. The only functionality that you really lose using this technique is renaming. You can't single-click to transform the filename into a typeable text box so that you can edit the name. To rename, you can either pause to select and then press F2, or you right-click and choose Rename from the context menu. To turn on Web-style clicking, choose Folder Options from Explorer's Tools menu, and then click Single Click to Open an Item.

> **Tip:** You can use a single Explorer, or permit multiple Explorers to open, one after the other, each time you open a new folder. Specify your preference by choosing Folder Options in Explorer's Tools menu. In the General tab of the Folder Options dialog box, look at the Browse Folders section. Select Open Each Folder in the Same Window or Open Each Folder in its Own Window. I prefer the former; if you are using the latter approach, however, your desktop can get cluttered pretty fast when you're looking for a file located down deep in a set of subfolders.
>
> Here's a cool trick you can use to quickly close all those folders simultaneously and clean up your desktop fast. Either press Windows+M or click the Show Desktop icon on the Quick Launch toolbar.

Folders: A Primary Organizational Tool

I really hate it when someone creates a new name for something I have been using for a long time. It's like throwing out a perfectly useable set of clothes because fashion has changed, or giving someone a new title to be politically correct. That's how I used to feel about the use of the term *folders* under Windows 2000. As far as I was concerned, it was just a new name for directories. Nothing could be further from the truth. Folders are not identical to directories: They might look similar and provide about the same functionality when viewed from a certain perspective, but folders do provide features that directories don't. I'm still not as happy as I could be about the name switch, but at least it makes sense.

How do folders help you work efficiently? Figure 8.1 shows one way: Folders support a context menu. As with most of the objects in Windows 2000, you can open and explore them. This isn't really all that surprising by now. You may be a little surprised, however, that you can copy and paste folders just like any other object. Putting a group of files in a folder enables you to move an entire project from place to place or to make a copy of the entire collection for someone else to use.

> **Tip:** One of the ways that using NTFS rather than the FAT file system helps is that you get two additional context menu entries: Compress and Uncompress. Their purpose is pretty clear: You can use these options to compress a folder until you need it later. Choosing the Uncompress option returns the folder to its normal state. This particular feature isn't just for folders; you can use it for anything else on the NTFS drive as well.

Context menus differ. Yours probably won't look exactly like mine. If you are not on a network, for example, you will not see the Sharing option listed on the context menu; this option enables you to share the folder with other folks on the network. Chapter 27, "Client/Server Networking," covers this feature in greater detail.

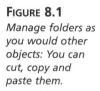

FIGURE 8.1

Manage folders as you would other objects: You can cut, copy and paste them.

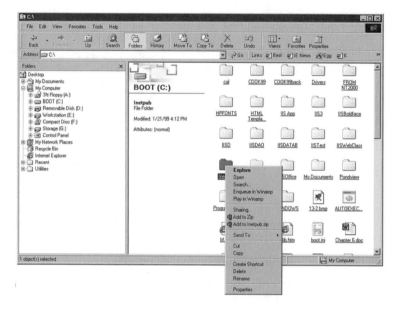

You also will find the Send To option useful. This option enables you to move the folder somewhere else. Default locations include the floppy drives and your My Documents. You can even send the folder to a mail recipient. Imagine how efficient it is to use email to send the folder to a partner or coworker who needs to see the information you have put together so far. Unlike past experiences in which I had to get all the files together and zip them up, this option is quite a bit more convenient and makes the work flow smoother. Of course, you will still want to zip files, particularly if you're squeezing a large file into the Internet's currently narrow pipeline.

I use the Create Shortcut option to create a link to the existing file. Then I move the shortcut to my desktop or some other convenient place. Each shortcut uses 1KB of memory, a small price to pay for the convenience it provides.

Chapters 5, "Exploring the Interface," and 24, "Peer-to-Peer Networking," cover the Properties option in greater detail. The Properties dialog box illustrates how files and folders share many of the same characteristics.

Desktop Tips and Techniques

I have moved to a totally docucentric approach on my desktop when it comes to projects. All I do is create a folder, give it a project name, and then gather shortcuts to everything I need for that project in that folder. It doesn't matter anymore where the data resides or what application I need to use to open the file. The only important element is that I have a data file that needs editing, so I open the project folder and click its icon to fire it up.

This docucentric approach is very important for managers. Think about the time you will save by putting one folder together and then mailing that folder to all the people who need to work on it. You control the location of the data and the type of access these people have. They need to know only that the data exists and that they can access it as needed.

Of course, like everything else under Windows 2000, all is not perfect with the totally docucentric approach. Even Microsoft agrees with me on this issue. It placed your Recycle Bin, My Computer, and My Network Places on the desktop for a reason. Sometimes you need to open an application rather than a piece of data.

I keep my communications program handy on the desktop; I can't really access any of its data from outside the application. My database manager also sits on the desktop, but that's for a different reason. I use Access to design databases more often than I use it for data entry, so, for me, it's really more important to work with the application in this particular case.

You, too, will probably run into situations in which the application is more important than the data. The bottom line is that you should try to work with the data first. If this proves to be an inconvenient solution, the docucentric approach probably isn't correct for that situation. The following is a list of some of the types of data I work with using the project-folder approach that I just described. You doubtless use some of these applications:

- **Word processing**— Word processor documents are ideal for the docucentric approach. The one minor inconvenience here is that Word always creates a new document using the Normal style sheet. This means that if I use the context menu to create a new file, I will probably want to change the template after I open the file. I like to use a variety of templates for different kinds of documents. It's a minor flaw, but an irritating one all the same.

- **Spreadsheet**—I seldom open just one spreadsheet. If I open one at all, I'm in there for hours. Therefore, I stick all my major files into a folder and place that folder on my desktop. That way, I can open a data file that will stay open throughout most of the editing session. I usually end up opening the other files I need by choosing File|Open.

- **Graphics**—I work with quite a few different types of graphics. This is one area where you will want to use the Thumbnails option on Explorer's View menu. Most graphics files are time-consuming to load. Having Thumbnails handy for the files it supports can really save you time.

Setups for a Multiuser Workstation

Workstations aren't usually private; someone might well use your Windows 2000 machine when you're not around. Multiple profiles enable everyone to customize a desktop to suit particular needs. Security keeps prying eyes away from your desktop and the data it contains. You aren't going to want to make every piece of data a secret, however, and installing applications more than once just so that each profile gets a copy seems like more of a nightmare than an aid to computing.

Windows 2000 has a solution. When you use Explorer to view the Profiles folder (or the Documents and Settings folder, depending on how you installed Windows 2000), you see an All Users folder that isn't really attached to anyone, as shown in Figure 8.2. Looking at this folder might give you a few ideas about how it's used. Think about ways to use common Favorites, Start, and Desktop folders.

Figure 8.2

The All Users folder contains generic settings.

Using the Start menu feature has pretty obvious benefits. When a network administrator completes a software installation, he just moves the Start menu entries for it from his profile folder to the All Users folder. The next time you log on to the workstation, you see the same application set everyone else does, derived from the All Users folder. Any additional applications appear in your profile folder only.

> **Tip:** Using the All Users folder to full advantage offers a couple added benefits you will want to consider. First, you won't spend nearly as much time setting up a new user on your workstation. All the common applications and data folders the user needs to start work will be available as a default. You will also find that this feature comes in handy when someone's profile gets corrupted. Instead of starting from scratch with a new profile, all you will need to add are any special applications or shortcuts the person had before the profile was corrupted.

I use the Desktop folder in a unique way. What if a lot of people are working on one project? Adding docucentric shortcuts to everyone's desktop would take a lot of administrator time. If you place that shortcut in the Desktop folder found in the All Users folder, however, everyone would see it on their desktops without any additional effort on your part.

Okay, so this particular setup has a problem. What if everyone who uses your workstation, except one person, needs that application or file? I'll show you a technique for assigning individual security to a particular folder or application in the section titled "Using the Security Page of the File or Folder Properties Dialog Box" in Chapter 28, "Security Issues." All you need to do is lock that person out of the folder or application. He will see it on his desktop, but he won't be able to access it. I'm not going to say that this is a perfect solution, but it does work and it reduces the amount of work you need to do without losing one iota of security.

On Your Own

Practice using some of the shortcut keys described in Table 8.1, particularly those you didn't know existed that can make your work more efficient.

Give the new Web-style (single-clicking rather than double-clicking) clicking a try for a couple weeks; I'm nearly certain that if you give it a fair try, you will find that you prefer it. After all, double-clicking was always kind of a hassle. (In Explorer, choose Tools | Folder Options, then select Single Click to Open an Item.)

Try adding a shortcut to the Startup folder on your desktop. Place any work you need to do tomorrow there tonight. Watch what happens when you start your machine tomorrow morning. You should get a desktop that automatically loads all the work you need to do.

Start separating your work into projects, if possible. Place each project in a separate folder on the desktop. Use separate folders, if necessary, to make it easier to find a particular kind of data. For example, you might need to place your graphics files in one subfolder to keep them from crowding the text files.

PART III

A Look Under the Hood

9

An Architectural Overview

Learning about a new operating system usually includes knowing a bit about the components that comprise it. You don't start learning about DOS by knowing that there are two hidden files (MSDOS.SYS and IO.SYS) and one visible file (COMMAND.COM) that make up its core, but you do learn about them later. It doesn't take very long for most people to figure out some of the things that take place under DOS as well. An in-depth knowledge of interrupts and vector tables isn't required, but a basic knowledge of what takes place is. Just about every user spends some time learning about ancillary system files as well. Everyone knows about the DOS configuration files—AUTOEXEC.BAT and CONFIG.SYS—because you can't do much without them when working with DOS (they aren't needed anymore with Windows 2000).

With this in mind, let's take a look at the Windows 2000 architecture and some its components. I looked specifically at the Professional version of the product while writing this chapter, but later verified that many of the pieces appear in the Server product as well. We won't go into bits and bytes during this discussion. In fact, we'll barely scratch the surface of what Windows 2000 contains. Still, you'll gain an appreciation of what goes on under the hood of this operating system. Having that knowledge can make it a lot easier to both configure and use Windows 2000 effectively.

A Short History of Windows 2000 Architecture

Windows 2000 started out, in part, from the ideas of some skilled programmers at Digital Electronics Corporation (DEC) . They were looking to build a new operating system (named *Mica*) that would feature more flexibility and more power than the current operating systems (namely UNIX and VMS). They began work, but DEC cut the project before it was completed. In an almost eerie coincidence, Microsoft was looking for a leader to develop its new operating system to compete with UNIX. It found that leader in Dave Cutler, who brought much of his Digital crew with him.

Microsoft wanted its new operating system to prepare the company for a move into the business-computing arena. Windows for Workgroups was clearly not up to the challenge of business computing. Microsoft's first attempt, prior to hiring the Digital group, was

OS/2, developed in tandem with IBM. OS/2 included some real improvements but didn't have the community support and some of the stronger features that Microsoft was hoping for in a business-level operating system. So began a four-year mission to develop a new Microsoft operating system, Windows NT/Windows 2000. In general, the goals of Windows NT/Windows 2000 were to deliver the following:

- Business-class reliability and fault tolerance
- True multitasking/multiprocessing
- Enhanced performance
- Increased security (later C2 security)

Microsoft's Windows NT (now Windows 2000) didn't really meet the goals of performance and reliability, or community acceptance, until version 3.51. At this point, the acceptance of Windows NT/2000 improved considerably. The interface was still based on the old Program Manager design. The latest version, Windows 2000 Professional, has an interface that's very similar to that of Windows 95/98 with a few subtle (yet important) distinctions. But don't be fooled by the common interface. Windows 95/98 and Windows 2000 don't share much more than a similar look and some application programming interface (API) sets.

Now that you know a little about what led up to the design, let's see what the system looks like on the inside. The remainder of this chapter is going to provide you with an overview of Windows 2000 from an architectural standpoint. It's important to understand that this is an *overview*—Windows 2000 is an extremely complex operating system that could take a considerable amount of time to write about from an in-depth architectural standpoint.

Windows 2000 As a Whole

I always like to take the grand tour of a new product before I get mired in details. Getting the big picture first gives you a better idea of how all the small pieces fit in. That's the purpose of this section—to give you the grand tour of Windows 2000. We'll look at how all the subsystems that I describe in later chapters fit together to create a comprehensive operating system.

Rings of Protection

Before I begin a discussion of individual Windows architectural components, I'd like to direct your attention to the "rings" of protection that the 80386 (and later) processor provides. There are four security rings within the Intel protection scheme, but most operating systems use only two (or sometimes three) of them. The inner security ring is ring 0. This is where the operating system proper is. The outermost ring is 3. That's where the applications reside. Sometimes an operating system gives device drivers better access to some operating system features than an application gets by running them at ring 1 or 2. Windows doesn't make any concessions; device drivers run at ring 0 or 3, depending on their purpose.

Windows uses these protection rings to make certain that only operating system components can access the inner workings of Windows—in other words, an application can't change settings that might cause the entire system to crash. For example, Windows reserves the right to allocate memory from the global pool; therefore, the capabilities needed to perform this task rest at ring 0. On the other hand, applications need to access memory assigned to them. That's why Windows assigns local memory a protection value of 3.

Think of each ring as a security perimeter. Before you can enter that perimeter, you have to know the secret password. Windows gives the password only to applications that it knows it can trust; everyone else has to stay out. Whenever an application does try to circumvent security, the processor raises an exception. Think of an exception as a security alarm. The exception sends the Windows police (better known as *exception handlers*) after the offending application. After its arrest and trial, Windows calmly terminates the offending application. Of course, it notifies the user before performing this task, but the user usually doesn't have much choice in the matter.

Figure 9.1 (described in the next section) gives you a pretty good idea of exactly whom Windows trusts. Applications and device drivers running at ring 3 (User mode) have very few capabilities outside their own resources. In fact, Windows even curtails these capabilities somewhat. Some of the activities that a DOS application could get by with, such as directly manipulating video memory, aren't allowed here. The reason is simple: Video memory is a shared resource. Whenever another application would need to share something, you can be certain that your application wouldn't be able to access it directly.

On the other hand, lower-level services such as those that control the CD-ROM or DVD-ROM drive on your machine operate at ring 0 (Kernel mode). These services require direct access to the hardware so that they can respond to application requests. Because there's only one service associated with each device, there isn't any concern about multiple accesses. Each access is controlled by one device driver even though there are many requests from multiple applications.

Now, on to the various components that actually make up Windows. The following sections break the Windows components into main areas. Each of these general groups contains descriptions of the individual components and what tasks they perform. Remember that this is only a general discussion. Windows is much more complex than it might first appear. The more experienced you become as a user, the more you'll see the actual complexity of this operating system.

Architecture

Several elements make up the Windows 2000 architecture, as shown in Figure 9.1. Each element takes care of one part of the Windows environment. For example, the Windows API layer lets applications communicate with Windows internals such as the file management system. You couldn't write a Windows application without the API layer.

Figure 9.1

Windows contains several major elements.

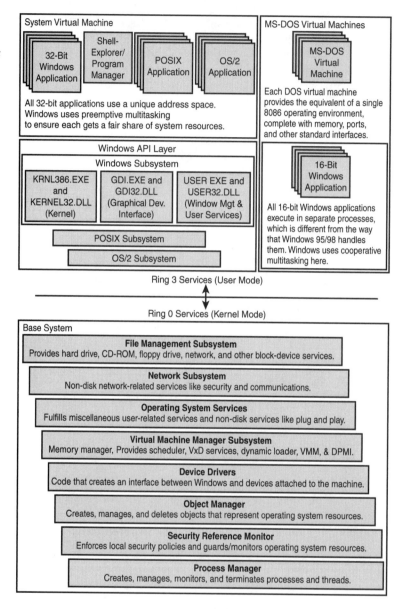

In short, Windows 2000 is built on layer after layer of operating system services. Each layer provides a different level of support and adds its particular capabilities into the mix. The interaction between the layers is important to the total operation of the system. It's like ordering from a catalog. The user is on the phone in his home (User mode system) . He makes a phone call to order some item. The phone is answered by the catalog center (Kernel mode service) . The user must be very explicit in his request; otherwise, he'll get the wrong item or nothing at all. The *catalog* is a published set of instructions for ordering an item. It contains item codes, colors, sizes, and options. The user must define each of these to get what he wants. The catalog center must also pass the information correctly to manufacturing and the delivery company to meet the order. This is essentially how the interaction between the layers occurs. The catalog that our little Windows 2000 operation typically uses is called the API set (Win32 API). I describe each of the main operating system components shown in Figure 9.1 in detail in the following sections.

System Virtual Machine

The System Virtual Machine (VM) component of Windows 2000 contains four main elements: 32-bit Windows applications, the shell, POSIX application support, and OS/2 application support. Essentially, the System VM component provides most of the Windows 2000 user-specific functionality. Without it, you couldn't run any applications. Note that I don't include DOS applications here. This is because Windows uses an entirely different set of capabilities to run DOS applications. It even runs them in a different processor mode.

There's one other thing you should notice about the OS/2 and POSIX support provided by Windows 2000. Notice that there's a client side to this support in the System Virtual Machine area of the diagram and a server side in the Windows API Layer part of the drawing. Windows 2000 uses a client/server approach to managing applications so that it can quickly adapt to applications designed for other operating systems. We really won't discuss this added support much in this book, but you should at least be aware that it exists.

> **Warning:** It may appear that you could run applications designed for different operating systems together under Windows 2000 and share their data. Although Windows 2000 will run more than one operating system's applications, it won't share data between them. For example, a POSIX application creates file handles differently than a Windows 32-bit application does. The POSIX file handle would be meaningless to the Windows 2000 application. The same idea holds true for any other type of data that an application may generate. In short, it's never a good idea to pass data from one application to another unless you use some documented method to do so.

There's another difference between Windows 2000 and Windows 95/98 when it comes to 16-bit Windows application support. Unlike Windows 95/98, which still contains a lot of 16-bit code in some support areas, Windows 2000 uses all 32-bit code. This means that Windows 2000 can relegate 16-bit Windows applications to the MS-DOS Virtual Machines area. In addition, unlike Windows 95/98, which use a shared memory area for all 16-bit applications, Windows 2000 runs each 16-bit application in a separate process. Using a separate process for each application means that, if one application crashes, it's less likely to affect other applications executing on the same machine.

The bottom line from a user's perspective is that Windows 2000 provides a higher level of protection for 16-bit Windows applications than its predecessors. You won't see many application-induced crashes. Even if you do, it's unlikely that the system as a whole will crash. The downside of this protection is that Windows 2000 is also less tolerant of older 16-bit Windows applications that might have broken some of the rules for running properly with other applications.

Theoretically, the System VM also provides support for the various Windows API layer components. However, because these components provide a different sort of service, I chose to discuss them in a separate section. (Needless to say, the distinctions between the client or System VM and the server or Windows API Layer parts of Windows 2000 architecture are a lot clearer than under Windows 95/98.) Even though applications use the API and users interact with applications, you really don't think about the API until it comes time to writing an application. Therefore, I always think of the API as a programmer-specific service rather than something that the user really needs to worry about. The following list describes the System VM components in detail:

COMPATIBILITY

- *32-bit Windows Applications.* Windows 2000 can use a wide variety of fully functional 32-bit applications, some of which won't run under Windows 95/98 because it uses the Win32 specification (a subset of the Windows 2000 API). A 32-bit application usually provides better multitasking capabilities than its 16-bit counterpart. In addition, many 32-bit applications support new Windows features such as long filenames, whereas most 16-bit applications don't. Also, 32-bit applications provide two additional features. The more important one is the use of pre-emptive, versus cooperative, multitasking. This makes your work flow more smoothly and forces the system to wait for you as necessary, rather than the other way around. The second feature is the use of a flat memory address space. This feature really makes a difference in how much memory an application gets and how well it uses it. In addition, an application that uses a flat address space should run slightly faster because it no longer has to spend time working with Intel's memory-segmentation scheme.

- *The Shell.* Unlike previous versions of Windows, Windows 2000 comes with only one user shell—Explorer. Explorer provides full 32-bit capabilities. It also sports the new interface shown in Figure 9.2. Explorer combines all the features you used to find in Program Manager, Print Manager, and File Manager.

- *POSIX Application.* I've never seen anyone use this particular feature, so I can't tell you how well it works. This is a government-specified form of UNIX that's supposed to be portable across a variety of platforms. It appeared in 1988 as IEEE Standard 1003.1-1988. Suffice it to say that you probably won't need to interact with this interface element unless your system is running a POSIX application. It's interesting to note that the current POSIX interface only supports character-mode applications. We'll talk about the intricacies of POSIX support later in the chapter.

- *OS/2 Application.* The OS/2 support under Windows 2000 is somewhat disappointing. The only things you can run with the current version of Windows 2000 are the character-mode programs used with OS/2 version 1.0. You can't run any of the Program Manager–capable programs. We'll talk about the intricacies of OS/2 support later in the chapter.

FIGURE 9.2
Windows 2000 sports a new interface that should make life a lot easier for the novice user.

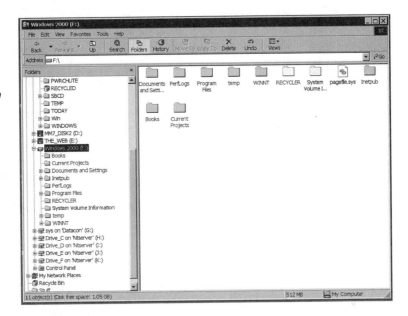

The Windows API Layer

Two Windows APIs are included with Windows 2000. The first API is exactly like the old one supplied with Windows 3.1. It provides all the 16-bit services that the old Windows had to provide for applications. An older 16-bit application will use this API when it runs. The other API is the 32-bit Windows API used by Windows 2000. The 32-bit API provides about the same feature set as the 16-bit API, but it's more robust.

You can physically see the two Windows APIs if you look in the right place. These two APIs exist side by side in separate files in your SYSTEM (16-bit) and SYSTEM32 (32-bit) folders. For example, all the common dialog boxes —such as the ones you use to open files and search for text in your document—appear in two files: COMMDLG.DLL (16-bit) and COMDLG32.DLL (32-bit). The 32 in a filename often gives it away as a 32-bit program. Using common dialog boxes gives your applications the consistent look you've come to expect. You'll find other pieces of the API in your SYSTEM folder as well. Microsoft groups various API calls together and places them in separate files to make it easier to update the operating system later. Using separate files also makes it easier to install upgrades to various operating system components and reduces the amount of hard disk space you lose to unwanted features.

LOOKING AHEAD

We'll take a look at why Windows 2000 has to use two different files for 16-bit and 32-bit DLLs in Chapter 11, "Memory Management." This is also the chapter in which I tell you all about the types of memory that Windows 2000 uses and how it affects you as a user. It's important to know about this issue because it affects the way that your applications interact with Windows. Knowing this information will also help you understand—at least a little better—why an application can't perform certain kinds of tasks even though it appears that the application should be able to.

To support multiple operating systems, Windows 2000 also has to provide multiple API layers. Microsoft calls these API layers (or subsystems) *servers*. The main server under Windows 2000 is obviously the Windows API that we just discussed—the other servers talk to it. The client (in most cases, an application) for a particular operating system calls the API that it can talk to. The API will then translate system requests (such as opening a file and printing a document) into something that Windows 2000 can understand. For example, an OS/2 client would call the OS/2 API, which in turn calls the Windows API. If you look at the block diagram in Figure 9.1, you'll see three API layers: Windows Subsystem, POSIX Subsystem, and OS/2 Subsystem. Even though this design is a lot different from the one used by Windows 3.*x* and Windows 95/98, the Windows 2000 32-bit API looks the same from a programmer's perspective (even though it does provide a wider range of calls). It's the actual operating system implementation that differs. To a user, the difference is completely transparent.

The Base System

The Base System component of Windows 2000 contains all the internal or low-level operating system–specific services. Some books call this the *operating system kernel*. This is the core of Windows 2000, the part that has to be operating in order for Windows to perform its work. You, as a user, will never interact with the Base System. In fact, few programmers even interact with this "hidden" part of Windows. The following list describes each part of the Base System in detail.

- *File Management Subsystem*. This particular part of Windows 2000 is examined in detail in Chapter 12, "The Windows 2000 File Systems: FAT and NTFS." Essentially, this part of the Base System provides an interface to all the block devices—such as hard, CD-ROM, DVD-ROM, and floppy drives—connected to your machine. It doesn't matter how the connection is made—physically or through a network. All that matters is that your machine can access the device. The Windows 2000 file-management subsystem also uses a hardware abstraction layer to allow it to run on multiple machine types (PCs that use processors other than the Intel 80*x*86 series of chips).

NETWORKING

- *Network Subsystem*. Windows for Workgroups was the first version of Windows to address the networking needs of the workgroup. It even incorporated networking as part of the operating system rather than as a third-party add-on product. Windows 2000 extends this capability. Not only can you run a Microsoft peer-to-peer network, but Windows 2000 provides protected-mode hooks for most major LAN products as well. In fact, you can keep more than one network active at a time. The modular nature of the Network Subsystem enables other vendors to add to Windows 2000's inherent capabilities through the use of VxDs. Up to this point, Windows 95/98 and Windows 2000 provide similar features; although, Windows 2000 does provide the superior form of security. There are two versions of Windows 2000. The version that we look at in this book is designed for workstation use. The Windows 2000 Server version is designed to act as a file server. In this respect, it acts more like the client/server architecture used by Novell's NetWare. We'll examine networks in detail in Part VI, "Networking with Windows 2000" (starting with Chapter 23, "Network Basics").

- *Operating System Services.* This is the part of the operating system that deals with features such as hardware profiles. It also fulfills miscellaneous user and operating system requests. For example, every time the user asks Windows 2000 for the time of day, he or she is requesting a service from this Windows 2000 component. Unlike Windows NT, Windows 2000 does provide an equivalent level of user-level services to Windows 95/98. In fact, this version provides fairly complete support for Plug and Play, which is a very nice change from Windows NT. Windows 2000 also provides a more robust hardware profile setup than Windows 95/98 does, thus allowing you to switch between hardware setups with ease. Except for the relatively steep hardware requirements for Windows 2000, you can use it equally well on both desktop and mobile machines.

- *Virtual Machine Manager.* Ever wonder where the exact center of Windows 2000 is? This is it; this is the component that holds everything else together. The Virtual Machine Manager takes care of task scheduling, and it starts and stops every application on the system (including any DOS applications that you might run). This operating system component manages virtual memory on your machine as well. Of course, your application uses the Windows API to make the request instead of talking with this part of the system directly. Because the Virtual Machine Manager handles all memory allocations, it also has to act as a DPMI (DOS Protected Mode Interface) server for DOS applications that run in Protected mode. When a DOS application makes a memory request, it's actually calling routines in this component of Windows. As with Windows applications, DOS applications can't directly access this component of Windows. The DOS application uses a DOS extender API to make its call. Finally, the Virtual Machine Manager is responsible for intertask communications. All this means is that all DDE and OLE requests filter through this section of the operating system.

- *Device Drivers.* Windows would never know what to do with your system if it weren't for the lowly device driver. This bit of specialty code acts as an interpreter. It takes Windows service requests and sends them to the Hardware Abstraction Layer (HAL) in a format HAL can understand. Note that it doesn't send the request directly to a device because a Windows 2000 device driver never knows what kind of machine you're using. The device driver thinks that it's talking to a device, but the HAL intercepts the request before the device actually sees it. Windows 2000 provides support for the Windows Driver Model (WDM) drivers.

These are the same drivers that are used with Windows 98 and above (there's a Windows 98 SE version available at the time of this writing). However, at the time of this writing, you still can't use a Windows 98 driver directly with Windows 2000 (and vice versa). This should change in the near future, making it possible for vendors to develop a single driver for all versions of Windows.

- *Object Manager.* This component of Windows 2000 creates, manages, and deletes objects. Most of these objects represent abstract operating system resources such as memory or a physical resource such as a hard drive. An *object* has properties, events, and methods. Think of a *property* as something you can use your five senses to detect. For example, an apple has red or yellow as a color property. Likewise, every component (such as a dialog box) that you see on your monitor has a color property. A *method* is what you can do with the object or something the object itself knows how to do. For example, you can eat an apple and the apple knows how to grow. Likewise, you can display a control, and the control can center itself on screen. An *event* is a reaction of some sort. For example, when you cut an apple in half, the inside turns brown as it reacts to the outside air. Likewise, buttons generate an event when you click them—some reaction occurs. The Windows 2000 environment is a lot more complex and it uses more modular components than Windows 95/98, so it needs this extra Base System component. (Windows 95/98 does use some object technology to implement many of the user interface components—Windows 2000 extends this to the operating system itself.) Using objects allows Windows 2000 to view its computing environment in much the same way as you view the world, thus making it easier for programmers to manage all the numerous pieces needed to make this operating system work. Every time you need to create a new system object, such as an icon or dialog box, you call the Object Manager.

- *Security Reference Monitor.* Windows 2000 provides a major feature that you'll never find in Windows 95/98—Class C2–level security, which restricts access to computer resources on a need-to-know basis. Implementing this level of security requires a lot of work on the part of the operating system, in general, and this module, in particular. You'll find all the qualifications for C2-level security in DoD manual 5200.28-STD. The security levels range from Class D (least secure) to Class A (most secure). In essence, this added level of security allows government agencies to use Windows 2000 in a secure environment. It probably won't affect you much as a user unless you work for the government. Windows 2000 also provides support for the new standards in security, such as Kerberos. Part of the System Reference Monitor's job is to monitor system resources. This prevents one process or thread from grabbing all the system resources, such as memory. The bottom line is that the module prevents the operating system from losing control for too long. An application is forced to work with the operating system in such a way that every process and thread gets a fair share of the computing resources. Finally, the System Reference Monitor provides statistical data that a network administrator can use to monitor system performance.

- *Process Manager*. Windows 2000 also supports a wider range of processing options than Windows 95/98 does. Multiprocessing environments require the use of heavier-duty process management techniques. The Process Manager creates, manages, and terminates both processes (applications) and threads (streams of execution within an application). It also allows the operating system to suspend and resume processes and threads, as needed, to keep the overall system stable. Like the System Reference Monitor, the Process Manager provides statistical data that a network administrator can use to monitor system performance.

DOS Virtual Machine

I've separated the DOS Virtual Machine component of Windows from the other components for several reasons. DOS applications have formed the basis for using the PC for a long time. In fact, for many years, nothing else was available. Yet most of these applications were written at a time when the standard PC ran one application and one application only. That one application had total control of the entire machine.

Each DOS application that you start under Windows 2000 runs on what Intel calls a *virtual machine*. Essentially, the processor fools the application into thinking that it's the only application running on your machine at the moment. Each virtual machine has its own memory space and access to devices on the system. The amazing thing is that you can have many virtual machines running on your one physical machine at a time. We'll take a more detailed look at the DOS Virtual Machine later. Suffice it to say that Windows 2000 has to literally perform back flips to make this whole concept work properly, especially when you consider Windows-hostile applications such as games.

It may sound like Windows 2000 would lose control of the system when it runs a DOS application. The truth is that each one of these virtual machines is still under the strict control of the processor. If the application makes a request that the processor can't fulfill, the processor raises an exception. Windows 2000 pays close attention to these exceptions and doesn't allow a DOS application to continue running when it sees one. Windows 2000 also monitors display memory and every device on your machine. It terminates any applications that try to access a device improperly. This higher level of monitoring explains why Windows 95/98 will run an application such as game programs when Windows 2000 won't. Windows 95/98 allows an application to continue as long as it can recover from an error; Windows 2000 terminates the errant application.

Remote Procedure Calls (RPC) and Local Procedure Calls (LPC)

Just as in mail-order transactions, an application running on your machine can place its order for operating system services in a variety of ways. With Windows 2000, for instance, the information and programs that you might want may not be on the local machine. In this case, Windows 2000 has the power to forward your request to a machine that can service the request—whether it's to run an application or to access data.

A couple of services running on Windows 2000 handle these requests. One is the Local Procedure Call (LPC) facility, which services many of the requests from the APIs and applications. The other is the Remote Procedure Call (RPC), which is a little more complex, but essentially allows for the redirection of requests to remote systems. (You'll see both LPC and RPC again in Chapter 15, "OLE, ActiveX, and DCOM," when it comes time to discuss how DCOM works.)

More than anything else, the way that this remote service is provided demonstrates some of the key design elements of Windows 2000. Recall the layering I mentioned earlier: Each layer knows only how to speak to the next and retrieve information from the layer below it. The user application has no idea that the Windows 2000 Kernel mode service has to go out to the network to, say, get an MS Access data file. The application knows only the name of the file and the directory (folder) that the user specified. You can see how this kind of protection benefits the overall stability of the system. This isn't a programming book, however, so let's move on to look at the architecture of the User mode components.

User Mode

When Windows 2000 was designed, it was built so that it could be integrated with other systems. Part of that integration is the capability to run programs and scripts from other operating systems such as UNIX and DOS. Microsoft needed to provide a way for such alien programs to believe that they were running on a machine of the type that they were originally programmed for. Environment subsystems provide virtual machines with functionality that simulates other operating systems. Of course, all the features of other operating systems aren't provided in the out-of-box OS. Some third-party vendors supply Windows 2000 with the added functionality.

The environmental subsystems provided in Windows 2000 Professional are POSIX subsystem (for UNIX compliance), OS/2 subsystem, and WIN32 subsystem. The WIN32 subsystem is the native subsystem that Windows 2000 32-bit code operates in. It's also the environment subsystem that provides compatibility with the 16-bit Windows and DOS applications. Much of the textual interface is provided through the Client Server Runtime (CSR) subsystem. Before discussing the Win32 subsystem further, let's address the other two subsystems first.

The POSIX subsystem was built for compliance with UNIX operating standards, primarily BSD UNIX. This makes sense when you recall that Windows 2000's developers came from Digital Equipment Corporation. DEC based its UNIX operating system offering on BSD UNIX, as opposed to System V UNIX, which IBM has chosen to base its AIX operating system on. The POSIX environment subsystem provides a character-based, POSIX-compliant interface primarily to be able to run scripts. Understand that although some of the more common UNIX commands are present when you open a standard command prompt, it's clearly not a complete set. If you require greater compliance and functionality to interact with UNIX operating systems, I suggest looking to third-party vendors. One product, called *OpenNT*, is capable of providing almost all the UNIX-based command set as well as XWindows functionality (XWindows is a UNIX/Linux graphical interface, much as Program Manager or Windows Explorer are graphical interfaces for Windows).

The OS/2 subsystem primarily provides compatibility for OS/2 character-based functionality. The OS/2 graphic operations aren't compliant with Windows 2000 operations. It would seem that OS/2 compatibility may be disappearing from Windows 2000 in the near future as well. With Windows 2000 Professional, we have seen the discontinuation of support for HPFS, the IBM file system. I suspect that in future releases we'll see the entire discontinuation of the OS/2 subsystem.

Both the aforementioned environmental subsystems actually rely on a Win32 subsystem running in User mode, called the *CSR*. This subsystem is responsible for all the character-based operations and is used by the OS/2 and POSIX subsystems to provide interaction with the user during nongraphical operations. Therefore, whenever you open a command prompt, you're actually running in the CSR, which provides a command set similar to DOS and UNIX. On any typical Windows 2000 workstation, you can open a command prompt and type **DIR**, for example. This will display a directory listing. If you install the Windows 2000 Resource Kit, which provides many common UNIX commands, you can also type **ls**, which is the UNIX command to provide a directory listing (it works much like DIR does). It may display in a slightly different format more customary to UNIX, but the result is generally the same.

When a program gets launched by a user in Windows 2000, it's provided its own little space—a personal playground to do what it likes. Applications are provided essentially 4GB of simulated memory to operate in. That is, each application has up to 4GB available to it. The actual amount that any one application uses is based on the amount of code and data it's storing in its memory space, called a *process working set*. Few applications, except for some high-level graphic design and simulation programs, will actually approach this limit. What's more, this 4GB "space" is virtual space—many people don't have 4GB available on their entire system (combining both their RAM and hard drive space). The 4GB limit for programs is essentially a theoretical limit today, but it provides a generous specification for possibly much larger future RAM and hard drive space. How Windows 2000 provides this amount of memory will be covered a little later when we talk about the Virtual Memory Manager. Each application is playing in its own little sandbox and isn't allowed to interfere with the other applications' sandboxes. Therefore, no application is permitted to read or write in another application's memory space. This is quite a divergence from the other Microsoft operating systems, in which any program could get or put information from or to any section of memory it so desired, sometimes with disastrous results. Windows 2000 was built to avoid these sometimes not-so-little disasters.

The Windows 2000 System (Kernel Mode) Files

The first thing you need to understand is what an operating system kernel is all about. Think of the kernel as the very central core of the operating system—the part that binds everything else together and provides a basic set of features. A programmer normally accesses the kernel using some special technique. For example, DOS programmers know you're supposed to gain access to the operating system using an interrupt service routine. These interrupts ask the operating system to perform a specific task. All the code for the interrupt routines appears in the system files. Under DOS you'd find these system files in COMMAND.COM, MSDOS.SYS, and IO.SYS. (Some people would say that you don't actually need COMMAND.COM, and you don't, but you do need some type of system shell, so I included the default here.) These three files load as part of the boot process and (except for COMMAND.COM) remain active the entire time you use DOS. This old method worked well in the DOS single-tasking environment, where the application was in control.

UnderWindows, the user is in control, and the old system of interrupt service requests won't work properly. Every Windows application gains access to the operating system using an API. Essentially, an API call does the same thing as an interrupt: It asks the operating system to perform a task. The code for the API appears in the system files, just as it does for DOS. Of course, this is a very simplified view of the API. An API is written using Protected mode code, unlike DOS, which is written in Real mode code. In addition, API code is reentrant, whereas the DOS code isn't. A "reentrant" piece of code allows Windows 2000 to process more than one call at a time. Under DOS, you couldn't reenter a piece of code—you had to complete one call at a time (a reasonable limitation because there was only supposed to be one application working at any given time under DOS). There are other differences as well, but the only people who really need to know about them are programmers. As we discussed in the preceding section, Windows 2000 actually uses two Windows APIs—one 16-bit API and one 32-bit API.

The API that most people are concentrating on under Windows 2000 is the 32-bit API. Not only are 32-bit system calls a lot more logical from a programmer's point of view (Windows 3.x was a programmer's nightmare; Windows 2000 is merely an inconvenience), but they also provide many more features as well. In addition, a 32-bit application enjoys the benefits that this environment provides. Of course, the biggest benefit that you'll hear most programmers talk about is the flat memory address space. Every application running under Windows—until now—has had to spend time working with Intel's segmented address scheme. A 32-bit application doesn't need to worry about segmentation any more. Every call is a near call; every call is in a single segment.

No matter which API your Windows application uses, it'll address three basic operating system kernel components. The 16-bit versions of these files are GDI.EXE, USER.EXE, and KRNL386.EXE. The 32-bit versions of these files are GDI32.DLL, USER32.DLL, and KERNEL32.DLL. The following list describes these three components in detail:

- *Windows Kernel (*KRNL386.EXE *or* KERNEL32.DLL*).* This is the part of Windows 2000 that provides support for the lower-level functions that an application needs to run. For example, every time your application needs memory, it runs to the Windows Kernel component to get it. This is the literal kernel of the operating system, but Windows wouldn't operate at all without the other two components. Think about this particular file as the "parts that didn't fit anywhere else" bin and you'll have a better idea of what it's used for. Obviously, the Windows Kernel component doesn't deal with either the interface or devices; it interacts only with Windows itself.

- *Graphical Device Interface (*GDI.EXE *or* GDI32.DLL*).* Every time an application writes to the screen, it's using a graphical device interface (GDI) service. This Windows component takes care of fonts, printer services, the display, color management, and every other artistic aspect of Windows that users can see as they use an application.

- *User (*USER.EXE *or* USER32.DLL*).* Windows is all about just that—*windows*. It needs a manager to keep track of all the windows that applications create to display various types of information. However, User only begins there. Every time your application displays an icon or pushbutton, it's using some type of User component function. It's easier to think of the User component of the Windows API as a work manager; it helps you organize things and keep them straight.

> **Note:** The other operating systems that Windows 2000 supports do so through the system of clients and servers that I talked about earlier. In other words, the server translates the calls made by the application into a Windows API call. In essence, they're using the same kernel components as any Windows application would even though they're designed for another operating system.

There are actually a few more pieces to the kernel, but it's better to think of them as you would the DOS loader. I didn't mention the DOS loader at the beginning of this discussion because no one ever uses it once the operating system is up and running. Likewise, Windows has to have some components that load it into memory and get it started. You won't hear too much about them because no one ever uses them once the operating system is started. We'll still look at the actual files in the section titled "A Look at the Windows 2000 Boot Sequence," later in this chapter.

Miniport Driver Support

What exactly is a miniport driver? This was the first question that came to my mind. A *miniport driver* is a device-independent way of moving data. It doesn't matter what form that data takes—it could be graphics, sound, or text. Windows 2000 uses the miniport driver concept for every subsystem on your machine. The benefit of using the miniport driver for your applications is improved speed. The application only needs to worry about the data it wants to output, not the format that the data takes.

Not only does miniport driver support mean a better and easier-to-use interface for the user, it also means a lot to software vendors as well. Under DOS, you have to write code for every little function. If you want to provide a File menu, you have to write all the code that the File menu requires. The same thing holds true for every other function a program might perform. Windows 3.*x* started a process in which the programmer didn't have to write so much code. Using the common dialog boxes is just one example. You no longer have to write a File menu, because Microsoft provides one as part of the Common Dialog DLL.

Windows 2000 takes this concept even further with the miniport driver support it provides. If you develop communications programs, you used to worry about the differences in control sequences for each modem type. Using Windows 2000 Unimodem support (a miniport driver), you open each modem and write to it like a file. The miniport driver takes care of details, such as control codes.

This approach has other significant advantages. For one thing, you no longer need to worry as much about how well an application will handle the details. Because each vendor is writing to the same interface, any changes to that interface will come from Microsoft. Using a common interface also means that every application will provide the same level of support for the various devices on your system. If one application supports a device, they all do (and at the same level).

LOOKING AHEAD We'll look at the specifics of miniport driver implementation as we visit each subsystem. Chapter 12 will cover the miniport driver concept from the file system point of view. Chapter 13, "Graphics Windows 2000 Style," will cover the same information on the video subsystem. Chapter 14, "Printing Under Windows 2000," covers printer support in much more detail. Details on network miniport driver support appear in Chapter 23. In most cases, I'll shorten *miniport driver* to *driver* in the rest of the book because a miniport driver is simply a special form of driver.

Win16 Support

By this time, you've learned much about the workings of Windows 2000. Let's now return for a slightly closer look at support for Win16/DOS applications. Initially, it took some convincing to make the developers working on Windows 2000 submit to even attempting to run DOS and old 16-bit Windows applications. Think of it, you've taken all the time and trouble to come up with a sleek, cutting-edge 32-bit operating system capable of running multithreaded, multitasking applications and someone comes along and says, "But, will it run the DOS EDIT.COM?". Nonetheless, adding this facility was a necessity. As consumers, we certainly weren't ready to run out and buy all new programs just for a new operating system. So, what they had to do was create an environment that simulated what the DOS and earlier Windows applications were used to.

Architecture

What resulted was the Windows 2000 Virtual DOS Machine, NTVDM.EXE. To Windows 2000, the NTVDM is just another 32-bit application. To a DOS application, the NTVDM is the whole computer! The NTVDM simulates a 16-bit PC environment down to the CPU ticks for timing and the old-style, segmented memory space. When a DOS application starts, an NTVDM is started by the Win32 subsystem. This NTVDM becomes the computer to the DOS application. Each DOS application will start in its own NTVDM; we have never heard of multiple DOS applications running concurrently (so the NTVDM, to be realistic, couldn't allow it). That's why each one starts an NTVDM of its own.

So now we have DOS. We still have to provide a 16-bit Windows environment. To do this, Windows 2000 launches another program called WOWEXEC.EXE (Win16 on Win32, or *WOW* for short). This program simulates a Windows 3.11 enhanced-mode installation. It's launched inside a running NTVDM, because Windows 3.11 runs on top of DOS. Therefore, if you start a 16-bit Windows application on your system, you can open up Task Manager and look at running processes. You'll see one NTVDM and one WOWEXEC.EXE with your Windows application showing up underneath one of them. The Windows application is really running as a thread inside one of the other applications. Shhh, don't tell the Windows 16-bit application though.

Running Win16 on Windows 2000

Whenever you start a 16-bit Windows application, Windows 2000 starts in a running NTVDM. If you start multiples, they'll all start in the same NTVDM; they won't each spawn their own, new NTVDM. Sixteen-bit Windows applications run in a shared memory space inside the same DOS machine, and this is how it is on Windows 2000 as well.

However, this can be adjusted. For a 16-bit application, you can tell it to "run in its own memory space." This will indicate to Windows 2000 that the application should be given its own NTVDM. This is especially useful if you have a misbehaving application. If you're running Windows for Workgroups and one of your applications hangs, what happens to the machine? Yep, it hangs, too. In Windows 2000, if one of the 16-bit applications fails, all the other 16-bit applications will freeze inside the WOWEXEC/NTVDM where the faulty app is. If you tell the faulty application to run in its own memory space, it won't affect the other applications. In fact, it won't know anything about them at all. It'll be in its own universe. It won't be able to share data directly with the other applications, either.

To make an application run in its own memory space, just right-click the shortcut or the item in Windows 2000 Explorer and choose Properties from the context menu. You'll see that you can click a little box marked Run in Own Memory Space. Notice that all 32-bit programs automatically run in their own memory space. The drawbacks of running a 16-bit application in its own memory space are that there's no communication with other 16-bit applications and more system resources will be consumed because you'll be launching new copies of NTVDM.EXE and WOWEXEC.EXE for each 16-bit application.

A Look at the Windows 2000 Boot Sequence

Getting your machine up and running after you turn the power on is called the *boot process*. It includes everything from the time that the Power-On Startup Test (POST) routines begin until the time you can start to use the machine. Under DOS, this boot process is relatively straightforward. Windows 2000 requires something a bit more exotic because we expect it to do more.

We'll look at the boot process from a user's perspective in the following sections. This means you won't get a blow-by-blow, "this-bit-does-this-and-that-byte-does-that" explanation. We'll just look at the highlights of the boot process.

> **Tip:** If you ever do want to see a blow-by-blow description of the entire boot process, create a BOOTLOG.TXT file by pressing F8 during the boot process and then selecting the BOOTLOG.TXT generation option. Once your machine is booted, you can look at BOOTLOG.TXT in the root directory of your boot drive. This file records every action that Windows 2000 performs during the boot process. However, it doesn't include a few of the initial actions, such as loading the Windows 2000 loader (NTLDR.BIN). At most, three or four actions take place before the log starts, though, so your chances of missing anything important are almost nonexistent.

Starting Windows 2000

Loading the initial system is fairly straightforward. The boot sector on the hard driver points to NTLDR.BIN—the program that the BIOS will call as soon as the POST routine completes, just as it would do with the DOS loader if you had DOS loaded. NTLDR.BIN calls the NTDETECT.COM program. This program displays the Windows 2000 splash screen.

NTDETECT.COM also begins a search for the computer's installed hardware. Once it gets a complete list, NTDETECT.COM displays the computer's hardware characteristics, such as what kind of hard disk it uses, and passes the information to other applications through the Registry.

LOOKING AHEAD   We'll discuss the Registry in full detail in Chapter 10. You'll be amazed at what kind of information is stored there—some of which used to appear in numerous INI files on your drive.

Once NTDETECT.COM completes its task, it passes control back to NTLDR.BIN. The next phase in the operating system boot process is to determine which operating system to load. BOOT.INI contains a list of operating systems installed on your machine—usually DOS and Windows 2000 or OS/2 and Windows 2000. It's at this point that Windows 2000 displays the screen that allows you to boot DOS or OS/2. If the countdown timer stops before you make a selection, Windows 2000 will then begin to load the default operating system.

> **Tip:** You can always interrupt the countdown timer by pressing the up or down arrow. This allows you as much time as you need to choose an operating system—NTLDR.BIN will simply wait until you press the Enter key to begin the loading process.

The next step in the process is to configure Windows 2000 at a basic level—much like CONFIG.SYS does for a DOS machine. NTLDR.BIN looks in two places for this information. The Registry contains all the hardware information it needs to configure the various devices on your system. In some cases, it also needs to look in BOOT.INI to see which devices to use. The BOOT.INI file also tells Windows 2000 which services, such as networking or a power monitor, to start.

This whole process works mainly with the Registry. Its whole function is to load some low-level executable files into memory to handle the rest of the loading process and configure Windows 2000 for use. It also allows you to choose another operating system before Windows 2000 begins to load. We're still using NTLDR.BIN to get the job done, but now we need to do something with the information that we've accumulated.

Loading the 32-Bit Core

We still don't have any GUI elements loaded into memory. The very first thing we need to do is get the core Windows 2000 operating system loaded. To do this, NTLDR.BIN loads an application called VWIN32.386. This little program loads the three 32-bit DLLs that form the 32-bit API: USER32.DLL, GDI32.DLL, and KERNEL32.DLL. Once it completes this task, VWIN32.386 returns control to NTLDR.BIN, which, in turn, calls the 32-bit kernel.

Now that all the core operating system components are loaded, Windows 2000 loads and initializes all the 32-bit virtual device drivers (VxDs). It also loads all the services. A *service* is just another form of VxD, but it's a form you can communicate with.

What precisely is a VxD? It's a *virtual device driver*—the protected-mode version of the device drivers you used under DOS. However, it's more than that because a device can be a lot more than just a piece of hardware under Windows 2000. To avoid getting into the bits and bytes of device management, let's just say that Windows uses virtual device drivers to manage all its low-level functions.

Once it completes this step, Windows initializes all those drivers. It starts with the system drivers first—all the drivers required to make the low-level functions in Windows work (such as the file system drivers). After the system driver, Windows 2000 initializes any services you've requested. The device drivers come next. Now that the 32-bit part of Windows 2000 is up and running, it creates one or more virtual DOS machines (VDMs).

Loading the 16-Bit Core

Now that there's a place for 16-bit Windows to run, Windows 2000 starts a copy of it in memory. To do this, Windows 2000 loads the three 16-bit shell components: USER.EXE, GDI.EXE, and KRNL386.EXE. It also loads some additional drivers and a few other components such as fonts. The 16-bit driver load-and-initialization sequence is the same as for the 32-bit portion, so I won't go into it again here. Now Windows 2000 has a completely functional, 16-bit–mode version of Windows available to run older applications. It doesn't have an interface yet, but every other component is present.

Somewhere in all this, Windows 2000 asks the user to provide some input in the form of a name and password. It checks this against the contents of the appropriate PWL file. If the password checks out, Windows 2000 completes the boot process.

Finally, Windows gets the Explorer interface up and running (it was loaded before but wasn't running). It displays all the required objects on the Desktop and initializes the taskbar. This is the point where it also looks at your Startup folder to see which applications you want to start automatically. You're set up and ready to compute.

On Your Own

I always find it interesting to see exactly what my computer is doing. Take a look through the BOOTLOG.TXT file on your boot drive to see which drivers Windows 2000 is loading and in what order it loads them. See if you can find all the drivers in your SYSTEM32 folder. You might be surprised to find that they don't all appear there. Which files (if any) does Windows 2000 place in other locations? Why do you think it places them there?

Check out your BOOT.INI file; then make a minor change using either the System or Services applet in CONFIG.SYS. How do these changes look? Knowing how Windows 2000 makes entries into this file could make it easier for you to recover if there's ever a problem in getting your system to boot. (I've never run into one that Windows 2000's automatic recovery couldn't fix, but you never know.) Make sure you return any settings to their previous conditions before you exit Windows 2000.

Look at System Monitor and see how opening applications affects memory and the disk. Using counters such as Memory: Page Faults/sec and Logical Disk: Disk Reads/sec, explore the symbiotic relationship between the disk and memory. Also, you can use Task Manager to observe memory use, file system cache sizes, and pagefile use.

Spend some time in the SYSTEM and SYSTEM32 folders trying to find various API elements. How do the 32-bit names differ from their 16-bit counterparts? Right-click the API components and select Quick View from the context menu. Do you recognize any of the exported functions that the DLL provides?

Peter Norton

Understanding the Windows 2000 Registry

In this chapter you'll see how to manipulate, safeguard, and manage the important Registry—a repository of preferences, setup details, system configuration, and other essential information. You'll also learn how to modify the Registry, making some kinds of changes that are otherwise impossible.

Prior to Windows 95, the Windows 3.x Registry was so simple that most people never gave it a second thought. About the only things it contained were some file associations and a few OLE settings. You might have found a few bits and pieces of other information in there as well, but for the most part, even Windows itself ignored the Registry. But it was a sleeping giant.

Today, Windows 2000 contains a Registry that's filled with (on average) 12MB or more of data. The Windows 2000 Registry contains every piece of information about everything the operating system needs to know. The Registry holds initialization conditions, preferences, and uninstall data for applications and the Explorer shell; system-wide settings and permissions for networked computers; file extension associations; descriptions, statuses, and properties of hardware components; performance counters and other low-level system status information; and much more.

In addition to your computer's local Registry settings, network administrators can also implement company- or enterprise-wide Registry settings, also known as *system policies*. The network-wide Registry settings are automatically merged with your local Registry whenever you log on to the network. Only the network administrator can change these policies—any changes you make to your local Registry will affect only your particular computer (or the particular computer you log on to, if you're working from someone else's desk temporarily). What's more, the system administrator can selectively allow some users to modify particular sections (keys) within the Registry or force a key or keys to be read-only. Overall, the Registry brings into a single location—and provides a degree of security and standardization for—all the configuration data that was previously scattered among various INI files. The Registry stores information about an entire network as well as individual applications, individual users, and individual computer systems (servers or workstations).

The Windows 2000 Registry also replaces two files that have bad reputations under Windows 3.x. Anyone who has spent time working with Windows 3.x knows about the fun of working with the SYSTEM.INI and WIN.INI files. The WIN.INI file holds Windows environment settings; it changes the way Windows interacts with the user. The SYSTEM.INI file contains hardware and device driver configuration information; it changes the way Windows configures itself during startup. Of course, the distinction between these two files is somewhat blurred (The WIN.INI holds the serial port and printer configuration information, for example).

These two poorly organized, cryptic files held the vast majority of configuration information for the Windows 3.1 system. Every time the user adds an application to Windows 3.1, the application adds its own heading or two and some additional entries to both files. On the other hand, when the user gets rid of an application, the entries stay right there, helping to bloat the INIs. These legacy configuration entries just sort of hang around and slow system performance. Some entries can even cause error messages or, in extreme circumstances, a system crash. Windows 2000 still supports these rather archaic and difficult-to-understand files, for backward compatibility with legacy applications that still use them. However, Windows 2000 prefers that applications use the new Registry.

Note: Windows 2000 copies the contents of SYSTEM.INI and WIN.INI into the Registry whenever possible. The only reason these two files exist is to meet the needs of Windows 3.x applications. You can, in theory, remove both files from your hard drive if you don't have any older applications that use these files. But it's best to leave them as is; they're probably quite small anyway, and WIN.INI in particular likely contains important information even now.

The Registry is a complex database. Windows 2000 can't boot without a clean Registry. Any corruption in this set of files will cause a host of problems even if Windows 2000 does manage to boot. Of course, the fact that you can't edit this database at the DOS prompt is itself a potential problem. (The other side of the coin is that the Windows 2000 Registry Editor, Regedt32 or Regedit, is a lot easier to use than the old Windows 3.x combination of WIN.INI and SYSTEM.INI. To edit or look at the old INI files, use Start, Run, Sysedit.)

Peter's Principle: The Two Registry Editors

There are two Registry Editors: Regedit and Regedt32. Regedt32 is the original Windows 2000 Registry Editor and features some special network-related capabilities such as auditing tools and a Security menu permitting you to control aspects of Registry access and security. You can selectively (or totally) exclude users from modifying the Registry. Regedt32 also includes an older-style multiple document interface, like the one found in Sysedit. What's more, where the newer Regedit features right-click context menus, Regedt32 does not.

continues

> Regedit originally appeared in Windows 95, but it's now also included with Windows 2000. Aside from its more contemporary user interface features, such as the context menus, Regedit includes superior search facilities: Regedt32 limits searches to keys alone; Regedit can search everything—keys, values, entries, and data.

As is so often the case with software, which Registry editor you prefer will likely depend on which one you first learned to use. I choose Regedit for most Registry-editing tasks and use it in this book whenever I demonstrate how to modify or examine the Registry. But feel free to use Regedt32 if you prefer. You'll notice that when describing several of the hands-on examples in this chapter (such as editing a remote Registry) I suggest switching from Regedit to Regedt32, because the latter is the superior tool for these tasks. One minor point: Regedit does not represent all Windows 2000 Registry data types correctly. In particular, the multistring data type shows up in hexadecimal rather than ASCII format.

Working with the Registry

Why should you bother with the Registry? After all, the Control Panel and individual applications enable you to make many changes and adjustments to the ways the operating system and the individual programs behave. In most cases, it's better to look for the standard way to customize some setting rather than working within the Registry.

There are two primary reasons for learning to work with the Registry. First, some useful changes to the operating system's behavior cannot be made any other way than by directly modifying the Registry itself. Second, learning about the Registry increases your understanding of the inner workings of Windows 2000, thus providing ideas that may help you troubleshoot hardware and software problems in the future.

Knowledge of the Registry can be invaluable if you're responsible for supporting your computer yourself. If your computer is part of a company network, however, check with the network administrator before modifying your Registry. Indeed, you may be locked out of making changes to the Registry by the network administrator unless you're granted special privileges or are logged on to your own machine and are posing as the administrator. Each computer's hard drive contains its own Registry file.

If you have the privilege of editing the Registry on your hard drive, you can do the following (among other things):

- Remove the My Computer icon (and other icons) from the desktop.
- Rename or remove the Recycle Bin.
- Adjust the speed at which menus pop out.
- Change the default Explorer icons for EXE, File, Drive, and so on.

These and other aspects of the operating system have been, for one reason or another, hidden from the ordinary user. In this chapter, we'll explore the structure of the Registry. I'll explain the purpose of the various sections and show you how to manipulate the Registry. I'll also illustrate various elements of the Registry with useful examples you can try. You'll doubtless find items you'll want to adjust yourself as you meander through the many megabytes of data within the Registry.

> **Caution:** One warning, however, cannot be repeated often enough. It's possible when working with the Registry to destroy or damage essential startup information, thus causing Windows 2000 to behave strangely or even preventing it from successfully launching. Therefore, when making changes to the Registry, take care that you don't, for example, delete an entire branch or otherwise edit the Registry in unintended ways. Also, make no changes until you've created a safety backup as explained in this chapter.

The Registry Editor, Regedit, features a split window and looks remarkably like the Explorer. Indeed, the two panes serve similar functions in both utilities. On the left side of Regedit window, you see the path, a set of nested keys (like an Explorer path with nested folders) that assist you in locating keys and values within the Registry. In the left pane, you click the plus sign (+) next to a key to expand the display to show its subkeys, just as you would click the plus sign to expand an Explorer folder and display its subfolders. You can also click the minus sign (–) next to a key or subkey to collapse the view of the subkeys it contains. You can click (select and highlight) a subkey from the left pane to see its contents—the name(s) and value(s) in the right pane.

In Regedit's right pane, you see the equivalent of a filename, the name of a particular piece of data. The data is also sometimes referred to as the *value* that's stored in the name. This bifurcation between name and data is hardly limited to Regedit. It appears throughout computer programming and database storage. It's the same distinction found between a variable's (or field's) name and the contents of that variable or field as well as between a specific address in memory and the contents at that memory location. Indeed, a great deal of mental activity, both animal and human, can be divided into these two categories: the distinction between the symbol (name) of something and that something itself.

This arrangement of primary keys (we'll call them *categories*) and subordinate keys that end up pointing to particular data in the Registry permits Windows 2000 to very quickly bounce along the branches down to the correct location to retrieve whatever information it's looking for. This database-optimization technique is essential because the Registry grows and grows and becomes a truly huge database.

Searches of the entire contents of the Registry, piece of data by piece of data (like a text search), would seriously retard Windows 2000's performance. It would be as if you had to look for a file on your hard drive without benefit of the clues you get from folders and subfolders. Without some kind of organization, some tree structure, or some other method of categorization, data management is, to say the least, cumbersome. You end up checking every item in a simple list rather than the far more efficient method of using a path of categories taking you rapidly to the data you're after.

Peter's Principle: Editing the Registry: What If You Make a Mistake?

Windows 2000 stores the current Registry settings for each user in the NTUSER.DAT file found in each user's profile folder. The Default User folder contains the standard Registry entries that Windows 2000 uses to create a new user. Because each user has his or her own personalized copy of the Registry, any mistakes you make while editing the Registry affect only that user. You have several ways to recover from an error in editing. You can just reverse the mistake while still in the Registry Editor. If you make a mistake and can't access the user's account when you try to enter it from the Log On dialog box, you can always log on as the administrator and copy the Registry file for a similar user to the damaged user's profile folder. You can also delete the user and add him or her back, which copies the Default User's Registry to the new profile folder. I suggest, however, that you avoid this delete/re-add approach. Deleting a user can have some serious consequences relating to file and folder ownership. I think the best solution is to substitute somebody else's NTUSER.DAT file. A fourth option is restoring a copy of the damaged Registry file from a backup. You'll make a backup of the Registry, won't you? I show you how to copy the NTUSER.DAT file to a safe location shortly.

Obviously, there's one particular user whose Registry file you'll never want to edit. Because just about every form of Registry access requires an administrator account, damaging the administrator's Registry file (\PROFILES\ADMINISTRATOR) is one good way to lock yourself out of the system. With that in mind, I always make sure that every machine has two users with full administrator rights: the administrator and myself (or a designated representative). Note that \PROFILES is replaced by \DOCUMENTS AND SETTINGS if you did not upgrade from NT4, but instead did a fresh install of Windows 2000.

Technical Note: Recall that the Registry is actually a database made up of several files. Also, as you've seen, the Registry is divided into several sections (HKEY_CURRENT_CONFIG, HKEY_LOCAL_MACHINE, and so on). These various sections are not equally dangerous. If you mess up some of the entries in the HKEY_USERS section, the result is usually relatively harmless. The worst that could probably happen is that a user might not be able to log on. Normally, if the NTUSER.DAT file is corrupt, Windows 2000 merely discards it and creates a new copy from the default NTUSER.DAT file. (The Default User folder—such as C:\WINNT\Profiles\Default User\NTUSER.DAT—contains the standard Registry entries that Windows 2000 uses to create a new user.) If you mess up HKEY_LOCAL_MACHINE, however, you can truly cripple the machine.

Caution: Unlike in Windows 95/98, the version of Regedit that comes with Windows 2000 doesn't provide any form of command-line (that is, DOS) interface. *You can't edit the contents of the Registry without a running copy of Windows 2000.* In addition, the Registry in Windows 95/98 is incompatible with the one in Windows 2000. Don't attempt to use the Windows 95 version of Regedit to modify the Windows 2000 Registry from the command line (from the DOS prompt). You *can* use the Windows 95/98 version of Regedit to edit the Windows 2000 Registry from a remote location in its GUI mode—from within Windows. Likewise, you can use the Windows 2000 version of Regedit to change a Windows 95 Registry.

Knowing that the Registry contains a lot of information and is easy to edit still doesn't tell you what it can do for you. When was the last time you used Explorer to check out your hard drive? I use Explorer a lot because it provides an easy way to find what I need. In turn, the Registry can help you customize Explorer to make it easier to use.

Note: You might want to add Regedit (or Regedt32, if you prefer) to your Start menu before proceeding. It helps to look at the actual Registry entries as you read about them. I also present some exercises that will help you better understand the inner workings of the Registry. See Chapter 5, "Exploring the Interface," if you need information about adding new applications to the Start menu.

A Centralized Database of Setup Information

It's time to take a look at how the Registry is organized. To start Regedit, just open Regedit as you would any other application on the Start menu, assuming you added Regedit to the Start menu as mentioned in the preceding Note (or you can use Start, Run, Regedit). You'll probably get a lot more out of the detailed discussion that follows if you open Regedit now. Working with Regedit to see how Windows 2000 arranges the various entries can make using it a lot easier in an emergency.

Note: Windows 2000 provides a higher level of security than other versions of Windows. You might find that one or more of the Registry entries I describe in this chapter are missing from your Registry display if the network administrator made them inaccessible to you. In fact, the network administrator can make the Registry entirely inaccessible to you if he or she wants to do so. Make sure you have the necessary permissions before you attempt any procedure in this chapter. Note that Regedt32 is the tool of choice for administrators—it has security features missing in Regedit.

The Registry is a single database; however, its data is nonetheless contained in several different files on the hard drive. The primary Registry file, though, is NTUSER.DAT.

I always step lightly when it comes to the Registry. I urge you to back up the Registry before you go any further. To create a copy, follow these steps:

> **Caution:** Regedit is an application designed to assist experienced users in changing Windows 2000 and associated application behavior. Although it enables you to locate important information, enhance system performance, customize many aspects of your OS, and make applications easier to use, it can cause unexpected results when misused. Never edit an entry unless you know what that entry is for. Failure to observe this precaution can result in data loss and even prevent your system from booting the next time you start Windows 2000.

1. Choose Start, Run, Regedit.

2. In Regedit, choose Registry, Export Registry File. You should see an Export Registry File dialog box similar to the one shown in Figure 10.1. You can type any name you want into the Filename box. I selected Regback.

3. Make sure that the All option button is selected in the Export Range group. It's not selected by default, and if you don't select it, only a portion of the Registry will be copied.

FIGURE 10.1

The Export Registry File dialog box enables you to save your current Registry settings.

4. Click the Save button to place a copy of the Registry on disk. The Regback.REG file you just saved now contains a complete copy of your current Registry. This is a text version of your Registry, and it's likely to be larger than Notepad can handle. However, you can view it if you wish using WordPad. (My backup file is 27MB.)

> **Tip:** If you right-click the backup registration file's filename in Explorer, you'll see the Merge option. Choose this and the backup will be merged with the current Registry.

If you experience problems starting Windows 2000—particularly following the installation of a new application or driver, try a partial restore of the Registry. This technique only restores the Registry key HKLM\System\CurrentControlSet. (From here on, HKLM is short for HKEY_LOCAL_MACHINE. You'll also find similar acronyms used for the other major keys in the Registry throughout this chapter.) The rest of the Registry remains untouched. Here's how:

1. Choose Start, Shut Down. Choose Restart and then click OK. (You could also simply turn on the computer's power if it's off.)

2. Press F8 as soon as you see the message Please Select the Operating System to Start.

3. Use the arrow keys to move to and select Last Known Good Configuration; then press Enter.

4. Select the Windows 2000 operating system and then press Enter.

(There is another screen after step 4, the Hardware Profile/Configuration Recovery Menu, where you can choose a recovery Profile if you have more than one.)

An Overview of the Registry

You can use the Regedit utility to view or change the contents of the Registry. Although the Regedit display might seem a bit difficult to understand at first, it really isn't. The major difference between the Registry and the Windows 3.x alternative of SYSTEM.INI and WIN.INI is that the Registry uses a hierarchical (*tree*) organization and plain-English descriptions that you'll find easy to edit and maintain. Also, the Registry, though quite a bit larger, is far more efficiently searched. Every application you add, as well as every new user profile, will add entries to the Registry file, but the file's organization makes it easy for an application to remove the entries when you uninstall it. Even if you install an older application that doesn't understand the Registry, you can still remove its entries with ease.

The Windows 2000 Registry uses five types of entries to maintain its organization: categories, keys, subkeys, names, and data; this organization is similar to the way information is organized in Explorer's view of the files on your hard drive (see Figure 10.2):

• Categories are similar to the drive name (C:\).

• Keys and subkeys are like folders (WINNT) and subfolders (WINNT\SYSTEM32).

• Names are like filenames.

• Values are the data in those "files."

Think of a key as the main heading that tells you what a particular section contains. Looking at all the keys provides an outline for a particular topic. The topics could range from the setup of each drive in the system to the file associations needed to configure the machine. The key at the top of the hierarchy usually contains generic information. Each subkey underneath it provides more detail about that particular topic. Keys always appear on the left side of the Regedit window.

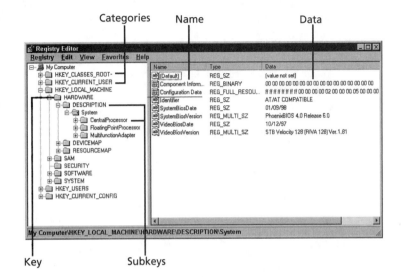

Figure 10.2

Information is stored in the Registry in a way that's similar to the organization of a hard drive.

Underneath subkeys are names that identify individual pieces of data (the values). A value can contain just about anything, but it's usually a single word (or phrase) or a single number. The value for a file association key can tell you which application Windows 2000 will start when you double-click a file that has that extension in Explorer, for example. A value could tell you which interrupt and I/O port settings a piece of hardware uses as well. You'll find the value you need using the keys, but you'll find the actual information you need by reading the names and data. The three types of data are binary, string, and DWORD. Usually, only applications use the binary and DWORD value types, sometimes containing configuration data in a format that can't be understood by humans. Some applications use DWORD or binary values to store data. You might find the score from your last game of FreeCell here, for example. String data (text) provides a lot of information about an application and how it's configured. Hardware usually uses string values as well for interrupt and port information. The name and the data it points to always appear on the right side of the Regedit window.

> **Technical Note:** A *DWORD* (double word) is a space for data that's 4 bytes large. Because of the way computers store information, a space this size permits storage of any number between –2,147,483,648 and +2,147,483,647. Technically, you could say that the Registry also includes some other data types, although some would argue that they aren't really separate "types" so much as variations of the types already mentioned—the REG SZ (actually text) and REG MULTI SZ (multiple lines of text) types, for example.

Key entries also have a superset. I differentiate these particular keys from the rest because they're the major headings in the Registry. During the rest of this discussion, I refer to these special super keys as *categories*. Think of categories as the chapter titles in a book. You need to go to the right chapter before you can find the right type of information. Information in one category might appear in the same order and at the same level in another category. The difference between the two occurs when Windows 2000 uses the entries in one category versus another.

Categories are the five main keys under the My Computer key. Categories divide the Registry into five main areas:

- HKEY_CLASSES_ROOT
- HKEY_CURRENT_USER
- HKEY_LOCAL_MACHINE
- HKEY_USERS
- HKEY_CURRENT_CONFIG

Each category contains a specific type of information. Although Windows 2000 still has to use the infamous SYSTEM.INI and WIN.INI files for antiquated applications, the use of the Registry for all other purposes does reduce the user's workload. Eventually, all applications will use the Registry to store their configuration data. The next few sections of this chapter describe the primary Registry sections (the categories) in detail.

Technical Note: You might be wondering how big your Registry can get, given that installing new applications can add large amounts of data to it. You might also be wondering whether you can you define its size. The answers to these questions are very big and yes. The maximum size is 80% of the paged pool (which itself has an upper limit of 128MB). A *paged pool* is a zone in RAM that, when not needed, is saved to the hard drive. The pool contains system information.

Therefore, the Registry can be 102MB large. By default, the maximum Registry size will be set to 25% of the paged pool. You can specify a different maximum Registry size by locating the key HKEY_LOCAL_MACHINE\SYSTEM\CurrentControlSet\Control and adding a new DWORD name: RegistrySizeLimit. Double-click this new name and, for its data, type in whatever size, in megabytes, you want to specify.

Windows 2000, however, will notice if the Registry is threatening to overflow, and it will warn you with a dialog box that suggests you might want to increase the maximum size in this situation.

A second way to specify the maximum Registry size is to click Start, Settings, Control Panel and then double-click the System icon. On the Advanced tab, click Performance Options, and under Virtual Memory, click Change. At the bottom of this dialog box you'll see the current Registry size and the maximum size. You can edit the maximum size. You should realize, however, that just specifying a maximum size doesn't ensure that the Registry will ever be allowed to grow to that size. Also note that the *minimum* Registry size is 4MB. (Note that you must be logged on as an administrator to change this setting.)

HKEY_CLASSES_ROOT

The HKEY_CLASSES_ROOT category has two distinct types of entries. The first key type (remember, a key is a Regedit topic) is a file extension. Think of all the three-letter extensions you've used, such as DOC and TXT. Windows 2000 still uses them to differentiate one file type from another. It also uses them to associate that file type with a specific action or set of actions. Although you can't do anything with a file that uses the DLL extension, for example, it appears in this list because Windows 2000 needs to associate DLLs with an executable file type. The second entry type is the association itself. The file extension entries normally associate a data file with an application or an executable file with a specific Windows 2000 function. Below the association key are entries for the menus you see when you right-click an entry in Explorer. It also contains keys that determine the type of icon to display and other parameters associated with a particular file type. Figure 10.3 shows the typical HKEY_CLASSES_ROOT organization.

FIGURE 10.3

A typical HKEY_CLASSES_ROOT display. Notice the distinct difference between file extension and file association keys.

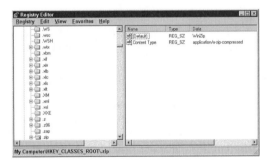

Don't let the deceptively simple appearance of this category fool you; it's one of the truly well-designed areas of the Registry. Let's take an in-depth look at the two more obvious key types. The following sections describe these entries in detail.

> **Tip:** You should always modify your application file entries to make your working environment as efficient as possible. You should never change an executable file association, however. Changing an executable file extension such as DLL could make it hard for Windows 2000 to start your applications, or it could even crash the system.

Special Extension Subkeys

Although some file extensions such as TXT provide a ShellEx subkey, the most common subkey for TXT and DOC items is ShellNew. The term *ShellEx* means "shell extension." I like to think of it as an automated method of extending the functionality of Windows as a whole. When you right-click the desktop and choose the New option from the context menu, all the types of files you can create are the result of shell extensions. Although ShellNew is the most common type of shell extension, a variety of other shell extensions is available. The actual number is limited only by your application vendor. Microsoft Excel provides no less than three different shell extension entries for the XLS file extension, for example.

A *shell extension* is an OLE hook into Windows 2000 (see Chapter 15, "OLE, ActiveX, and DCOM"). Only an application that supports OLE 2 extensions can place a ShellEx key into the Registry; don't add one of these keys on your own. When you see this key, you know that the application provides some type of extended OLE-related functionality. If you double-click a shortcut to a data file that no longer exists, for example, an application with the ShellNew shell extension asks whether you want to create a new file of the same type. (If you look at the values associated with ShellNew, there's always a NullFile entry that tells the shell extension what type of file to create.)

> **Tip:** Sometimes a file type won't appear on the context menu even though the application provides support for it. Most of the time, it happens with 16-bit applications that don't install correctly. You can use the shell extension behavior to create new files as if the context menu entry did exist. All you need to do is create a temporary file, place a shortcut to it on your desktop, and erase the temporary file. (Make certain that the application provides a ShellNew shell extension before you do this.) Whenever you double-click the shortcut, your application creates a new file for you. This behavior also works if you place the file shortcut in the Start Menu folder.

The Registry also has other, more generic shell extensions. The * extension has a generic ShellEx subkey, for example. Below this, you'll see a PropertySheetHandler key and an all-digit key that looks like some kind of secret code: {1F2E5C40-9550-11CE-99D2-00AA006E086C}. Actually, the key is a secret code. It's a reference identifier for the DLL (a type of application) that takes care of the * extension. As you can see, shell extensions are a powerful addition to the Windows Registry. You should never change or delete shell extensions; let each application take care of them for you. OLE 1 and 2 are, like Windows 2000 3.x, essentially ancient references.

HKEY_CURRENT_USER

The HKEY_CURRENT_USER category contains a lot of "soft" settings for your machine. These soft settings tell how to configure the desktop and the keyboard. It also contains color settings and the configuration of the Start menu. All user-specific settings appear in this category, as well as settings for installed applications.

The HKEY_CURRENT_USER category is an alias of a corresponding section in the HKEY_USERS area of the Registry database. When a user logs off, Windows 2000 saves all the settings to the user's Registry file.

This is the area where Windows 2000 obtains new setting information and stores any changes you make. As you can see in Figure 10.4, the keys within the HKEY_CURRENT_USER category are pretty self-explanatory in most cases. All the entries adjust some type of user-specific setting, but nothing that affects a global element such as a device driver. It's theoretically possible for drivers to maintain user-specific settings. This isn't done very often, but there's no reason it cannot be done. An example would be printer setup, which is maintained by a function provided by the printer driver. The dialog box for setup is also provided by the printer driver.

FIGURE 10.4

*The HKEY_
CURRENT_USER
category contains
all user-specific
settings.*

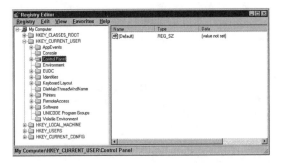

> **Note:** Windows 2000 uses a common setup for all users. Therefore, the HKEY_CURRENT_USER settings automatically reflect the default setting in the HKEY_USERS section of the Registry. See the section titled "HKEY_USERS" for more details on these settings.

AppEvents

Everyone likes to add a few sounds to his or her system to make it more interesting. The AppEvents key defines these sounds in a number of ways. Take a look at the AppEvents subkeys. This key has two subkeys: EventLabels and Schemes. The EventLabels key holds a list of events. Each event key contains the long name of a sound event. The EmptyRecycleBin event, for example, uses Empty Recycle Bin as a long name. This is what Windows displays in the dialog box you use to set the sound value.

> **Tip:** This Registry entry provides the only way you can change the strings displayed in the Sounds Properties dialog box. You might want to use this option after changing the name of the Recycle Bin or other Windows components.

The Schemes key is also one you'll probably want to explore. It has three subkeys. The Names key's subkeys hold the full names of the various sound schemes you might have defined. The Apps key contains major subkeys for each kind of application that defines special sounds. The default sounds are the beeps and other general Windows noises you hear on a daily basis. If you look at the values for each of the minor keys, you would see the name of a sound file. Finally, there's a NewSchemes category, evidently intended to hold any additional default schemes that make it into the final version of Windows 2000.

Console

Console applications require a DOS prompt to work. A DOS window requires settings to work, just like any other part of Windows 2000 does. When you change the default DOS window settings, the changed settings appear under the Console key of the Registry.

Control Panel

The Control Panel key is probably the most easily understood Registry key. Figure 10.5 shows all the subkeys this key contains. As you can see, the Control Panel key doesn't contain subkeys for each icon in the control, but it does contain keys for all the icons that permit user-specific settings.

FIGURE 10.5

The Control Panel key contains subkeys for every user-specific feature on the Control Panel.

The following list describes these subkeys in more detail:

- Accessibility. This subkey contains all the settings for the accessibility features, such as StickyKeys and a high-contrast monitor. You can find a complete description of these features in Chapter 16, "Exploiting Your Software."

- Appearance. This subkey contains the current display's color settings. It includes both a text description and the custom colors. This value doesn't include the actual color values. Below this key is the Schemes subkey. It contains the text descriptions and actual color values for all the color schemes you've defined.

> **Tip:** If you want to share your color schemes with someone else, you can export this key using the same procedure you use to save the Registry. Instead of saving the entire Registry, save only the Schemes branch. Be sure that your Schemes key is selected (highlighted); then from Regedit in the Registry menu, choose Export Registry File and make sure the Selected Branch option button is active (has a black dot in it). When the other user imports your partial REG file, he or she will have the same color schemes you do, but none of the user's other settings will be affected.

- Colors. This subkey contains a list of object types and their associated colors. Windows 2000 uses these settings to determine the colors used for all the standard Windows elements displayed. Notice the three numbers in most entries in the Data column. These are the RGB values specifying a color by its amount of Red, Green, and Blue content.

> **Tip:** The Colors subkey settings provide a level of flexibility you can't get using the standard Display Properties dialog box. Clicking the button displays the 3D object settings, for example. These settings don't provide the same precise control as the button values in this key.

- Current. You'll find the current scheme setting here. This entry will tell you which scheme Windows is currently using for user settings.
- Custom Colors. The values of any custom colors you define appear here. This entry might not appear in the Registry, depending on the display adapter you're using and its capabilities.
- Desktop. All your desktop settings appear in the values of this key. It includes the current wallpaper, background, and screen saver settings.
- Don't Load. This subkey key lists any icons that are not to be displayed in the Control Panel (.CPL is short for Control Panel).
- Input Method. This subkey key contains definitions of any hot key combinations you've defined to switch between input locales (English versus, say, Greek). This is a feature of the Keyboard applet in Control Panel.
- International. This subkey key contains the current country code.
- IOProcs. Leave this particular setting alone. It identifies the DLL Windows 2000 uses for some types of input and output.
- Keyboard. This subkey contains all your keyboard settings. It includes the amount of delay between key repeats and the speed at which Windows accepts input. You might not find this entry in some cases. Windows appears to add it if you modify the keyboard settings or use any of the keyboard-related accessibility features.

- Microsoft Input Devices. At this time, this subkey defines special mouse behavior when used with Internet Explorer or Microsoft PhotoDraw.

- Mouse. This subkey contains the standard mouse settings, not the Accessibility mouse settings. It determines how the mouse reacts when you're using a standard setup.

- Patterns. Windows uses this area to store all the desktop patterns you define on the Background page of the Display Properties dialog box.

- Power Config. Here are your specifications for power savings, such as letting your hard drive sleep after a certain amount of inactivity.

- ScreenSaver. Each screen saver you load as part of the Windows 2000 installation makes an entry in this area. It stores whatever settings it needs to display properly. In most cases, you'll find it easier to modify the screen saver settings through the Display Properties dialog box; there doesn't appear to be any "hidden" settings for the default screen savers provided with Windows. You might find some settings for non-Windows screen savers.

- Sound. Here you'll find the sound settings, such as extended sound and beep. This area doesn't contain the names of the WAV files associated with specific system events.

- Sounds. The name of the Sound Scheme is stored here.

Environment

The Environment key contains the DOS environment settings. The data is available via a USERPROFILE path. It uses these values when you start a DOS session. Windows applications can request this information as well.

EDUC

The EDUC key contains information about various typefaces for supporting various languages, if available on your machine. For example, there is a Japanese EDUC, and a separate definition for Chinese.

Identities

This location holds the Identities feature new in Windows 2000. See Chapter 21, "Outlook Express," for a description of this feature.

Keyboard Layout

The Keyboard Layout Registry key provides information about the keyboard currently attached to the machine. It doesn't really change from user to user unless one user needs to use a different language or keyboard layout. The Preload key under the Keyboard section reflects the different languages in use. The Substitutes key reflects the keyboard layout. You could use English (United States) as a language and English (Dvorak) as a layout, for example. The `Toggle` key tells you which control key combination you can use to switch between languages.

If you have added other keyboard languages, you'll see an `IMEtoggle` key as well.

Peter's Principle: Using Two Keyboard Layouts

I ran into an interesting situation the other day. Two friends were using the same machine. One uses the Dvorak layout, and the other uses the standard layout. Windows 2000 enables you to install multiple languages and switch between them using the International icon on the taskbar, but you can't switch between different layouts of the same language. So, how do you get around this?

Start by installing two languages using the Standard Keyboard dialog box. Make certain that the languages are at least compatible. To make life simple, I installed English (United States) using the standard layout and English (British) using the Dvorak layout. If you look at the HKEY_CURRENT_USER, Keyboard Layout, Preload key, you will notice two subkeys. The value for one is 00000409 (United States), and the value for the other is 00000809 (British).

Look at the Substitutes key. You'll see a subkey for 00000809. The value in this key reads 00020409. If you look up this value in the HKEY_LOCAL_MACHINE, System, CurrentControlSet, Control, Keyboard Layouts, 00020409 key, you'll see that you're using the standard Dvorak keyboard KBD driver. (Your key might read 00010409; 00020409 is for United States-International.)

The only thing left to do is change the International icon list so that it matches what the machine actually has installed. If you look at it right now, it says that you have an English (United States) and an English (British) keyboard setup installed. What you really have is an English (Dvorak) keyboard installed. You need to look at the HKEY_LOCAL_MACHINE, System, CurrentControlSet, Control, NLS., Locale key. Find the 00000809 value and change it from British to Dvorak. Close Regedit to make sure that the change is recorded.

Network

Unfortunately, most of the Network key's contents are network-specific. Essentially, this key provides the user-specific network information your machine needs. In fact, if you are using Windows 2000 on a standalone desktop machine unconnected to a network, this key won't even be in your Registry at all.

Printers

This key contains data about any printer(s) available to your user profile. It includes information about drivers and default attributes you've selected.

RemoteAccess

You might not find the RemoteAccess key in your Registry. It depends on what features you installed with Windows 2000's Setup utility. Within the key itself is an area code value and a DWORD configuration value for the Make New Connection Wizard.

Below this key, you'll find one subkey that holds the addresses you define. Each address you define has one binary value. These values include all the configuration information for that address. Obviously, you won't want to edit this value outside the Dial-Up Networking application.

Software

The Software Registry key should contain configuration information for some of your applications. The SSC section contains information related to the viewers. The Microsoft section contains keys for a variety of applications, regardless of whether you have them installed.

The Registry provides the Software key and a similar key in HKEY_USERS to replace many of the entries you used to have in WIN.INI and SYSTEM.INI. The hierarchical structure of this key makes it easy to remove application-specific information from your Windows 2000 installation. Of particular interest is the HKEY_LOCAL_MACHINE\SOFTWARE\ Microsoft\Windows NT\CurrentVersion key, which contains the user's name and company information. Applications look at this entry during installation. This is the only place you can change this information in Windows 2000. If you need to change the username for software installation purposes, this is the place to do it.

UNICODE Program Groups

Anyone who works with Windows 2000 for very long soon realizes that it supports Unicode at the lowest level. What exactly is Unicode? It's an expansion of the older ASCII code. ASCII characters were represented by a code number ranging from 0 to 255 (a single byte), but Unicode is the new standard, and it uses 2 bytes per character. This vastly increases the amount of code numbers, thus allowing Unicode to include languages such as Chinese that have thousands of characters. This particular Registry entry identifies program groups that use Unicode entries rather than the older ASCII 8-bit character codes.

Volatile Environment

The Volatile Environment area identifies the location of user application data and the name of the current machine. It's called a *volatile environment* because the settings will either become permanent or Windows 2000 will disregard them the next time you boot. Permanent settings are written to another area of the Registry.

HKEY_LOCAL_MACHINE

The HKEY_LOCAL_MACHINE category centers its attention on the computer's hardware. This includes the drivers and configuration information required to run the hardware. Every piece of hardware appears somewhere in this section of the Registry. If a piece of hardware doesn't appear here, Windows 2000 can't use it, even if the hardware is physically installed on your machine. (HKEY_LOCAL_MACHINE also includes software information.)

A lot of subtle information about your hardware is stored in the HKEY_LOCAL_MACHINE category. This category contains all the hardware-configuration information about your machine, for example. It also provides a complete listing of the device drivers and their revision levels. This section might even contain the revision information for the hardware itself. Windows 2000 stores that difference in the Registry.

The HKEY_LOCAL_MACHINE category does contain some software-specific information of a global nature. A 32-bit application stores the location of its Setup and Format Table (SFT) here, for example. This is a file the application uses during installation. Some applications also use it during a setup modification. Applications such as Word store all their setup information in SFTs. The only application information that does appear here is global configuration specific, such as the SFT. The following sections describe each key in detail.

> **Tip:** Some changes you might make to HKEY_LOCAL_MACHINE, such as ACLs (Access Control Lists, a security feature that specifies who has permission to access an object), will be lost the next time you boot your computer. Parts of the LOCAL_MACHINE section of the Registry are re-created by Windows 2000 at boot, and editing of them is therefore lost. Other sections of LOCAL_MACHINE are not reconstructed at boot. Changes to the HKLM\Software section, for example, will survive a reboot.

Hardware

Unlike Windows 95, where you can safely ignore the Hardware Registry key, Windows 2000 uses this key to store everything it needs to know about your hardware—the physical device, not the drivers that we'll discuss in a few moments. This includes everything from the processors your machine uses to the devices attached to the disk drive controllers. The following paragraphs describe the major entries in the Hardware key in detail:

- Description. One of the few Registry areas shared by Windows 95 and Windows 2000 is the Description subkey. Its primary function is to list the communications ports, processor types, and any floating-point processors attached to the machine. This key doesn't contain any actual configuration information—no information you would want to change, that is.

- Devicemap. This is another subkey the two operating systems share, but you'll find that the way they use this key is quite different. The Windows 2000 version of the Registry places an entry here for each device in your machine that maps it in one of three ways to the system. The first entry type points to the device entry itself. In fact, the name actually starts with the word Device, like this: \Device\Video1. These are devices that don't require additional definition before Windows 2000 can use them. A second type of entry points to another place in the Registry. Its data begins with the word REGISTRY, like this: \REGISTRY\Machine\System\ ControlSet001\Service. You'll find this kind of entry attached to display adapters and mouse devices, both of which require additional drivers to do their work. Finally, the third type of entry is SCSI specific. It maps a controller to each drive in your system. The mapping can get quite complex and depends on what kind of adapter you're using, so I'm not going to get specific here. The one interesting point about this particular entry is that you'll see it applied to some types of complex IDE controllers as well. Although it's an IDE controller, Windows 2000 still uses the SCSI keyword.

- Resourcemap. Every device on your system requires specific resources to work. The entries in this section talk about those resources. Unfortunately, most of this is setting information that uses binary values. Most of the settings deal with the various device modes. A serial port supports both raw and transmitted modes under Windows 2000, for example. You probably won't be able to gather much useful information about your system here. The one interesting entry you'll find in this section contains the HAL settings.

SAM

This entry holds Security Accounts Manager (SAM) data. It is the local user account authentication database. It can be empty if the feature is not in use.

Security

The Security Registry key is network specific. Refer to your network manuals for additional information. As a general rule, it contains pointers to files holding account and other network security-specific information. In some cases (usually with peer-to-peer networks), you won't see anything here, even if you have a network connected to your machine.

Software

The Software Registry key contains device driver and global application information. Notice that the subkeys include a variety of vendor-specific information.

One of the interesting subkeys is Classes. Opening this key reveals a list of file extensions and associations just like the list in HKEY_CLASSES_ROOT. The purpose behind this set of keys is totally different, however. Windows 2000 uses this list to locate application- or device driver–specific files instead of creating links for Explorer or providing

OLE configuration information. Changing any of these keys won't affect your Explorer display. Unfortunately, it might affect how some of your applications work. The bottom line is that you should not change any of these settings unless you have a good reason to do so and know exactly how the change will affect your setup. (Technically, HKEY_CLASSES_ROOT is an alias of HKLM\Software\Classes; they're the same thing essentially. The HKLM will be a superset of HKCR.)

Unless you have a Microsoft mouse, you'll probably have a mouse-specific entry—even if your mouse doesn't provide Windows 2000–specific software. Installing a Logitech mouse adds a Logitech key that provides mouse setup information as well as the driver version, for example. Usually, the key provides values that determine which buttons are assigned to various mouse functions.

> **Tip:** Using the Registry to edit a hardware configuration setting almost always gives you more control over all the features of a peripheral than adjusting the more limited Control Panel settings. What if you want to gain some additional control over your three-button Logitech mouse, for example? The default setup program enables you to assign a left- or a right-handed setup to the mouse. What if you want to exchange the right and middle button functions, essentially creating a two-button mouse? You can do so by transposing the MappingButton2 and MappingButton3 Registry values, even though the Control Panel's configuration utility doesn't provide the means to do that.

The Microsoft section of the Software key provides some useful information as well. One of these keys is the New Users Settings key. Most 32-bit applications and some 16-bit applications can provide an entry in this area. A new user inherits these settings when you set up a new logon on the machine. In essence, this key contains the initial global settings everyone uses with this application (at least until they customize their setup). This key also provides the location of shared tools and any global network settings required to make the application work.

If you install any applications that support open database connectivity (ODBC), all those settings appear under this key. ODBC is Microsoft's method of enabling you to access information in foreign data formats. Its original main purpose was to allow access to mainframe databases, but you'll find it used to access other sources of information, including those commonly found on a PC. Most programmers look at ODBC now as a method for generalizing access to any kind of database. You'll also see the 32-bit ODBC settings here. The strange thing is that they aren't identified using separate keys, even though the 32-bit settings appear as a separate icon in the Control Panel. Every ODBC connection and its configuration appears under the ODBC\ODBCINST.INI key. The two important values are the name of the ODBC driver and its version. Most 32-bit drivers include "32" somewhere in the filename. This enables you to separate the 32-bit drivers from the 16-bit drivers in this area.

The SCC key contains information about the viewers, if you installed them. Otherwise, you won't see this key. At first glance, you might not think this key has anything worthwhile to see. The bottom of the hierarchy has two keys that both use descriptive value entry names, such as Element 1. If you double-click one of these entries, however, you'll find the name of the DLL that controls it embedded in the binary data that each value contains.

One entry you might find here that you won't find in a Windows 95 Registry is a Windows 3.1 Migration Status key. Under this key are two entries: IniFiles and REG.DAT. The first key tells Windows 2000 whether it has taken all the INI file data and placed it in the Registry. The second key determines whether all the Windows 3.x Registry data was incorporated into the Registry.

System

The last Registry key in the HKEY_LOCAL_MACHINE category is also the most destructive when edited incorrectly. This section is a lot more complicated in Windows 2000 than the one you'll find in Windows 95, because Windows 2000 has security and multiuser constraints to worry about. However, Windows 2000 does offer the same flexibility through Plug and Play that Windows 95 does; therefore, everything about peripherals doesn't have to be defined as part of the setup for each device.

> **Caution:** Watch out! A bad entry in any value under the System key can kill your installation.

The main purpose of the System section is device control. Complex devices require additional information to make them work. That's what you'll find in part in this subkey. Remember the Registry value I told you about as part of the Devicemap key? The values in that section appear as keys here. Each one of those device maps appears in this section along with the current device map—the one you're using right this second.

Obviously, the System key has other types of information, too. Microsoft split these control set keys into four categories: Control, Enum, Hardware Profiles, and Services. Take a look at the Control key first. It contains all the subkeys that change the way the user reacts to the system. (You may see more than one control set.)

> **Caution:** Exploring the System key part of the Registry is somewhat risky. Some settings won't harm your system much; they might just change the text in a list box or under an icon. Other settings will damage your Windows 2000 installation beyond repair, and still others will prevent access to your system. Wandering through this section and seeing what will happen when you change a setting is one sure way to make your system unusable. Always make a backup of your Registry before you make any change to this section. Alternatively, you can also be safe by using Regedt32 rather than Regedit for explorations into this kind of dangerous territory. Choose Read-Only Mode in Regedt32's Options menu.

One of the keys you'll see under the Control key is the Nls (national language support) key. Remember the keyboard setting I mentioned before? This is where all the language settings come from. If you had the correct driver, you could add support for Martian by changing the value of one of these keys. The network administration–specific keys appear under the Control key as well. One of the first keys you'll see is the computer name used to log on to the network. Several subkeys give the advanced user an opportunity to tune system performance.

The third subkey under the System key is Hardware Profiles. You'll find one or more sets of configuration keys under this key that are identified with numbers. Along with these configuration keys is a Current key that contains the current configuration. When you select a hardware profile in the Control Panel, what you're really doing is copying the contents of one of these numbered keys into the Current key, thus changing the configuration of your system. Each of the configuration keys contains the setup information for the hardware you're using. You'll find the resolution of your display adapter here, for example. You won't find a complete hardware listing in this area; only the hardware with configuration settings appears in this section. For most people, that includes their display adapter and not much more.

The Services subkey is full of keys and data, and appears to cover everything within a Control Set. The Disk and MountedDevices entries include information on hard drives and partitions.

HKEY_USERS

The HKEY_USERS category contains a listing for all the users of this particular Registry file. If you change the appropriate section in HKEY_USERS, Windows 2000 will instantly change the mirror section in the Registry named HKEY_CURRENT_USER. Also, when the user logs off, these settings will be written to that user's NTUSER.DAT file. When the user logs on the next time, the settings will be there. It's very interesting to note that Windows 2000 services that are logged on have profiles loaded. Also, note that the .Default settings in HKEY_USERS are not the default settings for new users on the system. The .Default section in HKEY_USERS is data about what the operating system uses when no one is logged on. Change, say, the background entry in Default User and when you log off to the logon screen (press Ctrl+Alt+Del and then choose Log Off), the screen background will be set to whatever you indicated in this .Default section of HKEY_USERS.

Windows 2000 does not actually maintain multiple Registries in a multiuser configuration. The NTUSER.DAT file described earlier in this chapter, in combination with the folders listed by username in the WINNT\Profiles directory, collectively make up each user's profile in Windows 2000. Technically, the NTUSER.DAT file is known as a Registry *hive*. A hive is a file containing one or more Registry sections. (Remember that although the Registry should be thought of as a single database, its data is nonetheless contained in several different files on the hard drive. Also note that if you installed Windows 2000 directly rather than upgrading on top of an NT4 installation, you'll see a \Documents and Settings path rather than \Profiles.)

When a user logs on to Windows 2000, his or her hive is loaded into the HKEY_USERS section of the Registry, and that hive data is used to build the environment in which that user works. (The user's choice of keypress repeat speed, for example, is an aspect of that user's environment.) When the user next logs off of Windows 2000, the user's configuration information in HKEY_USERS is then saved to his or her profile or to his or her NTUSER.DAT Registry hive.

If you use the Regedt32 utility, you can load a hive for a user that is not currently logged on to the system. This way, you can change settings for a user who's not around. On Windows 2000 Professional, 10 is the default number of user profiles allowed on the system. After that, Windows 2000 starts deleting them based on how long it has been since a particular user last logged on.

Figure 10.6 shows a setup that includes the default and one user-specific key. Each user entry contains precisely the same keys, but the values will, of course, differ from user to user. When a user logs on to the network, Windows 2000 copies all the information in his or her profile to the HKEY_CURRENT_USER area of the Registry. When the user logs off or shuts down, Windows 2000 updates the information in his or her specific section from the HKEY_CURRENT_USER category.

Figure 10.6

Windows 2000 creates one entry in the HKEY_USERS category for each user who logs on to the machine.

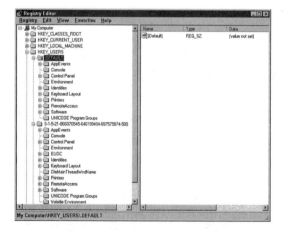

Where does the original information for the system defaults come from? The Registry contains one entry called .Default. (Notice the period in front of the keyname. Default without a period is a username.)

A default user profile is stored on the hard drive in Winnt\Profiles\DefaultUser\ NTUSER.DAT. When a new user logs on for the first time, this file is copied to a directory with that user's logon name, such as C:\WINNT\Profiles\YourLogonName. This data is then also loaded into the HKEY_USER section of the Registry because it has now become the basis for that user's profile.

The subkeys and values under the `.Default` key are echoed in the `HKEY_CURRENT_USER` category, so I won't discuss the settings again here. (The initial logon does more work than create a simple Registry entry, but this chapter doesn't cover that.) You should follow a few Registry-related tips when setting up your network:

- Always configure the workstation for the minimum possible access rights for the `.Default` user. This enables you to create new users without the risk of circumventing network security.

- Make a backup of all the `NTUSER.DAT` files for safety, in case you have problems later.

HKEY_CURRENT_CONFIG

The `HKEY_CURRENT_CONFIG` category is the simplest part of the Registry. It contains two major keys: `Software` and `System`. `HKEY_CURRENT_CONFIG` is where hardware profile information is stored. Hardware profiles are created in the Control Panel's System applet (Hardware tab) and are similar to user profiles, permitting a single machine to be configured different ways based on who logs on or which hardware profile is selected. After a hardware profile is created, it describes the drivers and services available to the machine. You can select among existing hardware profiles each time Windows 2000 starts running. When you reboot the machine, you're offered the choice of profiles after you see the Last Known Good message, but before the cyan screen shows up. You select the hardware profile, and Windows 2000 reacts by loading its various drivers and services. The differences between normal hardware settings and any custom hardware profiles are stored in `HKEY_CURRENT_CONFIG`. For details on the purpose and employment of hardware profiles, see "Peter's Principle: Using Hardware Profiles" at the end of Chapter 22, "Mobile Computing."

Essentially, these entries are used by the GDI API (described later) to configure the display and printer. (You might find other devices here, such as scanners, in some cases.) In most cases, the `Software` key won't contain any entries unless your display adapter or printer requires special software to do its jobs, or unless some simple Internet settings are required (such as whether autodialing is enabled).

The `Services` subkey under the `System` key contains the current settings for the system's video. In most cases, you'll find the display resolution and number of bits per pixel here. The bits per pixel value determines the number of colors available. For example, 4 bits per pixel provides 16 colors, and 8 bits per pixel provides 256 colors.

My Favorite Registry Tweaks

Here are some cool tricks you might want to try out. But remember, use the Regedit program's Registry, Export Registry File feature before messing around in the Registry.

Some changes you make to the Registry require rebooting before you will see the effect. This is because Windows 2000 loads that information (such as Recycle Bin's name) during startup. Other information is looked up as needed (for example, file associations such as the .ASC extension for launching Word or the icon used for My Computer on the desktop). In the case of file extensions, the change will happen right away because Windows 2000 forces a refresh when you make that change. The other kind of Registry editing—changing the My Computer icon for instance—only requires that you refresh the desktop. Click the desktop (in a blank area on your wallpaper, not on any icons or within any windows); then press F5. If you don't see an effect after modifying the Registry, try pressing F5 before going to the trouble to reboot.

Speed Menus

Now I'll show you how to make a change to the Registry to modify the speed at which menus appear. This option isn't normally available from the Control Panel or, indeed, anywhere other than the Registry. To observe the default menu speed, click the Start button and then move your mouse pointer up to Programs. A second menu pops out. Move your pointer to Accessories on this second menu, and a third menu pops out. As shipped from the factory, Windows 2000 inserts a 400 millisecond delay (about a half second) before a submenu pops out. Do you want these menus to pop out instantly? Here's how to make it happen:

1. Start Regedit. Your target is HKEY_CURRENT_USER\Control Panel\Desktop. Click the Desktop subkey so that its folder icon changes into an open folder. In the right pane, you should see the settings for various Control Panel options.

2. If you don't see a name under the (selected) Desktop subkey named MenuShowDelay, you'll have to create it. To add a new item "name" and its associated data to the list of names for the Desktop subkey in the right pane, right-click the Desktop icon in the left pane so that it's highlighted. (You can also right-click any empty part of the right-hand pane.) A menu appears.

3. Click New and then click String Value.

4. After you choose the New, String Value command, a highlighted new entry will appear in the right pane. Type in MenuShowDelay as the name of your item. Click some other entry or the blank background of the Registry to "set" the new item. This removes the focus from the new item (it's no longer highlighted.)

5. Now you want to give it a value (data). Select MenuShowDelay by right-clicking it to highlight it and display the shortcut menu; then choose Modify (or just double-click the name). An Edit String dialog box appears.

6. In the Value Data text box, enter a number between 0 and 1,000 (it's in milliseconds)—in other words, no delay at all, up to a delay of a full second. (Don't use quotation marks around your number. They'll automatically be inserted because you've stated that this is a string value. The word *string* is used in computerese to mean text, and text variable values are always surrounded by quotation marks.)

7. Type in 0 if you want the menus to really pop out instantly.

8. Click the OK button to close the Edit String window.

9. Shut down Windows 2000 and restart it to see the effect.

You've now told Windows 2000 how quickly you want pop-up menus to appear. Anytime you want to adjust this setting, go back into Regedit and right-click `MenuShowDelay` and then choose Modify. Some people find a zero setting causes alarm; I find it's rapidity a welcome feature.

Auto Logon

Perhaps you would prefer not having to log on manually (pressing Ctrl+Alt+Del and typing in your password each time you turn on your computer), but before the boot process lets you in to Windows. (I'm assuming that you didn't choose the Auto Logon option during setup.) Here's how to force Windows 2000 to log you on automatically.

Note that anyone who turns on your computer will also be logged on automatically—no password will be required of him or her either. Note also that an enterprising user who knows where to look in the Registry can read your password, as explained a bit later. Therefore, this trick is intended for those who work alone in a small office or at home, or who wantonly disregard security fears:

1. To force an automatic logon, locate this key:

   `HKEY_ LOCAL_MACHINE\SOFTWARE\Microsoft\Windows NT\CurrentVersion\Winlogon`

   Look for the entry named `AutoAdminLogon`. If it doesn't exist, create it.

2. Double-click the word `AutoAdminLogon` and change its value from 0 to 1.

3. Right-click a blank area in the right pane and choose New, String Value. Give it the name `DefaultPassword`.

4. Double-click the word `DefaultPassword` and type in your password, whatever it is. If you use an empty (blank) password, that's fine, just don't enter anything in the `DefaultPassword` field, although do create the new name `DefaultPassword`.

5. Close the Registry and shut down Windows 2000.

When you restart your computer, you'll see Windows 2000 go through the usual startup process, except it will not request that you press Ctrl+Alt+Del or enter your password to log on.

If you've made an error when typing your password into the Registry, Windows 2000 will report that it cannot log you on automatically because the password is incorrect. You'll then be given a chance to type in the correct password. Restart Regedit and again locate the `DefaultPassword` entry. Double-click the word `DefaultPassword` and type in the correct password this time.

To restore the default startup process, just right-click `DefaultPassword` and choose Delete. Then right-click `AutoAdminLogon`, select Modify, and change 1 to 0.

> **Tip:** If you hold down the Shift key while the machine is logging on, you'll stop the autologon process and the familiar dialog box will display.

Customized Startup

Here's how to display a custom message box to anyone logging on to your computer—a message they cannot ignore because they have to click the OK button to close it:

1. In the same location as described for the preceding tip (HKEY_LOCAL_MACHINE\ SOFTWARE\Microsoft\Windows 2000\CurrentVersion\Winlogon) locate the entry named LegalNoticeCaption.

2. Double-click the word LegalNoticeCaption and type in whatever you want to appear as the heading in the title bar of your message box (perhaps WARNING!).

3. Locate the entry called LegalNoticeText.

4. Double-click the word LegalNoticeText and type in the body of your message (perhaps Unless you are authorized to use this computer, access is forbidden!).

Next time you run Windows 2000 on this computer, you'll see the message box displayed at startup. To reverse this, double-click the words LegalNoticeCaption and LegalNoticeText and delete the text from both entries.

Renaming the Recycle Bin

For some reason, you're permitted to rename the Inbox, the Network Neighborhood, and even the My Computer desktop icons. Just right-click one of these icons on the desktop and then choose Rename and type the new name. However, you aren't allowed to rename the Recycle Bin. Odd isn't it? Registry to the rescue.

To rename the Recycle Bin desktop icon, follow these steps:

1. Start the Registry Editor. Make sure, by clicking it, that the top item in the left pane, My Computer, is selected.

2. Use the Edit, Find command (or press Ctrl+F), type Recycle Bin in the Find What text box, and click Find Next. Your first hit on this target should be the path HKEY_CLASSES_ROOT\CLSID\ followed by a long string of numbers. In the right pane, you should see (Default) in the Name column and Recycle Bin Cleaner in the Data column. Press Ctrl+F for your second hit, which is the Recycle Bin proper.

3. Double-click LocalizedString. Notice that at the very end of this file path is the name Recycle Bin.

4. Change the Value Data text box entry in the Edit String window to a suitable (and refined) term of your choice for this dumpster; then click OK. Don't change the rest of this string—just change the name Recycle Bin at the very end of the string.

5. Now click your desktop or wallpaper to set the focus to the desktop; then press F5 to make the change take effect.

6. Change the InfoTip (tooltip) text if you wish, too.

While we're at it, here's how to change the icons used to represent an empty and a full Recycle Bin. Search for "Empty" until you locate something like this:

```
Empty "C:\WINNT\SYSTEM32\shell32.dll,31"
Full "C:\WINNT\SYSTEM32\shell32.dll,21"
```

> **Note:** If you don't find these entries in your Registry, check to be sure you've checked the Keys, Values, and Data check boxes in the Find window. Also, uncheck the Match Whole String Only check box. Instead of C:\WINNT, you might find %SYSTEMROOT% (the ordinary default for %SYSTEMROOT% is WINNT).

The tags Empty and Full describe the locations of the two icons representing the two states of the Recycle Bin. In the preceding example, the icon for the empty Recycle Bin is the 31st icon in the file C:\WINNT\SYSTEM32\SHELL32.DLL. (Any DLL or EXE file can contain icons.) To substitute a different icon, right-click the word empty and choose Modify. Now type in the path name of any icon file, even a BMP file (as long as its dimensions are 32×32 pixels, so that it will look right). If you're going to use a BMP file whose dimensions are larger than the dimensions of an icon, Windows will resize it and the result may not look nearly as good. Also, this resizing slows things down.

Removing the Recycle Bin

The Recycle Bin—there it sits on your desktop. You can't delete it. Some people like a clean, blank desktop with no distractions; others don't like the way the titles under some icons mess up their wallpaper. Whatever your reason, if you want to get rid of Recycle Bin's icon, here's how:

1. First, locate this branch in the Registry:

   ```
   HKEY_LOCAL_MACHINE\SOFTWARE\Microsoft\Windows\CurrentVersion\Explorer\
   Desktop\NameSpace
   ```

2. Click the plus sign beside the NameSpace subkey icon to display the subkey it holds. These subkeys represent the "permanent" icons on your desktop.

3. Click any of the folders under the NameSpace folder to see the name of the icon it represents on your desktop. One of them will be Recycle Bin.

4. At this point, you might want to save this particular branch of the Registry, just so you can restore the icons later if you wish. Click the NameSpace folder icon to highlight it. Click the Registry menu and then choose Export Registry File. Click the Selected Branch option so that you don't save the entire Registry. Then save it to disk.

5. If you want to be permanently rid of the Recycle Bin icon, right-click its folder icon (the one you located in step 3) and choose Delete from the pop-up menu.

To see the effect of some of the changes we're making to the Registry in this chapter, you must restart Windows. In this case, however, you can just click the desktop (to make it the "active" element in Windows, the element with the focus) and then press F5 to refresh it. You'll see the effect immediately.

To restore one or more of the icons removed using this technique, start the Registry Editor and from the Registry menu, choose Import Registry File. Load back in the REG file of this branch that you had previously saved, as described earlier.

Suppressing Animation

If you don't like the way Windows 2000 expands an application when you click it in the taskbar and visually reduces it back to the taskbar when you minimize a window, here's how to turn this animation off (and thereby speed up screen redraw):

1. Start the Regedit program and then scroll down until you find HKEY_CURRENT_ USER\Control Panel\Desktop\WindowMetrics.

2. Right-click a blank area in the right pane and, from the menu that appears, choose New String Value.

3. Type in MinAnimate and press Enter.

4. Right-click the MinAnimate entry and select Modify.

5. In the Value Data text entry box, type 0 and press Enter to enter the value.

Shut the Regedit program and restart Windows 2000 for this change to take effect. Now, when you minimize a program (and it goes down onto the taskbar) or you click its icon in the taskbar to restore it to normal or maximum size, no animation will take place. The window will just appear onscreen with no visual effects.

Eliminating My Computer

Unfortunately, the My Computer icon is not on the list of persistent desktop icons described previously because it's more tenacious than anything in Windows 2000 (other than the Start button). You just cannot take My Computer away unless you use the method described here.

Removing all desktop icons is possible with this technique. Even My Computer goes away. You get a really clean screen. (But as you might expect, there's a penalty.) For the absolute purist, here's how you can permit nothing to intrude on your desktop. You can move the Inbox and other desktop default icons into a folder on Explorer. You can also dump some of them in the Recycle Bin.

However, My Computer is the outermost shell of the system. You can't move it into a folder to hide it. That would be as fantastic as trying to store your garage in your car.

To make My Computer along with all other desktop icons disappear so that the desktop is entirely vacant, add to the Registry a NoDesktop setting, as follows:

1. Navigate the Registry using Regedit until you get to HKEY_CURRENT_USER\ Software\Microsoft\Windows\CurrentVersion\Policies\Explorer.

2. With the Explorer folder icon highlighted, click the Edit menu, choose New, and then choose DWORD Value.

3. When you see a new value entry in the right pane titled New Value 1, right-click it and select Rename.

4. Enter the name NoDesktop and press the Enter key.

5. Right-click the new NoDesktop name and select Modify.

6. Type 1 and click OK.

7. Now shut down the Regedit program by choosing Exit from the Registry menu. You've done it now!

You'll have to shut down and restart the computer before this change will take effect. When Windows 2000 starts up again, it will check the Registry and find your change. Voilà, an empty desktop. You'll notice another thing: You can no longer right-click the desktop to change things such as wallpaper and color schemes. However, it's easy enough to click on Start, select Settings, select Control Panel, and then double-click the Display icon to accomplish the same thing.

If you decide that you want to go back to the way things were, if you miss My Computer, it's easy enough to reverse the process. Just start the Registry Editor again and follow the method just described to get down to your NoDesktop entry. Right-click it to display a submenu; then select Delete and close the Registry Editor program.

Tip: If you find yourself using Control Panel often, you might want to put it on the Start menu. This is faster than clicking Start, Settings, Control Panel or going to it via the My Computer icon. Just locate the Control Panel icon in Explorer's left pane, then drag it and drop it onto the Start button.

Changing the My Computer Icon

If you want to do something less drastic than expelling the My Computer icon, you might consider just changing its appearance on your desktop:

1. In Regedit, click HKEY_LOCAL_MACHINE to highlight that section of the Registry. This will speed up the search.

2. Then press Ctrl+F, type in My Computer, and press Enter to start the search.

3. When Regedit locates the value, the folder in the left pane will merely be identified by a series of numbers; My Computer will appear in the right pane. (You
   might first hit something like "Outlook My Computer Management Module" or
   some other incorrect location. If so, press F3 to continue the search.)

4. In the left pane, double-click the folder icon and then click the folder named
   Default Icon.

5. Now, double-click the (Default) label and change the number at the far right. If
   you want the icon to look like a nice ink blotter and pencil and pad, for example,
   try this: %SystemRoot%\Explorer.Exe,3. You can provide any path to any file that
   contains an icon you would like to use, but the EXPLORER.EXE file has a nice variety of icons within it.

Press WindowsKey+M to minimize all open windows (giving your desktop the focus).
Press F5 to refresh the desktop. There's your new My Computer icon, all big and bold.

You can also change the My Computer icon by clicking the Effects tab in the Display
Properties window (right-click the desktop and then choose Properties). However, the
selection you're offered there is SHELL32.DLL rather than Explorer's rich collection of
icons.

An Easier Double-Click

When shipped, Windows 2000 defaults to 4 pixel double-clicking. This means that a double-click will be recognized only if the mouse doesn't move more than 4 pixels between
the two clicks. If you're a nervous, jittery type like I am, or your mouse is greasy and
slippery, you might find that some of your attempts to double-click have no effect. You
might have thought you were double-clicking too slowly or too quickly. With the Mouse
feature in Control Panel, you can adjust the double-click speed, and you might have tried
adjusting it, only to find that you're still getting ignored sometimes when you double-
click. Here's the solution:

1. In Regedit, go to HKEY_CURRENT_USER/Control Panel/Mouse.

2. Right-click the right pane and choose New String Value.

3. Type in the name DoubleClickWidth and press Enter.

4. Double-click this new entry and type in 15 or 30 or whatever generous amount of
   pixels you think will be comfortable for you.

5. Likewise, create a DoubleClickHeight entry and provide it with a generous 15- or
   30-pixel value.

Now you're likely to find Windows 2000 more willing to accept your slack double-clicking technique.

Changing Any Icon on the Desktop

You can make your icons larger or smaller than the default size (32×32 pixels). To do so, right-click your desktop and then choose Properties and click the Appearance tab. Drop down the Item list box and locate Icon. Then adjust the size to suit yourself and click the Apply button. To display high-resolution icons, click the Effects tab in the Display Properties window and select the Show Icons Using All Possible Colors option. Now that you know how to create large, colorful icons, you're probably wondering how to change the various icons already on the desktop. For shortcuts, there's no problem. Right-click their icons, select Properties, and then select Change Icon from the Shortcut tab. Select any icon or BMP filename and assign it to the shortcut. Changing other desktop icons, such as the Inbox icon, calls for Registry modifications. To change these icons, search for their names in the Registry. To change the Inbox icon, for example, follow these steps:

1. Run Regedit.

2. Press Ctrl+F.

3. Search for Inbox.

4. Click the plus sign next to the folder in the left pane (after Find locates it) to open the subkeys.

5. Click DefaultIcon.

6. Double-click (Default) in the right pane.

7. Type in the name of your BMP file, complete with path (for instance, C:\EYE.BMP).

8. Click the desktop and then press F5 to see the change.

When changing icons using the Registry, you'll sometimes find a strange path and file-name, followed by a comma and a number, like this:

%SystemRoot%\System32\Shell32.dll,31

This translates as "Use the 32nd icon located in the file named SHELL32.DLL, which can be found in the System32 folder within whatever folder Windows 2000, itself, resides." This is WINNT unless Windows 2000 was installed in a different location. The 31 means 32nd because the icons are numbered from 0 on up. What does that tell you?

To see the icons embedded in many files (DLL, EXE, and others), right-click any short-cut, select Properties, Shortcut. Click Change Icon and then click Browse. Locate the file you want to explore. Look in WINNT\System32\moreicons.dll, for a start. You can, of course, use any of these icons to replace default icons, if you wish. Just use Regedit to replace, for example, %SystemRoot%\System32\Shell32.dll,31 with %SystemRoot%\System32\Shell32.dll,12 to change an icon to the 13th icon in SHELL32.DLL. There are many other default icons you can change to your own BMP images. Just search the Registry for DefaultIcon, and you'll find, among others, Directory, Briefcase, Textfile, and Drive.

Changing All the EXE Icons in Explorer

Try this useful and interesting trick: Substitute a more vivid icon for EXE files.

Do you sometimes find yourself searching through filename lists (in Explorer, Browse, Find, and elsewhere) for runnable EXE programs amidst all the other kinds of files? You have to look for the .EXE extension. You want to run an application, but you don't have a shortcut for it, so you have to look in its folder and find the EXE for that application.

As shown in Figure 10.7, I created a small high-resolution shaded ball, named BALL.BMP, using a graphics program. I use it as the icon for all my EXE files.

The solution to this dilemma is to change the standard, default EXE icon for one that really stands out (see Figure 10.7). Of course, most EXE files use their own icon. But the following technique will replace those that don't—those that use the default Windows 2000 EXE icon:

FIGURE 10.7

When you give them this ball icon (or some other dramatic icon of your own devising), EXE files are then easy to spot in an Explorer listing, as well as in other lists such as the Windows 2000 Find utility.

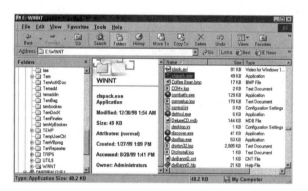

To make this change, search the Registry for Exefile. Keep pressing F3 to restart the search until you get to the key that has a DefaultIcon subkey. There's more than one reference in the Registry to Exefile, but you're looking for the first one that contains a folder (subkey) named DefaultIcon. You'll have to click the plus sign (+) to expand the Exefile keys and reveal their subkeys.

The current definition of an Exefile icon is %1, which tells Windows 2000 to use the first icon (there's often more than one icon buried in an EXE file) it finds within each EXE file. To change this to your custom BMP file so that all EXE files display your icon in Explorer or on the desktop, double-click the name (Default) and change the current reference from %1 to C:\BALL.BMP or the path to whatever BMP file you want to replace it with. Now, whenever you see a list of files in Windows 2000, you'll see EXE files with your glamorous new default image. Your graphic doesn't need to be a particular size, but make it relatively small and keep the aspect ratio square.

Note that this change (unlike adjusting individual icons for such items as the Inbox) requires that you shut down and restart Windows 2000 before you can see the effect. To reverse this, restore the %1 value.

> **Tip:** Be sure to adjust your Effects settings if you use a custom-made, high-resolution BMP file. To display high-resolution icons, click the Effects tab in the Display Properties window (right-click the desktop and then choose Properties) and select the Show Icons Using All Possible Colors option. Also, if you create your own BMP icon in a graphics program, be sure that the aspect ratio is square (for example, 32×32 pixels). That will look best.

Importing and Exporting Registry Data

One of the problems with using a Registry for everything is that all configuration data must be in a form that the Registry can accept. Quite a few mainstream applications create a Registry file (*.REG) that you can import into the Registry. Even the REG files created with 16-bit applications are compatible with the Windows 2000 Registry.

Importing Data

You can use several techniques to import your Registry information. First, you can open a copy of Explorer and find the Registry file you want to import. All you need to do is double-click the REG icon, and Regedit automatically enters it into the Registry. Notice that the REG file icon looks like the Regedit icon with a document behind it. After the Registry receives the new data, a confirmation message displays.

> **Note:** You can also run Regedit /s [filename]. This will install the REG file without presenting the dialog box at the end saying the information was put into the Registry. Note that you must use Regedit, not Regedt32, with this technique.

A second technique comes in handy when you have Regedit open. Just choose **Registry**, Import Registry File. The Registry Editor displays an Import Registry File dialog box. Click the Open button to complete the task.

Exporting Data

What happens when you want to save some configuration changes you made in the past? What if you add a new file extension to the Registry and want to save those entries for future use, for example? How about the custom color combinations you create—

wouldn't it be nice to save them before installing a new version of Windows 2000? You can export either all or part of the Registry by choosing the Registry, Export Registry File command in Regedit. When you export only a branch rather than the entire Registry, click the Selected Branch radio button in the Export Registry File dialog box. (Highlight the branch you want to save before you open the Export Registry File dialog box or just type the branch's path into the dialog box.)

All you need to do to complete the process is click the Save button. Regedit doesn't provide any kind of feedback after it exports the Registry to disk. You'll probably want to view the saved file before you make any changes to the Registry.

Viewing the Contents of an Exported Registry Entry

If you look at a saved Registry file (use WordPad), you'll see that the first line reads REGEDIT4, which identifies the version of Regedit that created the file. This prevents you from importing the file into an older version of the Registry. Application REG files normally don't contain any version numbers as part of the REGEDIT entry, which enables you to import them using any version of Regedit.

The second line of a Registry file contains a blank. Regedit uses this blank line as a delimiter between Registry key entries. The second line of text (the third line of the file) contains the Registry key. Notice that the key resembles a hard disk directory listing: Each backslash tells Regedit to create a new key level.

The final line of text contains the actual key value. The @ symbol at the beginning of the line tells Regedit that this is the default entry. Any other value begins with a value name. Quotation marks around the value itself tell Regedit that this is a string value. Binary values begin with the word hex followed by a colon, and dword values begin with the word dword followed by a colon.

Tip: You might find that you need to copy the keys from one branch to another branch in the Registry. You might want to use some of the OLE information from one file association when creating a new one, for example. It seems like Regedit should provide some type of cut-and-paste capability to take care of this task, but it doesn't. The fastest, most efficient way to add the contents of one branch to another is to export the Registry, use a text editor to cut and paste the values you need, and import the modified Registry file. Of course, you could find yourself with a machine that won't boot using this method. Make sure you keep an unmodified copy of the Registry handy just in case.

Peter's Principle: Using RegClean to Clean the Registry

Some applications are rude. You install them, but if you decide to remove them, they either provide no uninstall facility or a sloppy uninstall. In either of these cases, remnants from this kind of software are likely to be littered in your Registry. Over time, this not only increases the size of the Registry, it slows down performance. What to do?

Do a search of the Registry, looking for the software manufacturer's name or the application's name. If you locate a key or keys, you can delete them. If this action has any side effects, you always have your backup REG file (you made one, didn't you?).

A second housekeeping tool is a utility called RegClean, offered by Microsoft, which you can download from

`http://www.microsoft.com/NTServer/nts/exec/vendors/freeshare/Maintnce.asp#registry`.

This utility works with NT 4. Whether it will work with Windows 2000 is unknown at the time of this writing, but you should be able to find out by checking the URL address listed in the previous paragraph.

RegClean is to the Registry what CHKDSK is to your hard drive. RegClean looks at Registry keys and checks to see whether they contain correct data. With your permission, it will delete any keys it finds that contain bad data.

After you run this utility (which can take anywhere from 30 seconds to 30 minutes to complete its housekeeping job), it gives you two choices: Exit (no changes will be made to the Registry) or Allow RegClean to Go Ahead and Edit the Registry.

As a precaution, RegClean makes a backup of your Registry. If you want to revert to that backup version, you can just double-click it. The backup is located in the folder where RegClean resides and is named `UNDOYOURCOMPUTERNAMETHECURRENTTIME.REG`.

Multiuser Environment Considerations

Windows 2000 is a powerful operating system designed to meet a lot of heavy computer usage needs. Microsoft's original intent was to relegate Windows NT (2000's parent) to the needs of power users, such as engineers and programmers. Slow Windows 95 sales and a lot of conversation from its users eventually convinced Microsoft that Windows NT, with its superior stability and security, is the operating system of choice for corporate America.

Trying to manage all those computers, especially in a large company, can become a very difficult task. A network administrator needs the proper tools to get the job done. The Regedit utility might look like a low-level tool designed for use on the local computer; the first part of that perception is correct, but the second part isn't.

If you're an administrator, you can modify the Registry of another machine as long as you meet two criteria. To remotely edit a Registry you must be able to connect to the machine, have permissions on the target machine, and have permission to connect to the Registry, which can be altered. Regedt32 is a better tool than Regedit for loading hives and for connecting to remote machines.

Take a look at the first requirement. Windows 2000 doesn't automatically add the Remote Registry service as a default. In fact, Microsoft buries the documentation for this service on the Resource Kit disk and within a README file on the distribution disk. You won't find any mention of this service in the standard documentation. There's actually a good reason for all this secrecy. Just think about the power a user has when he or she has access to the local Registry. Now, what would happen if that same user gained access to all the Registries on the network? This chapter outlines all the settings the Registry contains, so it shouldn't take too much time to figure out why Microsoft keeps the Remote Registry service a deep, dark secret.

You will find the Remote Registry service files in the `\ADMIN\NETTOOLS\REMOTREG` folder of your distribution disk. Installing it is a snap.

> **Note:** If you want to access the Registry on a Windows 95 workstation, you have to set up the workstation for user-level access control on the Access Control page of the Network properties dialog box. Make sure you provide the name of the workstation's main file server. The workstation will use this file server as a source of users and groups. You must appear as an administrator on the file server you select.

The final piece of this puzzle is the Regedit utility. You'll find a Connect Network Registry option on the File menu. Choose this option, and you'll see the Connect Network Registry dialog box.

You can click the Browse button to display a list of machines currently on the network. All you need to do is select the name of the computer you want to see and then click OK to add it to the Computer Name field of the Connect Network Registry dialog box.

Click OK. Windows displays an hourglass icon for a few minutes while it makes the connection and downloads the other computer's Registry. When you finish, you'll see the other computer's Registry below your own. Notice that the other computer uses a different icon from your own.

Now that you have made a connection, you can make any changes to the remote Registry that you can make to your own[md]within certain limits. A network administrator can put certain areas of a Registry out of bounds for you. The next section looks at this particular issue.

The Windows 2000 Security Advantage

I'm not going to go through every security issue here; I cover a lot of these issues in the networking sections of the book (see Part VI, "Networking with NT"). My goal here is to make you aware of some features Windows 2000 provides that you won't find in Windows 95/98.

A network administrator can protect a Windows 2000 workstation in several ways. Some of these options are open to Windows 95 users as well. Because you can administer a Registry from a remote location, for example, you can just remove the copy of Regedit from a workstation. A user who doesn't have a copy of this utility can't edit his or her Registry. Of course, this won't work with a determined user, who'll just bring a copy of the program from home.

Modifying the Registry also requires certain rights under Windows 2000. As a default, only the Administrator group has these rights. A power user might be able to view the contents of the Registry, but he or she will receive an error message saying `Cannot open SECURITY. Error while opening key` if he or she tries to change it. Ultimately, this is the level of protection you'll need, giving rights to users only when they absolutely have to have them to get their job done.

Recall that Regedt32 is your best tool for dealing with Registry security issues. Regedt32 has all the security and auditing features that you'll need to audit a Registry. (You'll have to first set auditing in the Control Panel by way of Administrative Tools, Local Security Policy, Local Policies, Audit Policy.)

Peter's Principle: Using Registry Utilities

Microsoft's site offers a set of utilities you can use to work with the NT 4 Registry. Which of these will work with Windows 2000 is unknown at the time of this writing, but you should be able to find out by checking this URL address:

http://www.microsoft.com/NTServer/nts/exec/vendors/freeshare/Maintnce.asp#registry

Here's a list of some of the Registry utilities that Microsoft is currently making available:

- *ConfigSafe*. This utility tracks every change to the Registry and can restore previous settings rapidly. It also can be used to print reports of changes to system configuration.
- *DumpReg*. This displays all the Registry's keys and values in a scrollable list box and also permits you to view changes by time of last modification. Therefore, you can use it to quickly find which keys were modified while installing a new program or make changes to, say, a Control Panel applet.
- *RegWeb*. From ProStream, this utility permits Registry administration using standard Web browsers. Useful for system administrators who remotely manage Windows Registries.

continues

- *MultiReg*. This permits administrators to simultaneously modify Registries on multiple computers. This would come in quite handy if you have responsibility for maintaining a whole company's worth of workstations.
- *Registry Search and Replace*. This shareware utility simplifies the mass replacement of Registry strings, including those on remote machines.

On Your Own

Use Regedit to create a copy of your Registry using the procedure discussed in this chapter. Make sure you store this text copy of the Registry in a safe place.

Try replacing the icon used to symbolize EXE files. Remember that you can replace that icon for all files with the .EXE extension by making a single adjustment to the Registry. Try using icons embedded in other standard Windows applications such as those found in WINNT/SYSTEM.

To locate and view embedded icons, choose Folder Options from Explorer's View menu and then click the File Types tab. Click the Edit button and then click the Change Icon button. You'll be able to view all the icons in any application or DLL or other potential site by using the Browse feature of the Change Icon dialog box.

The Registry is a central part of Windows 2000. You can't do anything without it. Explore the Registry using Regedit. What do the values associated with each of the keys tell you about your system's configuration? Make sure you exit Regedit without making any changes to any of the keys.

If you're not bothered by the need to lock others out of your workstation, edit the Registry so that Windows 2000 will log you (or anyone else) on to the machine automatically: no Ctrl+Alt+Del, and no password required during boot. Also, fix the Registry so that your menus pop out instantly instead of each submenu taking four-tenths of a second to display.

Memory Management

Managing Windows 2000 is no different from most other aspects of life: You have to manage your resources carefully to get the biggest payback from your investment. On the other hand, if you spend all your time managing your resources, you won't get *any* return because you'll have spent everything before you start. Therein lies the challenge of managing resources without wasting them.

What are the resources you have to be so careful about? Memory and hard disk space are the two major concerns that come to mind. Of course, processor cycles are in there somewhere as well. You might not think about some resources right away, however. How valuable is your time, for example? Trading some memory or processor cycles for a big increase in your personal productivity can mean having more resources available for other people to use in the long run. For right now, let's take a close look at managing memory. We'll pursue the other topics later.

Peter's Principle: Management Versus Micromanagement

A good manager will often provide a little input and see what happens. If more input is required, fine; otherwise, the manager leaves his employees alone to get their jobs done in whatever way works for them. This is the kind of person everyone likes to work for, and he still manages to amaze his superiors with the amount of work he can accomplish. There isn't much of a secret to his success.

Spending your time getting your work done instead of doing someone else's work is always more productive.

The other kind of manager is the micromanager. He's the one you see following behind an employee at every step of every task. The only way to get the job done is his way. It might not be efficient—it might even be counterproductive for that particular employee—but at least he can always tell his superiors what the people under him are doing. This fellow will always fail to impress anyone. He might as well hang his motto on the wall of his office: "I want things done my own particular way, by someone else."

You might become a micromanager under Windows 2000 if you are not careful. A lot more tools are at your disposal, and it's easy to suppose that they are there for a reason. The truth of the matter is that even though you have more

continues

tools when using Windows 2000, the OS is actually better at managing its memory without any help from you. The tools are there so you can best determine what kind of limited input Windows 2000 needs.

When you're working with Windows 2000, the best principle is to provide a little input and see what happens. If more input is required, fine. If not, you have a fully tuned system that will get the job done for you. Let the system do the work it's designed to do until you see a good reason to provide that little bit of input.

Part VI, "Networking with Windows 2000," also shows that memory management in a networking environment requires a little more input from you. The Professional version of Windows 2000 requires only a little more input because you won't use it to maintain connections with a lot of other people. The Server version of Windows 2000 requires more input from you because you're usually trying to balance the memory load for a lot more people, and that load will tend to change a lot more over the course of the day than it would for a workstation.

The first thing you need to understand is that you must visualize two kinds of memory when you're working with Windows applications. You need enough system memory to load the application and any data files. Windows also needs enough system resources to load the windows, dialog boxes, and icons that your application uses.

Windows 2000 provides a lot of tools to manage your system resources. Chapter 7, "Performance Power," covers some of these tools. Windows 2000, however, remains a little complex in its management of memory. Many adjustments that can be made require Registry entries, which are a little outside the scope of this book. (We do cover some Registry tweaks in Chapter 10.) Take heart, however—Windows 2000 provides excellent memory management on its own and does offer some nice graphics methods for influencing memory allocation.

Unlike Windows 3.x, which has to have real-mode drivers, and Windows 95, which can use real-mode drivers for compatibility purposes, Windows 2000 doesn't have any real-mode drivers or TSRs you have to worry about. In a way, this makes Windows 2000 the easiest of the three products in which to manage memory: You don't have to worry about real mode creeping into your system. Yet, this convenience has a price. I have an older CD-ROM drive that works fine under Windows 3.x; I replaced it under Windows 95, not because I couldn't use it, but because I wanted to get rid of the real-mode driver. This same CD-ROM drive won't work at all under Windows 2000 because it *requires* a real-mode driver.

Technical Note: Windows 98 and Windows 98 SE both allow you to use real-mode drivers, but at a significant cost in performance. In some cases, I've noticed that Windows 98 will ignore a real-mode driver when there's a protected-mode driver available to perform the task. Microsoft says that this is a feature rather than a bug. My feeling is that Microsoft will probably disallow real-mode drivers in the next consumer version of Windows because that's the direction it appears to be moving.

Here's the crux of the matter: Under Windows 95, I had the *choice* of replacing the aging CD-ROM drive. Windows 2000 would not give me that choice; I would have had to simply replace that drive because Windows 2000 wouldn't accept the real-mode driver used by the drive. If you run into the same situation and your company doesn't have any plans to replace your aging equipment (at least not right this second), you could find that Windows 2000 provides less—not more—capability than its predecessors. The memory management you gain comes at the expense of potential lost equipment capability. When it comes down to it, you'll need equipment that's Windows 2000 compatible to truly get the benefits of Windows 2000's memory management power.

Memory Architecture (A Short Refresher)

The Windows 2000 operating system attempts to provide each application with up to 4GB of virtual memory. This allocation is based on what the application needs for its code and its data at any given time. This is accomplished through the use of *virtual memory*. The Virtual Memory Manager (VMM) provides virtual address ranges for the applications to access information normally stored in the physical RAM.

When an application requests an address to retrieve data or to load further code, the VMM responds with the correct information. Behind the scenes, the VMM is mapping to a physical address space. The physical address space certainly doesn't match the 4GB per process that's possible. VMM shuffles information in and out of physical RAM; this behavior is called *paging*.

Paging

The VMM is trying to keep data and code that isn't actively being used by a process out of physical RAM. *Paging* means that information goes out to a physical location on the disk called the *pagefile*.

After information is moved out of its original location in the physical RAM, there's one of two places that the information could be:either the file system cache or the pagefile. The *file system cache* (or system cache) is a location in memory reserved for information that has just recently been sent to disk or for information likely to be requested soon. When the VMM is asked to retrieve a piece of information that's needed, but not in physical RAM, it will trigger an event called a *page fault*. A page fault (technically, a *hard page fault*) requires that the information be retrieved from the physical hard drive (from the PAGEFILE.SYS file). However, information located in PAGEFILE.SYS is comparatively time-consuming to retrieve.

Tip: By default, Windows 2000 allocates a PAGEFILE.SYS file size on your hard drive that's equal to your total RAM, plus 12MB. Therefore, if you have 128MB, the default size for your PAGEFILE.SYS is 140MB. You can change this size, though, as you'll see later in this chapter.

Now that you have an idea of how paged information moves about in memory, let's examine a little more about how virtual memory is divided up.

The number of pagefiles and their location on the physical disk can greatly affect the overall performance of the operating system. Here are some quick tips:

- Multiple pagefiles on different physical disks help performance.
- Mirroring pagefiles hurt performance.
- Pagefiles and applications that use the disk heavily should be separated. Put the pagefile on another physical drive if possible.

Memory Pools

A *memory pool*, as defined in the Microsoft Windows 2000 world, is just the physical RAM divided up into logical units. Windows 2000 divides the total physical RAM into two logical groups:pageable memory and nonpageable memory. Nonpageable memory is memory that has been quarantined from being moved out to the pagefile. Being able to count on finding it in a predictable location is necessary for part of the kernel (API) and some other critical drivers in the operating system. The pageable memory pool is then divided up among the programs that are requesting memory. A section of the remaining available memory is then allocated to the file system cache. This part of the memory is again used to cache or store information that has been recently requested or written to the hard drive.

When an application starts, it requests a certain amount of memory called a *working set*. This is the memory needed by the application as it runs. Initially, the working set of an application is larger than what's actually needed once it gets started. After an application has loaded the necessary modules and data (such as splash screens and initialization pro-grams), it finishes its initialization and then no longer needs as much memory. The appli-cation will then be running with its normal working set. Whenever you request a new module, more information is added to the application's working set. If you open Word and start typing, for example, the application's working set will become fairly stable. If you stop typing and run the spell checker, however, the disk will run and a new compo-nent will be loaded into memory, thus increasing the application's working set for a time. If you don't use the spell checker for a little while, the system will consider paging that module out to disk and again reduce the working set of the application. The minimum amount of memory that the application requires for it to still be able to run is called its *minimum working set*.

File System Cache

The file system cache is dynamically adjusted by Windows 2000. From the moment the system starts and you run that first service or application, Windows 2000 is reevaluating the application's use of memory and the size of the system cache. In general, the file sys-tem cache is not permitted to exceed a size that would leave the system with less than 4MB of available memory. This allows Windows 2000 a little time to cope with large applications or heavy requests for memory. The file system cache can also be adjusted during those times when the system is undergoing heavy file transfers. In these situations, the system attempts to make disk access more efficient and, noting heavy transfers, will adjust itself so that larger amounts of information are transferred per write to the disk. On Windows 2000, the system cache size cannot be adjusted manually. This is yet another good reason to fill your computer with as much RAM as you can reasonably afford.

Memory Types

Windows 2000 utilizes a protected memory module. That is, it does not let any other application access the memory for another application. This is good for Windows 2000 and for operating system stability in general. However, it's not the way that many other DOS and Windows applications are used to working. Windows 2000 must therefore provide simulation of the various memory sections these applications are used to. The following list describes these memory types:

- *Conventional.* This is the original 640KB of memory that IBM set aside for DOS applications. Every DOS application needs conventional memory in order to run. Windows 2000 creates this kind of memory when it creates a virtual DOS machine. Windows 2000 uses a piece of code within the virtual DOS machine to provide a sort of heartbeat that simulates a process cycle. This heartbeat allows Windows 2000 to simulate BIOS/interrupt calls for DOS routines. If DOS needs to send data to the hard disk, for example, it still calls the same old BIOS routines. The Windows 2000 virtual DOS machine caches this call and takes care of it with its normal 32-bit routines.

- *Upper.* IBM set aside 384KB of the 8086 address space for ROM and video memory. In most cases, a system never uses all that memory. Windows 2000 ignores system BIOS in RAM. If this option is set in your CMOS setup for your machine, you should turn it off. It only wastes memory that Windows 2000 could use for something else.

- *High.* This is a magic 64KB block that actually appears above the 1024KB address limit. I discuss a topic called *memory segmentation* later in this chapter. Special memory-segmentation techniques make it possible for the processor to address this memory in real mode. Most users placed DOS in this area in Windows 3.11 to free more conventional memory.

- *Extended.* This is where DOS spent most of its time. A machine has to run in protected mode in order to access extended memory. This is the area beyond the addressing capability of the 8086.

- *Expanded.* Many game and some older business applications require expanded memory. At one time, you needed a special EMS card to partition expanded memory. Now, however, memory managers can convert extended memory to expanded memory on-the-fly.

Tip: If you look in your CONFIG.NT file, you'll likely find the line DOS=HIGH already there. The typical CONFIG.NT file contains the following information. You're welcome to modify it to suit your needs if you prefer DOS virtual machines under Windows 2000 to behave a particular way. The CONFIG.NT file contains several suggestions:

```
REM    Windows NT MS-DOS Startup File
REM
REM    CONFIG.SYS vs CONFIG.NT
REM    CONFIG.SYS is not used to initialize the MS-DOS environment.
REM    CONFIG.NT is used to initialize the MS-DOS environment unless a
REM    different startup file is specified in an application's PIF.
REM
REM    ECHOCONFIG
REM    By default, no information is displayed when the MS-DOS environment
REM    is initialized. To display CONFIG.NT/AUTOEXEC.NT information, add
REM    the command echoconfig to CONFIG.NT or other startup file.
REM
REM    NTCMDPROMPT
REM    When you return to the command prompt from a TSR or while running an
REM    MS-DOS-based application, Windows NT runs COMMAND.COM. This allows the
REM    TSR to remain active. To run CMD.EXE, the Windows NT command prompt,
REM    rather than COMMAND.COM, add the command ntcmdprompt to CONFIG.NT or
REM    other startup file.
REM
REM    DOSONLY
REM    By default, you can start any type of application when running
REM    COMMAND.COM. If you start an application other than an MS-DOS-based
REM    application, any running TSR may be disrupted. To ensure that only
REM    MS-DOS-based applications can be started, add the command DOSONLY to
REM    CONFIG.NT or other startup file.
REM
REM    EMM
REM    You can use EMM command line to configure EMM(Expanded Memory
➥Manager).
REM    The syntax is:
REM
REM    EMM = [A=AltRegSets] [B=BaseSegment] [RAM]
REM
REM    AltRegSets
REM    specifies the total Alternative Mapping Register Sets you
REM    want the system to support. 1 <= AltRegSets <= 255. The
REM    default value is 8.
REM    BaseSegment
REM    specifies the starting segment address in the DOS conventional
REM    memory you want the system to allocate for EMM page frames.
REM    The value must be given in Hexadecimal.
REM    0x1000 <= BaseSegment <= 0x4000. The value is rounded down to
REM    16KB boundary. The default value is 0x4000
REM    RAM
```

```
REM     specifies that the system should only allocate 64Kb address
REM     space from the Upper Memory Block(UMB) area for EMM page frames
REM     and leave the rests(if available) to be used by DOS to support
REM     loadhigh and devicehigh commands. The system, by default, would
REM     allocate all possible and available UMB for page frames.
REM
REM     The EMM size is determined by pif file (either the one associated
REM     with your application or default.pif). If the size from PIF file
REM     is zero, EMM will be disabled and the EMM line will be ignored.
REM
dos=high, umb
device=%SystemRoot%\system32\himem.sys
files=20
```

Conventional Memory

Some people still have some DOS utilities or games they want to run, and every DOS
application needs conventional memory. You could easily get mired in a lot of details
when running DOS applications under Windows 2000, but here's the quick view: You
can't use a memory manager under Windows 2000. The only way to gain more memory
is to change the way Windows 2000 allocates conventional memory. If you have an
application that wants more memory than Windows 2000 can provide, you'll need to
revert to Windows 3.x or Windows 95/98 to run it.

Upper Memory

Upper memory consists of six 64KB segments between 640KB and 1MB. Originally,
IBM called this area *reserved memory*. It was reserved for add-on peripherals and BIOS
extensions. The current term for this area of real-mode addressable memory is the *upper
memory block* (UMB). Microsoft invented the term *UMB* when programmers learned
how to circumvent IBM's original plan.

Expanded Memory

Anyone who has been computing very long will remember running into the need for
expanded memory (EMS) at some point in his or her career. EMS first appeared in 1985
as a means to bypass the DOS address limitations. Spreadsheet users were complaining
that they didn't have enough memory to run those gargantuan worksheets. These were
the same folks who kept expanding the memory envelope throughout most of the PC's
early history.

After much wrestling with various memory schemes for several years, EMS 4.0 finally
arrived on the scene. Under EMS 4.0, allocated expanded memory could be mapped as
conventional memory. The memory is usually divided into 16KB segments called *standard pages*. A program can use pages other than the standard 16KB size, however. These
pages are called *raw pages*. Obviously, determining the number of pages of memory
available is no longer a matter of just knowing how many 16KB segments are installed,
so EMS 4.0 also provides methods of determining the number of raw and standard pages.

Instead of only providing access to expanded memory through the page frame (as LIM 3.2 memory does), any number of standard or raw pages can be mapped between conventional memory and the RAM set aside for EMS. In addition, EMS 4.0 provides methods of moving memory regions between conventional and expanded memory. This makes it possible to execute multiple programs up to the full 640KB address range.

Using EMS with Windows 2000

The simple way to get expanded memory under Windows 2000 is to select the appropriate settings in the program's Properties dialog box. In fact, this is about the only way to get it short of adding HIMEM.SYS and EMM.SYS to your CONFIG.NT file. Chapter 17, "Exploiting Your Hardware," looks at this dialog box in detail. For right now, the important thing to remember is that Windows 2000 requires a different EMS strategy from previous versions of Windows. For one thing, you don't have the option of loading the Memory Manager before you start Windows—an option that still exists under Windows 95 (although I wouldn't even recommend using it there).

Extended Memory

There's one more specification to consider when managing DOS virtual machines under Window 2000:XMS. Microsoft's Extended Memory Specification (XMS) came into its own when, in 1990, Microsoft revised its HIMEM.SYS driver with the release of Windows 3.0. The scope of XMS memory was increased to include all of extended memory. This new release of Windows could use all of extended memory to multitask Windows applications. Disk caches, print spoolers, and RAM disks could now access extended memory through Microsoft's device driver. Formerly, any driver using extended memory had to provide its own scheme for switching in and out of protected mode. Microsoft established new terminology for all memory above 640KB:

- *Upper memory block* (UMB) became the term for the memory area above the 640KB boundary and below the 1MB boundary.

- *High memory area* (HMA) refers to the 64KB block of memory starting at the 1MB boundary (1024KB). This is the beginning of extended memory on 80286 and 80386 systems.

- *Extended memory block* (EMB) refers to the remaining extended memory (above the HMA) available to an XMS driver.

Virtual Memory

When you're running too many applications or an application's data is using up too much of the memory in your computer (that is, RAM), Windows 2000 uses virtual memory to make up the difference. *Virtual* generally means *nearly the same* or *seems like*. Windows 2000's virtual memory is a hard drive file named PAGEFILE.SYS. The Virtual Memory Manager (VMM), even before the computer's RAM fills up completely, looks for sections of RAM memory that haven't recently been used. Say, for example, that you're working on a document and run a spell checker. The spell checker module is loaded into RAM and run. After you're done, the module sits idle. VMM notices that you're not using the module activity and pages it out to disk. If you start to use the spell checker again, VMM quickly retrieves any portions on the pagefile and returns them to memory where they can be run. This swapping process is invisible to applications—they don't notice any difference with the exception of a slight pause, because access to physical RAM is quicker than to any disk subsystem. If you find yourself often waiting around impatiently while the hard drive grinds away (this is called *thrashing*) trying to swap between actual and virtual memory space, you may need to buy and install some more RAM memory.

Peter's Principle: How to Determine the Optimum Size for Your Pagefile

If your pagefile is too small, Windows 2000 continually and dynamically resizes it, trying to accommodate your memory needs. This generally will slow the system down. The word for this is *thrashing*, and it refers to a situation when the hard drive is wildly active, trying to respond to a flood of requests to store and retrieve memory pages. By default, Windows 2000 creates a pagefile that's 12MB larger than the amount of physical RAM you have installed. When setting the size of a pagefile on your system, you assign a range for the size. Although the maximum value is important, what's truly critical is the minimum pagefile size. The purpose of assigning a *range* is so that Windows 2000 can choose to dynamically expand this size from the initial size, if needed. Expanding the pagefile is costly in memory and processor resources. Making your pagefile the right size is important and will avoid forcing the system to waste resources expanding the pagefile to an appropriate size.

How to adjust your virtual memory—and how to chart how much of the pagefile you're generally using—is explained at the end of this chapter. In general, however, if you see that the current size of your pagefile is above RAM + 12MB, increase the minimum size of the page to 12MB + the peak size of the pagefile. If you're running SQL Server or IIS with a busy Web site, your minimum pagefile size should be close to RAM+32MB.

To see your pagefile setting, double-click the System icon in Control Panel, then click the Advanced tab, click Performance Options, and under Virtual memory, click the Change button.

Tip: This one's a bit iffy, but I've tried it on my machine with 512MB of RAM and it appears to work. A rumor has gone around that if you set your minimum and maximum pagefile size to the amount of physical memory in your machine, you'll get a speed boost because Windows 2000 spends less time micromanaging the pagefile. I tried this and it does appear to give a speed boost of about 5%, which is admittedly small (and one test case doesn't necessarily prove anything). I found that the speed boost is higher if you reset the pagefile right after you defragment your hard drive, because Windows 2000 will try to allocate the pagefile in a contiguous area of your hard drive. One of the things that concerns me about conducting this test on my machine is the fact that I do have 512MB of RAM, which likely skews the test and may not show the optimum size for the pagefile.

I've been telling you how great the automated features of Windows 2000 are and how they will make your life easier and provide more flexibility. I have even gone as far as to say you would be better off leaving them completely alone. Of course, you knew that wasn't going to last, didn't you? It's true that Windows 2000 does provide all those things, but I'm still talking about a piece of software that can't think independently the way you and I can. By default, Windows 2000 will put the pagefile on the same partition as the system files. This is not always the best scenario.

Take my machine as a case in point. I have two hard drives: a small, older model EIDE drive and a new larger, faster SCSI drive. The small drive, 1GB, contains some boot information, my DOS files, and a few other odds and ends. That drive has more than enough space left for a pagefile. The fact that I seldom change anything on it makes it the perfect location for a pagefile. Of course, Windows 2000 puts the pagefile on the larger drive where the system files are actually located.

So here's what I did. I rebuilt my machine (I can never leave well enough alone) and divided the 1GB hard drive into two partitions. The first is about 800MB; the second 200MB. I formatted both of these as FAT16 partitions. The 800MB partition ends up being my C: drive. This is where DOS, some applications that insist on being on drive C:, and my Windows 2000 boot files are located. The 200MB partition is the D: drive, which I left empty momentarily. On the other SCSI hard drive I installed Windows 2000 system files and converted it to NTFS. This is now my E: drive. I told Windows 2000 to remove the pagefile from the E: drive and put it on the D: drive. This helped my memory performance a great deal. There are several reasons why this configuration helped, so let's review them.

First, FAT16 is faster than NTFS on partitions smaller than 300MB. It's just a fact. NTFS is excellent on large volumes, where it will beat FAT hands down. On a small partition with not too many files and no requirements for security features, however, FAT is going to work faster. On my D:drive, I have only one file, the pagefile. It has no need for security because the file is basically always locked by the Windows 2000 operating system. The point is that the pagefile is on the partition by itself. Windows 2000 dynamically changes the size of the pagefile. (Note that if there are other files on the same partition, the pagefile can become *fragmented*. This means that the pagefile can actually be spread all over a disk in little pieces rather than in one nice, efficient, continuous file.) My configuration avoids fragmentation altogether. The pagefile is sharing the physical drive with a partition that's not going to be changing much. The DOS installation and Windows 2000 boot files are pretty rarely used. Therefore, the hard drive can concentrate on servicing requests to send information to, and get it back from, the pagefile.

> **Technical Note:** There's another reason why Windows 2000 wants to put PAGEFILE.SYS on the same partition as the Windows 2000 operating system files. In the event of a critical system failure (often called a *blue screen*), Windows 2000 can be configured to record crucial information about the error to a file called

the *memory dump file*. To do this, Windows 2000 must dump the contents of the memory to the pagefile and then process the information into a memory dump file when it reboots. If the pagefile is not on the same partition as Windows 2000, you cannot take advantage of this feature. Generally, I do not consider this much of a loss. I make the assumption that my system will be up and running and rarely, if ever, failing with a blue screen, so I configure my machine to work best while running. In the event that I start to experience some blue screen–type errors, I simply adjust Windows 2000 and put a pagefile sized to match the amount of physical RAM that I've installed on the same partition as the Windows 2000 system files.

Take a look at the process for changing your virtual memory setup:

1. Right-click My Computer and choose the Properties option. Then click the Advanced tab.

2. Click the Performance Options button in the System Properties dialog box shown in Figure 11.1.

FIGURE 11.1

The Performance Options dialog box provides access to your virtual memory settings.

3. Click the Change button. You should see the dialog box shown in Figure 11.2.

4. Select the drive you want to use and then the amount you want to allocate for virtual memory.

That's about all there is to setting the pagefiles for VMM. The two main things you need to worry about with Windows 2000's virtual memory is choosing your fastest drive (or using your least-crowded drive or partition) and making sure that it has enough space for the pagefile. Making sure that the drive stays defragmented is another way to ensure that you always get the best performance. Also remember to put the pagefile on a separate drive from the system files, if possible; avoid putting the pagefile on a fault-tolerant drive (a mirrored volume or a RAID-5 volume). Some fault-tolerant schemes are slow because data is written to more than one location. Finally, avoid putting multiple pagefiles in different partitions of the same physical disk drive.

Figure 11.2

Hand-tune your machine's virtual memory settings in this dialog box.

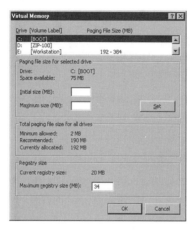

Peter's Principle: Managing the Secondary Cache

Windows 2000 sometimes makes an error when specifying the size of your L2 cache, so let's take a look at Windows 2000's assumption; if Windows 2000 is wrong, you can make your computer faster by correcting this specification.

A *cache* is memory (hard drive space) where recently used or soon-needed data is stored for quicker access than would be possible were it stored normally. Virtual memory is a kind of cache, but there are other caches, too, such as the collection Internet Explorer maintains of your most recently visited Web pages. There are even two small caches made up of RAM memory hyperfast caches right near the computer's CPU. Most computers have a bit of RAM memory called a *Level 1 cache* or internal cache as part of the CPU, itself, so it's an extremely fast cache but is also extremely expensive. The Level 1 cache is used to store low-level instructions awaiting execution or data that will be needed next, and the CPU looks there first for data. If it doesn't find the data there, it looks next at the *Level 2 cache* (external cache), which is RAM memory (usually 256 or 512KB) located on the motherboard. The Level 2 cache is slower than Level 1 but faster than ordinary RAM. When you see the term *512KB cache*, for example, in ads for computers, they're referring to the Level 2 cache. (These caches also sometimes work in the other direction. Rather than guessing what instructions or data will next be needed by the CPU, the cache is sometimes used as a temporary storage area for data intended to be saved to your hard drive when the machine is idle.)

To see what L2 cache size Windows 2000 has specified for your machine, press Start, choose Run, and then type in `Regedit` and press Enter. Locate the entry `HKEY_LOCAL_MACHINE\SYSTEM\CurrentControlSet\Control\Session Manager\Memory_Management` in the Registry. Double-click the `SecondLevelDataCache` entry. Click the Decimal Base option button and type in **256** or **512** or whatever amount of L2 memory your machine has (in kilobytes). Windows 2000 will default to 256KB, but you might have more. Click OK and shut down Regedit. Now reboot your machine. The actual effect of this particular Registry change has been debated much among many technical persons whom I've been in contact with. Although there is some debate on whether performance will actually be enhanced with this change, there is no disagreement that you'll not lose performance by changing this value.

Tip: If you want to quickly see how much of your RAM memory you're currently using, right-click your taskbar and choose Task Manager. Click the Performance tab and look at the Physical Memory report. Right now on my machine it says I have 130484KB (128MB) total (installed) and that 65204KB (a little over 60MB) is currently available (not being used). In general, the amount available should never go below 4000 (about 4MB); otherwise, you're forcing Windows 2000 to slow itself down unnecessarily. Add more RAM.

Architectural Details

We've examined the problem of memory management from various angles now, but that's not quite the end of the story. It's not enough to just say that you have certain types of memory available or that you know Windows 2000 has to use different methods to address it. Windows 2000 displays all these sources of information using a variety of window types. It looks like they're all in the same place working together.

Windows 2000 performs a certain "magic" to enable 16-bit and 32-bit applications to talk with each other. It also has to provide some method of reducing memory usage by optimizing the way it runs those applications. This section discusses both issues. Here, I answer the question of how Windows 2000 enables you to run so many applications together under one roof.

Getting 16-Bit and 32-Bit Applications to Work Together

Windows 2000 consists of a combination of perhaps some older 16-bit and newer 32-bit applications. Any older applications and device drivers you use now have to work within the same environment as the new 32-bit drivers and applications that Windows 2000 provides. You already know how Windows takes care of separating the two by using different memory schemes. The 16-bit applications work within their own virtual machine area. It would be nice if things ended there, but they can't.

Sometimes, 16-bit and 32-bit applications have to talk to each other. This applies not only to programs the user employs to perform work but also to device drivers and other types of Windows applications. Most Windows applications use a memory structure called *the stack* to transfer information from one application to another. Think of the stack as a database of variables. Each record in this database is a fixed length so that every application knows how to grab information from it. Here's where the problems start. The stack for 32-bit applications is 32 bits wide, which makes sense. It also makes sense that the stack for 16-bit applications is 16 bits wide. See the problem?

Of course, the problems are only beginning. What happens when you need to send a 32-bit value from a 16-bit application to a 32-bit application? The 32-bit application expects to see the whole value in the EAX register. On the other hand, the 16-bit application expects to see the value in a combination of the DX and AX registers. This same problem translates to pointers as well. A 32-bit application, for example, uses the SS:ESP register pair to point to the stack.

But wait, there's more! Remember that 16-bit applications use a segmented address space. An address consists of a selector and an offset. A 16-bit application combines these two pieces to form a complete address. On the other hand, 32-bit applications use a flat address space. They wouldn't know what to do with a selector if you gave them one. All they want is the actual address within the total realm of available memory. How do you send the address of a string from a 16-bit to a 32-bit application?

By now, you're probably wondering how Windows keeps 16-bit and 32-bit applications working together. After all, it must deal with a number of inconsistencies and incompatibilities. The stack is only the tip of the incompatibility iceberg. It's easy to envision a method of converting 16-bit data to a 32-bit format. All you really need to do is pad the front end of the variable with zeros. How does a 32-bit application send data to a 16-bit application? If the 32-bit application just dumps a wide variable onto the stack, the 16-bit application will never know what do to with the information it receives. Clearly, the data needs to go through some type of conversion. Windows uses something called the *thunk layer* to enable 16-bit and 32-bit applications to communicate.

The three components of the API layer also provide translation services in addition to the other services they perform. Each API component translates the data and addresses within its area of expertise. The two GDI components translate all graphics data between 16-bit and 32-bit applications, for example.

Most thunking is pretty straightforward. Windows just moves register data to the appropriate register, for example. The thunk layer builds a new stack to meet the needs of the application receiving it. Address translation takes a little more work. In addition, address translation is very expensive in terms of time. Every time Windows has to translate an address, it must perform several selector loads. The processor has to verify every selector load, so these translations can get cumbersome. Fortunately, you, as an applications programmer, won't have to worry too much about the actual thunk process. What you do need to worry about is making certain that the process actually takes place when calling a piece of code that needs it.

FIGURE 11.3

The thunk layer makes it possible for 16-bit and 32-bit applications to coexist peacefully under Windows 2000.

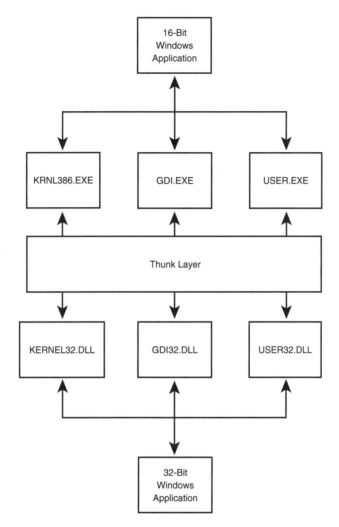

Windows and DLLs

Windows always has more than one task running. Somewhere along the way, someone figured out that if you have multiple applications running, there might be some duplicate code out there as well. The display routines used by one application are probably the same as the display routines used by another application at some particular level, for example. The same person probably figured out that you can reduce the overall memory requirements of a system if you allow all the applications to share these redundant pieces of code instead of loading them from scratch for each application.

The *dynamic link library* (DLL) is the culmination of just such an idea. There are two forms of linking under Windows (or OS/2 or UNIX, for that matter). The first link combines all the object modules required to create a unique application. That link cycle happens right after the programmer finishes compiling the code. The second link cycle happens when the user loads the application. This is where the DLL comes in.

Every Windows application has unresolved references to functions. Microsoft calls them *import library calls*. These calls load a DLL containing the code required to satisfy that function call. If the DLL happens to be in memory when Windows calls it, Windows increments the DLL's usage level to indicate that more than one application is using the DLL. When an application stops using a DLL, Windows decrements its usage level. When the DLL's usage count is zero, Windows can unload it from memory. The result: Using DLLs can save quite a bit of memory when you're loading multiple applications.

What does this have to do with the API? The Windows API starts with three files, as just described. These three files call other files, however (DLLs, to be exact). Instead of creating three huge files, Microsoft chose to reduce the size of the Windows kernel by using DLLs.

This capability also makes Windows more flexible. Consider printer support. All you need to do to add printer support for a new printer is copy some files to disk. At least one of those files will be a DLL. Every printer DLL contains the same entry points (function names), so Windows doesn't need to learn anything new to support the printer. The only thing it has to do is install a new DLL. Your application performs the same task when you tell it to print. It looks at the DLLs currently installed for the system. The application doesn't have to care whether the printer is a dot-matrix printer or a laser printer. All it needs to do is tell the printer to print; the DLL takes care of the rest.

DOS Applications on Virtual Machines

Enhanced mode is the name of the game if you want to multitask DOS applications under Windows. As I stated earlier, this is the only mode you get with Windows 3.11 and above (including Windows 2000). The underlying reason you can run more than one application is that the applications no longer load on the physical machine—instead, they load on a virtual machine. I have only one physical machine, so if I use it to run an application, there's nothing left to run something else. Virtual machines are different. Windows can continue to create new virtual machines as long as you have the memory to permit it to do so. Each virtual machine can run one DOS application. The capability to create multiple virtual machines means that you can always run more than one application.

What exactly is a virtual machine? I looked at many of the ramifications from an architectural point of view earlier in this chapter. Essentially, a *virtual machine* is a memory structure that acts like a physical personal computer. There used to be big gaps in this technology under Windows 3.*x*, but Microsoft greatly improved the virtual machine under Windows NT 4. It provided a protected-memory model, which prevents the accidental or insidious intrusion of one application into another application's memory space. NT 4 and Windows 2000 deal with this situation by terminating the application. The result is typically a Dr. Watson–type error (that is, general protection fault–type error). If this occurs in a driver or Windows 2000 Server, Windows 2000 halts and displays a memory dump called a *blue screen*.

From a memory standpoint, Windows 2000 creates each virtual machine from extended memory. After it sets aside the memory, it loads a copy of DOS from the phantom copy Windows 2000 keeps around just for this purpose. It then loads and runs your DOS application. As far as the DOS application is concerned, it's running on its own 8088 machine. Of course, this application can still request expanded and extended memory. It can even use Windows DPMI services to switch to protected mode and run itself as a protected-mode application.

After you exit your DOS application, Windows destroys the virtual machine it used. It returns the memory used by the virtual machine to the system memory pool. Each DOS application you load gets a new virtual machine to operate in. Windows just creates and destroys them as needed.

Getting Optimum Performance

Most of the following material is covered in other chapters. Nevertheless, this is a good place to summarize the various tips and techniques I've presented so far (or will present in Chapter 16, "Exploiting Your Software").

Most people get too little memory (less than 128MB), even though prices are so low now that systems are generally sold with 32MB or, at most, 64MB. You should buy or add enough RAM to reach at least 128MB, particularly if you ever work with graphics. Why? There are two fundamental reasons:

- More RAM means less paging—swapping data in and out of the relatively slow hard drive.
- Windows 2000 is designed to monitor performance, including memory issues. Windows 2000 is supposed to be, to an extent, *self-tuning*. In relation to memory usage, this means that Windows 2000 tunes your entire system dynamically, allocating any available extra RAM (not actively used by applications) to the general system cache. This improves both network and disk performance.

Technical Note: Another way to monitor your virtual memory is to run WINMSD.EXE, a utility you'll find in your SYSTEM32 directory. Click WINMSD's System Summary item and look at the bottom of that page to see your pagefile's total size, current usage, and peak usage. These results are reported in kilobytes rather than as percentages. If you notice that your peak usage (Page File Space) figure is higher than, say, 80% of your pagefile's total size, it's time to increase the pagefile. Click the System icon in Control Panel. Click the Performance tab and then click the Change button.

Here are my top 10 tips and techniques for tuning your system to make the best use of memory:

- *Always install Windows 2000 on a machine that can handle its advanced capabilities.* Trying to run Windows 2000 on an underpowered machine is the best way to sap performance. I suggest a minimum Windows 2000 configuration of a 266MHz Pentium with *at least* 64MB of RAM. The Microsoft-stated minimum will only frustrate you (and the person trying to get some work done).

- *Use your fastest drive for the pagefile, but don't starve Windows in the process.* A fast drive will improve performance in one respect. A small pagefile could kill that performance gain by reducing system stability and introducing some memory thrashing. Always choose the fastest drive that contains enough memory to hold the entire pagefile.

- *Manage your system but don't micromanage it.* I can already see that this will be a major problem area for some users. Tune the individual files for the performance you need. Tell Windows what you need to do but don't worry too much about how it gets the job done. Leaving Windows 2000 alone to do its work is about the best performance enhancement you can provide. (Of course, a little monitoring from time to time as your computing habits change wouldn't hurt either.)

- *Never run more DOS sessions than you need.* Windows 2000 does a much better job of managing memory when you have few DOS sessions going. In fact, you might even consider using all 32-bit applications—or at least as many as possible— to get the maximum performance benefits from Windows 2000.

- *Use the automatic memory settings whenever possible.* Sometimes, you have to step in and adjust them manually if you have an application that starts by grabbing everything available. In most cases, however, you'll be better off if you let Windows manage the memory for you. Letting Windows manage your memory provides a much greater degree of flexibility in the long run. That flexibility usually translates into increased efficiency and performance.

- *Avoid running games and other surly programs under Windows 2000.* Consider using Windows 95/98 if you plan to run a lot of programs that break the rules Windows 2000 tries to enforce. If you do find an application that just won't run using the default Windows memory setup, try creating an optimized environment for it using Windows 95/98's MS-DOS mode.

- *Enhance your memory usage by getting rid of the frills.* Wallpaper, screen savers, and other doodads can consume memory without giving you much in return. Entertainment is nice, but not at the cost of efficiency. The question you should always ask yourself is whether something relieves fatigue or merely consumes resources.

- *Increase your level of physical RAM as needed.* Windows 2000 can literally make as much RAM as you need from your hard drive, but there's a limit to how much performance you can get by doing this. See the preceding Peter's Principle for a simple way to calculate how much RAM you should install.

- *Get a faster hard drive.* Swap files are a fact of life under Windows 2000, and that means you're at least partially dependent on the hard drive's speed for overall system performance—even when it comes to memory. I find that a drive with a higher level of throughput is a better choice than one with faster access time when it comes to memory management. Windows tends to read from the pagefile in small, contiguous blocks. A drive with a higher throughput can deliver that data faster.

- *Kill those old applications.* If you're still using a lot of DOS applications, it's time to upgrade. Get rid of those old moth-eaten remnants. The only thing old DOS applications will do for you is slow down the system and cause reliability problems. Of course, 16-bit Windows applications aren't much better for the most part. Upgrading to the newer 32-bit applications helps you use memory efficiently and usually provides a speed benefit as well.

On Your Own

Open a DOS box and type MEM on the DOS command line to see what types of memory you have available. Also note the amount of each type of memory you have available. If you don't see that both expanded and extended memory are available, try to discover the reason why one or the other is absent.

Right-click the My Computer icon and then click the Advanced tab. Click the Performance Options button in the System Properties dialog box. Click the Change button and see whether the size and physical location of your pagefile is best for your system, based on the information you've received in this chapter.

Explore the other memory-tuning techniques detailed in the "Getting Optimum Performance" section. Can you use any of these tips to improve your machine's performance? Try different ways of implementing these changes to see what works best with your configuration. If Windows 2000 is a new operating system to you, you need to explore its weaknesses and strengths to see what you can do to improve your machine's capabilities. I think you'll find that many of the old techniques you used no longer work properly.

The Windows 2000 File Systems: FAT and NTFS

Should you use the New Technology File System (NTFS) or the older and more widely used File Allocation Table (FAT) for your file system on Windows 2000 Professional? The first answer that many people give is, "Well, I'm using Windows 2000, so I should use NTFS." Let's just say this approach to the question is a little shortsighted given the advanced capabilities that Windows 2000 provides.

NTFS is superior in many ways to the old FAT system, but if your hard disks are divided into volumes smaller than 1GB, FAT is actually the better performer. (FAT32, which is supported by Windows 2000, extends the performance advantage to at least 2GB.) Also, FAT is known to be superior to NTFS when engaged in random reads of a disk, no matter what the volume size. There are, of course, other issues beyond sheer performance—stability and security prominent among them. However, making the decision between FAT and NTFS is far from clear cut. Helping you make an informed decision on this issue is the main focus of this chapter.

When you look at Windows 2000, you're seeing an operating system that offers a choice of two base file systems: FAT/VFAT (Virtual File Allocation Table) and NTFS (also known as the NT File System). FAT file system support can be further broken down into FAT16 and FAT32. Likewise, there are two versions of NTFS support: NTFS 4 and NTFS 5. We'll talk about these varying levels of support as the chapter progresses.

File system support is affected by another factor that you might not have considered when working with Windows 95/98. Windows 2000 is designed to work on more than one hardware platform, which means that the actual level of file system support will be affected by the hardware platform you choose. As a user, you won't see any additional capabilities in the file system because of the multiplatform nature of Windows 2000, but the file system does need extra flexibility to make this all work. In addition, you won't get any form of FAT support when working with an Alpha machine—NTFS is the only option in this environment.

I want to mention a little more about the VFAT support provided by Windows 2000. You'll find it interesting to see that Windows 2000 supports long filenames as easily on a FAT-formatted drive as it does with any other drive. If Windows 2000 merely provided a true FAT file system, you couldn't use long filenames. I also found it interesting that these long filenames are as accessible from the DOS prompt as they are from Explorer. You'll also find that Windows 2000 uses many of the same DLLs that Windows 95/98 does (well, not precisely the same) to provide FAT file system access. Microsoft's documentation won't even mention VFAT, but I think that calling the level of Windows 2000 FAT file system support *VFAT* is more accurate. I'll get into the details of VFAT later in the chapter when I talk about the Windows 2000 architecture. Note that the "DOS command prompt" under Windows 2000 isn't true DOS; instead, it's simulated. That's why you can use long filenames in this "DOS" window. If you want to see true DOS, reboot the machine with a DOS boot disk. You won't be able to use long filenames in that case.

The purpose of this chapter is to tell you about the various file systems Windows 2000 supports. I'll describe the architecture first and then the individual differences between the various file systems. I think it's important to understand how Windows 2000 views the file system before you attempt to make changes to it. After I fully discuss the theory, I examine some user-related issues such as viewing files, and some of the new Windows 2000 additions such as LNK files. I also spend some time looking at the utility end of file system support. I discuss various methods you can use to protect your file system from data loss or corruption, for example, redundant array of inexpensive disks (RAID) and disk mirroring.

An Overview of the Windows 2000 File System

Let's take a tour of the Windows 2000 File System. Before you can begin to understand the file system support provided by Windows 2000, you need to understand why there's so much of it. My hard drives have a proliferation of file systems. Right now, I can boot both Windows 98 SE and Windows 2000 Professional. Both of these operating systems support the FAT16 and FAT32 file systems. Windows 2000 also provides its own file system in the form of NTFS.

Microsoft designed all these file systems at one time or another to meet various goals. The FAT file system, for example, is actually based on UNIX. Microsoft had to have a file system when it built DOS—the FAT file system is the result. Unfortunately, Microsoft's first attempt wasn't as good as it could have been. It used a 12-bit allocation scheme that seemed quite generous when DOS was young but soon caused problems when the size of a hard disk exceeded 32MB. The next version of FAT used 16-bit table entries, thus enabling the user to create much larger partitions. Eventually, even the 16-bit table entries provided by FAT16 proved too small, prompting Microsoft to create FAT32 for the Original Equipment Manufacturer (OEM) Service Release 2 (OSR2) version of Windows 95/98. FAT32 support has become standard in Windows 98. In reality, there are three different FAT schemes (12 bit, 16 bit, and 32 bit); from a user's perspective, however, there's only one.

When OS/2 came along, Microsoft decided that it needed something a bit faster than FAT; the answer was the High Performance File System (HPFS). One of the problems with FAT on a large hard drive is that the drive information is located at one end of the drive. Retrieving information located on the other end of the drive forces the drive to work harder and reduces overall performance. In addition, the linear list format FAT uses to store the directory isn't the most efficient way to find information. HPFS uses a B-tree directory structure that considerably speeds up access. A *B-tree* is a special software structure used by programmers for things such as database managers and files, wherein you need to search for something and find it quickly. I could dazzle you with a lot of statistics about just how fast a B-tree is, but all that you need to remember is that B-trees are faster than linear searches. HPFS also provides enhanced reliability. Because Windows 2000 doesn't support HPFS, I'll leave you with this bit of history and move on to something that Windows 2000 does support.

Windows NT (and now Windows 2000) offered yet another opportunity for Microsoft to fiddle with the file system. NTFS is an improvement from a number of technical perspectives that I describe later in this section. The two features that differentiate NTFS from HPFS are the capability to use larger files and partitions and the fact that NTFS is more fault tolerant. Anyone who has waited more than an hour for OS/2 to complete a CHKDSK command knows exactly what I mean. And HPFS doesn't handle power failures very well at all. The bottom line for you as a user is that Microsoft stressed both reliability and efficiency when it created NTFS.

There's also the matter of FAT versus VFAT to consider. When Windows 95/98 came along, users wanted the capability to use long filenames, but Microsoft needed a method for easily updating these systems, and that meant keeping the FAT file system. The compromise is the VFAT file system. VFAT doesn't require the resources that NTFS does, but it enables the user to use long filenames. If you take a good look at Windows 2000, you see that a good deal of the Windows 95/98 VFAT technology comes from the way that Windows 2000 handles the FAT file system.

What do you do with a system that's literally bogged down with incompatible file systems? You could take the easy way out—the way I originally took when I started working with OS/2. If you stick with the FAT file system, you'll certainly get all the operating systems talking to each other and run into a minimum of problems.

Tip: The primary reason that FAT remains the most popular file system even today is compatibility. For a long time, FAT was the only file system IBM PC users could employ. As a result, no matter which operating systems you now use, they can all access data from a FAT volume. You can have multiple operating systems on your computer, as I do, and, different as they are, none of them will have problems with a FAT volume. (Here's a list of the operating systems that can access FAT: MS-DOS, OS/2, Linux, Windows 3.x, Windows 95/98, and NT).

This solution has only one problem. If you stick with the FAT file system, you'll have compatibility, but you'll also miss out on the special features the other file systems offer.

FAT's weaknesses can be summed up in two words: inefficiency and exposure. FAT sets up its allocation table at one location near the start of the FAT volume. The FAT and the root directory must be located in a particular zone on the drive. There is, therefore, a distance penalty caused by the need to continually update the FAT (located at the start of the volume). With today's huge hard drives (8GB to 20GB is now common on new workstations), this back-and-forth travel to the FAT exacts a serious performance hit. It doesn't matter on small drives, but remember that FAT was designed when hard drives were about 1/500th the size they are today.

Technical Note: NTFS locates small files close to the NTFS directory on the drive. This is an intelligent approach to file storage. A hard drive head first has to go to the directory and then to the file. If a lot of small files are gathered around the directory, it's more efficient than placing files anywhere on a volume, willy-nilly, regardless of size or fragmentation, the way FAT does. Interestingly, NTFS uses what's called a *Master File Table* (MFT), a table that's a rough equivalent to the FAT. The MFT is divided into records like a database, and each stored file or folder has a series of attributes, including location, name, Access Control Lists (ACLs), and data. Data is just considered another attribute. If the data is less than 2KB, Windows 2000 will store it right there in the MFT itself, along with the other attributes of the file or folder. Also, the MFT is copied to several locations on the drive, depending on the size of the drive and the number of files and folders on the drive.

Another weakness: FAT locates files unintelligently. It just looks for the first available blank space and writes, never mind if this space is too small to hold the entire file and it has to be broken into linked chunks scattered here and there on the disk. In other words, write efficiency is the only consideration; how effectively this file archipelago will be read later isn't even thought about. The result: Severe fragmentation problems and a second major performance hit.

Both FAT and NTFS define a basic unit of organization called the *cluster*. FAT clusters are, well, too fat. No matter how much information you're storing in a file, that file will take up at least one cluster. If you're storing a Notepad TXT file that contains the word *Pam*, don't expect it to take up 3 bytes (or 6 bytes with Unicode) on your hard drive. Amplifying this wasted space problem is the fact that larger hard drives require larger cluster sizes. Table 12.1 provides you with some idea of just how inefficient FAT16 gets when working with large drives.

Table 12.1 FAT16 Cluster Size in Relation to Volume Size

Default Cluster Size in KB	Volume Size in MB
4	0–15 (12-bit allocation)
2	16–127
4	128–255
8	256–511
16	512–1,023
32	1,024–2,047
64	2,048–4,095
128	4,096–8,191
256	8,192–16,384

As you can see in Table 12.1, the smallest possible file stored under FAT16 will require a minimum of 2,048 bytes on a small, ancient 127MB hard drive and 131,072 bytes on a typical drive today. Compare the FAT cluster sizes to the NTFS cluster sizes shown in Table 12.2

Table 12.2 NTFS Cluster Sizes

Default Cluster Size(KB)	Volume Size(MB)
1/2 (512 bytes)	0–512
1	513–1,024
2	1,025–2,048
4	2,049 and bigger*

An NTFS volume can be as large as 2 exabytes. Exabytes isn't a word you'll hear very often because current technology can't offer hard drives smaller than a swimming pool with that much storage. An exabyte is 2^{64} bytes, or 17,179,869,184GB. (NTFS enables you to adjust the cluster size, but the cluster sizes listed in Table 12.1 for FAT volume are fixed and can't be adjusted.)

Finally, there's the fact that even dim-bulb spies have little trouble getting to the data on a FAT disk, and this can be a real problem for many businesses. There's personnel information, proprietary designs, business plans, and much more—all of which is exposed to the first person who boots off a floppy and then types C:\ at the DOS command line. This person might be interested in finding out information or destroying it. In either case, NTFS offers sophisticated security measures, whereas FAT includes only a simple, crude directory security and "hidden" files and "read-only" files that are, to anyone with a little knowledge, neither hidden nor unwriteable. NTFS offers improved reliability and a higher access speed than the old FAT file system.

Peter's Principle: A Method of Dealing with Multiple File Systems

After a lot of thought, I finally came up with a middle-ground solution to the problem of dealing with multiple file systems on one computer. This solution offers the maximum in compatibility yet lets me make the most out of what the other file systems have to offer.

The first thing I did was partition my drives. I set aside one partition for each of the operating systems installed on my machine. I had to do that anyway to get everything to boot correctly. Each operating system's specific partition uses the special file format it provides. This way, the operating system and its utility programs can benefit from the improved performance and reliability the new file system offers. I also stuck any operating system–specific applications in these partitions.

After I figured out where the operating systems would go, I installed them. Each installation required a bit of time and patience, but I got through it. It's important to test the capability to boot each operating system after you install a new one. Windows NT/2000 and Windows 95/98 like to overwrite the bootable partition marker. This means that whatever boot manager you've installed won't boot until you use a disk editor to set the active partition back to its original position.

After I installed the operating systems and tested the boot sequence, I had one large partition left (actually, I set a whole second drive aside). I labeled the partition on this drive COMMON and placed all my data and common applications there. It uses the FAT file system so that all the operating systems can access it. Obviously, you can use FAT32 if the two operating systems you plan to use are Windows 2000 and Windows 98 (or the OSR2 version of Windows 95/98). In some cases, I had to install each application once for each operating system. If you're careful, however, you can determine which files to copy from your Windows SYSTEM directory into each of the other SYSTEM directories. (DLLs and VxDs need to appear in the SYSTEM directory in most cases; otherwise, Windows won't be able to find them.) Is this a perfect solution? Not by a long shot. It's a solution that works, however.

Why did I go through this entire rundown of my system configuration? I think you might find yourself in the same dilemma. You have to test out all (or at least many) of the solutions available today, which means keeping multiple operating systems on your machine. This solution might be just what the doctor ordered when it comes time to test a Windows 98 or Windows 2000 solution that the entire company might adopt. If you don't test the advanced file system that comes with the operating system, can you really say you tested everything when the time comes to make a decision?

Technical Note: There's a third-party tool called *Partition Magic* that enables you to move partitions of different types around dynamically. There's another utility called *System Commander* that manages a multiple-boot situation very nicely. Together these programs can handle any combination of operating system and file system you can think of.

Now that you have a better idea of what the issues are, let's look at the file system architecture. Windows 2000 has a lot to juggle when it comes to file system access. Figure 12.1 shows you how it gets the job done.

FIGURE 12.1
The Windows 2000 File System has a lot to handle.

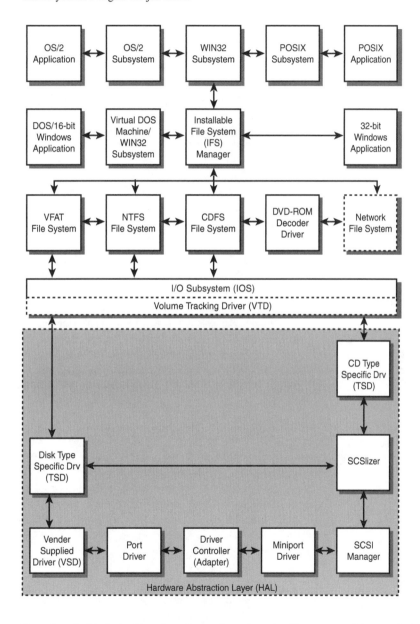

Even though this looks like a lot of ground to cover, the file system architecture isn't too difficult to understand if you break it into smaller pieces. The following list provides an overview of each of the architectural elements:

- *OS/2 Application, OS/2 Subsystem, POSIX Application, and POSIX Subsystem.*
  Microsoft has been saying for some time now that OS/2 support will be dropped
  from Windows 2000. However, Windows 2000 will still support Character mode
  OS/2 applications. What you won't find is support for the HPFS used by OS/2.
  POSIX support is being left to third-party vendors. If you're interested in strong
  UNIX support, look at OpenNT, a product that adds a UNIX subsystem supporting
  all the UNIX features: shells, services, and X11 (XWindows).

- *Win32 Subsystem.* Remember that Windows 2000 uses a client/server approach to
  taking care of the needs of the various applications it supports. It does this through
  the Win32 subsystem—a buffer layer that translates foreign operating system calls
  into something Windows 2000 can understand. Think about POSIX for a second.
  Filenames and other entities are case sensitive in that environment. Contrast this
  with the case-insensitive nature of DOS. You'll also remember that OS/2 is a 32-
  bit operating system, even in Character mode, which makes a big difference in the
  way its applications react. The actual number of differences between the various
  operating system applications are too vast to really discuss in detail here. On the
  other hand, it's always nice to know that these file system technology differences
  exist even if you don't need them.

- *Virtual DOS Machine (VDM).* Windows 2000 places each DOS application in its
  own VDM. The reason is simple: To provide the higher level of system reliability
  that Windows 2000 users demand, Microsoft had to make sure that each application had its own environment—an environment completely separate from that used
  by every other application. It's also important to remember that 16-bit Windows
  applications share one VDM. You need to remember that Windows 2000 always
  starts a VDM and then runs a copy of 16-bit Windows in it to service the needs of
  16-bit Windows applications. This effectively adds two layers to every interaction—one for the VDM and another for the Win32 subsystem. As with everything
  else, this additional layering is transparent to the user. You still use the same interfaces as before.

- *Installable File System (IFS) Manager.* This is the highest layer in the file system.
  The IFS is a VxD that provides the interface to applications. It doesn't matter
  whether the application uses the interrupt 21h interface or the 16- or 32-bit
  Windows interface; this is the component that receives application requests. It's
  the responsibility of the IFS to transfer control to the appropriate file system driver
  (FSD). Notice that Windows 2000 supports four different file system drivers.
  Chapter 24, "Peer-to-Peer Networking," discusses the network support.

- *File System Driver (FSD) Layer.* The most common file system driver layer component is the NTFS FSD. You can also use any of the other FSDs provided with
  Windows 2000, however, including VFAT, CDFS, and Network. Except for the
  Network FSD (which is discussed in Chapter 27, "Client/Server Networking"),
  these VxDs take care of all local hard drive requests. Besides file system–specific
  needs, each FSD provides the long filename support and Protected mode stability

that makes Windows 2000 better than its predecessors. Your machine might have several other FSDs, depending on the type of equipment you've installed. Notice that the block diagram shown in Figure 12.1 includes a CDFS driver, for example. This is a special driver designed to access a CD-ROM or DVD-ROM drive. The CDFS driver actually consists of three files on your system: CDROM.SYS, REDBOOK.SYS, and STORPROP.DLL (unless you're using third-party drivers). Windows 2000 only installs this driver when it detects a CD-ROM or DVD-ROM drive attached to your system. Note that under Windows 2000, the main difference from a user perspective for CD-ROM or DVD-ROM support is that there are additional decoder drivers for the DVD-ROM drive that allow it to play DVDs in addition to CDs. All the FSDs communicate with the IFS manager. They also send requests to the layers that directly communicate with the hardware.

> **Note:** The Windows 2000 CDFS driver is based on the ISO 13346 standard rather than the older ISO 9660 standard. The new level of support is required to support DVD-ROM drives in addition to CD-ROM drives.

- *DVD-ROM Decoder Driver.* Like CDs, there are two kinds of DVD: data and multimedia (movie) DVDs, both of which are handled by the DVD-ROM decoder driver. This driver is composed of several files on your system. The actual number depends on the DVD-ROM decoder hardware that you use. As a minimum, you'll find that DVDPLAY.EXE is installed for multimedia DVDs. This program further relies on new Windows 2000 features such as DirectShow and older features such as the media control interface (MCI). The DVD-ROM Decoder Driver also introduces a new executable file extension: .AX. The AX files all work with streaming media such as the kind found on DVDs, and they provide links to Microsoft's newer ActiveX technologies such as ActiveMovie. In most cases, there will also be special files such as AVSHELL.DLL, which allows you to set up your DVD-ROM drive for use in DVD mode.

- *I/O Subsystem (IOS) Layer.* This is the highest level of the block device layer. What do I mean by a block device? Any device that sends information in groups of bytes of a consistent size (such as a hard drive) is called a *block device*. A hard drive usually uses some multiple of 512 bytes as its block size. Other devices might use different block sizes. Network devices, tape drives, and CD-ROM/DVD-ROM drives all fall into the block device category. The IOS provides general device services to the FSDs. It routes requests from the FSDs to various device-specific drivers, for example. It also sends status information from the device-specific drivers to the FSDs.

- *Volume Tracking Driver (VTD) Layer.* Windows 2000 might not install this driver. It handles any removable devices attached to your system. If you have a floppy disk, CD-ROM, or DVD-ROM drive, for example, Windows 2000 will install this component. On the other hand, if you use a diskless workstation or rely on local and network hard drives alone, Windows 2000 won't need to install this component. The VTD performs one, and only one, basic function. It monitors the status of all removable media drives and reports any change in media. This is the component that will complain if you remove a floppy disk prematurely (usually, in the middle of a write).

- *Hardware Abstraction Layer (HAL).* This is another conceptual type of element in Windows 2000. Microsoft wrote the drivers and other software elements in such a way that it could easily move Windows 2000 to other platforms. That's how it moved Windows 2000 to the Alpha machines. The basic architecture of Windows 2000 is the same, but the low-level drivers—the ones that directly interface with the hardware—are different. Figure 12.1 shows the elements for an Intel processor machine. You might see something slightly different when using an Alpha machine. The important thing to remember is that, as far as your application is concerned, it's still running on an Intel machine. The only time you'll run into trouble is if you bypass the Windows API and go directly to the hardware.

- *Type-Specific Driver (TSD) Layer.* Every type of device needs a driver that understands its peculiar needs. The hard disk drive driver wouldn't understand the needs of a floppy disk drive very well, for example. This layer deals with logical device types rather than specific devices. One TSD handles all the hard drives on your system, for example, whereas another TSD handles all the floppy disk drives. A third TSD handles all network drives. After a data read or write leaves the TSD, it can follow one of two paths. Windows 2000 provides one level of handling for most standard drives such as IDE and ESDI. It provides a special level of handling for SCSI drives.

- *CD Type-Specific Driver (TSD) Layer.* This particular device gets a special entry because it has to handle multiple data types. The TSD works in a similar fashion to the one I described for a standard drive. Because a CD-ROM or DVD-ROM drive has to be able to play music CDs as well as read from (and, in some cases, write to) data CDs, it requires a special kind of a TSD—one that's more complex than a general drive requires. (Remember that DVDs are handled by the DVD-ROM Decoder Driver, which is a combination of TSD, player, and device driver elements.) The fact that a CD is a removable medium also serves to complicate the driver. Unlike a floppy disk drive, where a simple detection of a floppy disk change is needed, a CD not only has to detect the change but it also has to detect the media type. Also think of game and educational programs where the CD may contain both data and music—talk about a complicated situation. I don't want to get into the bits and bytes of CD data handling here, but it's important to realize that CD drives are a unique class of drives that requires special handling.

- *Vendor-Supplied Driver (VSD) Layer.* This is where a vendor would install support for a proprietary bus CD-ROM or a removable media device, such as a floptical drive. Windows 2000 provides a whole list of standard drivers that also get installed at this level. The IDE drive attached to your machine has its own VSD, for example. Every specific device type needs a driver that can translate its requests for Windows. This is the layer that performs those services. The VSD knows things such as the number of heads a disk has and the amount of time it needs to wait for a floppy disk drive to get up to speed.

- *Port Driver (PD) Layer*. The PD performs the actual task of communicating with the device through an adapter. It's the last stage before a message leaves Windows and the first stage when a message arrives from the device. The PD is usually adapter specific. You'd have one VSD for each hard drive type (such as IDE) and one PD for each hard drive adapter (a *port*, in Windows 2000 terms), for example. If your system uses an IDE hard drive, Windows would load the IDE PD to talk to the IDE adapter. A typical example of an IDE PD layer includes an ATAPI driver, the IDE driver, and an IDE extension for the PCI bus. In addition, there are drivers for each IDE channel that provide ATAPI support and display configuration property pages.

- *SCSIizer*. Don't let the strange-looking name for this layer fool you. The SCSIizer portion of the file system deals with the SCSI command language. Think of the command language as the method the computer uses to tell a SCSI device to perform a task. It isn't the data the SCSI device handles; instead, it's the act the SCSI device will perform. Windows 2000 has one SCSIizer for each SCSI device.

- *SCSI Manager*. Windows 2000 introduced something called the *miniport driver*. This is a platform-specific driver that enables you to use Windows 2000 on a variety of machines without making wholesale changes to the operating system. Before you can actually use the miniport driver, however, Windows 2000 has to translate its commands to a format the miniport driver will understand. The SCSI Manager performs this service.

- *Miniport Driver*. This is a device driver that provides support for a specific SCSI device. Only one device uses any given miniport driver. The miniport driver works with the SCSI Manager to perform the same task as a PD. Windows NT/2000 and Windows 95/98 use the same miniport drivers.

- *Drive Controller (Adapter)*. This is the physical device that provides disk services for the machine. Windows 2000 has to support a variety of controller types, including all those used by PCs, in addition to Alpha machines. The HAL makes communications between the internal portions of Windows 2000 and the drive hardware possible.

The FAT/VFAT File System

Now that we have some preliminaries out of the way, let's take a look at the VFAT file system provided with Windows 2000. I use the term *VFAT* because of the kind of support Windows 2000 provides; it's a lot more like the support provided by Windows 95/98 than the original form of FAT file system you used in DOS. As I said in an earlier chapter, one of the reasons for Windows 3.0's success was that the user could upgrade DOS to use it. In other words, the user could make the transition slowly without giving up a comfortable environment. Windows 2000 continues this line of reasoning, even maintaining a level of compatibility with the old FAT file system. (Unlike Windows 95/98, however, you can always choose the higher performance of the other file systems provided with Windows 2000.)

> **Note:** Unlike Windows NT, Windows 2000 provides support for the newest version of FAT: FAT32. This new version of FAT provides support for larger partitions and uses space on those partitions more efficiently that previous versions did. It's important to understand that FAT32 and VFAT are different. VFAT is an underlying technology used to access the hard drive, whereas FAT32 is a technology used for formatting the hard drive.

Why do we need yet another form of FAT file system when it's already out of date? People weren't satisfied with the old 8.3 filenames. They wanted long filenames, and the FAT file system can't provide this feature. On the other hand, trying to move some people from the FAT file system they're comfortable with to NTFS has proven less than popular. The VFAT file system represents an effort on the part of Microsoft to give people what they want and still maintain a level of compatibility with previous versions of DOS (and, more important, the applications that run under it).

> **Tip:** FAT (either FAT16 or FAT32) is actually the best file system for small volumes, such as floppy disks. As you might imagine, NTFS is overkill with small volumes. How much space would be left for actual data after NTFS's required security and other overhead? And FAT is a simpler system, which means that it's faster on small volumes.

Microsoft had another reason for adding VFAT support to Windows 2000. You can't use NTFS on a floppy disk drive (or some types of floptical drives). The only file system that works on this medium is FAT. Adding long filename support to FAT (making it VFAT) enables a user to move a file from one place to another without losing the long filename. Sure, it's a small consideration, but it's an important one as far as I'm concerned. I don't use floppy disks very much anymore—I can't even remember the last time I actually bought a new one. When I do use a floppy disk, however, it's usually to move data from my workstation to a notebook. Imagine how much of a hassle it would be to change the filenames of the files I moved just because my floppy disk drive didn't support the long filenames provided by the operating system. For this reason alone, I think VFAT will be around for the foreseeable future—at least until Microsoft finds a way to move NTFS to floppy disks, which seems unlikely. A more probable forecast is that the current 1.2MB disks will, at some point, be replaced with something like 100MB Zip disks or some other portable 100MB format.

The following sections provide you with a bit of history and then a current look at the way Windows handles file access (at least for the FAT file system). It's important to start at the beginning to see what you've gained with various versions of Windows. Even more important, this historical view will help you understand certain constraints Microsoft programmers faced when they designed the VFAT file system used by Windows 2000. It's easy to start out with a new product and design in all the features people want today. It's another story altogether to start with something that was fine yesterday and redesign it to meet today's needs. Windows 2000 isn't a completely new operating system; it still has to provide some compatibility with the older file systems used by previous versions of Windows. Fortunately, you aren't shackled with using those old file systems; you can move on to the next stage in computer development if you really want to. I've already covered some of this reasoning earlier in the chapter, so I won't discuss it again here. VFAT is probably the last stop for the venerable DOS file system.

A Look at Windows Under DOS

Everyone who has worked with DOS and Windows 3.x knows that they have at least one thing in common with other users: the FAT file system. That relationship between DOS and Windows 3.x also causes some problems for the user. Consider the speed issue many people bring up when you talk about using Windows. Because this older version of Windows rides on top of DOS, it must use some DOS services to access the hardware. The hard disk drive falls into this category. DOS provides all the file services Windows 3.x uses. In fact, this is about the only DOS service Windows 3.1 does use.

What using DOS to provide file services means to the user is that the system has to slow down every time Windows wants to access the hard drive. To see what I mean, look at Figure 12.2. Every time Windows wants to access the hard drive, it has to create a request in a format DOS will understand, switch over to Real mode so that it can access DOS, and then wait for DOS to get the job done. Meanwhile, all those applications that are supposed to do something in the background are suspended. Remember that the Intel processor can't multitask in Real mode; it can do that only in Protected mode. After DOS finds the bit of information Windows needs, Windows has to copy that information out of the conventional memory space into an area it can reach in Protected mode. It must then switch the processor from Real mode back into Protected mode.

FIGURE 12.2

Windows 3.1 needed to switch from Protected mode to Real mode to access the hard drive through DOS.

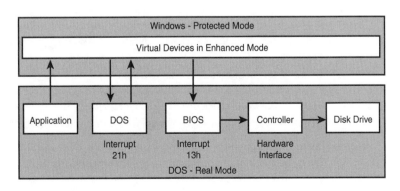

The transition from Real mode to Protected mode is only an inconvenience—it wastes time your machine could use to process information. There are more insidious problems with using Real mode drivers. Every time Windows has to make the switch from Protected mode to Real mode, it becomes vulnerable to attack from a maverick application. When the processor is in Real mode, the operating system can no longer track system activity. The processor won't alert the operating system when an application creates a memory fault. As a result, an application could crash the system before Windows 3.x even knows what's going on.

Unfortunate as it may seem, Windows 95/98 can still suffer from this problem if the drive being used requires a Real mode driver. This is one of the problems that makes Windows 2000 inherently more stable and reliable than Windows 95/98—users can't use Real mode drivers even if they want to. Under Windows 2000, all drive access takes place in Protected mode or not at all.

32-Bit Access Under Windows 3.1

Windows 3.1 provided a new feature called *32-bit access*. This feature reduces the possibilities of opportunity for system crashes and enhances overall system speed. Before I talk about how 32-bit access affects your computing environment, however, you need to understand what it is.

If you tried to figure out what 32-bit access is by its name, you might suspect that it's some new technique for accessing the data on your drive, 32 bits at a time. What 32-bit access actually provides is a little more complex.

Every time an application requests data from the hard drive, Windows intercepts the request to see whether it can be fulfilled using data in protected memory. Usually, the request asks to open a file or to read specific byte ranges of data. If Windows determines that it can't fulfill the request, it switches to Real mode and passes the request to the DOS interrupt 21h handler. This handler looks at the request and starts to take care of it by issuing interrupt 13h requests. You can look at interrupt 21h as the manager and interrupt 13h as the worker. Interrupt 21h gets the whole problem in one big chunk. It breaks up the problem into small pieces interrupt 13h can handle. As a result, each interrupt 21h call can result in a lot of interrupt 13h calls.

Of course, because Windows is monitoring everything, the system doesn't just stay in Real mode and take care of the entire disk request at one time. Windows intercepts each interrupt 13h call the DOS interrupt 21h handler makes to see whether it can fulfill the request using data in protected memory. If not, Windows switches back to Real mode, and the BIOS handles the call. The BIOS performs the work required to fulfill the call and passes the information back to Windows, which passes it back to DOS, which passes it back to Windows, which finally passes it back to the application. This might seem like a lot of work just to read a few bytes of data from the disk, and it is.

Figure 12.3 shows the 32-bit access method used by Windows 3.1x. Notice that the BIOS is completely cut out of the picture. That's because FastDisk (a 32-bit, Protected mode driver) emulates the BIOS using Protected mode code. This means not only that

Windows eliminates two mode transitions for every interrupt 13h call but also that it can effectively multitask during more of the disk access cycle. You lose only the DOS processing time rather than both DOS and BIOS processing time. This improvement accounts for part of the noticeable speed-up in Windows 3.1*x*. It also accounts for some of the improved stability that people experience.

FIGURE 12.3

Windows 3.11 provided a 32-bit access feature that reduced the opportunities for a system crash and enhanced system throughput.

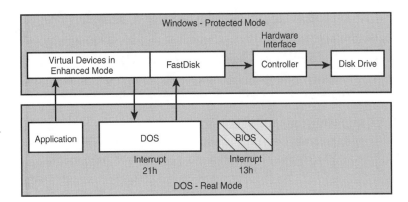

Windows 3.11 and Windows for Workgroups 3.11 add even more. In addition to 32-bit disk access, these versions add 32-bit file access. These versions of Windows use the DOS file-access features to search for files and to perform other file-specific activities. (This differentiates a file access from a disk access, which deals with reading and writing sections of data.) This means even fewer transitions to DOS because the file system no longer keeps the BIOS in the picture. The result is an overall improvement in system speed and reliability.

The Windows 2000 Alternative to 32-Bit Access

Windows 2000 gets around the entire Real mode access problem by incorporating all operating system functions into a 32-bit architecture. Microsoft has named this technique the *VFAT interface* for Windows 95/98; I've borrowed the same term for the service that Windows 2000 provides because, from the user's point of view, it's the same. The full name for this type of disk access is the *Protected mode FAT file system*. Figure 12.4 shows how this disk management system differs from the one used under Windows 3.*x*. Using Protected mode drivers means that there's less chance that a random application will cause a system failure because Windows 2000 is never unprotected for a long enough time. (In fact, unlike Windows 95/98, Windows 2000 is never in a state where it's unprotected because each application runs in its own memory space and Windows 2000 doesn't enable you to use Real mode drivers.) The VFAT file system always runs in Protected mode. Using Protected mode means the operating system constantly monitors every event taking place on the machine. It has the final say before a particular event takes place. This new system runs totally in protected memory, thus reducing to nearly zero the chance of system crashes due to disk-related problems and greatly enhancing disk-access speed.

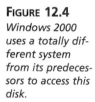

FIGURE 12.4
Windows 2000 uses a totally different system from its predecessors to access this disk.

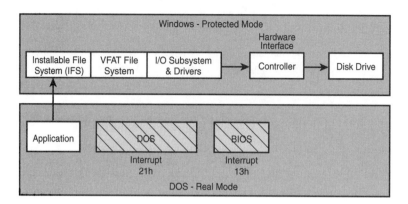

Figure 12.4 shows several discrete components in the Windows 2000 File System. Actually, Microsoft refers to these components as *layers*. The Windows 2000 File System has 32 possible layers, starting at the I/O subsystem. (The current configuration doesn't use all 32 layers.) Layer 0 is closest to the I/O subsystem, whereas layer 31 is closest to the hardware. The current version of Windows 2000 only requires a few (usually 12) of these layers to get the job done. The other layers are placeholders, available for future use. Each layer provides hooks for third-party software used to support custom file systems and devices. Adding a network driver to the file system layer enables you to access drives on other machines, for example. Unlike with previous versions of Windows, a vendor can retrofit the Windows 2000 File System to provide additional capabilities with relative ease. I already covered these various tasks as part of the architecture discussion (you can also see them in Figure 12.1), so I won't go into detail again here.

Windows 2000 Support for FAT32

There's one big change that many people are going to notice when it comes to Windows 2000: NTFS 5 provides support for FAT32. FAT32 is the file system that originally appeared in the OSR2 version of Windows 95 and now all versions of Windows 98. This means that you can use the more efficient FAT32 file system for dual-boot machines. Table 12.3 gives you some idea of just how FAT32 compares to FAT16 and NTFS.

Table 12.3 File System Statistics Comparison

Statistic	FAT16	FAT32	NTFS
Maximum partition size	2^{16}	2^{32}	2^{64}
Maximum file size	2^{16}	2^{32}	2^{64}
Cluster size	512 bytes+	4KB	512 bytes
Maximum volume size	2GB	2TB	16,777,216TB
Maximum file size	2GB	2TB	16,777,216TB

Note: Although NTFS can store 16,777,216TB (or 16 exabytes) on a single drive, there are practical limits imposed by the memory limits of current Windows 2000 technology (2GB for Windows NT 4, and 3GB for Windows 2000). Of course, given the memory capabilities of Windows 2000, it's doubtful you'd actually reach these practical limits, nor does Microsoft advertise them. Once a 64-bit version of Windows NT/2000 is released, these practical disk limitations will probably be removed.

As you can see from Table 12.3, FAT32 doesn't give you quite as much flexibility as NTFS does. However, it does allow you to get around the 2GB limit imposed by FAT16, which is very good news today considering most hard drives offer a minimum of 8GB of storage space. In addition, a 2GB drive will offer a minimum file size of 4KB under FAT32—the same file under FAT16 would take 32KB. Most people have realized significant space savings when using FAT32.

Windows 2000 Support for UDF

NTFS5 also supports the Universal Disk Format (UDF), which is based on ISO 13346. This file system replaces the older Compact Disk File System (CDFS), which is based on ISO 9660. There are a lot of low-level differences between these two standards. However, from a user perspective, the difference is very easy to understand. UDF supports both CD-ROM drives and DVD-ROM drives. This additional support allows you to gain the advantages that DVDs provide when it comes to choice of media and density of data storage.

Tip: The version of UDF used in both Windows 2000 (UDF 1.50) and Windows 98 (UDF 1.02) is read-only. The latest version of UDF is 2.0, at the time of this writing, and it wouldn't surprise me if you found this update in both Windows 2000 and Windows 98 sometime in the near future. You can find out more about this standard at the Optical Storage Technologies Association Web site at http://www.osta.org/. This site provides a lot of very interesting information about optical storage. For example, there's a paper available on multiread technologies.

Gaining Access to VFAT from DOS

You can access the VFAT interface in a DOS application. Microsoft incorporated a new set of services into the interrupt 21h handler. Table 12.4 shows the various calls you can make to this interface. Notice that the AL part of the service call corresponds to the current disk service call numbers. The contents of the other registers correspond to the old DOS register setups as well. If you know how to use the current set of interrupt 21h disk routines, using the new ones means a simple change in the contents of the AX register (in most cases). Microsoft recommends that you use the Get Volume Information (71A0h) to detect whether the current system supports long filenames. Set the carry flag before making the call. If the machine doesn't support long filenames, the carry flag will be unchanged on return, and DOS will clear the AL register. Never use the long filename calls on a system that doesn't support them. Remember that all these service numbers go into the AX register and that the values are in hexadecimal format.

Table 12.4   VFAT Interface Interrupt 21h Functions

AX Code	Function Name
7139h	Create Directory
713Ah	Remove Directory
713Bh	Set Current Directory
7141h	Delete File
7143h	Get/Set File Attributes
7147h	Get Current Directory
714Eh	Find First File
714Fh	Find Next File
7156h	Move or Rename File
716Ch	Extended Open/Create File
71A0h	Get Volume Information
71A1h	Find Close

The NTFS File System

For many of us, NTFS's best feature is its efficiency—it's fast. It's especially effective when used on large volumes (such as servers, graphics workstations, and power user's workstations). In general, you see the performance gains starting with volumes 1GB or larger. That's because the stability and security offered by NTFS don't come for free.

There's a lot of NTFS material to cover when it comes to Windows 2000 because Microsoft is always making this file system better. In fact, that's the first thing you need to know about NTFS; Microsoft designed it so that it could easily be extended without causing any backward compatibility problems. The ability to extend NTFS isn't just in the hands of Microsoft, either; every programmer can add new capabilities to what you see (I discuss this feature later in this section). This section of the chapter isn't meant as the end-all discussion of NTFS. What I give you is an overview of what makes NTFS special and why you should consider using it in place of the older file systems on your machine.

Layering and extending NTFS go hand in hand. I discussed this concept earlier as part of the layered approach that Microsoft uses in the design of the Windows 2000 File System. NTFS provides a lot more than just a layered and extensible file system, however. The idea of layering goes a lot further than that. You'll find that layering affects three areas of NTFS: multiplatform support, file attributes, and special features such as fault tolerance.

The multiplatform nature of Windows 2000 is one of the first ways that layering will help you directly as a user. I mentioned previously that Windows 2000 is designed to support a variety of operating systems in addition to working with a variety of CPU types. One of the ways it does this is by making the other operating system think that it's providing a specific service when it's really not. NTFS can mimic the capabilities of a POSIX file system, for example. One of these features is the capability to support case-sensitive names, so that FileName is different from FILENAME, for example. Under FAT, both names are the same because both file systems originally provided name support that wasn't case sensitive. Note that NTFS filenames are also not case sensitive, but NTFS has the capability to store filenames with their capitalization intact (this is called *case preservation*) in case it must deal with a case-sensitive operating systems such as UNIX.

Another POSIX-related feature in NTFS is the capability to support multiple timestamps. It doesn't take too long to figure out that if you can tell NTFS to mimic these features, other file system features are just as easy to add. File system features are one of the things that keep operating systems from working together, so this mimicry isn't just a minor addition to NTFS; it's something that'll probably help you create multiplatform links somewhere along the way.

> **Note:** The multiple-stream capability of NTFS does provide one unique feature that a lot of people will find handy. A Macintosh file contains two streams: one for data and another for resources. The data stream might include the creating application's name. The resource stream includes the file type and tells what icon to attach to the file. Until now, that data always got lost when a user transferred a file from a Macintosh to a PC. The multiple-stream capability of NTFS makes it possible for PC and Macintosh users to exchange files now without any loss of resource information.

Another form of layering comes into play with file attributes. NTFS permits programmers to assign their own custom attributes to files and folders. As more applications are designed to use NTFS, you'll find a lot of new attributes assigned to the files you use. A new attribute might be as simple as the name of the person who created the file or the version number of this particular file. Complex attributes might include things such as the resolution and number of colors for a graphics file.

Fault tolerance has become more and more important as companies place more of their critical data on PCs. Those of you who work with database management systems will recognize NTFS's crash-recovery strategy instantly. Windows 2000 stores some disk transactions in a log. It doesn't store all disk access operations in the log because that would result in a serious performance hit. Instead, Windows 2000 stores the *metadata*, which is information that could impact the integrity of the file system. This includes such events as changes to directory structures, changes to file or folder names, and the movement of folders to new locations. Less significant changes, such as resaving a Word DOC file, isn't transactionalized in a log and therefore can't be recovered by NTFS. Many applications, however, Word included, have their own data-recovery schemes.

What happens if a system crash occurs before a file transaction is complete? Windows 2000 can use the log entries to either reconstruct the file system's integrity or reverse any changes—it all depends on when the system error occurs. This technique even works for bad sectors because Windows 2000 uses the log to verify the contents of a file. The end result is a successful recovery—at least for events that the operating system can monitor—and the log strategy also protects against things that the operating system can't foresee, such as a power outage.

Security is another area where the file system comes into play. Chapter 28, "Security Issues," provides a lot more detail about this subject in the section titled "System Security and the Administrator." It's important to realize that the security I discuss in that chapter extends to the file system. Windows 2000 looks at every system resource—including disks, folders, and files—as objects. To gain access to an object, you must have the proper access token. Think of an access token as a key that consists of the password and other access features that Windows 2000 provides. In other words, to access any part of the NTFS file system, you have to have the right access. Unlike the FAT and HPFS file systems, you can't bypass this security by loading another operating system. Everything is under Windows 2000's control, which means that your data is a lot more secure.

Its superior security isn't the end of NTFS's special features list. You can add Unicode (16-bit) characters to a filename on an NTFS partition. This permits filenames in all languages. In addition, NTFS provides B-tree indexing. NTFS enables you to create indexes for all the attribute streams. This means that you can search a disk for the name of a particular document author or a version of a program used to create a data file. The possibilities are unlimited—something that you probably haven't heard from other file systems.

By now, it should be obvious why you'd want to switch from VFAT to NTFS. The thing to remember is that some of these features aren't in use today; you won't actually get to see them until application development catches up to the changes that NTFS provides. However, isn't it good to know that those capabilities are available and that you'll eventually be able to use them? I think that the future of computing is the NTFS file system—at least until someone thinks of a better idea.

NTFS 4 Versus NTFS 5

We've already covered a couple of the interesting changes to NTFS: FAT32 support and UDF. However, there are a lot of other interesting changes you should know about that affect NTFS 5 directly. For one thing, NTFS 5 supports *reparse points*. Essentially, this is a change in the way that NTFS handles file paths. Each step of the directory path is individually parsed and, if necessary, redirected to another location. For example, if you had a path of C:\Windows\README.TXT, the path would get parsed once for C: and again for Windows. This capability will eventually allow for multiple drive links into one. You could connect to any drive on your machine using a single drive letter. This feature is also extensible. A developer can create customized reparse filters that adjust the way that the file path gets parsed.

> **Tip:** This chapter won't cover all the intricacies of reparse points—at least not from a programmer level. However, Microsoft makes available a lot of detailed information about reparse points and other NTFS 5 features as part of the Installable File System (IFS) kit. The IFS kit is available at http://www.microsoft.com/hwdev/ntifskit/. This Web site also provides access to a mailing list that will keep you up-to-date on the latest IFS developments.

Another feature is per-disk and per-user quotas. The use of quotas will keep one person from consuming all the space on a server hard drive. Of course, this applies equally well to processes or any other object as well. Before the use of quotas, an errant application could fill an entire hard drive with log file entries, for example, and the administrator might not realize there was a problem before it was too late to do something about the problem. Once your machine runs completely out of hard drive space, it's susceptible to a crash from several different sources, including the inability to increase the size of the swap file and Registry. Quotas are based on the security identifier (SID) of the owner—whoever created the file is responsible for the space that it consumes. (If you don't know what a SID is, we'll cover it as part of the security discussion in Chapter 28.

NTFS also supports native property sets. The default property sets appear on the Summary tab of a file's Properties dialog box, like the one shown in Figure 12.5. This feature is like the property pages that you attach to a COM object. Property sets allow you to define attributes for a file. For example, you could attach a description of a graphics image to a graphics file using this technique. One of the perks of using this new feature is that Microsoft Index Server is set up to use property sets. Anything you attach to a file will be used to index it, which makes searches much easier for the user.

Tracking all the changes that occur to the file system is another NTFS 5 feature. You can record file creation, deletion, and modification, as well as changes to properties, security, encryption, and compression. In short, you can now actually track how the file system gets used.

You'll really like the new sparse file support in Windows 2000. When you're creating a normal file, the file size reflects every byte that you actually use. A *sparse file*, on the other hand, allocates a certain number of bytes but doesn't actually have to use them. This is known as *allocation on demand*. It allows you to create a file that'll provide enough space for what you need to eventually store, rather than allocate bytes as you use them. Fortunately, the system only "charges" you for the bytes that are actually in use. For example, you can allocate a 1GB file. When the user clicks that file, they'll see a 1GB file. However, if you've only place 64KB of data in that file, the quota system will see that you've only used 64KB of your allocated space on the drive.

NTFS5 Access Restrictions from Windows 2000

As previously mentioned, the file system is totally new for Windows 2000. Yes, Microsoft still officially classifies it as NTFS, but the version number has gone up to 5. Windows NT 4.0 uses NTFS 4. Needless to say, the two versions of NTFS aren't com-patible, so you can't really mix them without help. You must install Service Pack 4 (or above) on any Windows NT 4.0 machine that you want to use to access drives containing NTFS 5.

However, even if you do install the required support on your Windows NT 4 machine, there are still going to be limits to what you can do to maintain an NTFS 5 volume. For one thing, you won't be able to work with some new NTFS 5 features such as quotas from your Windows NT 4 machine—the support for managing quotas simply isn't available.

NTFS 5 also supports the idea of *super hidden files*, which we'll discuss in the "Understanding the Levels of Hidden Files" section of the chapter. Essentially, super hid-den files are those that are used for system purposes. The inability to remove these files (when needed) means that your ability to make changes to an NTFS 5 volume from Windows NT 4 is extremely limited.

Understanding the Levels of Hidden Files

DOS originated the idea of the hidden file. The main purpose of hiding a file was to make it invisible to the end user, even if the operating system could still see it. Anyone who's used DOS knows that the Hidden attribute did indeed keep files hidden from the casual user who only used DOS utilities designed to observe the Hidden attribute. It wasn't long, however, and people found ways to get around the Hidden attribute (most notably, the ATTRIB utility).

When Windows 95 came out with the Explorer interface, hidden files took another hit. Explorer made very little effort to hide files marked with the Hidden attribute. A simple change to the folder viewing options was all you needed to see any hidden files on your drive. In addition, it's easy to remove the Hidden attribute, making the file permanently visible.

Windows 2000 comes with a new type of hidden file that, for the lack of a better name, I'll refer to as a *super hidden file*. In essence, this is a protected operating system file. The two features that set super hidden files apart from their counterparts is that you can't remove the Hidden attribute from the file and you can't delete it using any of the normal methods. In addition, unless you make a special setting change to Windows Explorer (Tools, Folder Options, View tab and then Hide Protected System Operating Files), you really can't see a super hidden file (nor would you really want to, in most cases). An example of a super hidden file is the PAGEFILE.SYS file that's used for virtual memory and the primary Registry file, NTUSER.DAT. Even if you use the Windows 2000 search utility (Start, Search, For Files and Folders), you won't locate NTUSER.DAT if the Hide Protected System Operating Files option is selected.

Obviously, there are going to be times when you simply need to view the status of a super hidden file, such as when you monitor the size of the PAGEFILE.SYS file or make a backup of NTUSER.DAT. So, how do you see hidden and super hidden files if you need to? Both settings appear on the View tab of the Folder Options dialog box shown in Figure 12.6. If you want to see files that have just the Hidden attribute marked, then you'd select the Show Hidden Files and Folders option. If you also wanted to see super hidden files, you'd need to uncheck the Hide Protected Operating System Files (Recommended) option and select the Show Hidden Files and Folders option.

FIGURE 12.6

You have to make two settings changes if you want to see all the files on your system.

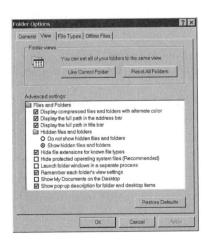

Volume Management

Windows 2000—both Server and Workstation versions—provides a lot more in the way of volume management capabilities than older versions of Windows. I find that working with Windows 2000 is a lot easier than what I've used in the past. Anyone who has spent time wandering the menus of FDISK when creating a complex system setup knows exactly what I mean.

> **Note:** This book is designed for the Professional version of Windows 2000. I'm not going to cover some of the features provided by the Server versions of the product, such as RAID. (Windows 2000 Professional does provide basic RAID Level 5 support but doesn't support other forms of RAID at this time.) I think that these are important features, and I hope Microsoft eventually adds them to the Professional product as well. For now, however, I'll cover the features that the Professional version of the product does provide. I think you'll still find that the features are well ahead of what you saw in previous versions of Windows.

The first thing you should do before you use this section is find the Computer Management snap-in for Microsoft Management Console (MMC), which appears in the Administrative Tools folder of the Control Panel. Within this snap-in are several utilities for managing your computer as a whole. Select the Disk Management folder and you'll see a display similar to Figure 12.7. Obviously, my disk layout is different from yours, so you won't see precisely the same things that I show throughout this section of the book. Just use the screenshots as a guideline for your own machine.

FIGURE 12.7
The Disk Management utility allows you to work with the hard drives on your machine.

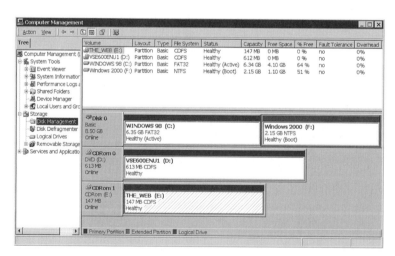

The initial view provided by the Disk Management utility shows a graphics layout of the disks and partitions on your machine. Figure 12.7 shows three kinds of partitions: CDFS,

FAT (FAT32 in this case), and NTFS. The are other designations for extended partitions, logical drives, and free space on the drive. For example, the NTFS partition in Figure 12.7 is on an extended partition, which represents a logical drive on that partition. Some special partition types include stripe set, stripe set with parity, mirror set, spanned volume, and RAID level 5 volume. The various spaces representing a partition provide a drive letter, volume label, partition type, and the size of the partition. You'll also find the total size of a drive and its designation on the left side of the display.

Above the graphic representation of your drives is a table containing precise data about the various partitions. You can determine the health of the drive, the file system that it uses, the amount of free space it provides, and whether this drive uses fault tolerance. In sum, this display provides you with just about everything you need to determine the current status of the drives on your system.

Now that you have a basic idea of how to view the information that Disk Management can provide, take a look at some of the other tasks you can perform with it. Windows 2000 enables you to do a lot of things that you can't under previous versions of Windows. The following sections cover the capabilities that the Professional version of Windows 2000 provides. You'll find that the Server version provides all these features and some server-related features such as full RAID support. (One of the new features of Windows 2000 is basic RAID level 5 support.)

Creating a Partition

The most basic operation you can perform with Disk Management is creating and formatting a partition. Windows 2000 supports two kinds of basic partitions: primary and extended. These are the same options that the old FDISK utility supported. The only difference is that you don't have to leave Disk Management and reboot the machine before you can access the new partition. The following procedure shows you how to create a primary partition. Creating an extended partition is the same. I'm assuming that you have Disk Management open to start this procedure:

1. Select a free space on one of your drives. The default Disk Management setup shows a free space as a black hatched area, as shown in Figure 12.8.

2. Right-click the free partition area and choose Create Partition from the context menu. You'll see the first screen of the Create Partition Wizard.

3. Click Next. The Create Partition Wizard will give you a choice of choosing a primary or extended partition, as shown in Figure 12.9.

4. Choose a partition type. Normally, you'll create a primary partition on a drive that doesn't already contain a partition. Extended partitions are usually added after a primary partition already exists on the drive.

5. Click Next. The Create Partition Wizard will ask you to choose a size for the partition. This dialog box also tells you the minimum and maximum sized partition you can create.

FIGURE 12.8

The Disk Management utility displays a free partition in black with a description of Unallocated.

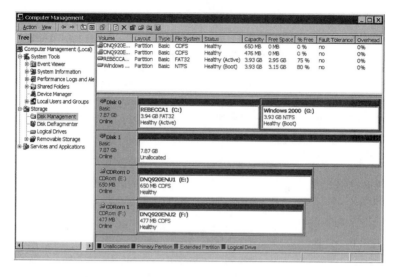

FIGURE 12.9

You can create either primary or extended partitions with the Create Partition Wizard.

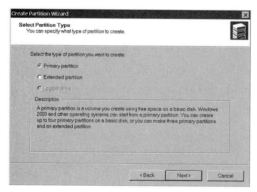

6. Type a partition size and then click Next. If you're creating an extended partition, you'll see a completion message—skip to step 9. If you're creating a primary partition, you'll see the Assign a Drive Letter or Path dialog box shown in Figure 12.10. This dialog box allows you to assign the standard drive letter to the partition, or you can access it from a folder on another drive. This is part of the new reparse point technology that Microsoft provides. The drive path is checked at each level and redirected as necessary. In this case, a reparse point will allow you to access the new drive from a folder on your existing drive, thus making the drive almost transparent in the process and allowing you to add the drive without worrying about the usual shift in drive letters. The advantage of using this technique is that you can add drive capacity to a machine without affecting the user environment—all the user will see is more drive space using the old drive setup. In addition, unlike a volume set (described in the next section), a failure of one drive won't affect the data contained on the remaining drives.

FIGURE 12.10

Reparse point technology allows you to assign a new drive to a blank folder on an existing drive.

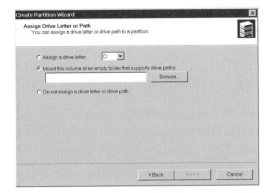

Note: Only NTFS 5 partitions support the new reparse point technology. If you want to assign a drive to a folder on another drive, you must select an NTFS 5–formatted partition as the place to put the redirection folder.

7. Choose a drive letter, an empty folder on an NTFS 5 partition, or neither option. Click Next. You'll see the Format Partition dialog box shown in Figure 12.11. This is where you'll choose whether and how to format the new partition that you're creating. The first choice you need to make is between NTFS and FAT (Windows 2000 will automatically choose between FAT16 and FAT32, depending on the size of the drive). You can also choose an allocation unit size (Default is the best choice if compatibility is a prime concern), a volume label, and the level of format to perform. If this is an NTFS volume, you can also enable file and folder compression.

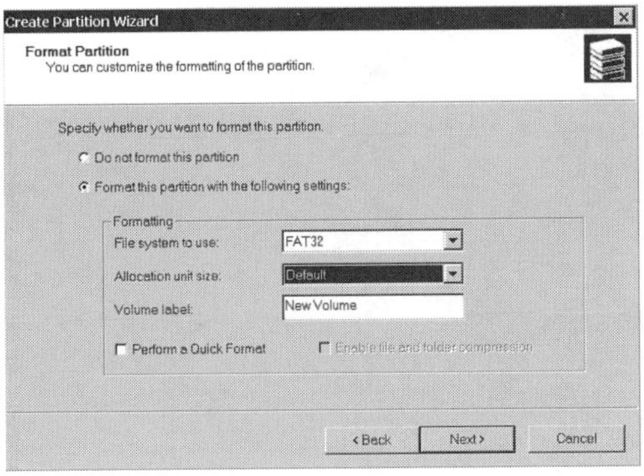

FIGURE 12.11

You'll get a variety of partition-formatting options when using the Create Partition Wizard.

8. Choose the partition format options and type a label for the partition. Click Next. You'll see a completion dialog box that contains a list of the formatting options you've chosen. It pays to double-check your choices before you complete the partitioning process.

9. Click Finish. Disk Management will create the partition and begin formatting it for you. Because Windows 2000 is a multitasking operating system, Disk Management will return control of the system to you and format the drive in the background. You can watch the progress of the drive format by checking the Disk Management display.

Data Compression

One feature of the NTFS file system that you might want to consider is data compression. Right-click any file on an NTFS drive and you'll notice the Compress and Uncompress options on the context menu. If you right-click a file stored on a FAT or HPFS file system drive, you won't see these entries. Unlike its predecessors, the NTFS file system doesn't force you to compress files using a third-party utility—at least not if you just want to save space on your disk. All you need to do is choose the Compress option from the context menu.

How well does this feature work? It's quick and painless. I decided to compress a graphics file to see how well it works. I didn't even notice any system activity and thought that the command had failed. Clicking the file and seeing that Explorer reported it was still the same size only seemed to confirm my suspicions. Opening the Properties dialog box showed the real story, however (see Figure 12.12). The file was compressed to nearly 34 percent of its former size—a substantial savings. The amount of space available on the drive also reflected the change in compression status.

FIGURE 12.12

The File Properties dialog box shows the result of compressing a file on an NTFS volume.

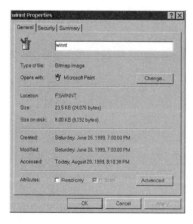

Technical Note: NTFS compression is highly flexible. You can compress individual files, whole folders, or even entire volumes. To compress an entire volume, just compress its root directory by right-clicking the volume you want to compress (in Explorer) and then clicking Properties from the context menu. On the General tab, click the check box at the bottom labeled Compress Drive to Save Disk Space. Click OK. Then respond to the dialog box by saying that you do, in fact, want all the subfolders compressed as well.

Don't get the idea that this on-the-fly file compression is free. It's possible to suffer a decrease in system performance when accessing a compressed file, so you may not want to use this feature with files you use a lot. For graphics or other large files that you use infrequently, however, the file compression provided by NTFS makes perfect sense. However, compression can be more than merely a way of conserving hard drive space (which used to be much more valuable than it is today, given the affordability of 8GB drives). Compression can increase performance in some situations, especially if you use small volumes (under 2GB). The trade-off is that the CPU has to work harder—so if you're frequently engaged in CPU-intensive behaviors, you might want to avoid compression—and the compressed files do remain accessible from the network by any client, including Windows for Workgroups, Windows 98, or whatever. The Windows 2000 disk drivers work with the I/O Manager to deliver the information in a format that the requesting system can read.

Tip: If you use the popular compression utility WinZip, you'll benefit in the same way if you're only interested in compressing on a file-by-file basis. WinZip also offers various additional features such as organizing archives and selective unzipping. WinZip provides context menu options as well.

Drive Indexing

Windows has included the ability to search for information in a variety of ways for quite some time. The two most common search criteria are specific filenames and files that contain a particular bit of text. You can also search by date, size, and other distinguishing characteristics.

In the past, these searches could take quite a while to accomplish if you had a lot of files to search. Windows 2000 includes the capability of indexing an NTFS drive—creating a database of key words. This greatly reduces the time to look for particular files, especially when you need to look for text within the files.

Note: The Indexing Service only provides full support with NTFS 5 drives. You won't get the full indexing capability with your FAT-formatted drive or with network drives that use other formatting schemes. In addition, there may be limitations to how much of a speed increase you'll get with NTFS 4 drives—it's normally better to use the Indexing Service with NTFS 5–formatted drives.

Indexing a drive takes time, but Windows 2000 performs the task in the background. I didn't really notice any performance penalty while Windows 2000 indexed my drive, but I did notice the vast improvement in search times later. All you need to do to start the indexing process is right-click the volume you want to index (in Explorer) and then choose Properties from the context menu. On the General tab, click the check box at the bottom labeled Allow Indexing Service to Index this Drive for Fast File Searching. Click OK. That's all there is to it. Windows 2000 will index the drive in the background. Although you won't be able to get the benefits of indexing immediately (it takes about two hours to index a 4GB drive, depending on the level of system activity and the amount of processing power available), you'll eventually see a vast improvement in drive search times.

New Extensions LNK Files

Pointers is a term familiar to programmers when used as a computer term. However, it's familiar to all of us when talking about a directional finder. Think of LNK files in Windows 2000 as pointers to something. They enable you to create an image of any Windows 95/98 or Windows 2000 object somewhere else. In most cases, the object is a file or a folder.

What good are LNK files? Suppose you're a manager and you need to get a bunch of files for the group that will eventually put a project together. A graphics illustrator has worked creating drawings for the last few weeks. A second group worked up all the figures and statistics with 1-2-3. Still another group worked on some text and charts to go with the other elements of the project. You're ready to get everything together for a full-fledged presentation.

You could copy all the files to one directory and print them out. After a lot of red lining during your meeting, each group could make the required changes. What an inefficient way to spend your week. This is the way a lot of places work, but I can't think of anything less productive.

Of course, some groups have become more modern. They place all the files in a directory on the network so that the group can work on them without making red lines. This is a bit better, but it's still not the best way because you have two copies of the files lying around now. This allows too many chances to make a mistake. Besides, what happens if George finds another change later? Does he try to find the correct file and make the change (or worse still, try to find the correct person to make the change for him)? Using double files is okay, but it's still not the right way to go. Double files create a version problem.

Windows 2000 offers an alternative. The manager can now create a project folder containing links (or pointers) to all the project files. The folder is easy to distribute to everyone who's working on the project, even if he or she isn't in the same building. The links (LNK files) make it easy for the person using the folder to access a single copy of the real file. No duplicates are needed. There's no chance for mislaid files or having to figure out which is the file with the latest edit; everyone can work on all the files as needed, and no one but the manager needs to know the physical location of the files. This is what a LNK file can do for you. (The only downside to using LNK files, and therefore a common data file, is that your application must be set up for file sharing.)

Of course, using LNK files can help a single user manage his or her work just as easily. In fact, I discuss some of these methods in the section titled "Working with Desktop Objects" in Chapter 5, "Exploring the Interface." I've found that I can manage all my work as projects and not really worry about applications or the actual location of the data. LNK files are a small idea with big implications. Take a look at some of the details.

Your Start Menu folder contains a ton of LNK files. If you think that any of your applications actually appear in the Start menu, you're wrong. Only the pointers (in effect, shortcuts) to those files appear here. If you erase a Start menu entry, all you erase is a LNK file, not the application itself.

Right-click the Start Menu icon on the taskbar and choose the Explore option. You now should see a dual-pane Explorer view of your Start menu entries. You can easily recognize the LNK files because they look like shortcuts (the icons with the arrow in the lower-left corner). Right-click any of the LNK files, and you'll see a display similar to Figure 12.13. (I chose the Windows 2000 Explorer LNK file, but any choice is acceptable for this discussion.)

FIGURE 12.13
A LNK file's Properties dialog box provides a General tab similar to that provided by other file types.

As with the General page of any file's Properties dialog box, you can set the file attributes: Hidden and Read-Only. This page also tells you the short and long filename and other statistics, such as when someone last modified the file. This is all interesting information, but you'll probably bypass this page, in most cases, to get to the Shortcut tab.

The following list outlines the four major fields on the Shortcut page along with the function of each entry. Of course, the two you'll use most often are the Target field and Run drop-down list box. I never use the Start In field, but you'll probably need it in some cases:

- *Target.* This is the name of the program you want to run. Of the two different types of target displays, the first type is for data files. The dialog box doesn't enable you to change the settings for that file. You must change the original file rather than the link. Of course, this makes sense when you think about it because each file could have multiple links pointing to it. On the other hand, in some applications you can change this entry. Notice that the Explorer entry also includes a system variable in place of a path. Windows 2000 makes more extensive use of environment variables than Windows 95/98 does in situations such as this one.

- *Start In.* Windows 2000 always assumes that everything the file will need appears in its target directory. This is probably true for data files. You might find that some applications need to use a different "working directory" from the one they start in, however. The term *working directory* should be familiar to users moving from Windows 3.x; it's the directory that Windows tells the application to check for data files. It's the same field you use in a PIF file to control where a program starts. This field does the same thing for Windows 2000. In other words, you're "in" the working directory (folder) when the application starts. In this case, Explorer will, when started, display a list of the folders and files in whatever working directory you specify.

- *Shortcut Key.* I covered this topic in Chapter 7, "Performance Power." The Shortcut Key field enables you to assign a key combination (Ctrl+Alt+*key*) to the particular LNK file. Using a shortcut key can dramatically speed access to your favorite applications or data files. You also saw other methods of speeding access to your data in the section titled "Customizing Your Desktop" in Chapter 4, "Installing Windows 2000 Professional: A Setup Primer."

- *Run.* Windows provides three run modes for applications. You can run them minimized, maximized, or in a window. I find the default setting of Window works for most of my applications. (In the majority of cases, this is a maximized window.) I start data files maximized for certain jobs. This is especially true of my word processing files because I like to get a full-screen view of them. How you set this field is solely determined by the way you prefer to work.

That's all there is to LNK files. Chapter 8, "Customizing Windows 2000 for Maximum Productivity," gives you some usage tips for LNK (or shortcut) files. You should read about the various methods you can use to create shortcuts to your data files and applications. Chapter 4 also discusses this topic from a Desktop point of view in the section titled "Working with Desktop Objects." The Desktop is where you can really benefit from using these productivity enhancers.

VxDs and DLLs

Object-oriented programming (OOP) is the fashion these days. Programmers will tell you the reason for favoring OOP is that it results in software that's easier to maintain and understand. It can also be easier for groups to program together using OOP techniques, particularly encapsulation (data hiding), so that one programmer can't get inside and fool around with the code or data hidden by the programmer who created the object. Likewise, side effects are minimized, if not eliminated. Those are all perfectly good reasons, but they don't really tell you much as a user. The impact of OOP on a user has to do with memory. It takes a lot of code to tell your machine how to get anything done when using a GUI such as Windows 2000. More code always translates into more memory. If every application had to contain the code for every task, such as displaying a dialog box or menu, the memory shortage you'd experience would dwarf the current problems.

Another user benefit of OOP is that you get, for example, a single spell-checker that works with all your applications. That not only saves memory (each application doesn't have to load its own spell-checker), but it also makes it easier for you to learn to use the utility and to create a custom dictionary for it.

Windows 3.*x* started the dynamic link library (DLL) and virtual anything device (VxD) craze for a good reason. Creating a Windows program is a complex undertaking, and programmers needed tools to get the job done quickly. A modular approach also ensures that items such as dialog boxes look the same no matter which application you use. The important reason for the current discussion is memory, however. People were already starting to complain about the huge memory footprint of Windows. Even when applications could share some code or data, it still took a lot of memory to get anything done. A GUI always requires more memory than a character-based operating system. If Microsoft had taken a DOS view of programming when designing Windows, we would all be using OS/2 today.

A program calls a DLL or VxD to perform specific tasks. Essentially, both files contain executable code—often in the form of a library of procedures, similar to a mini-API. When Windows sees the request, it loads the program (DLL or VxD) into memory. Both DLLs and VxDs contain entry points. Any number of applications can simultaneously access the program file and use whatever parts are needed. You might have noticed that the File, Open command in most applications produces the same dialog box, for example. This dialog box is actually part of the COMMDLG.DLL file located in your SYSTEM directory. An application makes a call to COMMDLG.DLL to display the File Open dialog box. Windows loads the DLL, looks for a specific function number, and then lets the DLL do its work.

Take a look at that COMMDLG.DLL file. Open Explorer and then the WINNT\SYSTEM32 folder. Right-click the COMMDLG.DLL file to display the context menu and choose Quick View. Page down until you see the Exported Functions entry.

Looking at this table, you'll notice two columns. The first column tells you the function number. The second column (the one that you're interested in) tells you the function name. Notice the kinds of things that a programmer can do with the COMMDLG.DLL. Especially important are function 1, which opens a file; function 2, which saves a file; and function 20, which displays the Print dialog box.

You can check out some of the other DLLs in the SYSTEM32 directory using this same method. Learning what the DLLs do for you can help when something doesn't work the way it should. What would you do if the File Open dialog box suddenly stopped working, for example? It might seem a very unlikely prospect, but data corruption can affect any file on your system. (If you were a Windows 3.*x* user, you might have found out about your system files the hard way when your system would stop working unexpectedly; DLL and other system file corruption was a fairly common problem for some people.) Knowing the File Open dialog box appears in the COMMDLG.DLL file could help you fix the system with just a few minutes' worth of work. All you'd need to do is restore a good copy of this DLL file from your backup. What DLLs do for software, VxDs do for hardware. When part of your system needs to access a piece of hardware, it usually calls a VxD. Of course, drivers can also work with software components but from a different perspective than DLLs. Drivers always provide some type of interface to a system component. Some types of memory allocation are performed with a VxD, for example. This isn't a function most users would worry about, but it's very important to the proper functioning of your system. One of the most-used VxDs on your drive is VMM32.VXD. It combines the functionality of a lot of the older files you found under Windows 3.*x* into one file. (Most of these entries appeared in the 386ENH section of SYSTEM.INI.)

> **Tip:** If you right-click a VxD file, you'll notice that it offers no Quick View option. To view the file, make a copy and give it a .DLL extension. You can now use Quick View to see the header of this file. This same technique works with other executable file types as well. Unfortunately, about the only things the file header will tell you is the amount of memory that the VxD requires to load and some programmer-specific information, such as the size of the stack the VxD creates. In most cases, it isn't worth your while to look at the file heading unless you're low on memory and you're looking for a peripheral to unload from your system. Unloading a peripheral device can free memory that you can use for applications. (Make sure that you back up any drivers that you unload using the procedures at the end of this chapter.)

Viewing File Contents

We've already taken a long look at the process of viewing files in quite a few of the chapters in this book, so I won't bore you with a lot of details here. It's important to realize that Windows 2000 does come with some built-in, file-viewing support. Most of the major applications you'll use are already entered in the Registry. Other levels of file support come from Registry entries made by your applications during installation. Even if your applications aren't successful during installation, you can always import the REG files they create to add support to Windows 2000. Chapter 10, "Understanding the Windows 2000 Registry," discusses all these types of file-viewing support.

You can also add support to the Registry for your own file extensions. I outline one way to add it for existing files in Chapter 10. Chapter 5 shows you still other ways to add support for viewing files. The method you use to add file support isn't important. The important thing to consider here is how efficient the new support makes you. Customizing Windows 2000 to the way you work is the best way to use all the added speed this product can provide. Using your old work methods means that you'll actually ignore those new features—a major problem for some people who have tried Windows 2000 and have been disappointed in its performance.

Here's a practical example of another type of file support that you can add to Windows 2000. I found that the level of Explorer support for DOC files didn't meet my needs, so I changed it. That's one of the first rules you'll need to learn about Windows 2000. Nothing's cast in concrete as long as you have some idea of what to look for in Explorer or the Registry. In this case, I just modified an Explorer entry to suit my needs.

Figure 12.14 shows the context menu I designed for DOC files. Of course, you could just as easily do the same thing for PCX or any other file extension, for that matter. Windows 2000 doesn't care how you customize your system; all it cares about is interacting with you and your applications when you get through.

FIGURE 12.14

Data viewing is fully configurable under Windows 2000 if you know how to use the Registry.

Notice that I can open DOC files with Word or WordPad. I can also use the Quick Viewer to display the files when necessary. Another entry enables me to use Word to print the file without opening it first.

Now that you've seen the results, look at the implementation. You can use this example as a basis for making your own custom context menu changes. All I did was open the Options dialog box by choosing the Tools, Folder Options command in Explorer. Then I selected the File Types tab and the DOC extension (Microsoft Word Document). Clicking the Advanced button displays the Edit File Type dialog box.

The WordPad entry is simple to make. Click the New button to add a new entry to the list of actions. Type the information shown in Figure 12.15. That's all there is to it. Click OK three times to save your new entries, and you'll have a custom context menu for your DOC files.

FIGURE 12.15
Adding new options to the context menu for a file extension is as simple as entering an application's path in this dialog box.

Formatting Disks

Formatting floppy disks is one of those tasks that everyone must perform from time to time. In Windows 2000, all you need to do is right-click the drive where you want to format from within Explorer. Choose the Format option, and you'll see the Format dialog box. Note that Windows 2000 has no way to make a DOS boot floppy disk. If you need to make a DOS boot floppy disk, you'll have to find a DOS-based machine, and that's getting harder and harder to do these days.

> **Tip:** Always use the Quick Erase option to format floppy disks that you know are good. This option formats the floppy disk in a little more than one-tenth the time a full format takes.

All you need to do now is select the options you want and click OK. Windows 2000 does offer a few nice surprises in addition to the interface. For one thing, it works very well in the background. I didn't experience a single problem when working on something else while a floppy disk takes its time formatting.

> **Tip:** You can double or even triple your formatting capacity by selecting network floppy disks to format under Windows 2000. A peer-to-peer connection enables you to use the floppy disk on another machine if you have access. Using two machines in close proximity in one office doubles the number of disks you can format simultaneously.

> **Tip:** The Windows 2000 pagefile (virtual memory) is one of the most important factors when you're trying to optimize a Windows 2000 installation. But which chapter does it belong in? Is it a disk topic, or is it a memory topic? I chose to discuss it as an aspect of memory, so you'll find an in-depth discussion of how to manage this significant feature of Windows 2000 in Chapter 10.

> **Peter's Principle:** Choosing Your File System: The Bottom Line
>
> Which file system you decide to use is up to you. Now that you know the trade-offs, you can make an informed decision. What do I recommend? Unless you have small volumes (below 1GB), I would use NTFS. NTFS offers security in two ways: Outsiders can't get to your protected data, and disk restoration and activity logging make maintenance easier. NTFS also boasts advanced cluster size efficiency and other efficiencies mentioned in this chapter. It's true that disk repair is less well developed for NTFS (FAT is an old, old system), but you can find good utilities out there to work on an NTFS drive if something goes wrong. What's more, you really need not worry whether you remember to keep updating your Emergency Repair Disk on a regular basis (as well as keep a boot disk and regularly back up your data).
>
> As you've seen, FAT works better on disks and removable drives—you can't afford the overhead NTFS must have in these relatively small spaces. Also, some experts have advised that you should always install a small but bootable FAT partition on your hard drive so that you can "get to" the drive if you have an NTFS crash of major proportions. I disagree. You seriously compromise one of NTFS's major strengths: its capability to keep your data secure from prying eyes as well as those who might want to damage or delete your files or introduce viruses.
>
> Put a bootable FAT on your drive and you might as well hang a "Visitors Welcome" sign on your machine. Added to that, if you do install a FAT partition, you've instantly violated C2 security. Hackers can access your system and, as one possible kind of havoc, post all your secrets on the Internet for all to see.

On Your Own

Try working in various ways with files to get an idea of how compression affects your system. First compress and then copy the files from one folder to another. Also try moving files rather than merely copying them. Take a look at how the compression of a file affects the properties in the context menu of various files and folders. Try compressing a folder and then see what happens when you copy an uncompressed file into that compressed folder.

If you're an experienced Windows 2000 user, you can even try compressing executable applications such as Word and then use System Monitor to see whether there's a difference in loading speed and processor time when you run a compressed (versus an uncompressed) version of Word.

If you own a CD-ROM drive, spend some time optimizing the VCache now that you know a little more about how it works. What size CD-ROM cache seems to use memory most efficiently? How much of a speed difference do you notice between a large and small cache when using applications directly from the CD-ROM drive?

Graphics Windows 2000 Style

The computer's primary output device is its video monitor, but monitors and the video boards that support them differ widely in their capabilities and prices. Prices for video cards (or boards or graphics adapters) range from less than $100 to more than $3,000. At the high end is a video capture card targeted to those who need to take snapshots of motion video; at the low end are no-nonsense business applications, such as plain text word processing. And you will likely buy a video system somewhere between these extremes. This chapter will help you make an informed decision about what monitor and graphics board best fit your situation.

Applications aren't the only issue. Sometimes, it is a matter of user perception. Someone with poor eyesight will want larger text and a high refresh rate—anything less won't do the job. Likewise, someone such as a programmer with a lot of data to display will want a high-resolution setup that provides maximum flexibility when it comes to character size.

Even environmental factors come into play. Have you ever seen a display that seems to flicker a great deal when used with fluorescent lighting? The problem might not even be with the computer, the video adapter, or the monitor. It might just be a sign of a bad ballast, a failing light bulb, or some other situation beyond the control of the person using the computer.

The first step to understanding what's going on with your display is knowing how Windows displays data. It also helps to know the kinds of graphics standards and what types of things you should look for when buying your equipment. This chapter addresses all three of those areas.

Looking Ahead

This book covers a variety of user-related graphics subjects as well. Check out Chapter 17, "Exploiting Your Hardware," if you want to know how to install a video adapter or monitor. You can find out about fonts in Chapter 18, "Fonts and Printing," which also talks about how fonts affect your display. If you work with multimedia, read Chapter 19, "Windows 2000 Multimedia," to see how multimedia support in Windows 2000 will affect your display. Finally, for those times when your display isn't cooperating with you, look to Chapter 31, "Solving Hardware Problems," for troubleshooting information.

The Windows 2000 Graphics Architecture

Video is the most noticeable architectural component of Windows. The underlying combination of hardware and software enables you to see the graphics, dialog boxes, icons, and other elements that make Windows worth using. Under DOS, text and graphics were separate elements and used different video adapter display modes, for the most part. Windows displays everything in graphics mode, so it would seem that the problem would be simpler, not more complex.

The truth is much different from what most people expect. That dialog box is an object, not just a picture. An object has properties and maintains its separate identity. When Windows draws a dialog box, it is building the representation of a screen object, not drawing a picture. The same holds true for all the other graphics you see onscreen. The graphical device interface (GDI) is ultimately responsible for managing all these graphics components that a programmer uses to create the applications you use every day.

Let's begin with a look at the three elements I consider crucial to an understanding of the GDI architecture. You need to consider intercomponent communications (a statement of video display problems and interfaces); current standards used to create the GDI (methods used to define solutions to various display problems and a description of the interfaces); and the GDI itself (the implementation of the standards). We'll look at two of these areas in the following sections. You should have a good understanding of what the GDI does by the time you are through.

Communication: The Key

Intercomponent communication is key to making the Windows GDI work properly. The problem isn't just one of displaying a picture onscreen—that would be easy to manage. The problem is one of communicating among the various elements that create and manage the picture in the first place. You need to remember that the GDI has a lot more to worry about than your application—or even all the Windows applications running on a machine, for that matter. The GDI must manage every application that Windows is running, no matter what environment that application is running in. The following list illustrates some of the Windows communications problems:

- **Application video emulation modes.** As previously stated, Windows 2000 provides a minimum of five different application levels: DOS, Windows 16-bit, Windows 32-bit, OS/2, and POSIX. DOS applications usually think they are alone in the world, so they violate just about every imaginable rule for displaying information. In fact, this lack of control prevents some DOS applications from running under Windows 2000. Game programs are the worst in this area. You can count on them to change the display adapter registers in unusual ways and to write directly to video memory with no thought that anyone else might be using the system. Their goal is speed, and anything they can do to increase speed is considered fair play. Although 16-bit Windows applications are a bit more conscientious than their DOS counterparts, they still use an older interface to draw to the display. Newer

32-bit Windows might offer the ultimate in available features right now, but they're often hampered by other applications running on the machine. Windows 2000 also must manage OS/2 and POSIX applications. Fortunately, these programs tend to be better behaved than their DOS counterparts, so the amount of additional management needed is fairly minimal.

- **Device driver.** I own an older display adapter that drives me crazy when I use Microsoft Word. There's not really a problem with the adapter; there's a problem with the drivers that support the adapter. If the display driver doesn't correctly interpret the commands issued by applications running under Windows, or if those applications use undocumented command features, miscommunication will probably ensue. With my faulty setup, the adapter misinterpreted some of the commands that Word and a few other applications used, resulting in an unreadable screen. Also, if you are thinking of buying a new video card, find out how mature the Windows 2000 drivers for this card are. How long has the manufacturer been refining the drivers? Are you buying hardware that has just been released and the drivers are still in beta testing? It is no use buying the finest high-tech video card if you have to put up with a driver that's slow or full of bugs. Get a video card with some track record; check the magazine reviews. You can use a search engine such as Yahoo! to locate the manufacturer's home page on the Internet. Also look for reviews on the Internet: ZDNet is a good source of current and archived reviews.

- **Adapter.** In the beginning, IBM set the tone and the baseline for all display adapters (video cards). Its leadership was responsible for the somewhat standard way in which the CGA and EGA display adapters worked. By the time VGA came around, IBM was starting to lose its leadership position. Then came SVGA (super VGA), and IBM had no standard to follow. For a while, vendors didn't have any kind of standardization for the extended modes that they built into their display adapters. The result was total chaos. How do you build a set of standardized drivers for an operating system with no standard to follow? I discuss how this problem finally was resolved a little later in this chapter.

- **Monitor.** Monitors have less of a standardization problem, but it is still an issue. The problem manifests itself in setups in which one monitor works fine but another doesn't. The problem lies in the signals coming from the display adapter. With today's ergonomic concerns, make sure that your monitor and board (if you are buying new ones) can work together to achieve a 75Hz refresh rate at the highest resolution and greatest color depth you will use. This rate is important to achieve a stable display and to reduce eyestrain. Some monitors and cards just can't handle the increased frequency requirements. Furthermore, there's some level of ambiguity on the part of vendors. I will never get over the fine-print problem with several monitors I considered. One monitor supposedly supports 1024×768 mode, but when I looked at the fine print, it became obvious that this support was good only in *interlaced* mode. This led to a problem when I installed Windows 2000. I saw the upper half of the picture just fine, but the lower half disappeared. The problem was some combination of adapter, driver, and monitor. If the monitor had supported 1024×768 noninterlaced mode, I would not have had a problem.

Now that you have a better idea of the communications problems that Windows 2000 must overcome, you might wonder why it works at all. Windows 2000 uses something called a message loop to talk with an application; each Windows 2000 session has its own message loop, and there is one loop for the system itself. This series of message (event) loops enables every application running within Windows to communicate with each other and Windows itself. In addition, Windows doesn't allow an application to draw to the real display buffer; it actually draws to a virtual buffer. When you switch from one environment to another—say, from Windows to DOS—Windows takes away one virtual screen and replaces it with another. The combination of an event loop and constant redrawing enables Windows to keep your display up-to-date, even if small amounts of miscommunication do occur.

The Windows 2000 Graphics Architecture

Now that you have some idea of the problems Microsoft (and any other vendor) faces when it comes to providing something for you to look at, it is time to discuss how they do it. Display adapters and monitors have both moved beyond the simpler requirements of the time when IBM was at the helm. In the interim, we have seen the emergence of even higher resolutions and an adapter called the XGA. The SVGA standard is also continually being improved. It used to be that 640×480 resolution and 256 colors were something to whistle about. Today, an adapter is considered almost inadequate at 1024×768 resolution and 24-bit (16.7 million, or true color) colors. Windows 2000 endeavors to handle this wide range of capabilities using the same centralized control mechanism that it uses for printing: a combination of the minidriver and device independent bitmap (DIB) engine.

One of the main architectural components is the GDI. This is the part of the graphics architecture that your application will interact with. The GDI has been tuned and retuned throughout the various incarnations of Windows. It is no surprise that Microsoft has spent so much time in this area, because many benchmark tests focus on graphics performance. In fact, what users notice most is the way the graphics engine performs. Microsoft did some more tuning of the GDI for Windows 2000, but I would call this tuning more incremental than major. The following list provides details on some of the more significant improvements that have been made to the GDI in the past few years:

- **GDI component duplication.** Chapter 11, "Memory Management," discussed the use of a thunk to convert 16-bit data to 32-bit format. Thunks cost time. This isn't a big deal in most cases because a thunk can be a lot less expensive than a transition to real mode to handle a device need. Some operations are performed so often that Microsoft decided to provide both a 16-bit and a 32-bit version in Windows 2000, however. This places the speed potential of this Windows 2000 component on par with that found in Windows 95/98.

- **Path support.** Windows applications once created complex objects using a lot of standard objects, such as squares, triangles, and circles. All these little calls could eat up a lot of processor time if the program needed to create a complex object. Using paths enables a Windows 2000 application to describe a complex shape in one function call. The GDI can then figure out the most efficient way to present it. The result is that the programmer spends less time describing the object, and the user sees a performance improvement as well.

- **Metafile support.** A metafile contains drawing commands that describe the drawing mathematically instead of actually providing a bitmap (a pixel-by-pixel copy) of it. Each command is called a record. The GDI processes records to reconstruct the image. The advantage of a metafile is that it can easily be scaled to any size. (Resizing bitmaps is both relatively slow and also causes loss of resolution when they're blown up.) Windows 98 offers metafile support, mainly for printing. Windows 2000, too, provides a full range of metafile commands that really enhance performance.

- **Bézier curve drawing.** A Bézier curve is drawn using a set of points. A curved freeform line connects the points. The idea isn't to necessarily touch all the points, but to draw a line that most nearly defines a shape that flows from point to point. The line is automatically smoothed, so the curves look correct. Some advanced graphics applications support this feature right out of the box. Windows 2000 adds this feature so that an application can describe a curve using points and allow the GDI to figure out how to draw it.

- **Image color matching (ICM 2.0).** It wasn't all that long ago that everyone used green screens and black-and-white printers. Today, the cost of a color printer is dropping rapidly, and color displays are standard on every machine. Trying to get the color on your screen to match the color on your printer, however, can be a problem. For one thing, the two devices use different methods to create colors. Another reason is that it is nearly impossible to create some colors on certain devices. The technical details of all this are keeping several standards groups busy, so it is impossible to say how the problem occurs or what to do about it. Still, the problem remains. With the emergence of color as a major new component of computing, Microsoft saw the need to provide color matching between devices. Although it is not a perfect solution, ICM 2.0 is a good start for people who can't afford professional publishing equipment.

Note: The Windows 2000 GDI has an interesting feature: It is one of the few pieces that Microsoft wrote mostly with C++. (The rest of Windows 2000 uses a combination of C and C++.) Why would Microsoft take this step? In my opinion, the reason is twofold. First, using C++ makes full use of the Microsoft Foundation Class (MFC) support built in to C++. Second, using objects rather than procedural code tends to make the GDI easier to maintain (especially in a multiplatform environment such as Windows 2000).

Windows 2000 overall architecture plays a role in how video works. I won't get into bits and bytes here, but I will tell you about the basic components required to display something on screen. Figure 13.1 is an overview of the Windows 2000 architecture.

FIGURE 13.1

Here's an overview of the Windows 2000 graphics architecture.

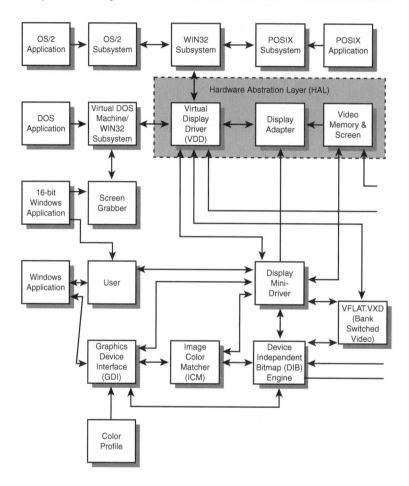

The following list tells you what task each of the components performs:

- **WIN32 subsystem.** Remember that Windows 2000 uses a client/server approach to taking care of the needs of the various applications it supports. It does this through the WIN32 subsystem, a buffer layer that translates foreign operating system calls into something that Windows 2000 can understand. Think about POSIX for a second: Filenames and other entities are case-sensitive in that environment. Contrast this to DOS, which is not case-sensitive.

- **Virtual DOS machine (VDM).** Windows 2000 places each DOS application in its own VDM. The reason is simple: To provide the higher level of system reliability that Windows 2000 users demand, Microsoft had to make sure that each application had an environment that was completely separate from that used by every other application. It is also important to remember that, unlike Windows 95, 16-bit Windows applications use individual VDMs. Windows 2000 always starts a VDM and then runs a copy of 16-bit Windows in it to service the needs of the 16-bit Windows application. This effectively adds two layers to every interaction: one for the VDM, and another for the WIN32 subsystem. The use of a separate VDM for each application also means that Windows 2000 can more accurately detect when a DOS application is about to take control of the display area. It notifies the User module and the screen grabber so that they can preserve the graphics system status information. As with everything else, this additional layering is transparent to the user. You still use the same interfaces as before. Note that, by default, every Windows 16-bit application runs in a VDM. Therefore, even if many 16-bit applications are running concurrently, they still all run together within a single VDM.

- **OS/2 application, OS/2 subsystem, POSIX application, and POSIX subsystem.** Windows 2000 provides support for OS/2 and POSIX. I included these four elements so that you know they're there, but I don't plan to say much about them because many of you won't use them much unless you're a developer, in which case you might use POSIX. Windows 2000 provides only character-mode support for OS/2 and POSIX applications. Note, though, that some developers are now using POSIX when building certain applications. You might want to look into it to see if it would be useful to you.

- **User.** I have already discussed the uses for this module extensively. (The Windows API functionality of User was discussed in Chapter 9, "An Architectural Overview.") This module tracks the state of all the display elements, such as icons and dialog boxes, in addition to drawing them. That's why it needs to be informed before a DOS session comes to the foreground: so that it can take a snapshot of the current state of these components. As stated earlier, the disk actually has two User-related files: a 16-bit and a 32-bit version.

- **GDI.** This is another module that we have spent a lot of time discussing. (Chapter 9 covered the Windows API functionality of User.) Like the User module, the GDI has two physical files: one for 16-bit and another for 32-bit needs.
  The GDI module works with the display driver and the DIB engine to produce the graphics components of a Windows display. The DIB engine used to be a separate component of the display subsystem, but is now included within the GDI.

- **Display Miniport Driver.** With Windows 3.x, every video signal goes through the virtual display driver (VDD). The VDD processes the signal and sends it to the display adapter. Windows 2000 can use a combination of the display minidriver and the DIB engine for adapters that can support them. Using this driver combination results in a speed increase from 32-bit code. The name of this file varies, depending on the type of display you are using. On my system, it is named ATI-RAGE.SYS. Unlike the VDD, which performs all video processing, the display miniport driver takes care of only device-specific details. The DIB engine takes care of graphics rendering. A miniport driver contains a lot less code than a full-fledged VDD, reducing the amount of code that a vendor must write.

- **Display Adapter Driver**. The module supports any special rendering features that
  your display adapter provides. With so many different display adapter processors
  on the market today, it's important to support these special rendering features. The
  name of the file associated with this module varies by display adapter. On my
  machine these functions are contained in the ATIRAGE.DLL file.

- **Video Port Driver**. Microsoft is moving toward a system of drivers that are completely generic. This driver represents part of that effort with regard to the display
  adapter. It contains functions that allow the User and GDI modules to perform
  general display adapter tasks like moving data from one point to another in memory. There are also status functions like one that checks the VGA setup of the display adapter and others that work with AGP port setups. The functions that are
  carried out by this module normally appear in the VIDEOPRT.SYS file.

- **Color profile.** This data file contains the color capabilities for your output device.
  It doesn't matter whether the device is a printer or a display adapter; the type of
  information is the same. The purpose of a color profile is to provide the ICM with
  the information it needs to keep the display and other color devices in sync. That
  way, when you select dark red on the display, you get the same dark red on your
  printer. I discussed some of the problems with color matching earlier, so I won't
  go into them again here. You will find all the color profile files in the
  \System32\spool\drivers\color folder . All these files have an .ICM extension. The
  Properties dialog box associated with each one gives you many more technical
  details about the actual profile.

- **Image color matching (ICM 2.0).** The whole process of matching the output of
  your printer to what you see on the display is complex—much too complex to
  really cover here. (The problem of color matching was discussed earlier in this
  chapter.) The ICM is the module that actually performs the work. It subtly changes
  the output of your printer and display so that they match. The GDI, display
  minidriver, and ICM work together to compare the current color set and translate it
  into something that will work on both devices. This is not a perfect solution, but it
  works, for the most part. The results are very close, but not absolutely the same.
  Most of us wouldn't notice, but a professional artist might. Of course, this solution
  can't take into account the many details that a professional would, such as temperature, humidity, and other environmental aspects beyond the control of Windows.
  The files that contain the ICM include ICM32.DLL and ICMUI.DLL; both appear in
  the System folder.

- **Virtual display driver (VDD).** Windows 3.x uses this module as its sole source
  of communication with the display adapter. Windows 2000 provides it for compatibility purposes and for DOS applications. In most cases, the name of this file contains some part of the name of the display adapter vendor. You will find it in the
  System32 folder. This driver converts drawing commands into signals that the display adapter can use. It also manages the display adapter and performs a variety of
  other tasks related to the way that all the applications on your machine share the
  display adapter. In essence, it is a 16-bit version of the display minidriver and DIB
  engine combination.

- **Hardware Abstraction Layer (HAL).** This is another conceptual type of element in Windows 2000. Microsoft wrote the drivers and other software elements in such a way that it could easily move Windows 2000 to other platforms. The basic architecture of Windows 2000 is the same, but the low-level drivers—the ones that directly interface with the hardware—are different. Figure 13.1 shows the elements for an Intel processor machine. The important thing to remember is that as far as your application is concerned, it is still running on an Intel machine. The only time you will run into trouble is if you bypass the Windows API and go directly to the hardware.

- **Display adapter.** This is the physical hardware in your machine, the video card or board, as it is called.

- **Video memory and screen.** Video memory is where the electronic form of the image you see onscreen is stored.

- **VGA Boot Driver** (Not shown in Figure 13.1). The VGA Boot Driver is normally used only in safe mode, when the main graphics system has broken down for some reason. This is a very generic 32-bit driver that any Windows friendly display adapter can use to display information at the low resolution of 640×480. It's the driver that the system uses before it identifies the display adapter in your machine during the installation process. For the most part, this driver is used during installation and troubleshooting only. It usually stays in the background, which is why I chose not to include it in the figure. You'll find this functionality stored in the BOOTVID.DLL file.

Keep in mind that this was just a quick tour of the video subsystem. The actual inner workings of this part of Windows 2000 are a lot more complex than you might think. To give you a better idea of the way things work, think of Windows 2000 as having three video paths (although it's more complex than that, don't get mired in too much detail at this point): one 16-bit DOS, one 16-bit Windows, and one 32-bit Windows. The path Windows 2000 uses depends on the applications you are using, the type of adapter you have, and the video performance settings you select in the Display Properties dialog box. The 16-bit DOS path consists of the VDD, display adapter, and video memory. The 16-bit Windows path adds WINOLDAP, the screen grabber, User, and the GDI. The 32-bit path includes User, the GDI, the display miniport driver, display adapter driver, video port driver, the DIB engine, and video memory. Both Windows paths can include the ICM and the associated color profiles. This depends on your setup, the drivers that Microsoft eventually includes, and the capabilities of the devices you are using.

Graphics Standards

The third major part of the GDI architecture triad is standards. You should think about standards as a very important part of any graphics decision you make. Many different standards organizations help keep things running smoothly on your computer. Several competing standards affect how your modem works. One of these organizations, the CCITT (International Telegraph and Telephone Consultative Committee), has become a major contributor. Another organization, the EIA (Electronic Industries Association) , defines specifications for the various port connectors, serial and parallel, that attach your machine to the outside world and peripheral devices. The standards organization you want to watch—for display adapters and monitors—is the Video Electronics Standards Association (VESA). This organization does a lot more than just define the electronics behind a monitor or display adapter; it also defines the programming interface. When IBM wouldn't publish the specifications for the 8514/A display adapter, for example, VESA got together with several other companies and published one in IBM's stead. When a company creates a device driver for Windows, it uses the VESA standards when designing the hardware interface section of the code. Your application indirectly interacts with that driver through the GDI. When you ask Windows to tell you the capabilities of a particular device, it can do so because the display adapter and its driver use a standard interface that Windows can understand.

> **Tip:** VESA can provide you with detailed specifications for a number of display adapter and monitor standards. You can usually get copies of these standards on the Internet at http://www.vesa.org/. The standards also sometimes appear in the manuals that come with your adapter or monitor. You can contact VESA as follows:
>
> Video Electronics Standards Association
> 920 Hillview Court, Suite 140
> Milpitas, CA 95035
> Phone: 408-957-9270
> Fax: 408-957-9277

I first discovered VESA in 1989, but it was probably around a while before that. IBM had dropped VGA in favor of its proprietary 8514/A display adapter. Without a leader in the field to dictate a standard, the entire display adapter arena fell into a state of disarray. At the time I first heard about VESA, the organization was working on a standard to fix the SVGA problem. Of course, the resolutions and number of colors were severely limited in comparison to what you can get today.

The main difficulty facing the graphics community was communication. Before this time, every display adapter used the same programming interface, in the form of a BIOS call, to change display settings and otherwise control the display adapter. All the old display methods worked, but vendors chose to differentiate their products by implementing the VGA extended modes differently. The resulting chaos made it impossible for any programmer to write an application that used SVGA modes without writing a different driver for each adapter.

VESA stepped in to make sense of all this chaos. The results of its initial efforts were several VESA standards and some additional software for each display adapter. That VESA driver you load for some applications is actually a BIOS extension that enables display adapters to use a standardized SVGA interface. The extension translates VESA-standard BIOS calls into something adapter-specific. As a result, an application can use one set of BIOS calls to configure and control the display adapter. Newer display adapters no longer require you to load a special driver; their BIOS chips come with VESA support installed. VESA works on a whole array of additional standardization efforts as well, such as industrial guidelines for the manufacture of computer components. Its most famous display standard unrelated to video is probably the VL bus. This was such an important standard at one time that in 1993, Dell wanted to take VESA to court over the matter of who owned the standard.

Video Boards

While I have your attention focused on the complexities of the video subsystem, take a quick look at video boards. You might have missed a few performance clues tucked away in the discussion of architecture. Did you notice that VFLATD.VXD supports only 1MB of address space? What happens if your display adapter contains 4MB or more of memory? (Today 8MB is a typical amount of video card onboard RAM.) Don't worry: Windows 2000 will completely support the entire range of memory provided by your display adapter. It might have to rely on the display minidriver more to do it, however. This means a lot more calls and perhaps a few more thunks between various display components. The end result is a slight loss in performance, from a purely display subsystem point of view.

You gain from having more video memory in several ways. First, more memory means more colors. A higher number of colors results in improved resolution and makes possible photorealistic-quality images. The second advantage is that a large video frame buffer can speed up the frame rate of motion video because the display can be slapped onto the monitor page by page rather than in smaller chunks. No matter which way you look at it, however, more colors and high resolution cause a performance hit. With today's special video acceleration features such as DirectX version 7, MMX, and AGP, however, you will likely not notice the hit. The Accelerated Graphics Port (AGP) is a standard that increases the PCI bus bandwidth.

Note: In 1997, Intel announced an improvement to their processors, named MMX. Nobody knows for sure what the acronym stands for (although generally taken to stand for "MultiMedia eXtensions"), but the effect of this technology on video throughput is impressive. MMX adds 57 instructions to the Pentium line of microprocessors. The instructions operate on 64 bits simultaneously, allowing considerable increases in efficiency when the processor is burdened with the huge job of displaying animation and motion video. Beyond that, the Pentium's L1 (onboard) cache size is doubled to 32KB. (For more detail about the two processor caches, see Chapter 11.)

Note: DirectX version 7 improves your system's various multimedia features, particularly video. The video card drivers are optimized for 3D animation and high-resolution color. The DirectX technology is made up of Application Programming Interfaces (APIs). With these APIs, programs can directly access many of your computer's hardware devices. Programs want to do this for precisely the same reason that DOS games were so notorious for directly writing to the screen hardware: added speed and control. The DirectX Foundation layer detects your computer's hardware capabilities and then makes sure that applications' behaviors respond appropriately. This way, various applications can fully exploit any high-performance hardware you might own, such as 3D graphics acceleration chips. You will find a deeper discussion of DirectX 7 in Chapter 19.

In spite of all these improvements in video standards, nobody can repeal the laws of physics: Moving the video window around takes a little time; allowing the frame buffer to manage more than 1MB of video memory takes even more. Each layer of management you add to the video subsystem chews up processor cycles. How do you get around these problems? Consider these suggestions:

- **Dual-ported video RAM (VRAM, or Video RAM).** Many display adapters come with this feature, but some do not. VRAM is a Texas Instruments innovation that was first introduced with their TMS340x0 series of processors. The reason that it is called "dual-ported" is that it actually makes use of two ports and can thus simultaneously send and receive data. A serial buffer enables the display to read the contents of video memory. A parallel buffer allows Windows to simultaneously write to video memory. Dual-ported memory gets rid of one of the constraints an application had with the display adapter: You could write to video memory during only part of the display cycle. (For more discussion of VRAM and related issues, see the following Peter's Principle.)

Peter's Principle: Remember that the capabilities of your graphics card can be quite modest if the computer will be used for standard business applications. Word processing, for instance, certainly doesn't justify the extra cost of replacing an older card with a new one containing high-speed VRAM memory. For many business applications, you can easily get by with the simplest of the older-style video boards with slower memory such as EDO DRAM (Dynamic RAM). But if you plan to work with graphics in any fashion, or if you expect that you will need to display multimedia, play games, or visit the many visually advanced Internet sites, insist on VRAM memory.

- **Display coprocessor.** Quite a few display adapters also come with a coprocessor. Windows 3.x doesn't make use of this feature; it sort of ignores that it is there. Windows 2000, on the other hand, has coprocessor support built right in. It offloads as much of the display processing as possible to the display coprocessor instead of using the DIB engine. This speeds performance in two ways. First, because offloading part of the graphics processing responsibility frees processor cycles, you will notice an overall improvement in system speed. Second, the display processor is usually a special-purpose state machine. It processes the graphics instructions much faster than the DIB engine could. Think of it this way: The math coprocessor in your machine is a state machine. It can't replace the general processor for most purposes. It is incredibly fast when it comes to performing some types of math calculations, however.

- **64-bit display adapter.** Graphics routines process a lot of data; there's no way around it. To display an image, you have to move data, and that requires time. You can reduce the amount of time by using a wider data path, however. Some display adapters come with a 64-bit or 128-bit internal path. (This refers to the data path for the video board's internal accelerator, not to the interface with the motherboard, which in the case of PCI can be either 32-bit or, with PCI 3.0 bus, 64-bit.) These 64-bit cards will work in PCI, AGP, and local bus machines (see the next point if you own one of these machines). Just the increase in internal data width will improve graphics performance.

- **AGP, PCI, or local bus.** Modern buses have a lot to offer. For one thing, it is not unusual to see a PCI or local bus video card running at 30MHz or above rather than the 8MHz used by older buses. Quadrupling the bus speed doesn't necessarily quadruple graphics display speeds, but you can be certain that it does have an effect. In addition, most PCI or local bus video cards produced today use a 128-bit internal path. For more on AGP versus PCI, see the following section.

- **OpenGL, Open Graphics Library.** This API, originally developed by Silicon Graphics (SGI), allows a Windows 2000 Workstation to be as swift and efficient as a dedicated graphics workstation, such as SGI. A number of vendors who create high-end CAD, 3D design, animation, multimedia, and other demanding applications have written their software for OpenGL. OpenGL has become the de facto graphics API for two main reasons: It is relatively easy to write hardware drivers for it, and it is scalable—you can see it on the fastest, best dedicated-graphics ultracomputers and also on humble, unaccelerated PC cards. (Of course, it will display lurching animation at best with these cards, but at least it works.)

Want to see what OpenGL can do, even on your humble workstation? Right-click your desktop, and then click Properties. Select the Screen Saver tab and, in the drop-down list box, choose 3D Pipes (OpenGL). Click the Preview button (see Figure 13.2). Impressed? And you don't even have an OpenGL-dedicated card. An API can work through any card, but to really appreciate the extreme speed and smoothness of 3D rendering OpenGL is capable of, you need a card that includes a coprocessor with wired-in OpenGL commands. Don't expect to pay little for this. Also, as dramatic as Pipes is, there's quite a processor performance hit while it runs. Luckily, it usually runs when nothing else is happening!

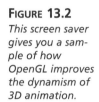

FIGURE 13.2

This screen saver gives you a sample of how OpenGL improves the dynamism of 3D animation.

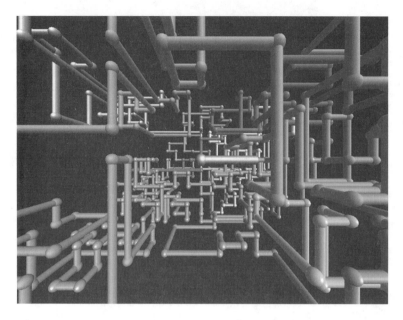

Peter's Principle: For a Workstation, You Should Usually Buy the Best RAM for Video

Several flavors of Video RAM (VRAM) exist. Some even employ more than two ports, such as 3DRAM used on higher-end 3D cards. Beyond that, a relatively new RAM type called WRAM is dual-ported like VRAM, but it can run at higher frequencies and offers approximately 30% better performance than VRAM. My recommendation is that you refuse to settle for anything less than VRAM or WRAM (Windows RAM), and that you also get a minimum of 8MB of it while you are at it. You never know when you will want to take advantage of the increasingly video-rich applications and Internet sites that require excellent graphics cards to support their cutting-edge images.

Is it possible that you could be asked to contribute to multimedia authoring or to join a group developing an Internet site? We're talking about workstations in this book. If you are buying a video system for a server that sits in the closet and whose monitor is rarely even turned on except to check memory dumps or logs during a network crash, you don't need anything beyond an old, cheap card and an old, cheap monitor. For workstations on which work is actually done and on which the display is an important feature, however, you want it to be a strong, stable image. SDRAM and EDO DRAM are the latest "in" video RAM chips.

Buying a New Video Board: PCI Versus AGP Versus UMA, and Other Considerations

Today, you must make this primary decision when buying a video card: Do you want AGP or PCI (the connection between your video card and the motherboard)? Unless your motherboard supports AGP, there is no point in getting it on the video board. The two must work together, or nothing happens with AGP. Of course, if your motherboard does support AGP, go ahead and get it rather than PCI. AGP is the superior connection and will likely replace PCI eventually.

PCI's latest bus is 66MHz and 64 bits wide, but bandwidth is the name of the game with graphics-intensive applications. You want the video card's internal processing to be 128 bits, if possible, and, likewise, you want the bridge between the card and the motherboard (the bus) to be as many bits wide as possible. Even though AGP is a 32-bit bus, it ratchets up the bandwidth by various arcane techniques (passing signals using the two edges of each contact, pipeline memory, and demultiplexing). The result? You get a connection superior to PCI 3.0.

Another bus also is designed to give AGP a run for its money: Unified Memory Architecture (UMA). Its primary advantage is that it eliminates the need to employ the computer's primary chipset when the graphics card calls the computer's RAM or the video frame buffer. To give you an idea of the relative difference in transfer rates, older PCI busses typically transfer data at an average of 100MBps; AGP and UMA work at about 500MBps. Is this futurology? No—most of Dell's systems now ship with AGP graphics.

If you are buying a new board, also make sure that it has at least 8MB of RAM and that it includes both scaling and video acceleration.

> **Tip:** If you plan to connect your computer's video to an ordinary TV, you will have to make sure that your video card has this capability. Often called *TV-out*, this connector enables you to display the computer's screen on a large-screen TV if you want. This can be useful for business presentations and can be fun when you are playing games as well. However, you will likely have to use a lower resolution on TV than you are used to on your PC.

Be sure to look through the list of devices that Windows 2000 supports with native drivers before you buy a new display adapter. The hand-tuned Microsoft drivers will almost always work better than those you get from the vendor because they are tested more extensively. They will definitely work better than the 16-bit drivers that come with some older display adapters. Buying a new adapter that sports a Windows 2000 logo (or, in most cases, the Windows 95/98 logo) will probably cost you more but won't buy you that much, other than a label. Looking through the supported hardware list will probably net you a great display adapter at lower prices, yet retain all the capabilities that Windows 2000 provides.

Windows 95/98 used to offer a feature that was missing in Windows NT 4: Plug and Play. However, Windows 2000 does include this important feature. You gain a lot from having both a Plug and Play-compatible monitor and a display adapter. Not only are these devices self-configuring, but they allow a greater level of flexibility as well.

Peter's Principle: More Than Enough Graphics: What Resolution and Color Depth Do You Need?

You will probably be very tempted to go out and buy the first display adapter that offers 16.7 million colors and 2,048×2,048 resolution. That might be a good way to build for the future, but it might be a little too much for today if you are using the computer strictly for business. Go ahead and get the tomorrow solution today; that only makes sense from a financial perspective. After you do get a high-performance display, however, think about the way you will actually use it. In some cases—word processing for example—a 256-color display provides enough color. If you are planning on using the computer for any kinds of graphics, including multimedia or games, however, get True Color (16.7 million colors). You will be glad you did.

One serious problem with only 256 colors shows up in gradients, where colors must smoothly range from, say, light blue to dark blue, as they would on a billiard ball. Unfortunately, a total of only 256 colors offers not nearly enough different shades to produce a smooth gradient, so you end up with a sad, crude-looking banded compromise as the computer struggles to simulate what it cannot truly reproduce, as shown on the right ball in Figure 13.3. Note both the crude bull's-eye shading and also the rough stair-step outline, both artifacts caused by just too few colors to do the job.

FIGURE 13.3

If you don't buy a graphics board capable of displaying enough colors simultaneously, you end up with ugly, compromised visuals, like the billiard ball on the right.

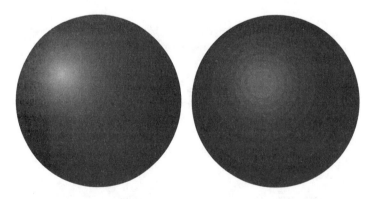

Tip: A 17-inch monitor supports a resolution of 1024×768 just fine, too. After you start going beyond this color and resolution level, your machine takes a performance hit because of the way Windows 2000 handles video memory.

continues

Using the higher level of display capability is fine if you don't mind giving up performance as well. I would rather squeeze every ounce of performance from my machine and use settings that are more in line with what I can actually use. Of course, that shouldn't stop you from getting a high-performance display adapter, but it should change the way you configure it. Always consider when you have enough graphics to meet your needs.

On Your Own

Try looking through the documentation for your monitor and video adapter. Which graphics standards does your equipment adhere to? It always helps to know where to find this kind of information before you go to a store to buy new equipment. Never take the salesperson's word for what a piece of equipment can do; verify that it meets the standards required to get the job done.

A variety of manufacturers now produce 3D video boards—video adapters specially designed to provide better performance when used with a game, CAD, or other graphics-intensive application. Try to find a computer store display that has a standard graphics and a 3D graphics machine side by side. How does the 3D adapter perform in comparison to the standard video adapter? Why do you think you either see or don't see an improvement in performance? (Hint: Many of these 3D video adapters do indeed provide better performance with CAD programs specially designed to use their extended command set. Windows 2000 itself isn't a CAD application, so it won't use this command set as a default. Some vendors see this as a potential problem and add other features to their 3D video adapters to give them a performance boost when used with standard Windows applications.)

Printing Under Windows 2000

Computers were supposed to create a paperless society where everything was done on a display rather than on hard copy. To some extent, computers have fulfilled that promise. However, until monitors can match paper in portability, resolution, and total image stability, paper will still beat displays, and printers will remain the most popular computer peripheral, after the video system and modem.

Printers do great things for us. We can now create documents that look right the first time—well, sometimes we can. The problem is partly human error, partly the fact that computers make documents so easy to produce, and partly a lack of standards.

Getting the output that you really want from a printer can be an exercise in frustration. Sure, it looks great onscreen, but when you get it on paper it looks totally different. WYSIWYG (what you see is what you get) was a catchphrase a few years ago; we still haven't achieved it, but we are getting close.

LOOKING AHEAD
Note that this chapter doesn't cover several printer-related topics. It doesn't cover the installation of a printer, for example. For details on installing a local or network printer, see Chapter 17 "Exploiting Your Hardware," which steps you through the various installation processes. Likewise, configuring printers and managing a parallel port, using the Printer Properties dialog box and the Point and Print feature, are covered in depth in Chapter 17. If you want to know how to use fonts and how to manage your print jobs, look at Chapter 18, "Fonts and Printing." In-depth information about ways you can physically connect printers to a machine's parallel (or even serial) port is available in Chapter 20, "Windows 2000 Connections."

This chapter focuses on the actual printing process, after the connection and installation are complete. This chapter helps you understand the problems you'll encounter getting a document from your word processor (or other application) to the printer in a way so that it actually looks as you expected it to. Therefore, we explore the Windows 2000 printer architecture. Then we take a look at some of the standards you should look for when it's time to buy your next printer. A printer that follows the standards might not always provide everything you need, but it will get you closer to perfection than a printer that doesn't meet the standards.

The Windows 2000 Print Architecture

The first stop on our tour of printers is a look at the Windows 2000 print architecture. Windows 2000 provides a lot more than Windows 95/98 (its closest relative in this area) in the way of printer support. It has to, because Windows 2000 has a lot more to support than Windows 95/98 does. Aside from the server considerations for Windows 2000 Server, even the Workstation version has more to worry about. The following points list some of the items you should be aware of before we begin the discussion of the architecture itself:

- *Portability*. Windows 2000 is meant to be portable, which means that Microsoft had to design it to run with a variety of operating systems on a variety of hardware with a minimum of changes. You'll also hear portability referred to as *platform independence*. You'll see later in this section how this affected the design strategy for the printing services in Windows 2000.

> **Note:** Portability isn't only an issue when it comes to printing. You'll want to look at the other architectural chapters in this book as well. The graphics interface is one area where Microsoft had to do a lot of work to make Windows 2000 as portable as possible. In Windows 95/98, for example, Microsoft's programmers were able to use some hand-tuned assembly code to speed up the rasterizer. The same can't be said of Windows 2000, where they had to stick with C++ as the development language (for platform independence). Assembly language is on such a low level (close to the hardware and highly machine specific) that it's not possible to easily port programs written in assembly language to other platforms or other types of computers.

- *OS/2 and POSIX support*. You can't provide support for applications designed for another operating system without also supporting the printing needs of those applications. Windows 2000 uses a client system to provide this support. Both OS/2 and POSIX have their own clients. This client architecture could conceivably enable Windows 2000 to support any number of operating systems. It represents a major difference between Windows 2000 and Windows 95/98.

- *Multiprocessor support*. Any time you introduce more than one processor into the computing picture, you have to also add code to handle it. Graphics is the largest consumer of resources on your machine, but printing on a network follows close behind. Not only do these two tasks require large quantities of memory, but they also require a lot of processor cycles. (That's one of the reasons why Novell suggests that you use a print server with NetWare—to offload part of the processing burden to another machine.) One of the bigger reasons why Windows 2000 has to provide support for using more than one processor is to complete graphics and printing tasks faster.

- *Improved reliability*. Reliability is a major concern with Windows 2000—much more so than with Windows 95/98. DOS applications that write directly to the video adapter and change its registers without much thought are a threat to security (think *games*). You'll find that Windows 2000 is a lot less tolerant of ill-behaved applications than Windows 95/98. Much of that intolerance is found in the GDI and other graphics elements.

Getting a print job from an application to the printer is no simple matter if you have multiplatform support and more than one application to worry about. An understanding of how printing works will often help you discover new optimization techniques or track down an equipment failure with ease. Each component of the Windows 2000 print architecture is described in the following list:

- *WIN32 subsystem*. Remember that Windows 2000 uses a client/server approach to take care of the needs of the various applications it supports. The way it does that is through the WIN32 subsystem—a buffer layer that translates foreign operating system calls into something Windows 2000 can understand. Think about POSIX for a second. Filenames and other text commands are case sensitive in that environment. Contrast this to the not-case-sensitive nature of DOS. You'll also remember that OS/2 is a 32-bit operating system, even in Character mode, which makes a big difference in the way its applications react. The actual differences between the various operating system applications are too vast to discuss in detail here, and you really don't need to know them to use Windows 2000. On the other hand, it's always nice to know that something exists even if you don't need it.

- *Virtual DOS Machine (VDM)*. Windows 2000 places each DOS application in its own VDM. The reason is simple: To provide the higher level of system reliability that Windows 2000 users demand, Microsoft had to make sure that each application had its own environment completely separate from that used by every other application. It's also important to remember that 16-bit Windows applications share one VDM. Windows 2000 always starts a VDM and then runs a copy of 16-bit Windows in it to service the needs of 16-bit Windows applications. This effectively adds two layers to every interaction—one for the VDM and another for the WIN32 subsystem. As with everything else, this additional layering is transparent to the programmer. You still use the same interfaces as before.

- *Graphical device interface (GDI)*. I discussed this particular element of the printing picture in previous chapters of the book. The GDI is the API that an application uses to talk to the printer. An application doesn't directly access a printer like DOS does. It uses the Windows services. This allows for centralized scheduling and control of print jobs—a necessary requirement of a multitasking environment. The Device Independent Bitmap (DIB) engine used to be a separate component of the printer subsystem but is now included within the GDI.

- *Print driver*. This is the third piece of the print page preparation. It interfaces with both the GDI and the DIB engine to produce printer-specific output in the form of journal records. Think of a journal record as the disassembled pieces of a puzzle.

All the pieces will eventually be put together, but each individual record is just a piece of that puzzle. Just like with puzzle pieces, you can look at them separately and recognize what they will eventually become.

- *Print processor.* The print processor accepts the printer-ready data from the printer driver. Its only function at this point is to despool the data to the print request router. In other words, it sends out the journal records single file in an orderly manner. Later, the print processor takes care of spooling the data to the local hard drive (spool files) if this is a local print job. This means that it takes all the puzzle pieces (journal records) and connects them into a single document.

- *Print request router.* This component routes the formatted data to the appropriate location. It determines whether the job is for a local or remote printer. If it's for a remote printer, the print request router sends the data to the network print provider. Otherwise, it sends the data to the local spooler.

- *Network print provider.* The network print provider is network specific. It's the interface between your machine and the beginning of the network data stream. Its job is to accept the journal records, connect them into a single document, convert the document into a network-specific format (if required), and transmit the converted data to the next component in the network data stream. If all goes according to plan, this data will eventually find its way to a network printer.

- *Local spooler.* The first job of this particular component is to hand off print jobs to the print processor. The print processor converts the journal records it receives into a document. The local spooler reads the data files the print processor stores on disk and sends them to the monitor. It also accepts messages from the monitor regarding the status of the printer. I discuss the types of information it receives when I discuss the monitor.

- *Spool files.* These are the physical files the print processor stores in the Spool folder in the main Windows folder. Each printer type has its own storage location in this folder.

- *Monitor.* The monitor handles all communications with the printer. It accepts data from the spooler and transmits it to the printer. The monitor is also responsible for providing the spooler with Plug-and-Play information about the printer. (Plug and Play is supported in Windows 2000.) Finally, the monitor provides the spooler with printer error information. Instead of giving you a `Printer not ready` message, printers that support a bidirectional port can supply an `Out of paper` or `Toner low` message.

- *Hardware abstraction layer (HAL).* This is another conceptual type of element in Windows 2000. Microsoft wrote the drivers and other software elements in such a way that it could easily move Windows 2000 to other platforms. The basic architecture of Windows 2000 is the same, but the low-level drivers—the ones that directly interface with the hardware—are different.

This might look like a lot of work just to get your document from an application to the printer connected to your machine—and you're right. If that's all the tasks Windows 2000 could handle, this architecture would be very inflated indeed. However, there's much more here than meets the eye. Using this kind of interface provides the user with a lot more freedom: It ensures that everyone gets equal access to the printer. Programmers benefit as well because it's easier to write print drivers. The DIB engine improves the quality of your output. I could go on, but I think the point is made. The printing architecture might be complex, but it makes printing easier from a user's perspective.

Print Process

Now that you know all the players, let's see what happens when we put them all together. In this section, I guide you through the actual printing process. Because this is a Windows 2000 workstation book and not a Windows 2000 Server book, the focus is on the client side of printing and not so much on the server side. The discussion also focuses on network printing. (For local printing, you just remove the network components and consider the workstation to be acting as a client and a server simultaneously.)

Also, the focus here is on Windows 2000. Although there are other clients such as UNIX and Macintosh that might print to a Windows 2000 server, those topics are beyond the scope of this discussion.

Let's begin by taking a more focused look at the printing process—particularly on the client side. An application prepares a print job using the WIN32 GDI, DIB, and the printer driver. A print job is more than just the data to be sent to the printer device. It's a collection of commands and code (such as PostScript or printer-specific code) that instructs the printer how to handle the printable material being sent. This preparation is usually called *rendering*.

Technical Note: Windows 2000 servers can integrate with other operating systems. For this reason, the printing process can be quite complex. This section focuses on the Windows 2000 Professional Print Client, although there are several other print clients (including the following):

- Windows 95/98 Print clients
- 16-bit Windows Network clients
- MS-DOS Network clients
- UNIX clients
- NetWare clients
- Macintosh clients

These clients will behave differently with the Windows 2000 server and use different components to complete the job. Essentially, however, the print process remains the same.

After this information is prepped, it's sent to the client-side print spooler. The client-side print spooler contacts the server and the print spooler on the server side. The server-side print spooler consists of three components: spooler, local print provider, and router. These components facilitate communication back and forth. The server-side print router contacts the remote print provider on the client machine. The information will be sent and spooled to the local hard drive.

Peter's Principle: How to Get the Best Performance from Your Spooler Files

By default, on a Windows 2000 server, the spooler location on the hard drive is `%SystemRoot%\System32\spool\PRINTERS`. This is usually fine. If printing traffic is exceptionally heavy, however, you may want to move this directory to another drive. Getting the spool files off of the system drive will help both the printing process as well as the overall performance of Windows 2000. To move the file for all printers, you need to modify the Registry in this location:

`HKEY_LOCAL_MACHINE\System\CurrentControlSet\Control\Print\Printers`

VALUE ENTRY: DefaultSpoolDirectory

Set this value entry to a directory that currently exists. Make sure you type the drive letter and the full path to the existing directory. In addition, make sure that all users (group name EVERYONE) have Change permission on that directory. Permissions for the directory are important here. If a user suddenly cannot print to a local printer, it may be that he or she has been messing around with permissions on various directories, including the spool directory. Therefore, if everything else seems to be fine, you might want to check permissions on this directory. Moving the spool directory to a different physical disk (a disk on a separate controller from the operating system's location or to a fast RAID disk system) will improve overall printer performance.

After the print job is spooled to the local hard drive, the local print processor will make a call to the printer monitor. Which printer monitors are used depends on the various types of printers that may be installed.

Standards

Technical Note: Windows 2000 can utilize several types of printer monitors to redirect output to various devices locally or remotely to other network printer servers or network print devices. Here's the current list of monitors Windows 2000 can employ:

- *Local Printer Monitor*. For local devices such as LPT1 and FILE.
- *Hewlett-Packard Printer Monitor*. For printing to network-connected HP printers. These printers usually have the proprietary HP JetDirect card installed.

continues

- *Line Printer Port Monitor.* Used for communicating with UNIX using LPR/LPD. (I discuss this in a little more detail shortly.)
- *Macintosh Port Monitor.* You guessed it—for printing to Apple LaserWriter printers.
- *LexMark Mark Vision Print Monitor.* Prints to LexMark printers. Incidentally, LexMark was the company that used to supply all printers with the IBM name on them. The company started producing printers under its own name just four years ago.
- *Digital Network Port Monitor.* Prints to DEC printers on the network. As Digital's printer division is disappearing, I anticipate support for this monitor disappearing shortly.
- *PJL Print Monitor.* This monitor is a generic printer monitor. It uses the Print Job Language (PJL) to communicate with devices that understand that language. PJL has been a standard for more than five years now. The language has undergone several revisions, primarily driven by Hewlett-Packard. The language, however, is widely supported by most printer vendors and remains strong competition for the PostScript printer language.

Windows 2000 selects the printer monitor based on the type of device you're printing to. This selection and the printer installation process are covered later in the book.

The printer monitor may have to communicate with the printing device locally or across the network. The printer monitor may adjust the print job as needed to better utilize some of the features of the printer itself. This is accomplished through both the printer driver and the miniport driver. The *miniport driver* is a small, specific piece of coding that's typically produced by the vendor and installed when you install the printer driver. The miniport driver communicates with the Microsoft print driver to provide the following data:

- Plug and Play information
- Hardware-specific settings and requirements
- Vendor value-added features

The print job has now finished its wild ride through the Windows 2000 roller-coaster-of-a-print-process. At last, it is delivered to the printer and put to paper.

TCP/IP Printing

Windows 2000 Professional has the capability to print using the TCP/IP protocol. This process is a little different from the one previously outlined, primarily because the receiving device is typically *not* a Windows 2000 server. When printing to TCP/IP, Windows 2000 will utilize what's called LPR/LPD (Line Printer Remote/Line Printer Daemon). (To use this process directly from a workstation, you need to install the TCP/IP Print Services. This is covered in Chapter 17, "Exploiting Your Hardware.")

The LPR functionality relies on the LPR printer monitor. This monitor is based on a version of UNIX called Berkeley UNIX (or BSD UNIX). Digital Equipment Corporation's Alpha UNIX is based on BSD; IBM's AIX is based on System V UNIX. At the point in the print process when the system needs to send the data to the printer, the LPR print monitor redirects it to another device on the network that's running and is also LPD compliant. The LPD is on the server side of LPR/LPD printing in UNIX.

It's important to note that the LPR/LPD printing implemented by Windows 2000 will not permit back-and-forth communication. Therefore, errors on the LPD side will all show up as general printer errors, but, alas, without giving you an indication of the nature of the error. You'll need to rely on the UNIX server, printer system (printers with printer network cards in them), or Windows 2000 Server to offer more information on the nature of the error.

The printing process should now be fairly clear, so we can turn our attention to the physical printer device, itself, the final target of all the previous activity.

Print Standards

Just out of curiosity, I sat down with a stack of printer technical manuals prior to writing this chapter. Usually, a vendor tells you what standards it's using to design a piece of equipment. For example, you'll find any modem manual packed with CCITT (Consultative Committee for International Telegraphy and Telephony; now ITU, International Telecommunication Union) standards that define how the modem is supposed to work at certain speeds. My network adapter manuals provide the same type of information; they tell me what standards it adheres to and, in some cases, how it cheats a little on them. The only standard I found in my printer manuals (all 15 of them) was the FCC Class B computing device label—even my telephone has one of those. How do you decide what kind of standard to follow when selecting a printer?

It's unfortunate that there aren't any standards committees to speak of when it comes to printers, at least no committees independent of the companies that lead in specific areas of the printer-vendor community. Because of this, it's probably smarter to ignore "standards" with printers and look at the companies that lead in specific areas. I think of three companies when I think of print standards: Epson, Adobe, and Hewlett-Packard. (All these companies do work with standards committees such as CCITT to define parts of the printer standard.)

Dot Matrix and Epson

Dot-matrix printing might seem like a dead issue, a technology that time has passed by, but I assure you that it's alive and well in database management systems (DBMS) and areas such as inventory control. You can still buy these printers most places where printers are sold. Every retail store I can name uses some form of impact printer to produce receipts. Also, think of ATM machines, grocery, post office, and credit card receipts, and all the other places where you hear a buzzing and snapping. A dot-matrix printout is ripped off the machine and handed to you.

I find that there isn't any substitute for a dot matrix when printing multipart forms. Some people try to replace the multipart forms with multiple copies from a laser printer, but it just doesn't work as well in some situations. If you want to know the standard for dot-matrix printing, look at Epson. Just about every dot-matrix printer on the market today provides some form of Epson printer emulation.

Ink-Jet Printing

Also, don't forget ink-jet printers, probably the most popular machines today for home and small business use. The reason for this popularity? Ink-jet technology offers afford-able color output. Ink-jet printers are available from Apple, Canon, Epson, HP, LexMark, Okidata, and other printer manufacturers.

Ink-jet printers work by spraying special ink onto paper. Magnetic plates are arranged so that they deflect the ink (which is ionized) in the correct pathways so that it splashes on the page, accurately reproducing an image. The accuracy is nearly as good as that achieved by laser printers, typically a resolution of 600dpi (dots per inch), although higher resolutions are now available on some models.

Ink-jet printers are lighter than competing technologies (good for portables) and on aver-age cost less than laser printers, too. However, there are a couple of drawbacks. Ink-jet printing is relatively slow, and you'll have smudging problems if you print on regular, inexpensive paper. The paper can cost, so check it out before you get into a situation where you avoid using your printer because it's become so expensive to buy that paper.

PostScript and Adobe

Adobe is the place to look if you're a PostScript user. Very few other companies have added much to the PostScript standardization. PostScript is a programming language that specifies how to print graphics and text. This "printing" can be on targets other than paper. It's device independent. (PostScript can be sent to a monitor, film, slides, or any other output device that can handle both text and graphics.)

Like the Internet's HTML, PostScript is a page-description language. It was first intro-duced by Adobe in 1985; now, of course, there are PostScript-to-HTML translators and, as the languages mature, it now seems that HTML is replacing PostScript altogether. PostScript, however, is still used by graphics departments and other graphics-intensive environments. Also like HTML, PostScript attempts to be relativistic in its specifications (big font rather than 28pt). This way, PostScript doesn't look wildly different on printers with different resolutions or pages of different sizes. That's the theory. In fact, device independence, like platform independence for computer operating systems, remains more of an ideal than a reality. You'll find some PostScript pages that do specify aspects required of the output hardware, for example, such as the kinds of paper trays that feed a printer.

Recently, Adobe, along with IBM, Netscape, and Sun Microsystems, submitted a Precision Graphics Markup Language (PGML) specification to the World Wide Web Consortium (W3C). Adobe perceives a need for a new 2D graphics language to describe printing, layout, color, and fonts on the Internet. If you're interested in learning more about the PGML specification, look at http://www.w3.org/Submission/.

> **Tip:** You can find out everything you need to know about PostScript by visiting the Adobe's home page at http://www.adobe.com/homepage.shtml. The site also features a group of user forums where you can share ideas with others.

Laser and Hewlett-Packard

As with the other two companies mentioned so far, Hewlett-Packard brings another dose of sanity to the world of printing. Its claim to fame began with the LaserJet III printer. Now, besides providing the language used to control a laser printer, Hewlett-Packard also champions a plotter language called PCL; not surprisingly, this language appears as part of the feature set for Hewlett-Packard's laser printers.

> **Tip:** Hewlett-Packard maintains an excellent Web site at http://www.hp.com/. Besides learning the specifications for a variety of laser and ink-jet printers, you'll find interesting pages on other topics. Needless to say, digging around doesn't hurt when you're looking for the latest on printer (or other) technology. Also, the HP home page is your gateway to the latest Hewlett-Packard drivers, enabling you to extract maximum efficiency when mating your operating system to your particular printer. If you have a different printer brand, be sure to check its home page from time to time to see whether a new, improved driver is available.
>
> HP has a new color technology called Color Layering Technology. It gives up to 1200×1200 ink-jet resolution using photo paper. One regular paper, you can get 600×600, which looks really nice as well.

By now, you're probably thinking that the whole area of printer standardization is pretty weak—and you're right. All I've done is mention three companies that seem to set the standard for dot-matrix, PostScript, and laser printers. I haven't even mentioned a leader for ink-jet printers. The problem is clear: There aren't any firm standards you can rely on when it comes to printers. What you should rely on is the vendor community that supports the technology.

Obviously, most companies are reluctant to base policy on the whims of a single, competing company. Look at what happened to the graphics standards after IBM lost its leadership position. It was a few years before VESA (Video Electronics Standards Association) stepped in and cleaned up the mess. How else can you minimize your risk besides buying a mainstream printer? I look for several things when buying a new printer:

- *Parts standards.* If you can't find a standard for the whole printer, looking for standards for the parts it contains is the next best thing. I mention a lot of different standards actually put out by standards committees throughout the rest of this book. Many different standards govern serial ports and graphics, for example. You'll find them in Chapters 20, "Windows 2000 Connections," and 13, "Graphics Windows 2000 Style."

- *Plug and Play compatibility.* You should also look for standardized features such as Plug and Play. A vendor who is on top of such things can probably be relied on to follow other standards as well.

- *Feature set.* Having a printer that also includes the necessary network connections so that you don't have to use a separate print server is also a plus. As with everything else I have mentioned to this point, the various network connections have standards. You can use this data point as one of the criteria you use when selecting a printer. Make sure that the vendor adheres to every standard you can verify.

- *Software compatibility.* Printers are notoriously late when it comes to working with anything. About the only reason Windows has plenty of drivers is that Microsoft wrote them. (To their credit, the three vendors mentioned in this section did provide their own Windows drivers and keep them updated on their respective Web sites.)

- *Specification compliance.* All the vendors I have mentioned in this chapter provide very precise specifications for their printers. Downloading these specifications and then comparing the features of the printer you plan to get with the established standards can save you a lot of time and effort tracking down problems later. (There is something to be said about buying a name brand printer in this regard— you know that it will follow the vendor specifications.)

- *Hardware quality.* There's something special about buying a Mercedes Benz, BMW, Lexus, or other luxury car. You can feel it in the heft of the door when you open it. The good, solid feel of the car as you drive it and the lack of road noise are other indicators of a quality product. Likewise, you can usually tell a quality printer by the various clues provided by your five senses. A lot of people were upset about the quality of the LaserJet 4, and for good reason: Hewlett-Packard ended up reworking the design of that printer a few times before getting it right. Look at the solidity of *some* of the recent LaserJets. I still remember a Panasonic printer I bought. In every way but one, it was just like getting an Epson. The one big difference was the quality of the print mechanism. I went through two Panasonic printers while my LQ-850 still chugged away. The Epson printer is still standing—I gave up on Panasonic long ago. (Does this make Panasonic a "bad" printer? Probably not, because some people won't use their printers heavily enough to warrant the additional cost of buying an Epson.)

As you can see, getting a printer is easy; getting one that will actually work well is another story. The lack of standards in the printer arena shouldn't prevent you from making a good buying decision, however. I find that spending just a little time to look for the right cues helps me avoid bad buying decisions.

One consideration: If you're looking for the very best print quality at a practical price, laser printers offer a very high-quality output and are also faster (8ppm is typical of even the least expensive models) and far quieter than most printers. For many, if not most, uses in an ordinary offices, a laser printer (at $250 and up) is your best choice overall if you can do without color. Also, don't forget, laser printers don't require that you buy special paper at 50 cents a sheet, or whatever. You use ordinary paper, which costs nearly nothing.

On Your Own

Spend some time looking through the vendor manual for your printer. Do you see specifications for the printer itself? If not, look for specifications that affect the component parts. If your printer includes an Ethernet card, for example, you should see some form of compliance with the Ethernet standards.

Look through the SYSTEM folder on your machine. See whether you can identify the various drivers used to make your printer work. Use the Windows 2000 View utility to look at the contents of the various DLLs. You should be able to identify some of the function names you see within the files as user components that you work with directly. You might see a function name that opens the Print dialog box or one that adjusts the print resolution, for example. Other function names will come from the User or GDI modules I talked about in Chapter 9, "An Architectural Overview."

Locate your printer's vendor's home page on the Internet and check to see whether there's an updated printer driver you should install.

Use your browser to look at some of the vendor Web sites I mentioned in this chapter. Do you see the variety of specifications these vendors provide? This is part of the basis for your printer-buying decision. Download one or more of the specifications. Reading through these specifications—at least glancing through them—will give you new insights into what you can expect from your printer and what you should expect in the future.

Peter Norton

PART IV

Advanced User's Guide to Windows 2000

OLE, ActiveX, and DCOM

You're going to run across three different terms when using Windows 2000: object linking and embedding (OLE), ActiveX, and Distributed Component Object Model (DCOM).
A fourth term, dynamic data exchange (DDE), may pop up from time to time, but you
really won't need to worry about it much. All four of these terms have one thing in common: They all provide methods of working with data in ways that make the low-level data
manipulation invisible to the end user. In other words, these technologies are all methods
of making you more productive when working with data.

DDE and OLE are methods for sharing data between documents. Of the two, DDE is
older and has fallen out of use in most application programs. There are two different versions of OLE. Windows 2000 supports the newer OLE2 standard, but that doesn't mean
your applications will.

The first thing you need to understand about OLE is that it's not just cut and paste. In
most of the chapters in this book, I talk about the objects that Windows 2000 uses to
make life simpler for the user. Would it surprise you too much to learn that these objects
are a form of OLE support?

One problem with OLE is that it's limited to documents you can access from the local
machine. In addition, you have to rely on the local hardware to perform any required
object processing such as modifying the appearance of the object or the data that it works
with. This brings us to the third entry in the title of this chapter: DCOM. OLE2 uses the
Component Object Model (COM) as the basis for creating compound documents (documents that contain other objects). When you embed or link an object using OLE, COM is
the underlying technology making it possible. DCOM, as the acronym implies, resides
not only on the local machine, but anywhere on the network as well. In other words, a
compound document could consist of objects created in a variety of places.

Why is DCOM important? First, it's the basis for new Internet-based technologies such as
the ActiveX controls used with Internet Explorer 3.0 and above. It's also the technology
that allows people to create Internet Information Server add-ons that execute only on the
server. The most common use for DCOM today is on intranets. Using DCOM on an
intranet allows users to make full use of network capabilities. DCOM is also used on the

Internet, where people want to share data over the World Wide Web. DCOM is embedded into Windows 2000, although it might be a while before you see it used for data sharing on your local network.

Microsoft has changed its stance on ActiveX several times since I first started looking at this technology. The term originally referred to COM/DCOM as a whole. Microsoft had envisioned using ActiveX as a moniker for a group of COM-based technologies. Today, ActiveX refers to controls specifically. A pushbutton on a dialog box is normally an ActiveX control. Microsoft is fond of the term *Active*; there are other Active technologies as well. For example, *Active Document* is a COM-based technology for applications that work with data. Active Document will allow an application such as your word processor to appear within a browser such as Internet Explorer. You'll be able to edit a document on the Internet just as easily as on your local hard drive, and you won't even have to switch applications to do it.

Compound Documents: The Microsoft Strategy

You need to speak the language of OLE to really understand it. The following list defines some of the terms you'll see in this chapter (and the chapters that follow):

- *Client.* This term refers to the application that holds a linked or embedded object. If you place a spreadsheet object in your word-processed document, for example, the word processor becomes the client.

- *Server.* The server is the application that originated an object. The server is the application that the client calls to manipulate an object. Embedded or linked objects are still in the native format of the application that created them. A client must call on the originating application to edit the object's content. In other words, if you double-click an embedded object to make changes to it, the server application starts running with the object loaded and ready for editing.

- *Compound document.* This is a document that contains one or more objects. Every OLE document is considered a compound document. We'll take a closer look at what this means a little later in this chapter.

- *Object.* An object is a piece of data that you move from one application to another in the object's native format. You can create objects from any data if the originating application supports OLE. This is the big difference between an object and cutting and pasting. You can do a lot more with an object because it contains intelligence that a simple piece of text does not. An object knows which application created it. (The term *object* is very widely used in computing today, but I'm using it here in the specific context of ActiveX components.)

- *Context menu.* We'll take another look at how to use this particular OLE menu later. This is the menu you use to change the contents of an OLE document, convert it, or perform any other operations the object allows.

- *Container.* A container is an object that holds other objects. Visualizing a folder, such as the ones used by Explorer, will give you a good idea of what a container represents. Instead of just holding files like a folder does, however, an OLE container can hold any kind of object.

Now that you have some idea of what these OLE terms mean, take a look at some actual examples. I use Microsoft Paint and WordPad for this example so that you can follow along if you want to. It isn't really necessary to do so; the important thing is that you understand the process.

The first thing you do is open both WordPad and Paint (Start, Programs, Accessories); then load a file named Santa Fe Stucco.BMP into Paint (you can find this same file in the \WINNT folder on your machine). You should see something similar to Figure 15.1. There isn't anything particularly special about these two applications, but they do both support OLE2—which will enable me to show you some of the things you can look forward to.

FIGURE 15.1

Using OLE starts with something as simple as opening two applications.

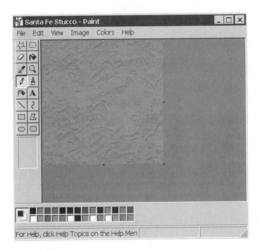

Choose the Edit, Select All command in Paint to select the entire image and then right-click it. You should see the context menu shown in Figure 15.2. Notice that you can't drag and drop this image because Paint doesn't support that particular OLE2 feature. If it did support drag and drop, you could just right-click the object and drag it where you wanted it to go in WordPad. We'll need to take a somewhat longer route, instead.

The context menu enables you to cut or copy the image. Notice the number of other editing options this menu contains. You might want to make note of what's available and compare it to the context menu after you copy the image to WordPad. For right now, choose the Copy option. Doing so places a copy of the object on the Clipboard.

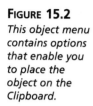

FIGURE 15.2
This object menu contains options that enable you to place the object on the Clipboard.

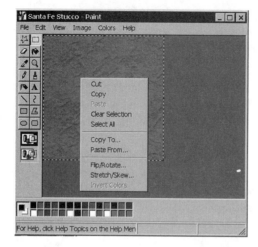

Note: You can use the Edit, Paste Special command in place of the context menu when working with WordPad (or other applications that provide this feature). In fact, some applications don't provide a context menu, so you have to resort to using the Edit menu. I demonstrate this method of linking or embedding an object later in the chapter.

Click WordPad to give it the focus. Right-click anywhere within WordPad's window. You should see a context menu similar to the one in Figure 15.3. Notice how this menu differs from the one you saw in Paint. Each context menu will have features unique to that application. A graphics application needs menu entries to help it manipulate graphics images, for example, and a word processor needs a different set of options to manipulate text.

FIGURE 15.3
The WordPad object menu differs from the one found in Paint because it needs to perform different work.

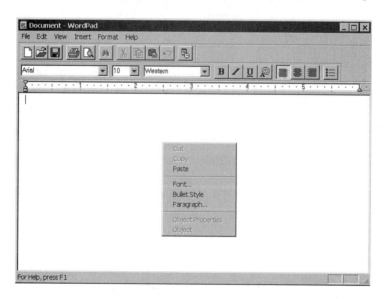

Choose the Paste option from WordPad's context menu. You should see a copy of the graphics image in WordPad. The first thing you should notice is the sizing handles around the image. These handles enable you to enlarge or shrink the object as needed. Now that the image is located in a WordPad document, go ahead and close Paint. You can always open it again if you need it later. Now right-click the graphics object in WordPad; you'll see a menu similar to the WordPad context menu you saw earlier. Notice, however, that the two bottom options are now activated: Bitmap Image Object and Object Properties. Highlight Bitmap Image Object to display a submenu.

The two options here are Edit and Open. Choose Edit if you want to perform in-place editing. The Open option actually opens an instance of the Paint application, which you can then use to edit the graphic as usual. The in-place editing feature is quite interesting: It transforms your current application (WordPad) into a hybrid application that combines aspects of both WordPad and Paint. To see what I mean, choose Edit now. You should see a display similar to Figure 15.4. Notice the hatched frame around the object. This is an OLE2 way of telling you which object you're currently editing. Also notice that the toolbar and menus changed to match those of Paint. This is what's meant by *in-place editing*. The application didn't change, but the tools in it temporarily changed to meet the editing needs of the object. Note that the title of this window remains Document WordPad.

FIGURE 15.4

In-place editing is one of the OLE2 features.

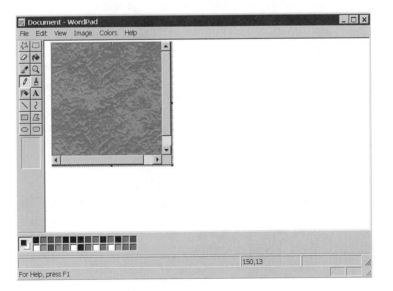

You can click anywhere outside the object to restore the original WordPad menu and toolbar. Whether you choose Edit (for in-place editing) or Open (to start the originating application) largely depends on personal taste, because the result of using either method is the same. The advantage of using the in-place method is that you remain in the same window all the time. This tends to increase efficiency and reduce the chance of losing your train of thought. You can also see the changes you're making in the context of any surrounding text or other objects. The Open method does require one extra step.

You need to tell Paint to update the copy of the graphic that's still in WordPad. Choose File, Update Document, as shown in Figure 15.5. Notice how this option replaces Save. In essence, the update process does save the graphic; the only difference is where the graphic gets saved.

Figure 15.5

Make certain that you update your document before you leave the server application.

Exit Paint and return to WordPad. Notice that the Exit entry on the File menu in Paint also says "Return to Document." Check out what that other context menu entry contains. Right-click the graphics object and choose the Object Properties option. You'll see the Bitmap Image Properties dialog box. About the only interesting entry on the General page is the Convert button. Clicking this displays another dialog box with a list of conversion options. In essence, this option enables you to convert the graphics object from one file type to another. Unfortunately, the only option is to transform the BMP file into a DIB file. Device-independent bitmaps are not widely used. This page also displays the file size and type.

> **Note:** Each object type provides a unique set of pages in the Object Properties dialog box. It's important to remember that each dialog box reflects a combination of the capabilities of the server applications and the needs of the data file format. Some file formats can't support some application features. As a result, some options might appear grayed out (disabled).

Click the View tab. You'll see the View tab of the Bitmap Image Properties dialog box, shown in Figure 15.6. This page has several interesting entries. The first is the radio button that determines whether the image displays as a graphic or an icon. You can make your machine run faster and use less memory if you select the icon option. Using an icon means that Windows doesn't need to load the actual image or the application required to support it unless you decide to edit it. Windows will suggest a default icon, but you can use the Change Icon button to select another.

Figure 15.6

The View tab of the Bitmap Image Properties dialog box enables you to change the appearance of the object.

The bottom part of this dialog box is fairly interesting too, even if you can't select it at the moment. It enables you to scale your graphic. The BMP format and application used to display it doesn't support the scaling option in this particular case. Close WordPad; you don't need it anymore for now. You don't have to save the image unless you want to.

This whirlwind tour presented some of the things you can try with OLE2. Of course, you haven't even come close to exercising every feature yet. Now it's time to take a step back and consider the meaning of DDE, a technology that preceded OLE and that contributes to OLE. (OLE, in its turn, preceded ActiveX and contributes to it, as you'll see at the end of this chapter.)

Dynamic Data Exchange: An Overview

Many people have the mistaken idea that DDE is dead. If DDE is so dead, why does it keep popping up in the Registry? Even Explorer, an application first designed for Windows 95 (and then incorporated into Windows 2000 among other things), provides DDE capability. The fact is that every OLE application uses a little DDE to make it run. Now that I have your attention, let's take a look at DDE. Using DDE has some significant problems. The most significant is that it creates a static link—one that won't change as the placement of the file on the hard drive changes. The fact that it provides a stable macro language that you can use to open files and perform other fancy maneuvers from the command line doesn't change the situation much.

DDE is a messaging protocol. It sends a message from one application to another and asks it to do something. Originally, DDE was supposed to provide the means to open another application and copy some data to the Clipboard. You could also get it to do other chores, such as printing files. A DDE macro contains part DDE and part application macro language. Prior to the standardized macro language, Visual Basic for Applications (VBA), that now appears in all major Microsoft applications, you had to learn the macro language of both server and client application. Making things worse, the client and server often used different macro languages. For example, Access Basic was different from Word Basic.

Note: The term *protocol* is often misused and very often misunderstood. As a minimum, a protocol when used in a computer environment is a set of rules that defines how two objects can communicate with each other. To put this in human terms, it would be the same as two parties agreeing to speak French during negotiations. You can only imagine what would happen on an international level if one side of a conflict spoke only German and the other side only Spanish, and there were no translators available to make sense of the conversation. Likewise, two objects on a computer have to speak the same language before any communication can take place. In addition to communication rules, a protocol could define other rules such as the method used to perform a specific kind of task. What other rules a protocol defines depends on the protocol—some protocols are communication specific.

Needless to say, DDE didn't get the kind of reception Microsoft originally hoped it would. DDE is just too complicated for the average user to consider using. In fact, even some programmers find it difficult to use (unless they use it on a regular basis).

OLE automation reduces or eliminates the need for DDE. One of the features OLE automation provides is a consistent macro language—the same macros work with every application. This means that a programmer can create a macro for an application that he doesn't even have loaded on his machine.

The problem with OLE is that few applications actually support OLE2 (although the number using OLE2 grows every day), and even fewer support OLE automation. I have 15 applications that support OLE automation on my machine right now—that's 15 out of 35 or so. (This is a lot better than even a year ago when a mere five of my applications supported OLE automation.) Considering that I have all the newest versions of everything on the market, that's not a very inspiring level of conformity. OLE automation, like DDE, was more of a local experiment within Microsoft's applications than a technology that caught the software developer world by storm.

Technical Note: Components built on OLE technology have the file extension .OCX (OLE Custom eXtension or OLE Custom Control, depending on whom you talk to). Just as the term *DDE* has largely faded into history as DDE sank beneath OLE and became merely an invisible support technology underneath OLE, so too is OLE sinking underneath the latest, greatest interapplication initiative from Microsoft: ActiveX. ActiveX components are, however, still called OCXs (although you can compile EXE- and DLL-specialized ActiveX components as well). I have much more to say about ActiveX at the end of this chapter.

Linking Versus Embedding

The concepts of linking versus embedding are important—they work in OLE as well as ActiveX. When you link a document, you are, in essence, creating a pointer to that file on disk. Think of a link as a road sign pointing to your house. As long as you don't move the house, everyone can find it because the road sign will point there. What happens if you do move the house, however? The sign still points to where it thinks your house is, but anyone who follows the sign will find nothing but an empty foundation.

Peter's Principle: A Time to Link and a Time to Embed

Some people get confused about when it's appropriate to use linking versus embedding. I break the two down into simple categories so that it's easy to determine when to use each type of OLE. The main problem is defining precisely what kind of compound document you want to create.

Embedding works best when you need to share a file with a lot of people. If the compound document is going to move around, you want to package it in such a way that nothing gets lost. An embedded object meets this criterion. Even though embedding is less subject to data loss, it does have a disadvantage: You can't easily share with other people the data embedded within your document independently of the document itself. The embedded data is sunk within your document like a diamond in a wedding ring—you must pass around both the object and its container document if you want to share the object with others.

On the other hand, linking does work well when you want to share data. If you plan to use the same file in more than one place, linking is the route to go. I almost always use this technique instead of embedding when working with logos.

The same principle holds true for links in compound documents. The link works fine as long as you don't move the document. The second you do move the document, however, you break the links. Of course, you can always reestablish the links, but that's a waste of time when not moving the file in the first place would require a lot less work.

Note: One of the improvements that Microsoft made for OLE2 was to make the linking process more stable. Instead of using a precise location, OLE2 uses a relative direction. What if you told your friends that you lived two blocks south of Joe, for example? As long as you and Joe maintained the two-block distance, people could find your house. (Of course, they'd need to know the location of Joe's house.)

Embedding is a different process from linking. Instead of creating a pointer to your data, embedding actually places the data object within the compound document. This means that wherever the compound document goes, the data will follow. This sounds like a great fix for the problems with linking. Embedding comes with several price tags attached, however. First, you'll find it very difficult to update multiple compound documents simultaneously. Suppose that your company just decided to use a different logo and it wants all the letters updated to reflect that change. If you had linked the logo file to the letters, the change would be simple. You'd need to change just one file.

Anyone who opened each document after that would see the new logo. With embedding, you'd have to change each document on an individual basis.

You'll also use a lot more disk space to store an embedded file. A link takes only a few bytes to create a pointer. An embedded object is complete. If the object is 4KB, your compound document will grow by a minimum of 4KB to accommodate it. Unfortunately, you won't get off that easily. In addition to the size of the object, some "housekeeping" data is included as well. The server needs this information to help you maintain the object.

Now that you know the difference between linking and embedding, take a look at how you'd implement them. Begin by opening a copy of WordPad. I'm going to explain another route you can take to link and embed objects in your documents. Choose Object from the Insert menu to display the dialog box shown in Figure 15.7. Notice that you can go two routes at this point: You can insert a new object or an existing one.

FIGURE 15.7

Use the Insert Object dialog box to embed or link a new or existing object into your document.

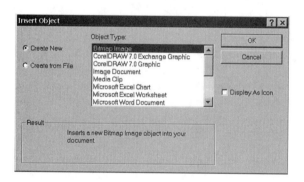

Click the Create from File radio button (the dialog box changes to the one shown in Figure 15.8). Choosing this option enables you to embed or link an existing file. Click the Browse button and find any BMP file you like. Double-click to select it. Click the Link check box. If you don't enable this check box, Windows automatically embeds the object instead of linking it. Your dialog box should match the one shown in Figure 15.8. Notice the Display As Icon check box. Clicking this displays the object as an icon rather than as a full image.

FIGURE 15.8

Use the Create from File option to embed or link an existing file to your document.

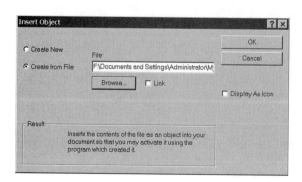

Tip: Sometimes it's better to display an object as an icon. You'll probably want to use this option as you design a document to reduce the load on the processor, for example. Every object you keep open reduces your capability to create a document quickly because the client application has to keep calling on the server application to display the information. After you complete the document, you can disable the Display As Icon check box to show the object in its original format. This enables you to print the document—complete with objects—after you finish putting it together.

Click OK to place a link to the object in the current document. A quick glance at this object doesn't reveal anything different from the last time you created a compound document. When you right-click the object, however, you'll notice that the menu entries are slightly different. The big difference is obvious when you try to edit the file. Instead of the in-place editing you could do after embedding the object, editing a link always opens the server (the originating application). You must edit the object in a separate window when using linked objects in place of embedded ones. If you really dislike seeing the other application start, you might want to use embedded rather than linked objects.

You should now completely understand the differences between linking and embedding. These differences are important for a lot of reasons. When there's a little overlap in functionality and it's acceptable to use either linking or embedding, select the method that appeals to you most. My favorite method is embedding because I prefer to use in-place editing when I can. From a practical standpoint, however, I often have to use linking now to reduce my workload later.

Clients and Servers

Every application that supports OLE/ActiveX provides one or more services. You might have noticed in both the examples that I used Paint as the server and WordPad as the client. The reason is simple: Paint cannot function as a client. It offers itself only as an OLE server. (Some programs only function as a server, some only as a client, and still others as both.)

This distinction is important because it affects the way you use an application. More than that, limitations of OLE support necessarily limit an application's value when you're creating a finished product.

Consider what would happen if you tried to use a graphics program to create a poster, but it didn't support OLE as a client. Would you just settle for cut and paste if there were a chance you'd need to modify the chart frequently? If Paint supported OLE as a client, you could create a chart for your poster in one application, the text in another, the graphics elements in a third, and then link them all together within Paint. However, the lack of client support means that you have to copy the text to the Clipboard. When you paste it into Paint, the text becomes a graphics element—part of the Paint graphics image. The text isn't an OLE object you can easily manipulate later using a word processor; it's a graphics element you have to erase and redo from scratch. This makes changes as small as using a different type style or font size a lot more difficult than they need to be.

Whether your application is a client or a server is an important consideration. You might find that it's less expensive from a time-investment perspective to get rid of an application with limited OLE support. You can follow some general guidelines when it comes to choosing applications.

Any application that will serve as a central location for all the objects in a project must support OLE. In most cases, you'll want to use a word processor or presentation graphics program for this purpose. They provide the greatest amount of flexibility when it comes to formatting your data. Charts and graphs might need the services of a graphics program. Unfortunately, most low-end packages won't work as clients, so you'll need to invest in a high-end package such as CorelDRAW! You'll definitely want a package of this sort to provide both client and server capabilities because you'll need to use both.

You can do quick-and-dirty edits with low-end packages. They usually have just enough features to get the job done and don't waste a lot of precious memory. Programs of this sort usually support OLE as a server but not as a client. No one would want the output from these programs; it just doesn't look professional. Microsoft Paint and other low-end graphics packages commonly fall into this category. You might see some note-takers here, too. In some cases, all you need is the text. A note-taker (such as the Notepad utility provided with Windows 2000) works fine for this purpose.

Finally, you'll never use some packages as servers because they just don't generate enough data on their own to make it worth your while to use them in that capacity. Some presentation graphics programs fall into this category. Because their output looks nice, you can use them as OLE clients without worrying about their server capabilities.

Differences Between OLE1 and OLE2

Microsoft introduced OLE1 as part of Windows 3.x. It provided a basic set of linking and embedding features that users soon outgrew. One of the biggest problems was the huge amount of memory that OLE1 required to create more than one or two links with other applications. OLE1 required the client to start every application that it had established an OLE link with—whether that link was actually displayed onscreen or not. If you had links with a spreadsheet, a graphics program, and a charting program, all three would have to be in memory when you opened the compound document. Most machines just didn't provide that amount of memory. The lack of speed was also a major concern. Keeping all those applications going at once made a real performance hit; most machines spent their time swapping out one application to disk and swapping in another as you moved from place to place in the compound document. In addition, the way that OLE1 managed links was inefficient.

OLE2 is supposed to remedy some of the OLE1 problems and provide much more functionality to boot. The following list gives you an idea of all the improvements Microsoft made in OLE2 (some of them are programmer specific, but everyone benefits from something that makes a programmer's life even a little easier):

> **Tip:** Most of the following new features require that both applications support OLE2. At the very minimum, the client must support OLE2 in order to make any of the features work. I discussed the Registry in Chapter 10, "Understanding the Windows 2000 Registry." Some vendors give you an idea of how to use OLE but don't really tell you how they support it. Looking in the Registry can provide important clues as to the type and level of OLE support that an application provides.

- *Visual editing.* One of the problems with OLE1 was that the user's train of thought got disrupted every time he or she needed to make a change to an object. The reason is simple: OLE1 loaded a copy of the server and displayed the object in the originating application's window for editing. OLE2 allows visual (or *in-place*) editing. Instead of opening a new window, the server merely overlays its toolbar, menu structure, and controls with those of the client. The user simply sees a change in tools, not a change in applications. As a result, the transition between documents is less noticeable. This method of editing has another benefit as well. Because you don't load an entire application, in-place editing is more memory efficient and reduces the load on the processor.

- *Nested objects.* OLE1 allowed you to place one object at a time in the container document. An object couldn't become a container; all the objects existed as a single layer within the container. OLE2 treats every potential container as just that—a container. It doesn't matter how many containers you place inside a container or how many ways you stack them. To get a better idea of how nesting will help you, look at the way Windows 2000 implements folders. You can treat OLE2 container objects the same way.

- *Drag and drop.* You used to cut or copy an object in the server application and then place it in the client using the Paste Special command. This option still works. OLE2 provides a new method of creating links to other documents, however. You can simply grab the object and move it wherever you want. It becomes linked wherever you decide to drop it.

- *Storage-independent links.* OLE2 enables you to create links to other documents, even if they aren't physically located on the local drive. It implements this using an LRPC (Light Remote Procedure Call) mechanism. Unfortunately, this linking mechanism has limitations. You'll find that it works fine with some peer-to-peer networks, for example, but it works only marginally with other network types. The next revision of OLE (the new Network OLE specification) is supposed to fix this problem by supporting RPCs (Remote Procedure Calls).

- *Adaptable links*. Many users screamed for this feature. If you moved any of the files required to create a compound document under OLE1, all the links got destroyed, and you had to re-create them. This older version stored the full path, including the drive, to the linked data. OLE2 stores only enough path information to maintain the link. If you create links between two files in the same directory, you can move these two files anywhere on the drive, and OLE2 can maintain the link. The only criteria for maintaining a link under OLE2 is that the relative path remain the same.

- *OLE automation*. Everyone knows about Visual Basic for Applications (VBA), right? It's the new programming language that Microsoft is trying to get everyone to support. OLE automation is part of VBA. VBA defines a standard interface for communicating with the server application, which enables the client application to send commands to the server that will change the contents of an object indirectly. OLE automation is the direct descendent of the DDE macro language that many applications still use. The big difference from the user's perspective is that DDE macros were difficult to write and very prone to error. VBA is the native language of the application and is consistent across platforms. The surprising thing is that even though many applications support the VBA interface right now, none of them support it as a programming language (except many Microsoft applications, of course). In essence, none of the application vendors have fully implemented this feature yet. (The rumor mill was correct about the new Microsoft Office products that came out about the same time as Windows 95 still not providing VBA programming support.) Most new versions of Microsoft products do provide this programming capability, however. Look for other programming languages—at least those with BASIC roots—to start coming out with this support as well. Once enough programming language products support VBA, you might begin to see it in a few applications.

- *Version management*. Have you ever received a document from someone only to find that part of it wouldn't work with your software? OLE2 can store the application name and version number as part of the link. If an application developer implements this feature correctly, a server (or client, for that matter) will detect an old version of a file and ask if you want to update it. This means that you'll never have an old file sitting around just waiting to make life difficult. Unfortunately, except for a few Microsoft applications and one or two other vendors' wares, this feature is largely unimplemented. I hope newer Windows 2000 versions of the programs you use will incorporate it.

- *Object conversion*. Your friend uses Excel and you use Lotus 1-2-3, yet you need to share OLE documents containing spreadsheets. One of you could go through the inconvenience and expense of changing to the other person's application and document format, but OLE2 can probably solve this problem without such a change. Object conversion enables Excel to act as a server for a compound document containing a Lotus 1-2-3 object. All you need to do is select the Convert option from the Lotus 1-2-3 object's context menu. At least, that's how it's supposed to work. Real life is a bit different. Conversion will work only if the other application already supports that data format. Of course, when you think about it, this restriction makes sense.

PERFORMANCE

- *Optimized object storage.* Remember the discussion about memory at the beginning of this section? Optimized object storage is part of the cure. It allows the linked documents to stay on disk until needed. That way, Windows doesn't need to load every application and data file required to support the compound document. In most cases, Windows uses a buffer-zone technique. A word processor might keep the applications and objects required for the preceding, current, and next page in memory. The rest of the objects stay on disk, thus greatly reducing the memory footprint of a compound document in some cases.

- *Component object model.* This is the programmer issue I mentioned earlier in this section. Essentially, it means that Microsoft simplified the application programming interface (API) for OLE2. An *API* is a set of tools that programmers use to create applications. Simpler tools mean programs with fewer bugs. This also means that the programmer can write at least part of the application faster.

You might think that all the changes to OLE2 would cause compatibility problems, but OLE1 and OLE2 can mix freely on your machine. When you examined the Registry entries in Chapter 10, "Understanding the Windows 2000 Registry," you saw that each application had a set of OLE1 and OLE2 entries. Compatibility is the reason for the dual set of Registry entries. The important thing to remember is that OLE takes a least-common-denominator approach. Everything is tied to the application that has the fewest capabilities. This means that if you have four OLE2 applications and one OLE1 application, everything would be tied to the level of support provided by the OLE1 application.

Application Interoperability

Getting two applications to work together might not always be as easy as it seems. The following list gives you some ideas about what to investigate if you can't get your objects to work properly:

- *Neither application is a server.* Remember that you must have a server and a client to make OLE work. One application must communicate needed changes to the other. The server then makes any required changes to the object and hands it back. One of the major purposes of OLE is to maintain this kind of communication.

- *Data corruption has ruined one or more OLE files.* This isn't very common, but it does happen. One of the causes of this particular kind of corruption is old data files. I've seen applications overwrite newer versions of OLE files with old ones. Even though the application can use the older files, other applications might not be able to. It's usually a good idea to record the time and date stamps on your OLE files. That way, you can always check for this special form of data corruption.

- *One program provides 32-bit services and the other provides 16-bit.* This problem isn't supposed to happen. I've seen it only once or twice, and when it did occur, I couldn't get the problem to repeat after I rebooted my machine. What exactly happened is debatable. If you do find that two programs that usually communicate with ease are suddenly hostile toward each other, it might be time to reboot the machine and see whether clearing memory helps.

- *Corrupted entries in the Registry prevent the application from working correctly.* I covered the Registry entries in detail in Chapter 10, "Understanding the Windows 2000 Registry." The bottom line is that if you have so much as a punctuation mark wrong, the Registry will balk and your OLE connection won't work.

- *Old entries in the Registry are confusing the application.* Even though the Registry is a lot better organized than the WIN.INI and SYSTEM.INI files used by Windows 3.x (and you'll definitely find it easier to maintain), you might have to remove an entry manually sometimes. Some applications get confused when they run across old OLE entries and end up trying to use the wrong files or settings.

- *Your network doesn't fully support OLE links.* Some networks require the use of special software when creating OLE2 links. Microsoft's network support supplied with Windows 95/98 and Windows 2000 use OLE without any additional software. A third category of network software seems to have trouble maintaining links. Banyan falls into this category. Unfortunately, all this assumes that you create exactly the same drive mappings every time you log on to the network. As an experiment, I tried a setup in which the user needed to use his old CD-ROM only occasionally. He didn't want to load the real-mode drivers every day because the driver lowered system stability. The days he didn't have the CD-ROM connected, all his OLE links worked fine. On the days it was connected, none of the OLE links would work. We finally traced the problem to changes in the drive mapping when the CD-ROM drive was active.

This list is just a sample of the types of problems you could encounter with a common setup. Add to these problems vendors who don't fully support the OLE1 or OLE2 standard. I encountered one piece of software that ended up providing some strange cross of support between the two standards (and I don't think this vendor was alone). These support problems only make the situation worse. If every application supported OLE perfectly, you could probably get past the other problems listed in this section. The combination of faulty support and less-than-adequate linking mechanisms does paint a grim picture for the user. It would be easy to point a finger and say that the vendor was totally at fault. Yet, anyone who has tried to read the OLE standards, much less follow them, will attest to the level of difficulty involved.

Before you get the idea that all is lost with OLE, I want to inject a dose of reality. I wanted you to be aware of all the problems you might find. In most cases, however, I don't have any substantial problems with OLE that I don't cause. Sure, sometimes I'd like to be able to do more than the applications I'm using will allow, but these are inconveniences; they don't make OLE unusable. The best thing you can do when using OLE is to thoroughly check everything before you make a huge commitment in time and energy to a specific solution. It always pays to check for potential pitfalls, and this is especially true of a technology as complex as OLE and ActiveX.

OLE Components

I previously mentioned that damage to the OLE information in a data file would prevent the objects you created from working properly. That's only part of the problem. You might also run into a situation in which someone created a document using a newer version of the OLE system files than you did. With all the work Microsoft is doing with OLE, this is a very real possibility. (Usually, Microsoft will make the updated files available on its Web site; WUGNet or some other Windows user group will make them available on online services such as CompuServe.)

Where do you find the OLE system files? You'll see a whole group of files that provide support for OLE in your \SYSTEM32 directory. The following list provides some details on the tasks each file performs. You can use this list if you ever run into a problem with corruption or you'd just like to know what level of support you can expect from a certain application. The presence or absence of these files might indicate problems with your installation as well. Missing OLE files means that you won't get the kind of support needed to make your system work efficiently. Here's the list:

- OLE2.DLL. If you see this file, you know that some part of the Windows installation on your machine supports the OLE2 standard. Windows 2000 always installs this file. This DLL provides some base functions.

- OLECLI.DLL. This file contains all the basic client code your application needs. Your application uses this file as a base for building its own client features.

- OLESRV.DLL. This file contains all the basic server code your application needs. Like the client code, this DLL won't provide everything. Your application uses it as a basis for building its own set of features.

- OLE2CONV.DLL. This file provides the generic routines a program needs to convert an object to the client program's native format. (You may see OLECNV32.DLL in place of this file.)

- OLE2DISP.DLL. Every OLE client application uses this program to help it display the objects it contains.

- OLE2NLS.DLL. Most versions of Windows provide National Language Support (NLS). This program helps OLE keep pace with the rest of Windows in providing support for other languages.

- OLE2.REG. You can import this Registry file into your Registry to install OLE2 support. In most cases, your application will do this automatically, so you don't need to worry about it. The only time you'll need to use it is if you can't get OLE2 to work and discover that the Registry doesn't contain the correct entries.

- MCIOLE.DLL. Sounds require special handling under Windows. Unlike with most objects, you don't display a sound. This special DLL provides the support an application needs to handle a sound object. (Your machine may have MCI-OLE16.DLL and MICOLE32.DLL instead of this single file.)

- OLE32.DLL. A whole group of OLE files in the \SYSTEM32 directory have "32" somewhere in their names. These files provide the same services to 32-bit applications as their 16-bit counterparts.

- MFCOLEUI.DLL. C++ programmers need every bit of help they can get. They use Microsoft Foundation Classes to make their workload a little lighter. This file (and any with similar names) provides the C++ interface to OLE. If you see a file with MFC in its name, you know that one of your applications uses the Microsoft Foundation Classes.

The Meaning and Uses of ActiveX

Just as DDE was converted into OLE, so, too, in its turn has OLE evolved into ActiveX. *ActiveX* is a broad term for component technology that relies on COM, although not nearly as broad as the original Microsoft meaning for the term. In most cases, ActiveX now refers to a component used to create applications. For example, all the buttons in your application could be considered ActiveX components. In some cases, the components are hidden, but they're still used to make the application function. For example, timers that you can't see are used with many applications. However, you can see the effects of these timers as you use the applications.

Microsoft is using the term *Active* in many ways. ActiveX is just one of those ways. The idea is that previously inert, passive, or static objects can come alive (and contain their own capabilities—such as methods for self-modification, animation, calculation). Objects are referred to as a combination of data with the capability to act on that data. This capability to act now is being distributed to locations that were previously static. Server HTML pages used to be simple page-description documents, for example. Now they can contain scripts (behaviors) that execute on the server side. (You're not surprised that they're called *Active Server Pages*, are you?)

But ActiveX did not emerge one day as a full-blown, new technology. It isn't new, nor is it a single technology. As you have seen, the earliest forebear of ActiveX popped up in 1990 with the name DDE, dynamic data exchange (also known as linking and embedding). DDE permitted two documents to share the same data. DDE-capable programs could trade information while they were running—exchanging text, pictures, and even some simple commands, with no user intervention. The user no longer had to select some text, click the Edit menu, click Copy, and then switch to the target application, click Edit, and then click Paste, because all these steps could now be automated. This automation—although primitive in 1990—had broad implications: In essence, it meant that one program could control the behavior of another. This was Microsoft's first major step toward object-oriented programming.

From 1990 to 1993, DDE quickly fell into the shadow of OLE, a technology that included DDE but expanded its features and added several innovations. Complex communication between applications became possible with OLE Automation. A Visual Basic application could access and trigger nearly all the features in Word for Windows, for example. This way, an application written in Visual Basic could, for instance, "borrow" Word's spell-checker, using it to examine the text in a text box. Beyond that, VB could make Word do nearly anything; VB had a relationship to Word that was similar to the relationship between puppeteer and puppet. This was true of any OLE client application—it could put any server through hoops.

In addition, the distinction between programming and data became less rigid. A new concept was introduced called *in-place editing*, as demonstrated earlier in this chapter.

Finally, the term *ActiveX* made its appearance in December 1995, as Microsoft was repositioning itself to address the exploding popularity of the Internet. ActiveX is an umbrella term that covers the various concepts and technologies of DDE and OLE, and it adds the idea that ActiveX controls (self-contained, usually smaller, specialized programs or libraries of data) can be used by traditional applications or can be embedded into HTML documents for use on the Internet.

Microsoft is committed to ActiveX and all that the term ActiveX implies. It's a technology, a set of operating system features (DLLs and API functions), a way of programming, and a collection of objects you can plug into your own programs or Web pages. ActiveX is therefore a generic term covering a variety of initiatives from Microsoft. Because this book is not about programming, this chapter is limited to aspects of ActiveX such as data sharing and the use of simple objects. It's important that you remember, however, that what used to be known as DDE and OLE is now being called ActiveX.

Networking with DCOM

It's time to look at COM with networking included. This section of the chapter will answer a lot of questions about DCOM. For example, many of you may not have any idea why DCOM is such a great architectural addition in the first place. We'll explore why an application you're using might require DCOM.

The next thing we'll discuss is what makes DCOM different from COM (other than the fact that the COM object executes on one machine and the application on another). It's important to have an overall understanding of what makes the technology work.

Finally, we'll visit the DCOM network protocol in detail. We'll get into the very depths of DCOM so that you can see how the various mechanisms it contains work.

Why DCOM?

There are a lot of reasons why some of today's applications use DCOM to enhance their functionality and flexibility. Of course, the simple reason is that it's one of the existing technologies that will allow a programmer to create distributed applications. (A *distributed application* is one where part of the application executes on one machine and part executes on another, yet the user sees just one application at work when it comes to the interface.) However, DCOM provides a lot more than just the ability to run COM objects from a remote location. The following list provides just a few reasons why using DCOM is essential in some situations:

- *Fault tolerance.* DCOM can endure both hardware and network failures. What this means is that you'll gain some level of reliability. Obviously, the amount of gain depends on your current network configuration and what you expect DCOM to do.

- *Scalability.* Theoretically, a programmer could write a single DCOM object and use that same object no matter how large a company gets. There are some practical considerations that anyone using DCOM would need to take into account, such as a multiple server scenario, but for the most part, DCOM is more scalable than COM.

- *Load balancing.* One of the problems with the desktop right now is that one machine might have an overloaded processor, whereas another is wasting processor cycles waiting for work to do. DCOM helps you balance the load on your entire network and make it more efficient by using more of those wasted resources.

- *Maintenance ease.* Placing a single COM object on the server and then allowing all the clients on the network to access it is one way to reduce the amount of time required to implement a solution. Initial releases and updates can now be performed by making one change to a single machine.

- *Flexibility.* DCOM hides many implementation details from the client. The client thinks that it always has a local connection to the server, which greatly simplifies the development process for the programmer. Any time a technology simplifies the development process, it means that you get to use new custom applications faster and the number of bugs in that application will be reduced.

- *Server hiding.* This facet of DCOM allows a network administrator to place the server where it's needed without asking the developer to rewrite any application code. Using DCOM also allows the developer and network administrator to tune the application, to a certain extent, for maximum performance by creating the best possible environment for both client and server. For example, a network administrator can move the server object from one machine to another when resources on the first machine become strained. All the network administrator will need to do on the client machine is make a simple configuration change in the Registry.

- *Connection management.* DCOM uses the same reference-counting mechanism as COM does to know when it's safe to release a component. (Every time a client requests to use an object, the object's reference count is incremented. Likewise, when a client no longer needs the object, the reference count is decremented.) However, DCOM goes beyond reference counting when it comes to the connection itself. Because network connections are uncertain at best, DCOM sends a periodic "ping" to the client (at approximately two-minute intervals). If the client doesn't respond for three consecutive pings, DCOM considers the connection broken and decrements the object reference count. This ensures the object only remains active when there are active clients to service—which means that server resources get used more efficiently. You'll also find that DCOM allows both client/server unidirectional communication and the peer connections required for two-way communication.

As you can see, there are a lot of good reasons to use DCOM in a distributed application environment. Of course, that begs the question of what a distributed environment is and what kind of applications it can support. A distributed environment occurs whenever two or more machines are physically involved with application execution. In other words, an application that relies on data stored on a second machine doesn't constitute a distributed environment.

There are actually two kinds of distributed environments, at least in the context of this discussion. The first type is where the application was designed from the ground up for a distributed environment and really wouldn't work any other way. Applications that fall into this category include teleconferencing and many forms of database management. The second type consists of two machines working together toward an end result. The application could just as easily execute on a single machine—the main advantage from distribution is to gain some performance advantage through load balancing.

Obviously, you don't get all the advantages that DCOM provides for free; there's always some cost involved with implementing any technology. These drawbacks will help determine when DCOM is the appropriate choice for a specific application programming need. For example, you wouldn't want to use DCOM in place of COM when all processing could be performed locally. The following list provides an overview of some of the problems with working with DCOM:

- *Security.* Any time you send data over a network, you take the risk of allowing someone to see it. DCOM not only deals with code, it also works with data. Because the component is executing on the server, the only thing that gets transferred over the network connection is the data, which is also the element you want to protect most. As with any distributed technology, DCOM presents many security issues that you'll need to consider before implementation.

- *Performance.* There are a lot of performance inhibitors when it comes to DCOM, so there isn't any way you can expect to get desktop performance from it unless the remote machine offers a great deal in the way of resources and you have a very fast network. The first performance problem is the connection itself. Using DCOM means that you'll go through more layers to create and maintain a connection to the server. Of course, the network connection, itself, adds further delays. Finally, you must consider server latency—the time the component waits for the server to allow it to execute.

- *Reliability.* DCOM normally relies on the User Datagram Protocol (UDP) subset of TCP/IP to transfer data when this protocol is available. UDP is a connection less protocol that relies on a combination of IP address and port number to get data from one point to another. Unfortunately, UDP can present a number of problems, including the inability to guarantee a successful data transfer. The use of acknowledgments does reduce the impact of using UDP. In addition, using UDP does allow DCOM to perform several data transfer optimizations by merging acknowledge packages with data and pinging (client keep alive) messages.

> **Note:** Although DCOM does prefer to use UDP when available because of the speed boost it provides, there isn't any rule that says your application must use UDP. DCOM is flexible enough to allow the use of other protocols—even custom protocols. Many of the shortcomings mentioned here could be overcome using custom protocols. For example, a developer could overcome the security issues by using a protocol that sends the data in encrypted form. Of course, this increase in security measures affects not only the speed but also the reliability of DCOM. Enhanced security adds extra processing steps, which means that there are more places that the data can get corrupted. It's important to understand that there's a triangle of factors that affect each other when it comes to DCOM: speed, reliability, and security. In most cases, an administrator or developer will increase one element of the triangle to the detriment of the other two elements.

- *Connection availability*. Any distributed application will need to deal with the problem of lost or garbled connections. Not only that, but there isn't any guarantee that a connection will be available when the user actually needs it. While solutions such as data caching do alleviate part of the problem, you still need to consider connection management when building a COM object for distributed use.

An Overview of the Connection

One of the main things you need to think about when working with a remote access protocol such as DCOM is precisely how the connection will take place. After all, without a good connection, many other considerations are rendered moot.

This section of the chapter answers several questions. First, we'll look at how the connection actually works. It's important to understand that there are a lot of things that need to take place before an application on your machine can use objects created on another machine. This first section will include both a block diagram and a simple run through of the various steps required to create a connection.

Second, we'll look at the question of how DCOM keeps the connection from becoming so mired in detail that the user gets tired of waiting for something to happen. For example, a poorly designed COM component will generate a lot of network traffic. This traffic could slow communication over the network to a crawl. Therefore, even though the client and the server machines are quite capable of taking care of application needs quickly, the network could slow or even halt the application.

Third, we'll look at some load balancing concerns—it's essential to know how DCOM scales as the load on one or more components in an application increases. From a user perspective, it's not important to know where an object is processing application requests. You shouldn't have to be bothered by DCOM with questions such as which server to use for processing. Therefore, there has to be something in the background that makes the decision of where to process your application requests when the server that you normally use is busy or even nonoperational. That's where load processing comes into play. It's good to know how DCOM decides where to process the information your application has requested.

How Does the Connection Work?

In this section, we'll take a bird's-eye view of how DCOM creates and manages a connection between the client and server. It's important to understand how this connection works so that you can troubleshoot problems in your own applications. Figure 15.9 contains a block diagram of the flow of data from the client to the server. The following list describes each of the diagram elements.

FIGURE 15.9
DCOM connection overview block diagram.

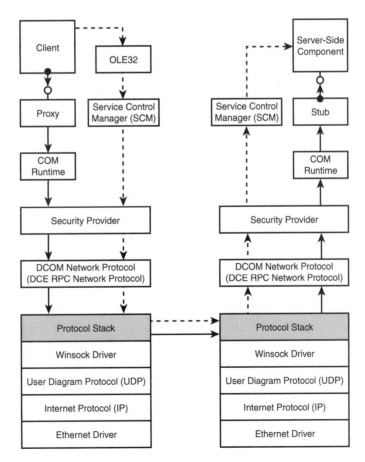

- *Client*. Originates requests to the server for resources and support.

- *OLE32*. A DLL containing the methods used to create an instance of an object (along with a wealth of other functionality). An application has to create an instance of an object before it can use the object. Developers have a variety of ways to create object instances at their disposal.

> **Note:** From a programmer's perspective, objects consist of three different elements: properties, methods, and events. A property describes something about the object. For example, you would use a property to describe the color of a pushbutton. Methods are pieces of code that allow the object to do something in response to input from another object. The methods that an object supports define what kind of tasks that it can perform. Finally, events are messages (or signals) that occur when something happens to the object. For example, a pushbutton outputs an event every time the user pressed it.

- *Service Control Manager (SCM)*. Creates the initial connection between the client and server. The SCM is only used during object creation. This feature gets implemented by functions in the RPCLTSCM.DLL file.

- *Proxy*. The server's presence within the client's address space. The proxy, which is actually a table of interfaces to the object that the client wants to use, is created and managed by the operating system at the request of the COM runtime. It allows the client to think that the server is local, even though the server is actually located on another machine. Windows uses functions (code that can perform a specific task) found in the RPCRT4.DLL file to create the proxy.

- *COM runtime*. Operating system elements that host objects and provide client/server communication. The COM runtime is part of any COM-related scenario—both in process and out of process, local and remote. (An *in-process server* is one that runs in the same process as the client, such as a pushbutton, whereas an out-of-process server runs in its own process, which could be on another machine. Out-of-process servers normally perform a variety of tasks in the background, such as giving the client access to a database on the server.)

- *Security provider*. The security provider logs the client machine into the server machine. Windows 2000 provides support for several standard security providers for both Internet and local network use. These providers include NT LAN Manager (NTLM, the standard Windows 2000 security protocol), Kerberos, Distributed Password Authentication (DPA, which is used by CompuServe and MSN), secure channel security services such as Secure Sockets Layer (SSL) and Private Communication Technology (PCT), and third-party distributed computing environment (DCE) providers. Some security providers will also ensure that all data transferred between the client and server is protected in some way—usually through the use of encryption.

Tip: It's important to understand that all objects are local as far as the client is concerned, so there has to be some underlying technology that makes remote objects appear local to the client. Windows uses the Remote Procedure Call (RPC) protocol to accomplish this task. However, Microsoft didn't create the RPC specification. This protocol specification was created by the Open Software Foundation. You can find out more about the distributed computing environment (DCE) RPC specification at http://www.osf.org/ or http://web1.osf.org/. There's also a good overview of how RPC works at http://www.ja.net/documents/NetworkNews/Issue44/RPC.html.

- *DCOM network protocol (DCE RPC network protocol).* Defines a protocol for creating a connection with a remote server for the purpose of using objects. In addition to implementing a component protocol, this block contains all the elements to implement the Object Remote Procedure Call (ORPC) specification at an application level. This particular component is known by several different names in the Microsoft documentation—the most popular of which is *DCOM wire protocol.* Only developers really need to know what's going on at this level. From a user perspective, this whole block of protocols simply allows your machine to communicate with the server and the remote object. Without these protocols, an application on your machine couldn't create an object on a server, much less ask that object to perform some work. Although it's interesting to know that there are a lot of different protocols at work in DCOM, all the work performed by these system components takes place in the background where you can't see it.

- *Protocol stack.* Actual network communication requires more than just one protocol—there are network-related protocols to consider as well. The protocol stack consists of all the protocols required to create a connection between the client and server, including network-specific protocols such as TCP/IP. Figure 15.9 shows a typical protocol stack consisting of a Winsock driver, UDP, IP, and an Ethernet driver. Not shown is the Ethernet network interface card (NIC) actually used to create the physical connection between the client and server.

- *Stub.* The client's presence within the server's address space. The stub is created and managed by the operating system at the request of the COM runtime. As far as the server is concerned, it's working with a local client. Windows uses methods found in the RPCRT4.DLL file to create the stub.

- *Server.* The COM object that the client has requested services and resources from.

There are actually two communication paths shown in Figure 15.9. The first path (the dotted line) is used to create an instance of the object. The second path (solid line) is used for normal communication between the client and the server. Creating a line of communication between a client and server normally follows these steps:

1. The client issues an object-creation method call to OLE32.DLL. The call contains information about the type of object that the client wants to create, along with the

name of the server that will be used to create it. (As an alternative, the server name can appear in the client machine's Registry, thus making the application, itself, machine independent.)

2. OLE32.DLL calls upon the client-side SCM to create a connection to the server machine because it can't service the call locally.

3. The DCOM network protocol creates the required packets to send information from the client to the server.

4. The server-side SCM creates an instance of the desired server-side object and returns a pointer of the object instance to the client.

5. The server-side SCM calls upon the COM runtime to create a stub for the object to interact with.

6. The client-side SCM calls upon the COM runtime to create a proxy for the client to interact with.

7. The SCM returns a pointer to the proxy to the client.

8. Normal client- and server-side component communications begin.

Connection-Oriented Data Flow Optimization

Sometimes, the development and placement of a component depends on just how much communication is taking place. Consider a situation where a client needs access to the contents of a database. A developer could place a component directly on the client machine that would access the database manager, gain access to the required data, and then format it for display within an application. However, this design would require a lot of network communication because the client would need to constantly communicate with the database manager and send or receive the data.

Most developers will divide the work the client expects the component to perform in two to reduce network traffic (creating two components instead of one). One component on the client machine could send data requests and format the incoming data. A second component on the server could make the data requests and deliver only the required information to the client. Using this approach significantly reduces network traffic, enhances both client and server efficiency, and makes the user more productive all at the same time.

DCOM does perform some connection manipulation on its own. One of the most important changes that DCOM will implement automatically is connection optimization. For example, if you have a server-side component that's manipulating a database using ODBC, DCOM will more than likely copy the component to the client and then get out of the picture. Because the connection to the database is through ODBC, neither the client nor the database manager notice any difference in the performance of the component. However, because DCOM is out of the picture, the component executes more efficiently. Obviously, this is a very specific kind of connection change and is only implemented when the client will see a significant performance gain.

Load Balancing Concerns

Load balancing is another connection-related problem. Normally, the developer will begin with all the server-side components required for an application loaded on a single machine. As people get added to the application users' list, the developer may have to move some components to another machine to avoid overloading a single machine. Breaking the component into smaller pieces may relieve some server stress as well. However, at some point, even a well-designed component may overload a single server. At this point, the developer will need to balance the component load across multiple servers.

DCOM supports two types of load balancing: static and dynamic. Static load balancing occurs when the developer assigns specific users to specific servers. Older versions of Windows normally rely on Registry entries to enforce the assignment of user machines to a specific server. Fortunately, administrators can use the remote Registry-administration features of Microsoft Management Console (MMC) to make any changes.

Another method to statically load-balance DCOM connections is to use a database containing usernames and the servers they're assigned to. Although this method does allow the administrator to make reassignments quickly, it also means adding some processing overhead to the connection and complexity to the application. The overhead comes into play in several ways—the most important of which is the time required for the client to look up the appropriate server prior to requesting component services. In addition, the client has to be rewritten to use the database, which may make the application unnecessarily complex and inflexible.

Yet another method of overcoming problems with static load balancing is to use a referral component. In this case, the client is designed to request the component's services from the referral component at the outset, so no extra programming is required. Once the referral component receives a request, it automatically makes the connection for the client, thus reducing the amount of overhead from using this technique. The obvious downside of this form of static load balancing is that the developer will need to write a special referral component.

Active Directory is the storage medium of choice for Windows 2000 developers. Instead of the DCOM entry being placed in the Registry, it appears in the Active Directory centralized storage. The actual storage location is called the *COM+ Catalog*, and it unites the COM and Microsoft Transaction Server (MTS) Registry entry methods. Obviously, this second method allows the administrator to make all required configuration changes from one location to a store that's always online rather than to multiple Registries, some of which may be offline because the associated machine is turned off. In addition, this second method allows the administrator to assign a specific user to a specific server, rather than assigning a machine to the server.

Both developers and administrators will be able to interact with the COM+ Catalog using the COM+ Explorer (which may be part of Component Services when you read this). In addition, Microsoft is developing a series of new COM interfaces that will allow the developer to interface with the COM+ Catalog directly.

Two of the major problems with static load balancing are that you need a predictable load as well as administrator intervention to implement it. In other words, static load balancing would probably work fine for an order-entry system where the same number of users would log in each day. It probably wouldn't work well for an Internet site where the number of users could vary by a large amount over the period of a few hours.

Dynamic load balancing can also rely on the referral component technique described earlier. However, in this case, the referral component would take factors such as current server load, past user request history, and current network topology into account when assigning a user to a machine, rather than assign the user based on a static list. Using this technique means that the referral component would require more time to get the job done, but the network would process requests more efficiently once the connection was made.

This approach has several problems. For one thing, the complexity of the referral component is greatly increased. Instead of just directing the user's request to another component, the referral component now has to make some decision as to which server to select. In addition, this technique relies on a database for storing user request history, the availability of server statistics (which must be refreshed for each request), and the availability of network topology data. In other words, dynamic load balancing is much harder to implement because you're essentially replacing the network administrator with some software.

Balancing a load at connection time doesn't necessarily mean that the load will remain balanced either. True dynamic load balancing needs to incorporate some type of reconnect strategy. As the load from a user on one machine increases and the load from a user on another machine decreases, it might be necessary to reconnect them to different servers to keep the load on both servers balanced. Unfortunately, DCOM doesn't provide any built-in functionality to implement a reconnection strategy, which means the developer will need to create yet another component that monitors the current situation and makes reconnection recommendations as necessary.

There's another load-balancing strategy for DCOM that relies on the new COM+ capabilities built into Windows 2000. This method assumes that you have a lot of users to manage and that the application you've created adheres to Microsoft's new Distributed interNet Applications (DNA) architecture.

Implementing the COM+ form of load balancing is relatively easy. The first thing you'll need is an application cluster—which is a set of up to eight servers that are capable of running the requested component. Once you have the application cluster servers loaded with the server-side components that you want to use, you'll need to add a load-balancing router to the picture. The load-balancing router sends client requests to one of the machines in the application cluster.

The client application won't access the application cluster servers directly. What'll happen instead is that client requests will get sent to the load-balancing router. The load-balancing router will use an algorithm to determine which application cluster server is least busy and then route the request to that application cluster server. Of course, the question that the load-balancing router will need to answer is what criteria to use for determining application cluster machine load. The default algorithm uses a response time algorithm to determine which machine to use.

Using the DCOM Configuration Tool

The DCOM Configuration Tool is a powerful utility that allows you to work with the components registered on a client machine. You can set the component to execute remotely or locally. In addition, this utility allows you to modify the security setup for the component.

Needless to say, this utility will also allow you to modify general DCOM operation on a client machine. For example, even though UDP/IP is the normal protocol used to create a connection between the client and the server, you can set it to any of the protocols that both the client and server support. This means that you could create a secure connection between the client and server by using an encrypted protocol instead of a plain text protocol such as UDP/IP.

This section of the chapter will show you how the DCOM Configuration Tool works and how you can use it to redirect execution of the component from the local machine to a server. We'll also look at some essentials such as security and the use of protocols in this section. Getting the right setup is important if you want your DCOM application to work as anticipated.

Setting Up the General DCOM Environment

Microsoft assumes certain defaults when setting DCOM up on your machine during the Windows installation process. Normally, these defaults work just fine, but you may find that you either need to change the features supported by the DCOM or the protocols used to communicate between client and server.

Obviously, the first thing you need to do before you can reconfigure anything is start the DCOM Configuration Tool. Just use the Run command on the Start menu to display the Run dialog box; then type DCOMCnfg in the Open field and click OK. You'll see the initial Distributed COM Configuration Properties dialog box shown in Figure 15.10. The Applications tab of this dialog box displays all the out-of-process servers installed on the client machine. The out-of-process server must be registered on the client, even if you intend to run it from a remote server. This dialog box will only reflect the out-of-process servers actually registered locally.

> **Tip:** The Active Directory support provided by Windows 2000 will obviate the need to register a component locally to use it on a remote server. The client workstation will download global Registry entries from the *domain server during login. These entries could include remote component Registry settings that will allow a client to access the component on a remote server. The advantage to this method is that the administrator will only need to make a single entry on the domain server for DCOM components.

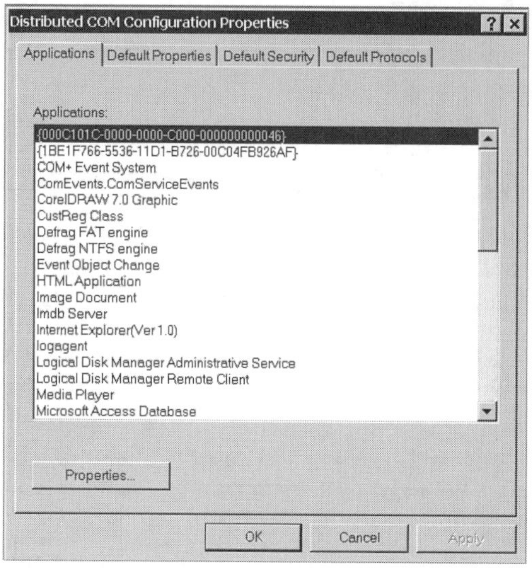

The Default Properties tab shown in Figure 15.11 allows you to change the general characteristics of DCOM on your machine. By default, Microsoft enables DCOM support on a client. This primary level of support will allow you to create trusted connections with servers on a local network. A second check box, Enable COM Internet Services on This Computer, will allow you to enable COM communications over the Internet.

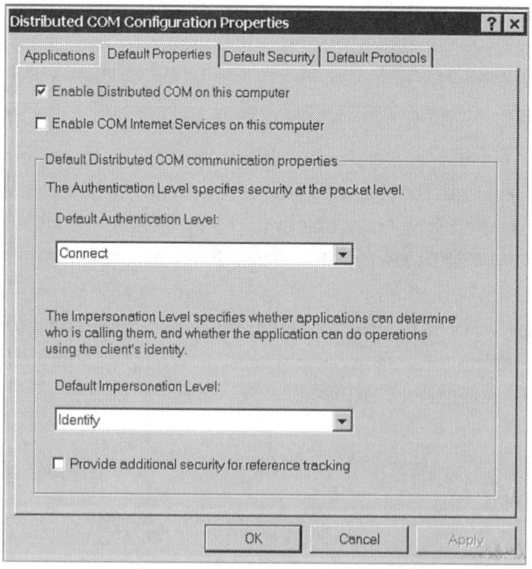

The Default Authentication Level list box controls how communication security is handled between the client and server. The default setting is Connect, which means that security is handled only once per connection. We'll talk more about how authentication level is used in the "Setting the Authentication Level" section of the chapter.

The Default Impersonation Level list box controls what the server can do on the user's behalf when it comes to identification. For example, this setting affects what'll happen if the server has to create another component to satisfy a user request. How is that component created? Is the component created in such a way that it looks like the user has created it directly? The matter of impersonation level affects what kinds of things the server can do for the client and how it does them. The default setting for this field is normally Impersonate, although some people have reported a default setting of Identity. The following list defines the various levels of impersonation that DCOM supports:

- *Anonymous*. This is the least secure impersonation level. The server performs processing tasks for the client without knowing the identify of the client application. Unfortunately, this setting limits the server to performing tasks that an anonymous user could perform—which means that many resources will be out of reach.

- *Delegate*. The most secure impersonation level. The server is allowed to perform all tasks as if it were the client. This includes requesting services and resources on other servers. Windows 2000 Server authentication service doesn't support this level of impersonation.

- *Identity*. Allows the server to identify the client application. What this means is that the client will gain full access to the resources and services available on the server as long as it makes the call directly. The server isn't allowed to impersonate the client, even for local service and resource requests.

- *Impersonate*. This is the highest level of impersonation level that the Windows 2000 Server authentication service supports natively. It allows the server to impersonate the client locally, which means that any services or resources that the server has to request to satisfy a client request will be done in the client's name. The Impersonation level only allows client impersonation on the local server; a server can impersonate the client on other servers.

The Provide Additional Security for Reference Tracking check box allows the server to track connected client application requests. Checking this option uses additional server resources—both memory and processor cycles. However, it does enhance server security because a client won't be able to kill the process prematurely. The effect of killing a process prematurely is that other clients will likely crash when they attempt to tell the server they no longer need objects that don't exist.

The last set of general settings for DCOM appear on the Default Protocols tab of the Distributed COM Configuration Properties dialog box shown in Figure 15.12. This tab shows the various protocols that DCOM will attempt to use in creating a connection between a client and server. In addition, the protocols get tried in the order in which they appear in the list. Figure 15.12 shows the default list of protocols that DCOM will attempt to use and the default order in which it'll try them. (This list may be affected by the protocols you have installed on your machine, so your display may not precisely match the one shown in the figure.) Notice that UDP/IP is at the top of the list because this is normally the first choice for DCOM communications, at least on a LAN.

FIGURE 15.12

The Default Protocols tab allows you to configure the protocols that DCOM will attempt to use to create a connection.

There are various controls on the Default Protocols tab that allow you to modify the protocols that DCOM will use. Clicking Add will display the Select DCOM Protocol and Endpoint dialog box shown in Figure 15.13. This dialog box contains a list of all the potential protocols and endpoints that DCOM will support, not necessarily the ones installed on the client machine. In other words, you have to use some care in choosing a new protocol and endpoint. Although nothing terrible will happen if you choose a protocol and endpoint the client can't support, DCOM will waste time trying to make it work, which will only delay the process of creating a connection.

FIGURE 15.13

The Select DCOM Protocol and Endpoint dialog box allows you to add a new protocol and endpoint to DCOM's support list.

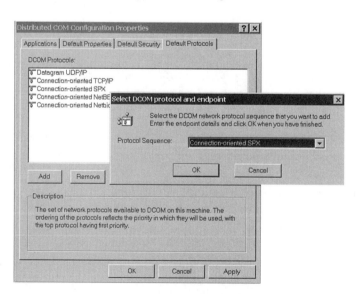

Some protocol/endpoint combinations also allow you to make some configuration choices. For example, highlighting the Connection-Oriented TCP/IP option and then clicking Properties will display a Properties for COM Internet Services dialog box like the one shown in Figure 15.14. This dialog box allows you to choose port ranges for various types of TCP/IP communication. You can choose one set of port ranges for intranet use only and another set of ranges for Internet use only. Security is the main reason to use this configuration dialog box—you need to set specific port ranges when using packet filtering with most firewall products.

Figure 15.14

Some protocol/endpoint combinations allow for further configuration using dialog boxes like this one.

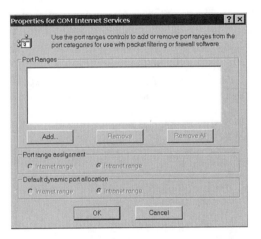

The order in which protocols get tried could make a big difference in some environments. For example, you might not want to use a connectionless protocol if there's a connection-oriented alternative available. To change the order in which protocols are tried, highlight the protocol and then click Move Up or Move Down as needed to change its order in the list. DCOM will attempt to use the protocols, in turn, starting from the top of the list and going toward the bottom.

Redirecting a Component

The whole purpose of using the DCOM Configuration Tool, at least from an administrator perspective, is to allow an application on the client to access a component that you've placed on a server. Distributed processing, coupled with multithreading programming techniques, allows two machines to work in tandem on a single problem. Overall, using DCOM should result in higher system throughput, efficiency, and security, while reducing overall network bandwidth.

This section is going to show you how to redirect execution of a component from the client machine to a server. If you follow along with the procedure, make sure you don't make the redirection permanent unless you really want to. Clicking Cancel instead of OK or Apply will reverse any changes you've made. Obviously, some of the particulars of my setup will vary from your setup. For example, your server will have a different name than mine does. However, except for the names, this procedure will allow you to redirect the execution of any component from the local machine to a server. Here are the steps to follow:

1. Start the DCOM Configuration Tool, if you haven't already done so.

2. Highlight the component you want to redirect on the Applications tab of the Distributed COM Configuration Properties dialog box. For the purposes of this example, we'll use the Media Player component. (If you don't see the Media Player component in the list, make sure that you installed this feature on your machine.)

3. Click Properties. You'll see a <Component Name> Properties dialog box like the one shown for the Media Player component in Figure 15.15. Notice that the General tab shown in the figure contains an Authentication Level list box. We'll talk about this list box in the "Setting the Authentication Level" section of the chapter.

FIGURE 15.15

*The initial compo-
nent Properties
dialog box shows
general compo-
nent information,
including authen-
tication level.*

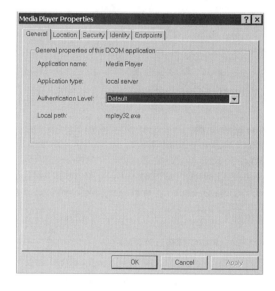

4. Choose the Location tab. You'll see a display similar to the one shown in Figure 15.16. This is where you'll choose where the component will run. The default setting runs the component on the local machine. There's also an option to run the component wherever the client's data is located. You'll find this option handy for database applications where a single client may need to access the same type of data on several different servers. Keeping the component on the server reduces network traffic because only query result information is sent back to the client. The option we're interested in for the Media Player component will run the component on a server, rather than locally.

Figure 15.16

The Location tab allows you to choose one or more places to execute the component.

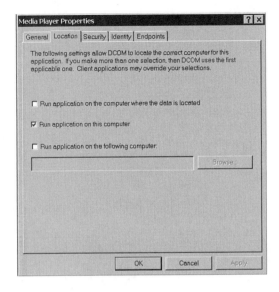

5. Uncheck the Run Application on This Computer option and check the Run Application on the Following Computer option. You can use the Browse button to find the server on the network. At this point, you could click OK to make the changes permanent. However, in many cases, you'll need to configure additional settings to actually gain access to the server.

Note: If you choose more than one location to execute a component, DCOM will look for the first viable execution option and execute the component there. The normal search order is to look at the local machine, then a server that you've specified, and finally the location where the client's data is located. If you don't want the client to attempt to execute the component locally, make sure you uncheck this option.

6. Choose the Identity tab. You'll see a display similar to the one shown in Figure 15.17. This is where you'll define the identity of the user who will execute the component on the server. The default option, The Launching User, works just fine in most cases (this is the identity you used to log into to the server, which is normally the same as your name and password for the rest of the network). The Interactive User option uses the name and password of the person who logged in to the workstation and started the client application. The This User option allows you to enter the name and password of a user who has the correct level of access to the server for executing the component. Finally, if you want to remotely execute a service (and not a component as we have here), you can choose to use the built-in system account for the server in question.

FIGURE 15.17

The Identity tab allows you to choose which user will log in to the server to request component execution.

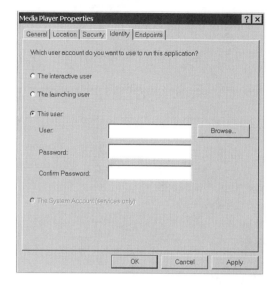

7. Select one of the identity options. As previously mentioned, the default option, The Launching User, works just fine in most cases.

8. Choose the Endpoints tab. You'll see a dialog box similar to the one shown in Figure 15.18. Normally, DCOM will simply use the protocols that were defined on the Default Protocols tab of the Distributed COM Configuration Properties dialog box. You can, however, choose to add additional protocols/endpoints, add a specific endpoint, or even disable a protocol/endpoint.

FIGURE 15.18

The Endpoints tab allows you to change the protocol/endpoint that DCOM will use to create a connection for your component.

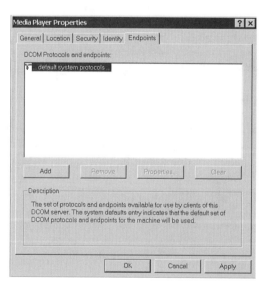

9. Click Add and you'll see a Select DCOM Protocol and Endpoint dialog box like the one shown in Figure 15.19. You'll see the same list of protocols here that you saw on the Default Protocols tab. However, in this case, there are several additional options for configuring those protocols/endpoints. The Disable Protocol Sequence option allows you to disallow a protocol/endpoint, even if DCOM would normally use it to create a connection. You can also use a static endpoint or the range of port addresses defined for Internet or intranet use. Finally, you can choose the Use Default Endpoints option, which allows DCOM to use the normal endpoints for the specified protocol. Selecting this last option allows you to change the order in which DCOM chooses protocols for making a connection. DCOM will always use the protocols/endpoints that you define for the component first and then move on to the general DCOM choices.

Figure 15.19

You don't have to use the default DCOM protocol/endpoint selections; this dialog box allows you to choose custom settings.

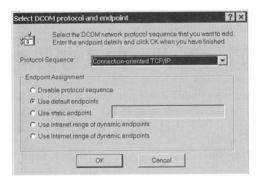

10. Choose a protocol sequence option and then add an endpoint assignment, if necessary, to control the protocol/endpoint configuration. Repeat this step for each custom protocol/endpoint required by your application.

11. Click OK to make the component choices permanent.

12. Click OK to close the DCOM Configuration Tool.

> **Note:** This procedure didn't address security. We'll cover security issues in the next section of the chapter. You'll need to check with your network administrator for security settings.

Creating a Secure Environment

Security is a major concern for any distributed application. The reason is simple: Making the application available over a network means that more than one person can and will access it. The more open your network environment and the more critical the data being transferred, the greater your need for robust security. You need to be sure that the right person accesses the application, while keeping others out. This is especially important in today's Internet-oriented environment where a company may want to allow remote access of critical company information using a standard Internet connection.

In previous sections, we saw some basic security measures you could take when configuring DCOM. For example, you can change the Default Authentication Level setting to ensure that each communication between the client and server is authorized. (This section will provide more detailed information on your authentication options.) The default authentication level only ensures authentication when the client connects initially (normally to create the object in the first place or add a reference to an already existing object).

This section of the chapter will show you how to use the DCOMCNFG utility to secure the components on your server. Using this utility will greatly reduce the external threats to your network.

> **Caution:** Securing the server and the components that reside on it still doesn't secure the data that gets transferred between client and server. Make sure you always use some type of secure communication protocol to transfer data from one point to another—especially when working on a public network. Check the various options in the "Setting the Authentication Level" section later in this chapter for details on how you can use built-in DCOM settings to make your data more secure (a good encryption product will only enhance the security you can get by default).

Using the General DCOM Security Options

Making sure that the DCOM environment as a whole is secure is the subject of this section. You'll find the general DCOM security settings on the Default Security tab of the Distributed COM Configuration Properties dialog box, as shown in Figure 15.20. Notice that this tab covers three main security areas: access, launch, and configuration. The Access area determines who can connect to your machine for the purpose of using DCOM in the first place. The Launch area determines who can remotely run applications on your machine. Finally, the configuration options determine who has permission to configure the DCOM settings on your machine. The following list will tell you about these areas in more detail:

> **Note:** None of the settings in this section will override application-specific settings. Windows 2000 will use the applications-specific settings first.

- *Default Access Permissions.* This option defaults to using the same access-level permissions provided by the system as a whole. In other words, if a person has permission to access your hard drive in some way, he or she usually has permission to access the applications found there as well. Of course, *access* doesn't necessarily mean the ability to execute. All that the Default Access Permissions option does is determine who can access the machine at all.

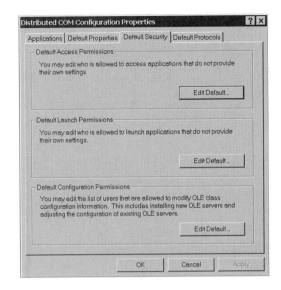

FIGURE 15.20

Three areas of security are covered by the options on the Default Security tab.

- *Default Launch Permissions.* Three groups are normally allowed to launch DCOM applications by default: Interactive Users, Administrators, and System. You must specifically assign a user to the Interactive Users or Administrators groups before they'll have launch permission. Only system-level services are allowed to use the System account. This particular dialog box also allows you to add specific groups that aren't allowed to launch an application.

- *Default Configuration Permissions.* Anyone who can work with the configuration of DCOM on your machine at all is in this list. Normally, the System account and the Administrators group are allowed full control over the configuration. Everyone else is only authorized to read the configuration. You have to allow read permission to anyone who'll launch or access applications because, otherwise, DCOM won't know how to interact with your machine. There's also a Special Access setting that allows you to customize settings, but this is a difficult entry to set up and normally you won't need to use it.

All three of these settings work the same way, so I'll discuss them as a single entity, even though each area affects a different area of DCOM communication. Clicking Edit Default will display a Registry Value Permissions dialog box like the one shown in Figure 15.21 for launch permissions. This dialog box allows you to add and remove users from the access list.

Click Add and you'll see an Add Users and Groups dialog box like the one shown in Figure 15.22. This particular dialog box shows the list of users and groups for the domain controller (you can also choose from a list for the local machine). There are advantages to using each list. Using the local machine's list allows you to individually control the security settings on a machine-by-machine basis. On the other hand, using the domain list means that you only need to change the settings on one machine to add a new user to a group that'll affect all machines running DCOM applications.

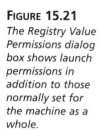

FIGURE 15.21

The Registry Value Permissions dialog box shows launch permissions in addition to those normally set for the machine as a whole.

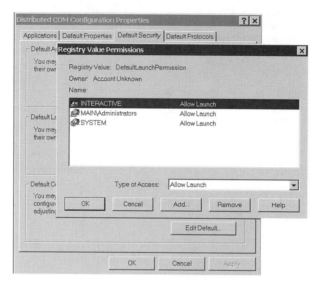

FIGURE 15.22

DCOM allows you to choose users and groups from the local machine or from the domain controller.

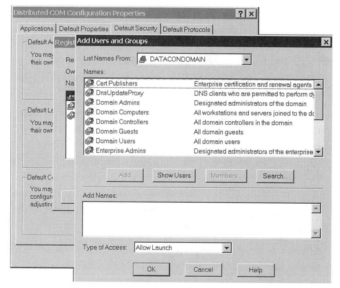

Working with Component-Level Security

Component-level security works much like the general security that we just talked about in the previous section. Figure 15.23 shows a typical example of a component-level Security tab (in this case, for the Media Player component). Notice that you can choose between general security and component-level security for all three areas that we talked about previously. If you choose the default security option, DCOM will use the options set on the Default Security tab of the Distributed COM Configuration Properties dialog box. Otherwise, you'll need to click the particular Edit button to set the security you want for that area of component-level security. Because the actual process of setting component-level security is the same as default security, I won't cover the various options in this section (refer to the previous section).

FIGURE 15.23

The major difference between the component-specific Security tab and the Default Security tab is default/custom option buttons.

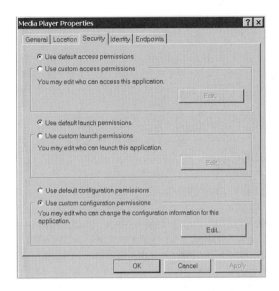

Setting the Authentication Level

There are two ways to set the authentication level for a component: at the DCOM level or at the individual component level. Both authentication-level settings determine the minimum-security requirements for the client and server to gain access to each other's resources. In other words, this setting determines how the client and server will exchange security information during a session.

You'll find the Default Authentication Level setting on the Default Properties tab of the main Distributed COM Configuration Properties dialog box. As previously mentioned, the default general setting is Connect. The component-specific setting appears on the General tab of the <Component Name> Properties dialog box. The default setting, in this case, is Default. These two settings represent a minimalist approach to DCOM security. There are other settings that may provide you with better security. The following list describes each of the Default Authentication Level settings:

- *None*. The client and server don't authenticate each other at all. You must use this setting when creating anonymous connections. However, this setting also comes in handy when working in a small workgroup network situation where physical security is high and there aren't any connections to the outside world. This setting reduces overall network traffic to the lowest possible level but also represents the greatest security risk.

- *Call.* Authentication occurs for every call while a connection is maintained. This is a moderately high security level that ensures the client and server verify each other's identity for each method call in the application, which may involve several packets. You'll notice a slight increase in network traffic when using this level of authentication, and there's no guarantee of complete security from third-party intrusion.

- *Connect.* One-time authentication takes place during object creation. The client and server verify each other's identity during this initial request. There's a good chance a third party could break network security when using this mode because the client and server don't have any way to verify either packets or requests. The advantage to this method is that initial authentication places limits on what the user can do. Also, network traffic is kept to a minimum.

- *Default.* At the individual component level, this setting means that the component will use the general DCOM setting. At the DCOM level, this setting means that DCOM as a whole will use whatever security the authentication method uses in general. For example, the default Windows 2000 Security Services uses Connect-level authentication. The results of using this setting vary according to the authentication method used.

- *Packet.* This is the first of three levels of truly secure DCOM communication settings. The sender's identity is encrypted and packaged with the packet. This means that the receiver can verify the authenticity of the sender with every packet; this greatly reduces the probability of third-party intrusion. However, this method also bloats the size of the packet and could greatly increase DCOM-related network traffic. This setting represents the most reasonable level of protection for a network that allows outside access.

- *Packet Integrity.* The sender's identity and a packet signature are encrypted as part of the packet. Using these two forms of authentication ensures that the sender is authorized and that the packet hasn't been modified in any way. However, this method won't ensure that a third party hasn't read the packet, and it does increase network traffic over Packet authentication. You only need to use this setting when the integrity of the data is absolutely essential and you don't care who reads the packet.

- *Packet Privacy.* In most cases, this is the paranoid level of security. Not only does the packet contain the sender's identity and a packet signature, but the packet itself is encrypted to ensure that a third-party can't read it. This level of authentication greatly increases network traffic and could actually slow communications to a crawl when used on slower traffic media such as a dial-up connection. However, this is the level of authentication you'd need to ensure safe financial transactions and the transmittal of critical confidential information from one site to another.

On Your Own

Test the OLE capabilities of the various applications on your machine. Which ones support OLE as a client? Which ones support it as a server? Of the various techniques I covered in this chapter for inserting an object in a container, which methods do you find easiest to use? Why do you think some applications support one technique and others support another technique?

Try dragging and dropping selected text between open applications. Which of your applications permit this, and which don't? How can you tell that a block of text is being dragged (hint: the cursor changes)? Also, create shortcuts on the desktop and see whether you like using that technique.

Open a copy of Explorer and use it to search your \SYSTEM and SYSTEM32 folders. Can you find all the OLE-specific files installed on your system? What do the names of the various files tell you about those files' purposes?

Spend some time acquainting yourself with how DCOM works; then look at the DCOM Configuration utility. You can even attempt to set up a component for remote execution on another machine (you'll have to ensure that the component actually exists on that machine and is registered for use—the Media Player is normally a good choice for remote execution tests). If you successfully set up a component for remote execution, applications that use it should still run as normal, albeit a bit slower than normal. You can see where the component is executing by looking at the Processes tab of the Windows Task Manager dialog box (right-click the taskbar and then click Task Manager to display the Windows Task Manager dialog box). The machine executing the component will have it listed in the Processes list. Therefore, if the component is remotely executing, you should see it in the remote list (the Processes tab of the Task Manager dialog box), but not on the list for your local machine.

Exploiting Your Software

I played with a lot of titles for this chapter before I finally decided to use this one. It probably best expresses the way some people manage their systems today. In fact, it should express the way you use your system. Of course, *exploiting your software* could mean a lot of things, so I'll take a few minutes to define what I mean.

Exploiting every possible feature of some of today's software products is impossible for the average user. The fact that some power users have a problem doing it really says something about current software *comprehensiveness*. Take Word 2000 as an example. Even if I decided not to install all the options, I would still have access to the mail merge feature, kerning, drop caps, a tables utility, an indexing utility, an HTML editor, and free lawn furniture—and that only scratches the surface. (Just kidding about the furniture.) The folks on the Word development team thoughtfully provided me with a huge amount of information and many, many features—most of which I'll never use. Obviously, exploiting your software doesn't necessarily involve using every feature it has to offer.

What do I mean by exploiting software so that you exercise every feature to its fullest potential? I use four basic criteria to measure my level of software exploitation. They're all interrelated, so you'll find that changing one element affects all the other elements. For me, it's a kind of game to see just how well I can get all these elements to work together. A fully exploited piece of software will do the following:

- *Accomplish the job at hand with a minimum of effort.* Everyone knows that learning to use a computer is both expensive and time-consuming. Add to that the cost of buying the equipment, itself, and you have a major investment before you see any kind of return. A fully exploited piece of software enables you to accomplish the same job as before but with less effort. Concentrating on the task rather than the means of performing it means you can be more creative in your work. I've always felt that computers should provide a way to remove the burden of work and leave the "fun" parts for us to accomplish. A fully exploited piece of software can do just that.

- *Produce results in a modicum of time.* It wasn't too long ago that people wondered why it was faster to do something by hand than to use a computer. I personally saw this problem often. What people were forgetting was that to use that older software to its fullest potential, you needed to set up the application only once. The computer could then automate the task for you so that it would take you less time to perform the task the second time. If you didn't set up your computer for rapid duplication of rote work (such as using macros), you weren't exploiting it. Fortunately, spending all that time to create your original document just isn't a problem anymore. I can use a variety of packages to write an application in a fraction of the time it used to take. Templates and other software add-ons make it faster to produce the first copy of a document, in addition to variations of that document later. The wizards provided with a lot of software packages give you a built-in ease of use that was unheard of only five years ago. A fully exploited piece of software today enables you to produce results faster than you could by hand in many cases.

- *Produce output that requires the least amount of system resources.* The amount of system resources you have is relative. Much of it has to do with the technology you have at your disposal. One consideration involves the money you have to spend on upgrades; however, I'll concentrate on the relative aspect of this picture. A fully exploited piece of software is optimized so that it uses a minimum of system resources. Chapter 15, "OLE, ActiveX, and DCOM," outlined a number of ways to embed or link an object into your document. Other chapters in this book show you various aspects of other forms of optimization. A fully exploited piece of software uses the least memory-intensive, yet fastest way to accomplish a task. Optimizing the way you use the software's features almost always results in reduced system resource requirements.

- *Produce the best results possible.* Optimizing your software to reduce system requirements, improving your techniques to reduce the time it takes to get the job done, and reducing the effort required to complete the task are all fine goals. It's the result of all this effort, however, that everyone will see. The boss won't care that it took you half the time to get something done if the final result isn't up to par. That's a problem for many people: They look for a quick fix to a problem, and that often isn't the route they really need to pursue. The test of whether you have successfully exploited your software is in the results you produce. Using the software and hardware available today should enable you to produce an end product superior in every way to what you could do yesterday. If you aren't getting that result, it's time to take another look at how you're exploiting your software.

Exploiting your software also means that you use the right tool for the task you're trying to accomplish. You can use a spreadsheet as a word processor (a lot of people do), but is that really exploiting your software or is the software exploiting you? Of course, few people can afford to buy every application on the market. There are limitations to what you can realistically use. If an inexpensive tool will do the job, that's the one you should select. It's a matter of defining the parameters of the job. Just how much work do you need to do? If I need to dig a small hole, I get a spade. A really big hole requires a backhoe. Perhaps your job is best done with a shovel.

To summarize, then, exploiting your software means that you get an application that's the right size and type for the job. You optimize its operation and environment. Then you sit back and watch the application do its job in the most efficient manner possible.

If this sounds impossible, read on. A lot of things seem impossible until you take the time to analyze the situation, break it into its component parts, and solve the small problems. Trying to take an entire project and solve it with one answer isn't going to do much, if anything, to make you efficient. Of course, you probably do all this with your current business. Most successful businesses take the time to get the most out of their employees and the resources they have available. Now what you need to do is apply these same principles to your computer.

Adding and Removing Applications

Have you seen the immense size of some applications today? I'm often appalled at how fast the applications I install can eat up a major piece of my 4GB partition, the c: drive. Installing Visual Studio—the full install—demands almost 2GB for itself! And if you have an older, smaller drive, sometimes you'll need to remove one or more applications you don't use much to make room for the applications you use often. Alternatively, you can consider compression.

Fortunately, Windows 2000 enables you to install and remove most applications with ease. The Add/Remove Programs feature keeps track of the DLLs, Registry or INI entries, support files, miscellaneous debris, menu icons, satellite utilities, and folders occupied during the original installation. Then, if you decide to uninstall, all the unique dependencies (files and data used only by the application in question and not shared with other applications) can be cleanly removed from all the places it resides.

The Windows 2000 Add/Remove Programs feature capability doesn't handle earlier NT–specific products—those designed for versions 3.5 and earlier. It also won't work with any Windows 3.*x* applications. To install and then later uninstall these products, you still need to use a third-party utility or try to delete items by hand.

Using the Add/Remove Programs feature, in theory, ensures that if you ever want to remove it, you can get rid of it entirely, including cleaning out the Registry and any unique dependency files used only by that application. That's the *theory*. In practice, this applet doesn't appear to do much and I never use it except to uninstall. It just lists 32-bit programs that are installed, and if you select from that list to remove the application, it merely locates and runs the application's Uninstall file to remove the program. (When you request installation, it finds the application's Setup file.) Most programs these days start their own install when the CD is loaded, completely bypassing the Add/Remove Programs feature (although the programs do appear in its list).

What's involved in removing an application after you've installed it? Every uninstall pro-gram should take the following five items into consideration. Uninstall programs handle each criterion to a different degree:

- *Application directory.* Every uninstall program handles this one with the same efficiency. For that matter, it would probably take you even less time to delete the application directory yourself when no longer needed. The problem is the applica-tion's data. Some uninstall programs leave it in place so that you can recover it later; others just remove the entire directory without giving much thought to the data it contains. I prefer the first approach because it keeps me from shooting myself in the foot and losing something I might later value. The second approach is a little too thorough in my opinion.

- *Windows directory.* Most older applications place an INI file in the Windows directory so that they can find this file easily (instead of using the Registry, as newer programs do). Some applications place two or even three INI files here. (I had one application place three different INI files here.) Each managed a different aspect of the product. I was surprised by the number of uninstall programs that don't take these files into account.

> **Note:** Although all your old applications will probably use one or more INI files, Microsoft discourages their use in new applications. In most cases, an applica-tion will use the Registry to store settings that once appeared in an INI file. Even if an application does use an INI file, you'll probably find it in the application's directory rather than in the Windows directory. The same principle holds true for many of the other items in this list. A new application, for example, is supposed to use its own directory for file storage rather than the Windows SYSTEM folder.

- *Windows system file modification.* It's a sure bet that Windows 2000 will have the same problem that previous versions of Windows did when it comes to spurious entries in WIN.INI and SYSTEM.INI. Even though Windows 2000 only provides compatibility support for these files, it does read them when you boot. Suffice it to say that some of the same problems you had in the past will still crop up when you try to uninstall 16-bit applications.

- SYSTEM *and* SYSTEM32 *directories.* Your SYSTEM directories have a ton of files, and there's no way of knowing which ones belong to your application. (If you have Microsoft's Visual Studio, though, check out the Depend utility that comes with it. It lists all the dependency files used by any application.)

  Even if an uninstall program tracks these files, it has no way of knowing how many applications use a particular file. This is especially true of DLLs. An appli-cation might install a copy of VB6DB.DLL in your SYSTEM32 directory, for example. When you install another application that also requires the same file, the second application might not add the file because it sees that the latest version of that file is already present. If an uninstall program removed VB6DB.DLL along with all the other files for the first application, the second application would also cease to work. How do you handle this situation? I don't know, and neither does your uninstall program. Some programs make a valiant effort to remove the less common files. When it comes to removing one, you're on your own—you have to delete the files from the SYSTEM32 directory by hand. An uninstall program will sometimes report that a DLL is not in use by any other application. In that case, it's safe to assume that the DLL is application specific and isn't shared by other applications. Therefore, go ahead and agree to have it removed.

> **Technical Note:** Windows 2000 maintains a \SYSTEM directory only for compatibility with 16-bit applications; all 32-bit applications use the \SYSTEM32 directory.

- *Common application directories*. Many applications try to reduce the number of files on your hard drive by placing files that more than one application could use in a separate directory. You'll find an MSAPPS directory on your machine if you use Microsoft applications, for example. The positive side of such directories is that they do indeed reduce the load on your hard drive. The negative aspect is that you really don't know which files to remove if you use multiple products from the same vendor and you want to remove only one product. In fact, I found that this common directory can actually confuse your uninstall program.

As you can see, trying to remove a Windows application from your machine isn't an easy task. A Windows application spreads files all over the place and makes entries in system files you might need, even if you do remove the application. (Multiple applications might need the same entry to run.) It's not too surprising, then, that Windows uninstall programs usually do a partial, not a complete, job of removing old programs from your system. Of course, a partial removal is better than nothing.

> **Tip:** Windows won't let you remove a file that's in use. Even if you close an application, Windows might not unload all its associated DLLs right away. Whenever you want to remove an application from your drive, shut down everything, reboot, and perform the uninstall routine with all applications closed. This ensures that the uninstall program can actually remove all the files it identifies as part of the application.

Installing or Uninstalling Standard Windows Applications

The latest version of Windows 2000 uses the same technique that Windows 95 and 98 do to ensure that you can add and remove applications with ease. All this happens because the install program gives the operating system much more information about what it installs, and why, than previous versions of Windows. That's why you can uninstall only applications specific to Windows 2000, NT 4, or Windows 95/98 with the new install/uninstall capability. Newer applications actually make Registry entries that tell the operating system what to remove later. This also allows Windows 2000 to look for common files and perform other types of analysis. When you can finally upgrade every application on your machine to a newer (Windows 95 or later) version, the install/uninstall program should work perfectly—theoretically, at least.

Now that we have all the preliminaries out of the way, the following paragraphs tell you how to use the install/uninstall program:

1. Open the Control Panel using the Start, Settings menu or Explorer.

2. Double-click Add/Remove Programs. You should see a dialog box like the one shown in Figure 16.1.

FIGURE 16.1

This utility has been redesigned for Windows 2000.

3. Click the Add New Programs button. The utility then searches the network, or you can specify that it should look on a CD-ROM or disk. In addition, you can choose Windows Update, which looks on the Internet for any bug fixes or feature updates to Windows 2000. If you select that option, you're taken to `http://windowsupdate.microsoft.com/`, and you'll see a screen like the one shown in Figure 16.2.

Tip: Interestingly, Internet Explorer 5 boasts a similar feature (Tools, Windows Update), but it's more comprehensive. If you use the IE 5 version, it takes you to a site that displays a list of updates to Microsoft software in addition to Windows 2000:

`http://windowsupdate.microsoft.com/default.htm?page=productupdates`

4. Click the Add/Remove Windows Components option on the left side of the Add/Remove Programs dialog box. This launches the Windows Components Wizard, as shown in Figure 16.3.

FIGURE 16.2

Here's where you can have Windows 2000 automatically update itself.

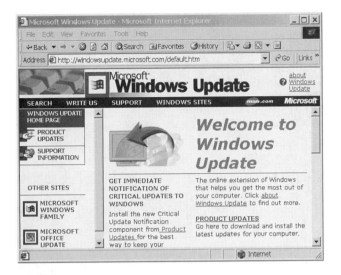

FIGURE 16.3

Use this wizard to add Windows 2000 features (or remove them).

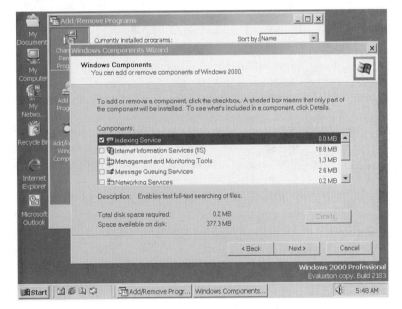

Fortunately, the previous confusion caused by blending Windows components and accessories into the same list as all other applications has now been cleared up. When you use the Windows 2000 Add/Remove Programs utility, you have buttons that clearly indicate what they do.

5. Close the Windows Components Wizard dialog box and in the Add/Remove Programs dialog box choose Change or Remove Programs. Then try an intriguing new feature. Click the Sort By list box to drop it down and then choose Frequency of Use, as shown in Figure 16.4.

FIGURE 16.4

Use this report to avoid deleting a program that you use frequently.

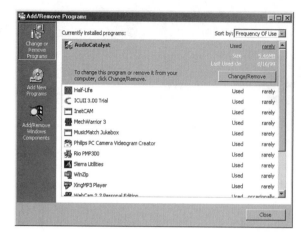

Warning: You probably know how often you use your various utilities and applications. However, if you need to free up disk space for some reason, it would be helpful to see your programs listed by frequency of use.

6. Click the Add New Programs button on the left pane of the Add/Remove Programs dialog box to try to install a new application. Put the application's CD in your CD-ROM drive. Click the CD or Floppy button; then when the Wizard appears, click Next. The install utility searches for an installation program (`setup.exe` or `install.exe`). If it doesn't find one on your floppy drive or CD-ROM drive, it permits you to browse those devices to manually locate the setup or install program. Double-click the name of this program and then click Finish to begin the installation process.

7. Windows 2000 launches the Setup application. Follow the vendor instructions for installing the application. You won't come back to the Install Wizard when you get done.

Uninstalling an application is just as easy, if not easier, as installing one. The following procedure shows you the steps you'll follow in most cases. Remember that you also have the option of using the application's uninstall utility. Of course, the tradeoff is that the application might not remove all the Registry entries that Windows 2000 made when you installed it.

To uninstall, follow these steps:

1. Open the Control Panel using the Start menu or Explorer.

2. Double-click Add/Remove Programs. You should see a dialog box like the one shown previously in Figure 16.1.

3. Select the application you want to uninstall and click the Remove button. You're asked whether you want to remove the application.

4. Click Yes.

   If the Uninstall utility cannot remove all the files, it provides you with a list and
   suggests you later remove these files by hand. Some uninstall applications *will* tell
   you when they're finished and provide you with a report. So, sometimes you do
   get feedback, but not usually.

5. The utility does not inform you that it has uninstalled the application—you're
   merely shown a list of currently installed applications, with one of them (the one
   you just uninstalled) no longer in the list.

If you open the Add/Remove Programs dialog box and see an item in the list that just
will not uninstall, you'll want to remove the item from the list at least. Run Regedit (see
Chapter 10, "Understanding the Windows 2000 Registry") and locate this Registry entry:

`HKEY_LOCAL_MACHINE\SOFTWARE\Microsoft\Windows\CurrentVersion\Uninstall`

Then remove the key for the program from the Registry. (Before fiddling with the
Registry, read the Warnings at the start of Chapter 10.)

Special Considerations for 16-Bit Applications

You'll find that your network probably has a few 16-bit applications hanging around.
I have a special application I wrote that I use for printing labels; I could recompile that
application in a 32-bit format (because I wrote it, I've got the source code), but most of
you won't have that option. What do you do with those old applications? After you see
the ease with which your new Windows 2000 applications install and remove, holding
onto these hard-to-manage applications will take more than a little self control. Let's face
it: The new applications you install will definitely make those old (but necessary) applications look completely out-of-date, in various ways.

The best way to resolve the situation is to see whether there's a new 32-bit version of the
product that will work with Microsoft's Add/Remove Programs utility. You're probably
going to find that some applications just don't fall into that category, however. Custom
software is especially prone to this problem. Another way to resolve the problem is to
find an update or patch that includes its own uninstall program. At least you could
remove most or all of the program that way (the actual capabilities of these uninstall programs vary widely).

How can you guard against wasting disk space when you try to remove a legacy application? One way is to look through the vendor documentation to see whether it provides a
list of files that an application requires. Make a note of which files you installed. You can
also make notes on the state of your machine before and after the install.

You'll need to protect your installation by looking for odd entries in both WIN.INI and
SYSTEM.INI. If an older 16-bit application relies on device drivers or DLLs to get the job
done, you'll almost certainly have problems getting the application to work properly.
I had a problem application that relied on a replaceable graphics driver to get the job
done. You can just imagine the mess it created when it replaced the 32-bit driver used by
Windows 2000 with its own 16-bit driver.

Special Considerations for DOS Applications

I haven't found a lot of gray areas when running DOS applications under Windows 2000. Either it works or it doesn't; there doesn't seem to be a lot of middle ground. Unlike 16-bit Windows applications, a DOS application won't interfere with the operation of Windows itself when you install or remove it. In fact, removing a DOS application usually consists of a single step: removing the directory that holds the application. If you use a separate directory for your data, you shouldn't run into any problems if you decide to reinstall the application later.

I cover DOS applications pretty thoroughly in the "DOS Application Performance Tips" section in Chapter 7. Rather than repeat information, let me just mention the bottom line: Windows 2000 runs DOS application a bit better than NT 4 did, but not as well as Windows 95/98.

Optimizing Windows Applications

After you install a new application, you need to optimize it for your use. Notice I said "for your use." The difference between an optimized and an exploited application is simple: The optimized application might run fast, but the exploited application is more efficient for you. Windows applications provide a wealth of settings that enable you to tune the way they work. Not only do these tuning steps affect the application's speed and memory requirements, but they also affect the user interface. I look at both elements in the following sections, because they're both important for fully exploiting your applications. Make sure you read the entire section before you start tuning your applications. Some elements involve a tradeoff: You need to select one or the other. I cover the most common choices, but you might need to make some decisions based on your application's specific setup.

Installation Options

Installing your new application is an important part of the tuning process. The decisions you make here will affect the way you view the application in the future as well as determine how the application performs. The following list should help you make some of the difficult decisions that will come up during installation:

Hard Disk Space Issues

If hard disk space is at a premium, you might need to limit the number of installation features you choose. Very few applications come without a fully functional tutorial now, for example. Generally, the tutorial makes use of the multimedia features Windows provides to reduce the time it takes to learn the product. All these features come at a price, however. Learning to use the product from the manual might not seem as efficient as using the interactive tutorial—in fact, I'll tell you right out that it isn't—but the disk space you save could make room for another option you'll use long after the need for the tutorial is gone. Theoretically, you could install the tutorial and remove it later; some people invariably forget to do this, however, making the resulting loss of disk space permanent. If you install the tutorial, make sure you remove it when it's no longer needed. Also, if the application comes with a large collection of fonts, clip art, graphics, or other such files, consider leaving these off your hard drive. Graphics, in particular, are disk hogs.

Nowadays, many larger applications permit you to select which portions of their software should be loaded onto your hard drive (for speed and easy access) and which should be accessed from the CD (you'll be asked to insert the CD if you choose one of these features). Use your own judgment about which items you need frequently and which you can use off the CD.

Uninstall Capability

You'll find that some applications provide a custom uninstall capability. Even if your application provides only a stock uninstall capability, you could install it fully once to learn how to use the product, uninstall it, and then install it partially a second time to get what you really want.

Solving Memory Problems

This particular item, of concern, applies to graphics programs for the most part because they're the biggest users of memory, but some other applications are equally guilty. Have you ever noticed that some applications seem to gobble every spare bit of memory on your system? The problem might be your installation choices and not the way the application works. Graphics programs, for example, often ask what types of filters and other "utility" elements you want to install. A graphics application might include a laundry list of application files it will import from and export to. Also, a graphics program might have many megabytes of sample photos and such.

A database manager might include an autodial feature, and spreadsheets are rife with background problem solvers. It might seem like a good idea to select them all. After all, you might need them sometime. From a memory standpoint, however, this decision could be problematic. Some badly behaved applications load all those fancy utilities and filters whenever you start them. Each filter or other add-on costs memory that you could use for some other purpose. If you need that product element, fine, but why pay a memory/performance penalty for something you don't need? The bottom line is that you should install only the filters and utilities you'll actually use later.

Interapplication Communication

I used to absolutely hate packaged applications. These suites of products usually contained things no one wanted—mini word processors with limited capabilities and a spreadsheet that could barely track your checkbook. Bundled applications suffer a lot less from this problem now and have improved in one other area as well. If you install a suite of products, such as Microsoft Office, rather than separate applications, there's a much better chance that the separate parts will communicate seamlessly or offer other efficiencies, such as sharing a spell checker between them.

I used to use products from different companies to get the best that each category had to provide. With today's huge applications, however, getting enough features is no longer a consideration for the most part. Unless there's a very good reason to do so, you'll probably want to go with a one-stop-shop solution to fulfill the better part of your applications' needs. Also, some of the "docucentricity" and ActiveX technologies built into Windows 2000 make interapplication communication far more simple that it used to be. (See Chapter 15, "OLE, ActiveX, and DCOM," for details.)

Miscellaneous Support Options

Some applications provide features that don't relate directly to how they work but instead manage how they react in a given situation. I just installed a new utility that gives me a thumbnail-sketch view of several files on my system. One of the installation options was to add that utility to my Startup folder. I had the memory required, so I said yes. It seemed like a straightforward decision, but I still needed to make it. Some of the other decisions aren't quite so straightforward. One application provided the capability to track my OLE links across the network, for example. This isn't the same as the distributed common object module (DCOM) specification. To do this, it had to load a rather large piece of code and allow it to remain resident. Because I very seldom think about using such a capability, I didn't install it. These other support decisions will affect the way you work as well as the amount of memory an application uses.

The installation process that used to seem so straightforward is no longer so simple. You need to make some hard decisions before you embark on the actual installation process. The tips I just mentioned will help you make these generic decisions, but you'll find others more difficult to resolve. How do you balance workgroup and individual needs, for example? For some products, such as Lotus Notes, this is a major concern. Using products such as these requires the administrator to make some decisions for the benefit of the group as a whole. Some users will definitely view the decisions as arbitrary and overly confining. When working with workgroup-specific applications, you'll probably need to consider some additional items:

- *Installation location.* Choosing where to put a workgroup application is a major decision. Placing all the installation files on the network makes it a lot easier for the administrator to manage and maintain the application. It also reduces the chance that someone will attempt to pirate the application, because the network usually provides better security for the server than it does for the workstation. A server installation also makes it easier to add new users and reduces overall application size, because not every workstation needs a copy of the common files, such as DLLs. The negative aspects of using a server installation are fairly substantial. The network will have to handle a lot more traffic as the application requests DLLs and other support files from the server. The users won't get as many configuration options as they would using a workstation installation in many cases.

- *Gateway options.* Many network-specific applications include gateway support. The decision about which gateways to support is fairly obvious, unless your network is in a state of transition. If you're in a state of transition, it might be a good idea to wait and install the new application when the network is stable. (A *gateway* is a way to link two different kinds of networks. It can involve both hardware and software that allow the networks to communicate.)

- *Local support for network features.* Many network products secretly invade the user's system and steal workstation statistics on a regular basis. This covert form of monitoring the user probably has its uses (and I don't mean to start a "Big Brother" rumor). Unless you're the sole administrator for a very large network, however, you have to weigh the importance of such a feature against the memory it will use up in each workstation. Windows 2000 is fairly memory hungry to begin with. Adding the burden of unneeded drivers will only make things worse.

Now that we've examined some of the things you need to consider when installing an application under Windows 2000, the need to plan that installation becomes a lot more obvious. Add to the installation problems the need to upgrade each user's machine and the cost of administrator time in doing so, and you begin to understand why some companies don't like software updates. Overall, a planned installation should provide you with a solid foundation on which to build your fully exploited application later.

Settings

Very few applications use the same settings. You'll find that applications of a particular kind (such as all word processors) might share a few of the same settings; for the most part, however, you'll need to spend some time reading the user manual to figure them out. I won't discuss the actual process of changing your application's settings in this section; you'll need to read the vendor manuals later. I present some general principles you can use to make your life easier. You can start looking at these areas for potential speed, memory, and efficiency gains.

Tip: Everyone's first inclination is to get into the application and complete this part of the setup immediately. However, this might be a bad idea. Software settings change as you learn how to use the application more efficiently. As your knowledge about the application increases, the feature that seemed important yesterday might appear almost foolish today. The settings I use for my applications are in an almost continuous state of flux. A little change here or a little tweak there can make a big difference in how well the application works for me. Take the time required to go through the tutorial first and then make any setting changes you think will help. I usually keep Notepad handy to record any ideas I have while running the tutorial.

Changing your settings is largely a matter of personal preference. Even a small change can make a big difference in the way you use an application, however. You can do something as small as customizing a toolbar and reap a fairly large increase in efficiency, for example. Not using an application's autocorrect feature might enable you to focus on your writing and leave spelling correction until a later, less intrusive time. Often it's not the major changes you'll notice the most but rather the little extras you add that make a difference in your computing environment. The following tips will help you get the most of out of your applications:

- *Toolbars*. A toolbar represents one way you can greatly increase your efficiency in exchange for a very small increase in memory usage. Remember that every icon you allocate uses some additional system resources, but if you have a reasonable amount of memory (128MB or more), don't worry at all about toolbars and icons. The amount of memory an icon uses is very small, usually less than 1KB. When setting up my toolbar, I don't assume that the vendor provided something even close to my optimal arrangement, so I try to track the commands I use the most. The commands that you use a lot should appear on the toolbar. It takes less time to click a command on the toolbar than it does to locate it within a menu, so placing common commands on a toolbar is one way to improve your efficiency. Seven icons should appear on nearly every toolbar: Open, Close, New, Print, Cut, Copy, and Paste. (However, if you memorize the keyboard shortcuts Ctrl+X, Ctrl+C, and Ctrl+V, you can leave off Cut, Copy and Paste.) You might want to add Print Preview to this list as well. Make sure you remove any standard toolbar buttons that you don't use. Microsoft Word sometimes adds links to its other products on the toolbar, for example. I usually remove these icons because I don't use the links in that way. You'll find much more information about these kinds of customization in Chapter 8, "Customizing Windows 2000 for Maximum Productivity." In most cases, you can modify a toolbar by right-clicking it and then choosing Customize from its context menu.

- *Printer settings*. Every application I own (with the exception of a few small utilities) enables me to set the printer configuration separately from the Windows general configuration. I usually set my printer configuration to match my use of that application. I use my word processor for final output in most cases, for example, so I use the best letter-quality resolution available. On the other hand, I never use one of my graphics programs for final output, so I select draft there. A draft printout might not seem acceptable—and it isn't if you plan to send the document to someone—but it's a lot faster when you just want a quick look at your document. (A minor benefit of using draft output whenever possible is that you'll use less ink, making expensive toner cartridges last longer.) You can also vary the print resolution. A low-resolution, letter-quality printout might work fine for workgroup presentations, but you'll want to use the highest quality available when making the same presentation to a larger audience. The resolution you use will affect the amount of memory and time required to complete the printout.

- *Macros*. I like to think of macros as "canned keystrokes." However, macros are actually small computer programs that, these days, can be extraordinarily powerful and complex. Many applications include a macro language every bit as powerful as traditional computer languages. But you can make them simple. For example, think about the steps you take to create a letter. Every time you do so, you probably add a heading with your company name and other information. Wouldn't it be nice if you could tell the program to do this for you automatically? That's what a macro can do; it can replay the keystrokes you would usually make by hand by recording them in a separate area of memory. A macro recorder works just like a tape recorder. It records your keystrokes and enables you to play them back later.

  Macros are one area where you might find it difficult to make a concrete rule for settings. I almost always create a macro for each repetitive task I perform with my main applications. The investment in time required to create the macro is always much more than paid back in improved efficiency. If I perform a task manually nearly every time I use the application, that's a repetitive task. I really don't need to perform that task if the computer can do it equally well in a lot less time. A main application is one that I use at least eight hours a week. If you spend less time than that in an application, you have to wonder when you would have time to use the macro (the main problem can be remembering which buttons or shortcut key combinations trigger these less-often-used macros). Also, some tasks work better as macros than others. I always set up my word processing files using a macro, for example. It makes more sense for the computer to do the work than for me to do it. In fact, I use this macro so often that I've attached it to my toolbar as an icon. This is another decision you'll need to make. Attaching a macro to a toolbar button is always a good idea if you use it a lot. Other tasks don't work well as macros. I always thought that changing the format of a document would make a great macro, for example, but implementing it proved frustrating. It takes a human mind to perform some tasks. But also remember that most applications enable you to assign macros, menu items, and all their other features to shortcut keys. That way, instead of using menus or even having to click an icon, you can trigger an application's behavior by merely pressing Alt+Z or some such combination. Give macros a try. You'll be happy you did.

- *Style sheets and templates*. One thing you can never have too many of are style sheets and templates. I always use a style sheet for my documents if the application supports them. The reason is simple: A style sheet doesn't take more than a few minutes to create, but it can save a lot of time later. Templates are the same. They take only a short time to create, but they'll definitely reduce the time it takes to create useful output later. Templates and style sheets also provide one other benefit: They tend to enforce uniformity in the format of your document. This is important whether you're part of a group or working as an individual. I view consistent output as one of the marks of a professional, and most other people do, too. In addition, if you spend less time worrying about how to format your document, you'll have a lot more time to work on its content. Also, many applications include various predesigned style sheets and templates, formats created by professional designers that you can customize to suit your particular job at hand.

- *Autocorrect.* The autocorrect feature provided by many applications is a source of much consternation for me. On the one hand, it provides a valuable aid: autocorrecting misspelled words or other types of user input. The problem is that most autocorrect features interrupt your workflow and the ideas you're trying to build as well as the transitions and connections you're making (the large view). They drop you down into the fact that a word isn't quite right, and you can lose your train of thought (at least I do). It's really a matter of personal preference. I usually turn off my autocorrect features and rely on my spell-checker (or other tools) to find all those mistakes at one time, after I've got the main ideas down in the document. Whether this approach is efficient for you is based on how you prefer to work. Actually, the resources used by autocorrect aren't that significant. What's more, the CPU is largely idling, particularly when you're using a word processor.

> **Tip:** Autocorrect can be used for other purposes than correcting spelling. It can enable you to save typing time: You can type in an abbreviation and have it extend automatically to a frequently used full word or phrase. Let's say, for example, that you're using Word 2000 and you're writing an article on Microsoft's Visual Studio. You'll be using the words *application, Visual Studio,* and *properties* quite often in the article. You can save a lot of time by choosing AutoCorrect from Word's Tools menu and then assigning abbreviations, such as *app, vs,* and *pr* to these terms. Then, whenever you type *vs* followed by a space, Word will automatically replace it with *Visual Studio.* Also, you might want to similarly abbreviate your name (don't use your initials as an abbreviation; you'll want to type them sometimes as is). Also, you can abbreviate your address, phone number, and other words and phrases you frequently have to type.

- *Autoload.* This feature goes back to those utility and filter programs I mentioned in the "Installation Options" section. Some programs, such as Microsoft Access and Lotus 1-2-3, enable you to autoload some of your favorite utilities and filters. This enables you to access them more quickly. However, there's a tradeoff for the convenience of instant access: You have to give up some memory and perhaps a few processor cycles to do it. The middle ground is to autoload only the features you know you'll use every time. It takes only a few seconds to load the other features, so you'll want to do that manually in most cases.

Peter's Principle: My Settings Won't Work on Your Machine

We're all individuals. Nowhere is this more apparent than in the way we use software. I might think the way you do something is absurd; however, if it works for you, it's probably the right way to go (at least until you learn better).

The world of applications does have some constants, and the wealth of available tip and technique books prove it. You can probably buy any number of tip and technique books to help you get your application set up in a very short time with a minimum of effort. On the other hand, you need to make just as many, if not more, personal decisions. I usually include the Insert I Comment command in Microsoft Word on my toolbar, for example, because I use this feature a lot. I suggested the same thing to a colleague and he found it a waste of time because he used a different technique for making annotations.

I find that the same thing holds true for just about every type of user setting; however, you might have to give up some autonomy in workgroup situations. I usually use three different user dictionaries: Common, Computer, and Jargon. This enables me to keep some words separate so that they don't contaminate my general-purpose dictionary. In a workgroup situation, you might find that everyone needs to use the same dictionary to ensure consistent results for a project. The same thing holds true for other user settings, such as templates and style sheets. A group project usually requires the individual to defer to the group's needs to enforce a certain level of consistency.

The point is that you need to work with an application long enough to build a rapport with it. After you figure out how you want to work with the application, you can start changing some of those personal settings to meet your specific requirements. In fact, you might find that some of your settings end up working for the group as well. Experimentation is a prime ingredient in finding the settings that work best for you.

Setting up an application is, in truth, an ongoing process. Exploiting your software is often as much a matter of using the software in the best way you know how as it is a matter of optimizing memory and speed settings. Don't give up personal comfort for a perceived memory or speed benefit. You have to weigh the time a specific feature will save against what it will cost. That's what you do in other business decisions; evaluating your software is no different.

Running 16-Bit Windows Applications

Chapter 9, "An Architectural Overview," looked at how 16-bit applications run. That should clue you into some of the problems you'll encounter when running them. Windows 2000 does a better job in some regards than Windows 95/98. Under Windows 95/98, all 16-bit applications share one address space. This means that they have to share the system resources required to display windows, icons, and graphics elements of all sorts. That same 16-bit application running under Windows 2000 executes in its own address space, thus making more memory available for graphics and other needed program resources. Windows 2000 has its own problems, however. I've actually seen some memory-intensive, 16-bit applications grab more resources even though they didn't need them because they aren't running in a shared environment. There's always a tradeoff involved in whatever environment you use. For the most part, I think you'll find the Windows 95 versus Windows 2000 tradeoff for 16-bit applications works in favor of Windows 2000.

Technical Note: In Windows 2000, a 16-bit application is actually running in a 32-bit shell called NTVDM (Virtual DOS Machine). It gets just as many processor cycles as 32-bit applications. There can be an efficiency hit, however, when multiple 16-bit applications run simultaneously. By default, they'll all run in a common NTVDM as independent threads. This puts them in competition for the virtual resources that the NTVDM is providing.

Some earlier Windows applications display an Invalid Dynalink Call error message when you try to run them. This means that they're incompatible with a new Windows 2000 version of a DLL. You have two choices. Upgrading the application is the best alternative because you'll replace that old product with something that will work better with Windows 2000—a 32-bit version of what you used in the past. If upgrading isn't an option, reinstall the application, reboot Windows 2000, and try it again. You have to reboot to reload the DLL into memory. Otherwise, you'll see the same error message because the Windows 2000 version is still in place. If you still get an invalid dynalink call message, there's some incompatibility between the application and a basic Windows 2000 system file. You absolutely must upgrade in this case because you can't replace those common files to meet the needs of one program. One or more Windows 2000 applications might cease to function if you do (including the operating system itself).

If you're migrating to Windows 2000 from Windows 95 or 98, the same types of optimization techniques you used before will probably work under Windows 2000 as well. However, you'll want to consider some issues that do, in fact, require different techniques. If you switch from the FAT to NTFS file system, for example, you'll have an opportunity to fine-tune your disk drive's behavior, even to the point of specifying cluster sizes (for in-depth detail on this topic, see Chapter 12, "The Windows 2000 File Systems: FAT and NTFS").

You'll still need to keep in mind the cooperative multitasking aspect of any 16-bit applications when running certain types of applications in the background. You'll probably find it difficult to run your 16-bit database and your communications program at the same time at high speed, for example. The "cooperative" nature of these applications means that the database will probably take control of the system for that one second longer than the communications program can hold data in the buffer. The result is lost data. Windows 2000 is superior in this regard to Windows 95/98, but it still isn't perfect because the applications it runs aren't perfect.

Tip: Some 16-bit applications give you a choice between storing DLL files locally or in the Windows SYSTEM directory. Choose the local option to make it easier to remove the application later. This also reduces the chance that the application's setup routine will accidentally overwrite a Windows 2000 version of a file.

Running 32-Bit Windows Applications

I've tested a lot of 32-bit applications and discovered a few interesting facts. Overall, a 32-bit application is larger and just a tad slower (when you view a single section of code) than its 16-bit counterpart. It's larger because you're using 32 bits for everything, even structures that might not require 32 bits. In addition, 32-bit code is typically larger than its 16-bit counterpart. Does this mean that 32-bit applications are memory hogs that you shouldn't use? Not by a long shot.

I want to explain the slower part of 32-bit application performance a little better. A 32-bit application starts out a tad slower than its 16-bit equivalent, but it ends up faster for a number of reasons. Most of these reasons have come from using a flat address space and the other architectural benefits of a 32-bit format. Yes, it takes more time to process 32-bit code than the equivalent sections of 16-bit code because the 32-bit code is larger. There's still a big speed benefit in the long run, however, because of the way a 32-bit application executes.

Running a 32-bit application has definite benefits in terms of speed. For one thing, it supports true multitasking. I found that background repagination in the 16-bit version of Word usually meant that I had to wait anyway until the application finished the task. Under the 32-bit version, Word spawns a task that really does run in the background. I seldom notice that anything is happening; the document just gets repaginated without my thinking about it. This is how multitasking should work from a user perspective. Email should download, Active Desktop items should update, and other background tasks should silently, invisibly activate while you remain unaware that they're even taking place.

Multitasking also helps you perform some tasks, such as printing, a lot faster than you could using a 16-bit application. For one thing, Windows can make better use of idle time with a 32-bit application. You'll notice that you regain control of the system faster. After a 32-bit application spawns a print task, it can return control of the computer immediately. It doesn't even need to slow you down as it checks on the status of the "background" print job like a 16-bit application does.

> **Warning:** Every time a 32-bit application spawns a new task (called a *thread*), it uses some system resources. Some applications can create so many threads that your system begins to slow to a crawl and Windows runs out of resources. The second you run completely out of resources, the machine usually freezes. Although Microsoft did increase the size of some memory areas and moved others to the 32-bit area, Windows 2000 still isn't perfect when it comes to managing 32-bit resources. The best thing to do is avoid the situation altogether. Don't try to run every feature that a 32-bit application can provide at one time. Limit the number of tasks you ask an application to perform in the background to a reasonable level. Finally, run what was previously called the Resource Monitor (now it's the Performance tab in Task Manager) from time to time just to see
>
> *continues*

how you're doing on system resources. You might find that you need to adjust some of your techniques to compensate for limitations in the Windows 2000 design. It's good at multitasking, but the tasks are basically happening serially. Your computer hasn't broken the laws of macro-level physics and started operating simultaneously in multiple states. It's still switching between operations, but gracefully.

The big performance-tuning tip for Windows 2000 and 32-bit applications is to use as many automatic settings as possible. The more room you give Windows 2000 to compensate for changing system conditions, the better. Chapter 7, "Performance Power," contains quite a few tips you can follow to optimize the environment. I discuss the need to monitor the swap file size to ensure that you don't end up wasting processor cycles in thrashing, for example. After you optimize the environment for a 32-bit application, you have essentially optimized the application itself. All you need to do is check out the section titled "Settings," earlier in this chapter, to make the application as efficient as possible during use.

Optimizing DOS Applications

It will be a time yet before you see the demise of all DOS applications. It's true that almost no American commercial application vendors are updating their DOS products anymore, but that isn't the total picture. The DOS scene offers more than just commercial applications.

One of the biggest areas where DOS used to be used was games, particularly those created for or by people overseas. Why were games such a hot DOS item? The DOS environment gives the programmer more direct access to more of the hardware (particularly the video) and enables him or her to write a fast and visually stimulating program. Windows is notorious for grabbing system resources and running games at a slower pace when compared to a DOS version of the same program. Microsoft has, however, essentially obviated this problem with several strategies, including DirectX, that make Windows more attractive to game vendors. These days, you won't find many games—for the U.S. market anyway—involved with DOS.

In addition to DirectX and other technologies, video board manufacturers have made improvements, too, in how their technology handles processor-intensive 3D action graphics. Yet, it's unlikely that all users want to give up their favorite old games either. Some games have an amazing shelf life when you consider the technology they use. I know people who still like to play the original ZORK series, for example—a text-based DOS game with a great plot but no graphics at all!

However, there's still one area where DOS remains king of the hill and unconquered: custom applications. But it's for a different reason than game programmers used to like DOS. A custom application can cost thousands of dollars. The consultant who writes the program has to charge that much because the chances of his selling even a few copies are slim at best, depending on how "custom" the application is. Because custom applications usually manipulate very sensitive company data that's hard to move to another application, people are going to think twice before attempting to move that data somewhere else. Fortunately, I see this particular class of DOS applications coming to an end as Windows tools become easier and faster to use. A consultant can be a lot more productive now, so the cost is less for creating a new application in some cases.

Yet old habits die hard. Some people are accustomed to using DOS utility programs, so that's what they will continue to use. I have to confess that I still use the Norton Commander for some kinds of file manipulation and text file reading. I've been using it since it came out over a decade ago, but I know it so well that it's efficient for me. These applications have perfectly acceptable substitutes in most cases—substitutes that are easier to use and that actually run faster—but some people just won't use them. This is the third group of people who will make at least some use of DOS under Windows 2000.

I explore a variety of DOS options in the following sections. In most cases, I show you the best methods first and later add a few marginal methods you can use in a pinch. Of course, my advice is to move to a 32-bit Windows 95/98 or Windows 2000 application as soon as possible. DOS isn't dead, strictly speaking, but it does have far more than just one foot in the grave. Remember that these are, after all, applications that no commercial vendor continues to support.

Understanding DOS Emulation

You use MS-DOS under Windows 2000 through the MS-DOS emulation mode. What actually happens when you run a DOS application is that Windows 2000 makes a copy of the phantom DOS session stored in memory, spawns a new Virtual 86 session (a *virtual machine*), and places the copy it made in the new session. What you see is either a windowed or full screen DOS emulation. All you need to do to open a DOS window is to choose Command Prompt from the Start, Programs, Accessories menu. You'll also trigger a DOS session whenever you choose a DOS application from Explorer or the Start menu.

As with almost everything else under Windows 2000, you can get a context menu for a DOS window. Right-click its title bar. It contains three entries that are important to you as a user: Close, Edit, and Properties. The Close option enables you to close the DOS window without typing Exit and pressing Enter at the DOS prompt. The Edit option enables you to mark, copy, or paste text from the DOS screen to the Clipboard. The Properties option displays the Properties dialog box shown in Figure 16.5.

As you can see, this dialog box contains four pages. I cover most of these settings in the following "Settings" section, but let's consider the Font issue here.

The Font Size list box enables you to choose the size of font used to display information in the DOS window. It defines the number of horizontal and vertical pixels used for each character. You need to find a balance between readability and the capability to view the entire screen at once. I usually use a font size that displays 25 lines of text in a dialog box that takes up about one-third of the screen area, because it offers the best of both worlds. Of course, the font size you choose is partially determined by the resolution of your display. A DOS window usually defaults to the Auto setting. This means that Windows 2000 attempts to find the proper font size based on the number of lines of text in the DOS box and the resolution of your display. If you choose an 80-character-by-25-line display mode and your screen provides 640×480 resolution, for example, Windows 2000 selects the font nearest to 8-by-19.2 pixels. To get these numbers, I divided the horizontal resolution by the number of characters (640/80) and the vertical resolution by the number of lines (480/25). In this case, Windows 2000 would probably default to the 8×16 font listed in the Font Size list box. I usually find that the Windows 2000 setting makes maximum use of the display but isn't the best setting for my needs. Optimizing the setting to meet your particular needs is the best way to go. Of course, if you have a higher-resolution screen setting, you can afford more readable font settings.

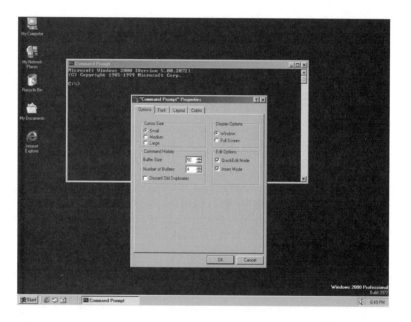

FIGURE 16.5

The "Command Prompt" Properties dialog box is where you can configure a DOS window on the fly.

Let's now switch to the Edit option on the Command Prompt context menu. There are three main options to consider: Mark, Copy, and Paste. A fourth option, Scroll, enables you to scroll the screen as needed during a capture. It only becomes active if the window buffer size is larger than the actual window. The following list covers these three options in detail:

- *Mark.* Use this control to select an area of the screen for copying. Windows 2000 places the selected area on the Clipboard after you choose the Copy command so that you can use it in other applications. The selected area is highlighted, as shown in Figure 16.6. You can use either the cursor keys or the mouse to select the desired area.

FIGURE 16.6

Use the Mark button to copy part of the DOS screen into the Windows 2000 Clipboard, and thereby have it available to applications in Windows 2000.

- *Copy*. The Copy button places the area you highlighted using the Mark button on the Clipboard.

- *Paste*. You can also paste information from a Windows application into the DOS box. Obviously, you can't paste anything other than text unless the display is in Graphics mode. Even then, your capability might be limited by the DOS application running at the time.

After you get past the fancy display, you'll see that DOS is unchanged. It doesn't really provide a lot more than you had in the past. One feature it does provide is long filename support. Use the DIR command if you want to see what I mean. Also, the Edit feature now provides the capability to modify more than one file simultaneously. I cover the specific changes in DOS utility support in the next section.

> **Tip:** You can also use long filenames when typing commands. The only requirement is that, in a few cases, you might be required to use quotation marks to enclose the long filename or directory, as in this example:
>
> ```
> DIR "Some Long Directory Name"
> ```

DOS Versus Windows 2000 Commands

Microsoft must have expected people to use the DOS "command prompt" for a while longer; otherwise, it wouldn't have improved some of the utilities in it. I discussed one of those utilities earlier, so I won't describe it here again. I really don't have room here to explore all the DOS commands, so I'm going to give you the highlights. The following list shows the changes that DOS (running under Windows 2000) provides:

> **Note:** The Windows 2000 approach to DOS includes a number of differences from the approach used by Windows 95/98 because of some assumptions that Microsoft made. You'll find, for example, that Microsoft kept many of the DOS

continues

> disk utilities in Windows 95/98, even to the point of providing batch file substitutes for them. The reason is simple: There's a good chance that someone using Windows 95/98 will want to maintain a dual-boot setup. He or she will at least want to know why a particular command in MS-DOS mode can't be used (a feature that Windows 2000 doesn't support). You also need to remember that DOS is a much larger part of Windows 95/98 than it is of Windows 2000. Windows 95/98 is built upon and around DOS, and Windows 95/98 is also designed to be flexible—to enable you to use those older DOS applications. Windows 2000 assumes that you'll spend all or at least most of your time within Windows itself.

- EDIT is a standalone command now. It also provides the means for editing more than one file.

- The NET command can be used to determine a wealth of information about your network from the DOS prompt. Typing NET VIEW, for example, displays a list of computers and other resources currently available on the network. To learn more about this command, type NET ? at the DOS prompt.

Although DOS under Windows 2000 includes features unavailable in the old, non-Windows versions of DOS, you won't find a few of the old features that were traditionally part of DOS. DOS under Windows 2000 doesn't include any of the following commands:

	INTERLINK	RAMDRIVE.SYS
ASSIGN	INTERSVR	
BACKUP	JOIN	REPLACE
COMP	MEMCARD	RESTORE
DOSSHELL	MEMMAKER	ROMDRIVE.SYS
EDLIN	MIRROR	SHARE
EGA.SYS	MSAV	SMARTMON
FASTHELP	MSBACKUP	TREE
FASTOPEN	POWER	UNDELETE
		UNFORMAT
GRAPHICS	PRINTER.SYS	VSAFE
	QBASIC	

Microsoft's reason for removing the majority of these commands is that they aren't compatible with the long filenames available with Windows 95/98 and Windows 2000. Other programs were removed because Windows 2000 supposedly makes them obsolete. I still would have liked to see Microsoft retain some of the commands. An enhanced version of QBASIC would have been nice for running those old BASIC utilities that I still have hanging around (one of which I use to calibrate my joystick). Obviously, there wasn't any reason to include some DOS utility programs, such as MEMMAKER, because Windows 2000 can't use them. Needless to say, some users will be unhappy about the absence of these commands and utilities.

Creating a DOS Session

You can create a DOS session using a variety of methods. Double-clicking a DOS application from inside Explorer creates a DOS session. The session ends as soon as you end the application.

Like previous versions of Windows, Windows 2000 includes a DOS prompt. All you need to do is click the Command Prompt option found in the Programs, Accessories section of the Start menu. If your DOS window is full screen, you'll need to type exit and press the Enter key to end this session and close that DOS virtual machine. If the DOS window isn't full screen, you can click the Close (X) button. However, you usually have to click an End Now button on a second dialog box as well.

Settings

A DOS application's Properties dialog box contains a lot more than most Windows applications' Properties dialog boxes. The Properties dialog box shown in Figure 16.7 enables you to change every setting involving the DOS application. In fact, Windows 2000 provides several new features for DOS applications that make running them a snap.

FIGURE 16.7

A DOS application has a larger Properties dialog box than most Windows 2000 applications.

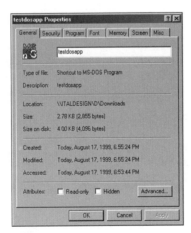

One of the things that differentiates Windows 2000 from Windows 95/98 is that the Windows 2000 Properties dialog box can contain several additional entries. Windows 95/98 doesn't provide a Security page, for example. In addition, not every DOS application uses all eight of the possible property pages (the Summary and Security tabs may not appear with your DOS object's Properties dialog box). Some programs only need six

pages because they don't provide version information, nor is the Security page necessary.
A few others only use three pages because they don't enable you to configure things such
as the amount of memory they use. The following sections describe each possible page
of the Properties dialog box in detail.

> **Tip:** If you want to increase the environment size, edit `CONFIG.NT` using
> Notepad. Either create or modify an existing `SHELL` line within `CONFIG.NT` so that
> it looks like this (assuming Windows 2000 resides in your `WINNT` directory):
>
> `SHELL=C:\WINNT\SYSTEM32\COMMAND.COM /e:512`
>
> This effectively doubles the default 256 bytes allocated for the environment;
> you can, however, set it as large as 32KB.

General

You'll find that every application under Windows 2000 provides a General page. This
page tells you the full name, type, location, and size of the program. It also tells you
whether the program is compressed if you click the Advanced button.

The only user-configurable settings on this page are the file attributes. In most cases, the
only attribute you'll see checked is the Archive attribute. This tells you that the file hasn't
been backed up since you installed it. Click the Advanced button to see the archiving
options.

Summary

Not every application provides the Summary page. You can use it to fill in vendor-
specific information about the current program—something that comes in handy when
you make a support call to the vendor. You can also include any other information you
find useful.

Security

You can individually protect applications under Windows 2000 using the Security page.
There are also options for auditing a file—determining when specific groups of people
perform specific tasks with the file. Finally, there's a setting for determining who owns
the file.

Program

The Program page enables you to change the way Windows executes the program (see
Figure 16.8). At the very top of the page, you'll see an icon and a field containing the
application's name. This is the name you'll see in Explorer.

The next three fields determine what application to run. The Cmd Line field contains
the name of the application you want to run. It must end with an `.EXE`, `.COM`, or

.BAT extension. In this case, I'm running a copy of the Norton Commander, my favorite overall DOS utility. The Working field tells Windows 2000 what directory to start the application from. In most cases, you'll start the application from either its home or its data directory. The choice depends on what kind of information the application requires to start. I use Commander for many general disk-access tasks, so I start it in my main working partition, E:. The third field, Batch File, was new to Windows 95; Microsoft has added it as an enhancement to Windows 2000 as well. It enables you to designate a batch file that runs with the application. With the command processor, for example, you could include a batch file that sets up the path and prompt and loads any TSRs you might need.

FIGURE 16.8

The Program page is where you can change the shortcut, the default directory, the name shown in Explorer, and other elements of the DOS application.

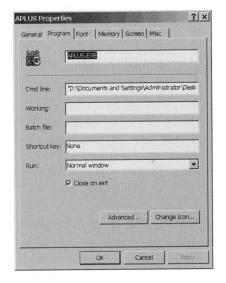

The Shortcut Key field enables you to assign a shortcut key to the program. Chapter 8, "Customizing Windows 2000 for Maximum Productivity," covered this, so I won't discuss it again here. I use *D*, for DOS.

Use the Run drop-down list box to select how you want Windows 2000 to display the application. The three choices are Normal Window, Minimized, and Maximized. The first two choices affect both windowed and full-screen sessions. The third choice starts windowed sessions maximized.

It's usually a good idea to close the DOS session as soon as you get done. Enabling the Close on Exit check box does just that. You quit Norton Commander by pressing F10, Enter—and that's easier than typing EXIT.

Clicking the Change Icon button displays a dialog box from which you can choose 38 alternative icons that are more specific than the arty, R. Crumb–like default DOS icon. Is Microsoft trying to tell us something about its opinion of our resorting to funky old low-tech DOS? After all, this icon is uniquely hand-drawn, contrasting it with all the other sleek, shaded, high-tech icons used for everything else. See the comparison in Figure 16.9.

FIGURE 16.9
The MS-DOS icon on the left is suggestive of old-fashioned technology. The icon on the right, by contrast, is typical of Windows 2000 icons: sleek, shaded, sharp, and techie.

You can select the icon used to identify the application within Explorer and the Start menu. Windows 2000 provides a greater variety of choices as do earlier versions of Windows. You can also choose from custom icon sets by clicking the Browse button. Clicking the Advanced button displays a dialog box that enables you to change the AUTOEXEC and CONFIG files used to start the application. The default setting is to use AUTOEXEC.NT and CONFIG.NT, but you can choose any file you want.

> **Tip:** I kept a copy of my old DOS AUTOEXEC.BAT and CONFIG.SYS files handy for older applications that need a little extra help getting started. All you need to do is carefully prune from these files any programs or device drivers that aren't compatible with Windows 2000 before using them. I think you'll find that a little editing is a lot faster than trying to re-create these files from scratch.

The Compatible Timer Hardware Emulation check box enables you to compensate for the needs of older programs. I've encountered more than a few of them that won't work on newer machines because they depend on timing loops. This check box changes that by emulating the timer hardware for the application.

Font

The Font page enables you to change the appearance of the fonts used to display data in a windowed DOS application. These settings don't affect a full-screen session.

This dialog box contains four main sections. The first section controls the type of fonts you get to see in the Font Size list box. You'll usually want to use the fullest set of fonts available by selecting Both Font Type. The only time you might want to switch to one font type over another is if your display has problems displaying a certain type of font.

The second section contains the Font Size list box. It contains a list of the font sizes you have available for the DOS window. The numbers represent the number of pixels used for each character. A higher number of pixels makes the display more legible. A smaller number of pixels makes the window smaller.

The Window Preview section shows you how big the window will appear on the display. The Font Preview section shows you the size of the print. You should combine the output from these two displays to determine how large a font to use. It's important to reach a setting that balances the need to see what you're doing with the need to display the entire DOS box at once.

Memory

The Memory page, shown in Figure 16.10, is the most important page in the Properties dialog box from a tuning perspective. Notice that it has only five list boxes and two check boxes, but the decisions you make here affect how the application runs. More important, they affect the way Windows runs. Chapter 7, "Performance Power," discusses many of the effects this particular page has on Windows, so I won't go into them here.

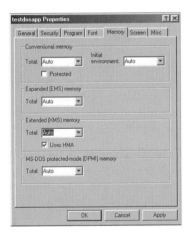

FIGURE 16.10

The Memory page enables you to modify the way Windows allocates and manages memory for your DOS application.

> **Tip:** In most cases, you'll want to keep all the list boxes set to Auto and both check boxes unmarked on the Memory page. Windows usually performs better if you let it manage memory. The default settings might include enabling the Protected check box, but unchecking this box results in better application performance.

The first group of settings affects your conventional memory. The Total drop-down list box enables you to select any value up to 640KB. You absolutely won't get more than 615KB of conventional memory, so don't try to set the conventional memory any higher than that. Windows usually allocates a 1024-byte environment for your DOS application. This is enough to handle most situations. I usually set mine to 4096 to provide space for all those environment strings required by real-mode compilers, however. The Protected check box is another diagnostic aid. Enabling it tells Windows 2000 to monitor the application for memory-protection errors. The only problem is that you'll suffer a performance loss when using it. If your application tends to corrupt memory, by all means check this box to keep your environment stable. Otherwise, consider leaving it unchecked for better performance.

The second group of settings contains a single drop-down list box that controls how much expanded memory Windows 2000 allocates for your application. If you change the default None to Auto, MEM (the DOS command that displays how much of various kinds of memory you have) will report expanded memory up to the amount of memory your machine has installed. Windows 2000 will make only 16MB of it usable if you have more RAM than that installed. The only time you should change the Auto setting is if the application grabs every bit of expanded memory it can find. Some older DOS applications get a little greedy, so you need to provide some controls for that greed.

The third group of settings controls the amount of extended memory available to your application. The Auto setting allocates the full amount of RAM installed on your system. This isn't an unlimited amount of memory, but it could be fairly high—much higher than the automatic expanded memory setting. As with the expanded memory setting, I usually change this setting to some specific number if the application gets greedy or if it has problems coping with the full amount of extended memory available on my machine. I usually leave the Uses HMA (High Memory Area) check box disabled because I load DOS in the high-memory area. If you don't use the HMA, however, you can always choose to load all or part of an application there by checking this box.

The final group of settings enables you to determine the amount of DPMI (protected mode) memory available to applications. Windows 2000 usually sets this to a value that reflects the current system conditions. There's little reason to change this setting from the default.

Screen

The Screen page is where you can specify the screen settings. The first group of settings, Usage, determines the screen mode and number of display lines. You should set the number of display lines here before you set the options on the Font page of this dialog box. Otherwise, a setting that worked well at 25 lines might not work at 50.

The second group enables you to change the window settings. It doesn't come into play if you use full-screen mode. Usually, the entries are good only for that session. I prefer that Windows remember my settings from session to session, so I check this box.

The third group of settings on this page affects your application's performance. I was a little surprised that this is the only section Microsoft chose to label as Performance, considering the number of other settings that affect the way your application will run. The first check box, Fast ROM Emulation, acts just like shadow RAM. It allows your application to use a RAM version of your display ROM. If an application had trouble with shadow RAM under DOS, it will also have trouble with this setting. Otherwise, you'll want to leave this checked to get maximum performance from your application.

The second check box in the Performance group helps Windows more than it helps the application. This setting allows Windows to retrieve some of the memory that the DOS application uses for Graphics mode when it goes into character mode. This modicum of memory isn't much, but it can add up if you're running a lot of DOS sessions. As with so many other settings, giving Windows the flexibility it needs to fully control the memory on your system is usually a good idea. The only time you would want to remove the check mark from this setting is if your application spends all or most of its time in graphics mode.

Misc

The Misc (Miscellaneous) page mainly provides settings that determine how Windows interacts with your application from a functional point of view (see Figure 16.11).

FIGURE 16.11

Put these options to work to define the interaction between the Windows OS and your DOS session.

The Allow Screen Saver check box doesn't really have much of an effect when you're using windowed applications. It determines whether Windows can interrupt a full-screen session to run a screen saver. Some full-screen applications really get confused if you allow the screen saver to operate. This is especially true of graphics applications and those that use RAM fonts. (A RAM font provides the check box and radio button controls you see in some character-mode applications.)

The Mouse group contains two check boxes. The QuickEdit check box enables you to use a mouse within a DOS window, just like you would with any Windows application. This means you can select, copy, and paste with a lot less trouble than you could before. The Exclusive Mode check box gives a windowed application exclusive control over the mouse. The consequences of doing this on a permanent basis are pretty severe. This means that you can't use the mouse with your regular Windows applications as long as this application is active. It would probably be a better idea to run this application in a full-screen session if it has this much trouble sharing the mouse.

Some of the settings on this page can provide subtle performance control over your application. The Background and Idle Sensitivity controls fall into this category. Enabling the Always Suspend check box does more than suspend the application when it's in the background. It frees resources for Windows 2000 to use with other applications. If you're using a DOS application for data entry or some other task that requires continuous input, it pays to check this box and use those resources for other applications. The Idle Sensitivity setting also controls how Windows allocates resources. Usually, Windows tracks the amount of activity from an application. If it determines that the application is sitting there doing nothing while waiting for input from you, Windows 2000 reduces its CPU resources. This is fine in most cases, but sometimes Windows doesn't give the application enough resources to complete the task it's performing. If this is the case, lowering the Idle Sensitivity setting gives the application the resources it needs at the expense of other applications running on the system at the time.

The Warn If Still Active check box in the Termination group displays a message if you try to terminate the DOS application window without ending the program first. Usually, you'll want to keep this checked to prevent potential data loss from a premature application termination.

Another performance enhancement, albeit a small one, is the Fast Pasting check box. You should usually keep this box checked so that Windows can use a high-speed method of pasting information into your DOS application. The only time you should change this is if data is damaged during transition when you're using the fast paste mode.

The final group on the page controls the use of Ctrl+*key* combinations under Windows 2000. Checking a box in the Windows Shortcut Keys group enables Windows to use that key combination. Unchecking a box allows the application to use the key combination. Obviously, you'll want to keep as many key combinations checked as possible. The only time you really need to change these settings is if the application needs them for some purpose and you can't change the application's settings.

On Your Own

Make a list of tasks that are repetitive and that you must frequently accomplish. Then see if you can record macros for any of them.

Find a DLL for one of the smaller applications installed on your machine. Use the procedure in Chapter 8, "Customizing Windows 2000 for Maximum Productivity," for viewing the contents of files to determine which DLLs and other system files this application needs to work. After you make the list, see whether other applications require the same files. You might be surprised by what you find. Windows 2000 reuses a lot of the same files.

Try fiddling with the many and various DOS properties, to see the effect and to choose settings that please you and are more efficient than the defaults.

Exploiting Your Hardware

Chapter 16, "Exploiting Your Software," examined some of the things you can do to maximize the effectiveness of your software. This chapter focuses on getting the most out of your hardware.

Installing and Deleting Devices

Windows 2000 usually detects all the hardware on your machine during setup. Windows 2000 now provides what Windows 95/98 have had for some time: Plug and Play support. Chapter 4, "Installing Windows 2000 Professional: A Setup Primer," covers this entire process. That chapter also covers some of the things you can do if Windows 2000 does not detect your hardware, so I won't repeat that discussion here. What happens if you install a new piece of hardware *after* installing Windows 2000, however? And what do you do with old devices? These are the topics I cover in this section of the chapter. I also outline troubleshooting procedures you can follow if Windows does not act as expected.

Installing Printers

Before you can use a printer, you have to install and configure it. I used to hate doing this because it seemed as if every printer was just different enough to make life difficult. It was a nice surprise to see how easy this process is under Windows 2000. This section provides the details required to install a printer. It also includes some productivity tips.

Even if you don't have any printers installed on your system, you'll have a Printers folder in the Control Panel. At a minimum, this folder will contain an applet that enables you to install a new printer. I'll show you how to install a local printer in this section; look at the next section for tips on connecting to a remote printer. We'll take a look at some configuration details in this section as well. Here are the general steps for setting up a printer:

1. Choose the Start, Settings, Printers command to open the Printers folder. You might see one or more printers already installed in the folder, along with the Add Printer icon.

2. Double-click the Add Printer icon. Click Next. You'll see the dialog box shown in Figure 17.1. In this dialog box, you have the choice to connect to an existing printer on the network or to use a local printer.

FIGURE 17.1

This wizard makes it easy (usually) to install a new printer. Try the automatic detection feature first.

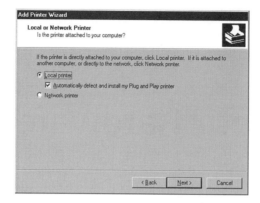

3. Select the Local Printer option to install a local connection; also choose the Plug and Play option. Click Next. After a brief pause—while Windows searches for a printer plugged into your local computer, you either see a message that no printer was detected or that your printer was found. If the printer is Plug and Play capable, you're done. The installation is automatic. If not, you see the message shown in Figure 17.2.

FIGURE 17.2

An incorrectly attached or non–Plug and Play printer produces this result.

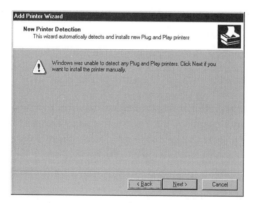

4. If Plug and Play doesn't see your printer, click Next. Usually, you'll see the dialog box shown in Figure 17.3, which asks you to select a printer port. In most cases, you'll see only the local ports if you haven't used a network printer port before. You can click the Create a New Port button to add a network port if needed. I'll show you how to add a network printer port in the section titled "Configuration." We'll also look at a problem with using network ports with Windows 2000.

> **Tip:** You can create multiple connections for one printer. I usually add a file connection, at minimum, so that I can delay printing until later (select File from the Use the following port ListBox in the "Select the Printer Port" page of the Add Printer wizard. A fax connection is also a good idea for supporting applications that don't provide a fax connection. (Note the Fax icon next to the Add New Printer icon in the Printers folder. It works automatically with most applications—displaying a Fax queue when you click it.)

FIGURE 17.3

Choose your printer port here—it's almost always LPT1.

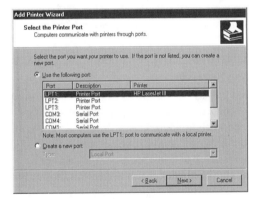

5. Select a port. Click Next to continue.

6. If you haven't yet defined the printer, you see a list of manufacturers and their printer models.

7. Click Next. Windows 2000 asks whether you want to keep the same driver. Click Keep Existing Driver if you want.

8. Click Next. You see the Name Your Printer dialog box. You have two decisions to make in this dialog box. The first is what to name the printer. The Add Printer Wizard usually suggests something appropriate, and you can accept this name if you intend to create only one copy of the printer. You might want to use a more descriptive name if you plan to install multiple configurations of the same printer, however. The second decision is whether to make this the default printer. Windows applications use the default printer unless you specifically select a different one. You should make the default printer the one you'll use most often.

9. Click Next to continue. You should see a dialog box that's interesting from several perspectives. The main purpose of this dialog box is to enable you to choose between shared and nonshared mode for this printer. Sharing your printer means that a certain number of processing cycles will always be used to monitor the printer port, thus reducing your machine's efficiency. Here's the interesting part of this situation: Suppose you installed a printer but used a network connection rather than a local port in step 5. That means the printer isn't attached to the local machine; it's actually attached to some other workstation Professional on the network, or it's a standalone printer with its own IP address. As you'll notice, this dialog box enables you to select more than one print driver type—it includes Windows 95 and other versions of Windows 2000. Windows 95 does not include this feature, so if you share a printer connected to a Windows 95 machine, you need to install a driver on every machine that uses it. On the other hand, you could create a connection to that workstation through a Windows 2000 Professional machine. Now, all the print processing will go through the Windows 2000 Professional instead of taking place locally. The processing burden for all the local machines is reduced, the amount of time spent looking for the right print driver decreases, and you'll have only one print driver to update when you change printers.

10. Click Next. If you chose to share the printer, you see a dialog box where you can specify location and comment.

11. Click Next to display the Print Test Page dialog box. I always send a test page to a local printer connected to an actual port. It makes little sense to print a test page for a file connection. Unless you already have your network connection configured, you'll need to test network printer connections later. Choose whether you want to print a test page, and click Next. You then see a summary of all the settings you've specified. Click Finish to complete the installation.

12. Windows 2000 displays a status dialog box as it copies any needed files to your drive. When it completes this task, you see the appropriate icon in the Printers folder. Double-clicking this icon enables you to view the current print jobs. Right-clicking enables you to see the context menu.

When Plug and Play Goes Well

If you choose to let Plug and Play do its thing, you can avoid most of the steps in the preceding printer setup section. When you first plug in a new device such as a new printer, Windows 2000 can detect that something *alien* is now attached to the machine. It automatically launches a Plug and Play routine. When this happens, you'll see the dialog box on the left in Figure 17.4.

It's thrilling to see the Found New Hardware message shown in Figure 17.4. You then know that you're probably in good hands and that the *Play* part of Plug and Play will most likely work.

FIGURE 17.4

If Plug and Play finds your new printer, you'll see this Found New Hardware message.

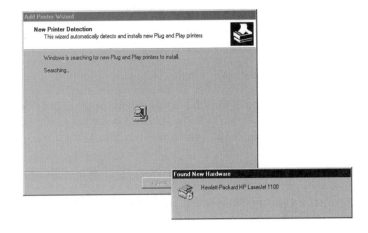

After whirring a bit, Plug and Play then displays the dialog box shown in Figure 17.5.

FIGURE 17.5

Print this test page and you're home free.

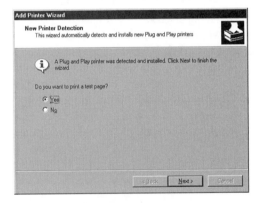

Choose to print the test page, as shown in Figure 17.5, and click Next. You then see the message displayed in Figure 17.6.

FIGURE 17.6

Once a test page leaves your printer—all is well. The new printer is up and running.

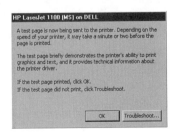

As you can see, installing a printer isn't difficult. The next section takes you through the process of connecting to a network port. After that, we'll discuss adding a port and then review the overall configuration procedure.

> **Tip:** If you *don't* see a test page or if attempts to print from your word proces-
> sor, Notepad, or some other source fail, try going to DOS (the command
> prompt) and typing this:
>
> `Dir > LPT1`
>
> If this prints a directory, your problem is most likely the driver (contact Microsoft
> or go to your printer's Web site to see if there's an updated printer driver for
> your printer). If the DOS test fails to print anything, turn off all power and
> reseat your printer cable on both ends. Then try printing again. If it still fails, try
> using a new cable.

Installing a Network Printer Connection

You should use the following procedure if you want to connect to a printer server on a network. In this case, Windows 2000 looks for another computer that contains the drivers and services it needs. You can get around the driver requirement. A Windows 95/98 workstation won't contain Windows 2000 driver files, for example, but you can still make an attachment using this procedure. Windows 2000 detects that the drivers it needs aren't available on the server and asks you to supply them. Usually, you would use this procedure in a server environment. Look at the services part of the equation: Windows 2000 also requires the remote workstation to process printing requests. A Windows 95/98 workstation can perform that part of the task. You need to share the printer on the remote workstation before Windows 2000 sees it and uses it. The following procedure takes you through the steps for adding a network printer connection to your system:

1. Choose the Start, Settings, Printers command to open the Printers folder. You might see one or more printers already installed in the folder, along with the Add Printer applet.

2. Double-click the Add Printer applet. Click Next. You'll then see the dialog box where you determine whether you want to connect to an existing printer on the network or use a local printer.

3. Click Next. You'll see a Locate Your Printer dialog box that lets you type a printer name or URL.

4. Select the Name option and then click Next. Now the Browse For Printer dialog box displays, as shown in Figure 17.7.

5. Select the desired printer and then click Next. A Printer Properties dialog box appears. The contents of this dialog box change to match the capabilities of the selected printer. This is your chance to make any local changes to the printer setup. In most cases, you should leave the settings alone.

FIGURE 17.7

This dialog box enables you to connect to a printer server.

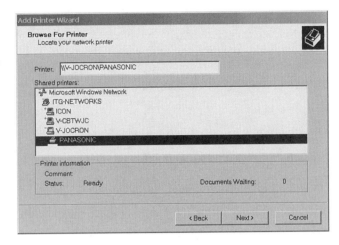

6. Click OK to clear the Printer Properties dialog box. You'll now see the final Add Printer Wizard dialog box.

7. Click Finish to clear the final Add Printer Wizard screen. Windows 2000 displays a status dialog box as it copies any needed files to your drive. After it completes this task, you see the appropriate icon in the Printers folder. Double-clicking this icon enables you to view the current print jobs. Right-clicking enables you to see the context menu. You should notice a big difference between this printer icon and any local printers in your Printers folder. Windows 2000 uses the network name for the printer rather than a pseudonym like you saw in the preceding procedure.

Tip: I should mention here that it's important to look at both the vendor documentation and any associated README files when setting up a printer. In some cases, you have to do some pretty weird things to get a printer to work right, especially if you're accessing it through a network connection. For example, my Epson Stylus 500 inkjet printer (which is connected to my NetWare file server) required me to open the Spool Manager 3 utility and check the Use Print Manager for This Port option. In addition, this particular network setup won't work unless the Spool to Local Printer option is checked. Unfortunately, absolutely none of this information appears in the vendor documentation—it only appears in the README file. You'll find the Spool settings by opening the Printers folder in Control Panel, then choosing File, Server Properties. Print Manager automatically opens when you start a print job.

Adding a Port

Adding a network port is very easy under Windows 2000. All you need to do is right-click the background of the Printer folder, choose Server Properties, and then select the Ports tab. Windows 2000 also enables you to access this page by right-clicking any installed printer icon, choosing Properties, and selecting the Ports tab. You should see a dialog box similar to the one shown in Figure 17.8. You can perform three tasks in this dialog box: adding, deleting, and configuring a printer port.

Figure 17.8

The Ports page of the Print Server Properties dialog box enables you to add, delete, and configure the ports your printer attaches to.

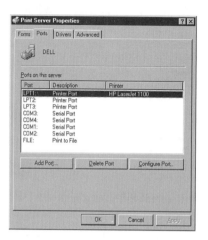

Clicking the Add Port button displays the Printer Ports dialog box. You can choose from two types of ports by selecting one from the Available Port Types list box: Local Port or Standard TCP/IP Port. You also can add third-party ports by clicking the New Port Type button. Windows 2000 asks you to supply a disk containing the MONITOR.INF file. The vendor should supply this file along with any drivers you'll need. The serviceability of the monitors varies according to the capabilities of the printer, the print server, or the network it supports. The default PJL Language Monitor gets its functionality from the PJL-MON.DLL file in your SYSTEM32 folder. It enables you to create local and digital network ports.

Let's begin with a quick look at the local option. Note that the following example is somewhat specific to a particular printer, so you may not see precisely what's described here during your installation. All you need to do in this case is highlight Local Port in the Available Port Types list box and click New Port. You'll see a simple dialog box where you just type the name of the local port you want to add and click OK to complete the action. Click Close in the Printer Ports dialog box, and you'll see a new local port added to the Ports on This Server list box in the Printer Server Properties dialog box.

Adding a TCP/IP port is a little more work than adding a local port. A wizard appears, and you must supply a name or IP address. This highlights some network identification fields for the port. Normally, you need to provide the network's name for the port and an address. The final piece of information you need to supply is a local name for the port in the Port Name field at the bottom of the dialog box.

After you configure your new port, click OK to close the dialog box. Click Close in the Printer Ports dialog box to complete the action. If you've filled out all the fields correctly, you'll see a new network port added to the Ports on This Server list box in the Printer Server Properties dialog box.

Configuration

Configuring your printer should be the next step after you assign it to a port. Most of the settings control the appearance of the output and the features the printer provides to the user. In some cases, a configuration option also affects the speed of printing. I'll point out the kinds of choices you'll be making as you proceed through this section.

Opening the Printer Properties dialog box is as simple as right-clicking the Printer icon and choosing the Properties option from the context menu. The first page you'll always see is the General page, shown in Figure 17.9. All this page contains is the printer name, a comment that other users can use to identify the printer, a location, and the name of the driver. You'll also find two buttons on this page: Printing Preferences and Print Test Page. The Comment field can contain any information you want, such as the days and times the printer is available for use. You shouldn't make any temporary comments because this field is copied only once to other machines that need to use the printer. In other words, the comment is permanent and won't change as you change the comment on your local machine. The Location field indicates where the printer is physically located. It appears on the Properties page for other Windows 2000 workstations and servers.

Clicking the Printing Preferences button is useful if you want to set defaults for the page orientation, the size of items such as letters, and the printing quality. You can click the Print Test Page button to test the connection to your printer at any time. Printing Preferences is also an option on the context menu for each defined printer (right-click a printer's icon in the Printers folder). You can also see the Preferences by choosing Sharing from the context menu.

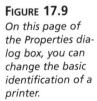

Figure 17.9

On this page of the Properties dialog box, you can change the basic identification of a printer.

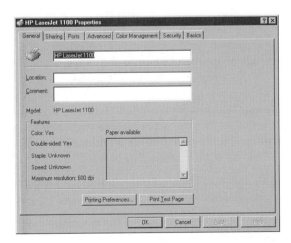

The Sharing page enables you to share the printer with other people. It contains two radio buttons. Selecting the Shared option enables other people to use the printer. You must provide a share name. If you share a printer, Windows 2000 adds a hand to its icon. This shows that the printer is shared, and it helps prevent any confusion over local and network resources.

> **Tip:** Sharing reduces your spooling options. In addition, using a shared printer imposes other speed penalties on the local user. I always create a second printer that isn't shared. This way, I get the best of both worlds: a shared printer for other people to use, and a nonshared printer that's configured specifically for my needs.

We've already discussed the Ports page of the Printer Properties dialog box, so let's take a look at the Advanced page. You can work with three different areas on this page. The Priority section is first. You can determine how much of a load a printer puts on the workstation by changing the printer's priority. Obviously, a high priority spools print jobs quickly, but it also noticeably affects the operation of any foreground tasks on the machine.

The second area determines when your printer will actually output data to its spool area of the hard disk (like a cache). The default setting is *spooling*; however, you can choose to avoid spooling and print directly to the printer. There are two main methods of printing. Spooling the data to the hard drive enables an application to finish its part of the job faster (you get control of your word processor instantly). The fastest way to spool is to send all the data to the hard drive first and then start printing it. That way, the print job won't have to take turns with the print spooler for processor cycles.

The last section of this page contains four check boxes. Enabling the Hold Mismatched Documents check box tells Windows 2000 not to print any jobs that are potentially damaged in some way, thus reducing the amount of time wasted with print jobs that it can't complete. Enabling the second check box, Print Spooled Documents First, tells Windows 2000 to ignore any print jobs that require dedicated printer access (those that you sent directly to the printer) in favor of jobs spooled by an application to disk. Enabling the third check box tells Windows 2000 to keep all the spooled print jobs when it finishes. That way, you can always resend a print job that was damaged in some way. The Enable Advanced Printing Features option (which is checked by default) controls features such as Page Order, Booklet Printing, and Pages Per Sheet, which are available under what's called *metafile spooling*. If you experience problems with your printer, try turning this check box off and see if that cures the difficulties.

The Printing Defaults button lets you change this printer's default document properties (orientation, page size, and so on) for *all* users who share this printer.

The Print Processor button allows you to switch to a different processor as well as select a different data type (EMF, RAW and so on). Normally you'll leave this setting alone.

The Separator Page button lets you define a feature that's sometimes useful when more than one person uses a printer. It sends a page containing your name and other identifying information to the printer before it actually prints your document. Using a separator page wastes one piece of paper for each print job, but it can make sorting through the printouts a lot easier when they all fill up a bin together.

The Security page is similar to those found on Properties dialog boxes throughout Windows 2000—it allows you, if you have the proper permission, to deny others access to the printer. If you have this ability, you doubtless know what to do with it. Deny everyone! (Just kidding.)

The final tab depends on your printer. Some printers show a tab called Device Settings, which lists Tray Assignments, Font Substitution Table data, and Installable Options. Another printer shows a tab named Basics, and it's a pretty strange page. You see disabled sections called Quick Sets, Page Protection, and Orientation, along with the Installed Memory and Copy input boxes, as shown in Figure 17.10.

FIGURE 17.10
This odd page displays, but prevents you from changing, a few elementary default settings.

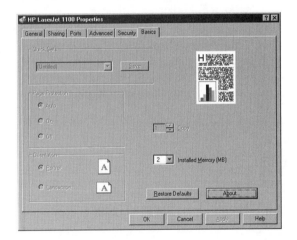

Point and Print

Point and Print is a Windows 2000 feature that enables you to perform several tasks. The most significant job it does is to simplify remote printer installation. All you need to do to install a remote printer from a Windows 95/98, Windows 2000, or NetWare network location is drag the icon from My Network Places into the Printers folder. Windows 2000 takes care of the rest. It might ask you to insert the CD-ROM so that it can load the proper drivers on your machine. Other than that, installation is as close to automatic as you can get.

Installing Graphics Adapters

Windows is filled with graphics; there isn't any doubt you'll need a good graphics adapter installation program to use the operating system. Of course, installing a new display adapter or monitor isn't the end of the process—it's just the beginning. You'll need to install software in the form of drivers as well, and that's what this section is all about. Chapter 5, "Exploring the Interface," contains a complete description of the five pages of configuration settings for the Display Properties dialog box, so I won't discuss them again here.

Adjusting Display Adapter Settings

If your adapter is Plug and Play compatible, Windows 2000 will install it automatically; if not, a standard driver will be supplied so at least you can see things. Manually installing a new display adapter driver can be very easy. Follow these steps:

1. Right-click the desktop and choose the Properties option. You should see the Display Properties dialog box.

2. Select the Settings page. Click the Advanced button and then click the Adapter tab. You'll see the dialog box shown in Figure 17.11. You should notice several features in this dialog box. First, it tells you the chip type and the DAC type (Digital-to-Analog Converter). You also see how much high-speed memory the card has. Click the List All Modes button to see additional data, as shown in Figure 17.11.

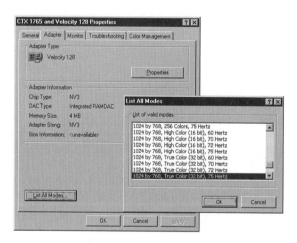

FIGURE 17.11

The Adapter page and the Modes list show you what your video system is capable of, regarding screen size, refresh rate, and color.

3. If you make any changes to the settings for size, refresh, or color, click the OK button. Windows might ask you to insert disks or a CD-ROM as it installs the new adapter. It also asks whether you want to restart your machine to make the changes permanent. Click Yes to restart your machine.

Configuring Modems

Communication is a major part of the job these days. It used to be that you could take care of everything with the office fax and a few phone calls. Today, a lot of people can't take the time to use the office fax; they need one close by to take care of their needs. The amount of electronic "paper" passing hands these days is amazing. A lot of people are busier in other ways, too. Playing telephone tag isn't fun, especially when you can leave a message for the person on email and expect a response later that day. And, of course, there's the pervasive info-weather that's always available on the Internet. Goodbye BBS, goodbye online services. The Internet has become the premier source of information for many people. I can usually get an answer to a networking- or application-related question far more quickly by going online than I could if I called a vendor support line. The differences are the fast search engines and the measureless amount of knowledge the Internet provides.

We've all also gotten used to downloading email or Web pages in the background—while using our word processor or some other application at the same time. Configuring your machine for optimum performance when using background communication isn't hard; it just takes a little time. You need to try a setting, communicate a little to see its effect, and then tune it a little more as necessary. Unlike other tuning tips I've presented in this chapter, there's no quick-and-easy way to tune your communications programs. The problem is that every machine is slightly different, as is every modem and every communications program that uses the modem.

Tuning Your Modem

To tune your modem settings, open the Control Panel and double-click the Phone and Modem Options icon. Click the Modems tab. Right-click your modem and then choose Properties from the context menu. You'll see a dialog box similar to the one shown in Figure 17.12.

FIGURE 17.12

Use this Properties dialog box to adjust various aspects of your modem.

In the General tab, you can adjust the speaker volume and specify the maximum speed your modem is capable of for accepting data *from applications* (not sending or getting data over the phone, for example). Figure 17.12 also shows an area called Dial Control with a single check box offering the option "Wait for dial tone before dialing." If your modem has trouble recognizing the dial tone, try turning this option off.

> **Tip:** Note that the Maximum Port Speed list displays the highest speed your modem can achieve when interacting *with your computer.* (This is not the maximum speed it communicates over the Internet or over other modem-to-modem connections—many factors can retard that speed.) For the greatest efficiency, choose the highest speed in this drop-down list that doesn't cause problems.

Click the Diagnostics tab to get technical information about (and test) the modem. If you're experiencing problems with your modem and you contact the manufacturer, you might be asked to use this page. Finally, the Advanced tab allows you to manually specify initialization commands (see your modem manual), or you can click the Change Default Preferences button to adjust the port speed, protocol, compression, and flow control. Furthermore, you can set how long to wait before canceling a call if you can't connect and how long to wait before disconnecting after a period of idleness (no activity). If your modem supports data compression, generally you should use it: This can boost your effective transfer rate as much as four times the usual rate. This Change Default Preferences button also offers an Advanced tab of its own, which shows Hardware Settings. The Advanced Port Settings buttons permit you to adjust the transmit and receive buffers. Normally, you'll leave both at their high settings for maximum speed, but if you're having problems with your connection, you can try lower settings.

> **Tip:** Sometimes data compression can actually hurt the efficiency of your transmission. Certain types of Telnet connections fall into this category, as do some BBS calls in which the host modem does not support your modem's protocols. If you're having trouble maintaining a connection or the data transfer rate isn't as high as you expected, try turning off data compression to see whether there's any improvement.

Configuring Ports

Ports provide the means for the processor and other devices to communicate with the peripheral hardware on your machine. Any data that a device requires to work goes through the port. Think of a port as the mailbox and the data as the mail. If everyone in town had the same address, the mail carrier would never effectively deliver the mail. It would all get jammed in the same box. The same idea holds true for your computer. If two devices use the same address, the computer won't know where to send the data.

A port conflict does more than just annoy the user; it can cause system instability or a malfunction of some type. The user might not be able to use part of the system or might experience "the slows" as the system tries to figure out which device it's supposed to use. A system with fully exploited hardware lacks any kind of port conflict. Each device has its own port to use.

Fortunately, there's an easy way to get rid of port conflicts. In Control Panel, double-click the Administrative Tools icon and the Computer Management icon; then click Device Manager in the left pane of the Computer Management dialog box. You'll see a list of your ports in the right pane. Double-click any of the ports, and you'll see the Properties dialog box for that port. On the General tab, click the Troubleshooter button.

A browser-style window opens (similar to the Windows 2000 Help window). You see advice in the right pane, and perhaps some hyperlinks to Windows utilities that can help solve your conflict. In some cases, you'll see a list of option buttons asking you to click the one that best describes the problem you're having.

The advice and hyperlinks you see will depend on whatever problem you have. One typical message is: `Device Manager Error Code 29. The device was disabled by a user through the BIOS setup program, or it has been disabled by the computer's BIOS because it is not needed in the current configuration.` Another message you may see is: `Is there a box with resource settings on the Resources tab? Checking the Resource tab for the device can help determine the type of resource conflict.`

Standard Port

If the Troubleshooter doesn't help solve a port configuration problem, try changing an I/O port in the following example. Communication is the name of the game in your computer. For communication to occur, there must be some way to exchange information. In the PC, the physical part of the communications path is called an *input/output* (I/O) *port*. If you want to send data from one area of the machine to another, your application must first tell the computer which I/O port (or address) to send it to. (I discussed part of this process earlier in this chapter when I examined hardware installation.) Usually, you don't need to change these settings, but sometimes you do. For example, if you have a board in your system that allows more than one setting and it happens to occupy the same address as a board that does not, you can change the address of the flexible board as needed.

The following procedure takes you through the process of changing an I/O port for a sound card on your machine:

1. In the Computer Management windows, click Device Manager to display the devices in your machine in the right pane.
2. Next to Sound, video and game controllers, click the plus sign (+) to display the list of devices it contains.

3. Right-click your sound board (audio card) and click Properties from the context menu. Next, click the Resources tab. Notice that this dialog box does not have the Use Automatic Settings check box enabled. You want to leave this box checked; however, when changing settings, you will need to clear it (letting Windows 2000 manage the settings for your equipment is always a good idea). This particular dialog box also contains some diagnostic information.

4. Disable the Use Automatic Settings check box. This should enable the Change Setting button and the Setting Based On drop-down list box.

5. Click the down arrow to access the Setting Based On list box. You'll see a list of basic configurations.

6. Try each setting in turn to see whether one will enable you to resolve the port conflict. Windows 2000 alerts you to any conflicts with registered devices. The error message tells you exactly which device you're conflicting with. This enables you to change that device's settings, if necessary, to resolve the conflict. Obviously, you'll want to keep the number of changes to an absolute minimum. The more you change the Windows 2000 setup, the greater your chances are of introducing unforeseen new conflicts.

7. If you try all the basic configurations offered and none of them work, reset the Settings Based On drop-down list box to its original setting. Otherwise, click OK twice to save the setting; then shut down and reboot your machine to make the new setting active.

FIGURE 17.13

Change port settings from the Resources tab.

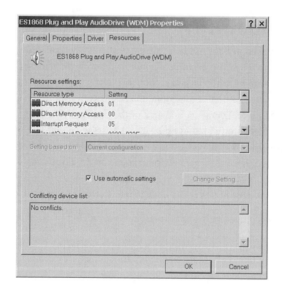

This procedure isn't limited to port settings. You can use it to configure any hardware setting. Windows 2000 won't enable you to change some settings. If you try to change one of these settings, Windows 2000 displays the appropriate error message. In most cases, a hardware limitation rather than a problem with the driver prevents you from changing a setting.

Serial Port

The serial port offers a variety of configuration options that go beyond address-conflict resolution. Several options control both the speed of the port and its compatibility with software. In the Device Manager, you select the port you want to change. You access it through the Computer Management window as described earlier, or from the System Control Panel applet, Hardware tab. Choose Start, Settings, Control Panel and then double-click the System icon. Click the Hardware tab and then click the Device Manager button. Open the Ports category and double-click the serial (or communications) port you want to change.

There's another way to set the serial port parameters. When you're using the Direct Cable Connection program provided with Windows 2000, you'll want to reset these settings to Maximum. Some users will miss this particular bit of irony because the utility never asks you to set the port settings. They just assume that the Direct Cable Connection program uses the maximum settings available. Experience says otherwise, however. You can actually slow data transfers from your notebook to a crawl by failing to observe this little "gotcha."

Windows 3.x provides all these serial port settings, as do most DOS applications. The one area where Windows 2000 rises above its predecessors is in the way it handles advanced universal asynchronous receiver transmitter (UART) chips. A UART contains the intelligence of the serial port, and some of the newer models contain features that allow better performance in a multitasking environment. It's this support that lets Windows 2000 provide a higher level of support for background communications than you might expect.

In the serial port's Properties dialog box, click the Port Settings tab. Notice that this dialog box contains several drop-down list boxes and an Advanced button. The list boxes control the current port settings. In the Advanced Settings dialog box, Windows 2000 automatically enables the Use FIFO buffers check box if it detects the proper port. This option is available only on the 16550 UART. Attempting to use it with an older 8250 UART will result in lost data. On the Resources tab of the port's Properties dialog box, you can change the I/O Port Address and IRQ settings for the port.

Before I go much further, I want to discuss the differences between certain UARTs. Earlier UARTs could store only one character at a time. This meant that the CPU had to retrieve that character immediately; otherwise, the next character the UART received would overwrite it. This is what people mean when they say their port dropped a character. It means that the CPU couldn't respond fast enough and the UART overwrote a character in its buffer as a result. Forcing the CPU to attend to the needs of the UART is fine in a single-tasking system such as DOS, but it isn't all that efficient in a multitasking environment such as Windows. After UART vendors realized that the older UARTs were a bottleneck when used in a multitasking environment, they started making new UARTs with a FIFO (first in, first out) buffer. The FIFO buffer can store up to 16 characters, giving the CPU time to complete whatever it was doing and then respond to the needs of the UART.

Parallel Port

The parallel port offers just one configuration setting as far as Windows 2000 is concerned: the Configure LPT Port dialog box. You access it through the Print Server Properties dialog box. Choose Start, Settings, Printers, right-click your printer's icon, and click Properties. Click the Ports tab and then select your LPT port and click the Configure Port button. As you can see, the parallel port configuration consists of setting a timeout interval. I usually maintain the default setting unless the port captures a network connection that needs more time to react. This transmission retry specification defines how long, in seconds, Windows 2000 will wait to notify you that the printer isn't responding. If you often send items to be printed but then must turn on the printer and wait 60 seconds for it to warm up, you might want to set this to a delay longer than the default 90 seconds—to give yourself time to run over and turn the machine on.

Configuring Your Mouse

A mouse is a necessity when using Windows 2000. Some tasks are difficult or impossible to perform through the keyboard alone.

Standard Mouse Configuration

Just as you should configure your keyboard for optimum performance (described next), you should configure your mouse as well. To do this, open the Mouse Properties dialog box by double-clicking the Mouse icon in the Control Panel. You'll see a dialog box similar to the one shown in Figure 17.14.

There are many ways to modify your mouse's behavior. You can switch between left- and right-handedness (this option reverses the behaviors of the two mouse buttons), and also specify that you want to move from double-clicking to single-clicking to activate applications, open folders, and trigger all the other actions that usually require a double-click. This is my preference—try it, you might like kissing double-clicking goodbye. (This same feature is available from the Tools, Folder Options menu in Windows Explorer.)

If you're *still* using double-clicking, you can try to find a comfortable timing of the two clicks by adjusting the slider at the bottom of this Buttons property page.

Figure 17.14

Fine-tune mouse behavior on this page.

The Pointers tab enables you to change the mouse pointers used to indicate specific events. In addition to the standard cursors that previous versions of Windows provided, Windows 2000 provides a few fancy cursors, such as reptiles. In addition to the static cursors, Windows 2000 also provides some cursors that move.

The upper section of this page enables you to save and load various mouse schemes. If you think of a mouse scheme in the same way you do a color scheme under previous versions of Windows, you'll have the right idea. Use the list box to select a previously saved scheme. Clicking the Save As button displays a dialog box that you can use to enter the name of a new scheme.

> **Tip:** Windows 2000 provides a wealth of mouse pointers, including some extra-large ones. The extra-large pointers are actually designed for use with some of the Accessibility options. However, they also come in handy on laptops, where seeing the mouse pointer can be difficult, as well as in presentations, where a larger-than-normal cursor helps you make your point with overhead projectors and such.

The lower section of the Pointers page contains the actual mouse pointers. The purpose of each pointer is self-explanatory. To change a cursor, highlight it and click the Browse button. Windows displays a list of cursors in the CURSOR folder (found within the main Windows 2000 folder). All you need to do is double-click the cursor you want. Windows replaces the current cursor with the one you selected. Notice that this dialog box also displays a preview of the cursor. Any animated cursors appear to move within the preview box, so you can see how they'll look when you use them in an application. If you ever select a cursor by accident and want to return to the default setting, click the Use Default button at the bottom of the Pointers page.

The Motion tab in the Mouse Properties dialog box affects the pointer's speed, acceleration, and snap-to settings. The pointer's Speed option determines how the mouse cursor tracks your hand movements with the slider at the top of the page. Setting the speed too high can cause jerky cursor movement and make it difficult to control some operations, such as drawing. Setting the speed too low causes you to make a large movement with the mouse to get a small movement onscreen. Acceleration changes the rate of speed of the pointer onscreen, relative to the speed of your hand when moving the mouse. This can be a valuable tool—I like to leave it at the default, low setting. The SnapTo option automatically moves the mouse pointer to the default button of a dialog box such as OK or Apply. That way, you can just click the mouse to choose the default option. I find this option frightening and always avoid it. There is also a final Hardware tab that lists the actual mouse and provides Troubleshoot and Properties buttons.

Keyboard

The Keyboard Properties dialog box has three tabs of selections that you can make regarding setup. Double-click the Keyboard icon in the Control Panel. In the first tab, Speed, you can change the repeat delay. The Repeat Delay setting adjusts how long the keyboard waits before it starts repeating keys. Setting this value too low could force you to undo a lot of excess keystrokes. You'll probably find this more of a problem at the end of the day. However, I prefer it very short. In fact, if the delay could be eliminated entirely, that would be fine with me!

The Repeat Rate setting adjusts how fast the characters repeat when you hold down a key. Setting a slightly lower rate will enable you to control repeated keys better. Microsoft thoughtfully provided a test area that you can use to check the combination of settings. Make sure you actually try the keyboard settings for a while before you make big changes in the settings. I found that even small changes affect the way the keyboard reacts. Again, though, as an experienced typist/writer, I would prefer an even faster rate than the fastest offered by Microsoft. You can *try* adjusting these settings in the Registry, but you'll find that boosting the setting for KeyboardSpeed, for example, from the default 31 to, say, 99 has absolutely no effect. Also, the KeyboardDelay setting is already 0 or 1, although there is a noticeable delay even at 0. (You'll find this Registry entry at HKEY_CURRENT_USER, Control Panel, Keyboard, but see the cautions at the start of Chapter 10 before fiddling with the Registry.)

Use the Cursor Blink Rate setting to change how often the edit cursor blinks per second. Some people like a very fast rate, and other people find that distracting and like it a bit slower. You'll want to use a slower rate on portables than you would on your desktop machine because it takes displays on these machines a little longer to react. A setting that works well on your desktop machine might make the cursor disappear on your laptop.

The Input Locales tab is discussed in the next section, and the Hardware tab contains only a description of the keyboard and a Troubleshoot and Properties button.

Multilingual Support

I partially covered the Multilingual Support feature in past chapters. More of the world is using Windows today, so it's not too surprising to see Windows come with a variety of language options. I was a little surprised by the fact that this language support is at least partially built into every copy of Windows. No longer do you have to perform strange rituals and manually edit your system files to get the proper level of language support. Windows 2000 has it built right in.

Installing a New Language

Multilingual support under Windows 2000 is a happy fact. Installing a new keyboard language is as simple as a few clicks. Take a look at what you need to do to install a new language on your machine:

1. Open the Control Panel. Double-click the Keyboard applet and select the Input Locales tab. Notice that English might be the only language listed in the Input Locales field. This field also provides other information you can use to determine the installed language type. In this case, it tells you the type of English (United States) and the keyboard layout (United States).

2. Click the Add button. It's important to consider which version of a language to choose. The English example is a good one. I currently have United States English installed. The selections for other forms of English might require different keyboard layouts. Pressing Shift+4 could produce a pound symbol rather than a dollar sign, for example. The choice of language also affects the way Windows makes assumptions about other setup needs. It affects the default selection for monetary and numeric formats, for example.

3. Click OK to complete the process. You should see a new language added to the Input Locales field. Completing this process also enables several other fields. You can now choose which Ctrl+*key* combination to use to switch between languages, for example. You can also choose whether to display the International icon on the taskbar. (I will show you how to use this icon later in this section.) There are actually two types of language switching: cycling through all your installed languages and switching to a particular language only. For cycling, you can't choose a Ctrl+*Any Key*; you must choose whether it's Ctrl+Shift or Left Alt+Shift. For particular languages, you can choose Ctrl+Shift or Left Alt+Shift, and a key of your choice. Note that you also have the ability to choose which of two methods turns off the Caps Lock key (on the Input Locales tab).

4. Choose a default language by highlighting it and then clicking the Set as Default button. You'll see the new default displayed with a check next to it.

5. You'll probably want to check the layout for your new language. Highlight the new language (I use German on my keyboard) and click the Properties button. The dialog box you'll see is a little deceptive. At first you might think that it's asking you to change the language again, but this isn't so. What it's asking you to change is your keyboard layout. Select a new layout to see for yourself.

6. Click OK to complete the process. In this case, I chose the Dvorak layout. Notice that the language remains the same; only the keyboard layout has changed. I'll use the Dvorak layout whenever I choose the German language from my list.

> **Note:** You might have noticed that this combination of language and layout provides the means to create a very customized keyboard layout. The folks at Microsoft call this *localization*. I call it a good idea for those of us who lived through the DOS code page nightmare. This elegant solution provides far greater flexibility than ever available in the past. If you need multilingual support, try the various options to see which setup is most comfortable.

7. Close the Keyboard Properties dialog box to complete the process. Windows might ask you to insert a disk or CD-ROM containing any files it requires. You can accomplish the same thing using the Apply button if you don't want to close the Keyboard Properties dialog box.

Changing your keyboard layout and language won't display prompts in the language you select. It affects only the way your keyboard reacts, and to some extent, it helps Windows 2000 provide better input in regard to other configuration selections.

Removing a Language

You'll probably encounter a situation in which you no longer require a specific keyboard layout. You might have needed to use a German layout for a while to type letters to another office, for example, but you don't need it any longer because that office closed. Whatever your reason for wanting to remove the language, Windows 2000 makes it easy. The following procedure shows you how:

> **Tip:** This would be a good time to use the procedures I showed you in Chapter 10, "Understanding the Windows 2000 Registry," for checking the filenames of the drivers used to support the language you want to remove. Windows 2000 won't remove these drivers, which means they'll clutter your hard drive until you decide to reinstall Windows 2000 from scratch—hopefully, a long time from now. Recording the filenames now, before you remove the name from the Input Locales page, means you'll be able to remove the driver files later. Make certain you shut down and reboot your machine first; otherwise, Windows 2000 will display an error message stating that the driver is in use.

1. Open the Control Panel. Double-click the Keyboard applet and select the Input Locales page.

2. You want to remove the German language support from your machine, so highlight that entry.

3. Click the Remove button.

4. Close the Keyboard Properties dialog box by clicking OK or Apply to complete the process.

Accessing a Language from the Taskbar

Whenever you have more than one language installed on your machine, Windows gives you the opportunity to automatically add the International icon to your taskbar.

You can use this icon in several ways. The first is to determine which language you're currently using. Each language has a two-character abbreviation. The taskbar is where this two-digit abbreviation is used.

A left-click on the International icon displays a list of languages currently installed on the machine. Notice that each entry is preceded by its two-digit abbreviation. This is one way to determine which language you're using if you forget what the abbreviation on the icon means. All you need to do to select a new language is click it, just like you would with any other menu. In addition to the list of languages installed, the indicator also shows what keyboard you're using in each language (if different from its default).

A right-click brings up a context menu. I was especially taken by the What's This? entry. It's apparent that no one at Microsoft thought the user would be able to figure out this icon for themselves. The associated help text is useful and could certainly help someone who's just starting to learn to use Windows 2000. I just wonder why Microsoft didn't include this help with the other icons for the sake of consistency, if for no other reason.

The Properties option of the context menu acts as you would expect. It takes you to the Keyboard Properties dialog box that we looked at earlier. Even though it automatically displays the Input Locales page, you can quickly switch to other pages as needed.

As with many of the other icons on the taskbar, you can also momentarily hold your mouse cursor over the International icon to get more information. Doing so displays the full name of the language you're currently using.

Access for Users with Disabilities

Windows 2000 provides special access features for people with disabilities. I gave you an overview of these options in Chapter 1, "Choosing Windows 2000." I also discussed some of the speed keys the Accessibility options provide in Chapter 8, "Customizing Windows 2000 for Maximum Productivity." I won't go over these details again here. What I will examine are the features and how you can use them to perhaps enhance productivity. The first thing you need to do to look at these features is open the Control Panel and double-click the Accessibility Options applet.

> **Tip:** In addition to the Accessibility features described in this chapter is Microsoft Active Accessibility, a set of operating system features that make it possible for third-party developers to add Accessibility features to their applications. These Accessibility features make it easier for people with disabilities to use the applications. Previous versions of Windows would only install the core Accessibility Option files if the user actually installed this feature. Unfortunately, this meant that a developer couldn't always depend on finding the feature installed, which reduced the number of applications that offered the Accessibility features. One example is video drawing operations using a new Display Device Interface (DDI) Redirector.

Special Keyboard Features

Windows provides three special keyboard features: StickyKeys, FilterKeys, and ToggleKeys. You'll find them on the Keyboard page of the Accessibility Properties dialog box, as shown in Figure 17.15. You can turn on any of these features by using the special key combinations that Microsoft provides.

All these features have one thing in common: They change the way the keyboard works independently of the keyboard driver. You must install the Accessibility Options feature to make them work.

FIGURE 17.15

Turn on any keyboard-accessibility features on this page.

Using StickyKeys

The StickyKeys feature comes in handy for a variety of purposes. It makes the Shift, Ctrl, and Alt keys act as toggle switches. Press one of these keys once and it becomes active. Press it a second time and it's turned off. I don't really use this feature a lot, but it does come in handy for a couple purposes.

One of the ways I use it is in graphics programs that require you to hold down the Ctrl key to select a group of items. It's kind of inconvenient to hold down the Ctrl key while you look around for objects to select. The StickyKeys feature alleviates this problem.

I also find that it's pretty handy when I want to type a lot of Alt+*key* combinations—for example, when I want to use the extended ASCII line-draw characters in a document. It's true that I could use the Character Map utility to do the same thing, but Character Map isn't always easy to access, and I might need only one or two characters.

Let's take a look at some of the options you can select. Click the Settings button to open the Settings for StickyKeys dialog box. The StickyKeys feature has several groups of settings. The first option, Keyboard Shortcut, lets you enable StickyKeys using the shortcut key. There really isn't any good reason to turn this off because it's unlikely that any application would use the same control key sequence.

The Options group contains two settings. Usually, the StickyKeys option works like a toggle. Checking the first box tells Windows to wait until you press the same control key twice before making it active.

The second check box is designed to enable two people to use the same keyboard. Pressing a control key and a noncontrol key at the same time turns off StickyKeys.

The Notification group also contains two settings. The first setting tells Windows to play a different sound for each unique control key that it makes active. This can keep you from activating a control key accidentally. The second option displays an icon on the taskbar so that you can control StickyKeys more easily. I usually select this option to make it easier for me to turn StickyKeys on and off.

Using FilterKeys

Do you ever find yourself making a lot of extra, accidental keystrokes at the end of a long day? I do. Sometimes, my words come out like "tthis" rather than "this." FilterKeys is a perfect solution to the problem of tired hands. I use it all the time near the end of the workday to filter out those extra keystrokes.

As with StickyKeys, you can adjust the way FilterKeys works by clicking the Settings button. The Settings for FilterKeys dialog box appears. Notice that the first option in this dialog box enables you to turn the shortcut key on and off. It works just like the same feature in StickyKeys. The Notification group at the bottom of the page should look familiar. The only difference is that rather than playing a sound, FilterKeys beeps when you activate it.

The Filter Options group enables you to select between two ways of filtering keystrokes. The first option filters keys that are pressed in rapid succession. This feature would filter the rapid typing of the extra *t* in the example I just mentioned. The Settings button displays a dialog box that enables you to select how long an interval must pass between the first and second times you press the same key. It also provides a field where you can test the setting. The second option in this group filters accidental key presses. You might press a key for a moment, not really meaning to. As with the StickyKeys option, clicking the Settings button takes you to a dialog box where you select how long you must press a key before Windows accepts it.

Using ToggleKeys

Ever start typing an email or message to someone, only to see later that you left the Caps Lock key on? It's time consuming to fix such a mistake, but you have to do it for formal documents and memos. A better solution is to be alerted each time you turn on one of the Lock keys. That's precisely what ToggleKeys does. It emits a tone every time you turn on the Caps Lock, Scroll Lock, or Num Lock key.

Special Accessibility Keyboard Shortcuts

The following table shows the keys to press to activate various accessibility features:

Table 17.1   Keyboard Shortcuts for Accessibility Features

Shortcut	Description
Left Alt+Left Shift+Num Lock	Holding down these three keys turns on the MouseKeys feature of the Accessibility options.
Left Alt+Left Shift+PrintScreen	Holding down these three keys turns on the High Contrast feature of the Accessibility options.
Num Lock (pressed for five seconds)	Holding down the Num Lock key for five seconds turns on the ToggleKeys feature of the Accessibility options.
Right Shift (pressed for eight seconds)	Holding down the Right Shift key for eight seconds turns on the FilterKeys feature of the Accessibility options.
Shift five times	Pressing the Shift key five times turns on the StickyKeys feature of the Accessibility options.
Windows+U	This key combination opens the Utility Manager where you can turn on the magnifier and the narrator disability features.

The Sound Tab

The Sound tab is helpful for people with hearing problems. It displays warnings when the system makes sounds. It can also tell applications to do the same, telling applications to display captions for any sounds that they make.

The Display Tab

This tab is helpful for people with vision problems: It uses a color scheme that features high-contrast graphics.

Special Mouse Settings

Have you ever been to the point of madness as you try to precisely position an object on a drawing screen using the mouse? It's difficult to do after a full day of drawing, especially if you aren't a graphics artist with the training and tools required to get the job done right. That's one of the reasons why some people sometimes resort to the MouseKeys feature. It enables you to use the arrow keys as a mouse. Instead of moving the mouse cursor with the mouse, you can move it with the arrow keys. Of course, this does not disable your mouse; it merely augments it.

MouseKeys has only one dialog box of settings. You access it by clicking the Settings button on the Mouse page. The first option, Keyboard Shortcut, lets you enable MouseKeys using the shortcut key. There really isn't any good reason to turn this off because it's unlikely that any application will use the same control key sequence.

The second group, Pointer Speed, is where you can optimize the performance of this particular feature. The first option enables you to set the fastest speed at which you can move the mouse cursor using the arrow keys. Set it to a slower speed to gain better control of the mouse cursor. Using a higher speed enables you to move around the display faster. The Acceleration setting determines how fast the cursor reaches full speed after you press it. Windows does not start the cursor off at full speed; it brings it there gradually. This enables you to make a small change without seeing the cursor take off toward the other side of the screen if you set the speed fairly high. The combination of these two settings determines just how much added control MouseKeys gives you over the cursor. Notice the check box in this group. Checking it gives you another option. Pressing Ctrl speeds up the mouse cursor; pressing Shift slows it down. You can use this option when you need a variety of speeds to get the job done.

The final group contains two settings. The radio button controls when MouseKeys is active. You must specify whether the Num Lock key should be on or off when you use MouseKeys. The choice you make depends on how you usually use the numeric keypad. The second option determines whether the MouseKeys icon appears on the taskbar. As with most of the special features that Windows provides, I keep this icon on the taskbar for quick access to this feature because it's more efficient.

The final tab, General, is in the wrong location: the General tab always comes first in a group of tabs. Anyway, on this page you can cause Accessibility features to turn off after a specified amount of idle time, notify the user by sound or message that a feature has been turned on, attach alternative input devices to the computer for people unable to use a standard keyboard, and cause these settings to be the logon default for this user or for all users.

The Onscreen Keyboard

An Onscreen Keyboard, shown in Figure 17.16, is a new Accessibility feature available in Windows 2000. It displays a virtual keyboard on the monitor for people with mobility impairments, making it easier to type using a pointing device or joystick.

FIGURE 17.16

The new Onscreen Keyboard makes typing easier when using a joystick or pointing device.

Turn on the Onscreen Keyboard feature from Start, Programs, Accessories, Accessibility.

The Magnifier and Narrator Utilities

Also available from the Start, Programs, Accessories, Accessibility menu are two useful assistants for people with vision challenges. The Magnifier opens a window that enlarges a portion of the screen (the portion under the mouse pointer or the button or other component that currently has the focus).

The Narrator feature provides a text-to-speech translation for people with vision difficulties. It reads both the user's typed input as well as the contents of the active window and menu items. Currently, it works with several Windows accessories and applications: Notepad, WordPad, Control Panel programs, Internet Explorer, the Windows 2000 desktop and setup.

> **Tip:** Anyone facing accessibility challenges should also run the Accessibility Wizard (Start, Programs, Accessories, Accessibility) and answer the questions to modify Windows 2000 to suit their needs. Provisions are made for various challenges including sight, hearing, and mobility.

On Your Own

Install several versions of your printer, each with different settings. Try each new installation for several weeks and see whether you notice the additional ease of use that several pseudo-printers can provide. Also try the various print settings to see whether you notice the variations in print speed and output quality.

Place a shortcut to your printer on the desktop and try the drag-and-drop method of printing. Just drag a file with your mouse pointer to the Printer icon and drop it. This is the easy way of sending output to the printer using the default setup. You might want to experiment to see which printer settings work best as a default setup for you.

Try all the different Accessibility options to see whether any of them provide features you can use. I provided suggestions on how you can use each feature in this chapter.

Install and try using the Dvorak keyboard layout. After you learn how to use this setup, you'll find that you can type more quickly with a lot less fatigue. This particular setup can also help you fight repetitive stress injuries such as carpal tunnel syndrome. Of course, nothing provides 100% protection. The Dvorak keyboard layout can't reverse years of abuse, but learning this new setup could help keep any problems you currently have from getting worse.

Go back to previous chapters—especially Chapter 8, "Customizing Windows 2000 for Maximum Productivity"—and practice using the various shortcuts I discussed with the Accessibility options turned on. Does using this feature with your standard shortcuts make a difference? Try a variety of combinations to create the fastest keyboard interface possible.

Fonts and Printing

It wasn't very long ago that you were a slave of the printer attached to your machine and limited to using only the fonts it contained. And if your printer didn't do what you needed it to do, you had to borrow someone else's machine to get your work done. Networks made more printers available to more people. Now many people have access to three or four printers (as a minimum) on the typical network.

But the major change was to the availability and quality of fonts. A *font* is a collection of characters (and symbols) designed to share a particular "look." The Arial font is clean and simple, with no curlicues or flourishes—just plain letters. This kind of font is often best for headlines and other large elements. By contrast, the Times New Roman font includes those extra curlicues and varying line thicknesses typical of classic body text fonts. I have much more to say about fonts presently, but first some background.

I still remember buying font cartridges for one of my printers and thinking I was lucky to have the two additional fonts they provided. Today, it's nothing for a typical user to have 100 or more fonts at his or her disposal. One product bundles well over 500 fonts and makes a special point of telling you so on the package.

Some people out there still have font cartridges. Another antiquated technology, fonts that you have to download into a printer before using them, are still available as well, although they're rare. You also don't see the old Adobe Type Manager (ATM) icons on people's screens anymore. Printers have become more flexible, and you have access to more of them; however, that flexibility comes at a cost in some added complexity.

This chapter will help you make sense of the confusing mass of available software options. I show you how to gain access to your printer and make the best use of the fonts on your hard drive. Even more important, I discuss some management techniques everyone should know when using a printer.

Quick Printing Techniques

Remember the context menus I've been talking about throughout the book? You won't escape them in this chapter either. Windows 2000 enables you to send a document to the printer in a lot of ways. I usually use the context menu shown in Figure 18.1 because most of my documents go to the same printer. Of course, you still have the usual

Windows defaults for sending a document to the printer, including the File, Print menu option for most applications.

> **Tip:** This book looks at docucentricity in a variety of ways. *Docucentricity* means shifting your focus more to documents rather than the applications used to edit them. One additional way to use docucentricity is to add another menu option to the context menu of your documents if you use more than one printer. This enables you to select something other than the default printer with the context menu. Your application must support the docucentricity feature for this option to work. Use the current Print entry as a basis for creating your advanced Print option.

FIGURE 18.1

The context menu for a document usually offers the choice of sending the document to the default printer.

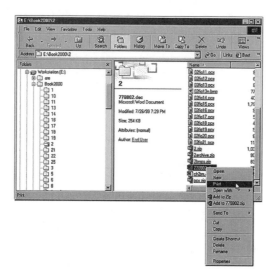

Another method you can use to send documents to the printer is to place a shortcut to the printer on your desktop. Then, all you need to do to print a document is drag it to the icon of the printer you want to use and drop the document. Of course, using this technique consumes some valuable desktop real estate.

Managing Print Jobs

Managing print jobs under Windows 2000 is fairly straightforward. Gaining access to the print jobs you have running is no problem. Whenever you print, Windows adds a Printer icon to the control area of the taskbar. Resting your mouse pointer over the Printer icon tells you how many print jobs are pending (see Figure 18.2). This provides a quick method of monitoring your printer status without opening any new windows.

FIGURE 18.2
The Printer icon on the taskbar tells you how many print jobs are pending. Right-clicking it tells you which printer is currently being used.

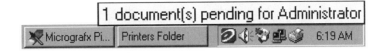

If multiple printers are in use on your workstation at one time, right-clicking the Printer icon displays a menu of available printers. You can choose to open one or all of them. The top menu item opens all active printers—those with print jobs. It doesn't matter whether the print job is paused.

The following sections describe the management tools Windows provides for printers. I discuss both local and remote printers.

Local Printers

The first type of printer we'll look at is the local printer. All you need to do to open a printer is right-click the Printer icon and choose it from the list. As an alternative, double-clicking the Printer icon displays the current print jobs for the default printer. The printer management display is shown in Figure 18.3.

FIGURE 18.3
Getting to the dialog box needed to manage your print jobs under Windows 2000 is easily accomplished from the taskbar.

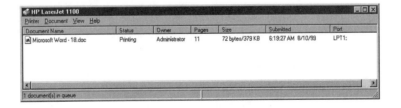

Note: Windows 2000 always defaults to a printer with an error. If you're having a printing problem, double-clicking the Printer icon displays the problem printer. The Printer icon also changes in appearance to alert you when there's a failure. This enables you to track the status of all your print jobs, even if the printer isn't in the same room as you.

Managing print jobs is fairly simple. After you open the printer management display, you can access all the print jobs individually. The Printer menu contains two options that enable you to control the printer itself: Pause Printing and Cancel All Documents. The

Pause Printing option enables you to stop the printer momentarily and restart it later. You could use this option to stop the printer for a quick ribbon change or to correct a paper jam. Cancel All Documents clears all the print jobs from the spooler. Use this option with care because you might accidentally remove something you don't want to. Note that a network printer display might display multiple print jobs that you cannot access because your network administrator hasn't given you permission to access other people's print jobs.

The Printer menu has several other options as well. The Set As Default Printer option enables you to maintain as permanent settings any configuration changes you make. The Properties option opens the Printer Properties dialog box discussed in Chapter 17, "Exploiting Your Hardware."

You can access the Document menu in one of two ways. The first method is to select a document and access the menu directly. The second method is faster: Just right-click the document you want to work with and choose the option from the context menu. The Document menu has five options. You can pause this document's print job using the Pause Printing option. The Cancel Printing option removes the document's print job from the spooler. The Restart option does just what it says. The Cancel option closes the menu, and the Properties option displays the currently selected document's Properties dialog box. Note that the primary difference between the Printer menu and the Document menu is that the latter only governs the behavior and properties of a single, selected document. The Printer menu governs *all* current jobs when you, for example, choose Pause.

One thing that isn't apparent when you look at this display is the fact that you can select a print job and move it somewhere else in the list. This enables you to change the priority of print jobs by just moving them around as needed. You can move groups of print jobs with equal ease. (Reordering job priority, too, depends on permissions if you're dealing with other people's print jobs on a network.)

Remote Printers

Managing a remote printer under Windows 2000 is nearly as easy as managing a local one. The only caveat is that the print server must be a Windows 95/98, NT 4, Windows 2000, NetWare, or other network that supports Point and Print. Otherwise, remote print jobs won't show up on your display. After you do establish a connection with the remote printer, you can exercise all the document-management capabilities you have with a local printer. (All this assumes that you have the access rights required to perform the task.)

> **Tip:** Point and Print is a technology that permits efficient installation of printers over a network merely by providing printer driver information. You just open My Network Places to identify a print server (open the printer's print queue). Alternatively, you can choose Start, Run and then type in the pathname to the printer's driver INF file. (You can even install a printer on a network by running the Add Printer Wizard found in the Printers utility in Control Panel.) Whichever approach you take, printer-specific data will be gathered from the network's server.

Remote printing does offer one opportunity that local printing doesn't. You can perform an offline print. Essentially, this is a form of pause. For remote printers, the Printer menu contains a special option called Work Offline. Checking the Work Offline selection pauses the printer and stores the print jobs on disk. When you uncheck this entry, all the print jobs are sent to the remote printer. A local printer can also be paused and then printed to later. Windows 2000 knows whether a print job is pending, even if you reboot. You'll be asked whether you want to start the print job.

Also, Windows 2000 boasts a new feature called Point and Print (AutoPublish) that can install a printer driver automatically on a client PC from any application. Here's how it works: If a user chooses File, Print in Word, for example, and browses the network and selects a particular printer—Windows 2000 will *automatically* install the appropriate driver on that user's workstation (after first checking to see if the driver is missing).

Font Types

You need to learn about only one type of font when using Windows 2000. There's a now out-of-date font type called *raster fonts* that provided you with nonresizeable bitmaps, and one used primarily with pen plotters called *vector fonts*. However, now nearly everyone uses TrueType (or the new OpenType, an extension of TrueType) an *outline font* that represents characters from line and curve commands rather than as bitmaps (a *bitmap* is a direct copy, analog version of the final output) or mathematical algorithms used in vector fonts.

> **Note:** When TrueType fonts are described throughout this chapter OpenType fonts are also included in the meaning, unless specifically excluded.

Vector fonts, being mathematical, are easily resized (you can multiply a math expression by 1.5, but you can't do that directly to a bitmap any more than you can mathematically multiply cheese). The following sections focus on the outline technology because nonscalable raster fonts have virtually died out and simply are not in use anymore, and Windows 2000 only supports three vector fonts: Modern, Roman, and Script.

Raster Fonts

Most people don't use raster fonts for printing purposes anymore because they're inconvenient: A raster font can't be resized. That means you have to keep one copy on disk of each font size you plan to use (or in a cartridge). In addition, you also have to keep one copy of each style: roman, italic, bold italic, and bold. Because raster fonts represent each character as a bitmap, the size of the file used to hold them also increases in size as the point size of the font increases. (They're analog analogies to the things they create.) You can soften the edges of rough-looking characters by using the Smooth Edges option in the Effects tab of the Desktop Properties dialog box. The Q on the right in Figure 18.4 has been smoothed.

FIGURE 18.4
The Q on the left illustrates how rough a huge character can appear onscreen (it's 66pt).

Vector Fonts

Vector fonts are stored as mathematical formulae. These formulae specify how to draw each character in the font. A vector font doesn't contain a bitmap that a device can use as output, so it must render the font each time the font is used. There is, of course, a slight performance hit caused by the necessity to calculate the character set for a vector font, but it's only a slight hit.

A vector font's rigid mathematical representation of how the font should look also results in potential problems. In particular, some vector fonts look good at one point size, whereas other fonts look best at a different point size. The problem is that even though a well-designed font is a refined representation of a set of characters, varying the number of pixels used to represent it allows discrepancies to creep in. A raster font vendor would hand-tune the character set at different sizes to get rid of the discrepancy or to at least fool the eye into thinking that it was gone. Vector fonts offer no such luxury. They are calculated, remember, not individually hand carved.

Consider this: Although they look identical to the casual glance, each column in the Parthenon is unique—they're not clones of each other. Each bulges slightly at the center, is a slightly different height than its neighbor, and is slightly tilted off center (inclined in individual, yet harmonic, ways). These and other fine-tunings of their shapes and positions contribute to the perfection of the result. Same thing with fonts: Characters should be fine-tuned to look their best.

Outline Fonts

TrueType and other font types such as OpenType use a feature called *hinting*. Like hand-tuning, hinting is mainly geared toward making small-sized fonts look better on low-resolution displays. Microsoft says that it carefully adjusts (hints) the following seven elements of a TrueType font set: color, readability, spacing, weight, alignment, symmetry, and "local aesthetics" (the actual bitmap shape for each character). The term *color* in typography refers to achieving a good balance between black character shapes and their white background. The idea is to avoid permitting letter combinations (words) that end up appearing blotchy (too much blackness when characters are combined) or contain pools of whitespace (too little collective blackness).

> **Tip:** If you don't like the look of TrueType fonts on your display, you can right-click the desktop, choose Properties, click the Effects tab, and then click the Smooth Edges of Screen Fonts option. This has the effect of blurring the edges so that you don't see a stair-step ragged outline when characters are large (as in headlines), as shown in Figure 18.4. This isn't the same thing as hinting, but it might be what's bothering you about your display fonts, if in fact you're bothered.

Now that hinting problems have been solved, outline fonts have a great deal to recommend them. Today they are the overwhelming choice for most computer work—both on the monitor display and for hard-copy printing. Their relatively small size enables you to keep many fonts on your hard disk without filling it up. In addition, you can resize an outline font to just about any point size, as well as rotate it. You can even create fractional point size fonts.

Understanding TrueType

TrueType (including OpenType) is a specific form of outline font. It comes with hinting and other features that mark it as an advanced font format. The important thing to remember is that TrueType is the native font format supplied with Windows 2000 (and many previous versions of Windows, for that matter). If you want to use other font formats, you need to install a third-party font manager. In most cases, you won't want to expend the resources to use a third-party manager. All the vendors who used to support alternatives to TrueType have now dropped that support because of the problems with supporting more than one font manager under Windows.

> **Note:** There's a big difference between printer fonts and third-party fonts. Laser printers sometimes include a number of specialized printer fonts you can keep on your hard drive that are downloaded to the printer as needed. You can still use these fonts with ease under Windows 2000. In fact, Windows has actually made the process of downloading easier. However, TrueType is so plentiful, well designed, and pervasive that few people bother with resident or downloadable third-party fonts.

Note: How can you differentiate between a TrueType font and any other font on your system? You'll see later that Windows 2000 provides different icons for the various types. Another way to detect the difference is by their extensions. TrueType fonts are superior to other font types in capability and appearance. TrueType and OpenType fonts normally use the .TTF extension.

Tip: Windows 3.*x* and earlier versions of NT required that a TrueType font use two files. The first had an .FON extension and pointed to the second file, which had a .TTF extension. Windows 2000 does not require the first file. As a result, you can erase any FON files on your hard drive without any loss of font data. Make certain, however, that the FON file really is an earlier Windows 3.*x* font file. Usually, these files appeared in the Windows \Fonts directory.

The final benefit of using TrueType fonts is the fact that Windows uses the same font for both screen and printer (WYSIWYG). Older font technologies used one font for the screen and another for the printer.

Installing Fonts

Just about everyone needs a new font from time to time—getting ready for a presentation, improving the readability of a Web site, following a new company policy, differentiating your work from someone else's, or just wanting a change. These are all motivations for trying new fonts. (See the "On Your Own" section at the end of this chapter for a good source of high-quality, free fonts.) Windows 2000 offers two ways to install a font. I'm going to show you both ways. The first method is the one that Microsoft recommends. The second method is the one that I use because it lets me look before I leap.

Note: Some programs, such as CorelDRAW!, include special versions of fonts used to store symbols. You have to use the application's installation program to add these fonts to Windows 2000. Otherwise, Corel's program won't recognize that the fonts are available. Just moving the font from the application's CD to the Windows font directory won't get the job done. Although such programs are few and far between, you do need to know that they exist.

The Standard Font-Installation Method

The standard method for installing a font is pretty straightforward, but it doesn't enable you to completely preview the font before you install it. It is, however, the safest approach because it's guaranteed to work every time. With that in mind, I show you the first method of font installation:

1. Open Control Panel and double-click the Fonts icon. You should see the display shown in Figure 18.5.

FIGURE 18.5

If you choose View, Preview, you can see this brief example of any font you pause your mouse pointer on top of.

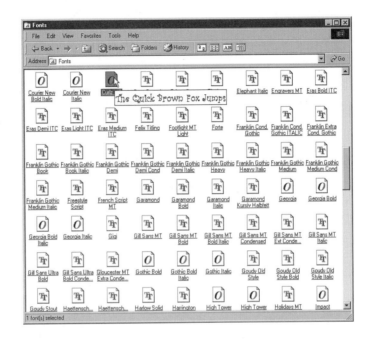

2. Choose the File, Install New Font command to display the Add Fonts dialog box shown in Figure 18.6.

FIGURE 18.6

The Add Fonts dialog box enables you to select fonts to add to your Windows installation.

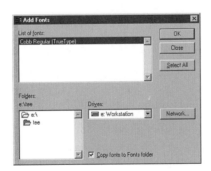

3. Browse your hard disk, floppy disk, or CD-ROM drive until you find the fonts you want to install. Highlight the desired fonts and click OK. You'll see the new fonts in your Fonts folder.

The Enhanced Font-Installation Method

I prefer a little more control when I install fonts on my machine. For one thing, I like to have a good idea of what they look like. Installing a font just so that I can view it seems backward. I found that this second font-installation technique is both easy and flexible. Best of all, it enables me to view the fonts before I install them. Follow these steps:

1. Open Explorer. Open the folder containing the fonts you want to preview.

2. Double-click a font (TTF) file to see what it looks like. You should see a dialog box similar to the one shown in Figure 18.7. Repeat this process until you find all the fonts you want to add to your font directory.

FIGURE 18.7

Double-clicking a font file displays the font in this window.

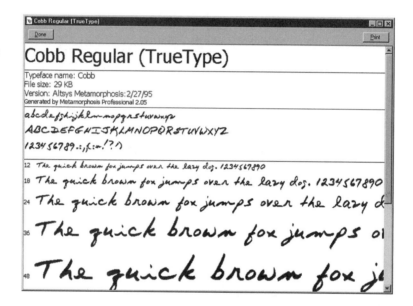

3. Use the scrollbar to move the FONTS folder into view in the right pane, but don't select that folder (look for WINNT\FONTS). Select all the fonts you want to move in the right pane and then just move them to the FONTS folder (drag while pressing the right mouse key) in the left pane where your WINNT\FONTS folder has been positioned.

That's all there is to it. See how easy that was? This technique works just as well as the more formal technique. I find that it's more flexible and faster, and I really know what I'm getting.

Removing Fonts

Removing fonts is very easy under Windows 2000. All you do is open the Fonts folder (either through Explorer or by double-clicking the Fonts applet in the Control Panel), select the fonts you want to remove, and press the Delete key. It is that easy.

You need to observe a few precautions. First and foremost, don't erase any font you're not sure of. Windows 2000 requires some fonts for its own system use, and erasing them could cause problems. Second, if you do erase a font, make certain you don't need it anymore or that you have a copy stored somewhere.

> **Tip:** Instead of deleting a font you no longer require, archive it. All you need to do is move it from the Fonts folder to a floppy disk or a network drive. This technique will save you headaches later if you're looking for the font you deleted and it's no longer available.

Viewing and Printing Fonts

The interface for the Fonts folder might be Explorer, but the options are different from typical Explorer options. The View menu contains some unique features you'll want to use to really examine your fonts. (I'm referring to the fonts themselves, not the files.) I'll show you what I mean.

Open the Control Panel and double-click the Fonts applet. (You can get to the same place using the Explorer technique I talked about earlier.) Open the View menu. Notice that Explorer now sports some new View options, as shown in Figure 18.8.

FIGURE 18.8
The Fonts folder provides font-related view options that will come in handy.

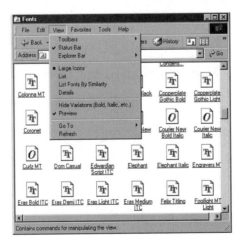

I like the List Fonts By Similarity option. It enables you to see which fonts you can use as substitutes for something else. What if you really like the font you're using for a particular purpose, but you want a slightly different effect? You could use this option to find the closest match in your directory or on a CD-ROM full of fonts. Figure 18.9 shows this display. Notice the drop-down list at the top of the display. This is where you first select the name of the font you want to use for comparison purposes. Then you click the List Fonts By Similarity option on the menu.

Another handy view selection is the Hide Variations option. You can use it with any of the display formats to hide the different files required to create a complete font family. If you turn on this option, for example, you'll see only one Arial font, even though there are typically 24 variations of Arial in the directory. Variations typically include bold, italic, and bold/italic versions of the font.

FIGURE 18.9

You can quickly find font families on a disk full of fonts by using the List Fonts By Similarity To drop-down list box.

It's very easy to print a sample of a font. All you need to do is right-click and choose Print from the context menu. As an alternative, you can always click the Print button or choose the File, Print command when viewing the font. The printout you get will look similar to Figure 18.7.

How Windows Matches Fonts

If you're designing a Web site, you must take into consideration that many thousands of people might visit that site. If you choose some odd font, very few of them will have that font installed and ready to use when displaying your page. What will happen when the user's machine cannot locate your font on the hard drive?

Windows uses a specific set of criteria to find a replacement font if the one you request isn't available. To get an idea of how this works, use the List Fonts By Similarity option in the Fonts folder. The results will tell you a lot about how Windows 2000 implements the rules in the font-matching table.

The font-matching table isn't actually a table; it's an algorithm Windows 2000 uses to compare fonts. Windows uses the following criteria to find a matching font: the character set, variable versus fixed pitch, family, typeface name, height, width, weight, slant, underline, and strikethrough.

A TrueType font is always replaced with another TrueType font, even if a raster or vector font is a closer match. This enables your application to maintain the flexibility TrueType provides. The drawback is that the output might not look even close to what was originally anticipated.

If the font you're trying to use is either a vector or raster font, Windows 2000 uses some additional methods to obtain a good match. The following list shows, in order, the sources Windows 2000 tries to tap:

- Printer ROM font
- Printer cartridge slot font
- Downloadable soft font
- TrueType font

Peter's Principle: Choosing the Right Typefaces

Regardless of whether you're designing a Web page or a company brochure, you'll want to follow some basic rules about choosing effective and appropriate fonts that have evolved over the years. It's especially important that you convey the right impression to your customers and potential customers in business publications. Therefore, if you're unfamiliar with the various issues involved in the selection and use of typefaces, the following suggestions may be well worth considering. Let's look at the four guidelines I consider key to helping you produce professional page designs:

- Use a sans-serif typeface for headlines, as shown in Figure 18.10, and a serif typeface for body text, as shown in Figure 18.11. Nearly all contemporary publications, ads, and other professionally produced documents follow this custom.

  The reason is that sans-serif fonts are harder to read at the small type sizes typical of body text. The curlicues (that's what *serif* means) and variations in line thickness of a serif face provide a reader with more visual cues than do the bare, simple sans-serif (meaning *without serif*) faces.

continues

- Most typefaces offer several styles, including boldface, italic, and under-lining, that are variations on the basic design. Boldface is most often used in headlines; it's big and thick. Only rarely do you see it within body text, where it jumps out at the reader and causes the bold words to be read initially as a group rather than within the context of their sentences.

  Use italic for emphasis. Avoid the bad habit of using boldface as a way to add emphasis to certain words in your body text. Also stay away from exclamation points, quotation marks, all-capital letters, underlining, or reversed, white-on-black characters—any of these tactics used to add emphasis reveal you as an amateur, ill-educated, or worse, a person with-out taste. These ways to add **"EMPHASIS!"** are an attempt to artificially add power to writing via typography instead of just writing powerfully. Let the words, not the typeface or punctuation, do the talking. If you must emphasize a word, italicize it. The italic version of a typeface is usu-ally attractive: It's just a slight variation, with a slight suggestion of hand-writing. It's not a brutally different look from normal text, yet different enough to subtly convey emphasis.

- Use proportional fonts. In addition to the primary division between sans-serif and serif, there's another elemental division: proportional versus nonproportional fonts.

  Courier and other "monospaced" fonts (Windows 2000 calls its version Courier New) are now rarely used. (Courier was the most popular type-face in the days of the typewriter but now is largely abandoned.) See Figure 18.12 for an example. Text is easier to read on paper if the letter widths vary. The letter i should take up less room in a word than the let-ter m. For mechanical reasons, however, typewriters had real trouble if the width of characters varied—hence nonproportional (or monospaced) fonts such as Courier.

  Typefaces such as Courier and Prestige are nonproportional: All charac-ters take up exactly the same width (consequently, there's considerable whitespace between the letter i and surrounding letters, for example). Computers, however, can easily produce varied spacing between letters. Why avoid Courier and other monospaced fonts? Studies have shown that proportional fonts can be read 30 percent faster (and incidentally use about 35 percent less paper) because each character takes up only as much room as necessary. Proportional fonts are easier to read because the varying width of the characters results in greater differences in word shapes. And that's one more visual clue (in addition to serifs and charac-ter line-width variations) that assists in reading. People who read well tend to gulp most words down whole—immediately recognizing the entire word, not piecing together individual characters or syllables within the word.

- Finally, keep it simple. Just because you have 30 typefaces available does not mean you should use all 30 in a single document or Web site. Two or three max; otherwise, you'll create the infamous "ransom note" effect.

Also, stick with classic, proven fonts such as Luncinda Sans, Helvetica, Arial, Times, Garamond, and Goudy. If you're new to fonts, you'll likely be tempted to use elaborate or eccentric fonts such as Gothic Germanic (see Blackletter in Figure 18.13), robot-modern (slashes through the zero are a clue), characters constructed out of hot dogs or pieces of wood, and so on. Even relatively tame fonts such as faux handwriting faces are jarringly overdone in nearly all circumstances. Script fonts (such as Lucinda Handwriting, illustrated in Figure 18.13) are almost always in bad taste.

Script typefaces, like other ornate typefaces, have extremely limited applications in contemporary typography—namely, wedding invitations and French restaurant menus. Script tries to look like fancy handwriting in the same way that many high school bands try to sound like music.

For several centuries, but ending in Edwardian times, it was possible to hire somebody to hand-letter your calling cards and the invitations to your balls. Talented cartographers can create text that's truly graceful. Mechanically imitated, however, the results are, at best, faux elegant. The family of script typefaces has joined the lace hanky in that museum of things that are too much trouble and too ornate for contemporary taste. Unless, of course, you throw balls.

FIGURE 18.10

A sans-serif type-face, such as Windows's Arial, is plain, stark (without curlicues), and has almost no variations in line thickness.

Arial is SANS. Plain. Even STARK

FIGURE 18.11

A serif is a small addition to a character—a curlicue that imitates the thinning line caused by lifting a pen from paper. Garamond and Times New Roman are typical serif fonts.

This Garamond, like Times Roman, is used for body text. The characters have varied shapes, extensions & thicknesses.

Courier is monospaced.
Times Roman is not monospaced.

FIGURE 18.12

A monospaced (nonproportional) typeface gives each character the same horizontal spacing.

Lucinda Blackletter
Lucinda HAndwriting

FIGURE 18.13

Unless you throw elaborate parties, avoid ornate, eccentric, or fussy typefaces like these.

On Your Own

This chapter showed you two ways to install fonts. Try both methods to see which works best for you. Many graphics programs include additional fonts. Fonts are often sold as collections in software stores, too. What's more, you can also download them from AOL and the Internet. Use this exercise to install the set of fonts that will get the job done for you. A really good site for high-quality, free (and shareware) fonts is `http://www.fontaddict.com/`. Take a look at it and see whether you want to download some of their wares.

Look in your \FONTS folder to see whether you can identify the various types of fonts Windows 2000 supports. How can you tell them apart? What purpose does each kind of font serve?

Finally, redesign your Web site, choosing typefaces following the guidelines offered in the Peter's Principle at the end of this chapter.

Windows 2000 Multimedia

You don't have to be a futurist, or even normally prescient, to realize that multimedia—sound and motion video—enrich computing and are its future. TV is going digital, and computers are getting more like TV every day. Just look at the best Web sites: They include rich graphics, animation, and sound. Now you can even use DVD (included in many of today's systems) to watch high-definition TV on your monitor. And don't bet against anyone who claims that Internet Explorer 6 will boast full-screen video.

Text-to-speech and speech-recognition technologies are already available and (almost) fully functioning. It's indeed a breakthrough when the computer can recognize what you say well enough to be able to carry out your wishes merely because you gave it a verbal command. Some manufacturers have begun shipping systems, including notebooks, with such software preinstalled.

> **Note:** Graphics and sound are discussed in other chapters in this book. You'll find considerable additional information about graphics in Chapter 13, "Graphics Windows 2000 Style."

Several additional technologies are contributing today to the multimedia features in Windows 2000 and Internet Explorer. To see one example of a new technology that's having an impact, consider DHTML (Dynamic HTML). Try this experiment. Open Notepad and type the following:

```
<HTML>
<HEAD>
<script language="JavaScript">
function wipeit(){
divzone.filters.revealTrans.apply()
divzone.innerText = "LOCAL ANIMATION & DISTORTION VIA DHTML EFFECTS"
divzone.filters.revealTrans.play()
}
</script>
</HEAD>
```

```
<BODY topmargin=50 leftmargin=50 onload=wipeit()>
<FONT SIZE=25 COLOR="BLUE">

<div id=divzone style="height:350;width:550;filter:wave(strength=14)
revealTrans(transition=2 duration=48)">
MULTIMEDIA EFFECTS ARE COMING TO A COMPUTER NEAR YOU.
</div>

</BODY>
</HTML>
```

Now save this file as EFFECTS.HTM. Choose Open from Internet Explorer's File menu and open EFFECTS.HTM. (This will work fine in Internet Explorer; it won't work in Netscape.)

If you get an error message, go through the Notepad file and replace all double quotes. They're likely open and close quotes (" ") rather than straight up quotes ("), and you must make them straight up.

This short, simple piece of programming (except for the scripting) is written in the classic Internet programming language HTML (Hypertext Markup Language). It's a page-description language, meaning that it describes where things are located, how big they are, and what colors are used as well as other font attributes. HTML is essentially a word processor kind of language, however. It is static.

The EFFECTS.HTM Internet page you typed in includes scripting and DHTML in addition to classic HTML. Scripting is essentially the same as ordinary computer programming. However, because scripts are downloaded to your computer, commands that can contact your peripherals have been removed from scripting languages. You don't want to download a script that has file-deletion and drive-formatting commands for obvious reasons.

LOOKING AHEAD	For details about the meaning and uses of HTML, see Chapter 25, "Using FrontPage Express."

The preceding script is written in JavaScript, but an equivalent VBScript is as easy, probably easier, to work with. In addition to the script (a little program that runs whenever this Web page is loaded into Internet Explorer or refreshed by the user pressing F5), there are DHTML features as well. Dynamic HTML means just that: Things happen, usually visual effects. The transition value used in the example is 2 (Circle in), but you can use any integer from 0 to 23, as shown here:

Transition Wipe	Value
Box in	0
Box out	1
Circle in	2
Circle out	3

Transition Wipe	Value
Wipe up	4
Wipe down	5
Wipe right	6
Wipe left	7
Vertical blinds	8
Horizontal blinds	9
Checkerboard across	10
Checkerboard down	11
Random dissolve	12
Split vertical in	13
Split vertical out	14
Split horizontal in	15
Split horizontal out	16
Strips left down	17
Strips left up	18
Strips right down	19
Strips right up	20
Random bars horizontal	21
Random bars vertical	22
Random	23

Tip: It's easy to revise and then test Web site programming. Just type in a change to the text in Notepad and then choose Save from Notepad's File menu. Press Alt+Tab to switch to Internet Explorer. Press F5 in Internet Explorer to reload the new, edited version of that HTM file.

These effects won't yet allow Internet Explorer to give ordinary TV a run for its money, but DHTML is way beyond word processing and the older static Web pages we had to put up with only a year ago.

Besides the Internet, the average user may use multimedia for training, for education, and (of course) for games. Many games provide intense graphic and sound presentations meant to thrill the user. It takes considerable hardware horsepower to run some of these games, and in fact, some of the more robust sales campaigns for multimedia hardware actually appear in gaming magazines.

Obviously, this isn't even the tip of the iceberg when it comes to multimedia. As voice-recognition technology improves, more people will use sound for feedback, for controlling their computers, and for storing and recording their own sounds. Because multimedia requires advanced hardware, we'll look at the hardware and software technologies you might need. By the time you finish this chapter, you'll have a better idea of what multimedia under Windows 2000 entails and how you can make it easier to use.

> **Technical Note:** What happened to the beep? You might remember the beeps and squawks made by the simple little built-in computer speaker that were used to alert you and often ended up frightening you. That speaker is still in computers sold today, but Windows 2000 has no driver for it. There's a simple reason: Preemptive multitasking doesn't allow the CPU to take the time to make the beep. The old DOS-style speaker buzzing was generated by borrowing the CPU exclusively to create—the sound and Windows 2000 doesn't permit the CPU's time to be usurped in this fashion. Even though the driver is missing, however, this doesn't mean that the little speaker never beeps under Windows 2000.

Multimedia Hardware

Here are some tips on what to look for in multimedia-ready hardware. Right now, it's hard to say which is ahead in the game—hardware or software. Except for high-quality digital sound boards using MIDI software, neither video nor recorded digital (WAV files) sound is yet ready for prime time. Sound files eat up huge amounts of space on your hard drive, and what motion video there is can be jerky (as the CD or Internet connection tries to catch up with what you're seeing), jumpy (too slow a frame rate), or tiny (a little window on your monitor). Nevertheless, compression tricks and other bandwidth boosters are improving all the time.

MIDI Re-creates Music on-the-Fly

Purely digital recordings (such as WAV files and digital video) use up a lot of space on a hard drive. Fortunately, there's an alternative to digital sound storage. Nearly all sound cards sold today are MIDI capable. MIDI (Musical Instrument Digital Interface) re-creates music on-the-fly. In other words, the sounds are stored in a MIDI file (.MID)—a kind of sheet music description of the notes (how loud, what pitch, what duration, the instruments that should play those notes, and subtleties such as vibrato). This kind of description takes up much less space than a digital recording. A high-quality MIDI-capable card holds brief digital recordings of many instruments (or a wavetable that can synthetically imitate the timbre of many instruments). Therefore, all a MID file has to contain is a brief text specification such as: `Play a middle C trumpet sound for three seconds`.

The quality of the result, however, greatly depends on how well your sound card can re-create musical instrument sounds. There's a great range—from the boring, unvarying honks and tweets of a toy organ to the accurate timbres of actual instruments recorded and then stored on ROM chips.

MIDI is a standardized computer-music description language that was established in the mid 80s. In addition to the pitch, a MIDI file describes the tone (timbre, the difference between a trumpet playing middle C and a French horn playing the same note), duration (or *sustain*, and any fading of the volume, also called sustain), vibrato (rapid changes in pitch), tremolo (rapid changes in loudness), and dozens of other aspects of music.

Duration and sustain are different. Duration is simply the amount of time that passes. Sustain is a downward ramp describing the loss of volume over that time. Some instruments fade in a linear way. Others, like a xylophone, have a rapid falloff, followed by a long, slow leak of volume as the tube rings. There is an actual shape to the sustain, and it differs from instrument to instrument.

A computer can store and manipulate sound in two ways: symbolically (coded, such as the MIDI descriptions of a sound) and imitative (sampled, such as a WAV recording of an actual sound). You can see this same distinction in the visual domain. WMF (Windows Metafile) images are mathematical descriptions of pictures—shapes, textures, and colors—and they're re-created on-the-fly when the file is brought into the computer from disk to be displayed. BMP files, by contrast, are sampled copies of an image, and they're merely displayed line for line, bit for bit, across the TV monitor. There's no drawing or calculating necessary—the color and shade of each dot on the screen is already saved in the BMP file.

This distinction parallels the difference between analog (imitative) and digital (descriptive) recording. Note, however, that both WAV and MIDI are stored digitally. Analog is also sometimes stored in an analog storage format on vinyl records or as patterns on audio tape. These patterns are more or less a carving, like a sculpture, of the sounds. If you could shrink yourself until you were walking along in the groove of an old vinyl record, drums would be huge bumps on the walls of the groove valley and a cymbal would appear as a series of many small ripples. These shapes are direct imitations, analogies of the sounds they store.

The goal of an imitative approach is to accurately reproduce the sound or image. The goal of a descriptive approach is to create a recognizable symbol of the sound or image. A photograph is imitative, for example, whereas a caricature is symbolic. Imitative (BMP and WAV) files more or less store and then reproduce the original; symbolic files (WMF and MID) more or less suggest or re-create the original. That is why a photo of President Clinton looks like him, and an editorial cartoon exaggerates his features.

The primary benefit of symbolic data storage is its efficiency; it just takes a lot less space to store the symbols for "two minutes of middle C played by a guitar" than to store that two minutes as an actual digital recording. MIDI stores a description.

The Multimedia Microprocessor: MMX

MMX (which some people translate as *Multimedia Extensions*) is an improvement to multimedia performance developed by Intel and built into recent Intel microprocessors as well as chips from Cyrix and AMD. (All Pentium II and later microprocessors (including Celeron) include MMX; a Pentium Pro chip does not, but Xeon chips do.) MMX adds 57 additional graphics-related instructions to the Pentium line of microprocessors. Some sound-specific instructions are included as well. These instructions operate on 64 bits simultaneously, allowing considerable increases in efficiency when the processor is burdened with the huge job of displaying animation, motion video, and other multimedia-related special effects (such as DSP).

DSP stands for *digital signal processing*, a way of manipulating digitized graphics or sound. One example of DSP would be adding echo to music. DSP also involves data compression. As you might imagine, DSP requires heavy-duty math, and having an efficient instruction set in an MMX chip assists the microprocessor with this kind of processor-intensive load.

In general, MMX contributes the most to the quality of games: both game animation and "movies" shown on your monitor. In both of those cases, the motion becomes smooth (or at least less jerky) because the number of frames (still images) per second can be increased beyond what non-MMX chips are capable of. In addition to the improved instruction set, the Pentium's L1 (onboard) cache size is doubled to 32KB. (For more detail about the two processor caches, L1 and L2, see Chapter 11, "Memory Management.") MMX is based on SIMD—the single instruction, multiple data technique. Note, however, that like most DirectX technology, MMX doesn't do anything for software that isn't written using the special MMX programming instructions.

The Video Board's Bus: AGP, UMA, and PCI

Most video cards sold today are relatively rich in memory and include graphics acceleration features. (If you buy a new board, try to get one that has at least 8MB of RAM and that includes both scaling and video acceleration.) There's another consideration, however. It doesn't matter much if your video card is lightning-fast internally if its bus (its connection to the motherboard) is narrow and slow.

Today, a primary decision you must make when buying a video card is whether you want an AGP (accelerated graphics port) or PCI bus. First, unless your motherboard supports AGP, there's no point in getting it on the video board. The two must work together; otherwise, nothing happens with AGP. Of course, if your motherboard does support AGP, go ahead and get it rather than PCI. AGP is the superior connection and will likely replace PCI eventually. There's also another bus designed to give AGP a run for its money: UMA (unified memory architecture). Its primary advantage is that it eliminates the need to employ the computer's primary chipset when the graphics card calls the computer's RAM or the video frame buffer. To give you an idea of the relative difference in transfer rates, PCI buses typically transfer data at an average of 100MBps; AGP and UMA transfer at 500MBps. For a discussion of these competing bus standards, see Chapter 13, "Graphics Windows 2000 Style."

Video Compression: MPEG Support

MPEG (Motion Pictures Experts Group) is a method of compressing VHS video into a small format that will fit on a CD-ROM. The VHS used by Windows 2000 is the same format that your VCR uses. The technical term for the type of functionality that MPEG provides is a codec (coder/decoder). Think of a codec in the same way you think of a modem. It enables you to send and receive video data using a standard medium. Instead of a telephone wire, you're using a CD-ROM drive. In place of digital data, you're receiving video images.

Windows 2000 can currently display VHS-quality images in a 640×480 window at 30 frames per second. That's about the same frame rate that you see on television. You're supposed to get this level of performance from a double-speed CD-ROM drive, but when tested with faster CD-ROM units, results are barely acceptable. Of course new computers are now typically being sold with 24× or faster CD-ROM drives, so that bottleneck, at least, is widening. I suspect that part of Microsoft's assumption is that you won't be running any other applications when using the multimedia capabilities, but that probably isn't valid. Some people will want to use multimedia for training, which means that they will probably have another application open. However, a 24× CD-ROM drive will probably provide the level of support you really need to use MPEG video.

Suffice it to say that if you want to fully exploit your machine's hardware capabilities, make sure you get more than a minimal system. Otherwise, you'll probably be disappointed with the performance that low-end hardware will provide.

A New Kind of CD: DVD-ROM

Digital Video Disc-Read Only Memory is a disc similar to a CD-ROM, but instead of a CD-ROM's approximately 680MB, a DVD-ROM boasts far, far more. How much? We'll get to capacity shortly.

DVD can provide digital video, and DVD players are now available for ordinary televisions that show prerecorded movies much like laser-disc machines. So far, DVD-ROM appears to be catching on with the public as a storage medium for movies. What's more, some CD-ROM manufacturers are planning to phase out CD-ROM production in the next few years in favor of the larger DVD-ROM format.

However, DVD isn't unsinkable—there's an iceberg up ahead by the name of HDTV. Nobody knows what impact HDTV will have on storage media—DVD included. DVD is backward compatible with CD-ROM but not forward compatible with HDTV. Probably around 2003, as HDTV begins to penetrate the mass market, the DVD-video format is likely to be boosted to a DVD-HD format. DVD-capable computers will likely be able to display HDTV because 2× DVD-ROM drives coupled with appropriate playback and display hardware can achieve the 19Mbps data rate needed for HDTV.

On the bright side, however, DVD is now in its second generation (called DVD-2). It can now read traditional CD-ROM discs at speeds up to 24×, so you don't need a separate CD-ROM drive. DVD can also read CD-R and CD-RW discs. (CD-RW means a CD that's rewritable over and over, as opposed to CD-R, which can be written to only once.) Some experts are predicting that DVD will eventually replace videotapes, laser discs, and CD-ROMs as the most popular storage medium.

You should understand the difference between DVD-Video and DVD-ROM. DVD-Video is hooked up to a TV and shows movies. DVD-ROM holds computer data and is read by a DVD-ROM drive hooked up to a computer. However, computers with DVD-ROM drives can also play DVD videos. This distinction recalls that between audio CDs and CD-ROMs. In addition to its playback capability, DVD-ROM also now embraces several recordable variations (DVD-R, DVD-RAM, DVD-RW, DVD+RW).

What about capacity? It depends. The DVD standard is rather flexible: a DVD disc can be single sided or double sided. In addition, each of the sides can contain one or two layers of data. The amount of video a disc can hold also depends on how much audio is stored and the degree of compression used. Recall that a CD-ROM holds about 680MB (a little over a half a billion bytes). Now compare that to DVD's current best. The most generous DVD format (DVD-18, currently under test only in laboratories) holds 15.9GB (17 billion bytes) and is a double-sided, dual data layer format. It will play more than 8 hours of quality video+audio. One hour of video uses up approximately two GB of storage space.

Sound Boards

There are all kinds of sounds and all kinds of hardware on which to play them. Windows 2000 provides the controls required to fully exploit the expanded capabilities that modern sound boards provide. All you need to do to start using these capabilities is adjust the settings found in the Audio Properties dialog box. To access this dialog box, right-click the Speaker icon on the taskbar, select Adjust Audio Properties, and click the Audio tab. You should see a dialog box similar to the one shown in Figure 19.1.

Windows 2000 will always play back any audio using the full capability of the sound board you select. However, there's a lot of room to customize the recording of sound. Microsoft thoughtfully provided three default recording selections. Each selection reflects the kind of sound recording quality these settings will give you: CD, radio, or telephone.

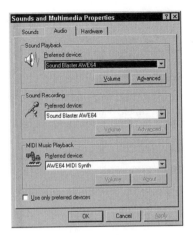

Figure 19.1

The Sounds and Multimedia Properties dialog box enables you to exploit your system's audio capabilities.

The actual level of quality you get has to do with the frequency (the number of samples of sound that Windows 2000 takes per second). The more samples it takes, the better the quality of the sound. Using stereo and 16-bit samples also improves the sound quality, as does the recording format. Before we go much further, I'll define a few terms:

- *Sample rate*. The number of times per second that Windows 2000 samples the microphone input line. A higher setting means that you get more samples. All things being equal, more samples always provide a better playback.

- *Sample size*. Windows 2000 supports two sample sizes: 8 bit and 16 bit. A 16-bit sample enables you to record a broader range of values. This means you can better differentiate between various sounds, resulting in a higher-quality recording.

- *Format*. There are several ways to store a sound, just as there are various ways to store graphics. Some formats take more space but preserve image quality better. Likewise, some audio formats are better than others at preserving sounds. You have to experiment to see which one sounds the best to you. Most recordings use the PCM (pulse-code modulation) format. Because this is the most common format, you'll probably want to use it when you need to exchange the recording with someone else, unless there's an overriding reason to do otherwise.

- *Number of channels (mono or stereo)*. You probably already know the implication of this setting. A stereo recording uses two microphones to record the sound from different perspectives. During playback, a stereo recording has greater depth than a mono recording of the same quality in much the same way that visual depth perception is greater with two eyes than with one.

Technical Note: Although the rate at which you sample audio or video is the more important factor, the size of each sample also contributes to the quality of the result. Using a movie analogy, think of the sampling rate as the number of frames per second and the sample size as the quality or *resolution* of each frame (how well the film displays fine detail and how many distinct colors it offers). In digitally recorded music, the sample rate is expressed in KHz (kilohertz), 1,000 per second (therefore, 8KHz means 8,000 samples per second will be taken during the recording). The sample size describes how many bits will be used to store each sample. The more bits used, the greater the silence between the sounds (resulting in crispness, definition of timbre, and quality high frequency). The bits-per-sample factor is usually called the *quantization level*. This factor is difficult to describe, but recording at low quantization produces a result similar to tape hiss. The purity of the silence, or absence of hiss, brings out the high frequencies of the cymbals, for example, because they then become contrasted against silence rather than partially blended into a background hiss. Try plugging a microphone into your sound card or playing a CD and recording (with the Windows Sound Recorder accessory) a sound, such as your voice. Adjust the bits per sample (BPS) from 4 bits per sample to 16 and play back the two recordings to hear the difference. (You can get down to 4 bits per sample by changing the Format option from PCM to Microsoft ADPCM.)

What's the best way to customize your recording settings? Remember that the better the quality, the higher the storage requirements. I tend to prefer stereo over mono recordings because the depth of sound can make up for a host of other problems. The trouble comes when you have only one microphone. In that case, selecting stereo is a waste of disk space because you can record only one channel of information. Selecting 16-bit sound improves quality a great deal for a small increase in storage size. You get a sample 2^{16} (65,536 possible combinations) versus 2^8 (256 possible combinations) for a mere doubling of disk space. Unless you're recording music, the highest sampling rate you need is 22,050Hz. In fact, using 11,025Hz for simple voice recordings usually proves sufficient.

Virtualizing Your Hardware

To make the best use of your hardware under Windows 2000, you must be able to access it. If absolutely necessary, you can use a real-mode driver to access an older device. DLLs enable you to access devices that provide Windows 2000 16-bit support but don't provide a Windows 2000/95–specific driver. This is better than using a real-mode driver but shy of the goal you want to achieve. The best driver to use is a Windows 2000–specific virtual "anything" driver (VxD). Using 32-bit Windows 2000 drivers is the best solution if you want to get the most out of your hardware. Windows 2000 isn't a perfect operating system, but it does provide enough advanced features that updating your hardware to use the new drivers is the best way to go. Using old drivers is just another way to introduce inefficiencies and stability problems into your system.

Software for Games and Multimedia

Because of a lack of operating system support, a dearth of multimedia standards, and poor documentation from vendors, early games were an exercise in frustration for anyone unlucky enough to install them.

Windows 2000 now provides much more robust support than earlier operating systems. You'll find that many of the features you need for playing a game or displaying a presentation are built right into the operating system. The fact that the operating system supports your hardware means that you have fewer problems getting single applications to work. Finally, there are more standards now, so it's easier to find drivers to get the job done.

There are some drawbacks to all this standardization and support from Windows 2000. Placing the need for driver support at the operating level is a good idea because you reduce the number of places to look when it's time to figure out why your hardware isn't working. However, it still doesn't reduce the problems you'll have getting the hardware to work in the first place. Multimedia software support under Windows 2000 is normally an all-or-nothing proposition. Buying standardized hardware and the associated drivers is one good way to make sure you'll have the fewest problems possible getting Windows 2000 to work with your software and recognize your hardware.

Windows 2000 isn't usually thought of as a games platform, but it can run games. It does a good job on many older games, for example, with Microsoft's Flight Simulator (Version 6 "for Windows 95"). If you buy games often, however, you'll likely find that some of them won't work on Windows 2000—and most software cannot be returned for refund after it has been opened.

You can take some steps to avoid getting games you can't use. First, look at the system requirements to see whether Windows 2000 is mentioned. That's your best insurance that the game has been tested and works on Windows 2000. Also, most of us wrongly assume that any game you pick up in the store is going to be on Microsoft's approval list. The one thing you should always look for is the Microsoft seal. This is your assurance that someone at Microsoft has at least looked at how the game is designed. There might be nothing wrong with a nonapproved game, but you don't know that.

On the other hand, a Microsoft seal isn't necessarily a guarantee that you won't run into any problems. All that the seal tells you is that the game was programmed in accordance with Microsoft's guidelines. In other words, the game meets certain minimal requirements. Whether that's enough to get the game to run on your machine isn't assured.

> **Technical Note:** One point to remember: Applications running on Windows 95/98 have the "capability" to directly contact hardware, whereas those running on Windows 2000 do not. Therefore, Windows 95/98 can run more games (many of which insist on direct hardware programming to get every last ounce of performance). This mainly applies to older games, however. Most newer games use an API, such as Glide or DirectX, to avoid writing directly to the hardware. Direct non-API hardware access is one of the main reasons people can't run games very well under Windows 2000 (although I still prefer Windows 98 for gaming because it does seem to handle game program differences better).

The following sections explore some of the software solutions that Microsoft provides for getting your hardware and applications to talk with each other.

Media Player

In essence, Media Player is Microsoft's method for distributing multimedia in a relatively small package. The Media Player enables you to play various kinds of multimedia files, including both audio and video files. Look for Media Player in Start, Programs, Accessories, Entertainment.

To find some things to listen to or watch with Media Player, try this Web site:

```
http://windowsmedia.microsoft.com
```

DirectX—The Solution for Today

Windows 2000 includes DirectX 7.0, making it every bit the multimedia player that its other Windows cousins have been for some time. Games particularly benefit from the various ways that DirectX permits direct contact with hardware—for added speed and flexibility.

If you want to find out the latest about Microsoft's DirectX technology, go to the following Web site:

```
http://microsoft.com/directx/
```

Understanding DirectX

DirectX is actually composed of several software layers. Each layer performs a specific purpose. The following list describes each layer and tells you what purpose it serves:

- *Components*. DirectX components represent the topmost layer of the DirectX hierarchy (most people would just call them *applications*). Obviously, any game or multimedia application that uses DirectX resides at this level. You'll also find that Windows 2000 comes with four DirectX components: Media Player, VRML 2.0, NetShow, and NetMeeting.

- *DirectX Media.* This is the layer that manages all your resources, such as video memory and access to a sound board. It's the application service level. You'll find several pieces of DirectX here, including DirectShow, DirectModel, DirectPlay, DirectAnimation, Direct3DRetainedMode, and VRML.

- *DirectX Foundation.* All the system-level services appear at this level. When the operating system needs to know what's going on, it talks to one of the pieces at this level. You'll find DirectDraw, DirectInput, DirectSound, DirectSound3D, and Direct3DImmediateMode at this level.

> **Technical Note:** The latest version of DirectDraw includes a feature that lets applications specify gamma levels for each primary color channel in full-screen mode, allows MPEG2 decoders to achieve a 20-to-40-percent frame rate increase, and can seamlessly match video frame rate to monitor refresh rate.

- *Hardware and Network.* None of this technology matters if you can't make your display present believable 3D graphics. DirectX is more than just software that helps you get the most from your games and multimedia applications; it also means getting hardware that you normally expect to find with your favorite stereo.

The Main Components of DirectX

Think of DirectX as a collection of libraries (DLLs) and drivers that improve multimedia (mainly games). Here's a brief description of the primary APIs:

- *DirectInput.* Handles joystick (and other peripheral) input. It's a highly flexible digital and analog joystick interface that can also be used for virtual reality input devices.

- *DirectDraw.* Speeds up the display of graphics.

- *DirectPlay.* Contains the information needed to facilitate game play over networks (as well as TCP/IP for play over the Internet).

- *DirectSound.* Provides drivers for music and sound, including such special tricks as 3D localization—an effect that's supposed to spread a stereo sound field beyond the speakers and, some claim, even behind the user. All without adding additional speakers.

- *Direct3D.* Helps speed up the complex rendering required when 3D objects must be drawn (and redrawn frequently during animation). All popular 3D video accelerator cards now support Direct3D.

The Latest, Greatest DirectX

At the time of this writing, DirectX has gone through several further iterations, and DirectX 7.0 is now included in Windows 2000. DirectX supports DVD playback, improved audio features, multiple monitors, and the new universal serial bus (USB). For more details on the USB, see Chapter 20, "Windows 2000 Connections."

The DirectMusic API adds a software-based synthesizer with wavetables for those whose sound cards don't include this high-quality feature. The result is passed through the sound card's digital audio playback. Microsoft claims that this feature doesn't burden the CPU much. Also included are improved MIDI, with seamless playback of MIDI streams, and DLSs (downloadable sounds), a MIDI specification for the description of sounds (instruments). These enable you to add new, custom sounds to those that ship with your sound card (if the card includes wavetable synthesis).

DirectX 7.0 boasts specialized boosters for hardware acceleration features and lighting effects using dedicated 3D accelerator hardware. This takes a burden off the computer's CPU. Microsoft claims that DirectX 7 facilitates "lifelike visual effects" such as reflections in a pool of water or light passing through a stained-glass window. Audio enhancements include support for so-called "3D sound" (fiddling with phase and frequency shifts to make it appear, psychoacoustically, that sounds are coming from beyond the stereo spread. Indeed, some people claim to hear such faux sound sources from above and behind them. Also, DirectX 7.0 is reported to run about 20 percent faster than version 6.1.

There's also an OpenGL 1.1 API standard that, itself, boosts graphics. OpenGL encapsulates geometric data and can handle multiple textures dynamically. If you want to develop high-performance, high-resolution graphics applications (modeling, animation, CAD/CAM, simulations, and so on), OpenGL can assist you in reaching your goals. The newest version of OpenGL boasts a beefy rendering pipeline that's two to four times faster than the previous OpenGL standard. Among other things, this provides improved frame rates when using texture objects.

Compatibility Issues

One of the most common problems with games involves old drivers. Some game installation programs won't bother to check which DirectX drivers are being used and will overwrite new files with the old ones on the CD. Other game installation programs misread the drivers and assume that you have whatever it takes to run the game when, in reality, you don't.

Another problem involves laptops. For whatever reason (I've heard more than a few conflicting reasons), the flat screen display provided with laptop computers doesn't react as well to DirectX as the displays used with desktop machines. As a result, I've had more than my share of video problems when running games on laptop machines. The thing you should do if you run into this problem is check with the laptop vendor for updated drivers. In many cases, someone else has already run into the problem and the laptop vendor has the fix you require.

You'll also run into problems that I place in the "strange" category. One game that I liked playing had a problem with IP addresses, for example. I could only contact another party on the Internet if the first IP number was two digits or fewer. I couldn't enter a three-digit beginning IP number. Fortunately, the vendor came out with a patch in short order and the problem was fixed. A good number of people assumed there was some problem with their machines, however, and went through all kinds of troubleshooting procedures before contacting the vendor. If you have a problem with a game, contact the vendor first (or at least a suitable newsgroup on the Internet) to see whether it's a common problem.

Finding Multimedia Software

Okay, you've used the suggestions in this chapter and you now have a multimedia power-house Windows 2000 system. What do you feed it? Games, of course. But if you're interested in sound or video, here are some places to locate good multimedia on the Internet.

There are a lot of MIDI collections out there, and many MID files contain high-quality renditions of popular as well as classical music. Because of copyright lawsuit threats, you'll find more classical music than popular music (that is, more music from dead composers than living ones).

For a collection of the entire Beatles oeuvre (try listening to And I Love Her from the Hard Day's Night album on a good sound card to see how good MIDI orchestration can sound):

`http://www.geocities.com/SunsetStrip/Towers/2838/index2.htm`

For beaucoup de Bach, and other great classical, try this:

`http://midiworld.com/cmc/index.htm`

Try this site to locate various MIDI files:

`http://www.midi.com/`

> **Tip:** If you see a MID file on a Web page that's clickable (it looks like a hyper-link, and probably is underlined), when you do click it, the Windows 2000 Media Player application (or whatever player application you've associated with MID files) will pop up and start playing the song. If you want to *download* the MID file to your hard drive instead, right-click the hyperlink and choose the Save Target As option on the context menu.

On Your Own

Spend some time checking your hardware and associated drivers. Most vendors have Web sites where you can download updated drivers. Hardware that uses flash ROM technology can benefit from downloads as well.

Visit various Internet sites to see how they use multimedia. You might even want to make some comments to the Webmaster about what you like and what you don't. Make sure you get the entire experience by using both sight and sound.

Try editing some of the values in the DHTML example source code I listed at the start of this chapter. You'll see new color and shape distortions applied to the text. The text is made wavy using this DHTML command: `filter:wave(strength=14)`. Try changing 14 to other values to see what happens. An even more dramatic effect is the wipe, just like transitions used between scenes or settings on TV. It's accomplished by the transition DTHML: `revealTrans(transition=2 duration=48)`. Also try some of these other dynamic transitions (listed under Transition Wipe) by substituting other numbers for the 2 in `transition=2` in the DHTML example.

Try to get a game running under Windows 2000. Some older games are a special challenge because you have to use special settings to get them to run. Make sure you take a close look at the game to see whether it's getting too old to run. As technology advances, it leaves some games behind, making it difficult to install or play them. You'll also want to check game vendor Web sites to see whether a patch is available for your game. In many cases, these patches fix Windows 2000–compatibility problems.

Check your game packages to see whether they all have the Microsoft seal. Which ones specify that they're Windows 2000 compatible?

PART V

A Look Outside

Windows 2000 Connections

Connections and communications make using the computer worthwhile for some people. It's not a matter of doing something faster; instead, it's a matter of being able to obtain and present information that drives them. Exchanging information with others means that you'll have to spend a little more time thinking about how you'll do it. Windows 2000 provides a lot of different types of connections, and each of them will help you communicate in some way.

I'm not going to tell you that every type of connection works well under Windows 2000. You'll need to address some real problem areas to make things work properly. Communications aren't always as clear as they could be. You'll find that not only do you need to learn new computing skills, but you need to learn a new way of talking with other people as well. This chapter takes you through the pitfalls you could experience and helps you avoid them.

This chapter has four distinctly separate parts. Two of them build on information discussed in previous chapters. The first part spends some time with physical details we haven't covered yet. Hardware connections are a necessary step in getting your machine ready for information exchanges of all types. I'm not going to spend any time talking about troubleshooting or network specifics here, but I do spend some time talking about common connections—the devices you use every day.

The second topic discussed here is software connections. Anyone who works out of his or her home knows the problems involved in keeping up with what's going on at the office. Sharing files and any other type of communication are problems as well. Previous versions of Windows NT left the user out in the cold when it came to these very necessary concerns. Windows 2000 takes care of that discrepancy by providing some very real assistance for the remote user.

LOOKING AHEAD

I'm not going to cover the particulars of online communication here. We covered that issue in Chapter 2, "Windows to the Internet." Network connections begin in Chapter 24, "Peer-to-Peer Networking." Make sure you look there for the ins and outs of that type of connection. We also cover troubleshooting in Chapter 31, "Solving Hardware Problems." Of course, these other chapters cover a lot more than just connections; they cover many user issues, as well.

When you combine the software and hardware connections that Windows 2000 provides, you'll find a somewhat complete level of coverage. I was appalled, however, at some of the areas where Microsoft skimped when it came to this important subject, and pleased at some of the new features Microsoft decided to include. Overall, Windows 2000 is an improvement, but perhaps not as big an improvement as you might expect. It's not time to throw away that third-party remote connection package yet, but perhaps in another few versions it will be.

This chapter also looks at two important technologies: Messaging Applications Programming Interface (MAPI) and Telephony Application Program Interface (TAPI) . The level of support you can expect is similar to that found in Windows 95/98. Windows 2000 even includes a couple utility programs that make use of these new APIs.

Next, we'll look at standards. Where would computing be without the standards we use today? If you really want to understand what's going on, you need to spend some time learning about those standards. The material in this chapter won't make you a communications expert, but it'll give you the resources you need to become one.

Making Hardware Attachments

As advanced as some users are when it comes to software, they're handicapped when it comes to hardware. Perhaps you've heard the story of the guy who placed a floppy disk in the space between the two drives because his machine lacked a 5 1/4-inch floppy drive. It's funny to think about someone actually doing something that silly. Of course, there's also the joke about people who use whiteout to cover up onscreen mistakes. Everyone has a favorite joke about someone who did something harebrained on his or her computer. My favorite is the quiet lady who called customer support and was told, "Now insert the 5 1/4-inch floppy disk and close the door." The customer service rep heard her click, click, click as she walked across the room and closed the door. My second favorite is the new executive assistant who was a bit afraid of computers and asked, "What should I avoid?" He was told "You really can't do any damage to a computer by anything you type in, unless you accidentally press the F11 key at the same time as the Enter key. Just avoid ever doing that and you'll be okay." Of course, he was told a few days later that this was just a joke. Nobody wanted him to dissolve into a nervous wreck trying to avoid this key combination.

Making the wrong connection in real life is another story. Finding that your printer or modem doesn't work when there's a critical deadline isn't funny at all. A frantic worker trying to figure out why his external SCSI drive or another device won't work without a terminator is enough to send chills up anyone's spine. That's the kind of serious connection work we'll talk about here. I won't bore you with stories of oddball incidents; I'm going to tell you about real-life connection problems and how to avoid them.

Any Port in a Storm

The first thing we need to talk about is the external ports on your machine. The problem for many people is not knowing where these ports connect or what they do. Some very different ports even look alike. There's the distinct possibility that you could confuse a game port with a thick ethernet port, for example, because they look exactly the same. Even though most ports are easy to identify given certain clues, just grabbing any port on the back of your machine isn't such a good idea. It's always better to mark the ports and know exactly what they do before you try to use them. You might end up costing yourself a lot of time if you don't. What if you have two nine-pin serial ports on your machine, for example? Which one is COM1? Just knowing what function the port serves might not be enough.

Technical Note: I've spent more than a little time trying to figure out foolproof ways to make sense out of that web of confusion on the back of everyone's machine—it can't be done with today's technology. Obviously, we need some new technology that'll clean up the mess sometime in the future. Just as obviously, any solution will make a big mess out of things for the interim.

Intel, Microsoft, and other companies have developed a standard that should help in the long run. The universal serial bus (USB) is available in both Windows 98 and Windows 2000. This standard, like Plug and Play, enables you to install all kinds of peripheral devices much more easily. In fact, you can already get several kinds of common devices such as a mouse, printer, joystick, monitor, and modem for your machine. With USB, you no longer need to worry about DIP switches, jumpers, DMA channels, I/O addresses, and drivers. There's a single connector type, and you just plug in the mouse, speaker, or whatever device, and the computer takes over from there.

When using USB, you can also chain devices and plug or unplug devices while the computer is on. With most devices a separate power plug isn't needed—the peripherals get their power right through the USB cord. Oh, and one other nice little feature: Data transfer is 10 times faster than current serial ports.

With USB, you can daisy-chain up to 255 devices to one port, eliminating the need for separate interrupt and port settings for each of those devices within your machine. A user will also benefit from the 32-bit data path this new standard offers because it exceeds just about any connection offered right now.

Until we all have USB devices, however, we can be thankful that at least some types of currently used ports are, fortunately, also tough to confuse. A 25-pin port with female pins, for example, is a parallel (printer) port. Nothing else on your system uses that configuration. A 25-pin port with male pins is a serial port; nothing else uses that combination either. And given their gender differences, you'll have a hard time plugging a female plug into a female port. (There are always odd exceptions to any rule, but mercifully they're few. I do have old SCSI cables that are 25-pin male, and I've installed SYNC cards to talk to SYNC modems that aren't a normal "COM" port. You're very unlikely to run into these items today.)

Of course, an external SCSI or other adapter is also pretty difficult to confuse. They usually contain so many pins that they fill the entire width of the expansion slot. Only SCSI plugs and porcupines plug into those. But that's the short list of the easy ports—the ones you can identify just by looking at them. The other ports require closer identification before you'll know what they do.

You can make several generalizations by looking at the back of your PC. Figure 20.1 shows the back of a typical PC with ports identified.

Table 20.1 contains a partial list of the clues I use to identify the ports on the back of my machine. You, too, can use these clues if there's some reason why you can't open up your machine. (Note that some warranty policies don't let you open your machine because the vendor is concerned about user tampering.)

FIGURE 20.1

You can identify the ports on the back of a PC by size, shape, position, and other cues.

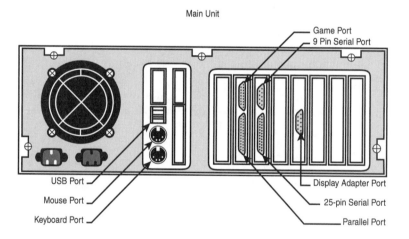

Table 20.1   Adapters and Their Associated Ports

Adapter	Port Description
ethernet	Today's predominant LAN port is the RJ-45 (Registered Jack-45) telephone-style connector. This is an eight-wire connector that you'll find everywhere these days making the connections between computers and LANs, particularly ethernets. The RJ-45 looks quite a bit like the RJ-11 plug used to connect telephones (in the wall jacks and in the phone proper) as well as the plugs that go into your modem. The primary difference between them is that the RJ-45 is a bit wider than the RJ-11.

Adapter	Port Description
	You might also see a "combo" card, with both RJ-45 and BNC connectors on it. (These cards never have DIP switches on them, although they almost always have lights.) ArcNet cards almost always have DIP switches on the back, because of the limited number of addresses.
	If you have legacy equipment, you might be using "Thicknet" connectors. True, it's getting harder and harder to find an ethernet card with the Thicknet connector on it these days. Almost everyone's now using the RJ-45 plug. However, in case you're working with the older connection, here's a description. The Thicknet adapter normally has a 15-pin thick ethernet port and a coaxial cable thin ethernet connector. The round coaxial connector is the same width as the slot and has two knobs on it for connecting the cable. The adapter might also provide DIP switches. Similar-looking cards include ArcNet adapters. However, they always lack the 15-pin port. ArcNet adapters usually include active indicator LEDs (lights) as well.
I/O port combo	The combination port card usually provides a 25-pin parallel port and a nine-pin serial port on the back of the adapter. The serial port is usually COM1 and the parallel port is LPT1. Be warned that the installer could have changed these default settings using the jumpers on the card or software setup. An I/O port combo adapter also includes either a 9- or 25-pin serial port and a 15-pin game port that attaches through the back of the machine. If your case doesn't provide the extra cable connector holes, these ports might appear in one of the expansion slot openings. Some older multifunction cards, such as the Intel Above Board, used this port layout as well. Fortunately, the ports served the same purpose.
SVGA display	Some older versions of these cards provide both a nine-pin digital and a 15-pin analog port. Note that this 15-pin port is the same size as the nine-pin port. The pins are arranged in three rows of five rather than the two-row arrangement used by the game port. They're also a little smaller than the ones used by the game port. The display adapter might include a mouse port for a PS/2-style mouse. Some adapters provide only the 15-pin port (a requirement for SVGA). Other features on the back of this card might include DIP switches or three high-frequency connectors to connect to a high-resolution monitor.

continues

Table 20.1 Continued

Adapter	Port Description
Game	This adapter usually contains two 15-pin game ports. The one nearest the top of the machine is usually the one you want to use. Game adapters almost always include a submini plug used for a variable-speed controller. This controller matches the speed of the game port to the speed of the machine.
Sound board	You'll usually see a 15-pin game port that doubles as a MIDI port when you select the right jumper or software settings. This adapter also includes three submini jacks that look the same as the earphone jacks on a portable radio. The precise arrangement of these jacks varies by vendor, but they serve the following purposes: output, microphone, and line input from an external source, such as a CD-ROM drive. Some older sound boards also include a volume-level thumbwheel.
External SCSI	You'll see a number of large connectors on the back of a machine. A 50-pin SCSI connector looks like a larger version of the Centronics connector that attaches to your printer. It doesn't use the same type of pins that the more familiar serial or parallel connector does.
External drive	A number of older CD-ROM drives used a 37-pin plug. It looks like a huge version of the parallel port. You might see this with other types of drives as well. It's never safe to assume anything about this plug. Always check it against the vendor documentation.
USB	This port is easy to spot because it normally appears near the keyboard plug in the back of the machine. The USB port is square in shape and will accept two plugs in the same hole (one on the top and the other on the bottom of the square opening). The USB port will eventually replace most, if not all, of the other ports on the back of your machine with one universal plug type.
Fax/modem	A fax or modem card usually provides two RJ-11 plugs. (They look like the ones on your telephone.) One plug enables you to connect the incoming cable, and the other plug is for your telephone. This adapter usually includes some external DIP switches, as well.

Besides all these combinations, a multitude of third-party adapters might look like one of the adapters in Table 20.1 but won't provide the same functionality. Fortunately, you'll probably know whether you have one of them installed, because you'll need it to perform some special task on your machine. The general rule to follow is this: If you see a port that you don't recognize, and it isn't marked, open the machine to identify it. You can tell by what board it's attached to as to what its function is. The second rule is that you shouldn't always believe the markings on the back of your machine. If you look back there and see that all the ports you do recognize are correctly marked, you can probably assume that the rest are correct, too. If you see a serial port identified as a parallel port, however, you should question whether any of the markers are correct.

> **Tip:** Always mark the ports on the back of the machines you maintain after you identify the ports. I use preprinted Avery or other vendor labels if at all possible. You can get them at any stationery store. Some computer stores also carry them. When I don't have any of the preprinted labels available, I use masking tape or a blank mailing label. Make sure you use a permanent marker, in this case, to prevent smudging. Also, don't just write down that something is a serial port. Specify COM1 or COM2 as part of the marking. Performing this little extra step can save you a lot of time later. You might want to follow this same procedure with cables, especially if the machine is connected to a workstation setup in which the cable source might become hidden. Trying to identify the correct cable when there are several possibilities is never a welcome task. It's easier to mark everything at the outset.

Printers

We covered the topic of printer installation and parallel port configuration in Chapter 17, "Exploiting Your Hardware," and Chapter 18, "Fonts and Printing," contains a lot of printer usage details. I'll cover printer connections in this chapter. Some people think there's only one way to connect a printer: through a parallel port. They're wrong. Every printer I know of provides a minimum of two connection types. You can always connect a printer using a serial or a parallel port. (Although it's true that you won't find many serial ports installed on printers these days as a default, you can usually order the serial port as an option.)

> **Tip:** Some printers don't provide a serial port as standard equipment; you have to buy it as a separate piece. Your vendor manual should provide details on buying the serial port option. Look to see whether the vendor also supports other connection options that might help in some situations. Many vendors now support a network connection as standard equipment; others support it as an optional module. The new USB connection type will become an important feature in Windows 98 and Windows 2000. Even though USB connections for printers are still rare, I have seen them. More common are USB-enabled mice, keyboards, speakers, scanners, digital cameras, and joysticks.

Choosing between these two connections isn't always easy, even though it seems like a no-brainer. A parallel port delivers the data eight bits at a time and at a faster rate than a serial port. Choosing the parallel port doesn't take too much thought if your machine has only one printer attached to it. But what if your machine acts as a print server for many different printers? You could easily run out of parallel ports in this situation. Just about everyone resorts to an A/B switch to increase the number of available connections, but there might be a better solution. Connecting your printer to the machine through an unused serial port will allow better access to it. No one will have to flip an A/B switch to use it. (Some A/B switches provide an automatic switching scheme when you send certain commands through the printer cable, but this means training the user to send those commands and a lot of frustration when the user forgets to do so.) The problem is that the access is slower—a lot slower than with a parallel port, which can make a big difference when you're printing a large report that needs to go out in an hour or so. Note that more and more printers are being built with an ethernet adapter right on the printer itself, so with them you don't have to worry about parallel ports at all. However, if a printer only has a parallel port, you can usually purchase an HP JetDirect card for it. This is a way to add it to a network.

Categorizing how people will use the printers attached to your machine is the next step. Placing a printer that the user is less likely to use or a printer that normally experiences a lower level of activity on a serial port shouldn't cause any problems. Just make sure you warn people that their print jobs could take a little longer because of the new configuration. I find that this enables me to connect at least four different printers to most machines. Of course, when you get to this level, you need to question whether you should dedicate a machine to act as a print server instead of trying to get by using a workstation on a peer-to-peer network. (A print server acts like any other server on a network—it accepts print jobs from a group of users and keeps them in a queue until the printer is ready to accept them.)

Tip: There's a point when it becomes difficult to support too many printers on a peer-to-peer network. I usually start to look at other solutions after the number of workstations reaches 10 users or the number of printers exceeds four. After that limit, the performance of a peer-to-peer setup diminishes to the point where it's doubtful that you can get any useful work accomplished. In these cases, you normally need to upgrade to a client/server setup like the one provided by Novell NetWare or Windows NT/2000 Server. There are always exceptions to the rule, but observing these limits usually provides the best measure of when it's time to upgrade.

These days, some printers (not too many, see the following Technical Note) come with a built-in network interface card (NIC). You can attach them directly to the network without using a workstation connection. The two most popular connection types are ethernet and AppleTalk. Of course, the appropriate selection depends on the network you're running. Whether this solution will work for you depends not on the NIC as much as it depends on the software included with the printer. The printer actually boots as a workstation or a self-contained print server on the network. You see it just as you'd see any other workstation. The only difference is that this workstation is dedicated to a single task: printing. You need to find out which networks the vendor supports. Unfortunately, the very nature of this type of connection excludes it from consideration until more vendors come out with Windows-specific products (any vendor that supports a Microsoft network should work). This really is a great solution for a peer-to-peer network, because it enables you to use the printer without loading down the workstation. Adding a printer this way also preserves precious workstation resources such as interrupts and I/O port addresses.

> **Technical Note:** Note that most printers don't boot as a workstation. Most printers are connected via an ethernet connection. Then you just have to install a proper protocol and communication interface to be able to talk to the device. Every single card I've run into supports TCP/IP printing, which uses the Line Printer Remote/Line Printer Daemon (LPR/LPD) protocol to handle the print job itself. To install such a printer, you only need to give it an IP address and then plug it into the network. The user installs TCP/IP Printing Services on Windows 2000 Professional or Server. Then the user creates an LPR/LPD port and tells Windows 2000 that that's where the printer is located. The most popular card by far is the HP JetDirect. You need two parameters to identify the machine and print to it: the IP address, which you enter as the name of the device, and the port number, which for a JetDirect card is 2100.

Printers also support some of the more exotic network connections these days, but you might be hard-pressed to find them. One solution that I see gaining in popularity is the wireless LAN. Just think—using this type of connection, you could unwrap the printer, plug it in, and perform a few configuration steps to get it up and running. In the future, adding a printer to the network might be even easier than adding it to your local workstation.

Modems

There are two fundamental kinds of modems: internal and external. I prefer an external modem for several reasons. The biggest reason is portability. I can move a modem in a matter of minutes by disconnecting it from the current machine, moving it, and reconnecting it to the new machine. It's a lot faster and easier than opening the machine to get at an internal modem card. About the only thing easier than moving a modem connected to a COM port is moving one connected to a USB port. In addition to allowing you to move it with ease, a USB modem will also automatically configure itself once you plug it into the new machine.

External modems also provide better visual feedback with their blinking lights, although some software is taking care of this now by displaying all the indicators that you normally see on an external modem. An external modem still has the edge when it comes to troubleshooting, because the light indicators you get from your software might not always reflect reality. In addition, most of the software out there doesn't accurately report the modem's connection speed—a necessary piece of troubleshooting information.

Some modems also generate a lot of heat and can affect system performance when installed internally. Although I've never run into a heat problem from using an internal modem, I've heard of other people running into this problem. On the other hand, modems have become relatively inexpensive, so you might want an external modem for troubleshooting and your portable computer, and an internal one for the convenience of having it always there.

> **Note:** The old 8250 UART chip won't provide a good connection beyond 9600bps. You must use a 16450 or 16550 UART with a 14.4Kbps or faster modem to ensure an error-free connection. Although there's nothing wrong with the UART itself, the lack of a buffer in the 8250 will cause data overflows. These overflows will, in turn, cause failures in the connection protocols.

After you get past the physical location of a modem, you get to the connections. The first connection is the telephone cable required to contact the outside world. Many offices don't have the RJ-11 plugs that a modem uses as standard equipment. They use a six-wire plug that looks like a larger version of the RJ-11. You can plug an RJ-11 jack into this plug, but I can guarantee that it won't work. Normally, you have to get an office wired for modems before you can actually use one. Of course, home users won't run into this problem because a modem uses a standard home telephone jack.

Modems are also rated by speed and capability. The speed that a modem can communicate at is increasing all the time. It seems that just a short time ago, a 28.8Kbps connection was considered the fastest around. Now most vendors offer 56Kbps modems, and there's talk of even higher speeds in the future. You'll also find that nearly all Internet providers offer access at a minimum of the 28.8Kbps rate. Because a modem can usually communicate with any modem at its speed or slower, there's never a good reason to buy a low-speed modem.

There are a ton of modem standards, most of which won't make a lot of difference to you as a user. There are some standards that you should know about, however. A lot of standardization has to do with the modem's speed, the way it corrects errors, or the method it uses to compress data. Knowing about these standards could mean the difference between getting a good buy on a modem and getting one that's almost useless. Table 20.2 identifies the more common modem standards, but you should also be aware of any new standards that develop around higher-speed modems (like those for ISDN and cable modems).

Table 20.2   Common Modem Standards

Standard	Description
Bell 103	The American standard for 300 baud modems. It was the rate that everyone used when PCs first arrived on the scene.
Bell 212A	The American 1200 baud modem included both this standard and the Bell 103 standard. European standards included enough differences to require a separate modem in most cases.
CCITT V.21	Defines the European standard for 300 baud modems. Like its counterpart, this standard is very much out of date.
CCITT V.22	The European version of the 1200 baud modem standard. It also includes the V.21 standard.
CCITT V.22bis	You might wonder what *bis* in this standard number means. Just think of it as revision B. In this case, it refers to the general standard for 2400 baud modems. (Bis is French for "second." Just think of it as revision B.)
CCITT V.23	A special 1200/75bps standard for the European market that sends data at one speed and receives at another. Modems don't support it unless they're designed for use outside America.
CCITT V.25bis	Defines an alternative command set for modems that you won't need unless your modem also supports an X.25 interface.
CCITT V.32	Defines the 4800bps, 9600bps, 14.4Kbps, 19.2Kbps, and 28.8Kbps standards.
CCITT V.34	Defines the data compression specifics for the 28.8Kbps standard. It also defines the 33.6Kbps standard.
CCITT V.42	Defines a data compression method for modems (also requires the modem to provide MNP Levels 2 through 4) that allows the modem to transfer data at apparent rates of up to 19.2Kbps.
CCITT V.42bis	The second revision of the modem data compression standard that allows up to a 4× compression factor or an apparent transfer rate of 38.4Kbps from a 9600bps modem.
CCITT V.FAST	This was a proprietary method of defining data compression for the 28.8Kbps standard. It's been replaced by the CCITT V.34 standard.
CCITT X.25	Some asynchronous modems also support this synchronous data transfer standard. You don't need it if your only goal is to communicate with online services.

continues

Table 20.2   Continued.

Standard	Description
MNP 2-4, 5, 10	Microm Networking Protocol, a standard method of error-correcting for modems. The precise differences between levels aren't important from a user prospective. A higher level is generally better.
x2 and K56Flex protocols	These are two rival standards for defining how 56Kbps modems work. A new 56Kbps standard will combine the features of both x2 and K56Flex standards into a single universal 56Kbps standard.
v.90	The combined x2 and K56Flex standards for 56 Kbps modems.

The main reason to worry about modem standards is if you're planning to use a modem in another country or if you're buying a generic, no-name modem that might offer a bargain price but no promise of quality. If you stick with name-brand, popular modems, you should have no trouble getting your modem to work with other computers.

Fax Boards

The section "Modems" introduced you to modem connections. Fax facilities are usually included with your modem (as in fax/modem). Windows 2000 supports a wide range of fax/modems. If all you plan to do is fax documents using Windows Exchange, you can do so without buying a lot of fancy hardware.

Every fax/modem transfer consists of five phases. The ITU (formerly CCITT) defines these phases in several standards, which we'll examine later. These five phases aren't cast in concrete, and each one could repeat during any given session. It all depends on the capabilities of your fax/modem, the software you're using, and the environment conditions at the time:

- *Phase 1: Call establishment.* Your computer calls another computer or a standard fax machine.
- *Phase 2: Pre-message procedure.* The sending and receiving machines select parameters that will allow them to transfer data at the fastest possible rate. These parameters also take into account the resolution, modulation, and other factors.
- *Phase 3: Message transmission.* This is the phase in which the actual data transfer takes place. If the initial group of parameters set in Phase 2 results in less than optimal results, the fax/modem performs Phase 2 and Phase 3 again, as required.
- *Phase 4: Post-message procedure.* Some software considers each page as a separate message. In fact, that's the way your fax machine works as well. Phase 4 allows the sending and receiving machines to evaluate the results of each message and then raise or lower the transmission speed as required. This is also the phase

in which the sending machine transmits a pagebreak marker. This is the same thing as a formfeed on a printer, except that the fax cuts off the page immediately instead of moving the paper to the top of the next physical page. Remember that faxes can be long or short, depending on the message needs.

- *Phase 5: Call clear down.* This is the easiest part of the conversation. The two machines hang up the phone after the sending machine transmits an end-of-transmission signal.

As with modems, several fax/modem specifications exist. You'll want a fax/modem that adheres to the ITU standards listed in Table 20.3 (most name brand modems sold today do).

Table 20.3   Common Fax/Modem Standards

Standard	Description
ITU T.4	Defines the image-transfer portion of the session used in Phase 3.
ITU T.30	Defines the negotiation and interpage phases (2, 3, 4, and 5). A normal multipage transfer uses T.30 only at the beginning of the call, between pages, and after the last page.
CCITT V.17	Defines the specifications for the 4800/1200bps speed. The slash shows that the fax receives at one speed and sends at another.
CCITT V.27	Defines the specifications for the 9600/7200bps speed.
CCITT V.29	Defines the specifications for the 14,400/12,000bps speed.
ITU V.34	Defines the combined voice, fax, and data standards for 28.8Kbps and 33.6Kbps modems.

Microsoft also provides for two classes of fax communication between fax/modems. Here's the user view of what these different classes mean. Class 1 communications send an editable fax to the other party. This means that the fax appears as actual text that the other party can edit in a word processor, rather than a graphic picture (a mere snapshot of a page). Class 2 communications are more like the fax you usually receive. They're graphics representations of the text and graphics in the document. This is the same format as Group 3 faxes, such as the ones you're used to seeing in the office.

The real-world difference between Class 1 and Class 2 fax/modems is really quite distinct. A Class 1 fax performs both the T.4 and T.30 protocols in software. This allows the additional flexibility Windows 2000 needs to create editable faxes. All data translation is performed by Windows 2000 drivers. A Class 2 fax performs the T.4 protocol in firmware—an EEPROM in the modem that does part of the work for the processor. This is a faster solution because it removes part of the processing burden from the processor. A Class 2 fax/modem should also be able to create editable faxes. This is where the plot thickens. Because the Class 2 standard isn't defined very well, Microsoft didn't have any dependable information on what to expect from a Class 2 fax/modem. It made the decision to restrict Class 2 faxes to the Group 3 graphics format.

Note: The Electronic Industries Association (EIA) approved a Class 2 standard that stringently defines what vendors need to provide in firmware. As a result, you'll see software that uses Class 2 fax/modems more efficiently than they used to.

Tip: If you're looking for Windows NT/Windows 2000-specific fax software, try this site:

http://www.ntfax-faq.com/

Making Software Attachments

After you get your hardware up and running, you have to get some software to talk to it in order to do any useful work. That's where some of the utilities you get with Windows 2000 come in. They don't necessarily provide the best capabilities, but they do provide enough for you to get going. In fact, you might be surprised at just how well they meet some of your needs.

The following sections describe several of the utilities that come with Windows 2000. These utilities won't help you "surf the Net" or download the latest industry gossip. I cover general communications in the next chapter when we look at online services. You'll find the Internet-specific utilities in the "Windows to the Internet" section of Chapter 2. Both sets of utilities help you make the necessary connections.

Peter's Principle: The Right Kind of Connection

It might be tempting to use a single type of connection to meet all your computing needs, but that wouldn't be the most efficient way to do things. You might view a direct cable connection as the panacea for all your portable data-transfer woes, but the direct cable connection is really designed for occasional, not daily, use. A direct cable connection works fine for those quick transfers from one machine to another when you have a fairly large amount of data to move. It works very well when you initially set up a portable, for example, and are transferring lots of data from your main desktop to the portable.

If you use a portable on a daily basis, using a direct cable connection is a waste of time. You'll want to find some other method of creating your connection to the desktop. A PCMCIA network card is one solution. It'll enable you to connect the portable to the network and use a much faster ethernet connection to make the data transfer. This works only if you have a network and a PCMCIA card, however. Some laptops also provide infrared ports that allow you to create a wireless connection to the network.

Windows 2000 also provides the Remote Access Server (RAS), which I cover at the end of this chapter. You can use it to dial in to your machine from another

continues

location. Of course, this assumes that your machine is online and that you have a modem with you on the road. The lack of proper phone connections in hotel rooms has become less of an issue in recent years, but you're still going to run into it. Make sure you check with your hotel before you count on connecting to your desktop machine while on the road. And also ask them about any extra charges for telephone use—some hotels really gouge you, even for local calls.

We covered the Synchronization Manager (the Briefcase replacement) in Chapter 5, "Exploring the Interface." This isn't a physical connection to your desktop machine, but it does do the job for smaller amounts of data. In fact, you'll find that a Briefcase can hold a substantial amount of data if you use it correctly.

Okay, suppose the network and synchronization options are out of the question because you're out of town. You can still make a connection to your desktop using RAS or the Dial-Up Networking utility. It won't be as fast as some of the other techniques, but it'll enable you to get the data you require while on the road or when working from home.

Windows 2000 provides a lot of different connections. You need to use the right one for the job, and that means taking the time to learn about the various options available to you. A connection that works well in one instance could be a time killer in another. Don't succumb to the one-connection way of computing; use every tool that Windows 2000 provides.

Using Dial-up Networking

Forget everything you know if you've used Dial-up Networking under Windows 95/98; the utility provided with Windows 2000 doesn't even bear a close resemblance to the Windows 95/98 equivalent. The Windows 2000 program is actually more flexible than the Windows 95/98 equivalent and allows you to create more connection types using a single utility: the Network Connection Wizard. You'll access this utility through the Make New Connection applet found in the Network and Dial-up Connections folder, as shown in Figure 20.2. Notice that the Network and Dial-Up Connections folder also stores any connections that you've already created. You can access this folder using the Start, Settings, Network and Dial-up Connections command.

FIGURE 20.2

The Network and Dial-up Connections folder is where you'll find any connections you create along with the Make New Connection applet.

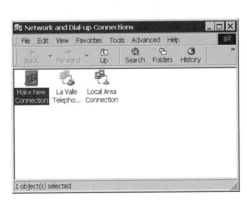

The default Network Connection Wizard setup will allow you to create five different network connection types, including three that are Internet related (the other two connection types deal with direct computer-to-computer connections). The following list provides a quick overview of the five connection types:

- *Dial-up to private network.* This option allows you to dial into a server from a remote location. However, just creating the connection won't be enough. The server has to be set up to accept the call, and you need the correct rights before the server will allow you to make a connection. You'd normally use this option to dial into the company network when working at home.

- *Dial-up to the Internet.* You'll use this option to create a standard connection to the Internet using a modem. It allows you to create a direct connection without accessing a proxy server or other intermediary first.

- *Connect to a private network through the Internet.* A lot of companies are creating Virtual Private Networks (VPNs) today to reduce costs. Calling into the company server using the telephone lines incurs long distance charges and relies on good phone lines between remote locations. Normally, the call through the Internet is accomplished for a lot less and is even more reliable in some situations. In addition, depending on how the client and server are connected, the connection can actually be faster than the connection speeds offered using standard telephone lines.

- *Accept incoming connections.* There are times when you may decide to allow other people to access your machine through the phone line. For that matter, you may simply want to access your work or home computer from another location. This option allows you to set up the various communication settings required for a remote connection from another machine. This option allows you to create connections using a phone line, the Internet, or a direct cable.

- *Connect directly to another computer.* A lot of people use a laptop on the road and another machine while at their company. This option allows you to create a direct cable connection between two computers that relies on a serial, parallel, or infrared connection.

Now that we have some of the preliminaries out of the way, let's see how you can use the Network Connection Wizard to create these five connection types. The following sections will guide you through the process of creating each connection type.

Dial-up to Private Network

The Dial-up to Private Network connection type allows you to call into your company's server from a remote location. All you need to use this option is a phone line and a modem. The company server has to be running some type of software, such as Remote Access Server (RAS), that allows it to accept a call from a remote location. In addition, your account on the remote server has to be marked to allow remote access. There might be restrictions on your account such as a callback requirement, where the server hangs up after it determines your identity and calls you back at a specific number. All this means is that you'll need to check with your network administrator before you can use this connection feature. The following procedure shows you how to set things up once you get the required permission:

1. Double-click the Make New Connection applet within the Network and Dial-up Connections folder shown in Figure 20.2. You'll see the initial Network Connection Wizard dialog box.

2. Click Next and you'll see a list of connection types you can choose from, as shown in Figure 20.3. As previously mentioned, this list reflects the default Windows 2000 configuration. It's theoretically possible that you'll see additional connection types.

FIGURE 20.3
Windows 2000 supports five default connection types.

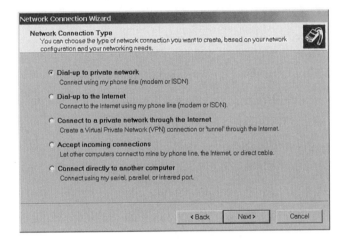

3. Choose the Dial-up to Private Network option and then click Next. You'll see a Phone Number to Dial dialog box that contains three fields and a check box. The three fields contain the area code, phone number, and area or region (such as the United States) that you're calling. The check box allows you to choose between using the phone number alone or using all three fields for dialing (as needed).

4. Enter a phone number as a minimum. You may also need to enter the area code and choose a region if you've chosen to use dialing rules. Click Next. You'll see a Connection Availability dialog box. This dialog box allows you to choose between making the connection available to everyone or keeping it private.

5. Choose either the For All Users or Only For Myself option and then click Next. You'll see a Completing the Network Connection Wizard dialog box.

6. Type a name for your connection. You may also choose to place a shortcut for the connection on your Desktop. Click Finish. Windows will create the connection for you and display a Connect dialog box.

Dial-up to the Internet

You'll use the Dial-up to the Internet connection type whenever you want to create a new connection to the Internet using your modem. The process for creating this type of connection follows the same first two steps as you saw in the previous section. Essentially, you'll start the Network Connection Wizard by double-clicking the Make New Connection applet. Then choose the Dial-up to the Internet connection type once you get past the initial dialog box. Once you make this selection, Windows will start the Internet Connection Wizard. This utility is covered in Chapters 2, "Windows to the Internet," and 21, "Outlook Express."

Connect to a Private Network Through the Internet

The Connection to a Private Network Through the Internet option will create a Virtual Private Network (VPN) connection for you. VPNs are something that many companies are considering today because they can get a long-distance connection for the price of a local call. There are a lot of other advantages as well. Depending on the situation, it's possible to create a high-speed connection without any special connections between companies. One company can use its high-speed Internet connection to dial another company without much problem. In the past, this type of communication would have required a special telephone connection.

Don't get the idea that VPNs are without problems. For one thing, there's the problem of creating a secure connection over the Internet, which means relying on data encryption and other protection methodologies such as digital certificates. In short, there's no free ride. The following procedure shows you how to create a VPN connection:

1. Create a dial-up connection for your ISP, if necessary. You'll need this connection later in the procedure. We covered the process of creating an Internet connection in the "Starting and Setting Up Internet Explorer" and "Making a Connection" sections of Chapter 2.

2. Double-click the Make New Connection applet within the Network and Dial-up Connections folder shown in Figure 20.1. You'll see the initial Network Connection Wizard dialog box.

3. Click Next and you'll see a list of connection types you can choose from, as shown previously in Figure 20.2. As mentioned earlier, this list reflects the default Windows 2000 configuration. It's theoretically possible that you'll see additional connection types.

4. Choose the Connection to a Private Network Through the Internet option and then click Next. You'll see a Public Network dialog box that provides the option of not dialing an initial connection or of automatically dialing one of the Internet connections that you've already created. The drop-down list box below this second option will contain a list of the currently defined connections on your machine.

5. Choose a dial-up option and then click Next. You'll see a Destination Address dialog box. This is where you'll enter the hostname or IP address for the server that you want to connect to. The IP address will likely be different than the one you use to access the server locally, so make sure you check with the network administrator before you enter a value in this dialog box.

6. Enter an IP address or hostname and then click Next. You'll see a Connection Availability dialog box. This dialog box allows you to choose between making the connection available to everyone or keeping it private.

7. Choose either the For All Users or Only For Myself option and then click Next. You'll see a Completing the Network Connection Wizard dialog box.

8. Type a name for your connection. You may also choose to place a shortcut for the connection on your Desktop. Click Finish. Windows will create the connection for you, offer to connect to the Internet (if not already connected), and then display a Connect dialog box to your server.

Accept Incoming Connections

Sometimes it's more than a convenience to access your desktop computer at work while on the road. Your laptop machine may not be able to hold all the data you need while on the road or you simply may want the option of downloading files if you forget something. Likewise, if you commonly work at home and at corporate headquarters, you'll want to have the option of transferring data from the other machine. That's where the Accepting Incoming Connections communication type comes in really handy—it gives you a lot of flexibility in communicating with a remote machine. Obviously, you can also use this option to allow other people to contact your machine for the purpose of exchanging information. The following procedure shows you how to set up this type of connection:

1. Double-click the Make New Connection applet within the Network and Dial-up Connections folder shown previously in Figure 20.2. You'll see the initial Network Connection Wizard dialog box.

2. Click Next and you'll see a list of connection types that you can choose from, as shown previously in Figure 20.3. As mentioned earlier, this list reflects the default Windows 2000 configuration. It's theoretically possible that you'll see additional connection types.

3. Choose the Accept Incoming Connections option and then click Next. You'll see a Devices for Incoming Connections dialog box like the one shown in Figure 20.4. This is where you'll choose one or more modems or other communication devices to accept incoming calls. The list shows all the devices that your machine can access. Checking the box next to the device allows that device to accept calls. Highlighting a device and clicking Properties will allow you to set the options for that device.

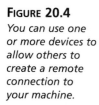

FIGURE 20.4

You can use one or more devices to allow others to create a remote connection to your machine.

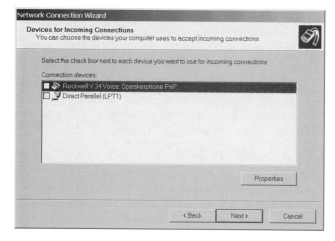

4. Check one or more communication devices. Set the communication properties for each device, as needed, and then click Next. You'll see the Incoming Virtual Private Connection dialog box.

5. Choose the Allow Virtual Private Connections option if you want other people to connect to your machine using the same technology as they would use for a VPN. (A VPN will also require a static IP address on the host machine.) Choose the Do Not Allow Virtual Private Connections option if you want to use standard data-transfer and user-verification procedures. This second option is a lot less secure than the first one, so you won't want to use it for critical company data. On the other hand, the second option is also faster.

6. Click Next. You'll see an Allowed Users dialog box like the one shown in Figure 20.5. This dialog box allows you to choose from a list of users that either your local machine or the domain controller will recognize. In short, the list will contain anyone who can be verified within your company.

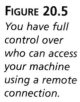

FIGURE 20.5

You have full control over who can access your machine using a remote connection.

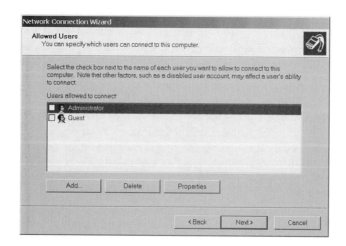

7. Choose one or more users to access your machine by checking the boxes next to their names. At this point, you need to configure each user who will access your machine.

8. Highlight a user who can access your machine and then click Properties. You'll see the General tab of the user Properties dialog box. This tab allows you to set a different password for user access than the user would normally use for accessing the network. Using an alternate password is a good idea because it reduces the chance of a cracker accessing your machine.

9. Change the user password, if desired, and then select the Callback tab. This dialog box has three options. You can disallow callbacks, which means that the user will connect and have immediate access to your machine. The user can also set the callback number, which means that your computer will record the number that the user is calling from and then test the validity of that number by hanging up and calling the user back. Finally, you can set the connection to call back the user at a specific number, which prevents anyone from dialing in from any location other than the one you specify. Of course, this third option also greatly reduces the flexibility of the callback feature.

10. Choose a callback option and then click OK. Click Next. You'll see a Networking Components dialog box like the one shown in Figure 20.6. This is where you'll use the protocols that the user will have access to when attempting to access the network from your machine. You can simply uncheck all the protocols if you want to completely restrict network access. Notice that this dialog box will also allow you to install or uninstall protocols and configure existing ones.

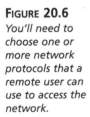

Figure 20.6
You'll need to choose one or more network protocols that a remote user can use to access the network.

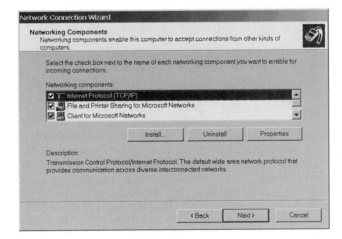

11. Choose and configure one or more network options and then click Next. You'll see the Completing the Network Connection Wizard dialog box.

12. Type a name for your connection and then click Finish. Note that there isn't any option for placing a shortcut to this connection type on your desktop.

Connect Directly to Another Computer

In this day and age, networks would seem to be the best option for connecting one computer to another. I can't think of any laptop computers that can't be fitted with a NIC. In short, this last option is for those occasions when you have no other way to connect two computers than using the tried-and-true serial port or parallel port option. (If you're using a cable connection, make sure you get a cable that supports a NULL modem connection. Yur computer dealer should be able to supply you with either a special cable or an adapter that makes a standard cable into a NULL modem cable.) This connection will also support infrared connections, which shows that it's essentially designed to meet the needs of laptop users who use a desktop while at home. The following procedure shows you how to create this connection type:

1. Double-click the Make New Connection applet within the Network and Dial-up Connections folder, shown previously in Figure 20.2. You'll see the initial Network Connection Wizard dialog box.

2. Click Next and you'll see a list of connection types you can choose from, as shown previously in Figure 20.3. As mentioned earlier, this list reflects the default Windows 2000 configuration. It's theoretically possible that you'll see additional connection types.

3. Choose the Connect Directly to Another Computer option and then click Next. You'll see a Host or Guest dialog box. One computer in the connection has to be the host, the other the guest. The host computer controls the connection for the most part, so you'll want to set the host to be the computer that you'll actually work at during the data transfer.

4. Choose the Host or Guest option and then click Next. You'll see a dialog box that asks you to choose a device for making the connection.

5. Choose a device from the drop-down list box. If you're creating a guest connection, skip to Step 7. If you're creating a host connection, click Next. You'll see an Allowed User dialog box like the one shown in Figure 20.5. This dialog box allows you to choose from a list of users that either your local machine or the domain controller will recognize.

6. Choose one or more users to access your machine by checking the boxes next to their names. At this point, you may need to configure each user who will access your machine. In most cases, however, you won't need to do anything but select a list of users because this is going to be a local connection. I've already covered the procedure for configuring a user in the "Accept Incoming Connections" section, so I won't cover it again here.

7. Click Next. You'll see the Completing the Network Connection Wizard dialog box.

8. Type a name for your connection and then click Finish. Note that there isn't any option for placing a shortcut to this connection type on your desktop. However, you can easily drag (holding the right-mouse button down) the connection from the Network and Dial-up Connections folder in the Control Panel, drop it on your Desktop, and choose the Create Shortcut Here option from the context menu.

TAPI and MAPI Support

Application programming interfaces (APIs) enable programmers to accomplish a lot of work with only a little effort. An API is a collection of procedures that come with an operating system and whose functionality can be "borrowed" by programmers. APIs ensure a standardized form of access to specific system resources and capabilities. Using a standard interface enables the operating system vendor to change the implementation details without "breaking" (messing up) too much existing code. Finally, an API also standardizes the results of using specific system resources and capabilities. Using the Windows API ensures that the user will see some of the standard types of interface components we take for granted, for example.

Windows 2000 provides two APIs of interest to us here: The Telephony API (TAPI) provides a standardized method of handling telephone services and the Messaging API (MAPI) provides a standardized method of handling online services and other forms of messaging. Both APIs provide standardized methods for using your modem more efficiently to conduct business. We've already looked at the effect of both APIs earlier in this chapter. This only represents the tip of the iceberg. Vendors make good use of these APIs; they're available in both Windows 95/98 and Windows 2000. The end result for you as a user is fewer problems getting your connections to work properly.

Besides the utility programs we examined in this chapter, you'll also see the effects of TAPI directly in the Phone and Modem Options applet in the Control Panel. It enables you to configure your modem in one place. Any application that supports TAPI will use those settings. This includes Microsoft Exchange and Microsoft Network as native Windows 2000 applications. It doesn't include older, 16-bit Windows applications. If you want the benefits of TAPI, you'll need to upgrade those applications as the vendors come out with new versions.

Microsoft Exchange is an example of a MAPI application. It enables you to access Microsoft Mail using a MAPI driver. A different MAPI driver provides access to CompuServe. Still another driver enables you to send a fax. In fact, you could have a MAPI driver to access each online service you subscribe to. The presence of these drivers would enable you to access them all using one application. The results are reduced training costs and the capability to move information from one service to another with the click of a button.

On Your Own

Look through the vendor manual that came with your printer. See whether the vendor provides any accessories for your printer that might make it more flexible to use. Especially important is the availability of alternative port options. You also might want to check for third-party solutions for your printer. Some third-party vendors provide port accessories for some of the more prominent printers, such as the HP LaserJet.

Identify the five phases of a fax transaction if you have a fax/modem attached to your machine. This is especially easy when using an external model. The lights on the front of the device help you detect when the various phases occur. Tracking this type of information can help you troubleshoot a faulty connection.

If you have a notebook computer, and both a network and a direct cable connection are available for it, try both methods of transferring a file. Most people have a serial connection available, so try that first. You should find that the network connection is a lot faster, but it's interesting to see how much faster. Try the same thing with a parallel connection (if possible).

Outlook Express

Outlook Express comes as part of the Internet Explorer 5.0 bundle, but it's actually a standalone application for handling Internet email and newsgroups. Although it's designed to work much like its predecessors, Internet Mail and News Reader, Outlook Express also includes many additional valuable features—for example, you can choose both plain text and HTML-based messages. You can also send URLs, graphics, and entire Web pages as well as use predesigned message "stationery" (theme templates) and modify your character font in numerous ways. Email from Outlook Express can be truly "rich text"; in fact, you can send, as email, anything that can be displayed in a Web site.

> **Technical Note:** If you're interested in a bit of history, you might recall legacy email/news products from Microsoft, including Windows Messaging, the original Exchange client provided with Microsoft Office, and the Exchange client that came with Exchange Server. Eventually, these three products fell into eclipse when Microsoft reorganized its messaging development team. The front-end GUI development people split off into one group and the back-end Exchange Server development team became a second, separate group. This split allowed the GUI folks to concern themselves with more than just Exchange, and the eventual result was Outlook Express, as we know it today.

Users of Microsoft Office might recognize Outlook Express as a streamlined version of Microsoft's messaging and scheduling application, Outlook. Although Outlook Express is a true email and newsreader in its own right, it doesn't include the scheduling and PIM features available in the Outlook application, such as a calendar, task management, and a full-featured contact database. What Outlook Express does provide is a highly effective set of email and newsgroup features, including an excellent, well-designed user interface.

In fact, in my view, and in the opinion of many national reviewers, Outlook Express is clearly the best email/newsreader available. Outlook Express is so packed with worthwhile features that, no matter how long you've been using it, I'm certain you'll find new tips and shortcuts in this chapter that you'll want to use. In researching this chapter, that's just what happened to me.

Launching Outlook Express

When you get ready to read news or mail, you can launch Outlook Express a number of ways:

- By clicking Start and selecting Programs, Outlook Express.
- By clicking the Outlook Express icon on the Quick Launch toolbar located, by default, on the left side of the Windows 2000 taskbar. (The icon looks like a smaller version of the Internet Explorer blue *e* in front of an envelope.)
- By clicking the Mail icon on the Internet Explorer 5.0 toolbar. (This assumes that you've put that icon in the toolbar.)

> **Tip:** If you're installing a new hard drive, reinstalling Windows 2000 from scratch (got a virus? bought a new machine?), or otherwise want to transfer your archived messages and Address Book, click a message section (such as Inbox) and then from the Outlook Express File menu choose the Export option. After you've set up your new installation of Windows 2000, choose Import from the Outlook Express File menu. In fact, you'll probably want to export your messages from time to time, just in case your hard drive crashes or some other disaster strikes. Losing your history of email is painful.

Using Outlook Express Mail

We'll begin by looking at how Outlook Express Mail works. At the top of the Inbox window is a toolbar containing eight icons, more or less, as shown in Figure 21.1. I say "more or less" because exactly which icons appear there is up to you. Right-click the toolbar and choose Customize to add or subtract icons as you wish. In the following list, I explain the primary icons most people cannot live without:

- *New Mail*. Clicking this button enables you to create a new message. You can insert graphics, format text, add horizontal lines, and otherwise go way beyond traditional email limitations. And, as you can see in Figure 21.2, there's a set of well-designed stationery-like greeting cards. The "cards" include a birthday card, party invitation, ivy, formal announcement, holiday letter, chess, technical, baby news, chicken soup, marble, story book, and tiki lounge themes. You can insert these theme backgrounds and designs by clicking the small arrow to the right of the New Mail button, or you can choose Apply Stationery from the Format menu after you begin working on a message. (Of course, for all this to work, your recipient must also have Outlook Express or a mail reader capable of displaying HTML.) Note that you can also create your own stationery in two ways. Either add a Web Page (the last option on the drop-down list displayed by clicking the small arrow) or choose Select Stationery (the third-from-last option on that same list). Then click the Create New button, and the Stationery Setup Wizard starts running.

FIGURE 21.1

The Outlook Express toolbar is completely customizable.

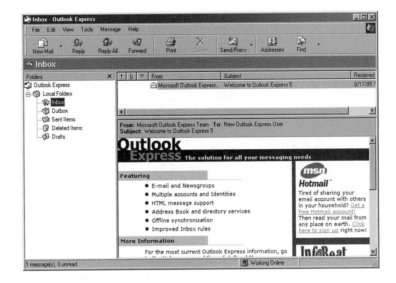

FIGURE 21.2

You can choose from a set of professionally designed "cards" that will seriously enhance your email.

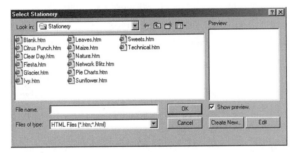

Tip: If you're mad about stationery—illustrated email with backgrounds and graphic designs—you're not limited to those included with Outlook Express. There's an entire Greetings Workshop where Microsoft, in partnership with Hallmark, offers additional stationery packs: Celebrate, Keep in Touch, Holiday Seasons, and Romantic. You can download these self-extracting packs, each with additional "cards" from `http://home-publishing.com/default.asp`. No need for your email to remain plain and boring.

Technical Note: Stationery is merely an HTM file. What does that tell you? You can send an HTML page *as email*. I show you how to do this later, but for now, note that when you choose the Select Stationery option from the drop-down list (click the little down-arrow symbol) under New Post (if you're in the Newsgroup section of Outlook Express) or New Mail (if you're in the email section), you're actually looking at a folder on your hard drive that contains the

continues

stationery (C:\Program Files\Common Files\Microsoft Shared\Stationery).
Obviously, you can use Windows Explorer to copy *any* .HTM file into the
Stationery folder so that it will become part of your stationery set, available
whenever you choose More Stationery. You can even create animated email,
but all this does make your email a bit larger in size.

Tip: You can send someone a Web page from Internet Explorer 5.0 by clicking
the Mail drop-down menu button (the small down-arrow icon) on the Internet
Explorer toolbar and then choosing Send Page.

- *Reply (to Sender).* Clicking this button enables you to respond to whichever
  incoming email message is currently selected (highlighted). This option sends the
  response only to the message's author, not to anyone else listed on the message as
  a recipient. The author is the person who appears in the From section of the message. If there are multiple email addresses listed in the From section of the message, your response is sent to all those recipients.

- *Reply All.* Clicking this button enables you to send a response to everyone who
  received a copy of the original message as well as to the author of the message.

- *Forward.* Clicking this button enables you to send a copy of the current message
  to someone else. If you click this, you see a standard email message dialog box
  with the forwarded message at the bottom. You can add your own additional text
  to the beginning of the forwarded message. This option also enables you to provide a CC: list.

- *Send and Receive.* Clicking this button enables you to send any messages currently sitting in your Outbox folder. It also looks on your ISP's mail server for any
  new messages not yet received. New messages appear in your Inbox folder. I talk
  about folders later in this chapter in the section titled "Working with Folders."

- *Delete.* Clicking this button places the selected messages in the Deleted Items folder. If you click this button while in the Deleted Items folder, the selected messages
  are permanently removed. This two-phase message-removal system should help
  reduce the number of messages you delete by accident, but it's also a little more
  work. You can have Outlook Express clean out the Deleted Items folder when you
  exit the program. Choose Tools, Options and then click the Maintenance tab.

- *Addresses.* Clicking this button opens your personal index of names and addresses.
  From the Address Book window, you can add new entries and edit and delete
  existing entries. You can also add information such as mailing addresses and
  phone numbers. You can send email directly to an Address Book entry by right-
  clicking an entry and selecting Action, Send Mail from the context menu. This
  opens a new message dialog box (it doesn't send the currently selected message).

- *Stop.* This one is really useful in two situations: when you're downloading a long,
  slow graphics file and you just don't want to see it, and when you started downloading something new but aren't finished looking over the current message or news item.

Connecting to a Mail Server

All this doesn't mean a lot if you can't get online. Fortunately, connecting Outlook Express is quite easy, provided you've already mastered the intricacies of Windows 2000's Dial-Up Networking or your local area network setup. It's even easier if you're already hooked up with IE5.

Setting Up Connections

If you have a working connection configured, all you need to do is tell Outlook Express about it. Presumably, you already provided this information the first time you set up Outlook Express, but if your connection situation changes or if you want to add a second account that works through a different connection, here's how you go about getting set up. Most users use Dial-Up Networking, but Outlook Express can deal with a variety of connections, including LAN access and proprietary dialers. You can adjust the connection properties of an existing account from the Account Properties dialog box, as follows:

1. Select Tools, Accounts and then click the Mail tab in the Internet Accounts dialog box.

2. Choose the existing entry you want to edit and then click the Properties button.

3. Click the Connection tab.

4. Click the Always Connect to This Account Using check box.

5. Click the Add button, and the Network Connection Wizard appears.

6. Select from the three option buttons as follows:

     • *Dial-up to private network.* Use this to automatically dial upon launching Outlook Express using an existing dial-up network setup. The Pick List item lets you select the dial-up setup you want to use.

     • *Connect to a private network through the Internet.* Use this if you use a Virtual Private Network or tunnel.

     • *Connect directly to another computer.* Use this for connections between two computers.

To see how to set up a new account, see the section "Setting Up Multiple Accounts" later in this chapter.

Updating General Information

In addition to configuring your dial-up settings, you can also edit your mail network settings. For example, you can update general mail information, as follows:

1. Select Tools, Accounts and click the Mail tab; select the mail account name you want to change and click the Properties button.

2. From the General tab, you can change the name of the active mail account by typing the new name in the text box at the top of the sheet.

3. Update personal information by typing your name, organization, and email address in the appropriate text boxes.

4. You can also specify a different return email address by typing it in the Reply Address text box.

Setting Up the Server

You can update the mail server from the Servers tab of the connection Properties dialog box. If you find that your initial setup failed to make a connection, the Servers page can help you correct things by letting you change vital items such as your mail and POP server data as well as your password and account name.

The following steps guide you through updating your server setup for a POP3 account:

1. Select Tools, Accounts and then click the Mail tab; select the mail account name you want to change and click the Properties button.

2. Click the Servers tab.

3. To change the address of your outbound server, enter the appropriate name in the Outgoing Mail (SMTP) text box. This often consists of the domain and suffix of your ISP, preceded by "smtp." or "mail."

4. To change the address of the inbound server, enter the address in the Incoming Mail (POP3) text box. The address is often the same as the one below it, although it may begin with "pop." rather than "mail."

You can also change the account information for the selected server in the Incoming Mail Server area. You need to enter your email account name and password in the appropriate text boxes. The password appears as a series of asterisks when you type it.

The Log On Using Secure Password Authentication check box sets up Outlook Express Mail to use a secure connection. If this option is activated, you might have to enter your account name and password when you log on with your ISP.

Finally, if your outbound mail server requires secure authentication, you need to check the check box item at the bottom of the dialog box. Then click the Settings button to open the Outgoing Mail Server dialog box. From here, you can select from the following option buttons:

- *Use Same Settings As My Incoming Mail Server*. The default setting is pretty self-explanatory.

- *Log On Using*. Enter the unique account name and password values in the corresponding text boxes, if needed.

- *Log On Using Secure Password Authentication*. Selecting this check box sets up Outlook Express to provide password access through a separate, secure resource.

Working with Folders

It's time to talk about folders—the primary way you organize your mail. Outlook Express comes with several basic folders, as shown previously in Figure 21.1. The purpose of each folder is as follows:

- *Inbox*. Receives all your new mail.

- *Outbox*. Holds messages you want to send to someone else. These messages are pending; they have not yet been sent.

- *Sent Items*. Holds copies of the messages you sent to other people so that you can refer to them later.

- *Deleted Items*. Contains messages you've deleted from other folders.

- *Drafts*. Enables you to hold onto unfinished outbound messages that you intend to complete later. Unlike the Outbox, messages in the Drafts folder won't automatically be sent the next time you click the Send and Receive button or when Outlook Express triggers a send/receive.

You can create new folders by selecting File, New, Folder or by right-clicking a folder item along the left side of the Outlook Express window and then clicking New Folder from the context menu. In the Create Folder dialog box, enter the name of the new folder you want to create. Click an existing folder in the list box to tell Outlook Express where you want your new folder to appear.

Creating folders enables you to organize your messages by project. Better yet, when you finish a project, you can quickly clean up by just deleting the associated folder. To do this, click the folder you created and select File, Folder, Delete. Outlook Express doesn't let you delete or rename its default folders.

You can rename your custom folders by right-clicking the folder and clicking Rename or by selecting File, Folder, Rename. Enter the new folder name in the Rename Folder dialog box and click OK.

> **Tip:** You can use project- or topic-related mailboxes to your advantage by creating a separate folder each time you need to separate a group of temporary messages. Outlook Express maintains a file for each folder you create in the \Username\Mail subfolder of the Outlook Express data folder on your hard drive. The file has a .DBX extension. You can just copy this file to a disk, backup tape, or other archiving device after you complete a project. If you need to look at the project messages later, just place a copy of the folder in your Outlook Express folder.

By now you should be wondering how to get your messages from the Inbox folder to a specialty folder. Here are a few ways to do it:

- *Manual*. Select Edit, Move To Folder. This displays a list of the folders on your machine. You can also select Edit, Copy To Folder to leave the selected message in the current folder and copy it to the new folder. (You can also right-click the Inbox message and use the context menu.)

- *Drag and drop*. Drag the item to the new folder and drop it there. If you hold down the Ctrl key as you drag, a plus sign (+) by the cursor notifies you that Outlook Express will copy the message to the new location instead of move it.

- *Automatic.* Select Tools, Message Rules, Mail. This displays the New Mail Rule
dialog box shown in Figure 21.3. Outlook Express uses rules (that you specify) to
determine how to arrange your folders. Whenever you get a message in your Inbox
folder from the ISP's mail server, Outlook Express looks through its list of rules to
determine whether the message meets certain criteria. As you can see, I've already
defined a few rules in the dialog box shown in Figure 21.3.

FIGURE 21.3

*This dialog box
allows you to
route incoming
messages.*

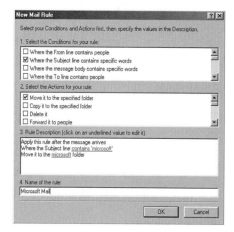

It pays to arrange the message rules in their order of importance because it can take the
Rules utility some time to look at each rule. If a rule you've just added will be used more
often than others in the list, just highlight this rule and use the Move Up button in the
Mail Rules tab of the Message Rules dialog box to move it. Likewise, if a rule tends to be
used infrequently, highlight it and move it using the Move Down button (see Figure 21.4).

FIGURE 21.4

*This is where you
can organize your
various message
rules.*

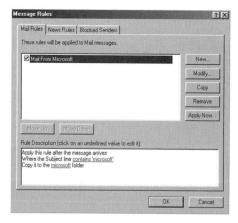

Notice the five buttons along the side of the Message Rules dialog box shown in Figure 21.4. Here's what each does:

- *New.* Clicking this button is the same as clicking the New Rules tab. (If you already have rules defined, you'll first see the New Mail Rule dialog box when you choose Tools, Message Rules, Mail. To get to the general Message Rules dialog box, click the Cancel button.)
- *Modify.* This button brings up the Edit Rule dialog box.
- *Copy.* This button makes a copy of the currently selected rule. Use this to modify a complex rule so you don't have to type everything a second time.
- *Remove.* Use this button to remove a rule you no longer need.
- *Apply Now.* This button enables you to specify which folder(s) the rule should apply to. If you don't apply the rule, it will disappear. (Or click OK in the Message Rules dialog box.)

Fight Spam

You've surely seen it. You've probably seen it today: messages in your Inbox that you don't want from people you don't know who send mail to millions hoping to get a few responses. Spam. There are ways to fight back.

Peter's Principle: Message Rules to the Rescue

The Message Rules feature (formerly called the Inbox Assistant) is a quite versatile utility, and some of its capabilities might not be immediately obvious to you. For example, you can use it to block spam. A few weeks ago I was getting two or three unwanted messages a day from a particularly persistent and mindless spammer. I first sent a message to the spammer's ISP, providing the spammer's return email address, but I was still getting this annoying junk email. If you find yourself in a similar situation, you can use Message Rules to bounce spam back to the server. Just choose Tools, Message Rules, Blocked Senders tab and click the Add button. Then enter the offender's email address.

You can also manage your email in many ways, some of them subtle, using the Message Rules feature. If you want to keep an archive of your email by putting it into a separate folder for each month of the year, for example, you can create a folder for this month and then click the For All Messages box at the bottom of the New Mail Rule dialog box's Conditions list box (you get to this dialog box by choosing Tools, Message Rules, Mail and clicking the New button if you already have rules). Then click the Move It to the Specified Folder option, specifying this month's folder.

Notice that you can also route messages based on their size, whether they have attachments, and many other qualities. Here's another point: If several people are sharing the same email account, you can use the Message Rules feature to route their individual email to individual folders. You can also assign more than one filter to a given action (for example, store all messages to Janice from Richard that are larger than 1KB in the BigFromRichard folder).

The order in which you list the rules can determine what happens to a given incoming email item. If you put a rule at the top that all email larger than 10KB goes into a folder named Large, for example, and you follow this by a rule that puts all email from Austin into a folder named Austin, a big email from Austin will go into the Large folder. If you want particular incoming messages always forwarded to someone, specify the criteria and then click the Copy To or Forward To check box. The Reply With action enables you to specify that a file be automatically delivered to the sender. This file can be any kind, including an email message (EML) created when you use Outlook Express's Save As option on the File menu.

There's one more matter to cover. What happens if you want to keep a rule, but you want to temporarily disable it? Notice that there's a check box next to each rule listed in the Message Rules dialog box. If a rule is checked, it's executed. Otherwise, the rule is ignored. Just uncheck any rules you don't need to use for the current session.

Technical Note: If you want to see *all* the detailed specifications about an email message, right-click a message in your Inbox and then choose Properties. Click the Details tab, and you'll see something like the following report (and if you click the Message Source button, you get even more detail):

```
Received: from olist.com ([209.2.164.231])
          by mtiwgwc08.worldnet.att.net (InterMail v03.0.07.07 118-134)
          with SMTP id <19990258090516.CFJG24922@olist.com>
          for <eothe@worldnet.att.net>; Wed, 28 Jul 1999 09:05:16 +0000
Received: (qmail 487 invoked by uid 780); 28 Jul 1999 09:05:15 -0000
Date: 28 Jul 1999 09:05:15 -0000
Message-ID: <93312715.434@olist.com>
To: eothe@worldnet.att.net
Subject: You have been added to dailyonline2@olist.com
From: Olist <dailyonline2-unsubscribe-264-eothe=worldnet.att.net@olist.com>
Mailing-List: list confirm@olist.com; contact http://www.olist.com
```

Peter's Principle: My Anti-Spam Attack Plan

Junk mail is bothersome, but you can throw it away pretty easily. Unwanted phone calls are extremely irritating, but you can just get an unlisted number (it worked for me). Somewhere in between these harassments on my Annoy-O-Meter is *spam*, unwanted email.

Here are some steps you can take to avoid becoming the target of those oblivious and rude people who make a living by broadcasting their tedious messages to millions, hoping to hit the odd respondent.

continues

Why does spam work? When I worked in publishing, we were planning a mass mailing to solicit subscriptions. I asked the circulation manager what percent of responses we could expect. He answered 2 percent: 1.5 percent representing people legitimately interested in the magazine and .5 percent representing people who for various reasons (confusion, loneliness, and so on) replied just to make a friend or because of a misunderstanding. In other words, no matter how preposterous your advertisement, if you send out 1,000,000 messages, you can count on perhaps 5,000 replies from lonely or confused people. Of course, the fact that we're dealing with email filters out some unfortunates. Email requires knowing how to use a computer, and that raises the bar somewhat regarding the confused. Nevertheless, spam works and always will. What can you do?

Rule 1: Never, ever reply to spam. Don't send it back. Don't send an angry letter, and don't fall for the "we'll be happy to remove your name from our lists if you just send us your email address…" line. That sounds courteous, but remember that these people make their living by *not* being courteous. If you respond in any way, chances are you'll be added to what they laughingly call among themselves a *hotlist*—a database of "quality respondents," which is a valued list of email addresses of people who are willing to reply (even if it's only to ask to be excised from the list).

Rule 2: Create a clone to attract spam. If you belong to AOL, create a second screen name. If you have a different Internet service provider, create a second email name. The idea is to have one name you give to business associates and friends, and they can use it to send email you actually want to receive. You use the other name when you are "out in public" and dealing with strangers— when you send messages to newsgroups, when you converse in "chat" rooms, and so on. Recall that spammers use automaton "agents," robots that scurry through chat rooms and newsgroups gathering email addresses that they add to their spam databases. The idea is that you can safely mass-delete messages sent to your "bad" public name, knowing that they're all illegitimate.

To create a second email address, click Accounts in the Outlook Express Tools menu and then click the Add, Mail button. A wizard will guide you through setting up a second email account. For more details, see the section later in this chapter titled "Setting Up Multiple Accounts."

Sending an Email Message

After you install and configure Outlook Express, you'll want to use it to send messages. To do so, just click the New Mail button on the toolbar to open a New Message window, as shown in Figure 21.5.

Tip: You can specify whether and how often your email is automatically updated. (*Updated* here means that new email is downloaded and put into your Inbox, and any email in your Outbox is sent.) Choose Options from the Outlook Express Tools menu, click the General tab, and then specify how often you want

continues

an update in the Check for New Messages Every X Minute(s) item. If you erase this box, leaving no minutes specified, email will be downloaded every 30 minutes, by default, or any time you click the Send/Recv button, press Ctrl+M, or choose Send and Receive from the Tools menu. Using these Send/Receive methods will download mail from *all* accounts you have set up. If you want to download mail from a specific account, choose Send and Receive from the Tools menu and select the account.

FIGURE 21.5

Here's where you create messages.

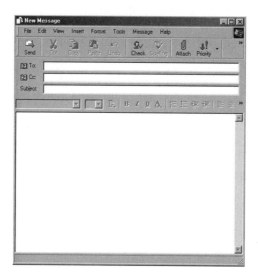

Take a look at the toolbar; it provides the features you use most often. The toolbar contains the following buttons:

- *Send.* Clicking this button sends the message you've just created or begins a spell-check if you've chosen that option. You must define a recipient in the To field before sending a message. In addition, Outlook Express checks the Subject field to make sure it's not blank; you can bypass this requirement, however, by clicking Yes when Outlook Express asks whether you want to send the message without a subject. Obviously, you should make sure the message contains some kind of information, even though Outlook Express doesn't check for this.

- *Cut/Copy/Paste.* These buttons work much like they do with any Windows application. You can cut or copy information to the Clipboard, and you can paste information from the Clipboard into your message.

- *Undo.* Outlook Express adds multiple levels of undo, thus enabling you to back up through many actions to the point you want. Its menu equivalent is Edit, Undo.

- *Check.* Checks the names in your address book. Suppose you don't want to try to remember a lot of email addresses when writing messages. All you need to do is type a word or even a part of a word and then click the Check Names button (or use the keyboard shortcut Alt+K). You'll see a Check Names dialog box that lists the names Outlook Express found in your Address Book that match in some way the text you typed. If you want to send something to one of the people at Seawel Bank, for example, and you have several people in your Address Book with the @SeawelR identifier as part of their email address, just type Seaw or something similar in the To field of the New Message dialog box and then click the Check Names button. When you see the list supplied by Check Names, double-click the recipient you want to use; Outlook Express adds the correct full email address to your message heading. If Outlook Express doesn't find the text you've typed into the To field, it gives you the option of adding the name to your Address Book.

- *Spelling*. Performs a spell-check. (To use this feature, you must first have a Microsoft spell checker available on your system—from Microsoft Office, for instance.)

- *Attach*. Click this button to attach a file (or several) to your message. Outlook Express displays a standard file browse dialog box, which you use to select the file.

- *Priority*. Lets you alert the recipient as to the significance of your message.

- *Sign*. This is a scheme that endeavors to ensure the security of email. If you attempt to sign a message, you'll be told you can't send it unless the recipient has a digital ID. In any case, the concept of a digital signature is an attempt to let recipients feel sure that you are who you say you are. Email doesn't include executables (macros), even though it can contain Web pages. *Reading* plain text cannot insert a virus into your system, but opening an attached file (even a DOC file) *can*. Therefore, some people want to ensure that the email they get comes from authenticated senders. You can check out this feature—if you feel you need it (don't do enough backups, do you?)—by looking at http://www.microsoft.com/ windows/oe/certpage.htm. You can get a free trial digital signature from VeriSign or some other provider.

- *Encrypt*. This option scrambles your email, but if you haven't bought a digital signature, you can't read the message in your Sent Items folder. If your recipients haven't purchased one, they can't read it either. What's more, if the recipients don't have digital IDs, Outlook Express won't send the email anyway.

    If you're not interested in these security measures—and most of us aren't—right-click the Outlook Express toolbar and choose Customize. Double-click Sign and Encrypt, and they'll be removed from the list of buttons on the toolbar.

- *Offline*. Disconnects you from your ISP.

If you're writing a message and you've added a name or two to your recipient list, you can type a subject for your message (if you don't, Outlook Express asks you if you want to add one when you try to send the message). The first thing you notice is that the title for the New Message dialog box changes to match the message subject. After you add some content to your message, click the Send button to send it. Your message is added to your Outbox folder. It's automatically sent the next time you click the Send and Receive button in the main Outlook Express window. If you've selected the Send Messages

Immediately option in the Send tab of the Outlook Express Options dialog box, however, email is sent the instant you click the Send button. The Outbox, then, is not used unless you're offline. Choose Options from the Tools menu and then click Send.

> **Tip:** What if you want to send an email message to various people simultaneously, but you don't want them to know who else is getting the message? It used to be easy: In previous versions of Outlook Express you just avoided the Cc and To fields and put their addresses in the Bcc field (Bcc means *blind carbon copy*). To use Bcc, click View, All Headers.

Managing Your Address Book

There are several ways to gain access to your Address Book, but the two most common methods are selecting Tools, Address Book from the main Outlook Express window and clicking the Addresses button on the Outlook Express toolbar (this is the quickest of the two).

You can create two kinds of email address entries in the Address Book dialog box. The first is a single entry, which has a Rolodex page as an icon. The second kind of entry is a group, signified by a Rolodex page plus two people (also note that the name of a group appears in boldface). Groups actually contain one or more of the single contacts you create.

Creating a single contact is easy: Just click the New button in the Address Book's toolbar and then New Contact to invoke the contact Properties dialog box. This dialog box contains the following seven tabs:

- *Name.* This tab contains all the personal contact information for the new entry, such as the person's name and email address. You can add even more than one email address to the list. Notice that one email address is designated as the default that you want to use; this is the address that Outlook Express uses unless you specify an alternative. You can specify a new default email address by highlighting the desired address and clicking the Set As Default button. Adding a new email address is easy: Just type it into the Email Addresses text box and then click Add. Likewise, you can delete old email addresses by highlighting them and clicking the Remove button. Highlight an email address and click Edit if you need to change an existing entry.

- *Home.* This tab contains all the personal information for your contact, including three personal contact numbers: home phone, home fax, and cellular. You can also enter the URL for a personal Web page. Clicking the Go button next to the Personal Web Page field enables you go directly to that person's personal Web page using your default browser.

- *Business.* This tab looks a lot like the Home tab. It contains three entries for business phone numbers: office phone, office fax, and pager. The Business Web Page field on this tab works just like the Personal Web Page field on the Home tab. Clicking Go on this page takes you to the business's Web page.

- *Personal.* Here you can enter personal information such as husband, wife, children, gender, birthday, and anniversary.

- *Other.* This tab, which contains little more than a single Notepad field, enables you to keep notes about your contact. Suffice it to say that there aren't any fancy gadgets for maintaining contact information by date. You'll probably want to reserve this page for long-lasting notes and use a contact manager to keep track of business information. The Group membership and Folder Location fields apply after the contact is created.

- *NetMeeting.* This tab enables you to enter information needed to make Internet-based phone calls and conferences using the NetMeeting program. Choose or type into the Conferencing server field the server name that you use for conferencing with this contact. In the Conferencing address field, choose the address or addresses for this contact. This address is usually, but not always, the same as the email address of the user you want to contact.

- *Digital IDs.* This tab enables you to verify that email messages are coming from a trusted source, using encrypted digital files associated with the sender's email address. For more information about digital IDs, consult the section titled "Understanding Certificates" in Chapter 28, "Security Issues."

Return to the main Address Book window. You can edit a group or single contact by highlighting the desired entry and then clicking the Properties button in the toolbar (or right-clicking an entry and selecting Properties from the context menu). Getting rid of an unneeded entry is just as easy: Just highlight the entry or entries you no longer need and then click the Delete button.

How do you create a group? Click the New button and then choose New Group. You'll see the Group Properties dialog box. The entries for a group include the group name and a list of members. When you send an email message to a group, every member gets a copy. Also fill in the fields at the bottom if you want to add someone not in your Address Book.

Here are the four buttons that appear along the side of the Group Properties dialog box:

- *Select Members.* Clicking this button displays a dialog box where you can select existing contacts or groups from your Address Book that you want to add to your member list for the group you're defining.

- *New Contact.* If you want to create a new Address Book entry and simultaneously add it to the group, click this button to open a Properties dialog box where you can define the contact.

- *Remove.* If you want to remove a member entry, just highlight the member name and click Remove.

- *Properties.* Highlighting a member name and clicking Properties displays the familiar Properties dialog box for that member, where you can edit the Address Book entry.

Customizing Outlook Express Mail

Outlook Express can be fine-tuned to your specific needs and preferences. You can alter the look of your email messages, change the interface layout and elements, and even turn Outlook Express into your email client for multiple accounts.

Setting Up Multiple Accounts

If you're like me, you have more than one email account, which forces you to dial in to two or more email accounts to retrieve your messages. Outlook Express provides relief through its capability to call up multiple email accounts automatically. Assuming you've already set up your main account, here's how you add a second mailbox to Outlook Express for a POP3 account:

1. Select Tools, Accounts and then click the Mail tab in the Internet Accounts dialog box.

2. Click the Add button and then click Mail in the fly-out menu.

3. Enter a name to identify the account.

4. In the next dialog box, enter the Internet email address of the account you're adding in the Email Address text box and click Next.

5. Enter the mail server name for this email address. In the Incoming Mail text box, you usually enter "pop." or "mail." followed by the domain and suffix of your ISP (for example, compuserve.com). Similarly, in the Outgoing Mail text box, you typically enter "smtp." or "mail." before the ISP information. Click Next.

6. Confirm that the information in the POP Account Name text box is correct (change it as needed) and then enter your account password in the Password text box. If your provider uses Secure Password Authentication, you need to click the bottom check box and follow the instructions. Click Next.

7. Click the Finish button to save the settings. You now have multiple email accounts registered with Outlook Express. Click the Close button to close the Internet Accounts dialog box.

Tip: In Step 5 above, if you are using Hotmail, you'll be working with an HTTP server rather than a POP3 style, so select HTTP from the dropdown listbox labeled My incoming mail server is a _____ server. With an HTTP server, you do not need to specify the *outgoing* mail server. Note that the same dropdown list also permits connection to an IMAP server. IMAP (Internet Message Access Protocol) and HTTP (Hypertext Transfer Protocol) are Internet protocols that allow you to send and receive messages that are stored on a server. These two protocols permit you to access your email from *any* computer that's connected to the Internet. One difference between them: HTTP accounts display all the available mail folders, but with an IMAP account you can choose to hide some of the folders if you wish.

You can do the same thing with news accounts. In the Internet Accounts dialog box, click the Add button and then click News. Follow the prompts to set up separate news accounts.

After you set up multiple email accounts, you can check them all at the same time by clicking the Send and Receive button on the main toolbar of Outlook Express. The program checks the accounts one after the other, sending and receiving messages for each. If you want to access only one of your accounts, select Tools, Send and Receive and then click the desired account name from the list on the fly-out menu.

Using Identities

New in Outlook Express 5 is the Identities feature. This feature makes it easy for more than one person to use the same computer while sharing an Outlook Express and Address Book. Each person creates his or her own identity. That way, all users get their own email and see their own address book rather than having to share these elements of Outlook Express.

To create an identity, choose File, Identities, Add New Identity. Type in the name for this identity. Add an optional password to prevent others from using or modifying the identity (although people with a little hacker in them can still locate and invade the files holding personal data). Click the OK button. You're asked if you want to switch to this identity now. If you do, you can use the currently active dial-up account. If not, choose No. If Outlook Express is running, it will shut down and restart. Otherwise, the next time you start Outlook Express, you'll see the new user screen with options Set Up a Mail Account and Set Up a Newsgroups Account. Choose one of these options, and the Internet Connection Wizard steps you through the process of specifying an email address, mail servers, and so on.

You can switch identities in Outlook Express any time by choosing File, Switch Identity.

Tweaking the Outlook Express Interface

Outlook Express enables you to adjust its interface to suit your tastes. I'll describe the three most interesting features: the View Bar, Contacts, and the Outlook Bar. Our first stop is the View Bar. Select the Layout option, which brings up several options. You can choose to display or hide most elements of Outlook Express. The Contacts option adds your Address Book to the panes in Outlook Express; the Outlook bar displays several icons (the Inbox, the Outbox, and your other folders) in a pane for easy clicking; the View Bar is for those who frequently change what messages they want displayed: hide messages already read, show downloaded messages only, and so on. The Preview Pane option lets you decide whether you want to see messages and newsgroup items always displayed or if you want to double-click each item to open it in a separate window.

If you're really into switching between views, you can create and name your own custom views. Choose View, Current View, Define Views, and you'll see a dialog box similar to the one you use to define rules for messages (see "Working with Folders," earlier in this chapter). You can define whether messages from a particular person should be displayed, for example.

If you want to reorganize your Toolbar, choose View, Layout and then click the Customize Toolbar button. Clicking it brings up a dialog box where you can add, remove, and change the order of the toolbar icons. Just select the desired items in the Available Toolbar Buttons scrolling list box and click Add to have them appear in the Current Toolbar Buttons box. (Alternatively, you can click a button and drag it over to achieve the same effect.) To change the order of toolbar icons, click the icon you want to move in the Current Toolbar Buttons scrolling list box and then click the Move Up or Move Down button. Again, you can also click the item and drag it to the place you want.

If you want to restore the Outlook Express defaults, click the Reset button. Click Close to affect the changes.

Selecting View, Columns displays a list of available and displayed column headers. To add more message header information, click the desired item in the list box. You can also remove displayed columns by clicking the applicable check box to clear it. You can reorder the displayed columns by selecting an item and clicking the Move Up and Move Down buttons (or by dragging the column in the Outlook Express window).

> **Tip:** You can reorder column headers just by clicking a header and dragging it across to the desired position. All the related information for each message appears in the new location.

Making More of Messages

You can enhance the look and layout of incoming and outbound email messages. Just be aware that others may use email clients that do not recognize HTML-enhanced text, so you might want to avoid using these features unless you know your recipient's capabilities. Some features that Outlook Express provides include the following:

- Using HTML formatting in outgoing messages
- Adding designs to outgoing messages
- Changing the font size and type in your message-browsing windows

Using HTML in Email

HTML is the universal language of the Internet, and more and more email clients are becoming capable of handling HTML-formatted documents. You can add visual punch to your email messages by sending them in HTML format. To enable this feature in Outlook Express, follow these steps:

1. Select Tools, Options.
2. Click the Send tab in the Options dialog box.
3. In the Mail Sending Format area, click the HTML option button.

4. Click the HTML Settings button to change how Outlook Express uses MIME encoding of messages. You can also tell Outlook Express not to send images (such as backgrounds) with your messages to reduce message sizes. You can also tell the program whether to indent existing text (the sender's text) when you reply to messages.

When you select HTML formatting, the New Message box includes a horizontal area above the text window that includes icons for font type and size, bold, italic, and underline formatting, and color, justification, bullet types, images, and links. You can use all these icons to add layout elements and items to your messages.

> **Caution:** Think twice before heavily formatting your HTML email messages, particularly if you're broadcasting to a large group of recipients. Not only do these enhancements boost the size of the message, but some email programs still don't support HTML email messages and cannot make sense of the formatting. Those recipients end up seeing a mess of HTML tags within the text.

One neat feature of Outlook Express is its capability to create links inside your messages. You can just type the address and it will be formatted as a link. Or you can click Insert, Hyperlink to type the address in the Hyperlink dialog box. A third approach is to select text and click Create a Hyperlink to open the same Hyperlink dialog box. When the message arrives at an HTML-aware email recipient, the user can click the link and go directly to the site using his or her default Web browser.

Changing Display Type

In addition to adding formatting to messages you send, you can change the way text looks when you compose and read email. The easiest way to set the font characteristics is from a message window (but this isn't available from the New Message window). To accomplish this, select View, Text Size. From the fly-out menu, choose one of the following:

- Largest
- Larger
- Medium
- Smaller
- Smallest

The text in the mail message grows or shrinks to the new size. In addition, the text size in messages you compose also adjusts to the new size.

> **Tip:** If you want to make a *persistent* change to the font style and size of your messages or news, choose Tools, Options and then select the Compose tab.

Searching Your Email

As a record of your correspondence, your collection of email is invaluable. If you're looking for a particular phone number or can't recall when a particular file was sent to someone, however, how hard is it to find these items in your huge archive of messages? As easy as can be. Outlook Express includes an admirably designed search utility with all the features you could want. Click one of the email folders, such as Inbox, and then Choose Edit, Find, Message. In the resulting dialog box, you can search for a word (or partial word or phrase) in the From, Sent To, or Subject field. (Choose Edit, Find, Message in this Folder to display just the basic Find dialog box. Click the Advanced Find button to see the Find Message dialog I describe above.)

You can also specify email that had attached files as well as any date or range of dates. You can have the search localized to a particular folder or subfolder or include all messages in Outlook Express. But best of all, you can enter search text for the message body; this causes the utility to inspect the contents of all the messages—a most valuable tool. To do this, type your search word or phrase into the Message text box. All the message headings that match the search criteria display, and you can then double-click any of them to see the full message.

Using Outlook Express News

Outlook Express also offers a newsreader feature, enabling you to read and respond to messages in newsgroups. A *newsgroup* is a public forum for discussing issues or for asking questions about a specific topic. One person begins the whole process by making a comment or asking a question. He or she uploads this information as a message. After you read the message, you can reply to it. A third person might see what you've written and respond to your message. Well, you get the idea. A series of messages on the same topic become what's known as a *message thread*. By reading the messages in a message thread in order, you can see the conversation.

Configuring Outlook Express Newsreader for Use

The first thing you need to do is configure Outlook Express for Internet newsgroups. To accomplish this, follow these steps:

1. Select Tools, Accounts and click the Add button. Then choose News from the fly-out menu.

2. Enter the name you want displayed in your newsgroup messages in the text box. Click Next.

3. If necessary, enter your email address. I would suggest you seriously consider whether you really want to give your email address in newsgroups. Several organizations send tireless spiders, rooters, and other automated robots that continually harvest email addresses from newsgroups so that they can create databases to sell to spammers. Click Next.

4. Enter the name of your news server. This usually starts with "news." followed by the domain and suffix of your ISP (for example, news.compuserve.com). Add logon information if your newsgroup requires it. Click Next.

5. The new account appears in the list of accounts in the Internet Accounts dialog box and in the list of folders on the left side of your Outlook Express window. You can right-click it at any time to adjust its properties.

6. Outlook Express prompts you to download the newsgroup list to your PC. This can take a while because there are tens of thousands of newsgroups.

7. The Newsgroups dialog box shows a list of all the available newsgroups in the scrolling list box. To gain access or to subscribe to a group, just double-click an entry. Repeat as often as you want to add as many newsgroups as you wish.

8. The newsgroups you've subscribed to appear under a folder with the name you entered for this account. When you click a newsgroup entry, you see the list of postings for that group.

Tip: Type in a word, a partial word, or a phrase in the Display Newsgroups Which Contain text box, shown at the top of the Figure 21.6.

Any time you want to change your subscribed newsgroups, just right-click the name of your account in the Folders List and choose Newsgroups from the context menu.

FIGURE 21.6

Locate your special interests quickly by typing in a key word in this text box at the top of the Newsgroup Subscriptions dialog box.

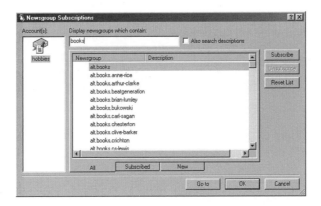

The All tab of the Newsgroups dialog box displays all the newsgroups you can join. After you find a newsgroup you think sounds interesting, double-click it to subscribe to it. After you do, you'll see a newspaper icon appear next to the entry. If you later decide that you don't need this newsgroup, highlight it and click the Unsubscribe button. Clicking the Reset List button downloads any new newsgroups from the ISP's news server. (Outlook Express will automatically inform you, after a certain number of new newsgroups have been created, that you might want to review the latest additions and decide whether you want to subscribe to any of them. However it doesn't do this by default. You must choose Tools, Options and in the General tab click the appropriate check box to turn it off.)

You don't have to subscribe to a newsgroup without looking at it first. Just highlight something that looks interesting and then click the Go To button. Outlook Express downloads message headers from the requested newsgroup and displays them in a way that's similar to the Inbox you use to view email messages. I describe how to use it in the next section.

The Subscribed tab looks just like the All tab, except it shows only the newsgroups you've subscribed to. (Subscribing to a newsgroup just means that Outlook Express keeps the newsgroup name available for quick access; there's no fee or signup process involved in subscribing to newsgroups.) The New tab of the Newsgroup dialog box enables you to quickly find new newsgroups. It's a really handy feature; imagine digging through the thousands of available newsgroups to see any new newsgroups.

Viewing and Subscribing to Newsgroups

By now, you should have Outlook Express's newsgroup reader configured and have a few newsgroups selected. The main window looks like the one shown in Figure 21.7. The easiest way to move between email and newsgroups is to use the setup shown in this figure. The left pane enables you to easily click any email folder or newsgroup, and then the titles of all messages are displayed in the top-right pane and the contents in the bottom-right pane.

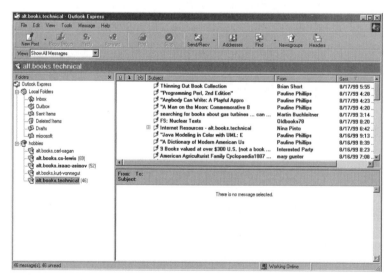

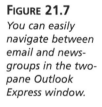

FIGURE 21.7

You can easily navigate between email and newsgroups in the two-pane Outlook Express window.

The pane containing the list of headings for the newsgroup shows you the message subjects you find in the newsgroup. If you've already read a message, the header text is no longer bold, and the yellow torn page with a red tack icon to the left is replaced with an open letter sheet with a yellow tack icon.

Like most Windows applications, Outlook Express includes a toolbar. The following list tells you what the various less-obvious newsgroup toolbar buttons can do for you:

- *New Post*. Clicking this button enables you to upload a new message to the newsgroup. It's almost like writing a message to someone using email. In this case, however, you're addressing the message to a group of people in a public forum. What's more, it's a message on a new topic of your own devising, not a response to an existing message thread. When you submit a "new post," you're starting a new thread.

- *Reply Group*. Click this option to send a reply to the currently selected message in the newsgroup. In other words, you're making a public response to a message someone else left. You can use this option to ask for clarification of the previous sender's message, ask a similar question of your own, provide an answer to the selected message, or just make a pertinent comment about the subject under discussion. In this case, you're continuing the thread.

> **Tip:** Good manners are as precious as gold. When you choose the Reply Group option, the previous message will be automatically included in the text box where you're going to write your reply. Obviously, because that happened to the previous message's author as well, the entire thread might be sitting there taking up everyone's space and taxing everyone's patience. To prevent messages from becoming bloated in this way by accretion, it's considered good manners to delete all but the most recent prior message before you send yours. In other words, only the message that prompted your response should be included in your new message.

- *Reply*. Sometimes a public response to a question isn't ideal. The author might specifically ask you to reply using email, for example, because he or she doesn't visit the newsgroup often or for some other reason. You might also want to use this option when providing personal information, answering a personal question, or providing information that the rest of the group isn't interested in reading. I find that this method of responding is a two-edged sword. On one hand, you might spare someone embarrassment; on the other hand, you remove the rest of the group from the loop. Not only does this prevent other people from providing additional information, it's contrary to the very concept of using a newsgroup in the first place.

- *Forward*. You might occasionally want to make a colleague aware of some information you've found in a newsgroup that he or she doesn't subscribe to. Clicking this option enables you to do just that: You forward a message from the newsgroup.

- *Newsgroups*. Clicking this button displays the Newsgroup dialog box described earlier.

- *Stop*. This button serves the same purpose here as it does within Internet Explorer: It enables you to stop downloading a message or a group of message headings from the news server.

- *Refresh*. Your ISP might disconnect you from a newsgroup after a certain amount of inactivity on your part. This doesn't disconnect you from the server—you're still online. If this newsgroup disconnection happens, you'll be notified by a message box. All you have to do to restore your contact with the newsgroup is click this button. This is not on the toolbar by default.

- *Find*. This utility works much like the email message Find feature described earlier in this chapter.

There's one additional piece of information you need to know: By default, Outlook Express Mail downloads only 300 messages at a time. To download the next 300 messages, select Tools, Get Next 300 Headers. You can adjust the default (300) by selecting Tools, Options and then clicking the Read tab.

Writing a Newsgroup Message

Getting a message uploaded to a newsgroup is much like writing a regular email message, but there are some differences. For one thing, you're addressing a public forum. You don't need to specify a recipient for your message because the entire group can look at it. I find it interesting that some people act as though they're addressing a specific person on a newsgroup, when in reality they can't. Make sure you always keep the idea of public versus private communication in mind when responding to a newsgroup message. It's also considered polite to avoid using all capital letters (which is considered SHOUTING) when writing your message. Also, remember to limit the number of previous messages included at the bottom of your message to one, merely the message in the thread you're actually responding to.

Take a look at a basic newsgroup message. Click the New Post or Reply Group button on the Newsgroup toolbar. You'll see a dialog box similar to the one for a standard email message. The following is a list of functions of the various toolbar buttons:

- *Send*. Use this option to post your message to the news server. You probably won't see the message appear right away. Some Webmasters monitor the messages they allow to appear on the newsgroup (some newsgroups are monitored, which is nice because they're not clogged with spam). Even if the news server posts messages without any form of monitoring (as they do on most newsgroups), it still takes time for your message to arrive at the news server.

- *Undo*. Clicking this button enables you to undo multiple actions.

- *Cut/Copy/Paste*. These three buttons work much like they do in any Windows application. You can cut or copy information to the Clipboard, and you can paste information from the Clipboard into your message.

- *Check*. Verifies the address of anyone you've added to the Cc (Copy To) text box.

- *Spelling*. Use this button to check your message for typos.

- *Attach*. Use this button to insert a file into your message. Outlook Express opens an Insert Attachment dialog box you can use to select the file.

- *Sign*. This is not your email "signature" (such as your name, address, and phone number). It's a digital signature, which is described earlier in this chapter.

- *Offline*. Lets you optionally disconnect and work offline.

Customizing Outlook Express News

Customizing the Outlook Express News view panes is identical to working with the Mail portion of Outlook Express. Column headers, for example, can be dragged to alter the order in which information appears in the heading window or to resize the columns. Each time you click a column header, you toggle the listing—for example, between the most recently sent and the earliest sent—or the alphabetization (from *a* to *z* or *z* to *a*). Likewise, you can select View, Text Size to enlarge or shrink the type used in the message window. Selecting View, Layout launches the Window Layout Properties box described earlier.

Other customization options are available on the Tools, Options menu item. In the General tab, you can make Outlook Express your default news reader, and you can alert yourself when new newsgroups are created. In the Read tab, you can define how long you can look at a message before it's marked as having been read. You can cause every message in each thread to be displayed (Automatically Expand Grouped Messages) or only display the initial messages that created a new topic. You can also choose to mark every message as read when you exit a group. More important, you can adjust the display font to make it the most comfortable font and font size for displaying text on your monitor.

Filtering Messages

You might be interested to know that you can prevent the downloading of certain messages—either email or newsgroup messages can be filtered in this way. They won't be sent to your computer or, of course, displayed as headings. To set up a newsgroup message filter, choose Tools, Message Rules, News and then click the New button. You construct the filter by specifying that you don't want to see messages by a particular sender, on a particular topic, longer than X lines, or older than X days. You can also highlight messages from a particular sender in green (or whatever color you like). You can also set up as many filters as you wish.

> **Tip:** Recall from the discussion earlier in this chapter about the Mail Rules dialog boxes that which dialog box you first see depends on whether you've previously defined a rule. The same advice applies to the two Newsgroup Rules dialog boxes. The first time you set up a new rule you're in the New News Rule dialog box (it doesn't have a New button). You just set up the rule and click OK. However, after a rule exists, you start in the Message Rules dialog box where there is a New button.

Another kind of filtering is available via the View menu. (In this case, you must first select a particular newsgroup before the option becomes activated on the menu.) This filter doesn't prevent particular messages from being downloaded, but it does enable you to define which message headers will be displayed. Click Current View on the View menu. You'll see a submenu menu that enables you to specify that only those messages meeting a particular criterion will be listed: unread, ignored, and so on.

> **Tip:** How do you know when some new email arrives in your Outlook Express Inbox? Take a look at the tray area on your taskbar. The tray is where the time is displayed, along with some tiny icons such as Volume, Dial-Up Networking, Printer (if you're currently printing), and so on. If you've got new mail, you'll see the mail icon (two twisted blue arrows superimposed on an envelope) shown in Figure 21.8. There's also an option that will cause Outlook Express to make a sound when new mail arrives. (Choose Options from the Tools menu and then select the General tab and click Play Sound When New Messages Arrive.)

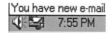

FIGURE 21.8
When you get new email, this icon appears in your taskbar.

On Your Own

Set up folders for each of your major projects and use the Message Rules feature to direct email messages into those folders. If you're bothered by junk mail from a certain source, set up a rule to move those messages to the Deleted Items folder automatically, or you can block them using the Blocked Senders List.

Set up a second email address for your "public" self, and use it to attract spam; keep your "good" email address private to your friends and business associates.

If you've been using another email client and decide you want to switch over to Outlook Express, check out the File, Import commands. They enable you to import email messages and Address Book entries into Outlook Express from several of the popular email client programs.

Configure Outlook Express to access the newsgroup server at your ISP and explore some newsgroups that interest you.

Mobile Computing

If you use a computer in your work at all, you likely also have a second, less powerful, but more portable version of your main machine: a notebook computer. In this chapter, I use the term *notebook* to refer to every kind of mobile computer. Of course, mobile computers actually range in size from the smallest PDA (personal digital assistant) to the luggable (they are too heavy to deserve the word *portable*) "laptop" dinosaurs I still see from time to time. But, for simplicity, I will stick with the term *notebook*, which is a fairly accurate metaphor for the size and heft of most of today's portables.

You might be saying, "Whoa! Windows 2000 on a portable, isn't that a bit of overload? Like putting a Harley engine on a moped?" A while back—during the days of 66MHz-, 8MB-notebooks—you would have been right. But today's portables—500MHz, Pentium III, 64MB RAM—are fully capable of accommodating Windows 2000 without slowing to a crawl under its weight.

Remember that although Windows 95/98 has a wider selection of tested, notebook peripherals (and their all-important, well-written, tested drivers), Windows 2000, when compared to Windows 95/98, always gives you greater stability and security. And it often gives you greater performance in the bargain. If you are using Windows 2000 Professional on your desktop, it's a good idea to maintain consistency by using Windows 2000 in your portable

Windows 2000 Professional is expected to sell surprisingly well on notebook computers. All the major notebook manufacturers will offer this combination of OS and machine, which would have been unthinkable in the early days of NT 4 (only a couple of years ago). This chapter covers three special mobile computing utilities built in to Windows 2000:

- Synchronize
- Dial-Up Networking
- Hardware Profiles

What's more, you will now find support from hardware and software manufacturers that enables you to do things with Windows 2000 on a notebook that were previously only possible using Windows 95. Plug and Play hot-swapping (you don't have to power-down to pull PCMCIA devices out or to plug them in), for example, is now available on machines from many manufacturers. They also offer hot-docking—you don't have to power-down either the notebook or the workstation when you dock or undock the notebook.

Finally, power management is now a sophisticated, workable feature on Windows 2000 notebooks. Windows 2000 supports both Advanced Power Management (APM) and also the Advanced Configuration and Power Interface (ACPI)—a new set of specifications supported by some of the latest machines. ACPI provides previously unheard-of control over a computer's power management features. However, not many existing laptops feature ACPI, so to use those new power management facilities of Windows 2000, you must upgrade the laptop's BIOS. Check with the manufacturer of your laptop to see if you can do this.

Given this increasing functionality and popularity of Windows 2000 in notebooks, let's consider your options if you work with Windows 2000 in the office and would like to take it with you on the road as well.

Before Windows 95 and Windows 2000 came along, many notebook computer users were still strapped to a desktop. What happens, for example, when you need to change a modem card in your notebook and replace it with an NIC to access the network? Unless you have some special setup software, you actually have to turn off the machine and reconfigure it. Time-wasting events such as this really frustrate people who use a notebook from time to time. Fortunately, Windows 2000 addresses these problems and many more.

Of course, Windows 2000 won't take your PDA (personal digital assistant) and make it into a desktop equivalent. I'm looking at machines that are really capable of running Windows 2000. This means that they have to meet all the installation criteria I discussed earlier in this book. To use some of the features that Windows 2000 provides, a notebook has to provide a PCMCIA (Personal Computer Memory Card International Association) slot or its equivalent. You also might want a notebook that can use a docking station. In other words, I really don't care how heavy or large the computer is, but it has to provide enough features to take the place of a desktop.

> **Note:** The PCMCIA card is often now referred to by the simpler name PC card, but that's a bit confusing because there are other cards that fit into a standard desktop PC when you remove its cover.

PCMCIA Devices on Your Notebook Computer

The first topic on the agenda is the PCMCIA bus. This is a "little" bus specially designed to meet the needs of the notebook computer market, but it is found in a growing number of desktop machines as well. The PCMCIA bus uses credit-card–sized cards that connect to external slots on the machine. This is perfect for a notebook because notebooks are notorious for providing few, if any, expansion slots. A PCMCIA bus makes it easy for the user to change a machine's hardware configuration without opening it. For example, you could take out a memory card to make room for a modem card.

This bus also supports solid-state disk drives in the form of flash ROM or SRAM boards. The flash ROM boards are especially interesting because they provide the same access speeds as regular memory, but also offer the permanence of other long-term storage media such as hard drives. Unlike SRAM boards, flash ROM boards don't require battery backup. Many people use solid-state drives to store applications or databases that change infrequently. This frees up precious space on the internal hard disk for data and applications that the user needs to access on a continuous basis. The popular removable Iomega Zip drives are a workable alternative to flash ROM, however, if you need non-volatile mass storage. And portable Zip drive hardware is so light that, with the right PCMCIA card, a good solution that hugely expands your permanent memory is to just take an outboard Zip drive and some Zip disks along with you on the road. They will only add a few ounces to your weight load—the drive is remarkably light. (Also, several companies make notebooks with Zip drives built in.)

There are a couple of cautions when you use a PCMCIA card:

- The most common problem associated with enabling enhanced support is that there are PCMCIA device drivers in CONFIG.SYS or TSRs in AUTOEXEC.BAT. Removing these entries should fix the problem.

- Windows 2000 normally tells you whether there is an I/O port address or interrupt conflict. To make sure, however, you should check the settings under the Resources tab of the PCIC (peripheral connect interface card) or compatible PCM-CIA controller Properties dialog box. (To open this dialog box, just right-click My Computer, select the Properties option from the context menu, select the Hardware tab of the System Properties dialog box, and click the Device Manager button.) Any conflicting devices appear in the Conflicting Device List field near the bottom of the dialog box.

- Always have a card in the slot while booting. If you don't, Windows 2000 might not detect the PCMCIA card slot.

- To ensure Windows 2000 supports your card, check it with the Add/Remove Hardware Installation Wizard in the Control Panel. (You can browse through the list of hardware presented on the third screen, and then click Cancel to exit the utility without installing anything.)

> **Caution:** You should always click on the PCMCIA configuration item on the taskbar and shut down the drivers to the device prior to removing that device. This prevents other errors on the machine that might occur if you just remove the card. Also, even if the card was originally detected, it will not operate properly if you remove it and then re-insert it. You will have to reboot.

> **Caution:** If you are considering buying a Windows 2000 notebook, check with the manufacturer to see that you will be getting all the support features you need. PC cards can be a problem; you still might have trouble locating Windows 2000-specific drivers.

Even if Windows 2000 doesn't support your PCMCIA slot, you can still use it by installing real-mode drivers.

Hot-Docking

Another Plug and Play feature you can now get with the latest Windows 2000 notebooks is called *hot-docking*. It enables you to remove a portable computer from its docking station without turning the power off. The portable automatically reconfigures itself to reflect the loss of docking station capability. Plug that portable back into the original docking station, or a new one somewhere else, and it automatically reconfigures itself to take advantage of the new capabilities that the docking station provides.

> **Tip:** Try not to move your computer with the power on. Remember that a hard drive spins faster than a neutron star and a sudden jolt could crash it. Or you could create surges or other electrical interference that could shorten the life of your machine. You could accidentally short something out, for example, when removing a notebook from its docking station. Moving your machine from place to place without turning it off is okay—it is a supported feature—but you need to consider the cost of exercising that option. And even if it is supported, I would avoid putting it to the test. Notebook hard drives are specially designed to absorb shocks and sudden movements, but even they are whirling at high speed so do try to be gentle.

Some other hot behaviors are quite useful when you are working on a notebook. If it is important to you, consider getting a notebook that permits hot swapping of batteries and even such peripherals as floppy disks or CD-ROM drives.

With hot-docking you can avoid having to reconfigure your notebook—you can just plug or unplug devices at will, or dock and undock the notebook itself into your workstation. You don't have to power-down, and you don't have to worry about configurations. The notebook will know when you have added a new battery or disconnected a PCMCIA memory card—you no longer have to boot to force the machine to take an inventory of the connected devices. It knows at once. As soon as you make a change, the initialization configuration takes place and the proper drivers are activated.

> **Caution:** Never touch the contacts of your PCMCIA cards when you remove them from the bus. Doing so could give the card a static electric shock that will damage it or shorten its life. Hot-docking doesn't mean you can abandon all caution and approach your machine senselessly.

Windows 2000 Mobile Computing Services

Microsoft added several features to meet the needs of notebook computer users with the release of Windows 95/98 and Windows NT 4. One of these features was the Briefcase, which enabled you to keep your files synchronized between your workstation desktop machine and your portable, and also facilitated sending files to other people across a network.

However, Windows 2000 offers Synchronization, which is a superior feature that replaces the Briefcase. Lots of travelers spend part of their time on the local area network (in house or via modem) and the rest of their time working offline. Naturally, this behavior creates a version problem—you want the latest versions of files you work on, no matter *where* you might have worked on them.

The Synchronization Manager is a powerful and effective tool. In Explorer (either Explorer, Windows, or Internet), go to Tools and choose Synchronize. You see the Synchronization Manager shown in Figure 22.1.

Figure 22.1

The new Synchronization Manager replaces the less-capable Briefcase utility, as a way of dealing with the version problem.

You can choose to automate the synchronization or you can do it manually. In either case, you can specify files or folders you want to maintain the latest versions of—then let Windows 2000 worry about which file or folder is the newer version. You govern when your offline files are synchronized with files on the network. Your choices are three:

- Every time you log on or off your computer (or both)
- At specific times
- At specific intervals

How does this work? The Synchronization Manager compares files or folders stored on the network with any files or folders that you updated (or even merely opened) while working offline. The Manager then removes any older versions—leaving the most recent version available on both your laptop as well as on the network. You can also choose to synchronize offline Web pages.

If you're concerned about security—strangers peering coldly at your data (or even copying it to a diskette!) while you're sitting unaware in a fool's paradise state in a meeting or something—you can choose to either keep your laptop with you at all times, or to take advantage of Windows 2000's Encrypted File System (EFS). You can specify that particular files or folders be encrypted, and only be decryptable via the proper public key. And don't be fooled by the word *public* here. Just as in Britain a *public school* is what we here in America call a private school, the idea of public key encryption is that in theory they can know the key, but still cannot decrypt the message. This level of security should suffice, unless you're working with incredibly valuable information that people will take great pains to decipher.

Remote Dial-Up (Dial-Up Networking)

I talk about the mechanics of using dial-up networking in Chapter 20, so I won't go through that process here. After you do get the software installed and configured, however, where do you go from there? If you are a notebook user, there are plenty of reasons to use this particular Windows 2000 feature:

- Document access—I have already mentioned how you can use dial-up networking to enable an entire group of people to work together. All you need to do is place a folder with shortcuts to the team's documents in a folder on the network. When a person calls in to the network, he can open the folder and see all the pieces of the project without looking very hard. I often place this folder in the user's home directory on the network. That way, I can personalize each folder as required, and the user doesn't need to memorize yet another location on the network.

- Application access—You won't need to access applications such as word processors or spreadsheets from a remote location (at least not often). But what about the custom database that your company uses as a contact manager? Unless you plan to either print the entire database or create a copy of it on your notebook's hard drive, you need to access it remotely. In fact, if the database contains sales or inventory information that you need to update later, this is probably the only way you could use this centralized application.

- Email—Many companies depend on email to keep employees apprised of important information, such as new access codes for the security system or opportunities to update W-2 forms. Losing this communication means that you are out of touch when you return from your trip. A few minutes of online time could keep you up-to-date and reduce that "vacation" syndrome that many people feel after a road trip.

- Emergency decisions—What if you are traveling in Europe and your company is in California? How do you find a good time to call them and make a decision that requires a 24-hour turnaround? The old way of doing things was waiting until the early hours of the morning to call your company during its normal business hours—either that or waking someone up at home. Using the company or an online service email to leave a message, and then checking for responses later, could give you those few extra hours of sleep at night.

* Missing-file syndrome—Notebooks almost always need at least twice as much hard disk space as they really have. How often have you cleared a bunch of files off your notebook only to find that you really needed them after all? If you are on the road, it is usually too late to regain access to those files, and you have to figure out a way to do without them. Or do you? A remote connection can let you grab some files that you didn't think you'd need. Placing a copy of your desktop machine's hard drive—or at least the data—where you can access it using a remote connection will save you a lot of trouble later. Make sure you ask the network administrator's permission before you do this, however.

These are just some of the common ways you can use dial-up networking with a notebook. You need to find the specialty technique that applies to your specific situation. In my particular case, for example, I find it handy to use dial-up networking to grab presentations. I have room for only one or two on my notebook at a time, but I might need several during the time I'm on the road. Using this feature enables me to call in and grab the next presentation in line. The result is that each presentation is fresh and specifically designed for the group I'm talking with—yet I don't have to lug around a monster-sized hard drive or other storage.

Peter's Principle: Tips for Dial-Up Networking

Windows 2000 includes additional functionality for dial-up networking by offering you the option of automatic dialing. You can establish remote connections virtually the same way you establish connections locally: Just click the object and the phone is dialed for you. This feature is most obvious on Outlook Express or Internet Explorer; just click one of their icons and—if you have configured this connection to be automatic—you will hear the modem dial out. If you are calling a network server, you can attach yourself to that network. In fact, you can use dial-up networking to contact shared files, client/server applications, the Internet, or remote databases. To set up a new phonebook entry, open My Computer, and then click the Network and Dial-up Connections link.

Remote Network Users

Networking is an essential part of any business today. I have already talked about dial-up networking to an extent, but now I take a look at some of the communication and other considerations decisions you need to make. Using dial-up networking is one thing; using it efficiently is another.

Let's begin by providing a little insight into one of the problems with using dial-up networking. Most people know that some telephone companies sometimes charge more for the first minutes of a long-distance call than they do for the time that follows. In these situations, people therefore try to keep their long-distance calls short and to the point. The telephone company capitalizes on this by charging you more when you make several short calls rather than one long one.

Given this trickery, imagine the cost differential of making one long computer call as compared to a whole bunch of short ones. It is easy to get into the habit of dialing the company every time you need a bit of information. Consolidating all your information needs into one call is better than making several short ones. You can save a lot of money by delivering all your mail during off-peak hours.

There are still times where it is impossible to take care of all your communication needs at one time. You will still find the need to make a few short calls during the day to gather information. You don't have to do that for message delivery, however. Delivering responses to email and performing other chores can always wait for off-peak hours, especially when you are overseas and the people who wrote the message won't see it until after you are in bed anyway.

The following sections describe some of the other methods you can use to reduce the cost of dial-up networking. Although these techniques don't always work because of your immediate need for data exchange with another party, they work in the majority of cases.

Local Communications

There are many forms of long distance communication, and some of them are local. Here's one scenario. You are in Detroit and your company is in Los Angeles. It is important that you send a file containing some new information about your client to an assistant for processing. You also need some additional information about another client that's stored in your company database. You have access to both dial-up networking and the Internet. Which do you use? Some people would use dial-up networking because it is faster and perhaps more convenient. In this case, however, the low-cost solution is the Internet.

Making a local phone call to your ISP is just as fast as transferring that file over the company email, and it costs you a lot less. In most cities of any size, your ISP likely requires only a local call. It is free in most quality hotels. This local-call efficiency is one reason to choose a nationwide Internet service provider, such as ATT or AOL. That way, you will find local numbers for many places to where you travel. Some smaller ISPs, however, solve this problem by offering you a toll-free number you can call from anywhere (although some hotels have the nasty practice of charging even for "free" calls).

Sometimes, however, the obvious choice isn't the one you should use. Suppose, for example, that you need to transfer the same files and get the same information. The difference is that this time you are in another part of the state rather than another part of the country. It will only cost about 40 cents to make the toll call to your company, so using dial-up networking is the right choice.

Dynamic Networking

Despite your best efforts, you will find that sometimes you need to work with the company database or other applications live. You can't solve every problem with email or a file upload. There are times when working with live applications or data is the only way to get the job done. You want to keep these times to a minimum, but keeping a local database management system (DBMS) current might override other cost considerations. Fortunately, your notebook still has a few tricks up its sleeve. The following list provides some of the ideas I have come up with, but you can probably think of others based on your unique set of circumstances.

- Internet access—Using the Internet still might provide the best means of working with live data. You need to overcome two problems. The first is gaining access to a local server that allows live connections. The second is that you have to make a TCP/IP connection and use a special modem to make this work. Both problems can be solved given enough resources. In the past, this solution might have seemed more like a dream than reality. Today, intranets (the private version of the Internet) abound. Even small businesses can occasionally write off the cost of using an intranet solution because it is less expensive than anything else I have covered here.

- Using a local office's PBX connection—Sometimes a local office will provide the long-distance call solution you need. It might mean a little wrangling with the local boss and perhaps a short drive, but this solution could save your company some money.

- Keeping notes—Even if your database doesn't support batch-mode processing, you could still keep notes and make all the updates at once. This enables you to make one phone call rather than many to record the required information. Of course, this solution still won't work with "live" data such as ticket sales and the like.

- Off-hour calling—This is probably the least likely solution. If your data needs are so time-critical that you can't afford to wait even a few minutes, off-hour calling won't work. However, you could combine this technique with batch-mode- or note-taking methods to work with live data on the network. You could even use this off-hour calling technique when using a local office's PBX connection. This reduces the local boss's objection to tying up the line to service your needs.

Tip: If you are using a custom DBMS, it might be possible to add batch-updating capability. This enables you to use a smaller version of the application on the road, create new records, modify existing ones, and make all the changes in batch mode when you return from your trip or as part of an upload to the company database. This is usually a less-expensive solution for inventory control or other types of sales databases than making live changes. There are two criteria for using a batch system: You need a fairly large outside sales force to make the change cost-efficient, and the company must be able to get by with daily or weekly database updates rather than real-time data. This works in most situations, but you couldn't use it for an airline ticket database, for example. Also note that Microsoft's new ADO database technology permits you to work with "detached" recordsets—recordsets that are not (yet) attached to any particular database.

Offline Printing

Remember in Chapter 18, "Fonts and Printing," when I covered printing? I talked about two techniques that the notebook computer user will love. The first is the idea of creating a printer for every purpose. You can create printers for all the local offices you visit during a trip. That way, you can print any notes or documents you need without worrying about whether you have the proper print driver to get the job done. You can also use this technique to print at client sites.

That isn't the only way you can print, however. You can also print to your hard drive using the offline printing technique explained in Chapter 18. All you need to do is set the printer to work offline. Everything you send to disk will wait on the hard drive until you send it to the printer.

What I didn't include in that chapter was something notebook-specific. Whenever you disconnect your notebook from the network printer or docking station, Windows 2000 detects the loss of printing capability and sets the printer to work offline automatically. Unfortunately, this doesn't work all the time. I experienced a few situations in which the printer disconnection wasn't detected. Either way, detection was consistent. Check your printer the first time, and you should be able to rely on the connection being consistent from that point on.

Power Management Strategies

The following list provides ideas on what you can look for on your notebook. Not every notebook provides every feature listed here, and you might well find some that are unique to your system. The first tip is to explore the vendor documentation that comes with your notebook. You will be amazed at the little tips you will find there.

- Forget fancy software—Screen savers probably eat more power on a notebook than most people imagine. Because most notebook computers come with a feature for turning off the monitor automatically, there isn't any reason for you to install a fancy screen saver. In fact, because most notebooks use flat screen displays, you might actually cause more harm than good by using a screen saver. A screen saver could inadvertently interfere with the automatic shutdown software and end up reducing the life of your screen, not extending it. Besides interfering with the normal way your notebook runs, some screen savers constantly access the hard disk, causing further drain on the battery. There are other culprits in this area as well. If you can, try to get by with a subset of your word-processing software. I installed the full version of my word processor the first time around and found that one of the features kept hard disk activity at a frantic pace. In an effort to provide me with the latest information on my files, the software was actually just eating power. I don't keep a lot of files on my notebook, so I always know exactly what I have available. Kill the fancy features of your software and you will find that the battery that normally lasts three hours will probably last three and a half.

Peter's Principle: Fear of Burn-In: Do You Need to Save Your Screen?

Notebooks use LCD or Active Matrix displays which are fundamentally reflective, so there is no way that a prolonged, static image could possibly *burn-in*. There is no danger that a notebook requires a screen "saver."

However, people have worried in the past about "burning" their ordinary computer monitors. Here's how the fear began: In theory, if an unchanging image is displayed on an ordinary desktop CRT computer monitor for hours and hours (like two days), the phosphors that coat the screen burn (or singe), which is like leaving a hot iron sitting too long on a shirt. You should get a ghostly image of the burn—whatever was on the screen during the burn-in is supposed to show up from then on, as a kind of faint image.

TV screens and conventional desktop monitors are lit from behind, by guided beams of electrons that strike against a coating of phosphorus that is painted on the inside of the glass. The phosphorus lights up. You see images!

Unremitting bombardment of the beams against the same locations on the phosphorus is supposed to discolor (burn) the phosphorus. The story goes that if you leave a word processor document sitting there overnight, you might come back the next morning and find that you can see faint outlines of the text no matter what other applications you switch to. Even after you shut down the word processor and look at your desktop wallpaper or a new fax or something, there they are, the characters of your overnight burn-in showing faintly in front of what you expect to see. And like rain specks on a window, you can't quite ignore them. They can drive you quite mad!

Fear of this screen burn-in phenomenon, however, is rather like the fear that if you don't cook bacon completely, you could get trichinosis. Nobody has ever known anyone to actually come down with trichinosis. Have you? What are the symptoms? Is it fatal?

Likewise, nobody has actually seen a burned-in computer screen, at least on modern color monitors (burn-in was certainly a problem with old early-80s monochrome monitors, and it can even happen when displaying static graphics like a video game on an ordinary television screen). However, today's color computer monitors—20 years later—are designed to prevent burn-in.

But none of us wants to be the first to have a dreaded condition. Therefore many people use screen savers. Besides, they often look nice and they have one other raison d'être, as well. Screen savers offer a certain degree of security. When you leave your desk, you may not want just anyone to be able to use your computer or examine your work in progress. Screen savers can be password-protected, whereby the screen saver can't be turned off without typing in a special code. Although this capability is not bulletproof security, it does provide a measure of privacy. Of course, a truly determined intruder could just turn off the power, then turn it back on, and gain access to your secrets (unless you have a log-on password for additional protection).

- Look for power-saving features—A lot of notebooks come equipped with a function key (FN on my system) that is poorly understood by the majority of users. In my case, there's a faucet at the top of the screen. Pressing FN+Faucet considerably reduces power consumption on my machine—yet I wouldn't have found this feature by just looking at the documentation. The vendor hid it in the screen section of the text; it wasn't in the power management section as expected. If you are in doubt about the function of any particular button or key on your notebook, keep searching the documentation until you find it. Most notebooks now come with a power-saving mode that you can use while on the battery. In some cases, you will discover programs run a little slower and that the backlight doesn't seem to work as well, but you will get a lot more life out of your battery.

- Change power-wasting habits and software configurations—I find that I occasionally develop a habit that is great in intent but short on true usefulness. When I start thinking about what I want to write, for example, I save my document. It sounds like a good habit to get into. After all, if you save during think time, power outages and other types of hardware failure are less likely to affect you. However, consider for a second that it is fairly unlikely that you will experience a power outage when working with a notebook unless you totally ignore the battery level or the machine is struck by a gamma ray. In addition, the hardware used in notebook construction is a lot less prone to failure than hardware of days gone by. Consider looking at your software configuration as well. I used to set the automatic save for my word processor to 10 minutes. That was just enough time for the drive to start spinning down. As a result, I wasted a huge amount of power starting and stopping the drive. Setting the automatic save to 20 minutes proved more efficient from a power perspective and I haven't lost a single bit of data as a result of the change.

- Turn off your sound—It is really nice having sound effects, but sound boards consume quite a bit of power and you have to ask whether you really need to hear any sounds while working on a document at 30,000 feet. In most cases, you can turn off your sound board with a simple setting in the Control Panel. Making this small change in configuration will not only save you power, it will make you more popular with the person sitting in the next seat. You will also want to avoid playing your latest music CD while on battery. A CD will keep the disk running almost continuously, greatly reducing battery life.

- Give it a break—I have seen more than a few folks eat lunch and work on their notebooks at the same time. Besides the risk of spilling something in the keyboard, working and doing something else (such as eating) at the same time probably isn't the most efficient way to use notebook battery power. Just suspend your notebook for the duration of your meal. Not only will you use battery power more efficiently, but you will also enjoy hot food for once.

- Avoid power-hungry devices and other disk-intensive applications. Also remember notebook CDs, floppy disks, and disk-intensive applications. In general, the notebook will turn off the drives when they are not in use. Windows 2000 is always using the hard drive, however, due to page-file activity. This is one of the reasons Windows 2000 uses up the battery power on notebooks so quickly. If you keep reading from a CD or floppy disk, however, you will drain power even more quickly.

> **Peter's Principle:** Using Hardware Profiles
>
> Don't forget that you can set up different Hardware Profiles in Windows 2000 (but you must be logged on to Windows 2000 as Administrator to be able to do this). This feature is particularly useful when you use a notebook. For instance, you might want to switch configurations in your notebook depending on whether you are currently docked to a workstation. Create a set of profiles; when you boot, you will see the list of profiles from which you can choose. It is also easy to toggle various services or devices using a single profile.
>
> To create a hardware profile
>
> 1. Right-click My Computer and choose Properties from the context menu.
> 2. Click the Hardware tab.
> 3. Click the Hardware Profiles button.
> 4. Copy an existing profile (you will edit the copy to define your new profile).
> 5. Select the profile you want to copy.
> 6. Click the Copy button and enter a new name for your copy.
>
> Now you can make any adjustments you want to this new profile by using the Device Manager (double-click the System icon in Control Panel, then click the Hardware tab and the Device Manager button) to disable or enable devices that are in the profile. If you disable a device in a hardware profile, its device drivers are not loaded when you turn on power to your computer.

Advanced Configuration and Power Interface (ACPI)

The new Advanced Configuration and Power Interface feature is actually an expansion of the power management features found in Windows NT 4. As a minimum, you will be able to control when your hard drive and monitor turn themselves off after a period of non-use. What will this mean to you as a user? Theoretically, you could leave your computer up all the time. Of course, this could lead to the security problems.

You will also find that Windows 2000 (via hardware vendors, as described shortly) supports two new features:

- Power schemes
- Suspend

Power schemes works just like the sound and appearance schemes you might have used in the past. A power scheme enables you to configure a method for managing the power on your machine. You select a power scheme based on your current activity. You might want to use one scheme at the end of the day to shut off your machine instantly, for example, and another during the day that provides a delay so that the machine doesn't turn off every time you stop to think.

Notebook users will already be familiar with the Suspend or Stand by features used in earlier Windows versions, but it is new for desktop users. The Windows 2000 Hibernate option found in the Shut Down Windows dialog box will enable you to electronically turn off everything on your machine without actually turning off the power. Your machine will go to sleep when you are not using it. If everything works as it should, your machine will use a minimum of power in this state—less than most nightlights use. To activate the Hibernate feature, open Power Options in the Control Panel, click the Hibernate tab (displayed only on machines that support it), and select the Enable Hibernate Support check box.

Power management is currently being supplied by hardware vendors for use with Windows 2000. Check with your notebook vendors about what kind of power management they might offer. As I mentioned earlier in this chapter, power management might require a BIOS upgrade. Although that sounds radical, it is, in fact, a fairly common adjustment to notebooks and is usually straightforward.

On Your Own

If you are thinking of buying a notebook and want to use Windows 2000 on it, make a list of all peripherals, PCMCIA cards, and other add-ons you will want to use with it. Then check with the manufacturer to be sure that these peripherals are available under Windows 2000—and that there are good drivers for them. Check out lists of compatible computers, hardware, and software at `http://microsoft.com/windows/ professional/deploy/compatible/default.asp`.

This chapter introduces many ideas on how a notebook user can use the capabilities provided by Windows 2000 to improve productivity while on the road. Of course, one of the big things I covered was the use of the PCMCIA interface. If you have a PCMCIA bus on your notebook computer, right-click My Computer and select the Properties option. Click the Advanced tab and then the Performance Options button to see whether your system is fully optimized. Make sure you double-check the bus.

Another productivity enhancement is the combination of Synchronize and dial-up networking. Split your projects into two categories: those that you are working on alone, and those that you are working on with a group. Use the Synchronize method with the projects that you are working on alone. Use the folder and dial-up networking combination for projects that you are working on in a group.

Make a list of the ways you can use dial-up networking to improve your productivity. I mentioned the most common ways in this chapter, but your company might have special needs that I didn't cover. It is important to use a little creativity when thinking about the ways Windows 2000 can help you. Keep the list handy for later and refer to it when you are looking for ways to solve a particular mobile-computing problem.

Add several Hardware Profiles to your notebook and your desktop workstation. Don't forget to set up separate profiles for your notebook in both its docked and undocked state.

PART VI

Networking with Windows 2000

Network Basics

Everyone needs a network, whether they realize it or not. At the very least, you need to dial out to some provider to join the Internet revolution. But beyond that, you can benefit from having a server around to manage certain operations anytime you have more than two workstations gathered together for work. Setting up a simple network requires no more than an investment of about $300, depending on where you find the parts, and hooking everything up into a network can bring significant benefits.

This chapter offers a brief technical background on networking, leading up to the issues of configuring a Windows 2000 Professional client to participate on a network. This chapter reviews the basic background on the following topics:

- Sharing resources with coworkers
- Building workgroups of users
- Redirecting drives
- Understanding the physical network and related software
- Understanding Windows 2000-supported protocols
- Using direct cable

Sharing Resources with Coworkers

The reason to build a network is to share resources and to communicate more easily with each other. Originally, this was a cool idea first implemented by a few engineers at the Xerox Palo Alto Research Center. They had a lot of workstations and a lot of know-how, and they basically grew tired of sharing information via disk or paper. So, these electronics wizards invented a way to communicate among machines electronically, which they called Ethernet. Xerox was not impressed with the way this concept fit into their business strategy, so the company never capitalized on the concept. In one of Xerox's fabled losses, however, an engineer named Bob Metcalfe left to form a company called 3Com, which brought Ethernet to the masses.

Why did the masses need Ethernet? Many businesses are based on sharing information. Accountants receive payments, write checks, and track expenditures, and unfortunately they can't all share the same workstation. In the days of big iron mainframes, they didn't share the same workstation. They used terminals connected to the mainframe via a network of sorts, and they shared the resources of the mainframe. They entered all their data into sequentially numbered accounts in an accounting system, selected items for payment, ran payroll, printed checks, and so forth using the shared resources of a single large computer.

With the advent of the personal computer and VisiCalc (a critical killer application in the 1980s), one accountant could perform a great deal of this work on a single personal computer. The computer model used was merely an accident; somebody happened to have an Apple II to give to the right people. VisiCalc was written by Dan Bricklin and Bob Frankston after Bricklin learned how to run the numbers using a room full of blackboards at the Harvard Business School. But VisiCalc enabled you to run the numbers in the virtual playspace of an Apple II, using the cells and grids of a spreadsheet rather than the cells and grids drawn on a blackboard.

If you had more than one accountant with this capability right on the desktop, you needed to be able to share and compare the results. You could share on floppy disk or on paper, but it was obviously easier to share electronically without an intervening physical medium.

If your eighth floor is devoted to accountants, they need a network desperately. Where are the time sheets? Where are the financial reports? They're all in a central location, accessible by anyone who must work with them over the network. Networking makes such sharing possible in ways that you could never accomplish using a physical medium. Run NetMeeting sometime and share an application. You can discuss your spreadsheet, allow multiple networked users to comment on it, and allow multiple users to edit different sections, all in the same session. The users can even be in different cities while sharing voice as well as video communication. You can have a worldwide meeting at a fraction of the cost of flying everyone to a central location so that they can show each other sheets of paper and colored transparencies.

Improving Communication

Sharing improves communication. Today that may seem like a no-brainer. Now that you can communicate with your child's teacher about homework assignments, absences, and what-have-you using email, the dramatic improvement in communication that networking brings can seem lost in the noise of its simplicity and efficiency. No one has to be there to answer the phone. You can broadcast your message to multiple recipients. You can communicate across the world, if you have to. You can send pictures, saving thousands of words, and you can search for the person you need to talk to in case you don't know his address. In fact, the original reason for building the Internet was to improve communication among the groups of scientists and contractors working with the Defense Advanced Research Projects Agency. These individuals used to fly to Washington, D.C., and read papers to one another at conferences. DARPA realized that they all had computers and could share information via computer. The origins of Internet email, FTP, and many commonplace means of communicating from one computer to another began with this insight. (For more about the history of the Internet, see Chapter 2, "Windows to the Internet.")

Note: The Internet is the global network that grew from the Defense Advanced Research Projects Agency (DARPA) implementation of a nationwide network. Intranets are applications of the same technology to build networks internal to a business. The primary purpose of an intranet is to use the Internet technologies, in particular the World Wide Web technologies, to share information within a business. Intranets are typically not connected to the Internet, although a business might have an intranet and be connected to the Internet as well. The intranet, however, will be isolated from the Internet in most implementations.

The decision to build a nationwide network to serve a particular research group wasn't based on economics alone. Communication also improved significantly. I could download my own copy from a central server, complete with the diagrams and supporting material. I could read the paper at my leisure, I could build archives of papers on my topics of interest, and I could search them easily to find what had been said about a particular concept.

These concepts have been applied to other situations with later-generation technologies. One of the important functions of the Secretary of State in any state is to receive registrations of corporations as well as to serve as a repository for the papers and reports required to be held on file by any given state. Of course, these are public documents of some note. Both lawyers and scholars, as well as interested individuals researching a stock purchase, might need access to the filings presented by any given corporation. The traditional means of retrieving this information on request is to send a clerk to a massive filing cabinet and have him search by hand, which is slow and painful compared to the alternative.

One consulting business founded in Kansas took on the problem of improving this particular act of communication between the Secretary of State's office and interested citizens. The company created images of all existing corporate filings on CD, indexed them, and designed search software to retrieve the indexed information. What may have been a month-long search by a legal clerk in the past can now be executed in seconds, thanks to networked CD-ROM towers. (CD towers are freestanding cases that hold multiple CD drives.) Share such towers on the Internet, and you have instantaneous access to the information for anyone who can connect to an Internet service provider. Communication definitely improves when you network, even if all you share is the employee manual in your small company. You keep one central repository updated, and everyone has the latest information.

Creating Cost-Effectiveness

The cost of networking can appear daunting, but that cost is deceptive under most circumstances. Consider this scenario of a three-person office: Assume that everyone needs a printer, a scanner, and a copier at their disposal. You can buy each person a printer, lease or purchase a photocopier, and provide some sort of central access to a scanner.

The cost of this configuration for a three-person office can easily reach $1,500 or more. This office can save money by networking. If you buy one Hewlett Packard OfficeJet Pro and share it using a $50 hub, $50 network cards, and three $10 cables, for example, you've provided the same services to everyone for at least $500 less.

Translate that into the cost of providing both black-and-white (fast) and color printing (vivid, but slow) to a large organization, and you can see how network wires cut costs. Where you might have provided one printer per user, you can provide one high-capacity printer for 20 users, reducing the cost per user for laser printing and color printing significantly. In addition, rather than providing large amounts of disk space for individual machines, with the associated cost of backing up multiple large drives in separate locations, you can provide a centralized drive array that requires only a single point of backup. This array can provide higher levels of fault tolerance and greater levels of loss protection at a lower cost per user than increasing the storage on individual machines.

Building Workgroups of Users

To simplify organizing users into working groups, you can arrange your network so that users who work on common projects share the same resources. In terms of networking, such a scheme is called building a workgroup. The operating system on each workstation contains a setting in which the workgroup can be identified using a name. As a result, users can log on to their workgroup by providing a username and password. They can then access the shared resources associated with that workgroup.

Boundaries between workgroups can be made relatively weak or relatively strict, depending on your preference. Workgroups are just logical (virtual) units on your network that enable you to organize access to resources. Using the security features of the operating system installed on the computers, you can give your logical workgroups the capability of seeing and sharing one another's resources, or you can take away this capability.

Such security is enforced under Windows 2000 using the concepts of permissions, rights, and abilities, as defined in the following list:

- Permissions govern actions that users can undertake with files or folders, such as reading and writing.
- Rights are actions that users can undertake to use the services of the operating system to modify their working environment, such as changing the system time, creating groups of users, or formatting the hard drive.
- Abilities are the same types of actions as rights, except Microsoft has preassigned them to certain built-in groups on the system. You may assign abilities to a user only by making the user a member of one or more of these groups.

Using permissions, rights, and abilities, you can build boundaries between workgroups so that they can't trample on one another's resources unreasonably and so that they can cooperate to achieve goals together efficiently.

Redirecting Drives

All networks require a mechanism that makes it possible for the user's computer to employ (use) network resources. This mechanism is known as redirection. The network could provide any means of granting access that its designers could imagine, but the one chosen most frequently is to make network resources look and feel like the resources on the user's machine. If you want to grant the user access to a folder on the shared network drives, you make it look like a drive on the user's machine.

Redirection is the process by which remote resources on the network masquerade as local resources on the user's machine. A component of the operating system, often called the redirector, undertakes this task. In the case of drives, the redirector assigns a drive letter unused on the user's machine to some node in the network file system shared by a computer whose function is primarily to share resources. This computer, known as a server (the physical device), has a component in its operating system known as the server (a special application). The server receives messages destined for the remote file system from the redirector and reinterprets them for the network file system. (Servers also have other responsibilities, such as security.)

This cooperation is functionally simple. The user wants to open a file on the M: drive. As far as the user is concerned, the M: drive is just like any other drive. It has a root folder, subfolders under the root folder, and files in the folders just like any other drive. The M: drive is really not on the user's computer, however. When the user accesses the M: drive using the Explorer, the redirector intercepts the access messages and sends them off to the distant server, where the server component receives them. The server component reinterprets a request to open a file in the first subfolder under the root of the M: drive as opening a file in a subfolder of a subfolder of a subfolder of the root of its C: drive. Then the server component opens the file and sends the result back to the redirector. The redirector presents the open file to the user as an open file on the M: drive.

The process of assigning a drive letter on a local machine to a node in the file system of a remote machine is called mapping. You map the M: drive to the shared folder Q on the remote server. From that point forward, the M: drive is the same as shared folder Q, as far as the local user is concerned. Q appears as the root of the M: drive in the Explorer, and the user needs to be none the wiser (see Figure 23.1). The redirector and the server components of the operating systems on the machines manage the entire conversation from the time the mapping is created forward.

Redirection and mapping can be used with other resources, most notably printers. With other resources, however, you assign a name to that resource, and the name serves as the mapping point. One of my printers, for example, is named Clarissa. When I map a local printer name to that name on the server where the printer is, I choose a name for the local printer that will masquerade as Clarissa on the local machine. The names need not be the same. On the local machine, I might name the printer Fred. However, I map Fred as a name on the local machine to the name Clarissa on the server. Whenever the user prints to the local printer named Fred, the redirector sends all output to the actual printer Clarissa, somewhere out on the network. The server on the computer to which Clarissa is attached receives that redirected output and sends it to Clarissa to be printed.

FIGURE 23.1

Windows 2000 enables you to map drives so that network resources appear in My Computer or Explorer as in any local drive.

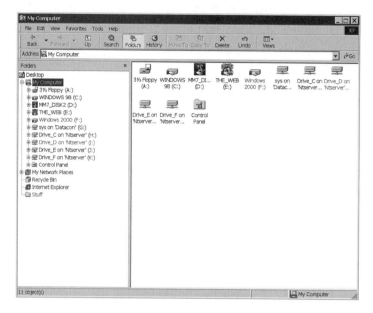

Understanding the Physical Network and Related Software

Redirection is a fundamental concept in networking for PCs, for a historic reason. In networking in general, redirection has been seen as the most efficient way to mirror remote resources on a local computer. When Novell invented the first PC-based network operating system, it chose to use redirection as a method and chose to represent remote file systems as drives. As a result, the drive metaphor for redirection in PC operating systems has been dominant. Other concepts are important as well, although not for the same historic reasons. These ideas have been associated with networking since the mainframe days, and they have standards that describe them and that have evolved along with them. This section of the chapter, therefore, briefs you on concepts general to networking.

Clients

Since the beginning, networks have been composed of two kinds of entities: servers, which provide services, and clients, which use those services. A client can be thought of as both the machine that you use to access networked services and as a software component in the operating system installed on that machine (see Figure 23.2).

In the early days of networking, a client was a dumb terminal: a screen and keyboard with just enough electronics to transmit and receive information between the terminal and the mainframe host computer. As dumb terminal hardware smartened up and evolved into the PC as we know it today, the term *client* also came to mean the software that emulated the role of the terminal. As Ethernet evolved and IBM created the Token-Ring Network, the client became the software that communicated with these new types of networks.

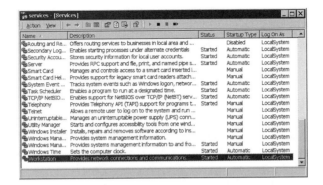

FIGURE 23.2
The client for a Windows 2000 machine is called the Workstation Service.

Note: A token ring is a networking scheme in which a computer can't transmit unless it has a token in hand that grants permission to transmit. The token is a packet that's passed around the ring of computers. It functions like the talking stick often used in training groups to communicate efficiently.

The client software is also known as the redirector. Its job is to interpret access requests and to determine whether they relate to the local file system or to the network file system. If they relate to the network file system, the redirector redirects the request to the network. The principal means of identifying whether an access request is for local or network resources is the name of the resource. PC networks use a convention called the Uniform Naming Convention, under which all network names begin with a double backslash (\\). This is the cue that causes the redirector to redirect the request.

Cabling

To redirect requests, the client must have a means of transmission between machines. Although all manner of methods can be imagined, from radio signals to waxed strings tied between the computers, PC networking settled on cabling as the transmission medium. Three types of cable are commonly used, and they adhere to a variety of standards. Any cable that runs through a ceiling must be certified as plenum-quality cable, which means that it can run through the space above the drop ceiling tiles (the plenum) and that it meets the fire retardancy and safety standards for materials that are to be installed in that space.

Perhaps the most common type of cable in use is twisted-pair, which uses connectors (called RJ-45 connectors) that look like oversized modular telephone connectors. This type of cable has eight strands of wire twisted into four pairs. This twisting eliminates crosstalk among the wires. Cable of this type comes in several grades, but the type you want to use is Category 5 cable because it supports transmission rates up to 100Mbps, the speed of Fast Ethernet. If you ever want to step up from standard Ethernet to Fast Ethernet, you need to have this type of cable in place. An upgrade to Fast Ethernet can be a major expense that you can avoid by going with Category 5 cable from the start.

The second most popular type of cable is thin coaxial cable, often called *thinnet*. This type of cable looks like the cable often used in cable television applications. It uses British Naval Connectors (BNCs) to connect to your computer, and it requires terminators at either end of the line to prevent signal reflections back from the terminus of the cable. One of the terminators should be grounded as well.

Another popular type of cable is fiber-optic cable. The advantage of this cable is that it's completely secure from anyone capturing the signal using a receiver that can amplify the signals that leak from other types of cables. This type of cable also supports virtually unlimited transmission speeds. It's less commonly used in most installations, however, because of its greater cost. Typically, you reserve the fiber-optic cable for a backbone and branch away from it using other, less expensive cable types.

Adapters

To communicate across the cable, you need a transmitter and a receiver. The network interface card (often called a NIC) has the electronics to transmit signals on the cable and to receive them. It also can buffer the information it receives and transfer it back to main memory for processing.

The transmission method used by the card determines much about the architecture of your network. Cards in use currently use one of two schemes. Ethernet uses Carrier Sense Multiple Access with Collision Detection (CSMA/CD) networking, also known as probabilistic networking. In this scheme, the transmitter listens to the wire to see whether it's quiet. If the wire is quiet, the transmitter transmits. If a collision occurs because another transmitter transmitted at the same time, there's significant noise on the wire. If the NIC detects such noise, it stops transmitting, waits a random interval, and tries again, until the transmission is successful.

IBM's Token-Ring strategy is different in approach. The NIC can't transmit unless it's in possession of a packet called the token. As a result, theoretically no collisions can occur on the wire because only one computer can transmit at a time. Computers on the network pass the token to one another (hence the concept of a ring, no matter what the actual topology of the network), and whoever has the token may transmit. The actual transmission takes place as an attachment to the token. A NIC's first response on receiving the token, therefore, is to check to see whether a message addressed to it is attached.

These two major networking schemas offer different transmission speeds. Ethernet originally transmitted at 10Mbps, and Token-Ring at 16Mbps. However, Ethernet now offers 100Mbps and promises to offer 1000Mbps in the near future. Token-Ring is moving toward a 100Mbps transmission speed. The speed is largely governed by the electronics of the NICs in use; the electronics in the hubs, switches, and routers; and the quality of the cabling. All of these, and the appropriate software, must be in place to take advantage of the highest transmission speeds.

NICs have a network address in ROM that's theoretically unique, although you occasionally hear of duplicates of these addresses appearing. This address is called the Media Access Control (MAC) address. It's the bottom-line address of your computer on the network. Novell, for example, uses this address as your only address on the network. Other schemes in which you assign your own addresses to network nodes do exist, as you'll see later in this chapter.

Packets

In discussing Token-Ring, I mentioned the word *packet*. Packets are the transmittable units of information on your networks. They run around 1500 bytes, depending on your networking software, and obviously represent small chunks of the total amount of data you need to transmit. As a result, to transmit data and receive data, your networking software wraps the chunk of data in a frame, which contains the routing information, sequence number of the packet in the total message, and similar information. On receipt, your networking software can then reassemble the original transmission in its entirety.

Protocols

Networking software manages the packing of packets into frames (as well as their transmission and reassembly) according to an agreed-upon format for the transmission of data between devices. This format is called a protocol. The protocol is usually enforced by a driver or a set of drivers residing on both the client and the server. These drivers control the orderly transmission and reception of the data. Protocols have been developed by independent vendors and have been standardized to permit diverse types of machines to communicate with one another.

Note: Although protocols are sets of agreements, you don't install and use a set of agreements. You install and use software that implements those agreements. There's a fundamental difference between a protocol and a networking model such as the OSI model. Protocols that have no software implementation literally don't exist because no computer can communicate using them unless the protocol is implemented in software. As a result, a protocol driver is often confused for the agreements it enforces. Here the term *protocol* is used to mean both the agreements and the software that implements them.

Understanding Windows 2000-Supported Protocols

Windows 2000 supports many protocols, but three are primarily used to allow communication between clients and servers on typical networks. In essence, you have your choice of three sets of rules for conducting communications, or you can even use multiple sets of rules, if you so desire. These three primary protocols are described in the next section, which gives you a sense of when you'd choose to run each one.

Microsoft Networking (to Windows 2000 Servers)

Historically, Microsoft has used a protocol called the NetBIOS Extended User Interface (also called NetBEUI) as its primary way of managing network communications. NetBEUI is the set of agreements that make up the protocol, and NetBIOS is the software interface to network components that implements the agreements. This protocol enables you to assign a name to each computer (just a text string in terms of its data type), and this name is used as the network address. To find another computer, the protocol broadcasts a message to every computer asking whether any computer recognizes the name. The computer that recognizes the name sends a message back to the MAC address on the original message, and this message has the MAC address of the sender on it. As a result, both computers are in possession of each other's MAC addresses, and they communicate to these addresses from this point on.

> **Tip:** You need to install NetBEUI as a protocol on your machine only when you intend to use it as a standalone protocol, as when you intend to use no other networking protocol. In the presence of other protocols, notably TCP/IP and NWLink, you need only install the NetBIOS component that communicates with these protocol drivers, and you have all the NetBEUI functionality you'll ever need.

NetBEUI is therefore called a broadcast-oriented protocol. It isn't favored for use on large networks because of the amount of needless traffic it creates—"needless" in terms of what traffic could be saved if all the broadcasts were avoided. Microsoft itself has rewritten NetBIOS, the API programs used to access this protocol, to be hosted by other protocols. As a result, you have little reason to use NetBEUI.

IPX/SPX

Internet Packet Exchange/Sequenced Packet Exchange is a protocol originally developed by Novell for its PC network operating system. This protocol uses the MAC address as the network node address, so each NIC is automatically addressed. Using this protocol, you have very little network configuration to do unless you run into problems. Addressing schemes and tables of names and addresses are built automatically. Servers also advertise themselves automatically. Microsoft recommends this protocol if you want an easy-to-maintain, self-configuring network. The company has built its own implementation, called NWLink.

TCP/IP

In contrast with IPX/SPX, the Transmission Control Protocol/Internet Protocol (TCP/IP), originally developed by DARPA for its intersite communication network, is neither easy to maintain nor self-configuring. To use TCP/IP, you need to master a significant amount of knowledge. This protocol uses a logical (user-assignable) address scheme. Because it's the protocol on which the Internet runs, you need to worry not only about having unique addresses on your own intranet, but also unique addresses on the Internet if you're connected to it. Because TCP/IP is the Internet protocol, however, it's probably the most widely used protocol at this time.

The main thing that you need to know now about TCP/IP is that it's actually a suite of related protocols. Each protocol in the suite manages a specific function. TCP manages connections and sessions, and IP manages addressing. Other protocols within TCP/IP include Address Resolution Protocol (ARP), which matches IP addresses to MAC addresses, when necessary; Bootstrap Protocol (BootP), which manages the booting of diskless workstations; Dynamic Host Configuration Protocol (DHCP), an extension of BootP that automatically configures network nodes; and the Domain Name System (DNS), which maps names such as macmillan.com to an IP address. Later chapters cover these and other protocols in detail. For now, just be aware of the names, buzzwords, and basic functions. (A detailed discussion of TCP/IP appears in Chapter 24, "Peer-to-Peer Networking.")

Using Direct Cable

So far, we've assumed that your network must be built of cables and NICs. Although that's the typical configuration, it's not the required configuration. Microsoft has provided two ways for you to connect two PCs and use networking protocols to manage communication without using NICs and cables. One of these is the Direct Cable Connection, and the other is the RAS connection.

Using Cable Connection

Suppose that you want to connect a laptop to a desktop to transfer a few files. In the past, you had to buy a program such as LapLink and a special cable. Windows 2000, however, enables you to connect a serial null modem cable between the two PCs and treat that cable as if it were a network connection managed by NICs at either end. (In many cases you can also use a parallel port and a special cable for connecting the two machines.) Microsoft accomplished this feat by building a virtual network adapter, called the dial-up serial cable modem, that's software only. Although it's just software, it manages the serial port as if it were the network card's connection to the network cable.

You install the dial-up features by clicking Start, Settings, Network and Dial-up Connections. This invokes the installation of the dial-up capabilities and management software. You must install a valid modem first, however. If you haven't done so, you'll be sent to the Modem Wizard to install a modem. The direct cable modem is first on the default list under Standard Modem Types. After you've installed the serial modem, you can use the RAS management software to connect the two machines (see Figure 23.3). Communication between the two machines is then managed by the network protocols installed on each. One machine in this partnership must function as a dial-up server, and one must function as a dial-up client.

FIGURE 23.3
The RAS software enables you to manage your direct cable connection.

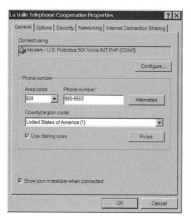

Using RAS

The Remote Access Service is the service that manages all dial-up connections. RAS is installed when you install the dial-up features in general. Its purpose is to provide management and dialing capabilities, as well as to answer remote calls. In the case of the serial cable modem, the RAS service initiates direct connections.

RAS cooperates with Windows 2000 security. It uses the networking protocols you've installed to initiate and manage connections. It can provide dial-back security, and it does use your machine's SAM database, the list of users who can log on to your computer, to validate callers. You can control whether a caller has access and also the caller's permissions, rights, and abilities. However, the dialed machine will function as a gateway to any network it's attached to. You may decide which protocol the RAS service uses for the gateway, but not which users may access the gateway.

Note: Under dial-back security, you dial up the server. The server then asks you for a number to dial back, disconnects the call, and dials you back. The server may also be set to dial a preset number only.

On Your Own

Right-click My Network Places, and choose Properties from the menu. Right-click each of the icons, choose Properties from the context menu, and explore your Windows 2000 network components. Try to identify the client and server components, and try to adjust their configuration using the Properties button. Locate the protocols that you've installed, and see what can be configured about them.

Check your computer to find the network adapter and cables. Identify their type. Can you tell whether you're on a Token-Ring or an Ethernet network? The properties of the protocols should help you figure it out.

Peer-to-Peer Networking

Just about every business—large or small—has a network these days. The benefits of linking a group of computers together, so they can share peripherals and files, are just too great to ignore. Even two- and three-person shops commonly have a network installed—if for no other reason than to share a printer and a few documents. I've been surprised at the number of home networks I see as well.

All this shouldn't be too surprising, however. Just think about the benefits to Mom and Dad of having a modern home workstation with a large hard drive, fast processor, and other new machine features. Using a peer-to-peer network allows the parents to give that old machine to the kids. Even if the kids' workstation only has a hard drive that's large enough for the Windows system files, their application files can reside on the larger hard drive of the machine used by their parents. Also, keeping the parents' machine separate from the kids' machine is a good way to keep your work separate from their play. In other words, even a simple network setup enables you to blend the capabilities of two or more machines, and to improve efficiency.

Regardless of the size of your network, you'll find some native support for it in Windows 2000. You can even install limited support for some of those older peer-to-peer networks on the market, as long as they don't use real-mode drivers. This does leave out older versions of LANtastic, however, as well as some of the other peer-to-peer offerings that worked well with Windows 3.x. On the other hand, the new Windows 95/98-specific offerings of these peer-to-peer networks seem to work fine with Windows 2000. Of course, a few of these older networks don't provide the same level of features they did under Windows 3.x, but at least they work well enough to get the job done. Unless that old network provides some indispensable feature not provided by Windows 2000, however, you'll probably want to get rid of it.

This chapter focuses on the peer-to-peer networking capabilities that Windows 2000 provides. For the most part, I purposely avoid talking about networks in general or even comparing the various options you have. The reason's simple: A single chapter can't possibly contain everything you'll need to ever know about networking. There are literally volumes of information about this topic—and some people think that even those are just barely adequate. We'll also look at the Windows 2000 networking architecture in this chapter—something that's common to both of the networking models it supports.

Looking Ahead

This chapter doesn't contain everything you'll need to know about Windows 2000 networking. It looks at the low end of networking alone: Peer-to-peer network support. Chapter 27, "Client/Server Networking," looks at the client/server networking model supported by Windows 2000. This is the kind of network that most medium-to-large businesses have installed. I've also devoted an entire chapter to security in this book; take a look at Chapter 28, "Security Issues," for details on this important subject. Obviously, both chapters look at the Windows 2000 view of things, with a spotlight on the user's perspective.

What are some of the special features of this chapter? I provide you with some insights into the way Windows 2000 provides network services—and that's something you'd be hard-pressed to find in one of those networking tomes. That's the whole reason for this chapter: To give you the Windows 2000 view of networking on a small, peer-to-peer scale. (I strongly suggest that you also spend some time learning about networks in general before you actually install one.)

This chapter also assumes a certain level of knowledge on your part. I'm going to assume that you've already spent some time on a network and know some of the basics. You don't need to be a networking guru to understand this chapter, but you do need to know what logging on is all about and some of the easier terms, such as network interface card (NIC). I've provided a complete list of the more obscure terms and acronyms in the glossary at the end of this book.

The Windows 2000 Network Architecture

This section of the chapter looks at the how of network support under Windows 2000. What can you expect, and why do things work the way they do? These are just some of the questions I answer here. Before we become too embroiled in some of the details of actually using Windows 2000's networking capabilities, I'd like to spend a little time looking at its architecture.

You need to understand a few things about Windows 2000 before you look at its architecture. The first thing you need to understand is that Windows NT/2000 always has had a strong peer-to-peer networking component. I'm talking from an architectural and usage point of view here (something called the network model), not the media point of view that often equates peer-to-peer to lack of power. Windows 2000 provides more than sufficient power to compete even with some of the client/server model networks on the market.

The second thing you need to understand is that Microsoft added the networking support for Windows 2000 to its I/O subsystem. In essence, the operating system views networking as extended I/O. This really makes sense when you think about it: A connection is still a connection, no matter how long the wire. Keep these two points in mind as you read the description of the architectural components. Figure 24.1 shows the Windows 2000 network architecture, which includes the following components:

FIGURE 24.1

An overview of the Windows 2000 network architecture.

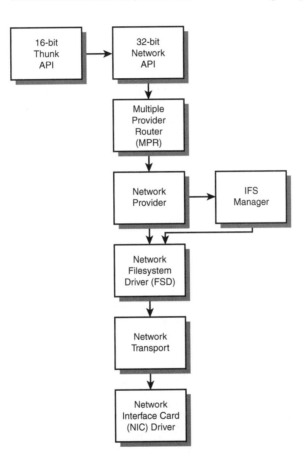

- **16-bit Thunk API**— Windows 2000 provides full network support using 32-bit code. However, there are still some 16-bit applications to support out there as well. This module replaces the Windows 3.x 16-bit API (known as Winnet16) with calls to the 32-bit API. It has to provide thunk support to do this. We looked at the thunk process earlier (in Chapter 9, "An Architectural Overview"), so I won't go into it again here.

- **32-bit API**—All application requests start at this module. I won't go into details about the API, but Microsoft has gone to great lengths to reorganize and simplify it. A user won't notice these details—except in the way that they affect network performance—but they'll have a definite impact on programmers, a positive impact. The API translates one application request into one or more standardized network requests. Quite a few files are involved in creating the network API under Windows 2000. Exactly which files get loaded depends on your network setup. The two most prominent files are NETAPI.DLL and NETAPI32.DLL. Loading NETAPI32.DLL also loads SECUR32.DLL (security), NETRAP.DLL (remote administration), SAMLIB.DLL (security account manager), WS2_32.DLL (32-bit Windows socket version 2.0), WLDAP32.DLL (lightweight directory access protocol), DNSAPI.DLL (domain name server), and WSOCK32.DLL (32-bit Windows socket version 5.0), which provide most of the low-level functionality the API requires. Obviously, these files load other, yet lower-level files. I cover some of the concepts in the "Understanding the Open Systems Interconnection (OSI) Model" section of this chapter.

- **Multiple Provider Router (MPR)**—You'll likely use more than one protocol with Windows 2000. In fact (theoretically, at least), you should be able to mix and match protected-mode drivers on the same network. You can mix NetBEUI and IPX/SPX on the same network, for example. In addition, some protocols automatically load when you request a specific service. The Microsoft data link control (DLC) falls into this category. It provides connections to mainframes and network printers.

  All network protocols require a network provider. The whole function of the MPR is to accept network requests from the network APIs and send them to the appropriate network provider (NP). Part of each request states which NP to use. This is how the MPR knows which one it should send the request to. Some requests are generic, however. A request for the status of the entire network, for example, falls into this category. In that case, the MPR calls each NP in turn to fulfill the application request. In still other cases, a request might not include enough information for the MPR to know which NP to use to fulfill the application requirement. In this case, the MPR "polls" the NPs to see whether one of them can fulfill the request. If none of the installed NPs can, the MPR returns an error message.

  You'll find that the MPR functions are located in the \SYSTEM32 folder in MPR.DLL. This DLL gets loaded by MPNOTIFY.EXE during startup. An intermediate file, MPRUI.DLL, provides a user interface. This is the DLL that contains the dialog boxes you see when you want to map or disconnect from a network drive. Interestingly enough, loading this set of DLLs also loads ADVAPI32.DLL. The MPR uses the functions in this DLL to view the contents of the Registry to determine which NPs and other network resources are available. The MPR also loads NETLOGON.DLL. This module (along with others, like SECURITY.DLL) checks for your password and performs other security-related activities.

- **Network Provider (NP)**—The network provider performs all the protocol-specific functions an application requires. It makes or breaks connections, returns network status information, and provides a consistent interface for the MPR to use. An application will never call the NP; only the MPR performs this function. Even though the internal structure of NPs varies, the interface they provide doesn't. This mechanism allows Windows 2000 to provide support for more than a single protocol. The code used by the MPR can remain small and fast because none of the NPs require special calls. If an NP can't fulfill a request because of a limitation in the network protocol, it just tells the MPR that the required service is unavailable. The NP also keeps the IFS Manager up to date on the current connection status. This is how Explorer knows when you've made a new drive connection.

- **IFS Manager**—When the IFS Manager obtains new status information from the NP, it calls the network file system driver (FSD) to update file and other resource information. When the NP tells the IFS Manager that it's made a new drive connection, for example, the IFS Manager calls on the network FSD to provide a directory listing. The same holds true for other resource types, such as printers. Besides this function, the IFS Manager performs its normal duties of opening files and making other file-system requests. The MPR doesn't know what to do with a path name, so it passes such requests through the NP to the IFS Manager to fulfill. Of course, applications also access the IFS Manager in other ways. The only time the MPR becomes involved is if a network-specific request also requires its intervention.

- **Network Filesystem Driver (FSD)**—Each server on the network could use a unique file system. NetWare and other client/server networks all use special file systems that the vendor thinks will enhance performance, security, reliability, and storage capacity. Windows 2000 doesn't inherently know about the special requirements of such storage systems. To access these other file systems, it needs a translator; to maintain consistency of access, it uses a translator for all network calls. The network FSD performs this task. It translates the intricacies of a foreign file system into something Windows 2000 can understand. A network FSD is usually composed of a file system-specific driver and a redirection driver. The second file provides the Windows 2000 interpretation of the file system specifics. Normally, there's only one network FSD for each NP. There's nothing to enforce this limit, however. An NP might require access to both a FAT and an NTFS network FSD for a Windows 2000 Server. If so, both drivers will be installed when you install network support. The IFS Manager also will call on the Network FSD for support. Although the NP usually makes requests for network status or connection information, the IFS Manager takes care of application needs, such as opening files and reading their contents. These two modules—NP and IFS Manager—work in tandem, each fulfilling completely different roles.

Note: You might wonder why Microsoft didn't combine the NP and the IFS Manager into one module. After all, from my previous comments, it would appear that the IFS Manager is just part of an access strategy for network drives. But you should remember to take the whole picture into account. The IFS Manager works with local drives as well as network drives. For each of these drives, a different file system might be in place. The whole point of the IFS was to allow for the possibility of new and unknown file systems communicating with Windows 2000. As a result, this two-part structure makes sense. The IFS provides access to any file system driver that's installed. Windows 2000 can then communicate with any file system for which there's a driver. Uniting the IFS with a single FSD would eliminate this flexibility by marrying Windows 2000 to a single file system. It's also worth pointing out that several networking components are actually applied as file system drivers. This way, local and remote access to various types of resources can be achieved through the same common component.

- **Network transport**—I placed a single module called network transport in Figure 24.1. Actually, this module is made up of many smaller modules and drivers. The number of pieces in a network transport installation is determined by the complexity of your setup and the requirements of the protocol. There are four elements within the network transport: the transport driver interface (TDI) , the transport protocol, the network device interface specification (NDIS) interface, and the NIC driver. (Make sure that you read the "Understanding the Open Systems Interconnection (OSI) Model" section of this chapter to see how these drivers fit into the bigger network picture.) The smallest network transport could consist of a mere four drivers. You could create a network transport for the NetBEUI protocol using the following files, for example: NETBIOS.SYS (the TDI), NBF.SYS (NetBEUI transport protocol), NDIS.SYS (NDIS interface), and NE2000.SYS (NIC driver).

Tip: If you work with both Windows 2000 and Windows 95/98, one of the first things you'll notice is that Windows 95/98 doesn't appear to use the same drivers as Windows 2000 does to get the network going. They do, in fact, use similar drivers and setups. (If you've upgraded to Windows 98, you'll find even greater similarity.) Just replace the .SYS extension on the first three drivers with a .VXD, and you'll start to see the missing drivers on your Windows 95/98 machine. Windows 95/98 also uses a NETBEUI.VXD in place of NBF.SYS—both files serve the same purpose. Both operating systems used the same name for the NIC driver.

NETBIOS.SYS performs the special function of virtualizing access to the protocol. This is the reason why more than one virtual machine running on your system can access the network drives at the same time. NBF.SYS performs the task of talking with the NDIS. It takes protocol-specific requests and translates them into smaller, standardized network requests. NDIS.SYS translates each Windows 2000-specific request into a call that the NIC driver can understand. Finally, the NIC driver talks to the NIC itself. The driver can take things such as port addresses and interrupts into account—everything needed to talk to the NIC. Of course, the NIC converts your request into an electrical signal that appears on the network.

Network transport requires other files as well. NDIS30.DLL, for example, provides the actual API support for NDIS.SYS. You'll find that NETBIOS.DLL performs the same function for NETBIOS.SYS. In essence, it takes a lot of different modules to create one transport. The reason for all these files is fairly easy to understand. What if you want to use a different NIC, for example? All you need to do is change the NIC driver, not any of the protocol-specific files. What if you want to use two different levels of NDIS support (Windows 2000 does support several)? You add an additional driver and its support files to the equation. To add TAPI support, for example, you need to load the NDISTAPI.SYS driver and its associated files. Adding the NDISWAN.SYS driver enables you to use the RAS support provided by Windows 2000. Instead of going into too much additional detail, let's close the book on the network transport for now. All you need to know is that the network transport takes care of the "transportation" details of your network installation.

- **Network Interface Card (NIC) driver**—I make special mention of this part of the Windows 2000 here for a reason. This particular driver is hardware-specific. It has to communicate with the NIC on a level the NIC can understand. Under Windows 2000, this driver is a 32-bit driver. Unlike Windows 95/98, you won't have to worry about the problems a real-mode driver creates when interfacing with a protected-mode operating system. You have one driver per NIC, and this requirement can lead to problems, especially when you change the NIC. I've run into situations, however, when I thought I had completely removed an old driver and installed a new one to support a new NIC, only to find that a piece of the old driver was hanging around. If the new driver attempts to access the file because of a similarity in name or a misdirected Registry setting, network calls can fail. The solution, of course, is always to make sure the old driver is gone. Remove it from the Network and Dial-up Connections Control Panel applet, and then reboot to make sure the Registry re-initializes completely.

All these files might seem like a lot of effort just to create a networked workstation, but that's only half the picture on many peer-to-peer installations. After you get past being a workstation, you have to take care of network requests as well. In the next section, I show you how Windows 2000 provides peer-to-peer network services. We'll look at Windows 2000's peer-to-peer support from a server level. We'll also look at a lot of the implementation details. How do you share your printer or local hard drive with someone, for example?

Understanding Peer-to-Peer Support

Peer-to-peer networking represents the easiest and least expensive way to get started in networking. Everyone starts with a workstation, just like you'd normally need in any business environment. You can share resources on standalone workstations; however, you need to connect them to do that. In the past, the standard method for sharing resources was to buy additional machines (called servers) and place the common components there. The investment in hardware and software for a full-fledged network can run into tens of thousands of dollars—prohibitively expensive for many companies. Peer-to-peer networks take a different route: One or more workstations simultaneously act as workstation and server. In fact, if you work things right and the network is small enough, everyone will probably have access to everyone else's machine in some form. This means that, except for the NICs, hubs (in some cases), and cabling you'll need, a peer-to-peer solution under Windows 2000 is free for the asking.

Windows 2000 (both Server and Professional version) provides peer-to-peer networking capabilities right out of the package. All you need to do is install an NIC on each machine, run some coaxial (or other network) cable, and add a few drivers to your setup. In some cases you may also need to add a hub, depending on the kind of network support you install. In fact, the Setup program is designed in such a way that adding network support requires almost no effort at all on the part of the installer. Of course, after you get everyone set up, you'll want to install a few extra utilities, such as a centralized calendar and email.

A Little History

Before we delve into all the details about how Windows 2000 supports peer-to-peer networking, let's take a brief look at the history of this networking system. The Microsoft end of peer-to-peer networking actually began with the introduction of DOS 3.1. Microsoft added the capability to lock files and records with that version of DOS—locking is a necessity for any kind of network. In the same year (1984), Microsoft released a product called MS-NET. Just in case you've never heard of MS-NET (it wasn't all that popular), Microsoft turned it into LAN Manager.

Apple actually introduced the first successful peer-to-peer networking in a covert manner in 1985. It included AppleTalk in every Macintosh sold. Most people didn't realize they were actually using a network when they printed a document using the LaserWriter.

Peer-to-peer networking continued to be a cult classic in the years that followed. Many companies wouldn't recognize peer-to-peer networking as much more than a kludge or a poor-man's network. Novell's NetWare used a client/server model that mimicked the big iron that corporations were used to using. It was comfortable using a network operating system that provided the look and feel of something substantial. In the PC world, many people thought it was client/server or nothing at all.

Note: Don't get me wrong. I'm not saying that peer-to-peer networking is the end-all solution for everyone. It's a very good solution for those on a limited networking budget who need to connect anywhere from 2 to 10 workstations. (I'm not talking about the domain server capabilities of Windows 2000, which make a much larger number of connections possible; I'm talking about an actual peer-to-peer network setup in this case.) You might even want to look at it for workgroup connections (the very reason that Microsoft came out with Windows for Workgroups). You can combine the benefits of a client/server network with those of a peer-to-peer network under Windows 2000. Although I'd probably set an upper limit of 10 workstations for a peer-to-peer network, it might also work for larger numbers of workstations if the network load is very light. Of course, if you're willing to dedicate a machine to act as a server, you can get the same kind of capabilities with Windows 2000 as you can with other client/server model networks like NetWare, but that's not a peer-to-peer network in the strictest sense of the word.

A group of companies began distributing peer-to-peer networking solutions for the PC. One of the bigger contributors to this groundswell of alternative networking technology was Artisoft, which still sells LANtastic today. Other vendors contributed products such as 10Net and TOPS. The Software Link even marketed a processor-sharing operating system for the 80386 called PC-MOS/386. This solution and others enabled people to share system resources without having to purchase a file server to do it. In addition, the cost of a peer-to-peer network operating system was a lot lower because these vendors faced stiff competition from Novell.

I'm not sure whether Novell helped or hindered the expansion of peer-to-peer networking with its introduction of NetWare Lite in 1991. This product was designed not to interfere with Novell's client/server product. NetWare Lite wasn't well designed or implemented. It couldn't even compete with other peer-to-peer products, such as LANtastic. The introduction of a peer-to-peer networking product by a major vendor such as Novell, however, at least put this type of networking on some people's agenda for the first time.

Things started to change for the better in the peer-to-peer market when Microsoft introduced Windows for Workgroups at the 1992 fall Comdex trade show. This show of support by Microsoft legitimized the use of peer-to-peer networking for some corporate applications. Of course, Microsoft didn't go as far as to say that you could use it for more than a few people. Still, it was a step in the right direction.

So, has everyone bought into the peer-to-peer networking technology? Not by a long shot, and I doubt that peer-to-peer networking will ever take over the market. Using a solution such as Windows for Workgroups, Windows NT Workstation/Windows 2000 Professional, or Windows 95/98 in the right place, however, could make a big difference at a very small cost. Both Windows 2000 and Windows 95/98 go a long way toward making dual solutions—a combination of client/server and peer-to-peer networking—a viable solution.

A Look at the Architecture

We've already taken a detailed look at what it takes to provide workstation support under Windows 2000. What happens if you also want your machine to act as a server, however? Providing server support means that your machine must accept requests from other workstations, process those requests, and return the requested information. Figure 24.2 shows the Windows 2000 peer-to-peer network server support.

FIGURE 24.2

An overview of the Windows 2000 Server architecture.

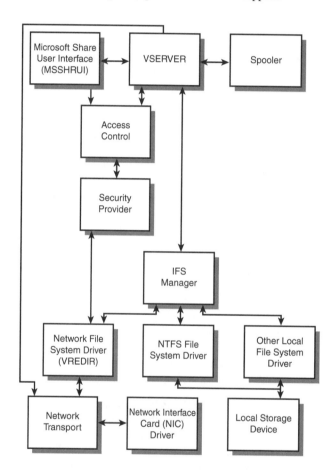

Now that you've seen the pictorial view of Windows 2000 peer-to-peer networking, let's talk about the various elements in detail. The following list describes each component in detail:

- **Microsoft Share User Interface (MSSHRUI)**—This module responds to external requests from the user for network resource configuration. Every time you right-click on a resource and tell Windows 2000 that you want to share it, this module fields that request. It works with the Access Control module to set password protection. An interface to the MPR and ADVAPI32.DLL enables the MSSHRUI to set the proper entries in the Registry. You'll find it in the NTSHRUI.DLL file in your \SYSTEM32 folder. (If you're using Windows 95/98, you'll find a corresponding file in place in the \SYSTEM folder named MSSHRUI.DLL.)

- **VSERVER**—The central point of all activity for the server is the virtual server driver. As with all the other drivers in this chapter, you'll find it in your \SYSTEM32 folder. This component provides direct access to all local resources for network requesters through the network transport. It works with the IFS Manager and Access Control modules to limit access to shared resources and to ensure that any access is performed properly. Each access to shared system resources is maintained in a separate thread. This means that access by one requester need not interfere with any other request. In addition, a single requester can make multiple requests. Of course, the number of actual requests is usually limited by the protocol settings you provide.

- **Spooler**—If you grant someone access to your printer, VSERVER sends any requests for print services to the spooler module. This module works just like it would for a local print request. As far as it's concerned, the request originated locally. There are four spooler-specific files in your \SYSTEM32 folder: `SPOOLSS.DLL`, `SPOOLSV.EXE`, `WINSPOOL.EXE`, and `WINSPOOL.DRV` (the `WINSPOOL.DRV` file may also appear in the \SYSTEM folder).

- **Access control**—Windows 2000 uses this module for a variety of purposes, not just network access control. Windows calls on this module to verify your initial logon password, for example, even if you don't request access to a network afterward. Unlike the other modules discussed so far, the Access Control module makes use of Registry entries (or data provided by a domain controller using Active Directory) to verify and set security; Windows 2000 bypasses the ill-fated PWL (password list) files used by Windows 95/98. You'll find access control in several files. The two main files are `NETAPI.DLL` (16-bit) and `NETAPI32.DLL` (32-bit) in the \SYSTEM32 folder. The Windows 95/98 equivalent for this file is `SVRAPI.DLL`, which you'll find in their SYSTEM folder. It's educational to compare a list of exported function calls in these modules. Windows 2000 provides a variety of security-related calls not available to Windows 95/98.

Tip: The security problems most people encounter with the Windows 95/98 PWL files are significant—enough to garner major media coverage during the early life of the operating system. You can get around part of this security problem by removing user access to all the PWL files on the drive. The danger is that PWL files are user-accessible. The encryption of passwords in the file can easily be attacked as a result. In addition, copying a PWL file onto another system and logging on as that user gives you access to all that user's resources.

- **Security provider**—Unlike Windows 95/98, Windows 2000 provides a single, centralized security provider. You'll find it in the SECURITY.DLL file in the \SYSTEM32 folder. Obviously, other files are associated with this one as well. The KERBEROS.DLL file provides the Kerberos security package, for example, but it's called by the SECURITY.DLL. You can always access the Windows 2000 Login module even if the network isn't running. The advantage to using it is that the Login module will always be available, even if you change the network setup or remove it altogether. The security provider performs two tasks. First, it's the module that asks you for a password. Second, it combines the user's logon name and the password he provides to verify any network requests.

- **NTFS File System Driver (FSD) and other local file system drivers**—I covered both these modules in detail in Chapter 11, "The Windows 2000 File Systems: FAT and NTFS."

- **IFS Manager, network FSD, network transport, and NIC driver**—I talked about these modules earlier in this chapter.

Understanding the server capabilities Windows 2000 provides is pretty straightforward from a conceptual point of view. After you get past theory, however, implementation becomes another story altogether. The problem isn't due to a poor plan, but to all the compatibility issues that come into play. Fortunately for the user, the design of the server capabilities makes all these details fairly easy to manage.

Understanding the Open Systems Interconnection (OSI) Model

I mentioned earlier that I'd talk about the OSI model a bit to give you a better idea of how all the architectural details we just looked at fit into the grand scheme of things. Figure 24.3 shows the OSI model and all the derivatives of that model that'll concern us in this book. I concentrate on the Windows 2000 model in this section, but I wanted to provide the NetWare and Internet models for discussion later.

What I'd like to do first is describe the OSI model itself. No one actually follows this model verbatim, but it acts as a guideline for the various layers of communications required to allow a network to transfer data from one point to another. (A layer is normally referred to by a variety of more specific names, such as protocol, but I want to keep things generic in this section.) I'm going to provide information about both the client and server side of the equation in the list. If you don't see a specific reference to either client or server, the text applies to both. The following list describes these default layers:

FIGURE 24.3

The OSI model is the basis for some of the architectural details in Windows 2000.

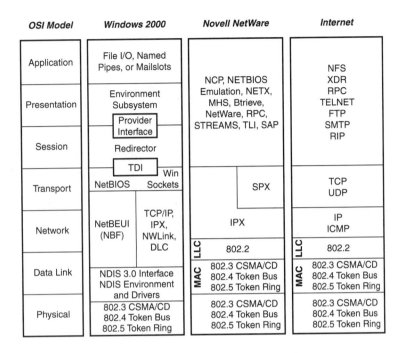

- **Application**—This is where the communication starts. An application makes a request for data contained on another machine. It can do so by any method the operating system allows; I'll describe this in a bit more detail shortly, but it's an important point. After the operating system verifies that the application is allowed to access the data, it passes the request to the Presentation layer. Obviously, only the operating system is involved at the server end of the communication. It verifies that the client application has access to the data again. The server also verifies that no one else is using the requested resource or that the resource is shareable. In essence, this is the layer you'll interact with exclusively. It's where you'll make the request and where the operating system will stop you if you don't have the required access rights.

- **Presentation**—This layer "massages" the data. In other words, it prepares it for transmission to the other computer. The presentation layer takes care of things like compressing the data to make it faster to transport. On the server end, the Presentation layer decompresses the file. The Presentation layer also encrypts the data, if required. Some networks also deal with things such as carriage returns differently than Windows or DOS does. (UNIX is one such. If you want to communicate with a UNIX server, the Presentation layer must convert the Windows form of carriage returns into something that UNIX understands.)

- **Session**—Each instance of an application on a machine is called a session. I've used that term before in this book, and now it's time to take a look at what that means in network terms. A network session manages one application. It takes care of things such as determining which application is talking and which is listening at any given instant. The Session layer also takes care of monitoring the other application. It's the part of the model that alerts you when you've lost the connection to the other end of the network.

- **Transport**—A network transports information in something called a packet. Think of a packet as an envelope and the data as a letter that you want to send. The Transport layer takes your letter and sticks it into an envelope. Unlike a regular envelope, a packet can only hold one page. If your letter is two pages long, you need two packets to hold it. If your letter does require more than one envelope, the Transport layer numbers them on the client side. The server side checks each envelope it receives and makes sure that they're in order before it puts the letter back together again. Some networks use a consistent packet size—others use a variable size. It's not really all that important to keep this in mind as a user, but it's important information if you're a network administrator. One of the subsidiary functions of the Transport layer is to shield the Session layer from changes in hardware. I'll show you in a few moments how Windows 2000 accomplishes this task.

- **Network**—This is the first layer that deals directly with the network topology. So, what's a topology? It's the physical characteristics of the network. Ethernet, for example, is a network topology, as is token ring. The Network layer manages the physical part of the network. It accepts the packets (envelopes) created by the Transport layer and puts an address on them. The address works just like the ones on the letters you send; it ensures that a specific workstation receives the packet you send. On the receiving end, the Network layer reads the addresses on the various packets as they pass by. It grabs any packets addressed to the server and gives them to the Transport layer. The Network layer also handles any conflicts on the network. It helps out when two workstations try to use the cable at the same time (called a collision), for example. Usually, the Network layers use different timeout values so that a collision isn't repeated.

- **Data Link**—The data link layer wraps each packet in a frame. I always like to think of this object as the delivery truck for the letter. It's responsible for making sure that the receiving computer acknowledges each frame it sends. If it doesn't get an acknowledgment, the Data Link layer sends the frame again.

- **Physical**—This is the easiest part of the OSI model to understand. The Physical layer contains all the things you can touch, such as a cable or NIC. It also describes the characteristics of all these physical elements. It defines how many pins the cable will have, for example, and what each of those pins will do.

Now that you have a better idea of what the OSI model is, the question is, how does Windows 2000 implement it? Look again at Figure 24.3, and you'll see that the various Windows 2000 elements often overlap one or more of the OSI layers. This tells you that the Windows 2000 elements actually accomplish one or more tasks. Notice that there are several paths through the Windows 2000 model. You can go from NetBIOS to NetBEUI to NDIS, for example. The one thing you should do about now is compare this figure to the description of Figure 24.1. You should start to see some similarities between the blocks on this figure and the levels of the OSI model. The MPR takes care of the environment subsystem level, which is the same as the Presentation layer of the OSI model. I provided a pretty complete description of all these elements in that discussion, so I won't go through them again here.

What I didn't describe in the architectural section was the Application layer. Windows 2000 provides three methods for an application to start a network conversation. The first type is fairly obvious. Any time an application decides to open a file that isn't on the current machine, Windows 2000 has to perform some type of network file I/O.

In addition to network file I/O, applications can make use of other mechanisms, called Interprocedure Calls (IPCs) to communicate with one another. These are highly specialized mechanisms that usually function at the thread level. The first, named pipes, is something you'll never deal with directly, but something that advanced applications use quite a bit. One thread of execution can pass information directly to another thread using a named pipe. The great thing about named pipes is that the two threads don't have to be on the same machine. Think about that for a second and you'll realize that what I'm really talking about is a distributed application. Essentially, one machine is using another machine's processor and resources to get work done. Obviously, Windows 2000 places severe limitations on this right now, but it's important to realize that named pipes do exist.

What if you need to send a message to more than one thread? Suppose that you're looking for a particular piece of data in a database application. If you use named pipes, you have to tie up the network for a long period of time as you send messages from one server to the next looking for the data you need. Mailslots are the solution to that problem. A mailslot allows a thread to send the same message to more than one thread—just as you can with email. You can also use mailslots in the opposite direction: to allow many threads to send a message to one thread. You might need to do this if a server is requesting the status of all workstations on the network through a network agent (a hidden application that monitors the status of a single machine), for example.

Understanding Domains

Domain—it sounds more like a term of conquest than something associated with computer networks. Think of a domain as a complex (or extended) form of workgroup. Essentially, a domain groups workstations and servers together into one unit. A domain enables you to access all the resources the domain provides (that you have the security rights to access) using a single logon. Resources, in this case, include things such as a system-wide security policy. A domain, then, is an all-encompassing version of the peer-to-peer network.

I want to take a very quick look at domains in this section. First, how do they differ from workgroups? Microsoft makes a distinction between the two concepts—one that's important enough for everyone to know. Second, I show you how the network looks at a domain versus a workgroup when it comes to configuration issues. You might not have a domain server available to you when you install your network. Joining a domain server later is relatively easy, but the dialog box for doing so is hidden in a place where some people won't easily find it.

How Is a Domain Different?

There are two user-specific elements—in addition to the things you normally associate with a workgroup—that make up a domain. First, a domain employs a common user database; Microsoft calls it a domain database. Second, a domain shares a common security policy. That's why you can access all the domain resources using a single password. The same security policy provides a consistent way for you to access resources on the system. It also determines which rights you have. From an administrator perspective, a domain also provides a common user list at all workstations. In other words, every workstation within a domain knows the rights and restrictions of all the users within the domain.

An administrator will see a lot of differences between a workgroup and a domain as well. The most important difference, as far as I'm concerned, is the fact that a domain provides better-centralized user management and setup. One of the advantages to this control is the capability to add users to the domain from a remote location; I'll show you how this works in a few moments.

I wanted to make a distinction between a domain and a workgroup for a simple reason. The Professional version of Windows 2000 can't act as a domain server; you need one of the Server versions of the product to maintain the centralized user and security database. The Professional version is also limited to a maximum of 10 simultaneous user connections, crippling its capability to serve large numbers of users. If your network consists of a combination of Windows 2000 workstations (using the Professional version of the product) and perhaps a few Windows 95/98 workstations, you don't have a domain available to you. You can only create a workgroup.

It's important to realize some of the limitations of workgroups, but it's also important to know that these limitations might not even affect you. If you're running a 5- or 10-person network, it's pretty unlikely that you'll be affected by the lack of centralized support in a workgroup setup. On the other hand, a network administrator responsible for 100 or more workstations would definitely notice the difference.

Joining a Domain After Setup

As a company adds new people to its staff, it usually must extend its network as well. After a time, a network administrator will find that the workgroup configuration that worked fine with five people and adequately with 10 won't work very well at all with 20. When you start getting to this level of complexity, you probably need to add a server and move to a domain, if only to work around the limitation on number of simultaneous connections.

I'm not going to spend time telling you about the relative advantages of a NetWare server over Windows 2000 (Server version). That's a topic that a lot of people are trying to tackle—and they're using a whole book to do so. This section assumes that, for whatever reason, you opted for the Windows 2000 Server.

After you have the server installed, you need to add people to it and reconfigure their workstations to recognize the server. In fact, what you need to do is join the new domain created by the Windows 2000 Server.

> **Tip:** Windows 95/98 uses a different setup from Windows 2000 in this regard. You're joining a domain when you select User Level Access Control and then type the name of a Windows 2000 domain server on the Access Control page of the Network dialog box. You access this dialog box by right-clicking the Network Neighborhood icon.

Follow these steps:

1. Log on to the workstation as an administrator; you'll need administrator rights to reconfigure the network. It doesn't matter if you log on using the administrator username, but it's probably the best way to ensure that you have all the rights you'll need to get the job done.

2. Right-click the My Network Places icon and choose Properties from the context menu. You'll see a Network and Dial-up Connections dialog box. Select the Advanced, Networking Identification command of that dialog box, and you'll see a display similar to the one in Figure 24.4.

3. Click the Properties button and you'll see the Identification Changes dialog box shown in Figure 24.5. This is where you select between workgroup and domain membership. If you choose Workgroup, you must type the name of a local workgroup. All computers having the same workgroup name will be able to share resources. Likewise, if you select Domain, you must type a domain name. In this case, the name you provide is the name of the domain created using a Windows NT/2000 Server.

FIGURE 24.4

The Network Identification tab of the System Properties dialog box tells you what workgroup or domain you're a member of.

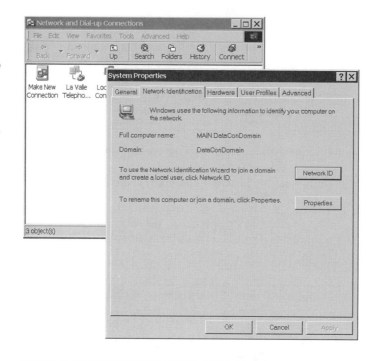

FIGURE 24.5

The Identification Changes dialog box enables you to choose between a workgroup and a domain association.

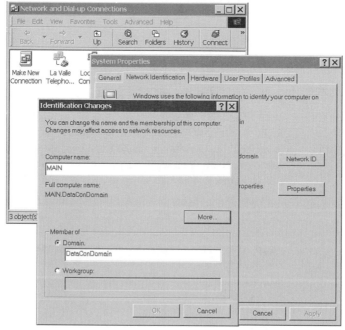

4. Click OK.

Windows 2000 searches for the domain server. If it finds the server, you're added to the domain. Otherwise, you see an error message. The important thing to remember if you do see an error is to check the domain name. I always verify the spelling of the domain name.

5. Click OK to close the System Properties dialog box.

> **Note:** Another way to accomplish this task is to click Network ID on the System Properties dialog. This will start the Network Identification wizard, which provides more complete help when setting up a new network identification. Just follow the prompts to join a new domain.

Sharing Drives and Printers

Sharing is the main reason to install a network. The very concept of networks came from the need to share expensive peripheral devices and files. Windows 2000 provides an easy-to-use interface that enables you to share just about everything on your network with a few clicks of the mouse. Let's take a look at what you need to do to share files and other resources located on your machine.

The first thing I like to do before I start trying to share files is to make sure I actually have the required support loaded. This is a no-brainer under Windows 2000 because you really don't have a choice about loading the support during setup. Someone could come along and remove the support later, however, so it's always best to check. Just open the Network and Dial-up Connections dialog box by right-clicking the My Network Places icon and choosing Properties from the context menu. Right-click the Local Area Connection icon in the Network and Dial-up Connections dialog, and choose Properties from the context menu. Look for the File and Printer Sharing for Microsoft Networks entry as shown in Figure 24.6. Make sure that this entry is both present and checked as shown in the figure.

After you make sure that the File and Printer Sharing for Microsoft Networks service is enabled, you need to select the items to share. Right-clicking any of your drive or printer icons and choosing Sharing from the context menu displays an additional Sharing tab like the one shown in Figure 24.7.

The first two radio buttons on this page enable you to determine whether the resource is shared. By selecting Do Not Share This Folder (Not shared for printers), no one can see the resource, even if he or she has other types of access to your machine. If you do select Share This Folder (Shared as for printers), some additional options become available. The following paragraphs provide the details on how to manage a drive under Windows 2000.

FIGURE 24.6

File and Printer Sharing for Microsoft Networks service enables you to share files and other resources under Windows 2000.

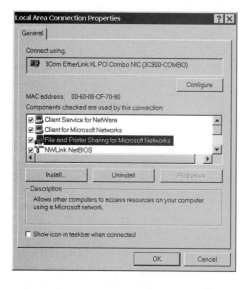

FIGURE 24.7

The Sharing tab of the printer or drive Properties dialog box enables you to define the level and type of sharing for that device.

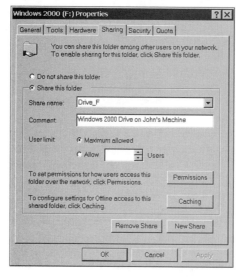

Note: Whenever your File and Printer Sharing for Microsoft Networks service starts, Windows 2000 automatically creates a default share for administrative purposes to all local resources. You'll want to leave this share alone and create a new share for your specific needs. If you don't want to have this default share active, you can turn it off by editing the Registry. Use the System Policy Editor to open the Registry for this purpose, because the option to enable or disable this option is a policy under Local Computer. Making the change is a matter of adjusting a check box.

Peter's Principle: Maintaining Control of Your System

Sharing doesn't always mean that you allow everyone to access every resource on your machine. It's easier to just provide access to an entire drive than it is to set the required level of security folder by folder, but the drive strategy might not be the best way to go when it comes to your company's health.

Many of us work with confidential information that we must keep safe, but we also work with other people who need to see some of this information. Someone working in the accounting department might need to share analysis files with a workgroup, for example. However, can you imagine what would happen if he also shared access to the payroll files? What about the new plans that your company might be working on? Even though you need to share access to the current project, you'll want to keep that new project a secret. A little bit of discretion can save you a lot of headaches later.

It's important that you provide the right level of access to everyone in your workgroup. I won't cover every bit of security in this chapter (we look at this in detail in Chapter 28), but you might want to put on your thinking cap now. Where are the potential security leaks in your company? It's a well-known fact that people complain when they don't have enough access to the network. Have you ever heard anyone complain about having too much access?

Finding the areas where people have too much access will give you the most trouble. Audits and other forms of security checking are just as important as the sharing itself on your network. Performing an audit takes time and resources that might be very difficult to defend, when management asks for an accounting. Of course, having a security breach is even more difficult to defend. Allow others to use the resources you have available, but don't allow misuse of those resources. It's up to you to do your part in maintaining the proper level of security on your network.

Creating a New Share

You can create more than one share name for a particular resource under Windows 2000. Each share name can have more than one group or user account associated with it and a variety of restrictions for that set of groups and users. To create a new share, just click the New Share button. You see the New Share dialog box, as shown in Figure 24.8.

Tip: Windows 2000 doesn't limit you to providing access to an entire drive or printer. You can define access to an individual folder or file as well. In addition, you can modify the permissions that individual users have to a file or folder, which means that some users may be able to write to the file or folder, while others may only be able to read it. I find it very convenient to set aside a temporary directory on my machine for file sharing. People can upload their files to a specific directory and avoid changing the contents of the rest of my drive. You can use the same principle for other resources. The key is to maintain control of your system.

FIGURE 24.8
The New Share dialog box enables you to define how you plan to share a drive or printer with other people.

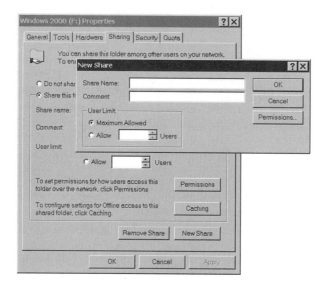

You need to provide a resource name in the Share Name field. This is how Windows 2000 will present the resource in dialog boxes, such as with the Drives field of the File Open dialog box. The optional Comment field enables you to provide a little more information to someone who wants to share the resource. I normally include the precise resource name and my name as part of the comment. This reduces the chance that someone will accidentally try to use a resource on my system.

After you define a resource name and assign it a comment, click the Permissions button to display the Permissions for resource name dialog box shown in Figure 24.9. The top list box shows who can access this resource. Highlighting an entry in this top list will show the kind of access the user or group has to the resource in the lower list box.

You can use the Add and Remove buttons to add or remove users or groups from the top list. Just check or uncheck rights as needed to give the user or group the proper access to the resource. You can provide four actual levels of access: no access (all check boxes unchecked), Read, Change, and Full Control. Read access enables someone to read from a resource but not modify it in any way. Change access enables someone to read and write to a resource, but not to create or delete anything. This enables you to set up a group of shared files where the users can edit a file but not delete it. Obviously, Full Control access enables the user or group to do anything you can with the resource. Use this option with discretion because someone can damage your drive or other resource if you give him or her full access. When you click the Add button to add a new user or group, you see the Select Users, Computers, or Groups dialog box shown in Figure 24.10.

FIGURE 24.9

The Permissions for resource name dialog box shows which user group or single user is allowed to access a drive or printer.

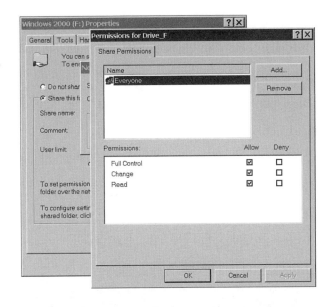

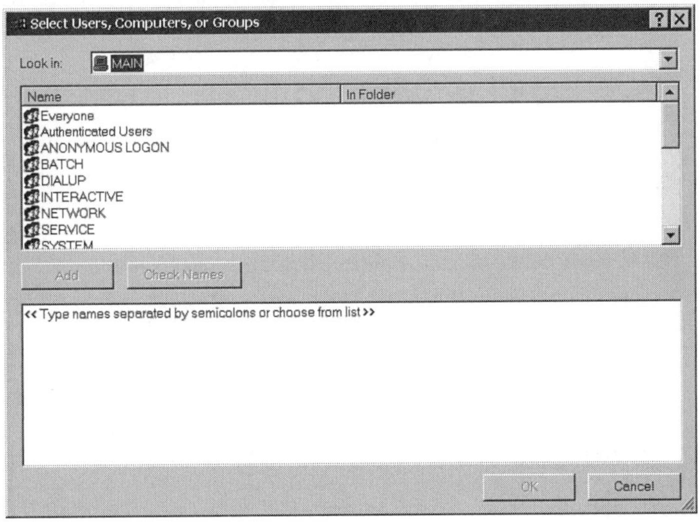

FIGURE 24.10

The Select Users, Computers, or Groups dialog box enables you to define who can access a particular resource.

The upper list box of the Select Users, Computers, or Groups dialog box lists the users, computers, and groups available from the source that you select in the Look In field. If you're working on a domain, the Look In field defaults to the domain controller that you're logged into. Otherwise, the list of users, computers, and groups will come from your local computer.

The lower list box shows all the new users or groups to which you want to give access. It doesn't show any existing user or group access. To add a user or group to this field, highlight that name in the Names list box and click the Add button.

> **Note:** Some products, such as Microsoft Word and most other word processors, require full access to a drive. That's because they create a backup file before writing any changes to the original word-processing file. You might have to limit word-processing files to one or two directories. That way, you can still limit overall drive access and provide better security.

After you select all the people you want to give a particular level of access, click OK. You'll see the new users and groups added to the top list box of the Permissions for resource name dialog box. At this point, you might wonder how to add password protection to your resource. Users will normally have to log on to your system before they can use a resource. That password acts as their key to gaining access to the resource, so Windows 2000 doesn't assign any added password to the resource here. In Chapter 28, I'll show you some techniques for adding more security to your system. To complete the action, click OK in the Permissions for resource name dialog box, and then click OK in the Drive Properties dialog box.

Removing a Shared Resource Name

A single resource can have more than one share name. You might need to remove one of those share names when a particular user or group no longer needs it. To remove a shared resource name, open the Sharing tab of the Drive Properties dialog box (refer to Figure 24.7). Select the shared resource name you want to remove from the Share Name drop-down list box. Make sure that it's the one you actually want to remove, because Windows 2000 won't provide much feedback in the way of an Are You Sure? confirmation box. Click the Remove Share button, and all the permissions associated with a particular shared name are marked for deletion. At this point, you can still recover them by clicking Cancel. If you click Apply or OK, the change becomes permanent.

Removing or Changing a User or Group Share

You'll eventually need to modify some details associated with a shared resource. If a user leaves the company, for example, you'll need to remove their access to your machine. To start the process, open the Sharing page of the Drive Properties dialog box. Select the name of the shared resource you want to change from the Share Name drop-down list box. Click Permissions to display the Permissions for resource name dialog box (refer to Figure 24.9).

Removing a share is pretty simple. Just highlight the share you want to remove, and then click the Remove button. I wish, in some respects, that Microsoft had made this a little more difficult or at least provided some additional feedback. Right now, you won't get any kind of feedback at all except for a missing line in the Name box. With this in mind, I always double-check a share before I remove it.

Changing a share is pretty easy, too. Just select the user or group you want to change, and then select a new level of access from lower list box. I described these various access levels in the "Creating a New Share" section, so I won't do it again here.

Click OK to exit the Permissions for resource name dialog box. You can still change your mind at this point by clicking the Cancel button in the Drive Properties dialog box. If you decide to make the change permanent, just click Apply or OK.

Adding New Services or Other Features

Windows 2000 provides a fairly complex and complete set of Transmission Control Protocol/Internet Protocol (TCP/IP) related features. Think of a protocol as a set of rules for a game. The rules tell you how to play the game and give you a basis for playing it with someone else. A protocol performs the same task on a network. It establishes rules that allow two nodes—be they workstations, mainframes, minicomputers, or other network elements like a printer—to talk to each other. TCP/IP is one of the more popular sets of network communications rules.

Windows 2000 also provides support for Point-to-Point Protocol (PPP) . Just like TCP/IP, PPP is a set of communications rules. In this case, however, the rules provide a method for conducting online (from one point to another) communications. Both of these features enable you to connect to a UNIX host or the Internet, or to enhance your dial-up networking capability.

> **Tip:** You might find that you don't need the full TCP/IP service package. Windows 2000 also provides a service-oriented TCP/IP package called Simple TCP/IP Services. You can install it using the same procedure that I'll describe in the "SNMP Support" section that follows. You'll find the Simple TCP/IP Services in the Networking Services folder.

In almost all cases, the support that Windows 2000 provides deals with remote communications. However, there are exceptions. The monitoring capability provided by SNMP, for example, could work in a local server setup. It's important to include this support as part of the operating system for two reasons. First, adding TCP/IP and PPP to the operating system makes it easier for software developers to write agents (special drivers or applications that use the rules these protocols establish to perform useful work). If you added either protocol as a third-party product, there wouldn't be any standardization, making it nearly impossible for other third-party vendors to write standard agents.

Second, adding this level of protocol support to the operating system means that Microsoft can incorporate an additional level of support as part of its utility program offerings. You'll find that both protocols are important when it comes to communicating with the Internet through Microsoft Network (MSN), for example. Before you can use TCP/IP, however, you have to install it. (Note that Windows 2000 automatically installs TCP/IP support for you in many situations, such as when you choose to perform a typical installation, so this support may already be available to you.)

> **Tip:** Installing TCP/IP support before you install dial-up networking will save you some extra steps later. The dial-up networking installation routine automatically installs the required protocols for you if you install TCP/IP support first.

Let's quickly go through a few of the things you need to do to install TCP/IP support:

1. Right-click the My Network Places icon and choose Properties. You'll see the Network and Dial-up Connections dialog.

2. Right-click the Local Area Connection icon, then choose Properties from the context menu. You'll see the Local Area Connection Properties dialog box.

3. Click Install, choose Protocol in the Select Network Component Type dialog, and then click Add. You'll see a Select Network Protocol dialog box like the one shown in Figure 24.11.

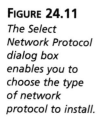

FIGURE 24.11
The Select Network Protocol dialog box enables you to choose the type of network protocol to install.

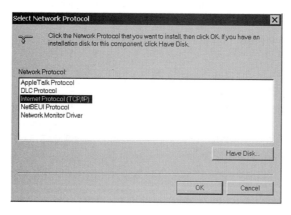

4. Select Internet Protocol (TCP/IP) and click OK. Windows 2000 will install the TCP/IP protocol.

Configuring the TCP/IP support after you get it installed is easy. All you need to do is select the Internet Protocol (TCP/IP) entry on the Local Area Connection Properties dialog box and click the Properties button. You'll see a dialog box similar to the one shown in Figure 24.12. (I discuss the various TCP/IP setup options in Chapter 4, "Installing Windows 2000 Professional: A Setup Primer.") Essentially, all the pages in this dialog box enable you to set the addresses and other TCP/IP properties for your machine. All the setup options available for automatic setup are present when you use this manual technique.

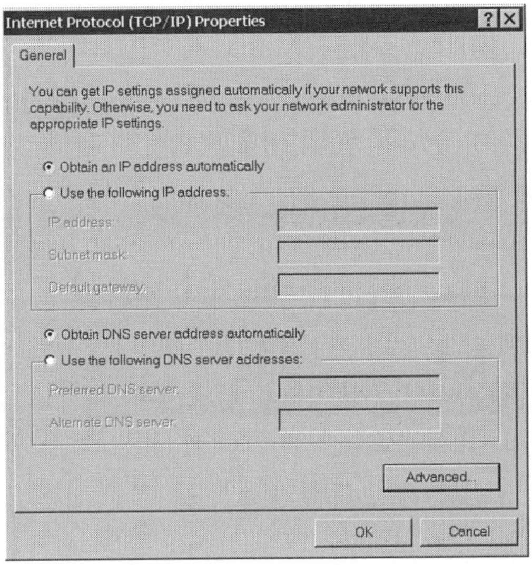

FIGURE 24.12

You can use the Internet Protocol (TCP/IP) Properties dialog box to configure TCP/IP support under Windows 2000.

Tip: You can click the Advanced button on the Internet Protocol (TCP/IP) Properties dialog to gain access to more TCP/IP settings for your machine. For example, you can use these options to disable DHCP support (which is enabled by default) or enter one or more DNS server addresses.

After you complete this initial installation process, you need to perform other installations to provide specific levels of support. You need to install dial-up networking, for example, and then the TCP/IP support that Windows provides before you can access that support for a remote connection. I already talked about the communications end of this support in Chapter 20. The following sections show you how to configure Windows 2000 to use both TCP/IP and PPP from a networking perspective. I also cover a few of the usage issues you need to know about.

SNMP Support

Windows 2000 provides remote monitoring agent support for agents that use the Simple Network Management Protocol (SNMP). SNMP was originally designed for the Internet. It allows an application to remotely manage devices from a variety of vendors, even if a device doesn't normally work with the managing device. A mainframe can use SNMP to send updated sales statistics to a group of satellite offices in a large company, for example. You can use an SNMP console to monitor a Windows 2000 workstation after this

support is installed. SNMP support under Windows 2000 conforms to the version 1 spec-
ification. Microsoft implements SNMP support for both TCP/IP and IPX/SPX using
WinSock (which I'll describe later). The following procedure enables you to install
SNMP support under Windows 2000:

1. Right-click the My Network Places icon and choose the Properties option. You'll
   see the Network and Dial-up Connections dialog.

2. Use the Advanced, Optional Networking Components command to display the
   Windows Optional Networking Components Wizard shown in Figure 24.13.

FIGURE 24.13
*Windows 2000
provides several
categories of
optional network-
ing components
for you to install.*

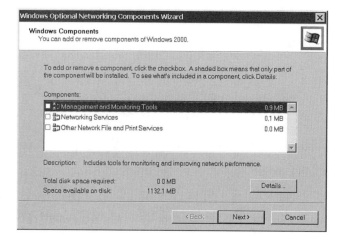

3. Highlight the Management and Monitoring Tools option, then click Details. You'll
   see a Management and Monitoring Tools dialog like the one shown in
   Figure 24.14.

4. Scroll through the list of services and highlight Simple Network Management
   Protocol, and then click OK. Click Next. Windows 2000 may ask you to insert the
   installation CD if you don't already have it in the CD-ROM drive. It will then
   copy some files to the drive.

At this point, the SNMP service is installed and running. However, before you can use it,
you'll need to configure the service. The way you do that is to double click on the
Services applet found in the Administrative Tools folder of the Control Panel. Scroll
through the list of services and find the SNMP Service. Right-click this entry, then
choose Properties from the context menu. The first configuration tab we'll talk about is
the Agent tab shown in Figure 24.15. The following list talks about the items on the
Agent tab:

FIGURE 24.14

SNMP is part of the Management and Monitoring Tools category.

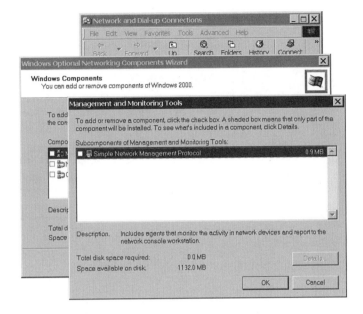

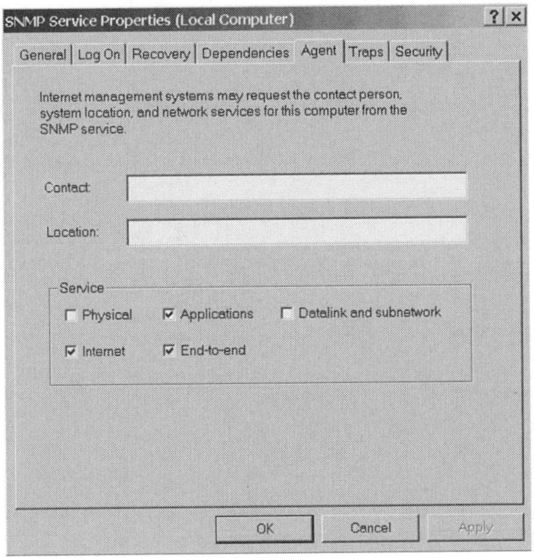

FIGURE 24.15

The Agent tab contains contact information and a list of services provided by SNMP.

- **Contact and Location fields**—These two fields tell whom to contact if you're using an Internet-based service. Someone calling into your workstation from the Internet will get this message, enabling him to contact you if he has any problems.

- **Service**—You can offer a variety of services using SNMP. Figure 24.15 shows the default settings. There are five services you can offer: Physical, Applications, Datalink and Subnetwork, Internet, and End-to-End. You need to enable the Physical check box if your Windows 2000 workstation manages any physical TCP/IP device, such as a repeater. The Applications check box refers specifically to TCP/IP-enabled applications, such as email. In most cases, you'll want to leave this check box enabled. Enable the Datalink/Subnetwork check box if your Windows 2000 workstation manages a TCP/IP datalink or subnetwork, such as a bridge. The Internet check box tells other computers that your workstation acts as an Internet IP gateway. Finally, the End-to-End check box infers that your workstation acts as an Internet IP host (an Internet server, in most cases). As with the Application option, you'll want to keep the End-to-End check box enabled in most cases.

On to the second page of our configuration: Traps. Figure 24.16 shows what this tab looks like.

FIGURE 24.16

The Traps tab of the Microsoft SNMP Properties dialog box enables you to deal with error conditions and security to a certain extent.

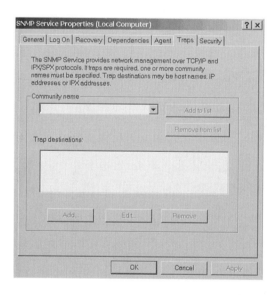

So what precisely is a trap? A few of you programmers should have a good idea. What happens on a remote communication if someone wants to access a community (the hosts that your computer can connect to) that doesn't exist? Let me put this in easier-to-understand terms. Suppose that you want to open a file, so you choose the File, Open command. Now, instead of typing a name of a file that exists, you either leave the filename blank or type the name of a file that doesn't appear on the drive. In a program, this produces an error condition. You'll see a message from Windows or the application saying that the file doesn't exist; some well-rounded applications will even give you a chance to create a new file with that name to get around the error condition.

> **Tip:** You're going to look at a lot of definitions for traps in a variety of books. Here's my short definition—the least complex way of looking at this complex topic. A trap is an automatic monitoring method. It automatically updates the host when specific events occur on your machine.

In SNMP terms, a trap (or error trap) is programming code that reacts to errors, perhaps fixing the problem, or perhaps merely displaying a message describing the problem. The process is a bit more complex than that, but this is a good starting point. There's also a certain amount of security involved here as well. If someone is requesting the name of a community that doesn't exist, you can assume one of two things: He either made a mistake or he's a cracker trying to break into your system. The trap has to be able to deal with both conditions. Now that we're all talking about the same thing, let's take a look at the fields in this dialog box:

- **Community Name**—This drop-down list box specifies the name of a community that you want to set a trap for. You'll see in the next section that you can set a variety of trap types. For right now, all you need to know is that this is a community name. After you enter the name of a community, click the Add to List button to add it to the list. Similarly, if you want to remove a community from the list, highlight it in the Community Name drop-down list box and click Remove from List.

- **Trap Destinations**—Use this box to define a list of host IP or IPX addresses that you want to send SNMP traps to. The IP or IPX address must be one of the machines in that community. All you need to do is click Add to add a new address. You'll see a Service Configuration dialog box, which asks for the IP or IPX address of the computer. This box also provides Edit and Remove buttons, which enable you to change or delete IP or IPX addresses from the list.

If you've been reading the trade press (or even the local newspaper) for the past few years, you'll know that security is a major issue. The next page in the Microsoft SNMP Properties dialog box should come as no surprise then (see Figure 24.17). This tab enables you to change the security for your SNMP configuration. More than that, it provides the means for creating connections to your computer—certainly a part of the security process. The following list provides a description of each option in this dialog box:

- **Send Authentication Trap**—Enabling this check box tells Windows 2000 to send an authentication trap whenever an authentication fails. This is one of those security-related features I told you about before.

- **Accepted Community Names**—This section defines the hosts from which your computer will accept requests. The default community name is Public. You can enhance security by deleting the Public entry and adding unique names of your own. Even though they aren't exactly the same, you could look at a community as a NetWare group or a Windows 2000 domain. Three buttons are associated with this field: Add, Edit, and Remove.

FIGURE 24.17

The Security page of the Microsoft SNMP Properties dialog box is one that you can't afford to ignore if network security is important to you.

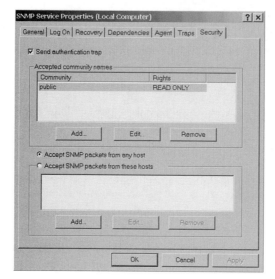

- **Accept SNMP Packets from Any Host**—This radio button enables your computer to accept packets from any SNMP host. This option provides a maximum of flexibility but a minimum of security.

- **Accept SNMP Packets from These Hosts**—Selecting this option reduces the number of hosts that can access your machine to the list in the box below it. You need to click the Add button to add some hosts to this list, or no one will be able to access your computer. Providing specific host names provides maximum security, but it does tend to reduce the flexibility of your configuration. As with the Accepted Community Names section, you'll find an Edit and Remove button here for managing your host list.

Once you've finished configuring the SNMP service, you can click OK to make the changes permanent and close the SNMP Service Properties dialog box. You can then close the Services dialog box and the open Administrative Tools folder. Even though Windows 2000 doesn't force you to restart the machine at this point, it's usually a good idea to do so to ensure the changes actually get implemented during the current Windows session.

Using the FTP Utility

Using the Internet requires some form of browser support if you want to download files or upload messages. FTP is actually a utility program that Windows 2000 installs for you along with TCP/IP support. It's a DOS application that uses a standard character-mode interface. The syntax for FTP follows:

```
FTP [-V] [-N] [-I] [-D] [-G] [<Host>] [-S:<Filename>]
```

The following list defines each FTP option:

-v   This switch disables the display of remote server responses. It comes in handy if you want the download to progress in the background without disturbing your foreground task.

-N   Use this switch to disable auto-logon upon initial connection.

-I   You can use this switch to remove interactive prompting during multiple file transfers. This enables you to automate the file-transfer process.

-D   Use this switch to display all FTP commands passed between the client and server. This enables you to debug script files.

-G   This switch disables filename globbing, which permits the use of wildcard characters in local filenames and pathnames.

<Host>   Replace this parameter with the name or address of the host you want to connect to for a file download.

-S:<Filename>   Replace <Filename> with the name of a text file containing FTP commands. In essence, this switch enables you to create a script for your FTP download. Use this switch instead of redirection (>).

The FTP utility provides a surprising array of commands you can use after you run it. There really are too many to list here, but you can get a list easily enough. All you need to remember is one command: the question mark (?). If you type a question mark, you'll see a list of all the things you can do with FTP.

Using the Telnet Utility

The Telnet is another browser utility program that Windows 2000 installs automatically when you install TCP/IP support. The strange thing is that Windows 2000 doesn't automatically install it in your Start menu. You need to add it manually. The Telnet utility always appears in your \SYSTEM32 folder.

When you open the Telnet utility by running Telnet.exe, you see a DOS window similar to the one shown in Figure 24.18. It's fairly simple to operate this application using DOS commands. To display the commands and see descriptions of their use, type ?/help after the Microsoft Telnet prompt, as shown in Figure 24.19.

Remote Procedure Call (RPC) Support

Remember near the beginning of this chapter when I talked about network transports and the way Microsoft implements them? I mentioned then just how complex a network transport could get if you added a few features. Remote procedure calls (RPCs) are a somewhat new concept for Windows 2000; Microsoft added them to Windows NT 4, but only now are the tools available to really make use of this technology. They're implemented as a network-transport mechanism using named pipes, NetBIOS, or WinSock to create a connection between a client and a server. RPCs are compatible with the Open Software Foundation (OSF) Data Communication Exchange (DCE) specification.

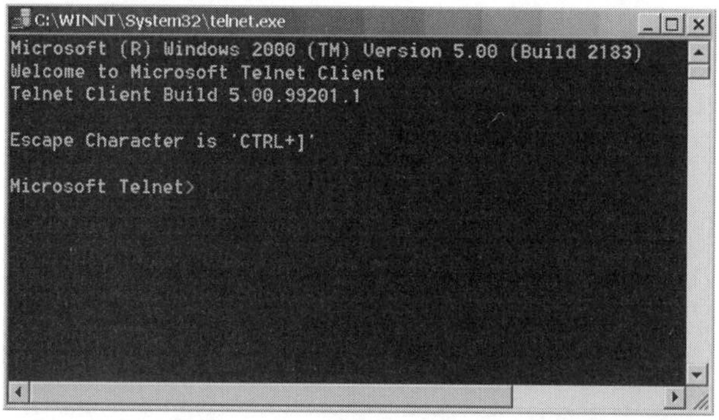

FIGURE 24.18

Telnet provides a very basic DOS window front end for a host connection.

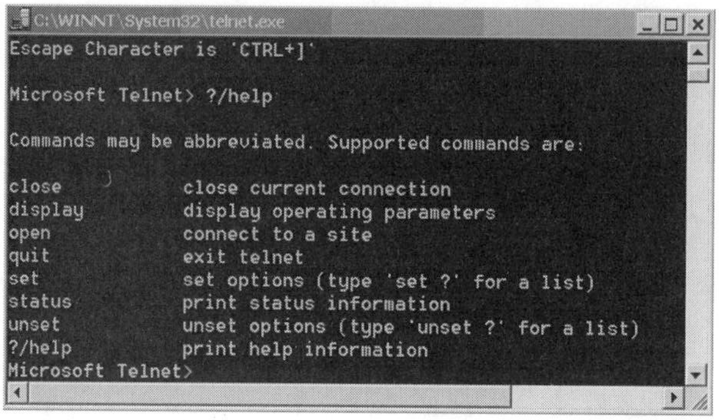

FIGURE 24.19

You use the several DOS commands to tell Telnet how and where to make a connection.

So what do RPCs do for you? OLE uses them, for one. Actually, OLE uses a subset of RPCs called light RPCs (LRPCs) to enable you to make connections that you couldn't normally make. I discuss this whole issue in detail in Chapter 15, "OLE, ActiveX and DCOM," so I won't talk about it again here. OLE is only the tip of the iceberg, however. There are other ways that RPCs can help you as a user.

Think about it this way: You're using an application that requires any number of resources in the form of DLLs, VxDs, and other executable code. Right now, all that code has to appear on your machine or in a place where Windows will be certain to find it. This means that every time a network administrator wants to update software, he or she has to search every machine on the network to make sure the job gets done completely. But what if you could "borrow" the DLL from someone else's machine? That's what RPCs are all about. An RPC lets your application grab what it needs in the form of executable code from wherever it happens to be.

Windows Sockets (WinSock) Support

Windows sockets (WinSock) started out as an effort by a group of vendors to make sense out of the conglomeration of TCP/IP protocol-based socket interfaces. Various vendors had originally ported their implementations of this protocol to Windows. The result was that nothing worked with anything else. The socket interface was originally implemented as a networked interprocess communication mechanism for version 4.2 of the Berkeley UNIX system. Windows 2000 requires all non-NetBIOS applications to use WinSock if they need to access any TCP/IP services. Vendors may optionally write IPX/SPX applications to this standard as well. Microsoft includes two WinSock applications with Windows 2000:

- SNMP
- FTP

Before I go much further, let me quickly define a couple of terms used in the preceding paragraph. You looked at what a protocol was earlier. It's a set of rules. TCP/IP is one common implementation of a set of rules. Think of a socket as you would the tube holder found in old televisions and radios. An application can plug a request (a tube) for some type of service into a socket and send it to a host of some kind. That host could be a file server, a minicomputer, a mainframe, or even another PC. An application can also use a socket to query a database server. It can ask for last year's sales statistics, for example. If every host uses a different-size socket, every application will require a different set of tubes to fit those sockets. WinSock gets rid of this problem by standardizing the socket used to request services and make queries.

Besides making the interface easier to use, WinSock provides another advantage. Normally, an application has to add a NetBIOS header to every packet that leaves the workstation. The workstation at the other end doesn't really need the header, but it's there anyway. This additional processing overhead reduces network efficiency. Using WinSock eliminates the need for the header, and the user sees better performance as a result.

Sockets are an age-old principle (at least in the computer world), but they're far from out-of-date. The WinSock project proved so successful that Microsoft began to move it to other transports. Windows 2000 includes a WinSock module for both the IPX/SPX and NetBEUI transports, for example.

Of course, WinSock is really a stopgap measure for today. In the long run, companies will want to move from the client/server model for some applications and use a distributed approach. This will require the use of an RPC interface rather than WinSock. You already looked at the implications of RPC in this chapter.

So what does it take to implement WinSock on your system? A group of five files in your \SYSTEM32 and \SYSTEM32\DRIVERS folders is used to implement WinSock. The following list tells you what they are and what tasks they perform:

- **WINSOCK.DLL**—This 16-bit application provides backward-compatibility for older applications that need it. An application such as Ping would use this DLL, for example.

- **WSOCK32.DLL**—32-bit applications use this DLL to access the WinSock API. It provides support for newer socket applications, such as Telnet.

- **MSWSOCK.DLL**—Windows uses this driver to provide both 16-bit and 32-bit TCP/IP and IPX/SPX WinSock support. It provides virtualized support for each virtual machine, enabling Windows to perform more than one WinSock operation at a time. This is the general driver used for both protocols. If Microsoft added more WinSock interfaces later, they'd all require this file for interface purposes.

- **TCPIP.SYS**—TCP/IP requires a protocol-specific driver. This file provides that support.

- **NWLNKIPX.SYS**—IPX/SPX requires a protocol-specific driver. This file provides that support.

On Your Own

Use the information in this chapter to determine which of your system resources are shared and which are not. You might want to create a written list of who has access and where for future reference. This enables you to plug any security leaks whenever someone leaves the company.

After you determine who has access to your machine, look for any security leaks. Make sure that you change passwords on a regular basis—especially after someone leaves the company. Check to see how the use of your system resources by others affects system performance and overall usability.

I discussed the network subsystem architecture in this chapter. Go through your \SYSTEM32 folder and see whether you can identify the components that comprise it. See whether your network needs any specialty components because it uses a different protocol than normal. You might also want to take this opportunity to look for any real-mode drivers that are still lurking around your hard drive.

Using FrontPage Express

You have probably heard about FrontPage, the Web site design program from Microsoft that has won several major awards. FrontPage Express is the "light" version of that same program, and it is available for free. It is "light" in the same sense that Outlook Express could be called "light Outlook," meaning that it is missing some of the features of the larger application, but is by no means crippleware. FrontPage Express (FPE) is a useful tool if you are interested in creating or improving a Web site of modest ambitions. It's more a visual design tool than a heavy-duty site builder (use Visual InterDev for complicated web sites). But for creating great-looking Web pages, FrontPage can't be beat.

You should find FrontPage Express on your Start menu; click Start, then Programs, then Internet Explorer. If you don't find it there, go to the Control Panel, double-click Add/Remove Programs, then click the Add/Remove Windows Components icon in the left panel of the Add/Remove Programs dialog box.

FPE is a WYSIWYG (What You See Is What You Get) editor for HTML documents that gives you most of the standard features of its more powerful sibling, FrontPage Editor. But describing it as merely an editor is reductive; it is more than that, as we will see. In general FPE enables you to create Web pages quickly and easily, often enabling you to use built-in, wizard-like dialog boxes, WebBots, and other efficient tools to avoid getting bogged down with tedious, unnecessary hand-programming. Of course, FPE does not include the site management capabilities of FrontPage 2000, nor does it include some advanced editing features such as the capability to create frames, predesigned themes, and GIF animations. But even with its (surprisingly few) limitations, FPE is a capable page designer and editor.

Peter's Principle: FrontPage Express, FrontPage 2000, Visual InterDev, or Visual Studio? Get the Tool You Need

If you are interested in developing a fairly sophisticated Web site, you will want to graduate from FPE and buy FrontPage 2000. The more advanced version of FrontPage includes several necessary tools for prototyping and maintaining a complex site with many pages and many internal links. FrontPage 2000 includes an automatic link repair feature that works in association with a Navigation bar WebBot to make life really easy for you if you reorganize the structure of a site

continues

(and you would be surprised how often this is necessary). Additional valuable features for use with larger Web sites include FrontPage 2000's scalable Site Diagramming and Link view. And if you need the ultimate heavy-duty Web site application, get Microsoft's Visual InterDev. It is targeted primarily to programmers, with features supporting Active Server Page debugging, scripting, and database connectivity. Visual InterDev also includes sophisticated group management and version control. It is capable of keeping things straight when a group of people work together to design and program an advanced Web site.

People are sometimes unclear about the relationship between FrontPage and Visual InterDev. Let's back up a moment and look at a marketing trend. Microsoft often releases applications in triads or quads. One thinks of the relationship between the Standard (or Learning), Professional, and Enterprise versions of such languages as Visual Basic. These three products are priced differently and they are nested, like a Russian puzzle box. The Enterprise version of Visual Studio includes absolutely everything; the Professional version includes a subset of the Enterprise features (it doesn't have Source Safe, for example). Finally the Standard/Learning version is a subset of the Professional version. Think, too, of the triad of applications formed by Notepad, WordPad, and Word—increasingly powerful word processing.

Often, the least powerful application in a set of tools is free (Visual Basic Control Creation Edition, Notepad, WordPad, Outlook Express, and so on). The expectation is that you will try the limited-yet-free (or inexpensive) version, and then purchase the more advanced tool if you find you need it.

This same tiered marketing tactic can be seen in Microsoft's several Web development tools: FrontPage Express; FrontPage 2000; Visual InterDev; and, the ultimate, Visual Studio, a megasuite of tools that includes everything but the kitchen sink: all Microsoft's RAD languages including Visual J++, Visual Basic, Visual FoxPro, Source Safe, and many other tools. Visual Studio also includes Visual InterDev. (Note that if you buy the standalone Visual InterDev, *it* includes FrontPage 2000.)

So what *is* the primary difference between Visual InterDev and FrontPage? Visual InterDev (VI) is targeted to site development administrators or site managers (the leader of a team working together to build or maintain a sophisticated Web site). VI is also targeted to programmers who write scripts (VBScript or JScript) for Web sites. VI includes many programmer's tools, including a full debugging suite. FrontPage, by contrast, is for everyone other than programmers and administrators: graphic designers, CEOs, writers, artists. In a word, FrontPage focuses on the surface, the content of a Web site. VI focuses on the engine room: the internals such as scripting and management.

Note: In addition to editing Web pages for the World Wide Web or a local intranet, you can use FPE to edit HTML documents that create the Web view for your folders. See Chapter 8, "Customizing Windows 2000 for Maximum Productivity," for details on customizing folders with Web views.

An HTML document is used for many things these days, but its main use is as a Web page. FPE is included in the Internet Explorer suite to give you a tool for creating and editing Web pages.

Creating Your Own Web Page

In Chapter 2, "Windows to the Internet," I looked at the Internet from a surfer's point of view. I answered the question of how to get the most information with the least amount of effort. But you would be wrong to think that the Internet ends there. The Internet isn't just about grabbing information. It is also about exchanging information and presenting your own point of view about issues that affect you most.

A lot of Web sites deal with everyday events and interests. I occasionally visit a Web site for dog owners, for example, and another to see what people think of the latest movies.

Suffice it to say that creating a Web page doesn't have to involve a commercial enterprise; you might just want to talk with someone about a topic of special interest to you. You could even go out and buy an inexpensive video camera and, like many people already do, leave it on 24 hours a day so that people can "live" your life along with you. If you envied Truman Burbank in *The Truman Show*, a live WebCam is for you!

> **Tip:** Building a Web page isn't the same thing as building an Internet site or even an intranet site. Some Internet service providers (ISPs) enable you to upload your own Web page to their server. The only requirement in this case is that you maintain the content of your Web site. The ISP takes care of the server and everything else needed to create the actual Internet site. Obviously, there are some limitations when you take this route, and you might have to pay for the privilege of displaying your own Web site. However, most noncommercial users will find the costs low and the constraints minimal.

Why Bother?

Most people are fairly excited at the thought of creating their own Web site. Then reality sets in. After all, maintaining a Web site can be a lot of work and the benefits (at least at the outset) can be minimal. In addition to the workload, some Web sites are so poorly conceived that other people won't even visit them. The typical response at this point is: "Why bother?" Creating a Web site that no one wants to visit wastes everyone's time.

Creating a good Web site requires first thinking it through. Ask yourself what you want to get out of the Web site you design and what you are willing to do to get it. A well-designed Web site normally begins with some really great ideas. If you can't come up with your own ideas, talk to other people with Web surfing experience. Better yet, visit other Web sites that appear to contain elements that you want to include with your site. Seeing what other people do can help you quickly figure out what you want to include.

There's another good reason to visit Web sites: You can quickly learn what works and what doesn't. If you find that you get annoyed waiting for a Web page to download, other people probably do as well. How does the Web page look from an aesthetic point of view? Is it inviting? Do you want to come back? How hard is the Web site to look at? Does it include glaring color combinations? Is the text easy to read? (Hard-to-read text ranks high on many people's lists of reasons not to visit a particular Web site.)

Determining Whether Your ISP Provides a Free Home Page

Just creating a Web page doesn't automatically make it available for others to see. For that, you must post your page on a Web server. Setting up a Web server is a major undertaking, but you don't need to do it on your own. Normally, you rent space on an existing Web server that belongs to an ISP or Web hosting service. In fact, many ISPs include a small Web site as part of the package when you sign up for an Internet access account. These free Web sites usually carry some restrictions, such as limitations on the amount of disk space your files can occupy and the amount of traffic your site can be allowed to generate (don't become *too* popular). However, they are usually adequate for most personal needs. You may already have a Web site and all you need to do is post your page on that site. If you don't have access to a free Web site as part of your Internet access account, your ISP will probably provide Web hosting service for a small fee. Another option is to check out one of the services that provides free Web sites in online communities; the service is free because the ISP hopes you'll interest advertisers, who then pay the ISP for the advertising space. One example of this kind of community is GeoCities (http://www.geocities.com).

Using FrontPage Express

After you finish the preliminary planning for your Web page, you will have a good idea of what you are trying to accomplish, what the page will look like, and where you are going to post it when it is done. Then you can open FPE and use it to create your Web page. To start the program:

1. Click Start.
2. Choose Programs.
3. Choose Internet Explorer. Note that there may be *two* Internet Explorer entries on your Programs submenu, but only one will be a folder.
4. Choose FrontPage Express.

Tip: If you want to edit an existing Web page instead of starting from scratch and creating a new one, you can start by viewing the page you want to edit in Internet Explorer. With the page displayed in the browser window, click the Edit button on Internet Explorer's toolbar. This automatically launches Notepad or FPE (depending on which you've specified as the default editor for .HTM pages) and loads the Web page you were viewing. Then you can use FPE to edit the page. This automatic loading happens only if you don't have another Web page editor installed on your system (such as FrontPage 2000).

When the FPE window first appears (see Figure 25.1), it looks rather like a word processor with a blank document in the work area. In fact, it behaves like a word processor in many respects. To enter text into the blank HTML document you are editing in FPE, you type in the work area just as you do to enter text into a blank word processing document. And you can use the Formatting buttons to enlarge or otherwise modify the characters.

FIGURE 25.1

The FPE editing window looks a lot like a word processor. You can start out with a few simple elements.

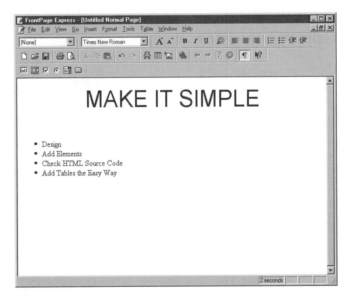

Tip: Many word processors and other programs can save documents in HTML format. That makes it a relatively simple task to open existing documents and convert them to documents you can use as Web pages.

Notice the *2 seconds* displayed in the status bar in Figure 25.2. FPE and FrontPage have a feature found nowhere else to my knowledge: The status bar tells you FPE's estimate of the download time required for the displayed page at the most common Internet transfer speed, 28.8Kbps. Add some heavy-duty, high-resolution graphics files to your page, and watch this estimate climb.

Note that you must check and ensure that your Web server has the FrontPage Extensions installed. These features require that it does. Many of the public Web servers don't. Find out what the Web server does support before your create a Web page using FPE. Otherwise, you could create a Web site that won't work once it's loaded on the Web server.

FPE may not have all the bells and whistles of the full-blown FrontPage editor, but it still has plenty of features for creating and editing Web pages. I can't possibly cover them all in detail in the space of the next few pages, but I can provide a get-acquainted tour of FPE that will give you a head start on your own explorations of the program. I'll start with the toolbars.

FIGURE 25.2

You can add backgrounds, custom elements, and other graphics to jazz up your site and make it look cohesive and professional.

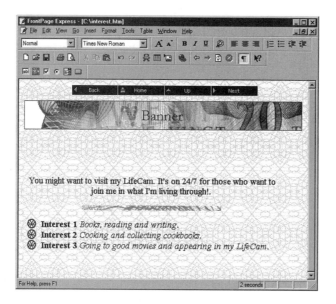

No doubt, many of the buttons on the FPE toolbars will look familiar; you have probably seen them before in a word processor or similar application. The first 10 buttons on the Standard toolbar (see Figure 25.3), for example, are New, Open, Save, Print, Print Preview, Cut, Copy, Paste, Undo, and Redo. These buttons trigger standard features common to many applications, and each does exactly what you expect. On the other hand, the next four buttons of the Standard toolbar are more specialized. They pertain directly to FPE's role as a Web page editor:

- Insert WebBot Component— Inserts a special FrontPage programming component into the Web page at the cursor location. These components contain all the programming necessary to accomplish a particular task—you don't have to write any

HTML or script yourself. Just drop a WebBot into your page and that's it. You can choose from WebBots that enable you to include another Web page, provide a Search feature, or timestamp your Web page. For the WebBots to work, they require support software on the server. (You need to check with your ISP to find out whether the Web server includes the FrontPage Extensions that are necessary for these WebBots to work.)

FIGURE 25.3
The Standard toolbar.

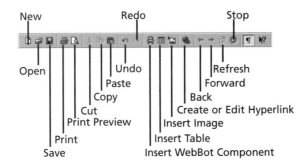

- **Insert Table**—Inserts a table at the cursor location. You can specify the number of columns and rows in the table by just dragging the pointer across a pop-up grid. Creating a table in HTML is awkward and time-consuming, but in FPE it is easy because you can essentially design it visually rather than having to program it.

- **Insert Image**—Inserts an image into your Web page at the cursor location. Clicking this button opens a dialog box where you can specify a filename or an URL for the image you want to insert, or you can choose one among the selection of clip art images that are shared by Microsoft Office applications.

- **Create or Edit Hyperlink**—Select some text or an image, then click the Hyperlink button to open a dialog box where you can define the target of the hyperlink. You can choose from any available bookmark on an available page, specify an Internet URL, or type the name of a new page that you then create with FPE. After you complete the hyperlink definition and return to the Web page, the selected text is a functional hyperlink.

The next four buttons of the FPE Standard toolbar are borrowed straight from a Web browser. They are Back, Forward, Refresh, and Stop. It should come as no surprise that clicking these buttons in FPE has the same effect as clicking their counterparts in a Web browser. The last two buttons on the Standard toolbar enable you to show or hide formatting marks and to access the FPE help document.

The Format toolbar (see Figure 25.4) also contains an assortment of buttons that look like they were taken straight from a word processor. In this case, however, looks can be deceiving. When you click a button from the Format toolbar, the effect on the document you are editing will probably be similar to the effect you get by clicking that button's counterpart in a word processor. Be prepared, however, for some subtle differences due to the characteristics of the HTML document standard and HTML formatting tags. When you make formatting changes in a word-processing document, you are usually directly manipulating the appearance of the selected text to achieve the look you want. However, you can't exercise the same degree of control over an HTML document. When you format a Web document with a paragraph style, for example, it is like giving generic instructions such as "make this a heading" and leaving it up to the Web browser to determine the heading's text attributes.

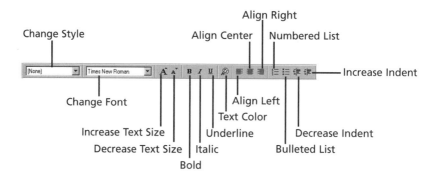

FIGURE 25.4
The Format toolbar.

> **Technical Note:** HTML is essentially a *relativistic* language, generally describing text size as Big, Bigger, Biggest rather than as absolute, specific sizes such as 12pt, 18pt, and 28pt. The reason that most measurements and position specifications in an HTML document are relative is because people resize their browsers in widely different ways. Not only can a browser window range from a couple of inches square to 19"×19", they can be dragged into various aspect ratios (the ratio of width to height). So, as you will notice, when you resize your browser window, an attempt is made to resize and reposition the contents within the window to accommodate your changes (within reason) before content disappears off one side and a scrollbar is added. Beyond size, position, and aspect ratio, there's also the fact that some people view Web documents with the graphics content turned off so no pictures are displayed. This also has an effect on the sizes and positions of text on the page.

Another example of browser-side calculation is text size. Instead of specifying a certain point size for text, you choose one of seven arbitrary sizes, such as Normal, +3, or –1. The user's Web browser determines the text size to use for Normal and each of the six standard variations. FPE displays your Web page using typical implementations of your formatting commands, but you must remember that the page might look different when it is eventually displayed in a Web browser. Here's a rundown of the buttons on the Format toolbar and what they do:

- **Change Style**—Assign one of the standard HTML paragraph styles, such as Heading 1, to the selected paragraph. Select a paragraph and then select the style from this drop-down list box.

- **Change Font**—Select some text on the page and then select a font from this drop-down list box. FPE displays the text in the chosen font. Other viewers don't see the same font when they view your Web page in their browsers, however, unless they have exactly the same font installed on their system. Theoretically, you can choose any font for the text on your Web page; as a practical matter, however, your choices are limited to a few common fonts (such as Times Roman, Arial, and New Courier) that are installed on nearly every computer.

Note: Users can override your choice of fonts and other elements in the Web page by choosing to enforce their own stylesheet on all documents rather than use your definitions or the browser's defaults for most HTML elements. Although this feature was designed for those with difficulty seeing, anyone can assign a custom stylesheet to Internet Explorer. To do this, go to Internet Explorer's Tools menu, choose Internet Options, click the General tab, then click the Accessibility button. Of course, you have to know how to design an HTML stylesheet—that's another book in itself!

Tip: Microsoft is promoting an expanded list of standard Web fonts by supplying those fonts with Internet Explorer and by making the fonts available for free download from the Microsoft Web site. The list of Web fonts includes the traditional standards as well as Impact, Comic Sans, Georgia, Trebuchet MS, and Veranda. You can download the fonts by going to http://www.microsoft.com/truetype/default.asp and following the links to the Web fonts.

- **Increase Text Size**—Clicking this button bumps the selected text up one size. Remember, text sizes on a Web page are defined as Normal (or as one of six variations from that Normal); the normal size in the viewer's Web browser might be different from what you see in FPE.

- **Decrease Text Size**—Clicking this button reduces the size of the selected text by one size.

- **Bold**—Select some text, then click this button to make it bold.

- **Italic**—Select some text, then click this button to make it italic.

- **Underline**—Select some text, then click this button to underline it.

- **Text Color**—Clicking this button opens a color selector dialog box in which you can click a color sample to apply that color to the selected text. Note that this color selection doesn't apply to the color of hyperlinks. Hyperlink colors are controlled from the Page Properties dialog box. (I explain the Page Properties options in a moment.)

- **Align Left**—Aligns the selected text with the left margin. Note that this applies to the entire paragraph.

- **Align Center**—Aligns the selected text with the center of the browser's viewing window (or with the center of a table cell).

- **Align Right**—Aligns the selected text with the right margin.

- **Numbered List**—To use this formatting option, you normally select several paragraphs and click this button to transform them into a numbered list. The browser automatically indents the paragraphs and adds sequential numbers.

- **Bulleted List**—To create a bulleted list, select several paragraphs of normal text and click this button. Like a numbered list, the browser automatically indents the paragraphs and adds a bullet in front of each one.

- **Decrease Indent**—Moves an indented paragraph one notch back to the left toward the left margin.

- **Increase Indent**—Click this button to indent a paragraph one notch from the left margin. Click again to increase the indent distance. You can adjust how far a paragraph is indented by indenting it a number of notches, but you can't control the size of those indentations.

Inserting Forms Components

The Forms toolbar (see Figure 25.5) gives you the tools you need to interact with people who visit your site (the users). With these tools, you can create onscreen forms for collecting information from visitors to your Web site. Clicking one of these buttons places a box containing the corresponding form element on your Web page at the current cursor position. Then you can type a text label beside the form element. After you place a form element on the page, you need to right-click it and choose Form Properties, Form Field Validation, or Form Field Properties to open dialog boxes where you can specify form handling instructions and define such things as default values for a field. (If you are not familiar with HTML forms, you need to refer to a good HTML book, such as *Sams Teach Yourself HTML 4 in 24 Hours* written by Dick Oliver and published by Sams Publishing. The topic is beyond the scope of this book, and the FPE help documents don't shed much light on the matter.)

FIGURE 25.5
The Forms toolbar.

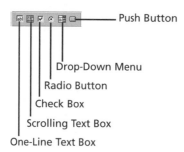

Push Button

Drop-Down Menu

Radio Button

Check Box

Scrolling Text Box

One-Line Text Box

Technical Note: In the last couple of years forms-handling has shifted from the traditional approach, in which the user clicked the Submit button to send information back to your server, and that information was then stored in a text file or perhaps appended to an existing text file. The problem with this approach was that you had to keep checking the text files on the server's hard drive or otherwise accessing the data in a fairly inefficient way. The more recent technique, which is preferred by many (particularly smaller sites that use an ISP's server), attaches your email address to the Submit button's form handler. That way, all user data is sent to your email account as a convenient, ordinary communication to which you can quickly view and respond. Of course, a site maintained by a large corporation has different needs and data streaming into files can be automatically manipulated, inserted into databases, or responded to without human intervention. The needs of a big corporation and a small individual differ, of course. For one thing, programming server-side incoming data streams is not for the amateur.

- **One-Line Text Box**—As its name implies, this button inserts a one-line text entry box into the form. You can stretch or shrink the text box horizontally.

- **Scrolling Text Box**—If you need a larger text entry area on your form, this is the button to use.

- **Check Box**—I Inserts a simple check box that users can check or clear to indicate yes and no answers. These are commonly used to permit users to specify preferences or indicate personal information (such as their age group).

- **Radio Button**—I Inserts a single radio button into the form. Normally you add two or more buttons in a column to give the user a choice of one of several options. FPE automatically groups adjacent radio button objects together.

- **Drop-Down Menu**—I Inserts a drop-down list box into your form. You definitely have to edit the properties of this form element to define the menu items that appear on the drop-down list.

- **Push Button**—I Inserts a button into your form that users can click to perform a task (such as submitting the data on the form, or resetting form fields to their default values). This is more commonly known as a command button.

Note: Although FPE can easily create Web pages that include HTML forms, you might not be able to use those forms on your Web site unless the Web server provides the necessary support services to collect and process the data that Web visitors enter into your forms. Before you invest time and effort developing forms, be sure to check with your Web posting service to find out if you can use forms on your Web site.

FPE toolbar buttons give you ready access to almost all the commands you'll need to create a Web page. One notable exception, however, is the important ability to define such characteristics of the page as the background color, background image, left margin, and so on. For that, you must go to the File menu and choose Page Properties. This opens the Page Properties dialog box shown in Figure 25.6. As you can see in the figure, the General tab is where you define the Title and other details such as Base Location, HTML Encoding, and Background Sound. The Background tab enables you to define a background or watermark image and colors for the background, text, and hyperlinks. The Margins tab enables you to specify the top and left margins for the page. (Web page designers often set these to 0 because otherwise the browser will insert a fairly thick margin.) The Custom tab is where you can specify system variables and user variables for the page.

FIGURE 25.6

The tabs in this dialog box enable you to define background effects and other characteristics of the page.

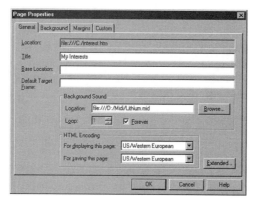

After you create a Web page in FPE, you will want to save it and share with others. Naturally, you click the Save button or go to the File menu and choose Save As. FPE responds by beginning the process of saving your Web page—that process, however, might include a few surprises. I know it surprised me the first time I used it. If you are like me, you probably expect the Save command to save the current document on your hard drive. However, FPE operates on the premise that the HTML documents you create are destined to become Web pages on a running Web server. The default action for the Save command is to first open the Save As dialog box shown in Figure 25.7. Then, when you enter the Page Title and the Page Location and click the OK button, FPE initiates an Internet connection and launches the Web Publishing Wizard (if installed). As you step through the pages of the Web Publishing Wizard (see Figure 25.8), the wizard gathers the information it needs to log on to your Web server and post your Web page and all its accompanying images and other files.

FIGURE 25.7

Supplying an appropriate title is an essential part of saving a Web page.

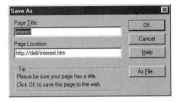

FIGURE 25.8

The Web Publishing Wizard prompts you for the information it needs to automatically post your Web page on the server.

When the Web Publishing Wizard works, it is great. However, not all ISP Web servers are compatible with the Web Publishing Wizard (they must have Microsoft's Internet Information Services installed); therefore the wizard isn't always a reliable way to publish your Web pages. If the Web Publishing Wizard doesn't work, you can save your Web pages as HTM files on the hard drive and then manually copy those files to the Web server. Fortunately, it is easy (but not very obvious) to save your FPE document as a file instead of posting it directly to the Web server. All you have to do is click the As File button in the Save As dialog box (refer to Figure 25.7). This opens a more traditional Save As File dialog box where you can select a folder, specify a filename, and click the Save button to save your work as an HTML document.

Tip: Although the FPE editor does its best to show you what your page will look like in a browser, FPE isn't, in the final analysis, a browser. There are some effects, particularly animation and WebBot behaviors, that require intelligence built in to Internet Explorer. This means that to really test your page you will want to save it as an HTM file, and then use Internet Explorer's File, Open feature to load the HTM file into Internet Explorer. For example, try adding a marquee to your page from the Insert menu. This is a scrolling bit of text that resembles the Times Square continuous news display. When you add it to your FPE page, however, it just sits there. After you save this page as an HTM file, however, and then load that file into Internet Explorer, the text comes alive and moves across the page.

Using IIS

IIS, or Internet Information Services, offers quite a bit of power. It has enough power to act as a staging area where you can develop a Web site on your local network. Then, when the site is polished, IIS deploys it to an Internet server.

IIS is Microsoft's robust Internet server system. IIS includes a utility, previously called Peer Web Services (on NT) and Personal Web Server (on Windows 98) that is useful when you want to build and test Web pages locally (within a corporate intranet or on a single desktop machine). As you know from the previous discussion in this chapter, you can test your FPE pages by saving them as HTM files, then loading them into Internet Explorer. IIS makes this testing possible because it can mimic a server, right there on your local hard drive—all without contacting an actual server.

Microsoft has positioned IIS as a powerful Web server that can handle high-volume traffic coming in from around the world on the Internet. The idea is that you can prototype and test your Web pages using IIS on a quiet, little, out-of-the-way workstation—then, when you are happy with it, you can deploy the site to your company's or your ISP's server running IIS.

If you don't have IIS running on your workstation, follow these steps to install IIS 5.0 (it is not installed by default, unless you *upgraded* from a previous version of Windows, and that previous version included PWS):

1. Go to the Control Panel and choose Add/Remove Programs.
2. Click the Add/Remove Windows Components icon in the left pane of the dialog box.
3. Follow the instructions to add IIS and its components.

For more information on IIS, see Chapter 26, "Working with Internet Information Server (IIS)."

Creating a Web Page

One of the best ways to test your Web pages or site while you're designing them is to use IIS as the "server" on your workstation and load the pages and navigate the site using Internet Explorer (just as if you were a visitor from somewhere out on the Internet). Do you have to upload your site to an official server? No, do it all within your Windows 2000 standalone workstation. Use Internet Explorer as the client. For the server, use Microsoft's IIS.

Of course you can save individual Web pages from FrontPage Express by choosing File, Save As, then choosing to save as a *file.* You'll save the page with an .HTM extension and it can be directly loaded into Internet Explorer and tested that way. However, if you want to test server-side behaviors (such as .ASP pages) or more complex Web site features, you must have your pages on a simulated "server" and that's where IIS comes in.

To use IIS, you have to set up a special folder on your hard drive to host your test Web pages:

1. Double-click the Personal Web Manager icon on your system tray (it should be on your Taskbar where the time is displayed). If you don't see it, see the instructions earlier in this chapter about how to install IIS.

You should see the Personal Web Manager shown in Figure 25.9. Note that my computer is named *DELL*. You should jot down the name of your computer—you'll need it shortly.

FIGURE 25.9

Use this dialog box to create special directories and manage PWM.

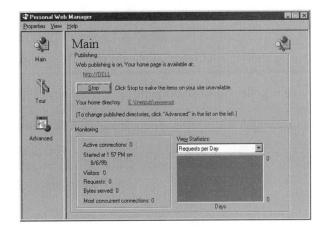

2. Click the Advanced button in the left pane of the dialog box.
3. Click the Add button to add a new virtual directory.

You'll see three checkboxes and three option buttons in the Add Directory dialog box. They are how you can specify the level of access that visitors have when they get to this directory. Read permission allows an .HTM page to be sent to the visitor's browser. The Write option permits them to save files in this directory. The Script option permits .ASP scripts to be executed. The Application Permissions section of the dialog box permit you to specify that scripts or executables (or neither) can be executed in this directory.

4. Click the permissions settings so you can execute everything and have full access.
5. Type MyWebTest as the Directory name. This name (or "alias") will later be used as part of the URL that you type into Internet Explorer to access this site.
6. Use the Browse button to choose the directory on your hard drive where you want to store the actual .HTM, .ASP or other Web files for testing. Remember the name of the directory so you can store your test pages there later. You might want to choose the inetpub/wwwroot directory so you can host it on the Web server.
7. Click OK. You see a warning message about how free and loose you were with the permissions. Click Yes, you bold person you.

8. The dialog boxes close and you should now see your new virtual directory (MyWebTest) listed in the Advanced Options page. Minimize the Personal Web Manager. You've now got a place to save and test FrontPage Express (or any other) Web pages.

On Your Own

Plan a Web page of your own, and then create it using FPE. Try some of FPE's more esoteric features, such as adding other components (Java applets or ActiveX controls) from the Insert menu. Also try your hand at writing script. Get a good book on DHTML, Dynamic HTML; you will be amazed at, among other things, what Internet Explorer can accomplish on the client side (in the user's computer) in the way of animation, wipes, and other special effects.

Test your new Web page using Internet Explorer, and then post it on your ISP's server if your account includes a Web site. After you post your Web site, view it using Internet Explorer and other Web browsers to see how the different browsers render your page.

Install IIS and practice creating a local Web site, or edit the sample template Web pages to get your feet wet. Create a personal or a corporate page, and then publish it on your local network.

Peter Norton

Working with Internet Information Server (IIS)

A lot of companies today are looking toward both Internet and intranet sites to provide the servicing capabilities they need for both clients and employees. A Web site can provide good access to data, take orders from customers, get input in the form of surveys, and help people find what they need in general—all without much in the way in human support. In short, a well-maintained Web site can reduce support costs and still make a company look more attractive to potential customers.

There are a lot of similarities between the Internet and an intranet. For example, you can access both types of server using a browser. However, there's one important difference between the two forms of Web site—at least for the purpose of this book. In most cases, an intranet site is private and local to the company that it serves. On the other hand, an Internet site is normally public (or at least accessible with a password) and open to the world as a whole.

The distinction between the two types of Web sites is important because it tells a lot about the value of IIS to the Windows 2000 user. Windows 2000 Professional provides a limited form of intranet server support in the form of Internet Information Server (IIS). This chapter will only provide information about IIS used in the capacity of an intranet server. If you really want an Internet server, then you need to install one of the versions of Windows 2000 Server.

> **Note:** No matter which tools you use to manage the intranet on your Windows 2000 Professional workstation, you're still working with IIS. It's important to understand that using higher end tools won't change the underlying Web server in any way. You'll still have the same limitations when using the tools in this chapter as you did with the tools in the previous chapter from a Web server perspective. What changes in this chapter is your ability to manage the capabilities of PWS.

In the previous chapter, we looked at what you could accomplish with Personal Web Manager (PWM). While this is a good start for a smaller company or a single individual, it's not going to provide you with enough flexibility for maintaining a larger Web site (remember, we're not talking a huge number of hits here or access to the Internet as a whole). That's where the IIS support that Windows 2000 Professional provides comes into play. It allows you to implement a fairly complex intranet Web site using a standard workstation. This Web site will use many of the same tools that the server version of IIS does, but it's important to remember that the Web server won't be able to service a large number of clients.

The following sections are going to help you understand the various tools that IIS provides for managing your Web site. All of these tools are accessible through MMC snap-ins available in the Administrative Tools folder of the Control Panel. You install them by adding subcomponents of the Internet Information Services component found in the Windows Component Wizard (Add/Remove Programs in Control Panel). We've already looked at creating content for your Web site in the previous chapter, so I won't cover that material again.

Default Web Site Setup

Windows 2000 automatically creates a default Web site for you as part of installing Web site support. You'll access the default Web site using the Internet Information Services MMC snap-in shown in Figure 26.1. This snap-in allows you to manage both local and remote Web sites. In addition, you can use it to manage other IIS features like FTP sites (which we'll cover in the next section of the chapter).

FIGURE 26.1

*The Internet
Information
Services snap-in
allows you to
manage all IIS
resources both
local and remote.*

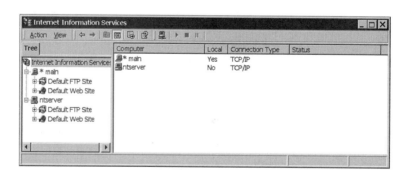

The new Web site created for you by Windows 2000 is more practical than functional (it's essentially a template). Figure 26.2 shows the default entries for the Web site, none of which include content that a user is likely to need (except for the IIS help files). The default Web site includes everything needed to create and manage a new Web site, but Microsoft leaves the creation of content up to you.

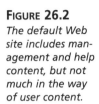

Figure 26.2
The default Web site includes management and help content, but not much in the way of user content.

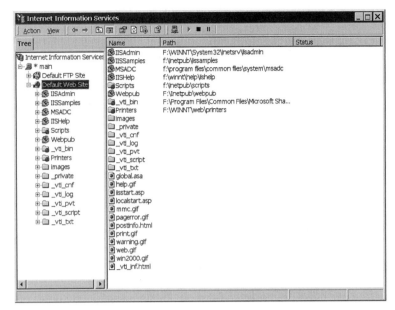

Now that you've seen an overview of the Internet Information Services snap-in, let's take a more detailed look at how you can use it to manage a Web site. The following sections will discuss a variety of Web site management issues, including how you can make printers attached to your machine accessible to others through an Internet connection. This particular feature comes in very handy for those times when you need to print something while on the road for someone back at the office.

Web Site Configuration

It's usually best to think about the configuration options for a Web site from a hierarchical perspective. The higher in the hierarchy that a configuration option appears, the more global the effect of any changes you make. You'll find many of the same configuration tabs at various levels within the Web site. This means that you can make the same change at different levels and affect a varying number of Web site objects. Obviously, the Web site itself is the highest level that you'll normally worry about when working with configuration options. However, there's one level above this one—IIS itself. Changing the IIS configuration options will affect all Web sites equally.

> **Note:** The Master Properties dialogs available through the server Properties dialog contains most of the same features that we'll cover in this section, so I won't provide separate coverage of the Master Properties dialog. It's important to realize that changing a property at the Web site level only affects that Web site, while changing it at the Master Properties level affects all Web sites in general.

Web Site Tab

Let's begin our tour of the Web site configuration options with the Web Site tab shown in
Figure 26.3. The first section is the identification information for your Web site. This
includes the Web site name and address information. Notice that there are two port
entries. The first is for anonymous contact with the server, while the second is for SSL
access. The SSL port entry represents one of the first concessions you'll find when using
the Windows 2000 Professional version of IIS. There's only one port address of 443
allowed—that's why this entry is grayed out.

FIGURE 26.3

*The Web Site tab
contains identifi-
cation, connec-
tion, and logging
information for
your Web site.*

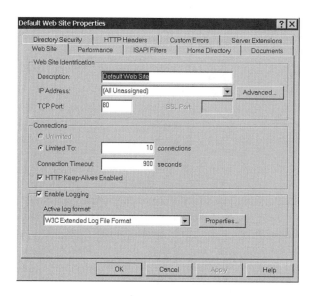

The next section contains connection information. This is where you'll find the second
limitation for the Windows 2000 Professional version of IIS. Notice that the Unlimited
option is grayed out. You are, in fact, limited to 10 connections when using this version
of IIS. The Connection Timeout field limits the time that an inactive user can remain
connected to your machine. Since you'll normally use this version of IIS with an
intranet, reducing this number should actually increase system performance and allow
people to access your machine faster when there are more than 10 people trying to do so.
Finally, you'll always want to keep the HTTP Keep-Alives Enabled check box checked.
This option enhances server performance by allowing a client to maintain an open connection with the server rather than creating an entirely new connection for each request.

The final section on the Web Site tab affects logging for your Web site. You have a
choice of enabling logging or not. In many cases, it pays to turn this feature off for an
intranet to conserve disk space. However, you'll never want to disable logging if you
have an outside connection—the logging feature could help you track down cracker
activity in the event of a break-in. IIS supports several different file formats, the most

popular of which is the W3C Extended Log File Format. This particular format is standardized across most Web servers, making it a popular choice for third-party tool vendors who create Web site analysis tools. You can also choose Microsoft IIS Log File Format, which is the text file format originally used by IIS; an ODBC format, which places the log file entries in a database; and NCSA Common Log File Format, which is another standardized file format used by several Web servers.

Performance

The Performance tab that you get with IIS for Windows 2000 Professional is the same as the one that comes with the Server version of the product. However, as you can see from Figure 26.4, most of the entries on this tab are blanked out. You don't have access to advanced features like bandwidth throttling.

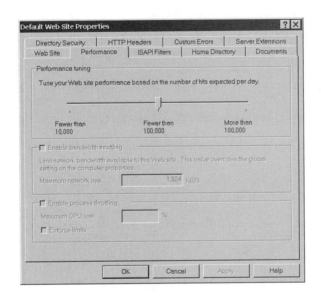

FIGURE 26.4
You don't get much in the way of performance enhancements with the Professional version of IIS.

The only option that works on this tab is Performance Tuning. I find it interesting that Microsoft didn't modify the default setting for Performance Tuning; it's extremely unlikely that someone using the Professional version of IIS will have more than 10,000 hits per day. This is one setting that you'll definitely want to change to save server memory and improve Web site performance. Make sure you choose the Fewer than 10,000 setting unless you're absolutely sure that your Web site actually gets more than 10,000 hits per day.

ISAPI Filters

ISAPI filters allow you to perform several different levels of background monitoring for your Web site. There are different types of filters for different purposes including security, URL mapping, and request header processing. In fact, ISAPI filters have the potential for being one of the most powerful methods of automatically monitoring your Web site and performing various types of automated processing.

Unfortunately, there isn't any third-party market for these applications, so your ability to use this technology is somewhat limited. ISAPI filters are usually custom designed for the Web site that they're intended to service. In addition, there's a rather steep learning curve for the programmer who wants to create them—most developers find scripting a much more attractive proposition, even if scripts are less flexible and provide far fewer features.

Essentially, you'll have to have a programmer on staff who can create the required application for you and then install it on the server. The ISAPI filter will be tested in place and you're very unlikely to have much to do with it. With this in mind, let's move on to the next tab.

Home Directory, Directory, Virtual Directory, and File

The Home Directory tab, shown in Figure 26.5, allows you to modify several elements about the location of files for the Web site. You can specify that the files for this Web site are located on the current computer or on a remote computer. In addition, you can redirect requests for information on this Web site to another URL, making it possible to create new links when the need arises. (I've seen this particular behavior several times on the Internet when a company changes ISP, but it's unlikely that you'll need it on a company intranet).

FIGURE 26.5

The Home Directory tab influences the location and accessibility of files for your Web site.

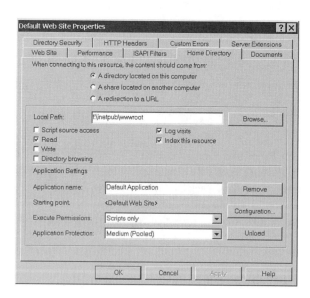

> **Note:** This same tab appears in different forms for directories, virtual directories, and files. The only difference is the features that each version of the tab enables. In addition, Microsoft uses a different name for each version of the tab. Since all four tabs are essentially the same, we'll cover all of them in this section of the chapter.

Once you get past the location of the files for a Web site, you need to consider the security used to protect them. In addition, you need to decide whether to index the files. Windows 2000 offers various levels of protection and monitoring for the files on a Web site as whole. Remember that you can also set the security and monitoring options for directories and files individually. The following list explains the various security and monitoring options, and how they affect file access.

- **Script Source Access**   This option allows the user to access the source code. You must also set the Read permission if you want to allow the user to view the source code, or the Write permission if you want to allow the user to modify the source code. In general, it's safe to allow a user to read the source code. Reading source code on other Web sites is one way that many Webmasters learn how to write scripts. Microsoft uses this setting for all types of scripts, including those found in ASP files. Of course, there may be proprietary data or other information in your HTML or scripting code, so check first to be sure that you want to permit everyone to see everything.

- **Read**   This setting allows the user to read and download the files and directories on your Web site. You must set this option to give the user even the most basic access to the content on your site.

- **Write**   Use this setting to allow the user to upload files to your Web site. This setting will also allow the user to change the content in Write-enabled files (this feature is disabled by default). The browser used to perform writing to a Web site must support the PUT feature of the HTTP 1.1 protocol. Internet Explorer is one of the browsers that falls into this category.

- **Directory Browsing**   Normally, the user needs to know the name of one of the files in a directory, or you have to set the directory up to automatically display a file when the user visits. This setting allows the user to see all of the files and directories contained within the current directory. Each file and directory entry looks and acts like a standard hyperlink, which allows the user to access the contents of the directory with a simple click.

- **Log Visits**   When you enable this option, Windows will make a log entry for each user visit to the directory. Using this setting allows you to see usage patterns on your Web site.

- **Index this Resource**   Select this option if you want Microsoft Indexing Service to include the directory within the search catalog. We'll spend more time talking about the Microsoft Indexing Service later in the chapter. All you really need to know now is that it speeds searches on your machine.

The final section of the Home Directory tab contains Application Settings. The most important settings in this are Execute Permissions and Application Protection. The Execute Permissions field determines what kind of applications the user can run. The default setting is Scripts only. However, you can restrict this further to none at all, or extend it to standard EXE applications as well.

The Application Protection field determines where the application is run in memory. The default setting of Medium (Pooled) runs the application in a separate process from the Web server, but in the same process as other Web applications. You can choose a lower level of application protection that runs the application in the same process as the Web server or set application protection higher so that each application runs in a completely separate process. The advantage of the lower setting is speed and memory usage. However, an errant application could cause the server to crash. The advantage of the higher setting is that your server and all of the applications running on it are totally protected. However, the performance and memory penalties are high when using this setting.

Documents

When a user enters a directory on your Web server, they either need to know the name of a file that appears within the directory or you need to provide a default file that executes if the user doesn't supply a filename. Otherwise, the Web server will generate an error message that the directory is inaccessible to the user (unless you have Directory Browsing enabled).

The Documents tab shown in Figure 26.6 allows you to define one or more default documents for the current directory. The documents are listed in order of preference, with the top file being displayed first, if possible. The file that the user actually sees depends on the availability of files within the directory and the capabilities of the user's browser.

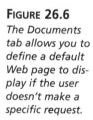

FIGURE 26.6

The Documents tab allows you to define a default Web page to display if the user doesn't make a specific request.

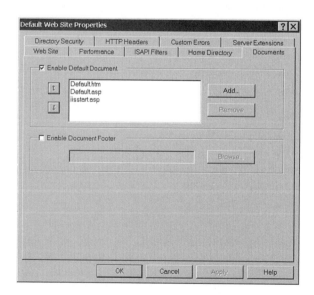

Note that defining default pages for the user to see won't make this feature active. You must also check the Enable Default Document option.

The Enable Document Footer option shown in Figure 26.6 allows you to also define a standard footer that will appear with each Web page. The footer isn't a complete Web page, it's merely a standard extension that you define for the sake of consistency. In most cases, a footer would contain items like a company logo, contact information, and a mail-to: entry. Obviously, you can place any content you like in the footer, but these are standard additions to consider.

Directory Security and File Security

IIS uses the same standard security tab no matter where you find it within the directory hierarchy. About the only two differences between the Directory Security and File Security tabs are the names and the scope of the security they affect. Figure 26.7 shows the Directory Security tab. Notice that unlike the Server version of IIS, you can't control access by IP address when using the Professional version.

FIGURE 26.7

IIS allows you to set security at both the directory and file levels so that you can completely control access to the Web site.

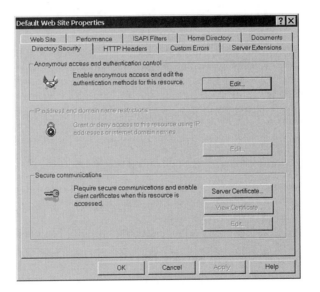

Click Edit in the Anonymous Access and Authentication Control section of the Security tab and you'll see an Authentication Methods dialog like the one shown in Figure 26.8. This is where you'll determine how the user gains access to the directory itself. Anonymous access means that anyone can access the directory, although you still have control over subdirectories and individual files. Even with anonymous access, the user is logged into the system using an account, which is normally the IUSR_<Computer Name> account (IUSR_MAIN in my case). The use of an account is important for providing specific levels of access to system resources—as we'll see later in the chapter in the section entitled "Making Printers Accessible."

FIGURE 26.8
Windows 2000 provides several levels of security for both directories and files on your Web site.

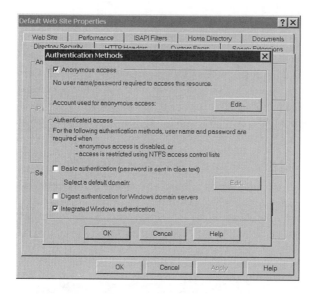

Caution: As long as you have Anonymous Access enabled for your Web site, someone will gain access to it, no matter what additional security measures you put in place. Once crackers gain access to your Web site, they can begin working on breaking the other forms of security you have in place. In sum, the only way to be sure your Web site is secure is to disallow any form of anonymous access. In addition, it's absolutely essential that you perform constant monitoring of the Web site to determine when a break-in occurs. We'll discuss security issues in greater detail in Chapter 28.

The remaining three levels of access require some type of identification on the part of the user before the user can gain access to the directory. When working with Basic Authentication, the user is asked to enter their name and password. The account is then verified using normal Windows 2000 security methods. The only problem with Basic Authentication is that the name and password are sent in clear text, which means that someone with a sniffer could intercept the data and gain access to your system using a legitimate password. (A sniffer is special hardware or software that's designed to intercept network packets—like those used to send user name and password information—and allow someone to read their contents.)

Digest Authentication for Windows Domain Servers is new for IIS 5.0, but isn't available with Windows 2000 Professional unless the workstation has a connection to a domain server. It works in a similar fashion to Basic Authentication. The user is asked to enter his name and password, which is then verified at the server. However, instead of sending the name and password in clear text, they're sent as a hash value (essentially encrypted).

This eliminates the possibility of someone snooping on the user's conversation and gaining unauthorized access to your Web site.

Integrated Windows Authentication goes an entirely different route to verify the identity of the user. Windows 2000 performs a cryptographic exchange with the user's browser. In short, this method relies on a digital certificate installed with the user's browser for identification purposes.

HTTP Headers

The HTTP Headers tab shown in Figure 26.9 actually performs a variety of tasks—each related to something called a response header. A response header is part of the content sent by the server to the user's browser that affects how the browser views the content it receives. The user normally doesn't see the response header.

FIGURE 26.9

The HTTP Headers tab controls the response header settings that affect how the browser views the data it receives.

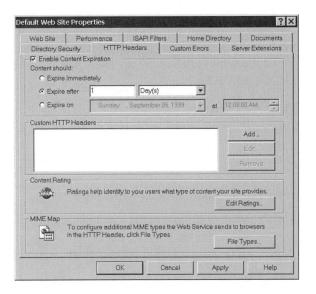

The Enable Content Expiration option allows you to set a time when the content of a directory is no longer valid. You can use this for time-sensitive content that the user will only need for a given amount of time. You can set the content to Expire Immediately, after a certain amount of time has elapsed (Expire After), or on a specific date and time (Expire On). The Expire Immediately option allows you to handle situations in which you want the user to see something like an advertisement only one time.

Custom HTTP headers allow you to control the browser. You'll normally use this area when the various Internet standards committees release response headers that a browser is likely to understand, but that were released after IIS was introduced in the market. In short, you'll need to know how response headers work to use this feature.

The Content Rating section is only important if your Web site contains information of an adult nature that you don't want all audiences to see. It allows you to define the Web site's content with regard to violence, sex, nudity, and language. Microsoft supplies a wizard that helps you determine what settings you should use for your site. In most cases, you won't need to worry about these settings in an intranet setting.

The final section on the HTTP Headers tab concerns special Multipurpose Internet Mail Extensions (MIME) settings for the files in the current directory. The only time you'd use this setting is if the content on your Web site relied on special file types. The MIME settings tell the browser how to react to these special files. In most cases, it means that the browser will load a helper application to display the special file.

Custom Errors

There's almost never a need to modify the contents of the Custom Errors tab. All that this tab contains is a list of standard HTTP error numbers and a Web page associated with that error. This Web page gets displayed when the error occurs so that the user knows that there's a problem with viewing the content of the Web site. Unless you have a good reason for changing the settings on this tab, you'll want to use the default error messages and their associated Web pages.

Server Extensions

The Server Extensions tab shown in Figure 26.10 determines some of the ways that your Web server reacts to FrontPage. We covered FrontPage itself in Chapter 25. What we'll cover in this section is the Web server end of the FrontPage Server Extensions.

FIGURE 26.10

The Server Extensions tab allows you to define how your Web server will react to FrontPage.

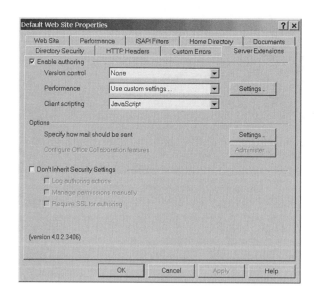

The first section of the Server Extensions tab allows you to define authoring settings. This includes Version Control, Performance, and the kind of scripting (Client Scripting) language used within FrontPage-generated Web pages. In this particular case, you have a choice between VBScript and JavaScript. You also can choose between no (external) version control or the version control built into the Web server. The performance options help you determine how the Web server will interact with FrontPage. In most cases, the default settings will work fine.

> **Tip:** Another way to access the FrontPage server extension settings for your Web server is using the Server Extensions Administrator MMC snap-in. This tool presents a hierarchical view of your Web site that you can traverse quickly. Right-clicking on any of the folders and choosing Properties from the context menu will display a dialog containing entries similar to the ones shown on the Server Extensions tab (Figure 26.10). If you have FrontPage installed on your machine, this snap-in will also allow you to open the various folders for viewing and modification—making the process of maintaining Web site content much faster and easier. In sum, the Server Extensions Administrator doesn't add much in the way of functionality, but it can make the Webmaster more efficient in handling changes.

The next section of the Server Extensions tab determines how automated email handlers work. You can define the Web server, contact, and SMTP email addresses. In addition, this section allows you to define how the mail is encoded and what character set it uses.

The final section allows you to control the security settings for the FrontPage Server Extensions. Normally, the same security settings get used for all directories. However, you may have a directory that contains sensitive information that you want to monitor with extra care. That's when you'd use this feature. The security settings include logging any authoring actions, setting permissions manually, and requiring an SSL connection before someone can author a Web page.

Making Printers Accessible

I was surprised to find one new feature in IIS 5: the ability to work with printers from a Web page. You can access this feature from the default Web page that Windows 2000 creates for you during installation by clicking the Web site link in the Web Printing section of the http://localhost/localstart.asp page. Figure 26.11 shows an example of what this feature looks like once you enable it. As you can see, this is one of those occasions when it pays to provide entries for the Location and Comment fields of the printer Properties dialog.

FIGURE 26.11

IIS 5 makes it possible to print documents from a browser, as well as manage your print jobs.

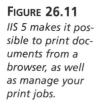

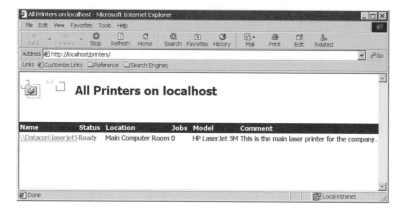

The Web page shown in Figure 26.11 will display all of the printers that you've decided to share through an Internet or intranet connection. Clicking on the printer link will display some addition printer information as shown in Figure 26.12. As you can see, you have full control over the printer as well as access to the same level of printer information as you would have at your desktop. The only difference between managing a printer through your browser and the local desktop is the Web page.

FIGURE 26.12

You get full printer management capability when using the new IIS 5 printer feature.

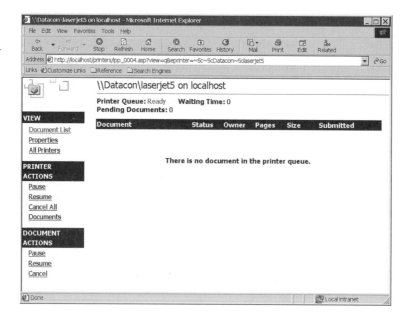

Before you get to use all of these new features, though, there are some setups that you need to take care of. The first problem is gaining access to the printer in the first place. To solve this problem, right-click the printer you want to share in the Printers folder, then choose Sharing from the context menu. You'll see the Sharing tab of the printer Properties dialog. Choose the Shared As option, then enter a name for your new share. The ability to share a printer isn't determined by a local or remote connection. The printer shown in Figures 26.11 and 26.12 is a network printer.

You'll also need to set up security for the printer. This means clicking the Security tab of the printer Properties dialog. The tab should include a list of users who have access to the printer right now. In most cases, you'll want to keep just this list of names if you're allowing access to the printer from the Internet—in fact, you may want to even prune it to those users who are on the road. However, what happens if you have no outside connection to your Web site and there are more users on your company's intranet than you want to enter? In this case, anonymous access is just fine, but you'll need to add a new user to get the right results. The user that you need to add is the IUSR_*Computer Name* user that I talked about earlier. This is the account that gets used for anonymous access to your Web site.

The final step in setting up printer support is to configure your Web site. You need to set the security for the Printers virtual directory to reflect the security you put into place at the printer itself. Right-click the Printers virtual directory entry, then choose Properties from the context menu. Select the Directory Security tab, then click Edit in the Anonymous access and authentication control section. What you'll see is the Authentication Methods dialog that we talked about earlier in the chapter. You'll need to select an authentication method that reflects the security you set for the printer, which may mean disabling any form of authentication and selecting anonymous access.

Default FTP Site Setup

Many of the configuration items that we covered for Web sites apply to FTP sites as well. However, since FTP sites are characteristically simpler in structure than Web sites, you'll find that they're fairly easy to configure. I'm not going to cover some elements of FTP site configuration in this section of the chapter because we've already talked about them in the Web server section of the chapter.

Security Accounts is the first tab of the Default FTP Site Properties dialog that you'll want to look at (see Figure 26.13). Most of the entries on this tab should look familiar from the Web site section. However, there's a new check box that allows you to set the FTP site to Allow Only Anonymous Connections. The main reason for this feature is to prevent crackers from gaining access to secure system resources using a name and password they may have gotten through some other means. In short, this is actually a security feature, even though it makes the FTP site itself less secure.

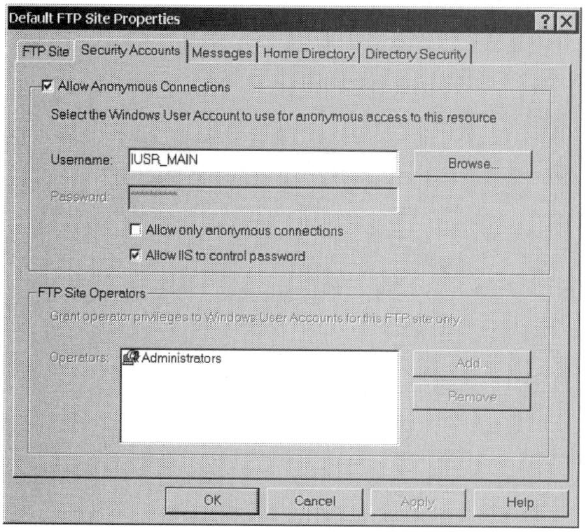

FIGURE 26.13

FTP Site security includes the ability to restrict access to anonymous connections.

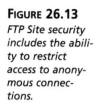

Notice that the Security Accounts tab also includes an FTP Site Operators section. This is another limitation of the Professional version of IIS—you can't select new operators. Only the network administrator is able to administer the FTP site. This particular limitation makes some sense considering the small site orientation of the Professional product.

The Messages tab shown in Figure 26.14 allows you to create a standard greeting, exit, and too many connection messages for your FTP site. You should supply one message for each condition.

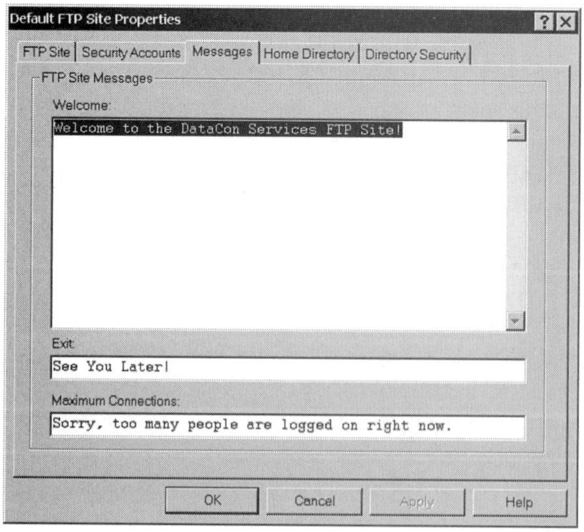

FIGURE 26.14

You'll need to supply Welcome, Exit, and Maximum Connections messages for your FTP site.

Microsoft Indexing Service

As hard drives and networks both get larger, it becomes harder to find the piece of information you need. Searching for the file you need isn't only time-consuming, but there really isn't any guarantee that you'll actually find it. There are situations when you'll actually bypass the file by the time you get to it because you're tired. In short, you need some fast and efficient method for finding files on your hard drive using a variety of search methods including word searches that rely on the content of the file. Microsoft Indexing Service is the latest addition to the user's arsenal for finding lost files. It allows your machine to build a search database in advance, which greatly reduces the time required to find a specific file, especially when you perform a keyword search.

You'll find the Microsoft Indexing Service within the Services and Applications folder of the Computer Management MMC snap-in (see Figure 26.15). Notice that this example shows two indexes that are called catalogs by the snap-in. The first is for the local hard drives in general; the second is for the Web server that we set up previously. Both catalogs are active at the same time.

> **Tip:** The quickest way to launch the Indexing Service is to press Windows+F, then click Indexing Service in the left pane. (You also can choose Start, Search, For Files or Folders.) When you see a dialog box, click the Advanced button (or Search Options link). The Indexing Service is such a handy utility that it's doubtless a simpler way to activate it will be made available—perphaps a shortcut on the desktop, or an entry in the Start, Search menu.

FIGURE 26.15

The first Indexing Service folder you'll see contains status information for the individual catalogs.

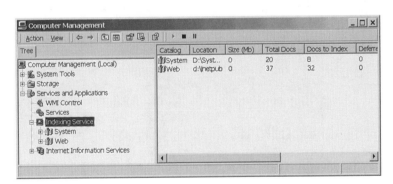

Catalogs are based on the directories that you tell the Indexing Service to look at. Figure 26.16 shows the Directories folder for the System catalog. Notice that you can use entries to include or exclude a directory from the catalog. Adding a new directory entry is as easy as right-clicking the Directories folder and choosing New, Directory from the context menu. You'll see an Add Directory dialog where you need to add the mapped path for the directory you want to add. (If you're using the Indexing Service dialog box rather than the MMC snap-in, double-click one of the folders in the Catalog column. This reveals the Directories and Properties folders.)

Figure 26.16

Directories determine what gets indexed to create a catalog.

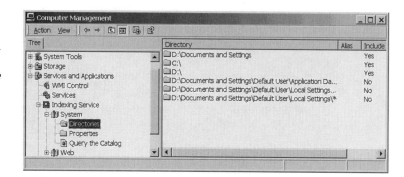

Obviously, there are a lot of document properties that you could index to create a catalog. However, trying to index them all would create a catalog that takes just as long to search as the files—perhaps longer. That's where properties come into play. The Properties folder shown in Figure 26.17 shows what appears to be gibberish. These properties actually define what kinds of data are entered in the catalog.

Figure 26.17

Properties determine what type of information is indexed for l inclusion in the catalog.

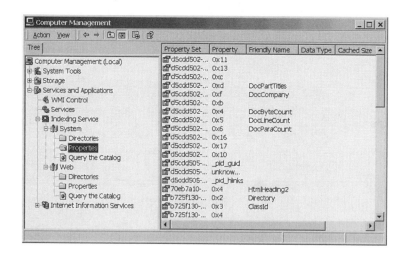

Notice that some of the properties in Figure 26.17 contain entries in the Data Type (the kind of property being indexed), Cached Size (the amount of space the property requires), and Storage Level (where the indexed property is stored in the catalog) columns. These are the active properties—the ones from the list of properties that actually appear in the catalog. In most cases, the properties that the Indexing Service uses by default will serve your needs. However, if you find that you're missing more files than you really want, then you may want to spend more time looking through the list of available properties to see if you need to add a new one to the list.

Now that you have some idea of how a catalog is created, how do you look for the files that it's indexed? The Windows 2000 Search feature relies on the catalogs and represents the easiest way to use them. You could also use a Web browser to perform the search. However, neither of these methods really uses the full power of the Indexing Service. To use the full power of this service you'll want to create a query using the Indexing Service Query Form shown in Figure 26.18. Notice that I've already searched for documents with an author of a specific name.

FIGURE 26.18

Using the Indexing Service Query Form allows you to better use the capabilities of this service.

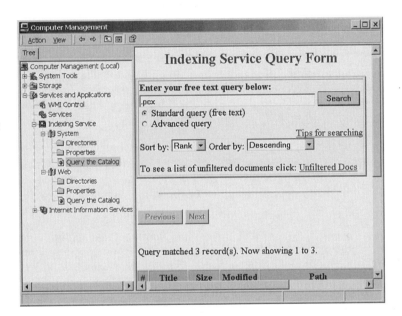

Creating a query for the Indexing Service is as simple as knowing which properties are indexed, then requesting a specific value for that property. For example, one of the standard properties for Indexing Service is the name of the last person who edited the document (DocLastAuthor). By asking for this property with my login name, I was able to find the documents on the local hard drive where I was the last editor.

Queries can get quite complex if you so desire. The Indexing Service supports a wide variety of query modifiers including full Boolean operator support. You can also specify that you want to see any document that contains at least part of the search criteria or that you want only the documents that exactly equal the search criteria. The Indexing Service will also allow you to enter free-form text statements (full sentences if you like). It'll take the sentence apart, try to determine what you're looking for, then deliver the results it finds. Obviously, this last method is less than precise, but it'll work in situations where you don't want to compose a formal query.

On Your Own

Spend some time learning to use the Internet Information Services snap-in to manage your Web and FTP sites. This tool will help you create new sites as well as modify the characteristics of existing sites. Make sure you learn how to connect to other machines (if there's more than one Web server on your network) so that you can manage other Web servers on the network from a single location.

Try setting up a printer that you can access from your Web server using the procedures found in the Making Printers Accessible section of the chapter. This new feature can be a real help to users on the road because it allows them to access the company printer just as if they were at the company. (Obviously, the ability to retrieve printed material is limited.)

As part of your FTP site configuration, add a greeting, exit, and too many connections message to the Messages tab. Make sure that the messages are informative. For example, the greeting message should tell the user which FTP site they've connected to.

Time some complex searches on your hard drive without Microsoft Indexing Services installed. Then, use the Microsoft Indexing Service to index your hard drive. Make sure you wait until the indexing process is complete (the column named Status at the far right of the folders view will say Indexing Paused rather than Scanning, Indexing Paused). Now, time the same searches again to see how much of a time reduction you see. In many cases, depending on the size of your hard drive or network, the time savings can be dramatic.

One of the ways to save time searching is to create specific catalogs for special needs. For example, I normally maintain a catalog of the network directories that contain my current project information. Another catalog I maintain is one of all my archived data so that I can find information that I worked with in the past quickly. Maintaining these special catalogs means that I'll only search them when needed. Think up some focused catalogs that you can create to make your data searches faster and more efficient.

Client/Server Networking

In the computer industry, several terms and concepts are so commonly used (and mis-used) that the exact definitions are foggy at best. Client/server is one of them. (Another is the term object, which can mean just about anything you want it to.) Nonetheless, in this chapter we're talking about the client-to-server relationship that networking in Windows 2000 uses.

We'll use a somewhat open-ended definition of client/server in this chapter. A client is a machine or service that's requesting data—think of it like placing an order at a drive-through window of a fast food place. An order is placed for some goods. The server side responds to the request and delivers the goods or services requested. In the previous chapter, you saw that even in a peer-to-peer network there's an underlying current of client/server architecture. Windows 2000 itself, as discussed in Chapter 9, "An Architectural Overview," has a client/server relationship between the environmental services and the executive services in Kernel mode. Well, enough review.

This chapter looks at client/server networking in a couple of different ways. First, I'll describe how the networking architecture is client/server-based. Then I'll discuss the various clients that you might want to use with Windows 2000 Professional. Out of necessity, I have to discuss the servers that you might want to connect to. As you can perhaps guess, we're working our way up from a base architecture into the realm of the user interface. I'll also discuss how you can use Windows 2000 client machines to take advantage of server resources, and even control the servers.

Windows 2000 Client/Server Networking

Recall that the Windows 2000 architecture itself is founded on a client/server strategy. Within that architecture, there's an environmental subsystem that essentially contains users running applications. These are the clients of the Windows 2000 architecture; in other words, they make the requests for information and operating system services. The servers in the Windows 2000 architecture are the Executive Services, such as the Virtual Memory Manager and the I/O Manager—taking requests and fulfilling them. This kind of philosophy is extended into the realm of networking. In the networking world, we also have a client/server relationship. The client side consists of a user and is primarily represented by the Windows 2000 component called the Workstation Service. The server is appropriately represented by the Windows 2000 Server Service.

The Workstation Service is basically in charge of issuing a request. When an application needs a resource on another machine, it's essentially asking the Workstation Service to retrieve the information. The Workstation Service (running under the SERVICES.EXE on Windows 2000 Professional machines) makes a request to the Kernel-mode driver, known as the redirector. The redirector, working with the I/O Manager, recognizes that the file is on another system. The request is passed to the other system and specifically aimed at the Server Service.

The Server Service waits around for requests from Workstation Services on other machines. It, too, starts under SERVICES.EXE on Windows 2000 Professional. SERVICES.EXE is essentially the service control. In the Kernel mode, the Server Service looks to the I/O Manager like a file-system driver, SRV.SYS. Therefore, it'll access the information from this service in much the same way that it'll access information from the network or the hard drive. After the data is collected, it's sent back to the requesting Workstation Service.

The process is relatively simple, but as you'll soon see, it gets complicated in an integrated network. Also, note that I haven't even mentioned the issue of protocols. These services don't really care much about the protocols they're using. They rely on the other services and drivers to handle that part of it.

Selecting a Client

Now that we have an idea of how the process works at the lower level, we'll want to move a little closer to where we usually operate—the user interface. Understand that we're now changing our view of client/server to a higher level. The client, at this point, can be thought of as any workstation that's requesting information across the network. The server is any machine that's fulfilling the request. This means that a "server" could be a Windows for Workgroup machine that has a shared directory. Or a Windows 95/98 machine sharing a printer or folder could be acting as a "server." Of course, most of the time our servers will be Windows 2000 Servers. However, they could just as easily be NetWare servers. It'll all depend on the size and complexity of your network. Just keep in mind that a "server," as we'll continue to speak of it in the remainder of this chapter, is a seller of information. The server is the guy selling newspapers on the corner. We're the consumers—the clients who pay the price and collect the information that they provide.

Of course, not all of us have time to read the paper. Some like to listen to the radio or watch CNN. There's a multitude of ways to get your daily dose of world news. In the world of networking, you have just as many ways to get information from servers. One of the first things that we need to do is to select a client and a proper protocol. Microsoft built Windows 2000 with integration in mind. The construction is reasonably open, to allow other vendors to build their own "clients" that Windows 2000 will use to communicate. A couple of the more popular clients are MS Client and NetWare Client.

Microsoft produces a couple of clients to permit you to connect to either Microsoft Windows 2000 Servers or NetWare servers. Both of them permit you to use the particular server for user authentication, printer sharing, file sharing, and application services.

Novell is working on a NetWare Client for Windows 2000 Professional as of this writing; there's already a client available for Windows NT machines. The Novell client allows you to perform more work with NetWare, but it also exacts a higher price in both memory and performance when compared to the Microsoft client. NetWare currently comes in several varieties including NetWare 3.x (an older operating system that's supported, but not marketed), intraNetWare 4.x, NetWare 4.x, and NetWare 5—so you need to get the right client for the task at hand.

> **Note:** One of the major reasons many network administrators preferred using NetWare in the past is the NetWare Directory Services (NDS) support that it provides. In fact, there's even an NDS add-on for Windows NT users that gives this older operating system NDS capability. NDS is essentially an object-oriented database that allows an administrator to manage an entire network using a single tool. Windows 2000 now includes this capability, as well, in the form of Active Directory, so it'll be interesting to see how larger companies react. We'll talk more about the NDS versus Active Directory way of managing a network later in the chapter.

If Windows 2000 detects a network during installation, it'll automatically install the Microsoft client. In most cases, Windows 2000 Setup will also install the Novell client if it detects a NetWare file server. There are some situations when you may need to install a client manually because Setup doesn't detect your complete network setup during installation. The following steps will get you started.

1. Open the Control Panel, Network and Dial-Up Connections applet. You'll see a Network and Dial-Up Connections dialog like the one shown in Figure 27.1.

FIGURE 27.1
Windows 2000 stores both network and dial-up connections in a single folder.

2. Right-click the Local Area Connection icon, then choose Properties from the context menu. You'll see a Local Area Connection Properties dialog like the one shown in Figure 27.2. If you already have the Microsoft and NetWare clients installed, your dialog will display both clients (as shown in Figure 27.2) and you can close the two dialogs that we've opened so far. Otherwise, you'll need to manually install the NetWare client.

FIGURE 27.2

Use the Local Area Connection Properties dialog to determine which clients are installed on your machine.

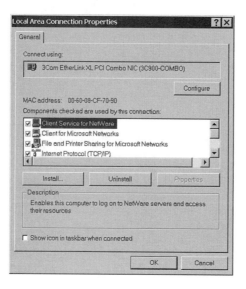

3. Click Install. You'll see a Select Network Component Type dialog.

4. Highlight Client, then click Add. You'll see a Select Network Client dialog.

5. Highlight the Client Service for NetWare option, then click OK. Windows 2000 may ask you to insert the Windows 2000 CD. It'll then install the NetWare client. Once the installation is complete, you'll see a Select NetWare Logon dialog like the one shown in Figure 27.3. Depending on your NetWare file server configuration, you'll need to choose either a preferred server (bindery emulation) or a default tree and context (NDS).

6. Choose a NetWare server connection option. You'll need to provide either a server name, or a default context and tree as well. Notice that this dialog also allows you to run the login script. This is the login script defined for your account on the NetWare server. We'll talk more about this issue later in the chapter.

7. Click OK. Windows 2000 will log you into the NetWare server using the location information you provided. You may be asked to provide a NetWare specific password. At this point, you can close the Local Area Connection Properties and the Network and Dial-Up Connections dialogs.

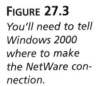

FIGURE 27.3

You'll need to tell Windows 2000 where to make the NetWare connection.

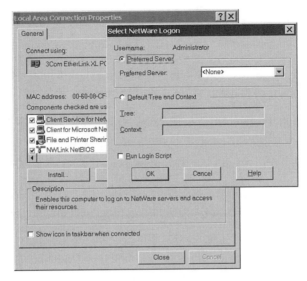

> **Note:** When using Windows NT, you needed to install support for Client Services for NetWare (CSNW). This support is now installed automatically with the client when working with Windows 2000. If you look in the Control Panel at this point, you'll see a CSNW applet. This applet allows you to perform NetWare specific configuration tasks like changing the way that documents get printed on NetWare printers. We'll cover the specifics of using CSNW later in the chapter.

Because the Novell client for NetWare was unavailable at the time of this writing, I can't tell you how it'll install. However, previous versions of the product came with an installation program that you could run to install the client. There's no reason to believe that Novell will handle things any differently this time around. Remember, this is a book on Windows 2000, not NetWare. Therefore, although I still believe both are very worthy of attention, I'll focus on the Microsoft Client Services for NetWare as opposed to the Novell NetWare Client.

> **Technical Note:** By default, when you install the CSNW or the GSNW for Windows 2000 it'll drag the NWLink protocol along with it. The NWLink protocol is Microsoft's version of IPX/SPX, a protocol that originated with Novell NetWare servers. In some cases, you won't need this protocol because the NetWare servers can run TCP/IP. You'll need to check and see which protocol you're running in order to configure the protocols correctly.

Getting Connected

Well, now that we have our clients installed, what can we do? Before actually using the client, we'll want to take advantage of the client/server paradigm. This generally goes beyond the peer-to-peer networking discussed in the preceding chapter. Here we want to either become integrated into a Windows 2000 domain or included in NetWare Services.

Connecting to a Windows 2000 Domain

A Windows 2000 Professional workstation connected to a network is either running in peer-to-peer mode (small network, 10 or fewer clients) or is part of a domain structure (large network). Windows NT/2000 domains consist of one or more Windows NT/2000 Servers running as domain controllers and a group of member servers and client workstations. Domain controllers currently come in two flavors: primary domain controllers (PDC) and backup domain controllers (BDC). In Windows 2000, all domain controllers (those servers that have Active Directory installed) with a domain are "primary" in that directory data is replicated between them all. These machines handle the user accounts and the machine accounts. The user accounts are just the names and passwords that we use to gain access to the resources that the servers publish on the network. The machine accounts are used behind the scenes by the Windows 2000 workstations and servers to let the domain controllers know who they are and what types of resources they may have that are of interest to other users. When you log on to the domain, you actually contact a domain controller and ask permission to enter. If you type in the right password, you're in the castle walls. Type in the wrong password, and you find yourself staring at the castle from across the moat.

Joining a Domain

For a workstation to join a domain, a few things need to be in place. First, you must have some type of networking installed to be able to communicate with the domain controllers. Hey, the phone's no good if it's not plugged in to the telephone company lines! The next thing you need is a valid username and password for the domain. Lastly, your machine must be granted permission to join the domain. Adding your machine to the domain normally occurs automatically when you request to join the domain. The following steps show one method for joining a Windows 2000 domain.

1. Open the Control Panel and choose Network and Dial-Up Connections. You'll see a Network and Dial-Up Connections dialog like the one shown in Figure 27.1.

2. Use the Advanced, Network Identification command to display the Network Identification tab of the System Properties dialog.

3. Click Properties. You'll see an Identification Changes dialog like the one shown in Figure 27.4.

FIGURE 27.4

The Identification Changes dialog allows you to modify the domain or work-group to which you belong.

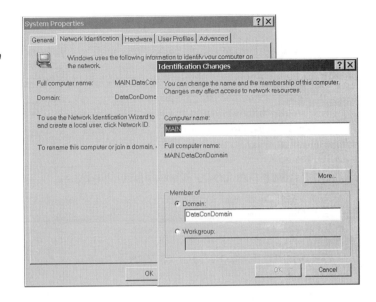

4. Type your computer name into the Computer Name field (if necessary).

5. Choose the Domain option, then type the name of the domain to which you want to belong.

7. Click OK. You should see a message saying Welcome to the whatever domain. Windows 2000 Professional normally doesn't require you to restart your machine. However, you may need to restart your workstation to properly complete the inclusion of the workstation in the domain.

Logon Options

After you've joined a Windows 2000 domain, your logon options change. You'll see that instead of the normal two boxes (Username and Password), a third will appear. This third box contains a list of available domains to log on to. The list of domains will include the name of the Windows NT/2000 Server that you joined and the local computer name. As you join other domains, the list will grow to include those domains.

User authentication is often a big point of confusion for beginners. Authentication is just the process of taking the username and password that's typed into the logon screen and comparing it against a database. In the Windows NT world, this database is the Security Administration Management (SAM) database. When working with a Windows 2000 server, your user and computer information is stored in Active Directory. The act of logging onto the server will look the same from a user perspective no matter which technique your server uses to store the login information.

When you belong to a Windows 2000 domain, you must use the domain account to gain access to server resources. But Windows 2000 gives you the flexibility to log on to the workstation locally, without authenticating against the domain controllers. This will leave you without the ability to connect to network resources, however. The third box on the logon screen controls which security database you wish to log on to. Both the workstation and the server include a security database. Normally, when you're in a domain you'll always use the domain security database; therefore, the third box will have the name of your domain in it. If your network is having problems, you may temporarily want to log on to your local workstation so that you can run MS Word, for example. In these cases, you'd make the third box display the name of your workstation. Notice that because these are two different security databases, you may or may not have a username and password to log on to the local machine. This will all depend on how your system administrator has set up the machines.

Connecting to a NetWare Server

NetWare machines don't include the concept of a domain. Most of the resources are controlled through the application of user rights. Therefore, we don't have the complications of joining a domain.

Preparing to Connect to NetWare

Connecting to a NetWare server is fairly easy under Windows 2000. First, you need a user account to access the NetWare servers, much as you had to do with the Windows 2000 domain. Your network administrator can do this for you. If you're the network administrator, you have to use the NetWare SYSCON utility to add a user if you're using an earlier version of NetWare. Newer versions use the NetWare Directory Services (NDS) utility, NWADMIN, to get the job done. (You can also use the NETADMIN character-mode equivalent from the DOS prompt, but I don't cover that utility in this chapter because the Windows version is easier to use. Note, however, that you must use the Novell Client32 for Windows 2000 to use NWADMIN. NETADMIN is the required choice if you're using the Microsoft Client for NetWare.) All you need to do is follow the instructions provided with your copy of NetWare to add the user account.

Obviously, this is a very brief version of the process you'll follow if you have to do things manually. I think that you'll find that accessing a NetWare server using Windows 2000 is a lot easier than what you went through under Windows 3.x, however. Your selection of NetWare Client (Microsoft's or Novell's) will determine the number of features you get with the connection. NDS support wasn't exactly present when the Microsoft Client first came out, for example, although it has since improved.

> **Note:** Just like any piece of software that you're going to install, you should examine the two NetWare clients and compare features yourself. The decision is largely personal taste, but it'll also depend on the more prominent network operating system as well as the type of applications and services used over the network.

Configuration Using the CSNW Applet

Installing NetWare support on your workstation also adds a new applet to the Control Panel: CSNW. The Client Service for NetWare dialog box (see Figure 27.5) appears when you open this applet. You've probably seen it before; Windows 2000 displays it during the client installation process.

FIGURE 27.5

The Client Service for NetWare dialog. After installing CSNW, you'll see a new Control Panel applet.

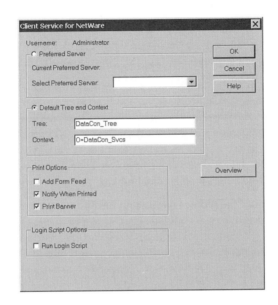

This dialog box contains three sections. The first section defines the way you'll log on to the network. You can choose to look for a specific server or to use the NDS-specific method of tree and context. The second section defines your print options. You decide whether to process a logon script in the third section. I cover the first two issues in this section of the chapter.

Selecting a Logon Method

Let's spend a few moments talking about how you can log on to a server. Obviously, the first method is for systems that use the user database called the bindery. All 3.*x* servers use bindery emulation. You have a choice between bindery emulation and NDS when you install NetWare 4.*x*/5.*x*. (Version 4.*x* doesn't use a bindery, but it can emulate one if necessary.) To exercise this option, specify a preferred server in the Logon dialog box. All Windows 2000 will do is request the nearest server with the name you specify. This is the name that appears when you type an SLIST command at the DOS prompt after making a connection to the file server. Fortunately, this is one of the few commands you can use without actually logging on to the file server.

If your NetWare 4.x/5.x server is set up for NDS, you need to select the second option. In this case, you need to enter the name of a tree and context in the Logon dialog box. The simple view for right now is that the Tree entry defines the server's position in the organization's hierarchy, whereas the Context entry defines how you'll interact with that server.

Defining Your Print Options

Now that we've gotten the logon process out of the way (at least for the moment), let's take a look at the simple Print Options the Client Service for NetWare dialog box provides. You'll need to consider three options: using form feeds, getting print-job-completion notification, and printing a banner.

In most cases, you'll want to disable the Add Form Feed check box. This option sends an extra form feed after a print job completes. Because most applications already do this, you'll just waste paper if you choose it. I used to have DOS applications that stopped printing when the text was complete; they didn't move the paper up to the beginning of the next page for you. It's been a long time since I've seen one of those applications, and I don't remember seeing one at all while working under Windows.

The Notify When Printed check box is pretty handy. Unlike the days of DOS, when your printer was attached to your workstation, networks tend to keep printers in one room. You no longer get auditory or visual cues when your print job is done. This option enables you to continue working until the print job is complete. Then you can go to the printer area to pick it up. This is one of those personal preference options. I normally enable it unless I don't want to be disturbed about a low-priority print job. You'll need to decide whether the interruption is worth it for you.

Network printers also share one other feature that you didn't have in the world of non-networked machines. Everyone on the network shares one or more printers, which means that you're bound to have confusion about print jobs from time to time.

The third print option, Print Banner, is designed to at least partially alleviate this problem. It sends a banner with your name to the printer. Because each print job is separated by a banner page, you can figure out who owns which print job. It's also easy for an assistant to put each person's print job in a mail slot for them to retrieve later. I always enable this option because there isn't any other good way to sort through the chaos otherwise. (This feature is sometimes referred to as a *separator page*.)

> **Tip:** There's a negative side to the Print Banner option: You waste a sheet of paper for each print job. Some environmentally-aware companies might view this as a real waste of trees and an easy way to fill our already overflowing landfills—in a way, it is. The alternative is pretty obvious. In this day of relatively reliable electronic mail, sharing information electronically rather than printing it is probably a better solution. Don't disable this check box if you want to save trees—the confusion just isn't worth it. Whenever, possible, use electronic mail rather than printing.

Logon Scripts

Windows 2000 provides several support mechanisms for logon scripts. Logon scripts are used to make additional settings to the client workstations. Often these are simple mapped drives on servers where the user can store or get information. Logon scripts can get much more complex, however. In either case, it's a great benefit to be able to run logon scripts.

Scripts in a Windows 2000 Domain

Windows 2000 provides basic scripting capabilities by enabling you to write logon scripts using a standard batch file processing familiar to users of DOS. There are no real options to adjust with Windows 2000 scripting; it's just installed when you join a domain. This particular scripting method is a little inflexible. There are alternatives, however. The Windows 2000 Resource Kit contains a toolset named Kix32. This language provides more features that allow for a variety of activities including referencing some valuable Windows APIs. For those UNIX crossovers, PERL scripting is available for Windows 2000 as well. Perhaps the most powerful scripting that has emerged is the Windows Scripting Host (WSH) , which you can download from the Microsoft Web site.

> **Tip:** The Windows Scripting Host is a method for doing some pretty fancy scripting. The Windows Scripting Host is available for install on any Windows 2000 Professional system using wscript.exe (for a windows-based version) or cscript.exe (for a command-prompt version). The advantage of the Scripting Host is that it enables you to write scripts in either VBScript or JavaScript, and it provides an object model for controlling the user environment and the operating system environment. In addition, you can use any installed object with the Windows Scripting Host, including applications like Word that expose their internal object model. You may prefer to launch such scripts from a Novell logon script. With the Scripting Host, you can almost say that you can script anything that Windows 2000 is capable of doing. (For additional information on the Windows 2000 Scripting Host, see Appendix A.)

Logon scripts are routinely used to set up environment variables for other applications, define printers, map network drives, and set the time on workstations against network servers. Scripting, however, is just the beginning of what can happen to your workstation in a Windows 2000 domain. When a workstation logs on to a Windows 2000 domain, it'll go to the nearest domain controller to authenticate the username and password. After your username and password are cleared for access, the system will look on the domain controller's NETLOGON shared directory. It's looking for several items:

- Logon scripts
- Default user profiles
- System Policies

Logon scripts have already been covered. User profiles are used to generate what the interface is going to look like. A user's profile defines the colors he or she sees on the screen, the position of the icons, and a variety of other user preferences. The default user profile on the domain controllers is used to create an environment for a user who has never logged on before. Systems Policies are a very powerful method of controlling the client machines. System Policies are just a collection of Registry entries applied to any workstation that logs on to the domain. The Registry entries generally control what the user can and cannot do on his or her workstation. With System Policies, you can make it so a user can't see his own hard drives or browse the network or even use the command prompt. For more information on these topics, I suggest a good book on Windows 2000 Server administration or Windows 2000 deployment.

NetWare Scripting

Windows 2000 automatically performs scripting when you log on to a Windows 2000 domain. For NetWare, you need to configure the CSNW to make it happen.

> **Tip:** You can reduce your need to use the MAP command (or anything similar) with the persistent mapping capability available by using Explorer or the context menu of My Network Places. I cover the Explorer part of the equation in Chapter 5, "Exploring the Interface." You'll find the My Network Places described in this chapter. Using the native Windows 2000 capability means less chance of error if an individual workstation's configuration changes.

To enable login script processing on the NetWare server, you need to check the Client Service for NetWare dialog box (refer to Figure 27.5). I already covered the basics of this dialog box in previous sections of this chapter, so I won't cover them again here. This dialog box has three functional areas. The one you're interested in is the check box that enables login script processing.

Enabling login script processing enables an administrator to maintain the pre-Windows 2000 security policy on the server. It also provides a means for creating automatic search mapping and other network operating system (NOS) specific features. You'll need to check the documentation that came with your network to see exactly what types of script file processing you can perform.

> **Note:** The system login script for a NetWare server using bindery emulation is stored in NET$LOG.DAT. You'll find it in the \PUBLIC directory. The individual user scripts will appear in their \MAIL directory.

> **Warning:** The Windows 2000 protected-mode script processor can't run TSRs. A TSR is a Terminate and Stay Resident program that runs in memory, waiting for some other event or program to trigger it into action. The TSR will start in a separate virtual machine, which will terminate with an error when the script file processing completes. This lack of TSR processing in your script files means that you'll have to wean yourself from DOS-style backup agents and other files that you normally install using the login script. In most cases, you'll find that Windows 2000 versions of such agents are available.

So, what does a typical NetWare script look like? Figure 27.6 shows one of the bindery emulation mode scripts I've created in the past. I usually keep mine very short and very simple. Remember that you don't need to use drive mappings anymore. Search mappings (essentially, the NetWare form of a path statement) are required. I also leave out the various greeting statements that a lot of administrators included in the past, because the user won't see them anyway. Why waste time processing a statement the user won't really get to see? If you take out the drive mappings, TSRs, and other nonessential statements, you'll end up with something very short and concise. I think you'll find that it's worth the effort to make the change, because the user will see a definite decrease in the amount of time required to log on to the network.

FIGURE 27.6

Sample NetWare script running in bindery emulation mode.

NDS scripts, like the one shown in Figure 27.7, offer a few more opportunities due to their object-oriented nature. You also get a nice Windows GUI interface rather than the DOS utility interface shown in Figure 27.6. Overall, however, you'll see little difference between an NDS and a bindery emulation script, except in syntax.

As you can see, this script provides the same search mapping as the script shown in Figure 27.6. There are some differences, however—some of which shouldn't be there. Novell decided to shorten INSERT to INS, for example, when it created the NDS script commands. I don't like to type any more than the next person, but it would've been nice if Novell had maintained compatible wording for those folks moving from NetWare 3.*x* to 4.*x*. As a result of these little changes, I ended up having to rewrite all of my scripts. Suffice it to say that if you're making the move from 3.*x* to 4.*x*, watch the wording of your scripts. Otherwise, you might get some unexpected results when users run the scripts you've moved from one environment to the other.

FIGURE 27.7
Sample NetWare script, running in NDS.

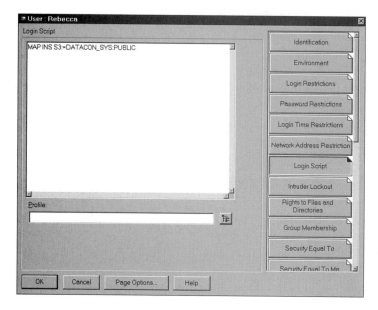

Exploring My Network Places

Now that we have connectivity to our domain, let's see what we can see. To view the network, we'll use a tool called My Network Places (which may not be installed if you don't have a network and don't use dial-up networking either). It sits right on your desktop and can also be seen from within the Windows 2000 Explorer. Let's open a copy of My Network Places. You can do this in one of two ways—much as there are two ways for most of the default icons Windows 2000 provides. The normal double-click method produces a single-pane view like the one shown in Figure 27.8. Figure 27.9 shows the double-paned view you get by pressing Shift while double-clicking the My Network Places icon. I find the second view a bit more helpful when I'm trying to find something. The first view is handy when I know what I'm looking for and need to do something like map a drive.

After you get past the machines that you see on the network, using My Network Places is much like any other Explorer activity. All you need to do is select a machine to view the drives it contains. From that point on, you can go through the directory hierarchy to find the file you need. Unlike Explorer, you don't have to map a drive before you see it in My Network Places. You automatically see all the resources at your disposal.

There's an important consideration here. My Network Places shows only the resources you can access. If you don't see a particular resource listed, it might mean that you don't have access to it. A check with the network administrator will tell you whether you have access to a particular resource.

FIGURE 27.8

The single-paned view of My Network Places provides more space for looking at the network itself.

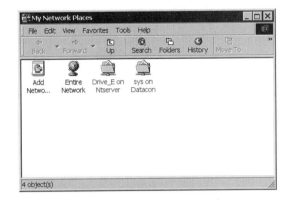

FIGURE 27.9

The double-paned view of My Network Places is great if you need to move around between local and network hard drives.

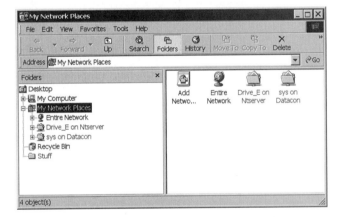

Managing Your NetWare Servers

Let's have a look at the various issues related to running our workstations in a NetWare environment. Integration is still key to the successful deployment of Windows 2000 Professional. The following sections will describe a few of the issues you need to be aware of when working with NetWare. One of the most important of these issues is how the data for your workstation gets stored so that you can access network resources. We'll also see how you can check on the current state of the network to ensure that those resources are actually available. In some cases, you'll use these techniques to manage network resources like printers.

Using Bindery Emulation

What's bindery emulation? Versions of NetWare prior to 4.0 used something called a bindery to store information about the network setup. The bindery contained a list of user names and their rights. In this respect, the bindery is nothing more than a database used by the NetWare operating system. You could compare it to the Registry used by Windows, but the content of the bindery is somewhat different. Think of the bindery as a security element within NetWare and you'll have a better idea of how it actually works.

When NetWare 4.*x* came along, Novell introduced NetWare Directory Services (NDS)—an object-oriented approach to managing network resources. It also introduced something called bindery emulation—a way to make NetWare 4.*x*/5.*x* look like it's using the older bindery rather than NDS. In essence, bindery emulation is a way for people to move from NetWare 3.*x* to 4.*x*/5.*x* with a few less problems. I get more into this topic in the next section. What you need to know for now is why Novell introduced NDS.

The bindery has more than a few limitations. It's machine-specific, for example. If you add a user to one file server, that user doesn't automatically appear on any other file server; you have to manually add him at each file server. NDS provides a global approach to network management: One utility enables you to view the entire network and add users with ease. Another problem is that the bindery requires special backup procedures. Even though Novell took great pains to protect the bindery from damage, the user still needs a backup copy for those times when damage does occur. There isn't anything the operating system can do about a failed hard drive, for example; you have to replace it, and then restore the bindery to reproduce your configuration. I'm not going to discuss every flaw in the bindery here; suffice it to say that NDS introduces some features that definitely make life easier for the network administrator.

Still, the bindery is a viable way to go for smaller businesses. If you have only one file server, adding users under bindery emulation isn't any more difficult than adding them with NDS. I also find that the earlier versions of NetWare are easier to understand from a user perspective—especially if those users moved from DOS to Windows over the past few years. Under bindery emulation, you log on to a file server without much more than your name and a password. NDS introduces some twists that some users find difficult, if not impossible, to get around. (One of the most common problems I've run into is trying to explain what a context is. I talk more about this topic in the next section.)

Peter's Principle: Between Procedures and Objects: Making the Bindery-Versus-NDS Choice

Technology is change—there isn't any doubt about it. I can even say that it doesn't always mean a change for the better, but it always involves change of some kind. A lot of programmers I know of fought the upgrade from C to C++ a few years ago. They saw C++ as a change for the worse because the programmer lost a little more contact with the hardware. On the other hand, proponents of C++ see it as a more natural way to write applications. Even though C++ offers a lot in the way of features, some programmers stuck with the older procedural language. The problem isn't one of shortsightedness, but of personal comfort. These folks felt very comfortable in the world of procedural languages, and the idea of moving to the world of object-oriented programming (OOP) scared them.

If programmers can run into difficulty when it comes to change, it's no wonder that the users of the products they create can run into the same problem. NDS represents a move from the world of the familiar DOS prompt to a new one that uses object-oriented technology. All those DOS utilities use a procedural approach to managing the network. Using NDS means learning a new way of doing things, and that makes some folks feel uncomfortable. When you use the DOS utilities, you see things in relation to the hardware. Likewise, using NDS means taking a real-world approach to viewing the network—one in which the hardware is a means to an end.

So what's the connection here? C++ and NDS both offer an object-oriented view of the computer world. Think about it this way: You deal with objects every day in the real world. Most people have an answering machine. Calls come in, it answers, takes a message, and plays it back to you. The answering machine is an object. Objects are said to have three *members*: properties, events and methods. Among this object's properties are the number of messages, length of recording time permitted, or the number of rings to answer on. This object will respond to events, such as a ring on the line or a button press to which it responds by playing a message.

The answering machine object will also have actions it may perform, called its *methods*, like playing back messages, deleting messages, or saving messages for later retrieval. You know that you're doing these things, but just how these things are accomplished on a low level inside the machine (the object) isn't important to you. Likewise, object-oriented technology helps you think about the computer in terms of the real world. You know that you have users, work-stations, servers, printers, and other resources. What you're really concerned about is the way that these various network elements interact with each other, not the process for allowing them to do so. A user has certain rights, and you need to know certain things about him, such as his location, name, and tele-phone number. All these things are the user's properties. How exactly the user may modify these network-related properties is determined by certain pre-established methods. You might decide that he could change his own password, but not anyone else's, for example. When a user does interact with the net-work—say, to log on—it's an event. NDS provides utilities for monitoring those events in a real-world way that makes a lot more sense than some of the audit-ing utilities you used at the DOS prompt.

NDS provides such a real-world view of the network—a view that corresponds to your spontaneous natural perception of the world. To gain the efficiency, knowledge, and other benefits of a real-world view, you need to give up a little comfort and learn a new way of doing things. I think it's worth it. Using bindery emulation when you have NDS available is like listening to all your mes-sages on the answering machine and writing them down on paper. NDS is your doorway to a new world of network management in which everything is pre-sented in terms that you can really understand.

For right now, let's take a look at some of the utilities that earlier versions of NetWare (pre-4.x) provide. I'm not going to give you a complete list of every utility because some of them aren't all that useful under Windows 2000. What I want to do is make you aware of them so that you can use the full capabilities of the file server. What I'm really giving you is a whirlwind tour of NetWare 3.x utilities. Make sure that you spend some time with the documentation, learning about their full capabilities.

Checking the File Server Status

Because the file server is the central core of everything you do on the network, it pays to know how to check it. There are two utilities that can get the current file server status: FCONSOLE and RCONSOLE. Each utility serves a different purpose under NetWare.

FCONSOLE enables you to view the file server status, but doesn't let you do much with it except shut it down. You can also use this utility to broadcast messages to workstations on the network. Figure 27.10 shows its main screen. Notice that there are actually two message-broadcasting options. You can choose to send a message to all the workstations on the network by using the Broadcast Console Message option, or you can send it to an individual by using the Connection Information option. You can also use the Connection Information option to view user specifics, such as network addresses and logon times.

FIGURE 27.10

Viewing file server status with the FCONSOLE *tool.*

The Status option of FCONSOLE enables you to determine the current file server time and date. You can also use it to enable or disable logons and transaction tracking. Disabling logons enables you to keep users out while you perform file server maintenance. The Version Information option tells you which version of NetWare you're using and how many users it supports.

Before you can use RCONSOLE, you have to load the RSPX.NLM at the file server console. This loads the required protocol drivers and interface module (REMOTE.NLM). After you load the file server console, you can load RCONSOLE. Figure 27.11 shows what the initial RCONSOLE display looks like. All you need to do is select one of the servers in the list and type a password. What you'll see next is the same thing you'd see if you were working at the file server console itself. You can load and unload NetWare loadable modules (NLMs) and use the MONITOR.NLM to check the complete status of your file server. If you don't see the server you want, make sure that you've loaded both RSPX.NLM and REMOTE.NLM at the file server console.

FIGURE 27.11
Using RCONSOLE *to administer NetWare servers.*

Using NetWare Directory Services (NDS)

The preceding section covered a lot of information about the command-line utilities NetWare provides, so I won't go through them again here. NetWare 4.*x*/5.*x* provides a lot more in the way of user aids than just command-line utilities, however. The big news, as far as I'm concerned, is the centralized management you get with NWADMIN.

Figure 27.12 shows what the NWADMIN utility looks like when you first open it. You'll see a list of network objects, including users, servers, groups, printers, and just about any other kind of organizational unit you can think of. You can even create an organizational hierarchy based on your company's current structure by adding departments. This figure shows an extremely simple layout; obviously, NDS is capable of a lot more than I'm showing you.

FIGURE 27.12
Using the NWADMIN *utility to manage NDS servers.*

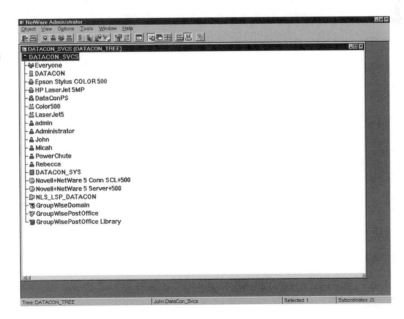

Peter's Principle: Keeping Console Commands Handy

It's pretty likely that if you're an administrator for a small network, you'll end up wearing several hats. Someone who only has to work on the network on an occasional basis might find it easy to forget all those long-winded console commands that Novell provides.

Very few people realize that you can create console batch files—just like the ones you use with DOS on your workstation. The difference is that you use an .NCF extension in place of the normal .BAT extension.

Suppose that you have a problem remembering the TRACK ON and TRACK OFF commands. Just stick them in a batch file and use a name you'll remember. When you need to use TRACK ON, just type the name of your batch file at the console prompt, and—voilà—you'll see the results onscreen.

You can make the batch files as long as needed and even display comments onscreen by using the ECHO command. The only requirement for using batch files under NetWare is that you place them in the SYS:SYSTEM directory to make sure they're always accessible.

It won't take you long to figure out that NWADMIN replaces all the old DOS utilities people used to use with one centralized management environment. Obviously, it replaces SYSCON and FILER without any problem; a simple glance shows that. Not so noticeable in Figure 27.12 is that it also replaces all your print-oriented utilities and enables you to monitor everything on the network with relative ease—although not in the way as the Windows 2000 monitoring tools I cover in Chapter 7, "Performance Power."

That brings me to what Windows 2000 4.x doesn't include. You won't find a graphics version of the RCONSOLE utility. Even though you'll find a menu entry for it in NWADMIN, RCONSOLE is still a DOS application that requires a DOS window to run in. You'll also find that NetWare 4.x/5.x is lacking the FCONSOLE utility, but let's face the fact that this utility was getting pretty close to useless in the 3.x version. It certainly didn't provide the functionality the 2.x version of FCONSOLE did, and for good reason—there are other ways for a network administrator to gain access to the file server console.

As with most good Windows products these days, NWADMIN provides a wealth of alternatives to using traditional menu-bar menus. Figure 27.13, for example, shows the context menu you'll see for most of the objects you can create with NWADMIN. This menu contains only six entries, but they provide access to most of the things you'll need to do within NWADMIN.

The NWADMIN context menu offers these options:

- **Details**   Displays a dialog box that contains a set of buttons on the right and the properties associated with the object on the left. You use this option to set up logon scripts and security for a user. It also includes user location and contact information.

FIGURE 27.13
Context menu for objects created with NWADMIN.

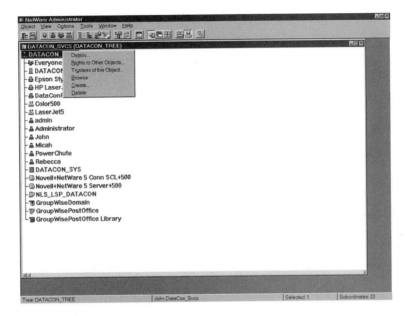

- **Rights to Other Objects** Displays a dialog box in which you can learn about the rights this object has to use or modify other objects. Remember that an object can include everything from a volume on the file server to a printer attached to a print server. It can also include nonphysical network objects, such as an organizational element or organizational role (a manager, for example).

- **Trustees of This Object** Lists the people or groups that can access and manipulate a particular object. Selecting a particular entry in the list tells you that person's rights and what he can do with the object.

- **Browse** Some objects within NWADMIN are containers for other objects. An organizational unit falls into this category, for example. The Browse option enables you to view the contents of a particular container object. Unlike when you double-click the object to expand the tree, however, you'll see the contents of the object in a separate window. I find that this feature comes in very handy when I need to view both the details of the NDS structure and the details of particular objects. All I need to do is minimize the Object Browse window until I actually need to see it.

- **Create** Any object that acts as a container also enables you to create objects to place within it. Choosing this option displays a dialog box containing a list of the object types the object container can hold.

- **Delete** Removes the current object. Be very careful when you use this option, because it also removes any objects the current object holds. If you delete an organizational unit, for example, you'll also remove all the users within that unit.

There are two DOS utilities that I would like to make you aware of. The first is NETUSER. The initial screen for this program appears in Figure 27.14. This is a user-oriented tool designed to make NetWare easier to work with. Most of the menu options are pretty obvious. The Printing option, for example, displays a list of printer ports and tells you whether they're local or captured to a network port. You can use the Messages option to turn broadcast messages on or off. It also enables you to send messages of your own to other users. The Drives option enables you to see your drive and search mappings.

FIGURE 27.14

Using NETUSER to manager users.

Things get a bit more complicated when you use the Attachments option. It displays a list of all the servers you're connected to. Each server provides the same list of configuration options. All you need to do is highlight a server and press Enter to see a list containing the option's login script, password, and server information. Each user is allowed to modify his own login script. You used to find this functionality in SYSCON. The same holds true for the Password entry, which enables you to change your password for that server. The Server Information screen replaces the one you used to find in FCONSOLE.

The last option is Change Context—the entry that confuses most users. Remember that NDS uses an object-oriented approach to management, so you have to provide it with a bit more information about your location within the structure on NDS. A context is where you're at in the hierarchy of the NDS tree. If your organization name is ABC_CORP and you're in the Editorial department, for example, your context might be Joe.Editorial.ABC_Corp. If you want to change your context—your location within the tree—to Sales, you might type Joe.Sales.ABC_Corp. Changing your context often means a change in the rights you have. A network administrator may choose to give you several contexts to reduce the amount of network traffic or to make it easier for you to navigate the network. Remember the view in Figure 27.12 when you think about what you need to type here. Each node on the tree begins with a dot (.), except for your name. All you need to do is trace your position in the tree, starting with your name, and type each node name as you go up to the root (the beginning of the tree). Obviously, you have to have more than one entry on the tree to be able to change contexts.

Let's take a look at the last utility: NLIST. This is a command-line program that enables you to list network resources like your current server or context. Figure 27.15 shows an example of the output from this utility. In this case, I displayed a list of users. You can also use this utility to display a list of groups, servers, printers, and other network resources.

FIGURE 27.15

Using the NLIST *utility to view network resources.*

```
Z:\PUBLIC>NLIST USER
Object Class: User
Current context: DataCon
User name= The name of the user
Dis      = Login disabled
Log exp  = The login expiration date, 0 if no expiration date
Pwd      = Yes if passwords are required
Pwd exp  = The password expiration date, 0 if no expiration date
Uni      = Yes if unique passwords are required
Min      = The minimum password length, 0 if no minimum

User Name                              Dis  Log Exp Pwd  Pwd Exp Uni Min
-------------------------------------------------------------------------
Admin                                  No   0-00-00 Yes  3-28-96 Yes 10
John                                   No   0-00-00 Yes  3-28-96 Yes 10
Rebecca                                No   0-00-00 Yes  3-28-96 Yes 10
A total of 3 User objects was found in this context.

A total of 3 User objects was found.

Z:\PUBLIC>
Z:\PUBLIC>
```

On Your Own

If you can, get a machine that's part of a domain and one that isn't. Look at the various logon differences and behavioral differences between the machines. If you're in a domain, try to log on to your local workstation using your domain username and password. See whether you can think through the response that you get and understand why it happened that way.

Windows 2000 is designed to work well with Novell NetWare. If you're attached to a NetWare server, spend some time learning about the utilities that are available for working with this product. Most important of all, if you're working with an NDS system, is the NWADMIN utility. Becoming familiar with this utility is an essential part of your networking experience.

Try using some of the NetWare-specific command-line utilities. NLIST in particular, can help you understand your rights on the NetWare server.

Use the native capabilities of Windows 2000 to avoid mapping drives through scripts. On the other hand, it does pay to become familiar with the scripting capabilities of both Windows 2000 and NetWare because these scripts can automate a lot of your networking tasks. Try creating some scripts that make it easier to get started when you log into the system.

WSH represents a vast untapped scripting resource that you can use to automate all kinds of tasks, not just those associated with the network. Spend some time learning how to use this relatively new product to automate a variety of tasks. See Appendix A.

Peter Norton | **28**

Security Issues

Security is a major thorn in most network administrators' sides. Even a small network with just a couple of servers requires some level of security planning, yet many managers fail to see the value of implementing the type of security they really need. Of course, I have seen the opposite side of the coin as well. Some administrators wrap the people who use the network systems in a tight cocoon of regulations and passwords. The chokehold on these people inhibits creative resource management and often impedes work as well.

This chapter covers many aspects of server security, but not so much on the topics of network or Internet security. Much of the planning and methodology that we use for our server systems will be applicable to network security as well. There are, however, entire books on the topic of security planning, network infrastructures, router configurations, and application firewalls. Here we stick mostly to securing servers.

It's difficult to create a bulletproof server setup that offers the level of flexibility most companies require. Adding a bit of flexibility normally means that you simultaneously open a security hole as a direct result. I find that a network administrator must reach an important balance. The first thing you need to realize is that there's no such thing as a bulletproof security system. There's always someone out there who has figured out (or will figure out) a way to access a system to which most people would not be able to gain access. Often the person's success has less to do with technical prowess than it does with having a refined understanding of how people behave and think, as you'll see shortly.

More important than physical security and password protection is the cooperation of those around you. I recently went into a client's office to check on their network setup. They enabled me to use one employee's desk to get the work done. Right in front of me was one of those yellow reminder pads. It contained not only the employee's password but his manager's password as well. Anyone could have just walked into the office and gained access to network systems because of this security breach.

This incident reminded me of the importance of the human factor in any security plan. You should take into account what users need to accomplish in their day-to-day work, as well as considering the inconvenience security will often cause users (and you, too). However, this human factor is just one of the issues you should think about when developing a security plan. Consider the following elements:

- **Physical security**—Place your file server in a locked room. I can easily break the security for a NetWare or Windows 2000 setup (or most other networks, for that matter) if I have access to a running file server. If you lock up the file server, I can't access it unless I have a key to the door.

- **Software protection**—Using passwords and other forms of software protection is your next line of defense. Make sure that all the right kinds of security measures are in place. I cover this particular topic in greater detail later, but this is one area where Windows 2000 can really help. It contains all the right features; all you need to do is implement them.

- **Cooperative security**—You can't secure the network by yourself. The larger your network, the more you'll need every user's cooperation. If you expect the users to cooperate with you, you'll need to actually talk to them and find out what's reasonable given their real-world, daily work activities. No one will use an unreasonable security plan. This cooperative strategy also extends to management. If you don't talk to management and tell them what your security problems are, they can't help. You also need to make sure management knows what kinds of security risks are present in the current setup. This reduces the chance of someone getting surprised later.

- **Training**—It's never a good idea to assume that users know how to use the security features Windows 2000 provides. With Windows 2000, you have a lot of choices in regards to security. You'll need to consider which security features to leave to the users' discretion and which to mandate. In any case, the users will not only need to be well informed about how to use the security features of their workstations but also about why they should go to the trouble.

- **A written security plan**—Even a small written plan is beneficial. At the very least, you can use it as a reminder of how you wanted to configure your network and systems. Besides, little networks often grow into big networks. As your network becomes larger, it becomes vitally important to get the rules down in writing. Otherwise, how will a user know what's expected or how to react in a crisis? Writing down everything will also make management aware of the security you have put into place. In addition, you can use the process of putting your security procedures down in print to test them and look for any problem areas before they occur.

This might seem like a lot of preliminary work to implement security, but it isn't when you consider the loss that a single security breach can cause. A pirate isn't going to steal last week's press release to the general public; he or she is going to steal something valuable and private. The more secret something is, the better the pirate likes it. Just think about what a competitor could do with your new marketing plan or the design for that new widget you plan to produce.

What's more, some pirates don't take anything. Rather, they leave something behind. What would a virus do to your network? It doesn't take too much thought to imagine your entire setup prone in feverish collapse as a virus infects it.

The next section of this chapter addresses network and systems security in the broad scheme of things. In other words, it actually goes a little beyond what you would need to implement in Windows 2000 itself. I'm including it because security needs to be cohesive. You can't create separate little security groups on a network. The entire network must be organized in a consolidated plan to ensure that your security net is consistent and that there aren't any holes in it. Anything less is an open invitation to whomever would like to circumvent your security.

After we get past these general guidelines, I show you the features Windows 2000 provides to help you implement a company-wide plan. We've looked at many of these features already, so I won't go into a lot of detail in some areas. (I tell you where the detailed information does appear in this book, however.) Even if you're running a small network, you'll want to read both sections. The first section tells you what to implement and the second tells you how to do it.

I'm also going to introduce you to a lot of theoretical areas of Windows 2000 security. There's a lot going on under the surface in the way of security, and it helps to know about some aspects of it. I'm not going to go into bits and bytes—that's the realm of programmers. What I do want to tell you about is the process Windows 2000 goes through to make your system secure. You could probably skip this section if it becomes too technical for you, but try to read as much as possible so that you have a complete understanding of how Windows 2000 works.

Creating a Security Plan

To run a network efficiently, you need to have a plan. Ad hoc solutions to any problem are just that: *ad hoc*. They won't go very far in helping you plug a security leak. Without a plan, you won't know what your security goals are or what steps you need to take to meet them. The problem that most administrators face is that they really aren't sure what goals a security plan helps them achieve. Figuring out what a security plan does for you is almost as important as creating it.

A security plan helps you achieve at least the following five goals:

- A security plan helps you define and organize your security system into manageable pieces. Divide and conquer is the technique used by many generals to win a war. Instead of trying to fight an entire army of problems by working on them all at the same time, take them on one at a time. You can win the war against security leaks by using this tried-and-true strategy. A network security plan is the map that shows you where to break the problem into smaller pieces.

- Most networks have security problems from time to time. An old employee leaves and a new one comes in, thus creating a potential gap in your security net. Someone gets promoted and you need to extend his or her rights on the network. Will that person know how to handle these new responsibilities if you don't provide any training? What about when people get transferred from one department to another? Do you really want them to have access to both departments' data? And as the network administrator, you might not even know that these problems exist. What if a manager inadvertently gives someone rights to a sensitive folder? One way to find problem areas quickly is to compare the current network state with a baseline state for that network. A network security plan can provide that baseline. It captures the network's ideal state rather than its current state.

- If you're like most administrators, users constantly ask why you implement one procedure over another. They might want to legitimately increase their freedom on the network. (Some users equate increased freedom with increased productivity— an inaccurate assumption on a properly designed network.) So how do you answer these questions? A network security plan can provide a historical context that tells why you implemented a specific procedure or network rule. Recording a rule and why you implemented it often helps you keep the network security plan up-to-date. Keeping old rules without any real reason is counterproductive. On the other hand, too much freedom is an invitation to security problems.

- You might find that the goals of management and the network's users don't reflect your goals as the network administrator. A network security plan provides an opportunity for you to express these differences. It also provides the means to discuss reasonable alternatives and compromises. Arguing a particular course of action after you study the ramifications of that action is the only way to create a network that everyone will enjoy using. Rules based on knowledge rather than personal feelings are the best way to later ensure that you know why the rule is in place.

- Evenhanded administration of the network means that you enforce the network rules the same way each time someone breaks them. Some network operating systems (NOS) even provide you with the tools required to detect security breaches in your system. (NetWare provides the Security utility for this purpose, for example.) It also means that you explain the rules the same way to everyone who uses the network. Unless you write down the rules, someone could legitimately say that you're biased toward certain network users or that you make arbitrary decisions regarding some infractions. Clearly written rules alleviate this problem by making the rules, the implementations, any penalties, and their historical context clear to everyone.

Tip: A small company doesn't necessarily need a formal written security plan. However, a simple plain-English statement of what you want security to be like on your little network is very beneficial. You should at least think these issues through before you start setting up Windows 2000, however. A peer-to-peer network needs some type of security plan, too. Trying to implement a security plan after installation is fine, but it will probably cost you extra time. Just as you plan your installation in advance, take the time to consider the security needs of your network, too.

As you can see, a properly designed and implemented security plan can change the way everyone views the network. There's always a group of people who fail to understand that a security problem on the network costs everyone money. A security plan can handle this situation as well. Even if some users don't agree with the implementation of a security feature, they won't want to face any penalties management assigns for failure to follow the rules. Of course, this is the last course of action you want to take. Assigning a penalty might show that a user failed to follow the rules, but it also shows that your plan failed to work in this instance. It's unlikely that you'll ever create a plan that everyone agrees with and no one disobeys, but getting as close as possible to this ideal is the goal. The following paragraphs provide more details about designing and implementing a security plan for your company.

Breaking the Company into Groups

Many companies use a combination of workgroups and a client/server architecture. The workgroup might use Windows 2000 to implement a small peer-to-peer network just for the people in that group. The client/server network might use NetWare or some other NOS. Networks allow the company to communicate as a whole.

Whether your company uses several small networks or just has everyone log on to one file server, you'll need to break a large network into smaller pieces before you create a security plan. This helps you organize your company into functional security areas. By breaking the security task into smaller pieces, you can reduce the overall complexity involved in making your system secure. There are many ways to break the problem into smaller pieces, and you'll probably need to employ more than one of them. The following list provides you with some ideas on how to accomplish this task:

- **Department/workgroup**—Because users who work together are apt to require similar access to the network, you can easily break the company into groups along this natural line. People working in software development, for example, are unlikely to require access to financial records. Similarly, the company's accountants won't require access to source code. This is the best way to go if your company already uses peer-to-peer networks to connect small workgroups.

> **Tip:** Always assign someone to manage every workgroup on the network if you have more than one. Let this person take care of some security details by enabling her or him to assign access for the local workgroup resources. It might also be a good idea to assign someone from the group to manage the print server if the group has one with more than one printer attached. You can't take the time to see to every networking detail, especially when a network starts to grow beyond 100 or so workstations. It'll take a lot of time just to keep the network applications current, keep the workstations up and running, and attend to the myriad other details a network administrator needs to worry about. Making someone in the local workgroup responsible not only reduces your workload but also helps keep any security measures in place.

- **Seniority/longevity**—Some companies assign tasks based on a person's seniority. When a manager leaves town for a few days to attend a convention, for example, she might assign the senior employee in that section to act in her stead. You might need to give that employee access to certain managerial areas of the network to enable her to perform these duties. Even though she doesn't need to have access to these areas as a result of a departmental or workgroup affiliation, she needs to have them as a substitute manager. As with many security considerations, this scenario is an exception to the rule.

- **Job function**—Another natural way to break the company into groups is by job function. Management might have one area set aside on the network for managers, for example. Another area might contain information of vital importance to people who maintain print servers on the network. A supervisor might require access to an area set aside for all the supervisors in the company. As you can see, some of these job-function areas cross department and workgroup lines.

- **Special designation**—Some companies give individuals special designations. You might have a person on staff who wears more than one hat, for example. He might require access to records from more than one department. You might need to accommodate the needs of a consultant from time to time as well. All these people fall outside the normal security boundaries. You need to list these special considerations.

> **Tip:** It's easy to get confused about the ways you need to split your company's various security needs into manageable pieces. Think of a workgroup in terms of a group of people working together on a single project. This is a key concept, because these people don't necessarily have to come from the same department to be in the same workgroup. Think of security groups as people with similar security levels. You can assign a person to more than one group. A person can be part of the engineering workgroup but also part of the managerial security group, for example. These ideas are separate, and you need to consider them separately.

Security Plan Considerations

After you divide a company into functional groups, it's a good idea to figure out the security needs for each group. Accounting will probably need more stringent security than someone who takes care of the company's correspondence. Sometimes you might be able to get by with read-only access for the accounting group. Usually no one would need to edit last year's accounting records, for example, but someone might need to refer to them.

You might need extra flexibility in an engineering division to promote the flow of ideas from one person to another. One engineer might have one piece of the puzzle, and that piece could trigger someone else's creative abilities to come up with yet another piece.

Inhibiting an engineer with a straitjacket of rules is never a good idea. A management group will need very tight security but will also need the maximum level of access within the group. You can provide management with a straitjacket and actually expect that they will use it. Hopefully, a manager will understand the need for tight security when discussing the company's future plans.

Besides these considerations, you need to think about special security items within your company. You'll also want to start implementing your security plan. The following steps will help you with both processes. They help you complete a security plan and present some additional ideas that you should consider as you implement it:

1. **Assess company tasks**—Even if you do a perfect job of identifying all the groups in your company, you might find that there are still a few tasks the company must perform that fall outside the purview of a group. In many cases, more than one group performs these tasks. Creating an end-of-year report, for example, might require the efforts of several departments in the company. Because this isn't a task the company performs every day, there's no need to create a special group to do it. You do need to consider this type of task when you create your security plan, however. Other examples of task-related groups include special committees and research groups. In this case, several specialists get together to work on a specific problem or idea.

2. **Appoint each person to one or more groups**—After you break the company into groups and decide what major additional tasks the company needs to perform, it's time to assign people to them. The finance group maintains accounting records, for example, and the personnel group maintains employee records. In many cases, the assignments you need to make are very straightforward. It's easy to see that everyone in the accounting department will easily fit within the financial group. There are some assignments you might not think about at first, however. You might have someone in personnel who needs assignment to both the financial and the personnel groups, for example. She might need to make entries into the financial program regarding employee raises or terminations.

3. **Brainstorm special user needs**—Other ways to look at your company's security needs are not merely organizational. Breaking the company into physical and logical units is fine for most security needs. Doing so enables the network administrator to work with both management and network users to make reasonable security assignments based on fact. In some situations, a lack of information prevents you from making reasonable assignments. What if a group is just starting a new project, for example? They may not know what type of access they'll require on the network because they have never tried to perform that task before. The manager might have a reasonable idea of what type of access the users require, but this is mere conjecture. You'll find yourself at a loss to make a reasonable assignment without more information. Unless you want to spend a lot of time retuning your network to compensate for these situations, you might want to first take the time to brainstorm the users' needs.

I would like to look at that third step in more detail. It's the last one you need to complete your security plan. After you do figure out special user needs, you have all the information required to make the plan work. Brainstorming is a think-tank approach to network management. It's a tried-and-true method used in many other ventures. Essentially, you define a task based on past knowledge of similar tasks and on future goals. You answer questions such as, "What do we plan to achieve?" and "How do we plan to achieve these goals?" You must consider what tools you have available on your network to get the job done. This includes both hardware and software resources. You should also throw out ideas for consideration. Someone might need to play the part of devil's advocate to make sure you consider both the positive and negative aspects of a particular decision. Of course, you want to use this approach only if there's insufficient information on which to base a decision using standard techniques. You can take a number of steps to make this process work properly:

1. **Break the user's task into logical elements**—What types of applications does the user need to use, for example? Each application involves a different set of security rights. Perhaps one or more groups already provide these rights on the network. Whenever possible, try to avoid making nongroup assignments. Nongroup assignment will tend to disrupt overall organization of accounts and user rights. Even in a small network, the assignments of rights and permissions—who can do what and where—can become unwieldy very quickly. When you don't have control of users' and user rights, you don't have control of the servers and their resources.

2. **Create a list of equipment the user needs to access**—Does the user need to use a fax or a special printer, for example? If the security system on the network limits access to these items, you might need to provide the user with the special access required to use them.

3. **Write down a list of tasks the user needs to perform**—Sometimes you'll see a special application or a piece of equipment the user will need to use to accomplish a task. Make sure you don't just list these tasks. Describe the tasks so that everyone is talking about the same task.

4. **Look for areas where the user might have too much access**—After you figure out where the user might need access, trim your list to areas where the user must have access to get the job done. There's no reason to give someone too much network access just because he or she is starting a new project.

As you can see, brainstorming a task can really help in a situation where you lack the information needed to make a good decision using just the available facts. You need to realize that your group bases such decisions on conjecture and derived information. Keep in touch with the users as they get further into the project. You might find that you can reduce access in some areas and that a user requires additional access in other areas. (Users normally will tell you when they don't have enough access, but seldom will they tell you if they have too much access.) Remember that it's your responsibility to make sure that the user has enough access, but not too much. Some users will try to convince you that they need additional rights to certain areas when they really don't. This isn't necessarily deception on their part: they might merely, and sincerely, anticipate that they'll need wider access than is actually the case.

Peter's Principle: Delegating Network Administration Tasks

You've installed your network and all the Windows 2000 workgroups are in place. So why are you still running around like the proverbial headless chicken? Windows 2000 provides a lot of tools to help the administrator manage a network. You learned in Chapter 24, "Peer-to-Peer Networking," that these tools pertain not only to Windows 2000 peer-to-peer installations but to other types of networks as well. You can install agents to monitor the status of a workstation remotely or through a local host. You can use all kinds of connections to get a bird's-eye view of your network. Yet, even with all these aids, you feel out of touch and barely able to maintain the system.

Some network administrators are under the impression that they can maintain the entire network themselves given enough time and tools to do the job. The truth is that only Superman (or Wonder Woman) can fulfill all the needs of some networks. This includes the area of network security. You might find that you require help to maintain a large network. How much help you need and what size of network can be defined as "large" are primarily matters of network complexity and whether you're a full-time network administrator. If management gives you a few hours each day to perform network duties and you wear another hat for the rest of the day, as few as 20 users could be considered a large network. Even a full-time administrator will begin to feel the pinch at around 100 users, especially if the company performs a wide variety of tasks with a conglomeration of equipment.

A few problems can arise when you allow other people to help you maintain network security. Centralized control of the network for security purposes is a real advantage. If one person is responsible to management for ensuring that network security remains high, there's little possibility that he or she will do a halfhearted job. In addition, centralized control means that fewer problems will slip through the cracks. Users will never wonder who they should ask for more rights on the network. They'll always know the one person who can help them.

I always follow a simple principle when it comes to network security: Always maintain control. When you can't maintain control, find out why. You might find that it's a problem with another administrator who is overwhelmed with requests for service and little time to really take care of the network. Don't kill the security plan that you worked so hard to create. Instead, give the network administrator sufficient help to get the job done.

Windows 2000 Security Basics

Now that you have an idea of what you want to do and how you would go about writing it down, let's see how Windows 2000 can assist you in implementing security measures. First, you must become familiar with the Windows 2000 security model. Then we'll move on to the next sections and discuss the details of actually applying security measures.

The Windows 2000 Security Model

The Windows 2000 security model is based on what is called *user-level security*, meaning that you assign permissions to files and even permission to perform certain actions, based on the user's account. This is a big departure from Windows for Workgroups and Windows 95/98. Windows 95/98 uses what is called *share-level security*. (This applies to peer-to-peer networking; if you're connected to a server you can use what's called user-level security). Share-level security focuses on shared directories and printers. As long as you have the password for the share, you can get in no matter who you are. A share is a folder or printer that has been configured for use over the network. Users can connect to the shared resource and utilize its contents or functionality. Also notice that on the Windows 2000 Professional logon screen there's no way to click a Cancel button that will give you local access to the machine. In Windows 95/98, if you click Cancel, you're allowed access to the machine (so much for security there). So what does all this get you with Windows 2000? Flexibility, tighter security, but increased complexity.

Let's examine this security model a little more closely. In any type of security system, computer or otherwise, you must have a key or token and a door protecting the room were your precious items are stored. Let's say, for example, you are a secret agent working with a super-secret agency. To get to headquarters, you must pass through a series of doors. Each door has an electronic card reader next to it. You must have your secret agent encoded card to open the doors within headquarters. As you approach each door, you swipe your card through the reader. Beep, whoosh, the doors open. If your card doesn't work, you don't get in.

This is essentially how Windows 2000 security is handled. When you log on to a Windows 2000 system, you supply a username and password. The authentication process is accomplished in two stages. First you request the logon; then your request is processed during a network authentication phase.

If you have a local computer account, the first thing that happens after you log on is that a local security account database—the Security Accounts Manager (SAM)—checks your logon data against its database. Both member servers and workstations can be used this way, but access is permitted only to the single machine where the user logs on.

If you have a domain account, the process differs. You enter your password (or swipe a smart card—a card with magnetic information stored in it) and it's compared to the sign-on credentials stored in the Windows 2000 Active Directory. If the logon succeeds, you get access to the domain and any other trusting domains.

Windows 2000 uses the Kerberos security system rather than the proprietary system that was used in NT 4. Kerberos is an Internet security protocol. One result is that passwords are not sent across the network in their plain, unscrambled form (the way you entered them during logon). Instead, passwords are first encrypted. This provides an added layer of security.

If you log on to a domain account with a password, the Kerberos system is employed to authenticate you. If you log on using a smart card, the Kerberos authentication with certificates process is used.

Following a successful logon, network authentication then verifies you to any network service that you try to employ. Windows 2000 supports a variety of network authentication technologies—for backward compatibility as well as flexibility. Supported technologies include Secure Socket Layer/Transport Layer Security (SSL/TLS), LAN Manager, and the new Kerberos V5 system.

Most of the objects in Windows 2000 can have security information called Access Control Entries (ACE) attached to them. Each ACE contains a list of users allowed to access the object and exactly what they're allowed to do (just read it, both read and edit it, or whatever).

A collection of ACEs is called an *Access Control List* (ACL). This whole process is generally called *discretionary access control*. This means that each object has an owner and that each object on Windows 2000 can have an ACL that will allow or disallow user access based on a process token.

The access token is more than just a name and a serial number; it describes a collection of a user's rights, abilities, and group memberships. ACLs are set based on the individual users or groups.

Now that you have some background, let's look at how to create users and groups, assign users to groups, and create the file/folder ACLs to govern access.

Managing User Accounts

Recall that the user gets assigned an access token when he or she logs on to the Windows 2000 system. Before the user can even log on to Windows 2000, however, he or she needs an account. Here we look at creating user accounts and groups. Our discussion expands on the summary topics of the previous section. More than just access tokens for shares and files, user accounts define the abilities and the rights that a person will have while on your workstation or network servers. You'll need administrator-level rights (permissions) to really use this section of the chapter because most user configuration options require it.

Let's start with a new security feature that beefs up the traditional NT security measures. We'll begin our detailed investigation of Windows 2000 security measures with WMI (Windows Management Instrumentation) security—an added layer of security beyond the basic operating system security features. Then we'll go on to review the more familiar, traditional security model.

The new WMI snap-in is used to let administrators configure WMI settings on either a local or remote machine. WMI allows you to authorize or set permission levels for either users or groups. You can even authorize persons to have control over WMI tasks and services themselves. Also use WMI to specify error logging (report errors only or the verbose alternative of reporting all actions). There is a repository available to WMI—a database containing all the objects that can be manipulated via WMI. The backup policy of the repository is something you can define.

Here's how to use WMI to add an existing user to a group: Open the Control Panel, Administrative Tools, Computer Management, as shown in Figure 28.1.

FIGURE 28.1
Add an authorized user to a group using Computer Management.

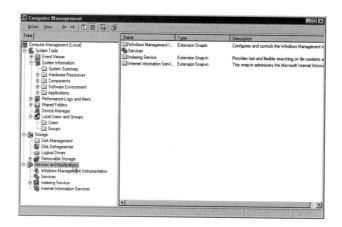

Next, follow these steps:

1. Look in the left pane for Services and Applications and double-click it to reveal the subfolders underneath it.

2. Right-click Windows Management Instrumentation (WMI) and choose Properties.

3. Click the Security tab and click the namespace that you want to offer access to.

4. Click the Security button. You'll see the Security dialog box shown in Figure 28.2.

5. Click Add. You'll see the Select Users, Computers, or Groups dialog box shown in Figure 28.3.

FIGURE 28.2

In this security dialog box, you can allow or deny various permissions to existing groups or individuals.

FIGURE 28.3

In this dialog box you can define individual users or groups.

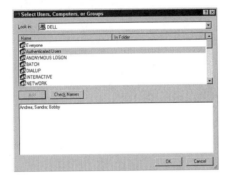

6. Click OK. The newly defined group or user will be added to the list shown in the Security dialog box (refer to Figure 28.2). The only permission available by default is *partial write*. You can of course change the permissions in the Security dialog box.

The WMI Security feature enables you to manage the users and groups of the local workstation or member server. If you don't have administrative rights, however, the Windows 2000 security dialog boxes will function as little more than glass windows on the front of a store. You might be able to see the goods, but you can't touch them.

Managing security under Windows 2000 begins at the group level. I'm not talking about workgroups here. A Windows 2000 user group is just a collection of user accounts. Put people into whatever "groups" help you, as the administrator, to keep things straight. User groups can be given permissions to access files, rights to perform certain actions on machines, and special abilities on the network.

A local user or group can be given permissions from your computer, but domain or global users and groups are not available to you on your local machine. Instead, they're managed by a network administrator. You have the ability (if logged onto your machine as an administrator) to add new local users, global users, and even global groups to your local groups. However, you can't add anything to the global groups.

As you'll see in the next few sections, you work with permissions and manage users with a new feature in Windows 2000: the Local Users and Groups feature of the Computer Management snap-in. The Local Users and Groups feature is not available on domain controllers, so global users and groups are managed on that level with the Active Directory Users and Computers feature.

Before continuing, I think it's important to make the distinction between rights and abilities. A *right* in Windows 2000 is some action or privilege that a user is allowed, but it can be taken away. A Windows 2000 right is much like the rights provided to people in the U.S. Constitution. You have the right of freedom of speech. Through legal action or incarceration, however, you can have this right taken away. It's much the same with Windows 2000. You can give a user or group the right to access the computer from the network or to change the system time, for example.

Abilities, on the other hand, are a special set of actions that can always, and by definition, be performed by select groups. An example is the ability to manage users and groups or to change the administrator password. Windows 2000's security model defines abilities, and they're hard wired. Even an administrator cannot modify abilities. We cover these topics again a little later.

Here's another point: The rights and abilities that you gain in one group are cumulative with the other groups that you belong to. If you belong to the Power Users group, for example, you can change the system time. If you're added to the Backup Operators group, you can also perform a system backup. It's important to know what kinds of access the various default groups provide. Table 28.1 provides a brief description of each group. Microsoft provides several predefined groups. As already stated, some of these groups have abilities that are found only within their respective group. In an effort to further provide assistance in setting up management of Windows 2000 systems, Microsoft also assigned particular user rights to these predefined groups. Recall that you'll be able to adjust the user rights, even on an administrator account, if they don't suit you.

Table 28.1 Default Windows 2000 Groups

Group	Description
Administrators	The best way to describe the Administrators category is *total access*. It's the only default (built-in) group that can do everything Windows 2000 allows. An administrator can act as part of the operating system, for example—a right no other group gets. You also have to be an administrator to add workstations to the domain. I always assign at least one person (preferably, two) this access level during the setup process.
Backup Operators	This is a standard user with the special rights required to perform a backup of the machine. The backup operator is the only one besides the administrator who can

Group	Description
	back up and restore files and directories. I'll show you shortly how you can also give power users the right to perform backups, but it's important to know that this group has a default right that you'll need to assign to the person who performs backups on your machine. Of course, in most cases, the administrator performs backups in all but the largest companies, so you won't have a problem in this area.
Guests	All this group can really do is log on to the machine and log back off. However, it can't just be overlooked— even a guest belongs to some special groups that we'll cover shortly. Guests can also connect to Windows 2000 from a separate computer and use shared resources such as printers and folders.
Power Users	A power user is someone you trust not to cause problems on the workstation. He or she is also a bit more knowledgeable than the average user. A power user can perform tasks such as profiling the performance of a single process and forcing a shutdown from a remote system. You'll want to assign this particular group with care; give it only to people who really know what they're doing. They'll also have access to various Control Panel options.
Replicators	Like Backup Operators, this is another specialty group. It allows the individual to perform file and folder replication within the domain.
Users	A novice user will start out in this group. It allows him or her to do the basic things needed to perform work within Windows 2000, without changing any of the system settings. In fact, this particular group can't even change the system time! I usually assign this group to new users with a low skill level. After a user becomes familiar with Windows 2000 and I know that I can trust him or her, I add that user to the Power Users group.
Everyone	This is a special group that doesn't appear in Figure 28.2. It's a supergroup that includes all the other groups. Every time you see this group listed somewhere, you know that it includes all the groups in this table and any local groups that you've defined. Keep in mind that the Everyone group includes the Guests group.

Now that you have a better idea about the basic categories of security under Windows 2000, let's look at some management specifics. The following sections provide additional details about managing users in Windows 2000. In NT 4, you run the User Manager to accomplish any of the procedures in each of the following sections. However, in Windows 2000, you instead open the Computer Management window (Control Panel, Administrative Tools, Computer Management). Then you work with the Local Users and Groups entry in the left pane under System Tools.

> **Note:** The groups and users mentioned in this chapter of the book are primarily workstation users and groups. Windows 2000 Server machines have some different default groups, depending on how they're set up (Domain Controller, for example). In turn, the Windows 2000 Server group Account Managers does not exist on Windows 2000 Professional workstations.

Adding New Users

One of the first things you need to learn as an administrator is how to add new users.

> **Technical Note:** The ability to create new users and groups is not limited to the administrator. Almost any user down to the standard "user" can create a new user or group on his or her workstation. Guest do not have this particular ability. This was done so that individual users could control access to resources on their machines. Remember, the reason for creating these workstation-only users and groups is so that you can then create shares to give people access to the information on the shares if you so choose. However, only an administrator can affect users and groups that he or she did not create.

When you install Windows 2000, there are only two users: guest and administrator. Before you add new users, however, make sure you have a security policy figured out and that you've determined which users to add. You'll also want to have an idea of what types of work they'll perform with their workstations, because that determines what rights they need.

To add a new user, follow these steps:

1. Double-click the Users and Passwords icon in Control Panel.
2. If it's not checked, click the Users Must Enter a User Name and Password to Use This Computer check box. That enables the Add, Remove, and Properties buttons. This dialog box is shown in Figure 28.4.
3. Click the Add button. You'll see the dialog box shown in Figure 28.5.

FIGURE 28.4

Add new users with this dialog box.

FIGURE 28.5

Fill in the user name and select the domain.

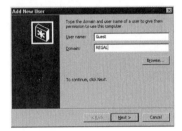

4. Click the Next button.

5. You'll see the dialog box shown in Figure 28.6. This is where you define the default group for this new user.

FIGURE 28.6

This page in the Add New User Wizard allows you to assign the new user to a default group. Note the drop-down list under Other.

6. Click the Finish button to finish the process of adding the new user.

An alternative way to add new people is via the new Local Users and Groups folders found in Control Panel, Administrative Tools, Computer Management (or you can click the Advanced Tab in the Users and Passwords dialog box and then click the Advanced button).

Either way, you can add new users in the Users folder shown in Figure 28.7.

FIGURE 28.7
Double-click the Users folder to see a list of all current users.

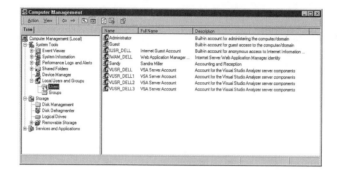

To add a new user, follow these steps:

1. Right-click the Users folder shown in Figure 28.7.

2. Choose New User from the context menu.

3. You'll see the dialog box shown in Figure 28.8.

FIGURE 28.8
Type in the necessary information about this user and then click the Create button.

4. The User Name field specifies how the user will log on to the workstation and how other users will see this person on the network. I've had users ask to use a nickname in place of their first name, and I don't see any problem with doing so. The Full Name field usually contains the user's full name; it's what the administrator uses to identify the user. Optionally, you can fill out the Description field, which is especially useful in a large organization.

5. Enter a password once in the Password field and then a second time in the Confirm Password field. I normally use a default password here, such as DAY*NIGHT. Notice that I don't use something silly, such as SECRET or MASTER. These passwords aren't secure if you provide outside access to a machine. Always use a memorable password but also ensure that it's not something obvious to provide a bit of security.

6. Select the password restrictions from the four check boxes at the bottom of the dialog box. I usually enable the User Must Change Password at Next Logon check

box to force the user to enter a new password the first time she logs on to the
network. (This is the default.) That way, she can't say that anyone (even the
administrator) has access to this account unless she gives her password out. I've
never figured out why Microsoft has added the User Cannot Change Password
check box, unless it's for some company with "Big Brother" syndrome. It's available if you want to assign the user a password and force her to keep it forever.
Notice that you can also disable a user's account—a handy feature if she has broken security in some way and you want to make sure that no one can access the
account. If you do select the top checkbox, the second and third options are
unavailable (gray). To make them available, deselect the User Must Change
Password at Next Logon check box. The Password Never Expires option overrides
any maximum time setting in Group Policy.

7. Click the Create button. The new user is created. Click the Close button to exit the
    dialog box.

8. Now you can see your new user in the Users folder, as shown in Figure 28.9.

FIGURE 28.9
Randy is now an accredited user.

Modifying a User's Properties

Once a user exists in the system, you can go ahead and add him to a group or groups,
edit his official name or password behavior, and define a User Profile and a home folder
for this user. All these things can be done by right-clicking the user's name in the Local
Users and Groups, Users folder and then choosing Properties from the context menu, as
you can see in Figure 28.10.

In the first tab, General, you can modify the user's name, description, and password
state. Note the Account Is Locked Out option. This prevents the user from even logging
on. You cannot select this option; instead, Windows 2000 sets it if a person attempts to
log on and his or her password fails more than the number of times permitted (as specified in the password policy of the Group Policy Editor). You can, if you wish, deselect it
though. Note that this differs from the Account Is Disabled option, which you can select
if you want to prevent the user from logging on—due to some other reason or security
infraction.

FIGURE 28.10

Right-click a user's name and choose Properties to modify the security status.

You'll then see the user's properties dialog box shown in Figure 28.11.

FIGURE 28.11

Use this Properties dialog box to adjust this user's security settings.

In the Member Of tab of the user Properties dialog box, you can add the user to new groups if you wish. Just click the Add button and select a group.

You'll want to spend some time learning about the rights and abilities of each group before you start assigning people to them. Most of the group names, as you saw in Table 28.1, are pretty self-explanatory. Notice that Windows 2000 provides a default group membership to the Power Users group.

The Profile tab includes two features. First, you can define the path to this user's profile. A *user profile* is essentially the user's desktop settings (display choices, network and printer connections, and so on). Here are the three types of user profiles:

- **Local**—This one is automatically created the first time the user logs on. It's stored on the local machine's hard drive and remains specific only to that particular machine.

- **Roaming**—System administrators create these profiles, which are network wide— no matter which machine you log on to, you see "your" desktop and its familiar icons, setup, and everything. A roaming profile is saved on the server.

- **Mandatory**—This is a version of the roaming profile, but it can be used for either individual users or groups of users. Again, only system administrators have the freedom to edit a mandatory profile. The purpose of the Mandatory feature is that it provides a consistent set of desktop settings that cannot be saved by the user (it's instead governed by the administrator).

You can also specify a logon script for this user in the Profile tab of the user's Properties dialog box.

Furthermore, you can define a location for the user's home folder—the folder the user lands in following logging on. If you don't specify a home folder path, Windows 2000 assigns a default location in \USERS\DEFAULT on the local hard drive where Windows 2000 is installed (if an upgrade) or in the root folder of a clean Windows 2000 installation.

Type the path and script name you want Windows 2000 to process each time the user logs on. A script contains any batch-processing commands you want Windows 2000 to perform. You can use a BAT (batch), CMD (OS/2 command), or EXE (executable) file for scripts.

> **Note:** Users who log on to a NetWare network don't need an entry here because you can perform script processing when they log on to the file server. Chapter 23, "Network Basics," has details on how to do this. There's nothing to stop you from processing both a Windows 2000 script and a NetWare script, however.

Don't confuse the home folder with the My Documents folder on the Windows 2000 desktop. Every user gets a My Documents folder; it's intended to be used as a desktop storage location for text documents. It's not the user's "primary residence" on the network.

Adding New Groups

Windows 2000 user groups are used in a couple different ways. First, they provide groups of users with some specific rights and abilities. Second, they're used to make it easier to manage access to files and folders.

I have found that the default groups Windows 2000 provides cover a wide variety of situations in regards to rights and abilities. There have been a few situations where I needed to define a few new groups. One company I worked with wanted a special Programmer group. This group had all the same abilities of a power user, with the added ability to back up files. They didn't want to use a combination of Power User and Backup Operator because the programmer wasn't supposed to restore files and folders. Programmers also needed some of the administrator-type rights to test security features in the applications they wrote.

User groups are also created to control access to shares, folders, and files. For example, here's something you can do:

1. Create a user group called Managers on your workstation.

2. Add all the managers' user accounts into the group.

3. Create a share called Budget and give the Managers group read/write access to the share on your workstation.

4. Tell the managers to put their budget spreadsheets on your machine at that share. No other users can access the share at all.

    This process is quicker and easier to manager than assigning each individual manager read/write access to the share.

Whatever the reason for adding a new group, it's pretty simple to do. Just follow these steps:

1. Right-click the Groups folder under the Local Users and Groups feature in Administrative Tools, Computer Management.

2. Choose New Group from the context menu.

3. You see the New Group dialog box shown in Figure 28.12.

FIGURE 28.12
Adding local groups.

4. Type a group name and description in the first two fields. Make sure that the group name is self-explanatory and that the Description field contains a summary of the access this group provides.

5. Click the Add button. You'll see a Select Users or Groups dialog box. This dialog box automatically displays a list of users on the local computer. You can use the Look In drop-down list box to select another computer as a source of names. There won't be any groups listed because you're adding members to a group.

6. After adding members, click the Create button in the New Group dialog box and then click the Close button. Now press F5 to refresh the list of groups in the Computer Management dialog box.

    You're not done yet; the new group you created doesn't have any rights except those available to the Everyone group. What you need to do now is add the appropriate rights to the new group.

7. Add rights to the new group using the procedure described in the "User Rights" section later in this chapter. Essentially, what you need to do is add the new group to each right separately.

Removing a User or Group

Removing a user or group is easy. All you need to do is right-click the user or group (in the right pane of the Computer Management dialog box). Then when the context menu pops out, choose Delete.

You'll see a dialog box similar to the one in Figure 28.13. Notice that this is the one you'll see when deleting a user; the group version is very similar to this one. Click OK to clear the warning dialog box, and the user or group will be gone. The warning shown in Figure 28.13 points out that the deletion will be permanent. Even if you re-create an account for this user with the identical properties to the deleted account—the system will see that user as a totally different user.

FIGURE 28.13
This warning appears when you try to delete a user or group.

Caution: Removing a user or group is permanent. Even if you create a user or group with the same name, it won't be the same. Windows 2000 actually tracks users and groups by a code called a *security identifier* (SID). Think of it as a badge number. These badge numbers are not permitted to be duplicated or recycled. Therefore, if you delete an account, you retire that SID forever. The permissions to files and folders are actually assigned by SIDs. The user names are only displayed to us poor humans who might have a hard time understanding that S-1-0-58674-4875928374-1123483298 is Sally Smith. It's a better practice to disable an account before you delete it. This often works out well. Suppose a programmer quits, and a new programmer is hired to replace her. This new programmer needs exactly the same rights and permissions as the old programmer. You can just rename the old user account to match the name of the new user and change the password. The access and rights, which are assigned to the SID, remain intact.

Changing a User's or Group's Properties

There are times, of course, when you must modify the properties of a user or group. To do that, right-click the entry and then choose Properties from the context menu to change the properties as needed. You'll see the same dialog box you used to create the user or group. Change the properties you need to change and click OK to make the changes permanent.

Technical Note: If you're trying to test changes that you've made to a user account or group membership, you need to do a couple of things to make sure you're actually testing the change. First, try pressing F5 to refresh the Computer Management window. Then close that window. The system won't actually commit the changes (that is, save them to the Registry) until you close the application. Therefore, leaving it open while you test access based on changes in most cases won't work. If a user is already connected to the system, he or she may need to log off and back on, especially in cases of group membership changes or changes to user rights. Generally, if you're only changing access to a folder, file, or share, retrying the operation of reading or writing will be sufficient.

Managing File/Folder Access (Access Control Lists)

Up to this point, we've been talking about creating users and groups. The whole purpose of this is to assign the users and groups the permissions to access shares, folders, and files. Right-click any file in Windows Explorer and you'll see a context menu. Choose the Properties option and select the Security page; you'll see something similar to the dialog box shown in Figure 28.14. This demonstrates that five access levels can be set for each file.

FIGURE 28.14
Controlling permissions for individual files.

Here's where this particular Windows 2000 feature can get time consuming. Think about the administrator who sets the security features for each file in a folder rather than taking a folder-wide approach to the issue. (It happens all the time.) An administrator will want to give one group access to file A and another group access to file B. Instead of putting the files in separate folders, the administrator will take the time to work with each file individually. Don't set yourself up for an administrative nightmare like that. Organize your files along application, usage, and security lines before you start to get into the configuration issues I cover in the next few sections.

If you choose Properties after right-clicking a *folder* in Explorer, you can click the Security tab and govern the permissions for that entire folder. If you choose Properties after right-clicking a *drive* in Explorer, you can similarly establish the access to that entire drive.

Working with Permissions

Perhaps the most common event for a network administrator is assigning permission to use a folder or file to a specific group. Windows 2000 provides a fairly broad range of capabilities in this area (file-level security is only available on NTFS-formatted drives). In NT 4, the File Permissions dialog box offered only a subset of the permissions available in the Folder (Directory) Permissions dialog box of Windows 2000. You can now set a full range of accesses for each file. The one option available in the Folder Permissions dialog box that's now missing in the File Permissions dialog box is List Folder Contents.

Setting Security Inheritance

Let's begin our discussion of permissions by looking at the check box at the bottom of the dialog box shown in Figure 28.14. If you organize your directories properly, Windows 2000 takes care of file security for you. As a default, Windows 2000 applies any changes you make to the files in the current folder.

Click the Advanced button shown in Figure 28.14. You'll now see two check boxes in the Access Control Settings dialog box, as shown in Figure 28.15.

FIGURE 28.15

The advanced Access Control Settings dialog box allows you to add or edit groups, individual users, and categories of users (such as Power Users).

If you decide you want to make the changes specific to the folder (whose dialog box this is), disable the check box Allow Inheritable Permissions. The first check box tells Windows 2000 that you also want to apply any changes in security to subdirectories. This enables you to make changes at one level in the folder hierarchy and then let them flow down throughout the remainder of the folder tree.

The second check box shown in Figure 28.15 resets all child folders (subfolders) and permits inheritance to propagate down through them from the current settings of the current Property dialog box. If you click the View/Edit button, your choices expand; the degree of refinement you can describe for the permissions for the folder grows to a total of 13, as shown in Figure 28.16.

Let's consider for a moment the issue of inheritance. When you create a new folder under an existing folder, the permissions of the existing folder are automatically applied to (inherited by) the new folder (when this check box is left checked, as it is by default). When you're looking at the security permissions for a folder, this is the first set of permissions in parentheses. If you create a new file in a folder, the file assumes the rights and permissions of the second set of permissions in the security permissions display for a folder. Let's look at a couple of cases. Consider the following information:

Folder:	`C:\My Documents`		
Permissions:	Users	(RWXD)	(R)
	Administrators	(Full Control)	(Full Control)
	SallyM	(RWXD)	(RW)
	CREATOR OWNER	(RWXD)	(Full Control)
	Everyone	(R)	(R)

R = Read

W = Write

X = Execute

D = Delete

Now let's say JohnS logs on to this workstation. He's not in the Administrators group. He's in the Users group. So what types of permissions does he have in this folder? Users' permissions. He has RWXD (read, write, execute, and delete permissions) in the folder. On any new files in the folder, he will have R, the second parameter. Of course, permissions can be set on a file-by-file basis. Therefore, if someone changes permissions on a particular file to allow JohnS access, he can get into it.

We must consider a couple of other items in this permissions listing example. The group CREATOR OWNER is a special group. It signifies the person who creates a file. Certainly it would be bad to allow someone to create a file and then not let him or her make changes to the file. Therefore, you use the CREATOR OWNER group to give special permission to the creator of a file. Let's look at JohnS again. He logs on. Normally, if he creates a file, the only permission he would have to the file would be read access. However, because he's the CREATOR OWNER of the file, he has full control of the new file. This does not change his permissions for any other files, only for the ones he creates and owns.

Here's another little scenario: JohnS has created a file in the `C:\My Documents` folder as specified previously. He has full control. Now, SallyM logs on to the machine. What permission does she have on the file? If you said read and write, that's correct. When the file was created by JohnS, it inherited all the permissions as specified for the folder permissions in the second column of permissions. SallyM has RWXD on the My Documents folder and all folders created under it. She also has RW permissions by default on all new files created in the folder. Of course, if SallyM creates a file, she's the CREATOR OWNER; she would get full control of the file she created.

Let's look at one more example. LarryJ logs on to the workstation. He's not in the Users or Administrators group. His account is in the Managers group. However, the Managers group is not listed. Therefore, he should not have access to any of the files or directories. Why do you suppose that is? Has security failed us? No. All users who can get on a machine or access it from the network are automatically included in the Everyone group. Therefore, LarryJ has read access to the folder and read access to the files.

Inheritance works on newly created files, but what happens if you copy a file or move a file into the folder. Copy and move are really two distinct operations in Windows 2000. Remember, first, that the permissions or ACLs are an attribute of the file or folder. The size of the file, date of creation, even the data in the file are all considered attributes of the file. When you copy a file, you're really creating a new file and copying the data attribute of the file and putting it into the new one. Therefore, if SallyM copies a file into the previously mentioned My Documents folder, the file will inherit the permissions from the folder as if she had created a new file. If you move a file, it's like uprooting a tree; you get the tree, the roots, the dirt around the roots, and the leaves. When you move a file, it takes all its attributes with it. Therefore, if SallyM moves a file into the My Documents folder, it carries its ACL baggage with it to its new home in the folder. Note that this means the file will not inherit the permissions from the folder into which it's moved.

> **Technical Note:** When copying a file, you need only R (read) permissions on the file and W (write) permissions in the folder where you're going to put the file. When you move a file, you need R (read) and D (delete) permissions on the file, RWD permissions on the folder the file is coming from, and W permissions on the folder the file is going to.

Changing Group or User Access Levels

The next thing you'll want to look at in the Folder Permissions (Advanced) dialog box is the Permission Entries list box. You can place group or individual user names here. I always suggest that people use groups because they're easier to manage. Obviously, there are exceptions to every rule, so the capability to add individual users is important. Notice that there's a permission level to the right of every name in the list. You control this level with the Permissions list of check boxes, as shown in Figure 28.16.

These access levels are expansions of the basic permission sets: read, write, execute, delete, permissions, and ownership. Read and write are simple enough to understand, and so is delete. Execute can have different meanings depending on the type of object. If the object is a file, for example, the execute permission allows you to run the file if it's a program. If the object is a folder, the execute permission allows you to enumerate (list) the subdirectories below the one you're at.

> **Tip:** Giving someone No Access can often be overkill, so use it wisely. If you do not want someone to access a folder or file, just make sure the user and any groups he or she belongs to do not appear on the ACL. It's like not being on the list for a dinner party. Look at the ACL from the last example. If the user LarryJ, who doesn't belong to any of the groups listed, tries to access the folder, he gets Access Denied just because he's not on the list.

Taking Ownership

Normally you must have full control to alter the permissions on a folder or file. Alternatively, you can be the *owner* of the folder or file. Within Windows 2000, you can be given the right to take ownership, which permits you to claim a file or folder as your own and therefore have the ability to change permissions on the file to give yourself access. The Administrator group has the special ability to take ownership of any object on Windows 2000. This group can give permissions to other groups to take ownership as well. You cannot give ownership; you can only take it. So what does this mean to you from a security standpoint?

Every time someone changes the permissions for a particular file or folder, he or she leaves a virtual "paper" trail behind. You can view the ownership of a file or folder to see who changed security for it last, even if it was the administrator. Therefore, you might have a file or folder that you do not want anyone to see, not even those folks in the Administrator group. You created the folder and files originally, so you're the owner. If a curious administrator wants to the see the files, he must first take ownership and then change permissions on the files to allow him to read them. He then changes the permissions on the files back so that you won't notice what he has done. Because he cannot give ownership back to you, however, the administrator remains the owner. Therefore, if you suspect that someone was looking at the file, check the ownership. If it has been switched, you know that someone was at least curious enough to take ownership and change permissions back and forth on the file.

Clicking the Owner tab on the Access Control Settings dialog box displays the Owner dialog box shown in Figure 28.17. Notice that it displays the current owner of the selected folder or file. One of the security-related tasks you should perform on a regular basis is checking this dialog box.

FIGURE 28.17

If the ownership of a folder or file has changed, you know that someone has changed a permission and you need to find out what that change is.

Adding/Removing Users or Groups

Tip: The best practice to follow when you're trying to maintain security is to be a minimalist. You determine the minimum amount of rights and the file and folder access that a user needs to get his work done. Therefore, if a user needs to access a shared drive, you don't give him full control on the share. You determine what he needs to do and assign the privilege.

You need to perform two operations with the Directory (or File) Permissions dialog box relatively frequently, even if you do set up security correctly. These two operations are adding and removing users or groups. Removing a user or group is easy. Just highlight the entry you want to remove in the Name list box and click the Remove button. I covered adding a user earlier. All you need to do is click the Add button. You'll see the Select Users, Computers, or Groups dialog box.

Enforcing Security Policies

The previous sections covered a lot about the mechanics of setting permissions on files, folders, and shares. Those sections also identified the rights and abilities users gain through membership in various Windows 2000 user groups. This section discusses setting account policies, establishing auditing of activities, and using domain features to control users' abilities on their workstations.

Account Policies

Polices provide a method for deciding how Windows 2000 sets up security on a global basis. In fact, it's the software equivalent of the security plan I previously discussed for a single machine. A policy affects everyone who might log on to a workstation, so it's important to carefully think about any changes you make.

I like to think of a security plan as the *specification* and policies as the *implementation* of that specification. Obviously, the security plan contains more information than you'll find in this chapter, but it does set the tone for what you'll do here. As is the case with most other items I've covered so far, you set policies within the Local Users and Groups dialog box (formerly known as the User Manager). With the Local Users and Groups utility, you create new users and groups, delete users from or add users to groups, disable user and group accounts, and reset passwords. To get to this utility, open the Computer Management feature in the Administrative Tools feature of Control Panel.

> **Technical Note:** Windows 2000 passwords are case sensitive. The user account name, however, is not case sensitive. For example, Total*Recall is a different password than TOTAL*RECALL. Make sure that your users realize this; otherwise, they won't be able to figure out why the computer won't give them access. I've had several situations in which the previous user left Caps Lock on and the next user experienced problems logging on because he or she had selected a lowercase password.

Click a user's name and choose Properties from the context menu. The first thing you'll want to check is the Password Never Expires setting. Typically you'll want a user to have the ability to change her password if she thinks it may have been compromised. However, you do not want the user to be able to change the password repeatedly (say, in a single day).

User Rights

Changing the permissions you give to a group or a user is handled with the Microsoft Management Console (MMC). However, you must first add a snap-in (accessory utility) to the MMC. The following steps show you how to do this as well as how to modify the rights that users or groups have:

1. Open the Microsoft Management Console by selecting Start, Run and then typing MMC and pressing Enter.

2. Choose Console, Add/Remove Snap-In.

3. Click the Add button in the Add/Remove Snap-In dialog box. The Add Standalone Snap-In dialog box appears.

4. Double-click Group Policy in the list box.

5. Leave the local computer as the Group Policy object.

6. Click Finish.

7. Click Close to shut the dialog box.

   You now see Local Computer Policy in the Standalone Snap-Ins list in the Add/Remove Snap-In dialog box.

8. Close the Add/Remove Snap-In dialog box.

The console now displays a Local Computer Policy entry in its left pane, as you can see in Figure 28.18.

FIGURE 28.18
The Local Computer Policy feature added to the MMC window.

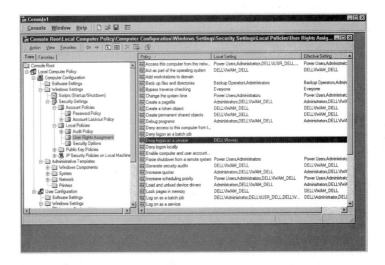

At this point, you need to open folders and subfolders as shown in Figure 28.19 until you get down to the folder User Rights Assignment. The path is `Local Computer Policy\Computer Configuration\Windows Settings\Security Settings\Local Policies\User Rights Assignment`.

To add or remove a right from a user or group, right-click one of the rights listed in the right pane in Figure 28.19. Then choose Security from the context menu. Click the Add button in the Local Security Policy Setting dialog box and you'll see a list of all users and groups, including any new groups you may have defined (see the section "Adding New Groups," earlier in this chapter).

Auditing

Auditing keeps track of whatever user account accessed files or other objects. It also tracks logon attempts, shutdowns (or restarts), and similar activities. An administrator specifies in Group Policy which activities should be audited. Setting the auditing feature is similar to setting permissions: You pick out the object (such as a folder or file) and then choose users or groups whose behaviors you want to track. Then you pick the behaviors you want tracked. The Event Viewer provides the log of activities for your inspection.

For instance, to set auditing for a particularly suspicious file, right-click that file in Windows Explorer, choose Properties from the context menu, and click the Security tab. Click the Advanced button and then click the Auditing tab. Click the Add button, click the name of the suspect (I mean, *user*), and then click OK. The Auditing Entry dialog box opens, as shown in Figure 28.19.

FIGURE 28.19

You can really get specific about how you want people followed and their actions recorded.

Like many things that were different in NT 4, you have to look in a new place for the Event Viewer so you can then see what auditing has recorded about the users' behaviors. In Windows 2000, the Event Viewer is accessed via the Computer Management icon located within the Administrative Tools icon in Control Panel. Got it?

Also note that before you can audit files you first need to set up Audit Policy (in the same tree as User Rights Assignment in Group Policy).

On Your Own

Take this opportunity to design your own security plan. Work with the network users and management to come up with a plan that's both fair and reasonably secure. Another good resource is Sams Publishing's *Peter Norton's Guide to Network Security Fundamentals* (ISBN 0-672-31691-9).

The plan you create should be analyzed for leaks and potential security risks. Make sure you tell management about these risks and their effects on the network. Also come up with contingency plans to plug the leaks if management decides that the risk is too great.

Spend some time training the users on your network about security. It's very important that you also take the time to explain what types of passwords are acceptable. Spend a little time with each user who has problems understanding the security plan.

If you're a home user, try setting up a variety of security options on your own machine. You might want to create a security profile for young users, for example, that allows them access to programs they can use but removes access to programs that could damage your machine. Try using the tools I described here to make the process of creating a home security plan easy.

Try using the auditing features Windows 2000 provides for a few weeks to see how they affect system performance and how many resources they use. It's important to know what to expect in the way of output and what you need to provide to make these auditing features work. You won't have time to work out these details when a hacker is busy trying to access your workstation.

Working with Microsoft Message Queue (MSMQ)

Microsoft Message Queue (MSMQ) is a new addition to Windows 2000 that will greatly affect how applications on your machine work while you're at work and on the road. The most important change for you, as a user, is that you'll spend less time worrying about the application's needs and more time on performing tasks with the application. A properly designed MSMQ application will work the same at the desktop as it does on the laptop. No longer will you need to worry about special procedures for communicating with the home office. In addition, an MSMQ application won't care if you lose the connection with the server—it'll act the same with or without that connection. In short, this is an exciting new technology that finally makes it possible for users to follow one set of rules when working with applications.

This chapter won't make you an MSMQ commando, but it'll help you understand this new technology and the potential it has for changing your current computing environment. We'll look at the theory behind MSMQ, the various things you need to know about working with MSMQ, the ins and outs of disconnected applications, and finally, the limitations of using MSMQ. In short, we'll take a good look at MSMQ from the user perspective, but it's also important to understand there are a lot of MSMQ programmer issues as well. Applications can't use MSMQ unless they're specifically designed to do so.

What Is MSMQ?

This section will provide you with a very broad overview of the theory behind MSMQ. What you should walk away with is a basic understanding of how MSMQ works. It's important to understand how MSMQ works so that you can better understand how MSMQ-enabled applications can help you become more productive.

Understanding Messages

In Chapter 15, "OLE, ActiveX, and DCOM," we spent a lot of time talking about DCOM and how it works. In some ways, MSMQ works similar to DCOM. What you're doing is creating a connection between a client and server for the purpose of information exchange. However, instead of creating a direct connection using a network protocol like DCOM does, MSMQ uses queues (think of a line at a bank) as an intermediary destination for the data that flows between the client and server. These queues are actually special places on your local hard drive that are used to hold messages, which is the method that MSMQ uses in place of the packets normally used by networks to transfer data.

The advantage to using the message as a basis for transferring information is that the client and server (the ActiveX components) don't need to exist at the same time. In other words, using MSMQ means that you can open your application and use it without checking for server availability first. If the application is written to use MSMQ correctly, you won't even notice if the server is available once the application is open. This kind of "detached" or "on-demand" interaction permits work to be done on a portable, in anticipation of its later interaction with a server. A similar feature is found in the "detached" recordsets now permitted in Microsoft's new ADO database technology.

Let's put this technology into a real world perspective. Right now, someone who works outside of the office on a regular basis is at a disadvantage because company resources aren't available. For example, a salesperson on the road is always out of contact with the company and that loss of contact can cause problems when it comes time to record new sales. Using MSMQ, a salesperson could record an order now, away from the office, then allow MSMQ to automatically upload it to the server later without modifying the methods that he or she would normally use. MSMQ makes the delivery in the background without any interaction on the part of the user. The orders that the salesperson creates while the connection to the server is severed are stored in a local queue as messages. Each message will normally represent a single order's data, although there really isn't a limit on how an application can format the messages. A message could hold more than one message or only part of a large order.

The disadvantage of using messages as the basis for data transfer is that there's some additional overhead. Obviously, there are more layers of processing now, which means that direct connect scenarios actually run a bit slower. In addition, there's a little additional coding and setup time for the developer when using MSMQ. However, the advantages far outweigh the disadvantages when the ability to use the same application in either connected or disconnected mode is a necessity.

There's one other important concept to grasp about messages. A message is an object, just like all of the other objects that Windows works with. It contains properties just like any other object. Since a message is an object, it isn't limited to just one kind of data. Obviously, many messages will contain text because that's going to be the main form of communication for application data. However, message objects can contain other objects (like sounds or pictures). In addition, message objects can be made up of complex forms of data. That's why you can transfer an entire database record using just one message rather than individual messages for each field in the record. Message objects are a new and very flexible way to transfer data within Windows 2000.

Understanding Transactions

We have to take a little detour in our discussion of MSMQ to talk about another new Windows 2000 feature, Microsoft Transaction Server (MTS). This isn't actually a new product—Microsoft used to market MTS as a separate product. However, Windows 2000 is the first operating system to include MTS as part of the product. In fact, when you hear the term COM+ mentioned with Windows 2000, what people are actually referring to is the combination of MTS and COM used in newer applications.

> **Note:** We aren't going to cover COM+ in detail in this part of the book. The only purpose of this section is to acquaint you with transactions. In fact, most of the implementation details for COM+ are so esoteric, that only a programmer would love them. If you want to learn more about COM and its derivatives from a user perspective, check out Chapter 15.

As the name implies, MTS deals with transactions. The first question you need to answer is "What is a transaction?" There are a lot of different definitions for this term floating around in the trade press, many of which are contradictory. Let's begin by looking at the one thing that most people agree on: A transaction is a way of packaging data and commands and then ensuring they reach their destination successfully. In other words, when you submit a form to the database and use a transaction to do it, you can be sure that either all of the data in the form will get added to the database or none of it will. In short, a transaction is insurance that your database (or other application) won't get erroneous data placed in it even if it means losing the data for a single transaction (which is normally an entire record for database applications).

MTS is the Windows 2000 component that ensures the data or objects (MTS can encapsulate anything, not just data within a transaction) you transfer from one machine to another will arrive in good shape and that they'll be fully executed. Execution may include a variety of things, even though most programmers look at transactions as being data oriented and used only within a database management context. A good way to remember what MTS transactions are all about is the acronym ACID. The following list provides an overview of what ACID is all about.

- **Atomicity**   All of the updates required to complete a transaction are grouped together. Either the entire package of updates succeeds and the change becomes durable (permanent), or the package fails and all of the updates are removed.
- **Consistency**   The transaction is a correct change of the system state. It preserves the state invariants, which means that you won't get unexpected results from the transaction once complete. In other words, the conditions for each transaction are tracked and maintained so that the data for the transaction is always handled in the same way.

- **Isolation**   Concurrent transactions can't see each other, and the results from one transaction won't affect other transactions running at the same time. Obviously, this is an extension of the principle of encapsulation for objects. Think of a transaction as a form for an object—all of the updates are encapsulated in such a way that the outside world can't see them.

- **Durability**   You could also term this bullet as fault tolerance. A transaction should be able to survive some level of failure. These failures might include obvious problems like server system failures or unexpected problems like communication failures.

ACID describes MTS in its perfect state, which is what Microsoft would have you believe is always the case. However, there aren't any foolproof technologies for the PC; you have to plan on some level of failure even if you use transactions. It's at this point that some people differ on exactly what a transaction fault tolerance means. For the purposes of this book, a transaction also infers the capability to roll back the addition of data or the execution of commands until the transaction reaches a point of stability, the point at which the last set of operations completed successfully. A transaction never completes until the receiver accepts the data or commands. The second that the data or commands are accepted, the transaction is complete and the event is over.

Of course, transactions are complicated by a number of environmental factors. For example, in a client/server setup the number of failure points is relatively limited. In the modern n-tier application world (one where the application can execute on more than one machine—including more than one server), a transaction may involve a number of clients and servers, any of which could fail. MTS views transaction completion as the point at which the original request is completed. If the original request fails, then all intermediate transactions are rolled back. This means that all of the machines involved in the series of transactions required to answer an original request must maintain state information until that original request is completed.

Another environmental factor that complicates matters is the Internet. Consider the fact that this medium is both unstable and prone to connection losses. In short, an Internet enabled application needs to consider transactional failures that aren't caused by the application or any associated components, but by the Internet itself. A connection failure could still cause the transaction to fail even if all of the required application code works as anticipated. MTS helps application programmers handle this kind of failure by maintaining connection information for the programmer. In addition, the use of MSMQ can make the state of the connection a moot point, as we'll see later in the chapter.

Some people also insist that transactions infer some type of data recovery. In other words, the receiver will notify the sender that the data or command wasn't accepted for whatever reason. While error recovery is a very important thing to have—especially when it comes to database managers—you'll find that some transaction methodologies won't allow for any form of recovery. If the data is lost, then it's gone. It's up to the sender to ensure that the data actually got added to the database or that the commands were executed on the server. Transactions under MTS do have a level of data recovery, although it's uncertain how robust that data recovery is and exactly what it'll protect. In most cases, you'll want to be sure that the MTS/MSMQ-enabled applications you use include some type of data recovery mechanism in addition to whatever Microsoft provides for you when it comes to critical data.

An Overview of MSMQ

So, how does a messaging application differ from DCOM? The data is most likely the same, which means that the way that information is entered in the application and then processed for the database will be the same. However, the delivery method is different. We're now using the idea of message objects to transfer data and a queue to hold those messages. (A *queue* is a sort of a mailbox for messages that exits as a special location on either the client or server hard drive—or sometimes in both locations.) At a minimum, there's a queue on the server that holds all of the messages that the server components will process. Each active component on the server has a separate queue. These components will pick messages up from their queue whenever processing on the current message is complete.

In addition to the server queue, some clients will have a queue as well for local processing. The local queue gets emptied into the server queue anytime there's a connection between the client and the server. In short, messages can be viewed as the packets that would normally get carried between client and server on a network. Obviously, this is a simplification of a more complex process, but it does help to start out with this perspective of the functioning of MSMQ and the messages that it uses.

The obvious advantage of using MSMQ in place of DCOM is the ability to perform disconnected application handling. The local client queue allows the client to continue processing information even when there's no direct connection to the server for handling the messages. (Obviously, you'll need to configure the client for independent use.) Using a local client queue allows the user to continue working as if the connection existed and without performing any special procedures to transfer the resulting messages from the client the server when a connection is made. MSMQ handles all of the message transfers in the background without the user's knowledge. Figure 29.1 shows the relationship between the client and the server and the kinds of queue setups that you can expect.

Notice that there are actually two client types:

- Dependent
- Independent

The main difference between the two is that the independent client also provides its own queue, while the dependent client relies on a direct connection to the server.

FIGURE 29.1

MSMQ allows the user to continue working even when no connection between the client and server exists.

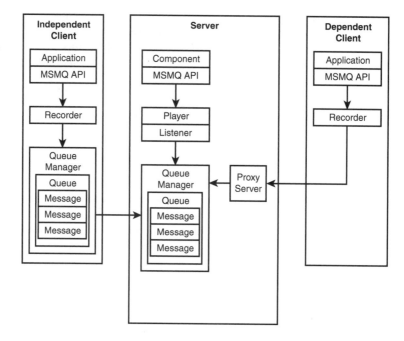

In most cases, you can choose a client type depending on the capabilities and needs of client, but there are exceptions where the choice of client is dependent on the type of machine being used. Obviously, you can't use a dependent client setup for a laptop computer that you intend to use on the road because the dependent client lacks a queue. However, a dependent client setup will work for a desktop machine that's located in the same building as a server or on a WAN with a reliable connection. Using a dependent client setup reduces the disk requirements for using MSMQ and can result in a slight performance boost because the messages are only placed in one queue rather than two.

There are three elements required for establishing and maintaining a message flow between the client and server:

- Recorder
- Listener
- Player

The recorder takes the client output, creates messages, then places those messages in either the local message or sends them to a proxy server on the server. MSMQ takes the message that the client creates and places it in the server's queue. When the listener sees a message in the server's queue, it removes the message and gives it to the player. Finally, the player takes the message and turns it into data for the server.

You can look at the data transfer process (message recording and playback) used by MSMQ as the same one that goes on with an answering machine in your home. When someone calls and finds that you're not home, they leave a message by talking to the answering machine instead of you directly. The answering machine stores the message. When you get home, an indicator on the answering machine tells you that you have one or more messages. Pressing a button on the answering machine normally plays the messages back for you, allowing to you to determine who has called in your absence. As you can see, the idea of disconnected communication isn't new, MSMQ represents a new implementation of an existing idea.

As previously mentioned, MSMQ and MTS are tied together, in most cases, to make applications work. MSMQ applications use a minimum of three transactions for every data transmission, even if it appears that there's only one transaction taking place. The first transaction occurs between the client application and the local queue. MSMQ creates a second transaction when it takes the message from the local queue and places it in the server queue. That's where the third transaction begins. As soon as the server removes a message from the queue, it creates a third transaction that tracks the message's progress on the server. This three-transaction approach makes it a lot less likely that an update will fail due to communication problems, which, in turn, makes the application more reliable. In addition, since there's a special MSMQ transaction for delivering data from the client to the server, you can be sure that each message will get successfully transmitted only one time, but that it'll get transmitted at least that one time.

Throughout the chapter, we'll address the topic of queues in several ways. There are two kinds of queues supported by MSMQ:

- Application
- System

The application queue is created by the application and is used for messages, administration, reports, and responses. Systems queues are created by MSMQ. There are two types: dead letter and journal. Queues can also be public or private. Public queues are available for anyone to use and are tracked by the MSMQ Information Service (MQIS). Private queues are normally used for one-to-one communications like a response from a server on a client machine. We'll be talking more about these queues as the chapter progresses.

Installing MSMQ

MSMQ isn't installed as part of Windows 2000—you need to install it as a separate item. Obviously, you'll only want to install this feature if you have MSMQ-enabled applications installed on your machine. Otherwise, MSMQ will sit in the background eating up processor cycles that you could use for other purposes. The following procedure will help you install MSMQ. It assumes that you're connected to a domain controller that can service the MSMQ messaging requests.

Tip: Windows 2000 comes with MSMQ version 2.0. This new version of MSMQ includes many new features, such as the ability to use Active Directory to store MSMQ settings. Many people installed MSMQ 1.0 on their Windows NT machine and experiences problems when upgrading their machine to Windows 2000 and MSMQ 2.0. Microsoft may have corrected these problems by the time you read this, but it still pays to know about any problems that you might encounter before you perform any upgrade. Make sure you read the Microsoft documentation thoroughly before upgrading your system, and pay special attention to any MSMQ 1.0 to 2.0 upgrade problems.

1. Start the Windows Components Wizard by double-clicking the Add/Remove Programs applet in the Control Panel, then clicking the Add/Remove Windows Components button in the Add/Remove Programs dialog. You'll see the Windows Components Wizard dialog.

2. Check the Message Queuing Services option, then click Next. Windows Components Wizard will ask whether you want to create a dependent or independent client as shown in Figure 29.2. Notice that an independent client allows you to specify a domain controller running MSMQ.

FIGURE 29.2

MSMQ gives you the option of installing a dependent or independent client.

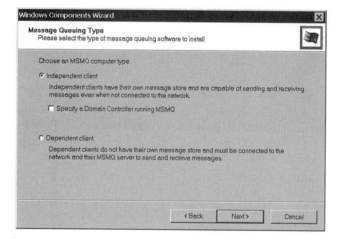

3. Choose either a Dependent or Independent client, then click Next. In most cases, you'll see the Message Queuing Server dialog shown in Figure 29.3 (unless you choose to create an independent client and Windows 2000 automatically finds a server for you to use). Notice that you can specify a MSMQ 1.0 server. Windows 2000 won't find this version of the server automatically, so you'll always need to specify it manually.

FIGURE 29.3

You'll use this dialog to specify the name of an MSMQ server, which may not be the same as the server you log into.

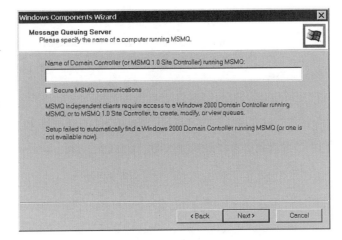

4. Type the name of an MSMQ server, then click Next. Windows Components Wizard will copy the files needed for MSMQ from your Windows 2000 Professional CD. You should see the Completing the Windows Components Wizard dialog once the installation is complete.

5. Click Finish. At this point, MSMQ installation is complete.

Configuring MSMQ

The applications on your machine will normally configure themselves for use. What this means is that any components, queued or otherwise, will automatically install and configure themselves as part of application installation. So, from a user perspective, MSMQ requires little, if any configuration.

However, it also pays to know where these components are and what they look like. You'll always find the MSMQ components for your machine in the Component Services MMC snap-in shown in Figure 29.4. You'll find this snap-in in the Administrative Tools folder of the Control Panel.

Notice that Figure 29.4 shows two QC (Queued Component) components. These are the two default components that MSMQ will always install for you and we talked about both components when working with Figure 29.1. The first is a listener component that will allow a server to respond to your application using messages that will be downloaded to your machine. The second is a player that creates messages based on your application's output. The messages will be placed in the Public queue. If a developer wanted to use a private queue or a custom public queue, then he or she would need to develop a component for that purpose and install it as shown in Figure 29.4.

FIGURE 29.4

MSMQ installs components that you'll find in the Component Services MMC snap-in.

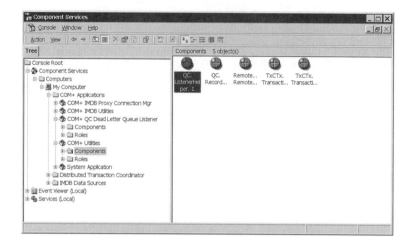

So, how can you tell if a component is working? Normally, a component remains still (as shown in Figure 29.4). You'll see a plus sign on the round ball icon that defines the component. If the component is currently performing work, then the round ball will appear to rotate. So, if you're expecting your application to do something and the component isn't rotating, there's probably something wrong with the component installation.

There's a third MSMQ component shown in Figure 29.4 that we looked at in the discussion of Figure 29.1; it's called the COM+ QC Dead Letter Queue Listener. The main purpose of this component is to handle messages that can't be delivered for some reason. This is one component that you don't want to see operating because it only has to work when there are errant messages on your system. If you see this component doing something, then it's probably time to have the administrator check out the applications installed on your machine.

Managing Message Queues

MSMQ uses messages to transfer data from one place to another. Those messages are stored in queues until the component responsible for handling them can react to the message. All of your message queues are managed with the Computer Management MMC snap-in shown in Figure 29.5.

These four default folders will contain the queues that hold the MSMQ messages. In fact, if you look in the System Queues folder, you'll see that there are at least three queues installed by default. There's one queue for journal messages and two for dead letter messages (one with transactions and a second without).

FIGURE 29.5
The Computer Management snap-in allows you to manage MSMQ queues.

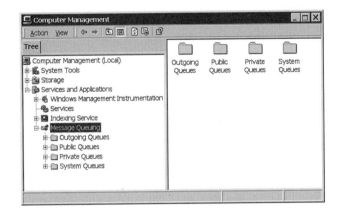

In most cases, the applications you install will manage the message queues automatically. However, it's educational to look in these folders and see what types of message queues your application uses. In addition, the Message Queuing Control Panel that gets created when you install MSMQ provides local administrative options that allow you to change where message files are stored, what level of security is used, and the ability to change sites.

Getting the Job Done with MSMQ

Now that you understand what's going on with MSMQ, it's important to understand how MSQM can help you in a practical business way. From a user perspective, the most important reason for using MSMQ is the ability to work with disconnected applications. Being able to complete transactions while the client is disconnected from the server is an important way to make applications reliable.

Of course, disconnected applications are really only the tip of the iceberg. What are the hidden benefits of using MSMQ in the business environment? The following list provides an overview of some of the business reasons to use MSQM in place of some of the other technologies that businesses may have tried in the past. (I've written this list from the administrator's perspective, which is the right view for a product of this type.)

- **User Training**   Right now managers and developers must train users to perform application-related tasks in at least two ways if they want to implement a disconnected application scenario for mobile computer users. Users have to use one technique when they're directly connected to the server and a second (two-step) technique when disconnected. The two-step approach is necessary because data is entered during the first step, then uploaded as a batch file in the second step. Of course, this means that a business has to invest more time and money training the user, which increases business costs. In addition, because there are two techniques for performing a single task, the probability of user confusion and the resulting user error is much higher.

- **Reliable Database Updates**   The mobile user is currently required to perform transactions in two phases. First, they take the order at the remote location from a new customer. Second, they must update all of their orders to the company database in some way. This two-step approach to working with transactions means that the potential for human error is greatly increased. Several problems can occur, including the loss of data between the time the order is taken and the time it arrives at the company server, the user simply forgets to upload his or her orders, the order is mangled during transmission, or the order gets transmitted more than once. Because of the way MSMQ is designed, the update process isn't only automatic, but the use of transactions also ensures data integrity. In short, administrators and developers will spend a lot less time troubleshooting errant database entries.

- **Application Scaling**   One of the MSMQ features that you might not notice immediately is that the disconnected processing scenario also allows the server to scale better. When using a direct connection the client requests have to be processed immediately or the client will notice a processing delay. Using MSMQ doesn't mean that the requests will get processed any faster, but placing the requests in a queue allows method calls by the application to return faster, which means that the user won't notice a processing delay nearly as fast. The user continues to work as if he or she had the server all to themselves. When the processing load starts to fall, the server can begin to process the messages contained in the queues at a faster rate. As a result, the server runs at a higher efficiency and the user is happier.

- **Non-Critical Path Processing**   A developer or administrator can also use MSMQ to prioritize the work that the server needs to perform. For example, the server has to be available to receive customer orders all of the time. Otherwise, you may lose an order to a competitor who is ready. However, once you have the order in hand, you don't need to process it immediately. You could check the customer's credit card validity during off peak times. In addition, order fulfillment can take place during the evening hours when the server is less likely to be busy. All this means that you get better efficiency out of your server investment by ensuring that the server is always busy doing some type of work for your company.

- **Fewer Error Messages**   Consider, for a moment, the cost of an error message to your business. The user has to call a support technician. If the support technician isn't available immediately, then the user sits waiting instead of processing orders for your business. The more error messages that a server generates, the greater the number of support technicians you require and the more time the user wastes waiting for an answer. Because MSMQ allows your server to scale better, the user will receive fewer resource related error messages, meaning that the ability to scale affects your bottom line in several easy to understand ways.

- **Human Processing Time Removed**   When you create a direct connection between the client and the server, the objects created on the server usually exist for the entire time the application runs on the client machine. This means that the server is allocating resources while the user is thinking about the data needed to commit a transaction. Using MSMQ means that the human part of the equation is removed from server resource allocation. The server side objects are created only long enough to process the transaction after all of the data is collected. As a result, the server uses resources more efficiently and can usually handle a larger processing load.

MSMQ Limitations

MSMQ won't fix every programming problem a developer will experience in creating applications for tomorrow. Of course, this means that the application you use tomorrow still won't be the perfect application everyone is looking to create. In fact, because of the way that MSMQ is designed, it actually introduces a few new limitations of which you need to be aware. These limitations will affect the types of applications that you can expect a developer to create for you. In short, MSMQ is another tool for a developer's toolbox, but it shouldn't be viewed as the only tool that a developer needs. What Microsoft is attempting to do is create an environment where more than one tool might meet a particular need and the developer needs to consider the pros and cons of each tool before he or she uses it. The following list will help you understand MSMQ limitations.

- **One-Way Message Transport**   Chapter 15 introduced you to the idea that most server components can create output as well as accept input. However, when working with MSMQ a developer can create components only with inputs and no outputs. The reason for this one way transfer of information is easy to understand: The client and server might not be available at the same time. As a result, the server might not have a client to send a response to. What this means to you as a user is that applications that rely on MSMQ may be less responsive than those that use other technologies.

- **HRESULT Value Limited**   This is a programmer-specific issue that you must know because it affects the kinds of feedback that the developer can add to an application. An HRESULT is a special kind of value that an application normally receives as the result of making a call to the server. This value can tell the developer if there were errors or other potential problems with the call. Because the client may be sending a message to the server in disconnected mode, client won't receive the same kind of HRESULT that it's gotten in the past. When using MSMQ a non-error return value may indicate that the data was received by the local queue instead of telling the developer that the transaction succeeded as a whole. This means that the developer has to limit any assumptions when designing the application. It also means that you won't receive as much feedback about the final state of any transactions you create. Since the HRESULT may only reflect the transfer of data to a local queue, the application may not be able to provide feedback on what happens when the data gets transferred from the local queue to the one on the server.

- **No Synchronous Result**   MSMQ provides asynchronous data transfer through messages. This means you can't expect instantaneous results from it. For example, you might query the database for recent customer orders. If the developer stores that information on your local hard drive, then you can expect to get a response even in disconnected mode. On the other hand, if the information appears only on the server, then you might receive some type of informational feedback instead of the data you requested. In a well-designed application, this feedback should allow you to retrieve the information you need. In short, there are some situations when a connection is required. The best the developer can do is to download a subset of the company's database to your machine. In most cases, this will include those records that the developer thinks you're most likely to need while in disconnected mode. This means that MSMQ applications require some level of intelligent download capability based on your schedule.

- **Complete Messages Only**   Since the requestor may be unavailable when the server begins processing a request, the messages an application sends to the server's message queue have to contain complete information. For example, if you want to enter a new order into the fulfillment database, all of the data required for that order has to appear within a single message. Unfortunately (despite assurances to the contrary), this might require the developer to perform some extra coding to get an application ready for MSMQ use.

As you can see, most of the limitations of MSMQ are based on the same thing that makes this technology so attractive in the first place. When a developer creates a disconnected application, he or she has to assume certain things about the client and the server, like the inability of the server and client to talk with each other. This means that the developer will have to think about the kinds of information both the client and server will require well in advance of the first trial on the road. It also means that you'll probably end up beta-testing that application for the developer for a much longer time than usual.

On Your Own

Now that you've spent a little time with MSMQ, you might want to learn more about it. Spend some time looking at the default queues created for MSMQ using the Computer Management snap-in in Administrative Tools folder of the Control Panel. Try to learn the purpose of each queue. (You won't find any messages in any of the queues until you install an MSMQ application.)

Use the Component Services MMC snap-in to view the default MSMQ components installed on your machine. Try to match the names of these components to their function in Figure 29.1

See if your company has any plans to use MSMQ as part of its application management strategy in the future. If so, you may want to volunteer for any pilot programs the company puts in place so that you can see MSMQ in action.

PART VII

Troubleshooting

Solving Software Problems

It would be nice to say that Windows 2000 takes care of every problem and that you'll never experience any kind of software error ever again—but that wouldn't be reality.

Of course, Windows 2000 does provide a level of safety you've probably never seen before. From a security standpoint, it's a lot better than Windows 95/98: If an application is ill-behaved, Windows 2000 kills it immediately. (In four months of extensive application testing, I didn't encounter a single general protection fault (GPF) or system crash under Windows 2000—either the application would run or it wouldn't.) However, that protection is a two-edged sword. Sure, you'll experience fewer software problems under Windows 2000, but part of the reason is that Windows 2000 is strict about what it allows, so many problem applications won't run at all.

Let's take a quick look again at Windows 2000 versus Windows 95/98. When you look at Windows 95/98, you're seeing the middle ground of reliability, not the best there is. Microsoft had to make some concessions to allow any legacy programs you used under Windows 3.x to run under Windows 95/98 as well. In addition, there was a problem getting enough security built into a package that must run in 8MB to 16MB of RAM. Space constraints make it difficult to take care of every kind of software-integrity problem.

Then Windows 2000 comes out and supposedly needs more RAM than Windows 95/98, although Microsoft's recommendations for the "minimal system" are frankly less than is really optimal for both of these operating systems. (We talk about the minimum requirements for a functional Windows 2000 system in Chapter 4.) In any case, much of the extra RAM in Windows 2000 is used to keep your machine from crashing when running marginal software. Not listed on the Windows 2000 package are all the applications it won't run at all because of the wealth of security features it provides. After Dark, a screen saver that runs fine under both Windows 3.x and Windows 95/98, for example, won't run at all under Windows 2000. Likewise, many games have problems with Windows 2000, violating good programming practice to squeeze out every possible 3D display efficiency. So far I can't get Civilization: Call to Power to work.

> **Note:** Windows 2000 does do a much better job of running marginal software than Windows NT did. I was surprised at the number of games that I was able to use. However, there are still many limitations to what you can expect to run under Windows 2000, for the reasons discussed in the preceding paragraphs.

So, how do these limitations affect you? First, you'll still have problems with GPFs when running a problem application under Windows 95/98, but at least the application will usually run. Windows 2000 provides a very strict environment for sensing programs that make illegal calls, and it recovers from them by just terminating the offending application. This won't quite work with some applications that depend on those illegal calls to run. As I've said several times throughout this book, you'll always have a trade-off: added flexibility with Windows 95/98, or added reliability with Windows 2000.

Another problem occurs with DOS support. In the Windows 95/98 environment, when your application switches to real mode to run, the operating system is vulnerable to attack. There's no real mode when using Windows 2000—the program builds a true virtual machine for your application to run in and never loses even a modicum of control. Windows 2000 handles DOS application problems by implementing a strict set of rules. A DOS application that breaks even the smallest of those rules gets terminated, just like its Windows counterpart. As with the Windows applications, Windows 95/98 relaxes these rules so that more applications can run. The result is that an errant application can crash the system. What does this mean in real life? Most of you who want to run games on your computer will be disappointed with the kind of support Windows 2000 provides (although you'll be less disappointed than when using Windows NT). On the other hand, I can get the vast majority of the games I've tried to run just fine under Windows 95/98. The trade-off is sharp, however, even for a business user. A lot of old graphics programs just didn't follow the rules. For example, an older copy of Harvard Graphics that works fine under Windows 95/98 won't even get past its splash screen under Windows 2000.

> **Tip:** The best advice I can give you is to test before you buy. If that old application is important and won't run under Windows 2000 in the store, no amount of fiddling will make it run on your computer at work, either. Take a look at Windows 95/98 before you make a Windows 2000 decision if you have marginal applications to run.

I've been testing Windows 2000 pretty thoroughly while writing this book. I've changed the Registry and tested what will and won't work. Setup also got a good workout as I added and removed applications. I even changed the network setup quite a few times to test different configurations. If Windows 2000 ever had a good reason to crash, it was while I kept changing its configuration. During this time, I didn't experience a single application-related crash (contrasted with about one per day with Windows 95/98 when I did a similar level of testing on it). However, I did experience several device driver-related crashes, one of which made my machine unusable. The culprits were old device drivers that Windows 2000 isn't equipped to run. It definitely pays to get hardware that includes device drivers designed to run under this new operating system. Fortunately, device driver problems are normally a one-time issue. Installing a new device driver usually fixes the problem permanently, unlike the myriad of application-specific crashes you'll experience when using Windows 95/98.

The bottom line? You don't get many things for free. That applies to operating systems as it does to most aspects of life. Windows 2000 is the best you can do when it comes to well-behaved, mission-critical applications. I don't think I'd settle for anything less when it comes to a data-entry program or inventory-control system. For those people who don't want an operating system that places their applications in a straitjacket and forces them to buy new applications, however, Windows 2000 is definitely not the answer. These folks will want something capable of running their old stuff well and their new stuff even better. That's what Windows 95/98 provides: tolerance, but at the cost of system stability. Of course, Windows 95/98 just doesn't provide anything close to the level of security provided by Windows 2000.

The next couple sections cover some of the problems you'll experience from a software perspective. I'll also tell you about some of the fixes that Microsoft provides to solve them. Will those fixes always work? Probably not. Fortunately, the fixes in this chapter *always* work. I can't say the same thing for Windows 95/98. During one incident, I had to actually reinstall Windows 95/98 and all my applications because the Registry got trashed beyond recognition. An application decided to overwrite some files that would have been fine under Windows 3.x but not under Windows 95/98. Suffice it to say that you'll experience fewer problems under Windows 2000 and that the cures Microsoft provides work most of the time, but thinking that they'll cure every problem just isn't realistic.

Setup and Configuration Errors

Configuration problems normally manifest themselves in several ways. The most devastating problems occur during system startup. Have you ever seen the infamous blue screen that appears when something really strange happens to the machine? (You may see a black screen instead of the infamous blue screen, in some cases, but the effect is the same.) If you reconfigure your machine as often as I do, you're definitely going to see it. Fortunately, Windows 2000 is a lot less prone to this problem than Windows 95/98. During similar periods of the same types of configuration changes (those required to write a book), Windows 2000 displayed the blue screen of death only one time, whereas Windows 95/98 displayed it four times.

> **Tip:** The blue screen problem is related to errors in Kernel mode. Applications don't cause blue screens; drivers, OS components, and system services cause them. Applications tend to cause Dr. Watson errors, which are commonly called general protection faults (GPFs).

The other types of configuration problems are a lot more devious. They usually rob your system of its flexibility or make some of its components unusable. You'll find yourself running in circles trying to identify the culprit, only to find that it wasn't any of the things you suspected at all. One of the problems I found in this category was my sound-board. I couldn't figure out what was wrong. The MIDI Balance setting kept getting out of whack. I looked at the driver—no luck. The same held true with the hardware itself. I thought there might be a problem in the way the CD software was working, so I disabled it. No luck there, either. After several days of searching, I found that the problem occurred only when I ran a particular multimedia program. Problems such as these can really make you want to pull your hair out.

Don't get the idea that configuration problems are always obvious. It's pretty easy to fig-ure out when your soundboard isn't working correctly—especially with my previous problems. Even my neighbors knew I had a problem with my soundboard. But what about the problem I was having with another application? It would work just fine—at least, just fine on most days. What would happen on the other days is almost indescrib-able. My machine would make a strange noise, the screen would look funny, and then one or more of my applications would just disappear. (The same problem under Windows 95/98 caused the system to reboot; disappearing applications are better than a reboot and are a testimony to Windows 2000's power to maintain control of the system even during serious perturbation.) I couldn't figure out what was going on. The solution to this prob-lem turned out to be a Control Panel setup problem. One of my applications had over-written the standard ODBC files. The new files were incompatible with this application in certain low-memory situations. I discovered that the problem always occurred when I had my word processor or any other large application open.

> **Tip:** I could have experienced a lot less grief fixing the ODBC file problem if I had recorded the time stamp for the files in that section or at least made note of the time stamp for my Windows 2000 files. You can do the same thing. Throughout this book, I've made every effort to tell you which files affect which functions. You can use this information when you're troubleshooting. It also comes in handy when you're recording information for a setup that works. When you get into a situation in which the setup no longer works properly, one of the things you can do is go back to your notes to find a potential source of trouble.

As you can tell, I've had a lot of fun digging up these real-life problems for you to learn about. The next few sections describe some of the types of problems you'll run into when your machine's configuration gets out of whack. I'll also provide you with some ideas on how to fix these problems.

Startup Problems

Startup problems are the worst kind of configuration problems to fix because you can't use the tools Windows 2000 provides to find them very easily. What usually happens is that the settings for one or more devices conflict, get lost, or are somehow incompatible with the device you're using. When a device conflict affects the display adapter or your hard drive, you see a blue screen. (Other, more insidious problems bring up the dreaded blue screen, such as a damaged Registry or a virus, but the most common problem is that of failed or misconfigured hardware, so I plan to cover these issues in this section.) That blue screen means that Windows 2000 can't recover from this sort of problem.

So, how do you get around this? The best way is to start the machine in Safe Mode. During the Windows 2000 startup, you can press F8 to display a list of Safe Mode startup selections. Highlight one of the options, and press Enter to return to the initial startup screen. At this point, Windows 2000 will start in Safe Mode rather than the standard mode.

Quite a few Safe Mode options exist, but all of them share some of the same characteristics. For one thing, your machine will default to using VGA mode, and the number of colors you'll see will be very limited. The easiest way to see if you're in Safe Mode is to look at the four corners of the display for the Safe Mode indicator, shown in Figure 30.1.

FIGURE 30.1
Windows 2000 indicates when you're in Safe Mode by displaying easily recognized indicators.

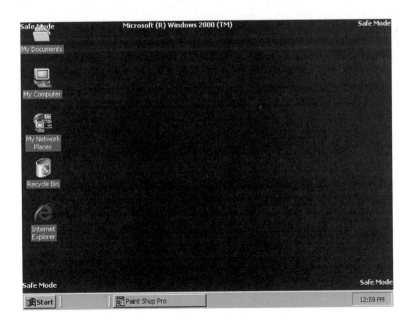

You'll notice some other differences during the boot sequence. For one thing, Windows 2000 displays more messages as it loads drivers. It also tests your hard drives for errors and performs other diagnostics (the hard drive tests are the most noticeable). Of course, the number and type of drivers installed depends on the level of Safe Mode support you request. The following list provides you with an overview of the various Safe Mode options and how they change the way that Windows 2000 starts.

- **Safe Mode**—This is the most restrictive of the Safe Mode options because it installs only basic device support. You won't be able to access the network or any special peripheral devices, such as soundcards. You'll normally use this level of Safe Mode support for catastrophic errors.

- **Safe Mode with networking**—In many cases, you'll need to gain access to the network to fix a problem with Windows 2000. This level of Safe Mode support allows you to interact with the network in a very limited way. At the time of this writing, you can access only Microsoft networks, which means that you won't be able to access other servers (such as Novell NetWare servers) using this mode.

- **Safe Mode with command prompt**—You can use a wealth of command-line utilities to fix problems with Windows 2000—especially those that affect the registry. When using this level of Safe Mode, you'll get a command window but no GUI. You'll need to press Ctrl+Alt+Delete to display the Windows Security dialog box and shut down the system when in this mode.

- **Enable Boot Logging**—This option allows you to start your machine normally. However, the boot cycle will take a lot longer because every action on the part of the operating system during the boot process gets recorded. This feature helps you to better determine exactly what command is causing the system to freeze, and it could help you restore the operating system to working order.

- **Enable VGA Mode**—Display adapters will always be a problem for any operating system because the technology they use is constantly changing. This option allows you to start your system normally, but your display adapter will use a very generic VGA driver instead of the one provided by the vendor. This option helps you detect problems with your display drivers with relative ease.

- **Last Known Good Configuration**—In a lot of situations you can reverse the effects of an errant device driver simply by restoring the last known good configuration. This option won't start you in Safe Mode, but it'll restore your configuration settings to those for the last good boot. In essence, any device drivers you installed during the last session will be ignored. However, they won't be uninstalled from your machine; you'll normally need to do that manually.

- **Directory Services Restore Mode (Windows 2000 domain controllers only)**—Even though this option is available, you can't use it with Windows 2000 Professional. This Safe Mode option is designed for use with domain controllers using one of the Windows 2000 Server versions only.

- **Debugging Mode**—This is a developer-specific mode that you won't ever need to use. It allows a developer to set the operating system up for low-level debugging, normally for device drivers.

Windows 2000 won't automatically boot in a fail-safe mode as Windows 95/98 will when there's a problem; Windows 2000 will boot with the configuration that you tell it to boot with. The only automatic startup behavior is the occasional disk cleanup. During the course of operation, Windows 2000 marks sectors as dirty or bad. During the next boot up, it runs a disk checker, similar in display to CHKDSK of DOS fame, to try to recover the data in these sections of the hard drive and mark them as unusable.

After your machine boots in Safe Mode, start looking for hardware or software conflicts. You might want to begin by removing all the applications and data files from your Startup folder. This is an especially bad problem area under Windows 2000 because its architecture almost ensures that some of your applications will have trouble running. Also, check WIN.INI to make sure that it contains no LOAD= or RUN= lines in it (click Start, and then select Run and type Sysedit). Go ahead and comment out (type REM at the start of the line) any lines you do find so that the application won't run the next time you start Windows. After you make sure that all the conflicts are resolved, start your machine again.

A second approach that's more efficient in some situations is to take a look at the Event Viewer. You'll find the Event Viewer in the Administrative Tools folder of the Control Panel (Start, Settings, Control Panel). If there's a device conflict, Windows 2000 will report it in the Event Viewer's System log during bootup. Event Viewer watches the memory allocation of the drivers and services at startup very closely. Of course, this could be done even before entering fail-safe mode, as long as the system doesn't go blue screen. Also, if a blue screen appears, the first and most direct method of determining the problem is to read the blue screen. It can be a bit cryptic, but you can probably figure out at the very least which driver caused the problem. After that, search Microsoft's TechNet (http://www.microsoft.com/technet/default.asp) to figure out who owns the driver.

As a final note, remember that WIN.INI, AUTOEXEC.BAT, and CONFIG.SYS have almost nothing to do with Windows 2000 unless you're running a lot of old applications. Those INI files and the other two startup files are left for compatibility, but most of their settings are actually translated by Windows 2000 into Registry settings. Take a look at them with Start, Run and then type Sysedit.

Hardware Configuration Problems

Hardware-specific configuration problems can become an extremely complex issue under Windows 2000, but you can do a few things to make life a bit easier. The first thing you should do is look at the log in the Event Viewer. Normally, it displays a message for each device that won't start. If you see two devices that didn't start, it's fairly certain that you have some kind of conflict between them, not a failure of one of them.

Figure 30.2 shows a typical Event Viewer display. It also shows the detailed description of one of the entries—normally, this text tells you what went wrong with the device's initialization and gives you a starting place for troubleshooting. The mechanics of using the Event Viewer were covered in Chapter 7, "Performance Power," so I won't cover them again here.

FIGURE 30.2

Hardware conflicts can become a thorny issue under Windows 2000; Event Viewer at least gives you a place to look.

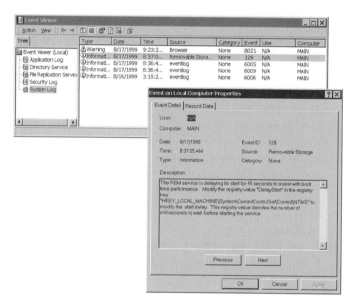

The Event log normally records every kind of hardware failure that's the result of an actual failure or some kind of conflict. In some situations, however, Windows 2000 won't record a problem. What happens if you've installed a new device, for example, but it doesn't actually get started? Double-click the System applet in the Control Panel, choose the Hardware tab, and click the Device Manager button. You'll see a dialog box similar to the one shown in Figure 30.3.

Notice that two defective devices are listed in the Other Devices folder in Figure 30.3. The first has a question mark with an exclamation point added to it—this means that the device isn't working for some reason. In most cases, it means that Windows 2000 detected the device but was incapable of finding a driver for it. In some cases, it means that the driver you provided won't work with Windows 2000. In still other cases, it means that the device failed. Whatever the cause of failure, you can double-click the device entry to get further information about fixing the problem. The Device status field on the General tab of the Device Properties dialog box will contain a message describing the problem.

FIGURE 30.3

The Device Manager shows you which devices either aren't working or are simply disabled.

The second entry in the Other Devices folder has a question mark with a red X on it—this means that the device is disabled. You must manually disable a device because Windows 2000 will never automatically disable it for you. Enabling a device is as simple as changing the Device Usage field of the General tab of the Device Properties dialog box.

Windows NT users will be familiar with the Services applet found in the Administrative Tools folder of the Control Panel. In the past, this applet would have listed all drivers for your machine; now it lists only the services that your machine provides, as shown in Figure 30.4. However, the lack or inclusion of a service on your machine can affect how the hardware runs. For example, the Print Spooler service (highlighted in Figure 30.4) provides background printing support for any printers attached to your machine. Figure 30.4 might look a little complex at first, but it's relatively easy to understand. Obviously, the first entry you'll look for is the service name and associated description. The next thing you should look for is a Started entry in the Status column. A blank tells you that the device wasn't started. This is where you figure out whether a service will start. Just highlight the device you want to test, and then click the Start Service button. If the device doesn't start, look in the Event Viewer for a potential cause of the problem. On the other hand, if it does start, you might have to look at the device's starting mode, which is listed in the Startup Type column of the Service dialog box.

Changing the Startup Type setting for a service is easy. Just double-click the service entry, and you'll see a Service Properties dialog box, like the one shown in Figure 30.5. The Startup Type field of this dialog box allows you to modify the way that the service gets started during the Windows 2000 boot process.

FIGURE 30.4

A device could look like it's malfunctioning when you just didn't start it.

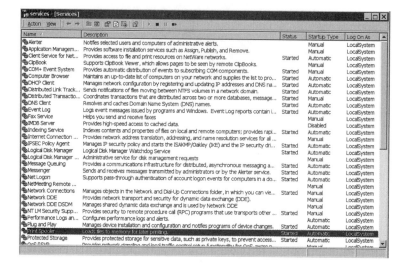

FIGURE 30.5

Windows 2000 provides three starting modes for devices; you need to select the right one to ensure that the device actually starts.

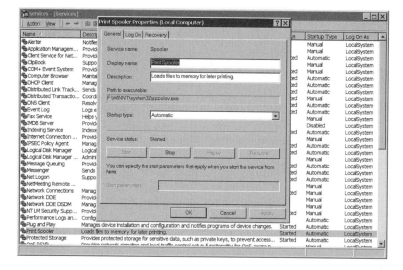

As previously mentioned, Windows NT provided both device and service support through this one utility. Windows 2000 needs to provide only service support, so there are fewer startup modes than before. You need to select one of the three starting modes described here for the various services installed on your machine:

- **Automatic**—These are services, such as the print spooler, that you'll need every time you start your machine. Any service that gets used every time you start your machine should be set to automatic. This includes services that are attached to a specific class of hardware. For example, if you have a smart card attached to your machine, you'll want to set the Smart Card and Smart Card Helper services to automatic. The default setting is manual.

- **Manual**—Some services don't get started every time Windows 2000 starts. This is especially true of services such as Windows Installer that don't get used every time you start the machine. Some hardware-related services fall into this category (although they're admittedly fewer than other service types). For example, you might have some special data-gathering device on your machine or a special hardware feature that's not essential to system operation. You can place either one of these devices (and the services that support them) in the Manual category. Dependent devices—those that rely on another device to start them—also fall into this category.

- **Disabled**—This is a special setting for services that are installed on your machine but that you won't use. A disabled service can't be started, even if you try to start it from the Services dialog box. In most cases, you'll never disable a service unless you're tuning your system and are absolutely certain that you won't need the service. Windows 2000 does use this setting for services that are installed and not implemented. For example, it always installs the Routing and Remote Access service but leaves the service in the disabled state until you need routing or remote access services.

Windows Software Configuration Problems

A Windows application configuration can go wrong in many ways. I recently installed an older 16-bit application that required Program Manager to install properly. For whatever reason, the setup application didn't signal its need for Program Manager, and I thought the installation was a success.

On the contrary, the setup program had actually quit before it completed the installation, so I was missing an important INI file. The result was a piece of software that kept freezing my machine. I fixed the problem by manually creating and installing the required INI file. The moral of the story is to install any old 16-bit Windows applications with the assumption that they may not work because of simple installation problems rather than application incompatibility with Windows 2000. That way, you'll avoid any problems.

Other Windows application problems can arise as well. Have you ever noticed how many applications want to modify your path statement in AUTOEXEC.BAT? Unfortunately, if the application actually does modify AUTOEXEC.BAT, the settings it needs won't appear under Windows 2000. You must set up the path in the System Environment Variables section of the System Properties dialog box (you access it by right-clicking My Computer and choosing Properties from the context menu). Of course, even intercepting these settings and making them by hand in the program's stead can cause problems. If you let every application have its way, you'll probably have a mile-long path. Many applications run just fine without a path statement. However, there are two ways in which an application can fail.

Typically, if an application is adjusting AUTOEXEC.BAT, it's a DOS or Windows 3.1 application. In these cases, when the application starts, Windows 2000 will run AUTOEXEC.BAT as part of creating the DOS session, and it'll add application-specific path information to the PATH statement for that session. You also can configure the system to allow for individual paths based on the shortcuts. You can have Windows 2000 run a batch file ahead of the application to ensure that all those DOS settings are made ahead of the application starting.

I ran across the first problem area by accident: I added the file association required for a new application I installed. Whenever I double-clicked a data file, however, I got a message that the application couldn't find the data file. The application started just fine, but it wouldn't load the data file. After a few hours of troubleshooting, I found that I could get rid of the problem by adding the application's location to my path.

Some applications fail in a big way if you don't add them to the path statement. CA-Visual Objects and some other large applications fall into this category. They usually provide some nebulous error message and quit before you can get them going—either that, or the application loads and then refuses to load any add-ons because it can't find them. You might see symptoms of this problem when an application can't remember any customizations or options you specify. Whenever you're in doubt, try adding the application to your path statement to see whether the problem goes away.

Shared-file (such as DLL) corruption is another problem area. The DLL might not actually contain any bad data—it might work just fine with several other applications. One application might require an older version of the DLL, however, because it uses an undocumented feature of that DLL or uses some bug to its advantage. Sometimes you'll need to keep the old version of a DLL on disk to satisfy the needs of a particular application.

But what happens if one application needs the new version of the DLL and another application requires the old version? In that case, you must decide which of these two applications to keep. In most cases, I use this situation as an excuse to upgrade my software. There usually isn't any reason to keep an old application around if it refuses to work with all your newer applications. In fact, an incompatibility of this type usually means that it really is time to retire that old application and get the newer version.

> **Tip:** A few applications will look for the DLLs they need in their home directory before they look in the Windows 2000 system directory. If you have an application that needs an old DLL to run, try placing the DLL in the program's home directory. The problem with this approach is that Windows will load only one copy of a DLL at a time into memory. This means that you'll have to reboot the machine after using the old application to clear the old DLL from memory.

I ran into a really strange problem with one application on my machine. This was a communications program, but I imagine the same thing could happen with any application. Every time I tried to open this application, it filled the screen—and then some. No matter what I did, as soon as the main application window appeared, the machine froze and I had to reboot. As it turned out, I discovered that the problem was caused by the fact that I had lowered my screen resolution to capture some screen shots for this book. This is yet another example of an application that failed because its environment was not set up correctly. The point that I'm trying to make is that the cause of failure isn't always obvious. You usually need to spend some time looking for the potential cause of a problem. Some of these causes can lead you down blind alleys into places you thought would never fail. You can also deal with this kind of problem by pressing Ctrl+Alt+Delete, choosing Task Manager, and then clicking End Task after selecting the offending program from the list of running applications.

DOS Software Configuration Problems

If you thought Windows software had a lot of failure points, you haven't worked with enough DOS software recently. You'll never get some applications to run under any version of Windows. Most of these applications fall into the game category, but I've seen others in this situation as well.

An application that assumes it has the machine to itself, combined with users who keep asking for better performance, equals a situation in which the programmer is going to access the hardware directly in ways that the programming community as a whole would never recommend. This is precisely the situation some game and utility program vendors get into. Users are always demanding faster games with better graphics and sound, yet they want to run these programs on very outdated hardware. The game programmers usually must resort to register-level programming to get the speed the user wants. Of course, this usually means that any mistake in programming—even a small one—results in a frozen machine or perhaps even, in rare cases, a damaged hard drive. Fortunately, Windows 2000 isn't very susceptible to DOS application-induced failures. Remember, Windows 2000 is a highly secure environment that's well defended from errant applications. On the other hand, it gets around the problem by refusing to run them at all.

> **Note:** Running DOS applications is one area in which Windows 95/98 exceeds the capabilities of Windows 2000, if that matters to you. Applications that fall into this category can be fixed in only one way: You must run them in Windows 95/98 MS-DOS mode or under native DOS.

So, how can you fix that errant DOS application? I usually look at the application settings to see whether I can find a potential problem. Here's one scenario: You have a game program that always freezes when you run it in Windows, but it works fine from the DOS prompt. What's the problem? I found several setting-related problems that can wreak havoc with a game. One of them is that you can't assume that the soundboard settings you use in DOS are the same ones Windows uses. Checking all your settings is an important part of getting a DOS application to run.

Other setting-related problems exist as well. Many of my games require that I add a SoundBlaster setting to my AUTOEXEC.BAT, for example. They read this setting and configure themselves appropriately. If you don't include the SET statement, the game freezes because it doesn't know what settings to use. As with every other environment setting under Windows 2000, you'll find the SET statements in the System Environment Variable section of the System Properties dialog box (click the System icon in the Control Panel, click the Advanced tab, and then click the Environment Variables button).

Speaking of settings, most DOS applications are very sensitive to the environment settings. I find that compilers are the worst culprits in this area, but other applications can be quite challenging as well. It's usually a good idea to run every application that requires a complex environment setup from a batch file. Add all the required environment settings to the beginning of the batch file, and make running the application the last step. You might have to change the program's environment size setting to make this work. See Chapter 5, "Exploring the Interface," for more details on the DOS application memory settings.

After you get past settings and strange hardware-access problems, you might face a few other problems. One of the big problems, especially with games, is a lack of conventional memory. This issue was covered fairly thoroughly in Chapter 5, but it pays to mention it again. Unlike Windows 95/98, you don't have any alternatives when a DOS application won't run in the conventional memory space that Windows 2000 provides. You have no Memory Manager solutions at your disposal, nor are there any Terminate Stay Residents (TSRs, little applets that sometimes caused problems in DOS) you can unload—as you see, Windows 2000 is all there is. If a DOS application won't run on your system because it doesn't have enough conventional memory, you must use native DOS or run it under Windows 95/98.

> **Technical Note:** Native memory is simulated in Windows 2000. Direct memory access is forbidden and thus may present itself as a memory resource issue, but it isn't. Each DOS application has plenty of memory to run. Other situations can also create problems that appear to be memory issues but that really aren't.

Memory-Related Problems

You can face quite a few memory-related problems under Windows 2000, and these fall into several categories. It's important to know which one you're dealing with before you attempt to fix the problem. The following list categorizes the various memory-related problems you could have when using Windows 2000. Go through the list to see whether you can find the symptoms that match your particular problem:

- **Memory leaks**—A few Windows applications don't manage memory properly. They grab a lot of memory from Windows and then don't release all of it when they terminate. The result is a gradual loss of memory capacity that you can actually track by using the Memory field of the application's Help About dialog box. You'll also notice that your other applications start to slow down after a while as the system starts using a larger swap file to make up for the memory loss. If you have an application that shows a gradual loss of memory, the best way to use it is to start it once and then leave it open the entire time you need to use it. Such an application still gradually bleeds memory from the system, but the loss is more gradual if you don't open and close it very much. Eventually, you'll need to reboot the machine to regain the memory; just restarting Windows won't do the trick. You actually need to restart the system from scratch (a cold reboot, so-called because you must turn off the power and then turn it back on). Logging data to the Performance Monitor is an alternative approach. See Chapters 7 and 11 for more information on how to use that utility. Also, try looking at the Task Manager's Performance tab, which will show you an overall picture of memory usage graphically, although the change in memory usage might be quite gradual.

- **Too many frills**—Some types of memory problems are created when you have too many frills on your machine. You might find that Microsoft Access or another large application is running very slowly or could even produce GPFs a lot after you add a screen saver or another frill to the system. Most people associate utilities with small memory requirements, but this isn't necessarily true. A utility generally accomplishes a more limited, narrowly defined set of tasks than a full-fledged application. However, you shouldn't assume that because the utility is more limited in its focus that it's necessarily limited in its memory requirements. DOS utilities had to stay small to keep their conventional memory requirements to a minimum, but Windows utilities have no such limitation. Their designers have fewer reasons to keep their applications small because Windows is designed to allow for better memory management. Also, people generally have much more memory these days, now that you can get 32MB for about $50.

- **Windows system space corruption**—I find it incredible that some vendors put so little effort into testing their products that this type of problem could actually go unnoticed. What usually happens is that an errant pointer in the application starts overwriting the Windows system area. Most of the time, Windows 2000 detects this problem and displays an appropriate warning dialog box. In fact, I've never actually seen this problem myself, but a few people have reported seeing it. Windows 2000 always recovers by terminating the application. On a few occasions, Windows 2000 doesn't detect the problem until it's too late and half its brain is gone; then it just freezes. In most cases, you'll want to contact the vendor about this kind of problem and see whether a workaround or fix is available.

- **Disk thrashing**—If you try to use an application that your system can't really support, you might experience something called disk thrashing. You'll know your system is thrashing if the hard disk light stays on for abnormally long periods of time and an application runs really slowly. Probably the best way to fix this problem is to add more memory (remember, memory is now relatively inexpensive). Of course, you can also look at some of the memory-saving techniques discussed in Chapter 7.

- **Display memory corruption**—Some older Windows applications might experience problems when writing to the display. Even though they use a different method than DOS, in some situations a Windows application can cause problems with the entire display. One of these situations is when it changes the palette (the display colors if you're using a 256-color setting or less) without regard for any other applications running on the system. You can't do much about this problem. The application window will probably look fine, but everything around it will use really strange color combinations that might produce unreadable text. The big problem occurs when an pplication leaves the display in this state even after it exits. You might see other forms of display corruption as well. It's possible for an application to corrupt the icon cache, for example. You'll see on the display icons that no longer match the functions associated with them, or your icons might disappear altogether. The fix for this condition is to exit the application and reboot the system. Sometimes even that does not work, however. If you find that the problem persists, you might have to erase the ShellIconCache file in your WINNT folder and reboot the machine. The ShellIconCache file contains an archive of the most recently used icons. Windows 2000 loads this file when it starts to reduce the time it spends reading the icons from disk. Some types of corruption become embedded in this file when Windows exits with a corrupted icon cache in memory. However, this problem is far more common in Windows 95/98 than in Windows 2000.

Probably other ways exist by which to corrupt memory as well. Windows 2000 uses other cache files, for example. Any of these caches could become corrupted and cause problems for your system. You'll need to spend some time looking for the particular cache files on your system. Besides the ShellIconCache, I also had a ttfCache, a FRMCACHE.DAT file, and several other caches on my system. The ttfCache affects the fonts listed in the Fonts folder (you may see it as FTNCACHE.DAT). You might find that the fonts listed no longer match the fonts actually in the directory if certain types of memory corruption occur. The same holds true for the FRMCACHE.DAT file. Erasing the corrupted file and allowing Windows 2000 to rebuild it during the next boot cycle easily cures any type of cache corruption. To locate the caches on your system, click Start, Search, For Files or Folders, type cache into the Search for Files and Folders Named field, and search your hard drive(s).

> **Note:** You're unlikely to run into this type of corruption, however. This caching information may appear in Windows 2000 only for compatibility with Windows 95/98 applications that might use them.

After you identify and clean up a memory-corruption problem, it's usually a good idea to find the application responsible. Most memory-corruption problems won't just go away. You'll find that the corruption occurs over and over again at the worst possible moment. After you identify the culprit, you usually must contact the vendor to find out whether a fix is available. If one isn't, you need to decide whether to live with the corruption problem or get a new application, one that hopefully doesn't exhibit the same memory-corruption problem you're trying to get rid of.

So, how do you find the culprit? You can't just assume that the culprit is the foreground application; it could be a background application. For that matter, it doesn't have to be an application at all. A device driver could be causing the memory corruption as you use a specific device. A third class of problem is some type of interaction between two applications or an application and a device driver. You have to start somewhere, however, and looking at the applications you have running is a good place to start. You can follow this simple procedure to find many, but not all, of the memory-corruption problems on your system:

1. Start a list of potential problem applications. I usually make note of all the applications I had running when a memory-corruption problem occurred. It's also important to make notes on any devices you had running. Of course, some devices are always running, so it doesn't pay to list those.

2. Run the suspected applications one at a time to see whether you can get the problem to repeat.

3. If you still don't find the culprit, go back to your normal setup and try various combinations of applications. You could be seeing some type of interaction problem.

4. Take a look at the Application Log in the Event Viewer to see whether there were any problems loading the drivers or any conflicts in resource usage. Windows 2000 is very particular about who can access memory and where.

5. Keep a running list of active applications each time the memory problem appears. Eventually, you'll see a pattern of one or more applications that always seem to be around when the problem occurs. Try loading just this group of applications and see whether you can get the problem to happen again. Keep whittling down the list until you end up with one or two applications that won't work together. The solution is to avoid running them at the same time.

This kind of testing by a process of elimination is time-consuming; if you do it right, however, you can usually track down a stubborn problem without enormous difficulty. Unfortunately, memory problems are inherently difficult to locate in an environment such as Windows 2000 because so many things are happening simultaneously. Each application and device driver interacts. You'll find that the hardest problems to find are those that result from three or four applications or device drivers working against each other. It always pays to take your time and do a thorough job of testing each potential problem area.

Of course, when you come to a conclusion, finding a permanent fix could prove to be the most difficult part of the journey. You've probably gone through this before: the waiting on the phone as each vendor points the finger at someone else. In reality, there might not be an easy fix for some types of memory problems; you might just have to avoid the situations that cause them in the first place. Get a newer version of the same application, or even go as far as to update your hardware.

On Your Own

Reboot your machine, press F8, choose Safe Mode from the resulting menu, then continue booting your machine. It's important to actually see how your display looks in VGA mode. Fortunately, unlike Windows NT, Windows 2000 does display a Safe Mode message that allows you to quickly determine the status of your machine.

Check out the contents of the Administrative Tools folder and System applet in the Control Panel. These two Control Panel entries contain most of the tools that you'll need to troubleshoot your system.

Use the Device Manager found on the Hardware tab of the System Properties dialog box to make a list of the devices that are currently installed on your machine. (Make note of any devices that aren't operational, and do what you can to make them functional.) You can use this list as a troubleshooting aid when you experience some kind of problem. Comparing the items on your list to those that are actually started during a crisis could help you pinpoint the source of the problem. You'll also want to note the startup mode for the device, just in case an application you install decides to change it.

If you have an old DOS application that you can't get to run, try to find out why. You might discover that the soundboard or other device settings you're using don't match those used by Windows. If there's a conflict, try changing the DOS application settings to those used by Windows to see whether that will enable you to run the application normally. Also check for environment settings (look at PATH or SET) that could affect your capability to use the application from within Windows. Run the Sysedit utility from Start, Run to check this out.

Devise a recovery strategy for your machine. If you're a network administrator, devise a strategy for all the machines on the network. Keep track of this strategy, and change it as necessary to meet changing user and machine needs.

31

Solving Hardware Problems

Under Windows 2000 (or any operating system, for that matter), hardware problems are usually less of an issue than software problems. The reason is fairly easy to understand. Hardware problems generally fall into two easily recognized groups: compatibility issues and catastrophic failure (the device simply won't respond).

> **Note:** Unlike other versions of Windows, Windows 2000 provides extensive system-monitoring features that you can use as part of your strategy for monitoring catastrophic failure. For example, an increase in the amount of network traffic for a particular workstation might not indicate anything more than a bad cable or a failing network interface card (NIC). The section "Monitoring the Results of Performance Enhancements" in Chapter 7, "Performance Power," covers the monitoring capability that Windows 2000 provides, so I won't cover it again here.

The fact that you can't use real-mode device drivers under Windows 2000 is a real problem for companies with older machines. Upgrading every piece of equipment can be an expensive proposition. Forbidding real-mode drivers, though, means reduced compatibility problems and a higher level of reliability.

I wish I could say that compatibility issues are a thing of the past, but I can't quite go that far. You'll still find NICs that won't work under Windows 2000, as well as a long list of ancient equipment that isn't supported by Windows 2000 at all. On the plus side, compatibility problems are fairly easy to fix under Windows 2000. You'll probably get a symptom like this: A device looks as if it failed, but later testing shows that it hasn't. I've already covered some of the solutions for this type of problem. For the most part, you'll find that they're easy to trace and fix.

The Importance of Maintaining a DOS Partition

Before the dart you're throwing hits my head, think about the Windows 2000 environment for a second. Why did you buy Windows 2000 rather than Windows 95/98? In most cases, it's because of the added robustness and security that Windows 2000 provides. It's more robust and it's able to do things on a larger scale than Windows 95/98. Running mission-critical applications, including acting as a Web server, is one of the biggest reasons some IT managers in corporate America didn't buy into Windows 95/98.

> **Note:** Windows 95/98 machines can act as Web servers of a sort, but you'll want to use Windows 2000 for mission-critical applications on an intranet or on the Internet. The Web server provided with Windows 95/98 is meant for small setups, and it lacks many of the features you'd need to implement a large site.

The same two qualities that make Windows 2000 such a pleasure to use (robustness and security) also hinder the diagnosis of hardware failures. I've actually worked on several machines where Windows 2000 led me to believe that one component had failed when the problem was actually something totally different. The fact that an application has no direct access to the hardware means that it can't really "talk" to the device and ask it what's wrong.

For that reason, I usually try to provide some type of alternative environment for troubleshooting hardware failures. Some diagnostic tools come with their own operating system or reside on a board that troubleshoots the system at the hardware level. In most cases, these diagnostic aids are a bit of a challenge to use, so I use DOS-based utilities as my first line of defense and reserve these other tools for situations in which the DOS-based products can't get the job done for me. Using DOS-based utilities also allows me to include hardware vendor–specific diagnostic aids with my tools. Many major display adapter vendors include a diagnostic disk with their product, and that disk is sometimes DOS based.

You don't have to maintain a DOS partition on your machine if you don't want to, but I consider it a good idea. I usually keep a small 10MB partition—just large enough to hold my diagnostic aids and a copy of DOS. As an alternative, you can always resort to using floppy disks to hold the diagnostic tools. Obviously, this isn't the most efficient approach—you'll spend some amount of time swapping floppy disks back and forth—but it works, too.

A Quick Look at Catastrophic Failure

Figuring out a catastrophic error usually takes a little time and a few hardware and software tools. You also have to know how to use these tools.

Here's a typical scenario. You start your machine in the morning, and Windows 2000 comes up fine, but you can't use the mouse. After a little looking around, you find that there aren't any conflicts and you haven't installed anything new recently. The probable cause of your problem is some type of hardware failure. At least, that's a good place to start searching for the problem. Device Manager allows you to quickly determine whether Windows recognizes a device failure. You can open Device Manager by clicking the Device Manager button on the Hardware tab of the System Properties dialog box (double-click the System icon in Control Panel to open this dialog box). A failed device will be marked with a yellow exclamation mark over the usual device type symbol. (Disabled devices are marked with a red ∞ over the device type symbol—you should always try to enable a disabled device before you assume that it's failed.)

All kinds of problems fall into the catastrophic category. For example, a crimped cable can cause some types of hardware failure. It might be as simple as a device that won't respond or a network connection that seems to work intermittently. Port failures don't happen often, but they do happen. You'll also find that NICs fail from time to time. Everyone knows that hard drives fail.

Part of the problem for a network administrator or a home user is figuring out how to find the problem for certain. Some people try a simple process of elimination: They just replace one component at a time until they locate the problem. Unfortunately, that's really not the best way to do things. Using diagnostic aids and other troubleshooting tools will save you a lot more time than they cost.

> **Note:** The process of replacing pieces of hardware until the problem is located is sometimes called *Easter egging* by people who frequently work with hardware. That's not to be confused with the other way the term *Easter eggs* is used in computing: That refers to software in which you can see special embedded messages by pressing certain key combinations. There are even special graphics found in some locations in Flight Simulator (try flying east of Cairo). These special items are put into software by the programmers for their amusement and for the enjoyment of those "in the know."

> **Tip:** Never discount the usefulness of hardware-specific diagnostic aids. Most soundboard and display adapter vendors include a complete, highly specific diagnostic for their product as part of the package. Some hardware vendors are starting to include this feature with motherboards and other major components as well. I even found one motherboard vendor—ASUS—that provides a diagnostic disk with its products. The diagnostic tests basic motherboard functionality and any installed memory. In addition, a real-time monitoring program constantly checks the power supply status, motherboard temperature, and cooling fan rotation speed. An alarm sounds if any of these monitored devices fail, allowing you to react quickly before any more damage occurs.

Let's look at some of the diagnostic aids I've found helpful in the past. The following sections aren't necessarily an inclusive list of every tool you'll ever want, but you might find that they provide enough help so that you can get through a repair with a minimum of effort.

Peter's Principle: DOS, Windows 2000, and OS-Independent Diagnostic Programs: How to Choose the Right One for Your Needs

It's easiest to use a diagnostic program that runs under Windows 2000. You just run it. This simplicity makes most DOS or lower-level diagnostic schemes look totally inefficient by comparison. After all, the efficiency of the GUI is the primary reason most people switched from DOS to Windows in the first place. And, in fact, you can rely on Windows 2000 diagnostics to provide vivid graphics, an easy mouse-based input style, and useful and easy-to-read information. These diagnostic utilities also locate a great majority of the hardware problems you could experience as well.

However, recall that for some kinds of problems there just isn't any reliable way to completely test your hardware from within Windows 2000. Although a product such as Norton Utilities for Windows 2000 provides you with a superior level of Windows 2000–specific information, you just can't count on it to offer the ultimate level of hardware analysis. The multitasking nature of the operating system makes this impossible. A thorough diagnosis demands total access to the hardware. Windows 2000 won't allow this kind of access. It requires that access be achieved through drivers (and drivers themselves can be the problem).

There's another issue with Windows 2000 diagnostic programs—something that won't occur to most people until it's too late. What happens if you can get DOS up and running but a hardware conflict or failure prevents Windows 2000 from starting? I've experienced this particular problem more than a few times. Using a DOS diagnostic means that if the system will boot at all, you can at least figure out what's going on. Using an OS-independent diagnostic is the purest approach of all, as you'll see in the discussion of #1-TuffTEST in a moment.

The bottom line? Most of the time, you'll find that a simpler Windows 2000–based diagnostic product works fine for a home user with only one PC to worry about and little capability of fixing some of the more difficult problems anyway. As soon as you move into a corporate environment and have more than one PC to work with, however, it's imperative that you work with something a little more broadly reliable. We'll examine two examples of this kind of Windows 2000 diagnostic utility later in this chapter.

Note: What about using a DOS session within Windows 2000? Are you kidding? You're going down into one additional level of abstraction. Although you could probably at least run DOS diagnostic products from within the Windows DOS box, the results you'll get are going to be inaccurate at best. Always run your diagnostic programs in a separate DOS partition; that way, you know you're getting a complete diagnostic check of the system. Windows 2000 allows you to maintain a separate DOS partition. If you do, Windows 2000 displays an option to start in DOS when you start your machine. Chapter 4, "Installing Windows 2000 Professional: A Setup Primer," tells you how to create a multiple-boot setup.

Microsoft Diagnostic (WINMSD)

Microsoft Diagnostic (MSD) has been around for a long time. Microsoft includes it with both DOS and Windows but doesn't install it to your hard drive with Windows 2000. What you get instead is a GUI form of the product named Windows MSD (WINMSD for short). WINMSD (also known by other names like System Information) has been around in various forms over the last few years, but I think you'll find the latest incarnation is actually the easiest to use because it includes the Explorer interface (as does everything else in Windows 2000).

Note: The version of WINMSD that comes with Windows 2000 relies on the Windows Management Instrumentation service to perform its work. (You can start it by using the Start, Run command to open the Run dialog, type WINMSD in the Open field, and then click Run. It also appears as an MMC snap-in called System Information found in the Computer Management applet of the Administrative Tools folder in the Control Panel.) This service is normally stopped by default and is set to activate manually. If you find that WINMSD can't read the status information of your local machine, you may need to check the status of the Windows Management Instrumentation service. You'll find this service in the Services applet in the Administrative Tools folder of the Control Panel. To start the service, right-click the service entry and then choose Start from the context menu.

WINMSD's original purpose was to provide Microsoft technicians and beta support staff with a full accounting of the capabilities that your machine provides. Figure 31.1 shows that this is still its main purpose. WINMSD helps detect any hardware you have installed on your machine. It also allows you to save this information to a file that you can use for future reference (use the Save As Text File or Save As System Information File entry on the WINMSD Action menu).

Tip: There's a popular trick being played on unsuspecting computer buyers today. Rapscallions and scoundrels have found that it's easy to open up a mom-and-pop computer store in, say, Outatheway, Florida. It's only $300 a month to rent a storefront in cheesy, run-down strip malls, and if you promise to hold their hand when they get confused, some people will prefer your style of "customer service" to the big players, especially mail-order. Sometimes buying hardware this way is a bad move. Many small computer dealers are honest; others aren't. The dishonest ones have been slapping 450MHz stickers on 133MHz machines, and worse. How does the average computer buyer know—aside from a vague sense that the machine is sluggish—what speed Pentium he or she has bought? WINMSD to the rescue: Double-click the System Summary folder, shown in Figure 31.1, wait a few seconds while it collects its data, and then you'll see the processor type, speed, and even the amount of memory installed on your machine. Hope you see what you expected to see! Better yet, run it in the store before you hand over your credit card.

FIGURE 31.1

The opening WIN-MSD (System Information) display shows the types of hardware WINMSD will detect for you.

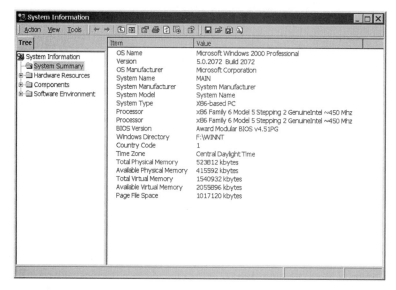

The main reason for using WINMSD is to detect all your functional hardware. The key word, of course, is *functional*. If you run WINMSD and find that it doesn't detect something, there's a pretty good chance that one of two things occurred. Either the driver required to turn on the device isn't present, or the device has failed. If you can eliminate the first cause, you have found the cause of a hardware failure.

Tip: You can use WINMSD across a network as well as on a local machine. Choose Properties on the WINMSD Action menu or click the Properties button (currently only available when executing WINMSD from the Run dialog box, not available from Computer Management). The Select Computer tab will allow you to choose the local computer or a remote computer. You'll be able to view the status of all the machines on your network this way, which is quite a bit easier when you're inventorying network-wide data and would prefer not to have to travel to each local computer.

WINMSD is pretty limited as far as diagnostic aids go, but you can use it in a pinch. It'll accurately detect serial port types in most cases—something the earlier DOS version had a problem doing. If you're maintaining more than one machine, I recommend you use WINMSD for its intended purpose—hardware inventory—and supplement that data with a commercial diagnostic aid that provides more information.

There's one additional way in which WINMSD can help that you won't find in most diagnostic aids. Let's say you check a piece of hardware using a DOS utility and it works fine. Unfortunately, the same piece of hardware is nonoperational within Windows.

You can use WINMSD to find out detailed status information about your device, including the version number of any specialty files (see Figure 31.2). (Driver file information is stored on the Driver tab of the device Properties dialog box accessible through Device Manager—just click the Driver Details button and you'll see a list of drivers and details such as version number and creation date.)

FIGURE 31.2
WINMSD allows you to detect status information about devices on your system.

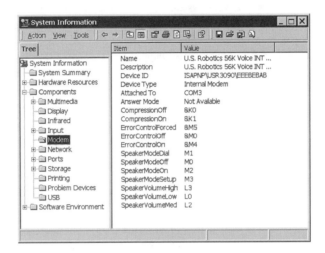

#1-PC Diagnostics Co. PC-Technician and TuffTEST

Running a diagnostic using any operating system is risky business. The problem is that the operating system can actually interfere with your ability to find a problem. This is less of a problem under DOS than under Windows, because the diagnostic can simply bypass the operating system, but the problem is real.

PC-Technician (which recently changed its name from Windsor Technologies, Inc.) takes an approach that solves this Windows 2000 OS interference problem: You boot from your A: drive with PC-Technician's disk in the drive; then it uses its own proprietary loader to load its own custom operating system. This allows PC-Technician to take complete control of the computer system. It's also able to diagnose the hardware no matter what OS is running on the various systems an office might include. The product has been well thought out. For example, it even relocates itself while testing memory, so all memory ends up getting certified.

PC-Technician (and its sister products described next) stands out from the pack for reasons beyond its useful OS independence. PC For example, the code is written in assembly language and is therefore compact; compare this approach with DOS-based diagnostic utilities written in C that can take up a huge chunk of memory. PC Also, instead of relying on existing device drivers, the utility employs its own device drivers—yet another way that this diagnostic analysis works directly with the hardware rather than going through (possibly problematic) existing drivers. All you do is place the floppy disk in a drive and boot the machine. The next thing you'll see is the PC-Technician display.

The fact that PC-Technician doesn't need an operating system is a big advantage in several ways. First, you can use PC-Technician on any machine, even if your company uses several different operating systems. Second, using this product means you don't have to have a functional hard drive to test the machine. Of course, DOS versions of diagnostic software can say the same thing. Third, you don't need to worry as much about viruses affecting the results of your tests. The non-DOS format of the PC-Technician disk makes it more difficult for a virus to infect it. Still, Windsor Technologies does provide some information on virus prevention that you should follow.

The product comes in four flavors. The full PC-Technician is designed for people who make their living servicing other people's computers. It comes with a carrying case for field use, a hardcopy handbook, a 3 1/2-inch and even a 5 1/4-inch disk, and text plugs for a nine-pin serial, a 25-pin serial, and a 25-pin parallel plug. An abridged version, PC-Diagnosys, includes much of the functionality of PC-Technician but doesn't have the carrying case and also doesn't include advanced, deep-level writing features such as CMOS update.

However, unless your job description includes hardware field repair, you might be more interested in #1-TuffTEST and #1-TuffTEST-Pro. These products are similar to their big sisters but can be downloaded over the Internet. If you want the ability to thoroughly test your serial and parallel ports, you'll need to purchase a set of test (loopback) plugs separately. Alternatively, you can build your own, following the pin descriptions provided in the tables later in this chapter in the section "Serial and Parallel Port Loopback Plugs." You can download either TuffTEST product from www.tufftest.com.

#1-TuffTEST is targeted at the average Windows 2000 user. It's said to be completely safe to use, even by novices, because it doesn't contain any tests or features that can overwrite hard drive data or otherwise change the system's settings. The utility requires no special knowledge or training. Just boot with a diskette containing the #1-TuffTEST software and sit back: The OS loads itself into lower memory and, unless you interrupt the process by pressing a key, the entire set of system analysis tests will run automatically. At the end of this process, OK or Fail is reported for each of the tests conducted. You can print or save this report.

The #1-TuffTEST Pro version is targeted to a different audience than PC-Technician (which is for field repairers and other support professionals). For example, unlike #1-TuffTEST's OK or Fail, the Pro version provides error descriptions for any problems it finds.

TouchStone CheckIt

Finding an inexpensive troubleshooting aid can be quite difficult. Running about $45 for the DOS or Windows version, CheckIt is more than a hardware inventory program. It also includes a variety of diagnostics, a virus scanner, a hard disk formatter, and a floppy disk alignment checker. In fact, you can place both of the DOS version CheckIt Pro 3.*x* 360KB floppies on one 1.2MB or 1.44MB disk and have plenty of room left over for the DOS boot file and your network drivers. The latest version, CheckIt 4.*x*, requires a bit more space, but you can still run it from a set of 1.44MB floppies (one boot, one for CheckIt, and a third for SysTest).

> **Note:** TouchStone has recently come out with the new 4.03 version of CheckIt. This version offers expanded test features that the original product doesn't include. The most important update is the ability to test advanced Intel Pentium II features. The amount of memory you can test has also increased, along with the capabilities of just about every other test. Of course, this version also includes updates for the CD-ROM test that was one of the new features in the 4.0 product. I'll concentrate on the new version of the product in this section. Be sure to contact TouchStone for the updated version at `http://www.checkit.com`. You can also call (714) 374-2801 or (800) 800-2467.

CheckIt Pro (or CheckIt Portable Diagnostics) is the venerable version that most people will recognize—it's been around for a very long time. The latest version of the product includes a much-enhanced version of CheckIt Pro and WinCheckIt in one package. However, even the original CheckIt (version 3.0) is still good enough for most purposes (you'll need the latest version, though, to test machines with Pentium II and above processors). You'll see in the sections that follow what the latest version has to offer since it's been out long enough for most people to get it.

> **Note:** TouchStone does produce a version of CheckIt for Windows. However, this version of the product is designed for use with Windows 9x. TouchStone doesn't recommend using the Windows version under Windows 2000. The reason is simple: There are just too many operating system limitations for the product to provide an acceptable level of troubleshooting information.

Using CheckIt 4.0

CheckIt, as shown in Figure 31.3, offers four basic tasks you can perform: Collect Data About Your Machine, Load an Existing Configuration File, Skip the Data Collection Process, and Exit the Diagnostic Program. In most cases, you'll want to select either the Collect or Load option because there isn't a lot you can do without knowing the configuration of the machine. (The Collect, Load, and Skip options all end up at the testing screen.)

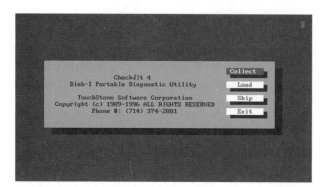

> **Tip:** Unlike its predecessor, CheckIt 4.*x* includes a separate burn-in and batch-testing utility named SysTest. It provides a lot more flexibility than the old combined version of CheckIt. The next section looks at this program.

If you do choose to use the Skip option, you go immediately to the testing screen. Fortunately, you can use the options on the File menu to either load or collect data later. Selecting the Load option displays a standard File Open dialog box that you can use to choose an existing configuration file. You have to collect data and save it to disk before this option will work.

The Collect option displays a dialog box like the one shown in Figure 31.4. This is where you choose what to collect and how in-depth to look. There are two or three columns of options for each device on your machine. The X (Exclude) column tells CheckIt not to look at the selected hardware feature. A Standard look provides an overview of hardware statistics such as hard drive settings—CheckIt looks exclusively in the system CMOS for this information. This is the option to use if you have problems when CheckIt takes a look at a specific piece of hardware. You can also use it when an in-depth look at the hardware isn't required. (For example, you might need to know only the basic settings for the hard drive.) Selecting the Advanced option (for devices that provide this option, such as the COM ports) gives you in-depth information about a particular piece of hardware. CheckIt actually tests the hardware to see what it can do. You'll get information such as the IRQ that the hardware actually uses (versus the setting that Windows may think it uses). Getting this information can take quite a bit of time, though, so you'll want to use the Advanced setting with care. In addition, because the Advanced option actually tests the hardware, you might find that there are conflicts with any software you have loaded.

Figure 31.4

CheckIt enables you to determine how much time you want it to spend collecting data.

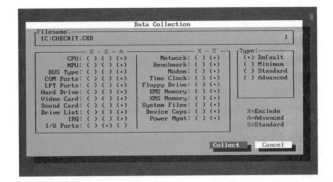

You'll also notice some preset defaults in the Type group. I find that the Standard option provides me with just about everything I need to know on a regular basis, without spending a lot of time to get it. I use the Advanced option if I need to troubleshoot a specific hardware-related problem. In this case, getting all the information you can is a good idea if you don't want to overlook the obvious. The Default setting in the Type group selects a combination of Standard and Advanced options that TouchStone feels most people will need. The Minimum setting obtains the level of information you absolutely must have to use CheckIt to its fullest potential.

After you choose the level of hardware information you need, click the Collect button. CheckIt displays a series of screens as it checks your hardware. What you'll see next is the testing screen mentioned earlier. Figure 31.5 shows a typical example, although your screen will contain different information than mine. At this point, you're ready to use CheckIt for a variety of purposes, such as single-component testing or verifying your hardware settings.

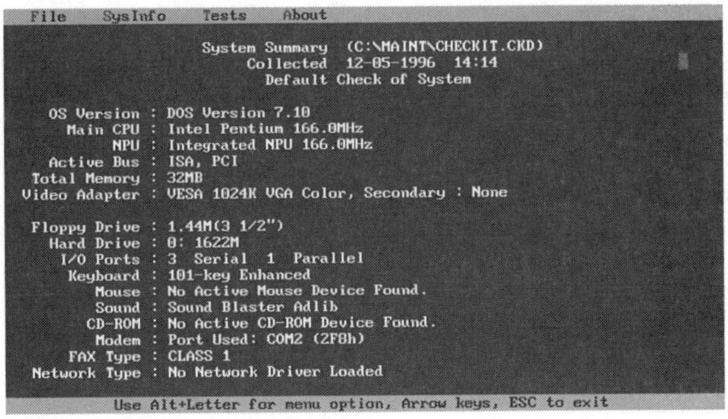

Figure 31.5

CheckIt provides an overview of the information it collected in the initial testing screen.

The two menus that we're most interested in are SysInfo and Tests. The SysInfo menu appears in Figure 31.6. It enables you to obtain concise details about the various facts that CheckIt collected about your machine. Figure 31.7 shows an example of what you might see for the modem. Notice that the check not only determines the address of the modem port, it also tells you whether buffers are available (an important consideration in a multitasking environment such as Windows 95/98). This screen also shows the results of various AT information commands.

FIGURE 31.6

You can get information about any part of your system by using the SysInfo menu options.

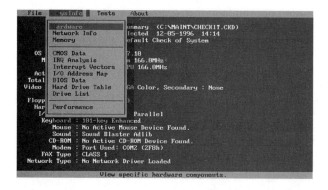

FIGURE 31.7

A typical information display provides every piece of information you need to know about the device in question.

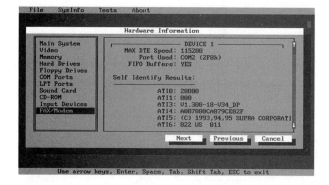

The Tests menu does a lot. It provides a list of tests you can run by using CheckIt. Figure 31.8 shows a list of the tests CheckIt currently supports. Notice that along with standard tests, such as those you'd run on the system board or ports, you can test your CD-ROM drive and modem.

Every test on this list is fully configurable. Figure 31.9 shows a typical example. In this case, you're looking at the Memory Test configuration dialog box. Notice that you get to choose the area of memory to test, along with the level of test you want to perform. Unlike the previous version of CheckIt, you can't choose a precise memory range to test. This is one of the few areas where the new version of CheckIt doesn't quite perform as well as the older ones, but the loss in functionality is minimal.

FIGURE 31.8

The Tests menu provides a complete list of the kinds of tests you can run with CheckIt.

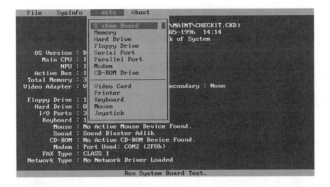

FIGURE 31.9

You need to decide how to run the various diagnostic tests.

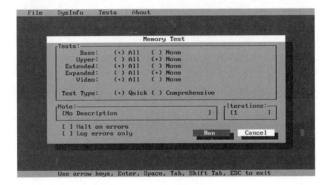

Burn-In and Batch Testing Using SysTest

The CheckIt disks now include a separate batch-testing program named SysTest. Figure 31.10 shows the initial display for this program. The main reason for using this program in place of CheckIt is for burn-in or certification testing. You can also use it to find intermittent problems with hardware. For example, you might have a memory problem that shows up only under certain conditions, or maybe a partially failed part is giving you problems. Batch testing can help find it. You might even want to use batch testing to verify that you've completely fixed a problem. There have been a few cases when two bad components caused a system failure, and finding the second component proved problematic after fixing the first one.

The menu system for this utility looks a bit more complicated than the one used for CheckIt, but you can break it down into four areas. The File menu enables you to look at reports. It's also where you select a custom batch file to run or change the location of program output. (You might want to use a printer rather than the screen for batch testing because the printer can provide a history of each test.)

FIGURE 31.10

SysTest enables you to perform burn-in, certification, and other forms of batch testing.

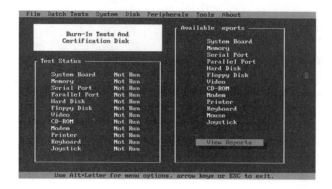

The next menu entry, Batch Tests, enables you to run and create various kinds of batch and burn-in tests. We'll look at this menu in a few minutes. Suffice it to say that this is the heart of the SysTest utility.

The next set of menu entries includes System, Disk, and Peripherals. These options work much like the Tests menu did for CheckIt. In fact, you'll find that SysTest uses the same configuration menus for the various tests. The only difference is how the tests are arranged on the menu. You use these menu selections if you want to test one hardware item multiple times.

Finally, there's a Tools menu. It enables you to save the contents of your CMOS to disk—a handy feature if you think you might run out of battery backup power sometime in the future (and who doesn't?). You can use this same tool to restore a CMOS configuration file that you've saved to disk. Figure 31.11 shows the Save/Restore CMOS dialog box that you see when using the Tools, Save CMOS command. The Tools menu also contains entries for the RAM Exam utility (an advanced memory-testing program) and Rescue Disk (which creates a boot disk you can use in case of emergency).

FIGURE 31.11

The Save/Restore CMOS dialog box enables you to save or restore your hardware configuration settings.

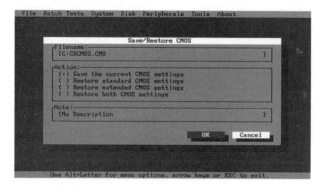

Now it's time to look at the meat and potatoes of this utility—the batch-creation utility. You use the Batch Tests, Custom command to display the dialog box shown in Figure 31.12. This is where you decide which tests to run and how. As you can see, there are two option groups. The first group, Select Test, selects a basic test, such as the System Board Test. When you select a test, you can choose it in the Configure Test option group. Normally, you'll get a dialog box just like the one shown earlier in Figure 31.9 for the memory test. Notice the FileName field in Figure 31.12. The output of this custom batch-testing process is a .BAT file. After you create it, you don't even have to enter SysTest or CheckIt to perform a standard test of your system. Simply type the batch filename at the DOS prompt, and you're ready to go. You lose the capacity to view reports within the CheckIt environment, but you can still use a standard text editor to view the test results file.

FIGURE 31.12
Creating a custom batch-testing job results in a .BAT file that you can run from the DOS prompt.

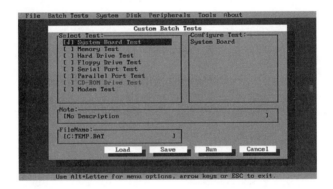

Serial and Parallel Port Loopback Plugs

You can't fully test the serial and parallel ports in a workstation without loopback plugs. These plugs pass the signal from the port's output back to its input. To create a loopback plug, you use a blank connector without wires and then connect wires between specific pins. Most of the high-end diagnostic programs you can buy (such as PC-Technician) provide these plugs. Table 31.1 provides you with the pin connections for a parallel port. Every parallel port uses a 25-pin male connector. Another designation for this type of connector is DB25P. You need to create two connectors to test serial ports. There are nine-pin and 25-pin serial ports. Every serial port uses a female connector. The designation for a nine-pin serial port is DB9S. Table 31.2 lists the pin connections for a nine-pin serial port. The designation for a 25-pin serial port is DB25S. Table 31.3 gives you the pin connections for a 25-pin serial port. You can find the blank connectors and wire you need at most electronics stores.

Table 31.1 Parallel Port (DB25P) Loopback Plug Connections

First Pin	Connected to Second Pin
11 (Busy +)	17 (Select Input –)
10 (Acknowledge –)	16 (Initialize Printer –)
12 (Paper Out +)	14 (Autofeed –)
13 (Select +)	01 (Strobe –)
02 (Data 0 +)	15 (Error –)

Table 31.2 Nine-Pin Serial Port (DB9S) Loopback Plug Connections

First Pin	Connected to Second Pin
02 (RD: Received Data)	03 (TD: Transmitted Data)
07 (RTS: Request to Send)	08 (CTS: Clear to Send)
06 (DSR: Data Set Ready)	01 (CD: Carrier Direct)
01 (CD: Carrier Detect)	04 (DTR: Data Terminal Ready)
04 (DTR: Data Terminal Ready)	09 (RI: Ring Indicator)

Table 31.3 25-Pin Serial Port (DB25S) Loopback Plug Connections

First Pin	Connected to Second Pin
03 (RD: Received Data)	02 (TD: Transmitted Data)
04 (RTS: Request to Send)	05 (CTS: Clear to Send)
06 (DSR: Data Set Ready)	08 (CD: Carrier Direct)
08 (CD: Carrier Detect)	20 (DTR: Data Terminal Ready)
20 (DTR: Data Terminal Ready)	22 (RI: Ring Indicator)

As you can see, the pin connections are relatively easy to make. Whether you buy commercial loopback plugs or make your own, this is an essential tool for your toolkit. Without loopback plugs, you'll never know whether the serial or parallel port you tested really works.

Using a Cable Scanner

Network administrators, especially those managing large networks, can spend a lot of time tracing cables. People are forever abusing cables in ways that would seem impossible unless you actually looked at the damage (for example, pushing a desk hard against the cables trapped between the desk and a wall). If you're a network administrator, a cable scanner is the most important tool you can get for your toolkit. An average cable scanner costs about $1,000, although you can usually find them a little cheaper.

Alternatively, you could build your own cable scanner using plans in some electronics magazines for about $200. One of the better cable scanners on the market is the Cable Scanner model from Microtest. (Microtest provides many other cable scanners with more features, but the Cable Scanner model provides the minimum feature set you need to maintain a network.) This product tests for opens, shorts, and improper terminations. It tells you the distance from your current location to the cable fault. In most cases, all you need to do is track the cable for the required distance and you'll find the problem. To help you trace the signal, the main unit outputs a signal that you can pick up on a remote unit. Instead of taking down every ceiling tile in your office, you simply use the remote unit to trace the cable.

You can send the data collected by Cable Scanner to a serial printer. The unit collects the data, stores it, and allows you to output it later. Cable Scanner provides both text and graphics output. This is a handy feature for maintaining records on your system. All you need to do is print the results of the cable check and add it to the network documentation.

Cable Scanner provides a few other unique functions that you might not use very often. It can detect the noise level of the cable on your system, for example. This means that you can reduce the number of packet errors by simply reducing the noise that the packet signal must overcome. You can also interface Cable Scanner with an oscilloscope. This allows you to actually monitor the signal that flows across the network. An experienced network administrator could use this information to troubleshoot problem installations.

> **Tip:** If spending hundreds on your business's potential cable problems seems a bit out of proportion, try a simpler solution. Just keep some extra cables around and, if you suspect a cable is causing difficulties, swap it out with one of the known good extras. Easter egg it, as the hardware pros say. Also, consider investing in a cable scanner—it can be a good investment. It reduces the time required to locate a problem, and it can also detect a wire that's going bad but isn't yet broken.

Incompatible Hardware

Windows 2000 can require you to buy updated hardware; there's no easier way to state it. The fact that Microsoft tries to ease the purchase of this new hardware by defining a Windows PC specification doesn't really solve anything—all it means is that the machine you buy to use Windows 2000 should work out of the package if it meets all of the specifications. Windows 95/98 is the hardware-compatibility king when compared to any version of Windows. For the most part, any hardware that was used under the DOS or earlier Windows environments will also run under Windows 95/98. Even if you have to use a real-mode driver, you should be able to use that old device under Windows 95/98 if you really want to. The same can't be said of Windows 2000. If you want the added reliability and security that any version of Windows 2000 provides, you need to pay for it. This means that any device you use has to provide a Windows driver—preferably, a 32-bit Windows 2000–specific driver. Old hardware just doesn't provide this kind of support in some cases.

Obviously, the issue of compatibility runs even deeper than simply having a workable driver. Windows 2000 has to be able to find the device's ROM routines in some cases. It always has to have access to the device's ports and interrupts. Windows 2000 really does try its best to figure out which interrupts and port addresses are in use, but it doesn't always succeed—especially if you have an eclectic mix of old and new hardware (and mixed 16-bit and 32-bit drivers). Fortunately, Windows 2000 does support Plug and Play, which eases matters considerably.

The very best way to avoid hardware compatibility problems today is to purchase Plug and Play hardware designed to work on a newer bus such as the PCI bus. If you can't get a PCI bus card, then a Plug and Play card designed to work on an ISA bus is the second best choice. Windows will still be able to detect the settings of such a card. If you really must use an older, non–Plug and Play device, you may need to perform some troubleshooting to get it to work properly under Windows 2000. The following sections are devoted to helping you achieve this goal.

Understanding the Problem with Older Hardware

When using older, non–Plug and Play hardware and drivers, no automatic checking of actual device settings takes place; every setup is a manual process on the part of the installer. Adding to this problem is the fact that some of these device drivers don't register themselves properly when you load them. A device driver is supposed to register itself in a device chain and provide certain types of information as part of that registration process. If it doesn't provide the right level of information, Windows 2000 can't fully detect it. (Yes, it knows that the driver is present, but it can't use the driver to access the hardware.) What happens next is inevitable, given such circumstances. If Windows 2000 doesn't see the device driver or it thinks that the device is using different settings than it really is, Windows 2000 might assume that the interrupts and port addresses the device uses are free. The result is that you might find two devices trying to share the same interrupt or port address.

> **Tip:** As of this writing, Microsoft is experimenting with signed drivers. A *signed driver* is one that has met Microsoft testing criteria and contains a special signature that Windows will check. Using a signed driver means that you'll experience fewer problems in getting your system up and running. However, you can still use older drivers if you really need to. The system will warn you that these older drivers aren't signed by Microsoft and may not work reliably.

One of the best ways to eliminate some of the problems of using older, non–Plug and Play hardware is to make a checklist of all your hardware and the settings each device uses. You need to include the port address, interrupts, and the DMA address. Physically check the settings on cards that use jumpers. You might want to use this opportunity to physically check the BIOS revision of your card; an undocumented update could make a big difference in the settings you'll need to use with Windows 2000. A software-configurable device usually includes the current settings as part of the setup dialog box in the Control Panel. (If not, you'll want to contact the vendor and ask how to determine the current settings.) All you really need to do is get out the vendor manual and determine what the settings mean.

After you get all the settings written down, check your list for potential conflicts. Windows 2000 might tell you that there aren't any, but it's possible that you'll find some anyway. Someone I know recently tried to install Windows 2000 but found that he could not do it. The machine he was using included two SCSI adapters. Windows 2000 recognized one adapter but not the other. The result: Windows 2000 didn't recognize the CD-ROM drive attached to the second adapter and therefore couldn't install itself properly. Removing the second SCSI adapter and connecting the CD-ROM drive to the first adapter solved part of the problem. At least Windows 2000 would install. Performance on the network was very slow, however, and the user still experienced some problems. A check with Windows didn't show any device conflicts. However, a physical check of the remaining SCSI adapter showed that it was using the same interrupt as the NIC. (Windows 2000 had claimed that the NIC was using interrupt 5 and the SCSI adapter interrupt 3.) Physically changing the SCSI adapter's interrupt setting solved the remaining problem.

At times, you might not be sure that you got all the settings right during the first check. You can also determine the equipment settings by viewing the port and interrupt addresses that a device uses with the MSD utility discussed earlier in this chapter or with a diagnostic program such as #1-TuffTEST or Norton Utilities. In fact, using this technique, along with physical inspection of your hardware, ensures that you have all the settings for each device. Even if there aren't any conflicts, you should still maintain a complete record of your hardware.

Unfortunate as it might seem, an ill-behaved device driver normally looks like a malfunctioning device rather than the software issue it really is. This normally doesn't happen with 32-bit drivers because they're newer than the 16-bit drivers that cause most of the problems. I was surprised when I found someone in this position with an old CD-ROM drive. Fortunately, I was able to get from the vendor a newer driver that did work. This is the solution you should try as well. Many vendors even allow you to download their upgrades directly from their Internet sites for free. Some older devices include their own BIOS. Sometimes, the BIOS routines conflict with Windows 2000 and cause various types of system failures. Most vendors upgrade their BIOS as time goes on. They fix bugs and perform some types of optimizations. I've never been able to understand why, but hardware vendors are notoriously reluctant to tell anyone about these fixes. If you have an older piece of hardware with a BIOS that's causing problems with Windows 2000, see whether the vendor has some type of BIOS upgrade that might fix the problem. Installing a new chip is usually cheaper than buying a new peripheral.

Tracking Down Non–Plug and Play Hardware Problems

By now, it should be apparent that hardware incompatibility can cover a lot of ground. Everything from misinterpreted settings to a poorly designed device driver can make it appear that your hardware is incompatible with Windows 2000. Let's take a look at the hardware-compatibility problem from a procedural point of view. To do so, follow these steps:

1. Get into a DOS partition and test the hardware to ensure that there's no problem with the device itself. As I stated previously, Windows 2000 has a bad habit of hiding problems because you can't really access the device. Using a real-mode driver and a vendor-supplied or third-party diagnostic program to check the hardware under DOS might seem archaic, but it's probably the easiest way to go.

2. Check the device settings to see whether there's a conflict with any other device. This is especially important when you try to mix older and newer hardware. (Get rid of any 8-bit boards, if possible, because you're just too limited in the range of settings they can use.) Remember that 16-bit drivers are old technology that's not necessarily reliable. After you compile a list of device settings, manually configure the drivers for the hardware that uses jumpers first and then complete the setup for hardware that uses a software-configuration technique.

3. After you determine that the hardware is working and that it doesn't conflict with anything, see whether the vendor documentation provides any insights as to the requirements for using the device driver. This is always particularly important when using 16-bit drivers. The vendor doesn't always document everything you need to know about the driver.

4. Check your BIOS revision level. Vendors provide a variety of ways to detect this information, so you'll have to check your documentation for details about your particular device. A display adapter I own has a program that I run to display the BIOS and setup information. Check with the vendor to see whether a newer version of the BIOS is available. You might have to send the device to the vendor's repair facility to get the BIOS replaced. It depends on the vendor's policy concerning sending BIOS updates to customers.

5. If all else fails, see whether replacing the board with a similar board from another vendor helps. You might find that a software or other conflict is disguising itself as a hardware problem this way. Recall that a problem with a serial port can disguise itself as a faulty mouse, for example. You might find that other types of problems disguise themselves as well.

Incompatible hardware rarely is, in itself, incompatible (except when you don't have the proper driver for it). There's usually some problem that you can define, given enough time and resources. The question you have to ask yourself is whether that old hardware is really worth the effort. In my case, I replaced the hardware that was giving me problems, which probably saved me time and frustration. Some types of expensive, specialized hardware might be worth the effort involved in looking for the cause of incompatibility, but make sure that you'll get some type of payback.

Getting Rid of That Old Device (Real Mode Not Spoken Here)

I've mentioned this particular issue elsewhere in this book, but it bears repeating. Windows 2000 doesn't speak "real mode." If you have an old device that you absolutely must use and it only comes with a real-mode driver, your best bet is Windows 95/98. The second problem is 16-bit drivers. Replace them with 32-bit drivers whenever possible. Still, you really don't want to get rid of those real-mode and 16-bit Windows drivers, and here's why. What happens if you experience some type of failure on your machine? Suppose that Windows 2000 can't start because of a corrupted file. You could restore it using Backup, but Backup needs Windows 2000 to run. So what do you do now?

Getting a new copy of the corrupted file from a floppy disk setup of Windows 2000 wouldn't be too hard, but you're using the CD version, and you need Windows 2000 to gain access to that, too. Now you're really in trouble—or are you? You really need a boot disk that contains all the drivers needed to activate your hardware. Make sure you include all the real-mode driver equivalents for your CD-ROM drive and soundboard. In fact, you'll want to include everything needed to make your computer fully functional on this disk. The Windows 2000 Emergency Repair Disk is one thing; your personal Disaster Repair Kit is quite another—a necessary other. You'll also want to keep a copy of those real-mode drivers around if you test your system using a DOS-based diagnostic program.

EISA Configuration Requirements

Under DOS, no one cared if you ran an EISA configuration utility. However, you really should run it in order for Windows 2000 to function properly (in fact, Windows 2000 is far more sensitive to this requirement than Windows 95/98). Part of the Windows 2000 startup sequence depends on being able to poll the EISA configuration to find out what kind of devices you have installed.

What does an EISA configuration utility do? It places information about each adapter in your machine in an area of CMOS. When you run the configuration utility, you see one blank for each slot that your EISA bus provides. An EISA configuration utility comes with a list of adapters that it supports. All you need to do is select a slot and then select a device from the list of available devices. This tells your motherboard the specifics of the adapter installed in that slot. The configuration utility automatically displays a device name in each slot you define.

After you tell the configuration utility the contents of each slot, you have to supply it with the interrupt, port address, DMA address, and any other configuration information for that device. This is the information Windows 2000 uses to configure your machine even if the device drivers or the adapter itself can't supply the required information. It also helps Windows 2000 locate some types of problems. If Windows 2000 can't detect a device that the EISA bus says is present, for example, it displays an error message telling you so instead of simply ignoring the device. The configuration utility also allows you to enable or disable some types of motherboard features, such as installed ports. You'll need to consult the manual that came with your motherboard for full details on how to use the configuration utility.

Will anything terrible happen if you don't run the configuration utility? It won't be terrible in most cases, but it'll hinder you from making full use of your machine. Without this information, Windows 2000 won't be able to perform some types of optimizations that it would normally provide for your system, and it could end up running slower as a result. (There are a few places where Windows 2000 will definitely holler if you don't provide the EISA configuration information; 32-bit EISA hard drive controllers constitute one of them.)

The problem for most people is that their EISA configuration utilities are out of date, and some peripheral device vendors don't provide the files needed to configure the bus. It's unlikely that you'll find a configuration file for your modem, for example. To solve the first problem, you'll need to contact the vendor to get a new set of configuration files and perhaps a new utility program as well. The second problem might prove a little more difficult. In some cases, your motherboard vendor will be able to help you with a generic file that will take care of the peripheral. In other cases, the vendor who designed the peripheral might have a configuration file that you can use; the vendor just didn't include it with the device. In some situations, though, despite your best efforts, you won't be able to find a configuration file. The thing to do, in these cases, is to manually configure all the devices in your machine to the best of your ability and hope that Windows 2000 recognizes the device without an EISA configuration entry (in most cases, it will).

PCMCIA Conflicts

The last kind of hardware I'll address in this chapter is the PCMCIA bus (also see Chapter 22, "Mobile Computing," for an in-depth discussion of this interface). There's been a problem with this bus since the day it came out. Some cards won't work with your bus. You might plug a card into the slot, and it won't work at all. Of course, when you take it back to the place you bought it from, they'll show you that it does work (this is one of the reasons you should take your machine with you if at all possible when you suspect some type of compatibility problem). Even worse, some cards will work with your bus, but only in a certain slot or only with certain other cards. You might find that a modem card works fine in the first slot but not in any of the others.

Most people have heard about the problems with getting PCMCIA cards to work properly. Fortunately, current standards help to make the cards compatible, so you'll find that most cards available today avoid these issues. Nevertheless, the best advice I can offer is to buy new cards from a vendor that actually allows you to test them with the other cards in your machine.

Make sure you run a thorough test, using several different combinations of cards to check the new one for compatibility problems. The test should include checking the card in several different slots.

Peter's Principle: The Heat and the Dust

Like high blood pressure in people, heat is the number-one invisible enemy of a computer's good health. Slowly, undetected, your chips weaken, until one day, pop!

In this chapter, we've covered various ways you can supervise your hardware to make it work when it fails and, in some cases, to try to prevent it from failing in the first place. But I've left one topic for the end, and it's the most important preventive medicine you can use. Nothing is more likely to cause your computer and its peripherals to degrade—and then fail—than overheating.

Of course, you don't pile paper on top of your monitor. You can see those necessary heat vents, and you wouldn't be thoughtless enough to block them. But there are other less obvious ways to bring about heat damage to your system.

I was once misguided, or perhaps a bit lazy. I had been installing and upgrading peripheral cards for several months and got tired of unscrewing all those screws and then having to slide the awkward case top off and then putting everything back on when I finished plugging in the new video card (or other device). I finally decided, after installing a new hard drive, that I would just leave the metal case off the computer. That would give it lots of air, my rationalization went.

So, I left the case off and did more damage than I would have imagined. The case is important for two reasons. First, it keeps out dust (and dust on chips acts like a blanket; you guessed it: more heat). Second, notice those little vents on the bottom of the case? They're part of the design of the machine. The locations of these openings are tested and calculated to maximize the draw of cool air over important components and then send that now-heated air out the other side of the computer case.

This air flow pattern was planned, and when you remove the cover, you're countermanding that plan. You're now relying merely on radiating the heat off the chips. Heat radiation is less efficient by far than directed air flow. You can prove this by sitting still for a while in a hot room, thereby trying to radiate yourself cool, and then turning on a fan.

continues

Which brings us to a couple of other issues. There's a fan in the computer, and it's usually up to the job, but if your work environment is particularly steamy (above 80 degrees), consider either directing a room fan toward your machine or adding a second, extra fan (see computer parts supply houses for this item). And watch out for carpeting. Suddenly, inexplicably, in the mid 1950s wall-to-wall carpeting became the rage. Of course, in the years since then, cooler heads have prevailed, and hardwood floors have been the fashion for over a couple decades now.

But if you must have your computer sitting on a carpet, put the machine on a solid surface such as a board that's cut to fit. The vents on desktop computers (as opposed to tower designs) are located at the bottom of the case and will suffocate in carpeting. And, of course, you won't want to block the vents in any other way, such as piling papers or books against them.

Also note that certain types of dust can even be conductive and can therefore short the motherboard and peripheral boards. (The dust that flakes off of certain kinds of shoe soles is especially conductive.)

My best advice? Treat your machine with respect and it'll last for a long, long time. (Then you can resell it in good condition.)

Note: There are, of course, a host of other environmental problems that can kill a computer beyond those just mentioned—dropping an anvil on it, for instance. But seriously, the one major problem I've not yet mentioned is power. If you could make yourself small and thin and then insert yourself into the computer's power cord to watch the power flowing into your computer, you'd find that there are shockingly frequent surges and sags. I always use a surge suppressor. And, if you can afford it, I also suggest you beef up your power smoothing with an uninterruptible power supply as well. (You'd be surprised at just how many problems a UPS can eliminate.)

Technical Note: As long as we're discussing dust, I also want to mention that technical people claim it's a good idea to try to get rid of as much dust as possible from the inside of the computer, even if it means just removing the cover and blowing on the innards real hard. Some say that it's worthwhile to blow out the dust anywhere from once a month to twice a year (the experts disagree).

Cleaning However, you don't want to get down and personally blow inside the computer. Even the air coming from your mouth is reactive—it can cause all kinds of problems, from shorts to contact corrosion. Instead, use an inert gas, such as the gas supplied in the cans of "air" sold by computer stores. An inert gas isn't reactive; it won't cause the problems that the damp air coming from your mouth or a compressor will.

On Your Own

Try WINMSD by selecting the Start, Run command, typing WINMSD in the Open field, and then clicking OK. Try the various features and take a look at the report it generates. Become familiar with your hardware components.

Buy a diagnostic program and completely test your system—especially the hard drives. Make sure you get a diagnostic program that's easy to use and tests everything your machine has to offer. Try using loopback plugs to test your ports, or you can build your own loopback plugs using the procedure in this chapter.

Download one of the #1-TuffTEST diagnostic utilities and see if its OS independence suits your needs. Perhaps you could start out with the smaller, automatic version and then decide if you want to upgrade to the Pro version.

Check any real-mode device drivers installed on your system. Make sure they're the most current drivers the vendor has to offer. Do the same with any peripherals that provide their own BIOS. This includes both modems and display adapters. You'll also find a BIOS on most hard disk controllers and many other devices installed on your machine. Using the most current BIOS not only ensures that you'll have the least number of bugs to contend with, but it could also mean a slight speed boost because of optimizations the vendor made to it.

Check around all your external peripherals—monitor, printer, whatever. Find all their air vents. If you've got a peripheral's vents backed up against a wall, blocked by a towel, covered with a stack of magazines, sitting on top of a space heater, or otherwise negating the device's air-cooling design, move it. Remember to open the case from time to time and blow out the dust with a can of pressurized air.

PART VIII

Appendixes

Using the Scripting Host with Windows 2000 Professional

In this appendix, we're going to explore the Windows Scripting Host (WSH) feature, which is part of the Windows 2000 operating system. I'll show you how to leverage this powerful tool to improve your ability to configure, control, and maintain machines. I'll cover the following main topics:

- What the Windows Scripting Host is and how it works
- How to run a script
- How to choose your scripting language
- How to create scripts

Before continuing, you must understand that writing WSH script doesn't require a fancy editor. Notepad will work fine. You do need to master a basic programming language, such as VBScript or JavaScript. Extensive programming experience is not required. I'll be focusing on VBScript due to Visual Basic's popularity and simplicity. However, if you prefer Java-style programming (JavaScript is actually very, very similar to VBScript), I'll give you a taste of that language as well. Often translation between the two means merely adding some extra symbols, such as braces ({), or reversing the normal order of operators to change VBScript to JavaScript. In general, if you can learn from examples, this appendix will get you started using the scripting host and your preferred scripting language. You can find the latest version (perhaps a Beta version) of WSH and additional information at `http://msdn.microsoft.com/scripting`.

> **Technical Note:** Technically, a *script* is merely programming, like any other programming. However, scripts are usually short and perform small, relatively specialized tasks when compared to the more complex programming that produces large utilities or applications. In fact, VBScript, for example, offers only a subset of the most useful and typical of the more extensive features you'll find in Visual Basic. Scripting is also used to add behaviors to Web pages, and VBScript and JavaScript (or JScript) are used in Internet scripting as well as the new WSH scripting.

Running Scripts

WSH is a language-independent scripting host implemented as an ActiveX object. As an ActiveX component, the host makes itself available to a scripting language as a set of objects. Essentially, you use the host by first instantiating a host's object and then manipulating its properties and methods to accomplish your tasks.

Because the WSH engines support programming languages with rich feature sets, you'll probably find you can do pretty much any task you want to. You run a script by launching the scripting host and loading the script. Under Windows, the scripting host has default actions registered for file extensions. Double-clicking a .VBS (Visual Basic Script) or .JS (JavaScript) file, for example, causes the host to load and execute the VBScript or JavaScript in the file. Under DOS, a command with arguments can launch the script.

The ability to work either from the GUI or from the DOS command prompt implies that the scripting host comes in two versions. In fact, it does. The Windows program is WSCRIPT.EXE, and the DOS version is CSCRIPT.EXE.

Using WSCRIPT.EXE

You can run a script using WSCRIPT.EXE in four ways:

- Double-click a script filename or right-click it and select Open from the context menu.
- Select the Run command from the Start menu, enter the name of the script file, and click OK.
- Run WSCRIPT.EXE with the filename of the script as a parameter.
- If you want to run a script at login, place a shortcut to it in your Startup menu or launch it as a part of your login script.

Tip: If you run WSCRIPT.EXE without any parameters, you gain access to the Windows Scripting Host properties page, just as if you had right-clicked a script file and selected Properties from the context menu.

With the Windows version of the scripting host, you can set two options. When you right-click a script file and select Properties, you see the Windows Scripting Host properties page, shown in Figure A.1.

Figure A.1

The Windows Scripting Host allows you to set two properties.

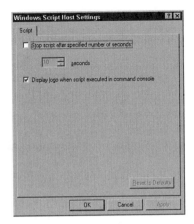

This dialog box allows you to control how long scripts run by allowing you to stop them after a specified number of seconds. This helps prevent any errant scripts from hanging around and using computer resources forever—or at least until you power off. The property options allow you to control whether a logo appears when the scripts execute in a DOS window. If you're running the scripts as part of some other process, such as part of the logon process, you may not want to bother the user with the logo information. Also, if the script might be running on a server when no one is logged on, having a dialog window trying to pop up could cause problems. Setting these properties affects the execution of all scripts.

Using `CSCRIPT.EXE`

The DOS version, `CSCRIPT.EXE`, provides you more options in running scripts and is therefore the more powerful method for launching scripts. Here's its command-line syntax:

```
cscript [//OptionsForHost] [MyScriptFileName] [/OptionsForScript]
```

Typing the command at a DOS command prompt and pressing Enter causes the scripting host to display a list of host options and its command syntax. Table A.1 defines the host options.

Table A.1   Host Options for the Windows Scripting Host

Option	Meaning
//B	Suppresses all output except that to the command prompt
//D	Enables Active debugging
//E:engine	Enables you use an engine to execute script

continues

Table A.1   Continued

Option	Meaning
//H:cscript	Sets the scripting host file to CSCRIPT.EXE
//H:wscript	Sets the scripting host file to WSCRIPT.EXE
//I	Allows input requests and output to be displayed under the GUI (opposite of //B)
//Job:xxxx	Enables you to execute a WS script
//Logo	Displays a logo banner
//NoLogo	Prevents the display of a logo banner
//S	Saves command-line options for this user
//T:seconds	Sets the number of seconds before the script is stopped by the scripting host
//X	Enables you to execute a script in debugger
//U	Enables you to use Unicode for redirecting I/O from the console

As you can see, the DOS version of WSH is more flexible than the Windows version. You can enter batch mode, save command-line options, control display of the banner, and set a timeout on the script. Note that these are all host options. They affect the running of the script on the host computer—the computer on which the script is running, not the computer where the script may be stored.

The options for the script that appear on the command line are defined by the script. These options are simply parameters passed to the script that it can make use of. All script options begin with a single slash (/), as opposed to the double slash (//) that begins the host options. An example of a script option would be a script that connects to a network drive based on the user's name. The user's name would be passed to the script as a parameter (or script option). Here's an example:

```
Cscript //Nologo mapnet.vbs /pnorton
```

In this sample script, the logo display is prevented by the script host option, and pnorton is the user's name passed to the actual script MAPNET.VBS that maps the network drives based on the user's name. Script options may affect either the host or a client.

The division between host and client processing is quite relevant when you consider scripts running on the Internet Information Server (IIS). If a script runs on the Web server, it may need to carry out certain actions, such as retrieving items from a database, on the server. The database used to display information on a Web page does not exist, typically, on the Web client. It may need, however, to carry out actions on the client as well, such as copying cookie files or initiating the download of a file.

This division is also relevant to running login scripts. Some processing in the script, such as mapping drives, primarily affect the client. However, other actions, such as updating log files, may affect the server only. As you work with scripts, therefore, you need to keep clear whether the code affects the client or server as well as whether the switches affect the script or the host. Confusing these targets is a common cause of bugs in scripting. If you experience such difficulties, check to make sure these distinctions have been clearly maintained.

The final method for running the script and controlling the options is to utilize a .WSH file. This file is a standard text file that controls the options for the script as well as indicates the script to be run. Here's an example:

```
[ScriptFile]

Path=C:\Windows\MyScripts\netmap.vbs

[Options]

Timeout=0

DisplayLogo=0

BatchMode=0
```

This file is organized much like the old INI files that you might recall from early days of Windows. The [ScriptFile] section allows you to indicate the script to be run. In this case, it's a VBScript called NETMAP.VBS found in the C:\Windows\MyScripts directory. The [Options] section lets you set the host options for running the scripts. When you double-click the WSH file, it will run the script indicated with the options specified. The options displayed in the sample file here are the only options currently available; however, additional features are being added to the Windows 2000 WSH. At the time of this writing, there's supposed to be support for sendkeys, stdin.stdout/sterr, addwindowsprinterconnection, and drag and drop.

You can also generate this file automatically from the Explorer interface by following these steps:

1. Right-click the script file in Windows Explorer.
2. On the context menu that appears, select Properties.
3. On the Properties page, choose the settings you want to take effect when the script is run.
4. Click OK or Apply.

WSH files are useful when you don't want to trigger the default scripting options.

Selecting a Scripting Language

Now that you know how to run scripts, you might want to begin creating scripts. Unfortunately, you really have to learn a scripting language in order to build scripts. First, decide which scripting language suits you best. You can accomplish just about anything in either JavaScript or VBScript—although neither language permits manipulation of peripherals (including no support for formatting hard drives, erasing files, and so on). Which you want to use probably should reflect your background with computer languages.

Java is very much like C++ in form and structure. If you're used to C programming or C++ class libraries, you'll probably find Java very easy to pick up. Java is generally considered to be a cross-platform language, although the goal of platform independence has been sought for over 20 years now and doesn't seem to be yet achieved.

VBScript is a subset of Visual Basic. Visual Basic is a feature-rich version of the BASIC language that we all learned if we wanted to program an Apple II or Commodore computer in the early 80s. Personally, I think Visual Basic's syntax is easier to master than that of Java, but I know plenty of programmers who disagree. Visual Basic also has the advantage of being tightly integrated in the Microsoft Office suite of products. Visual Basic for Applications (VBA) can be used in applications such as Word and Excel to write macros that automate or customize many tasks. Therefore, if you plan to write scripts that leverage Office integration, VBScript may be the language for you.

Microsoft supplies samples of using scripting languages on its Web site and on the Windows 2000 CD. Try going to this address:

```
http://msdn.microsoft.com/scripting/default.htm?/scripting/windowshost/
default.htm
```

You can use Notepad or a sophisticated programming editor (such as the one built into Visual InterDev), depending on how demanding your programming needs are.

WScript

WScript is the scripting engine, itself, from the programmer's point of view. To use the scripting engine, you must first initialize it and create it as an object, which you can do using the following lines in VBScript:

```
Dim wshshell

Set WSHShell = WScript.CreateObject("WScript.Shell")
```

Never mind what all this means—you just have to type these two lines in for each script, although you can display message boxes to the user without them.

Properties: The Qualities of an Object

The following sections detail the properties you can access once you've instantiated the WScript object.

Application Property

This property points to the script file itself. You can use it to identify which script is running.

Arguments Property

This property points to the list of arguments (or options) passed to the script file, either from the command prompt, from the Run dialog box, or from the shortcut properties. You can use this collection to identify which arguments you need to respond to in your script (if you allow the passing of arguments). Essentially, this will create an array for you that contains a list of any command-line switches that have been sent to the script. Let's look at a piece of code from EXCEL.VBS in the Windows 2000 sample scripts (note that at this point in the code, objXL has already been instantiated):

```
'

' Show command line arguments.

'


Dim colArgs

Set colArgs = WScript.Arguments

Call Show _
        ("Arguments.Count", colArgs.Count, "Number of command line "arguments")

For i = 0 to colArgs.Count - 1

    objXL.Cells(intIndex, 1).Value = "Arguments(" & i & ")"

    objXL.Cells(intIndex, 2).Value = colArgs(i)

    intIndex = intIndex + 1

    objXL.Cells(intIndex, 1).Select

Next
```

We'll look at the whole program shortly, so don't worry too much about the Show subroutine or the objXL.Cells variable. I focus on the use of WScript.Arguments to assign the command-line arguments to a variable, which essentially becomes an array of the items on the command line. Therefore, if you were to run the script with these command-line switches

```
WScript c:\Windows\samples\wsh\excel.vbs arg1 arg2
```

the result would be that an array called colArgs would have two items in it:

```
colArgs(1) = "arg1"
```

```
colArgs(2) = "arg2"
```

You could query this in your script with something like this:

```
If colArgs(1) = "blue" Then Label1.BackColor = "Blue"
```

Passing parameters to your scripts is very powerful. It allows you to write a script that can react to situations or the environment. For example, suppose you have a set of short-cuts that point to applications installed on servers that you want to place on a user's desktop. However, the icons depend on the user's job duties and which server is closest. If the user is a secretary, he or she needs Word running off server A. If the user is a manager, he or she needs MS Project running off server B. You could pass a script some parameters like this:

```
Cscript C:\Setshrts sec A or
```

```
Cscript C:\Setshrts mgr B
```

The script would then react to these arguments and create the appropriate shortcuts pointing to the correct servers.

FullName Property

This property contains the fully qualified pathname to the executable file on the host computer (starting with the drive letter and containing each folder up to the executable file). This property reveals whether WSCRIPT.EXE or CSCRIPT.EXE is executing your script.

Interactive Property

This property reveals whether the script is running in batch mode (return value 0), in which case the only output allowed is directed to the command line, or in interactive mode (return value -1), in which case users can interact with the script.

Name Property

This property contains the "friendly name" of the scripting host. You can expect it to contain "Windows Scripting Host" or a similar string.

Path Property

This property identifies the folder path to the scripting host executable file (WSCRIPT.EXE or CSCRIPT.EXE).

ScriptFullName Property

This property gives the full path and filename of your script file.

ScriptName **Property**

This property provides the filename of your script, stripped of the path information.

Version **Property**

This property contains a text string that identifies the version number of the Windows Scripting Host executable you're using.

> **Technical Note:** WScript offers the last seven properties just listed, but you may not find regular use for them in your scripts. These properties are primarily for the scripting engine's use. For example, the scripting engine needs to know where its executable file is so that it can load a bit of code as necessary. It finds the file using the Path property. One property, though, Version, is likely to be very useful to you as the scripting engine ages and is released in new versions. You can write code that accommodates new features using logic such as the following:
>
> ```
> If WShell.Version = "9" Then
>
>     'Code that supports version 9 features
>
> ElseIf WShell.Version = "8" Then
>
>     'Code that supports version 8 features
>
> End If
> ```

CreateObject **Method**

This method creates an object. It takes one parameter (in parentheses): the string name of the file for the program you wish to instantiate as an object.

> **Tip:** Remember to place text strings inside double quotes (" ") when using them as parameters for these methods.

Let's stop for a moment and take a closer look at the EXCEL.VBS sample script, found on the Microsoft Web site:

```
' Windows Scripting Host Sample Script

'

' ---------------------------------------------------------------------

'              Copyright 1996 Microsoft Corporation
```

```
'

' You have a royalty-free right to use, modify, reproduce and distribute

' the Sample Application Files (and/or any modified version) in any way

' you find useful, provided that you agree that Microsoft has no warranty,

' obligations or liability for any Sample Application Files.

' ...................................................................



' This sample will display Windows Scripting Host properties in Excel.



L_Welcome_MsgBox_Message_Text    = "This script will display Windows
➡Scripting Host properties in Excel."

L_Welcome_MsgBox_Title_Text      = "Windows Scripting Host Sample"

Call Welcome()



' ***************************************************************************

' *

' * Excel Sample

' *

Dim objXL

Set objXL = WScript.CreateObject("Excel.Application")

objXL.Visible = TRUE

objXL.WorkBooks.Add



objXL.Columns(1).ColumnWidth = 20

objXL.Columns(2).ColumnWidth = 30

objXL.Columns(3).ColumnWidth = 40
```

```
objXL.Cells(1, 1).Value = "Property Name"

objXL.Cells(1, 2).Value = "Value"

objXL.Cells(1, 3).Value = "Description"


objXL.Range("A1:C1").Select

objXL.Selection.Font.Bold = True

objXL.Selection.Interior.ColorIndex = 1

objXL.Selection.Interior.Pattern = 1 'xlSolid

objXL.Selection.Font.ColorIndex = 2


objXL.Columns("B:B").Select

objXL.Selection.HorizontalAlignment = &hFFFFEFDD ' xlLeft


Dim intIndex

intIndex = 2


Sub Show(strName, strValue, strDesc)

    objXL.Cells(intIndex, 1).Value = strName

    objXL.Cells(intIndex, 2).Value = strValue

    objXL.Cells(intIndex, 3).Value = strDesc

    intIndex = intIndex + 1

    objXL.Cells(intIndex, 1).Select

End Sub



'

' Show WScript properties
```

```
'

Call Show("Name",WScript.Name,"Application Friendly
Name")

Call Show("Version",WScript.Version, "Application Version")

Call Show("FullName",WScript.FullName,"Application Context:
Fully Qualified Name")

Call Show("Path",WScript.Path, "Application Context:
Path Only")

Call Show("Interactive",WScript.Interactive,"State of Interactive
Mode")


'

' Show command line arguments.

'

Dim colArgs

Set colArgs = WScript.Arguments

Call Show _
        ("Arguments.Count", colArgs.Count, "Number of command line arguments")


For i = 0 to colArgs.Count - 1

    objXL.Cells(intIndex, 1).Value = "Arguments(" & i & ")"

    objXL.Cells(intIndex, 2).Value = colArgs(i)

    intIndex = intIndex + 1

    objXL.Cells(intIndex, 1).Select

Next


' ********************************************************************

' *
```

```
' * Welcome

' *

Sub Welcome()

    Dim intDoIt


    intDoIt = MsgBox(L_Welcome_MsgBox_Message_Text, _

                     vbOKCancel + vbInformation,    _

                     L_Welcome_MsgBox_Title_Text )

    If intDoIt = vbCancel Then

        WScript.Quit

    End If

End Sub
```

There are many interesting and useful scripting techniques going on here. First, it calls the standard Welcome() subroutine that displays a message box, allowing the user to accept or cancel execution. Next, it uses the CreateObject method:

```
Set objXL = WScript.CreateObject("Excel.Application")
```

The "creation" of the object actually causes the registered application, Excel, to launch. This is how to launch an application from within your scripts. The next few lines first make the application visible (it's no fun if you can't see it, right?). The next lines then operate within Excel, adjusting column widths and preparing the Excel spreadsheet to be populated with data. Notice that we're referring to objXL and not Excel with these functions. When we assigned Excel.Application to the variable objXL, we told the WSH that we would be referring to Excel.Application as objXL for short. You'll see a subroutine call Show next. Show() populates the Excel spreadsheet shells with data. We get some of the data by using various properties of the WScript object, such as wscript.name and wscript.path. To get the command-line arguments, we use a For-Next loop to cycle though the array generated by the wscript.arguments method, which I've already discussed.

This script illustrates several scripting techniques:

- How to open an application such as Excel from a script
- How to address the opened application and alter it
- How to get command-line arguments and display them

- How to use `For-Next` loops and subroutines
- How to use WScript properties to acquire information

Not bad for one little script.

Methods: Things an Object Can Do

Now I'll list the methods of various objects. Methods are things an object knows how to do. For example, an Internet browser has a `Refresh` method that reloads the currently displayed Web page.

The following methods are presented roughly in the order in which they're used to familiarize you with which steps you need to take first, which ones come in the middle of the process, and which ones typically end a process.

GetObject Method

This method retrieves an existing object or objects. Its parameter is a comma-separated list of the string names or the full pathnames for the objects you want to use. Once you've created an Excel object, for example, you can assign it to a variable using this method. Once the object is assigned to an object variable, you can access its properties and methods. This is often done using the `CreateObject` method we just used.

However, sometimes the application is already running and you only need to assign it to a variable, such as `objXL` in preceding example, to be able to send the application instructions. Here's the syntax for assigning an object to a variable using this method:

```
Dim objXL

Set objXL = WScript.GetObject("Excel.Application")
```

You can tell whether an application is already running by checking for a null value in `objXL`. Under most circumstances, when you use this method, you're already certain that the application is running, either because your script just started it or because the application is running as a service.

Echo Method

Like the `echo` command in DOS, this method displays a string of text in a dialog box or on the command line (if you're running `CSCRIPT.EXE`). The text string follows the method and is not enclosed in parentheses. The syntax is as follows:

```
ObjXL.Echo "This text screen just echoed to the command line."
```

GetScriptEngine Method

This method gives you a script engine object (for JavaScript, VBScript, or some third-party engine for a different language) for a script engine present on your system. You'll use this only if you create a scripting engine and need to create a registration routine for it. The argument, in parentheses, is the string name of the script engine. Once you have an object reference, you can use the script engine's `Register` and `Unregister` methods to undertake registration or removal from the Registry. The syntax for this method follows:

```
Dim objXL

Set objXL = WScript.GetScriptEngine("MyScript.Engine")
```

Quit Method

This method ends the execution of the script. If you place an error code in parentheses, the method returns the code to the command line or in a dialog box. The syntax is as follows for an object variable named `WShell` and an error code of `9`:

```
WShell.Quit(9)
```

WScript.WshShellObject Object

The `WshShellObject` object gives you access to the Explorer interface for Windows 2000 or the operating system shell, as it's often called. You're likely to interact with this object extensively as you write scripts. It contains methods only, but they're very useful methods. A fine example appears in the `SHORTCUT.VBS` script:

```
Dim WSHShell

Set WSHShell = WScript.CreateObject("WScript.Shell")
```

Notice that before you can utilize any of its methods, you must first assign the shell to an object variable, as was done in the Excel application in the previous examle.

CreateShortcut Method

This method, obviously, creates a shortcut in the current folder. It takes the string path to the file object as a parameter, in parentheses. To use this method, employ the following syntax:

```
Dim WSHShell

Set WSHShell = WScript.CreateObject("WScript.Shell")

WSHShell.CreateShortcut("c:\winword\word.exe")
```

DeleteEnvironmentVariable Method

This method allows you to delete a single environment variable. It requires one object, in parentheses—the name of the environment variable. Optionally, you can place a second argument following a comma—the location of the environment variable. Possible locations are `System`, `User`, `Volatile`, and `Process`.

`System` refers to system-level variables. `User` refers to variables that are particular to the active user's environment. `Volatile` refers to variables that are currently in memory without affecting the permanent settings. `Process` refers to variables created by the current process.

Normally, you won't worry about what level the variable is at. However, on occasion, you may wish to temporarily adjust a parameter such as PATH to be different while your script executes but want it to return to the user's default settings after the script is finished. For a quick list of system and user environment variables, open a command prompt, type SET and press Enter. Use the following syntax with this method:

```
WSHShell.DeleteEnvironmentVariable(%Path%, "User")
```

GetEnvironmentVariable Method

This method retrieves the value of an environment variable. It takes the same arguments as the DeleteEnvironmentVariable method. Here's an example:

```
MyVal = WSHShell.GetEnvironmentVariable(%Path%, "User")
```

Popup Method

This method displays a message box. It can take four arguments, separated by commas and enclosed in parentheses. The first argument is required; it's the text to display as the message. The second is the number of seconds to display the message box. If this is nonzero, the box disappears after the number of seconds you indicate. If it is zero, the box requires that the user click a button to close it. The third argument is the title to display in the message box. If this is left out, the title is "Windows Scripting Host." The final argument, if present, is a number that governs which buttons and icons appear on the box. This must be one of the numbers shown in Table A.2 or a sum of several of these numbers.

Table A.2   Values That Determine the Style of a Pop-up Message Box

Value	Meaning
0	OK button
1	OK and Cancel buttons
2	Abort, Retry, and Ignore buttons
3	Yes, No, and Cancel buttons
4	Yes and No buttons
5	Retry and Cancel buttons
16	Stop Mark icon
32	Question Mark icon
48	Exclamation Mark icon
64	Information Mark icon

In addition, this method returns a value that indicates which button the user clicked to dismiss the message box. You can use this value to determine what action to take when the message box has been dismissed. Table A.3 shows the possible return values.

Table A.3   Return Values for a Pop-up Message Box

Value	Corresponding Button
1	OK
2	Cancel
3	Abort
4	Retry
5	Ignore
6	Yes
7	No
8	Close
9	Help

Here's an example of using the Popup method:

```
Dim wshshell

Set WSHShell = WScript.CreateObject("WScript.Shell")

'Popup with 2 buttons and no timeout

Dim respnse

respnse = WSHShell.popup _
        ("May I connect your network drives for you?","0","Little Network
        Helper","1")

If respnse = vbCancel then

   WScript.quit

end if

' code to setup users network drives

'completed message with 3 second timeout

response=wshshell.popup("Done",3,"Little Network Helper",0)
```

As usual, we begin this script by setting up the object WSHShell with the CreateObject method. Then the user is presented with a message box asking whether his or her network drives should be connected. This first message box prompts the user and will not close unless he or she selects an option. The options available are OK and Cancel; the last parameter is 1. Once the user responds OK, some action is taken to connect the drives. Another pop-up box is displayed indicating that the operation finished. This second pop-up box waits three seconds and disappears. The only button displayed is the OK button.

An alternative to the Popup method is the MsgBox function that's commonly used in Visual Basic. This function is used in the Microsoft sample files and is well documented in Visual Basic help files.

> **Tip:** You may notice the use of the SET command in front of the CreateObject statement, as shown in the following example:
>
> ```
> Set WSHSHELL= WScript.CreateObject(" WScript.Shell")
> ```
>
> You should also note that absence of SET in front of the response variable:
>
> ```
> response=wshshell.popup("Done",3,"Little Network Helper",0)
> ```
>
> Generally, use SET when you're setting or creating an object variable, as opposed to a regular text or numeric variable, such as response in this example.

Then next few methods have to do with retrieving and modifying Registry entries. Of course, the standard warnings apply. Make sure that if you write scripts that modify the Registry, you test them thoroughly on a machine that you really don't care about. Messing up the Registry is the fastest way to make a machine inoperative. (See Chapter 10, "Understanding the Windows 2000 Registry," for ways to reduce your risks when tampering with the Registry.)

RegDelete Method

This method deletes a key from the Registry. Place the key name as a text string following the method, but not in parentheses. The statement looks like this:

```
WshShellObject.RegDelete "HKCU\PMARegTopKey\"
```

> **Tip:** You can use the following abbreviations for Registry keys to simplify using them: HKCU for HKEY_CURRENT_USER, HKLM for HKEY_LOCAL_MACHINE, and HKCR for HKEY_CLASSES_ROOT.

RegRead Method

This method fetches the value stored in a value name. Place the value name as a text string following the method, in parentheses, as follows:

```
MyVar = WshShellObject.RegRead("HKCU\PMARegTopKey\Top key")
```

RegWrite Method

This method creates a key or a value or sets the value associated with a value name. Two parameters follow the method, and parentheses are not used to contain the parameters. The first parameter is the name of the key or value to set; the second is the value to enter. Optionally, you can specify the data type of the value to set, if you wish. The method automatically converts the value to the data type of the value if you omit the data type parameter. The statement for using this method looks like this:

```
WshShellObject.RegWrite _
 "HKCU\PMARegTopKey\PMAReg2ndKey\BinaryValue", 3, "REG_BINARY"
```

The REGISTRY.VBS sample script (also found on the Microsoft Web site) demonstrates how to add and remove entries from the Registry. Notice that the creation and naming of the keys and the values is the same process.

> **Caution:** One word of extreme caution: Windows 2000 and Windows 95/98 operate differently in regards to the deletion of Registry keys. In Windows 2000, if you ask to delete a Registry key that contains subkeys, such as HKLM\Software, it will generate an error. In Windows 95/98, it will happily delete the key and all of the subkeys below it. This, of course, would be devastating to the operation of Windows. Again, testing is important!

Run Method

This method runs a program, the path to which you specify as the first parameter, using no parentheses. You run the program, but you do not create an object for it. You can include up to three comma-separated parameters. The path to the program is required. The second parameter is an integer that indicates the window style: 0 for hidden, 1 for normal, 2 for minimized, and 3 for maximized. The final parameter indicates whether to return to the script or to wait for the program to terminate before continuing to run the script. Not specified or FALSE returns control to the script immediately. TRUE causes Windows 2000 to wait until the program terminates before returning to run the script. If the application is already running, whether you start a new instance of the program depends on whether the program itself allows multiple instances. The statement looks like this in its full form:

```
WSHShell.Run "c:\winword\word.exe", 1, FALSE
```

SetEnvironmentVariable Method

This method sets an environment variable. It takes three parameters, not enclosed in parentheses. The first parameter is the name of the variable, whereas the second parameter is the value of the variable. The final parameter is optional; it indicates the location of the variable. This parameter takes the same values as described for the other environment variable options.

WScript.WshNetwork Object

This object gives you access to network information relating to the current session. Use this object to find out what settings are in force and to carry out common networking functions. Much like using the WScript.Shell object, you'll need to use WScript.CreateObject("wscript.network") to create a reference object.

ComputerName Property

This property contains the NetBIOS name of the local computer. Use it to identify the computer engaged in the session.

UserDomain Property

This property contains the name of the domain the user has logged in to. Use it to identify the home domain for the session.

UserName Property

This property contains the username of the logged-in user. Use it to find out who is logged in for this session.

> **Tip:** Your primary use for the preceding properties will be to personalize scripts for users. You'll find yourself setting text boxes or background text controls to their values in order to communicate with users in a comfortable fashion.

The next few methods have to do with retrieving and modifying Registry entries. Of course, the standard warnings apply!

The AddPrinterConnection Method: One of My Favorites

This method creates a remote printer connection. It can take five parameters, the first two of which are required, and none of which are placed in parentheses. The first parameter is the text string that's the name of the local printer. The second parameter is the text string that designates the UNC name of the printer to connect to. The third parameter takes the value of TRUE or FALSE and indicates whether to store this connection in the user's profile so that it can be accessed again when the user logs in next time. TRUE indicates to store the connection; FALSE or not specified indicates not to store it. The last two optional parameters are text strings that represent the username and password for attaching to the remote printer.

This method is one of my favorites! In general, it's a real administrative issue trying to get users connected to the appropriate printer. Now you can use this method in a logon script to get them pointed to the right device. Here's some sample code:

```
Dim WSHNetwork

Set WSHNetwork = wscript.createobject(" WScript.Network")

WSHNetwork.Addprinterconnection "My Laser", "\\ServerA\HPLaser",TRUE
```

This example simply attaches to a printer on server A being shared as HPLaser. The printer in Settings, Printers on my desktop will appear as My Laser. Also, the printer will be saved to my profile and automatically connected whenever I log in.

Using the other methods and properties just illustrated, you can determine the user's domain, name, and machine name and select a printer from a list if you like. You can also check to see which printers the user is connected to and disconnect the user if the printer is no longer appropriate.

EnumNetworkDrives Method

This method fetches the current network drive mappings and places them in an object variable that you've previously created. You can then retrieve the mappings by examining `objectvariable.Item(ZeroBasedIndex)`, where each item in the collection contains a drive mapping.

EnumPrinterConnections Method

This method fetches the current network printer connections and places them in an object variable that you've previously created. You can then retrieve the mappings by examining `objectvariable.Item(ZeroBasedIndex)`, where each item in the collection contains a printer connection.

> **Tip:** The preceding methods take the following syntax:
>
> ```
> myObj = WSHShell.EnumNetworkDrives
> ```
>
> You reference the drive or printer connections using `myObj.Item(0)`, incrementing the index value to reference additional drives or printers.

MapNetworkDrive Method

This method creates a network drive map. It can take five parameters, the first two of which are required, and none of which are placed in parentheses. The first parameter is the text string that will represent the name of the local drive letter. The second parameter is the text string that designates the UNC name of the share to connect to. The third parameter takes the value of TRUE or FALSE and indicates whether to store this mapping in the user's profile so that it can be accessed again when the user logs in next time. TRUE indicates to store the mapping; FALSE or not specified indicates not to store it. The last two optional parameters are text strings that represent the username and password for attaching to the remote share. An example follows:

```
WSHNetwork.MapNetworkDrive strDrive, strShare
```

RemoveNetworkDrive Method

This method removes a drive mapping. It can take three parameters, the first of which is required, and none of which are placed in parentheses. The first parameter is the text string that represents the name of the local drive. The second parameter takes the value of TRUE or FALSE and indicates whether to force removal even if the resource connection is currently not in force. TRUE indicates to remove the connection; FALSE or not specified indicates not to force removal. The last parameter is also Boolean in nature, indicating whether to update the user's profile. TRUE means the mapping should be removed from the profile, and FALSE or not specified means to leave the mapping in the profile. Use the following example to guide your use of this method:

```
WSHNetwork.RemoveNetworkDrive strDrive, TRUE, TRUE
```

RemovePrinterConnection **Method**

This method removes a printer connection. It can take three parameters, the first of which is required, and none of which are placed in parentheses. The first parameter is the text string that represents the name of the local printer. The second parameter takes the value of TRUE or FALSE and indicates whether to force removal even if the resource connection is currently not in force. TRUE indicates to remove the connection; FALSE or not specified indicates not to force removal. The last parameter is also Boolean in nature, indicating whether to update the user's profile. TRUE means the connection should be removed from the profile, and FALSE or not specified means to leave the connection in the profile. Use this example as a guide:

```
WSHNetwork.PrinterConnection strPrinter, TRUE, TRUE
```

The final example we'll look at is NETWORK.VBS from the Windows sample scripts on the Microsoft Web site. This example illustrates how to use some properties and methods and also demonstrates two other scripting techniques we've not yet touched on: functions and the InputBox object. Let's start with how you use a function in VBScript:

```
Function TryMapDrive(intDrive, strShare)

    Dim strDrive

    strDrive = Chr(intDrive + 64) & ":"

    On Error Resume Next

    WSHNetwork.MapNetworkDrive strDrive, strShare

    TryMapDrive = Err.Number = 0

End Function
```

Up to this point, we've been using subroutines. We pass parameters to a subroutine, and then it does something for us. A function is the same, except it returns a value. (JavaScript uses functions only, no subroutines.) If you wish, the returned value can tell you whether the function's operation succeeded or failed. In the preceding example, the TryMapDrive function attempts to map the drive. If it fails, it's forced to return a zero. If it succeeds, a nonzero number is returned. To return the value, simply set the function name to the value you want to return:

```
TryMapDrive = Err.Number = 0
```

This particular example is a tricky little piece of logic that you may have to look at for a while to convince yourself that it works. If `ErrNumber` is 0 (that is, it's successful), the expression `ErrNumber=0` evaluates to TRUE.

The `InputBox` function, like the `MsgBox` function, is particular to Visual Basic and allows you to get input from the user:

```
strShare = InputBox("Enter network share you want to connect to ")
```

The user types in the share name, and the value is stored to the variable `strShare`.

> **Technical Note:** Recall that VBScript offers both functions and subroutines, but JScript only uses functions. It has no `Sub` structure.

Scripting in Visual Basic

When you're scripting in Visual Basic, often the first thing you must do in any script is to gain access to the Windows Scripting Host object itself. First, you must dimension an object variable, and then you must use VBScript's `CreateObject` method to give yourself a pointer to the WSH object. The following lines of code accomplish this task:

```
Dim wshShellObject

Set wshShellObject = WScript.CreateObject("WScript.Shell")
```

> **Tip:** If you need to gain access to an application such as Excel, you use the same syntax, going through the scripting host object to open the Excel object, using the following line of code:
>
> ```
> Set objExcel = WScript.CreateObject("Excel.Application")
> ```

Recall that when you work with the scripting host object, you manipulate its properties and methods. You can use the `SpecialFolders` method to return the path to any system folder by name. CreateShortcut method (WshShell object) You can use the `CreateShortcut` method to create a shortcut in any path you choose. The `ExpandEnvironmentStrings` method allows you to use environment variables maintained by the system when setting properties for the shortcut. The following code shows the use of these methods as well as sets three properties, including `WindowStyle`, for the shortcut:

```
Dim shctPMA, strStrDesktopPath



strStrDesktopPath = wshShellObject.SpecialFolders("Desktop")
```

```
Set shctPMA = wshShellObject.CreateShortcut _
        (strStrDesktopPath & "\Shortcut to notepad.lnk")



ShctPMA.TargetPath = WshShellObject.ExpandEnvironmentStrings _
        ("%windir%\notepad.exe")

ShctPMA.WorkingDirectory = WshShellObject.ExpandEnvironmentStrings _
        ("%windir%")

ShctPMA.WindowStyle = 4

ShctPMA.IconLocation = WshShellObject.ExpandEnvironmentStrings _
        ("%windir%\notepad.exe, 0")

ShctPMA.Save
```

You can use the Echo method of the scripting host to place text in a dialog box or to display text at the command prompt. The following line of code shows the simple syntax for doing so:

```
WScript.Echo "A shortcut to Notepad is on the Desktop."
```

The Popup method accomplishes the same goal. However, the Popup method will not work when you're not in interactive mode. The Echo method is therefore the general-purpose messaging method, whereas the Popup method is best used only in Windows, not DOS. The Popup method also lets you set a time limit on the display of the dialog box. The following line of code demonstrates the use of the method:

```
WshShellObject.Popup _
 "Create key HKCU\PMARegTopKey with value 'Top key'"
```

Using the Registry methods of the scripting host, you can create keys and values, write keys and values, and delete keys and values. You can specify the data types for values if you wish. Remember that if you do not specify data types, automatic type conversions occur for existing values. The following lines illustrate the various options you have—creating a high-level key, creating a subkey of the high-level key, writing some values, and deleting keys:

```
WshShellObject.RegWrite "HKCU\PMARegTopKey\", "Top key"

WshShellObject.RegWrite "HKCU\PMARegTopKey\PMAReg2ndKey\", "2nd key"

WshShellObject.RegWrite "HKCU\PMARegTopKey\IntegerValue", 1

WshShellObject.RegWrite "HKCU\PMARegTopKey\PMAReg2ndKey", 2, "REG_DWORD"

WshShellObject.RegWrite _
        "HKCU\PMARegTopKey\PMAReg2ndKey\BinaryValue", 3, "REG_BINARY"
```

```
WshShellObject.RegDelete "HKCU\PMARegTopKey\PMAReg2ndKey\BinaryValue"

WshShellObject.RegDelete "HKCU\PMARegTopKey\PMAReg2ndKey\"

WshShellObject.RegDelete "HKCU\PMARegTopKey\"
```

As noted in the description of the methods, you can make use of constants (predefined integer values) to determine what appears in a dialog box as well as to set window styles. In the shortcut code, I showed you how to set a window style using an integer value.

The next example illustrates an alternative way to use constants. I'll also demonstrate that you can use any VBScript statement in your code as well as how the Quit command works. Note the use of constant names, such as vbOKCancel and vbInformation. These are predefined names in Visual Basic that are associated with dialog box styles. vbOKCancel is equivalent to 1, whereas vbInformation is equivalent to 64. Adding these two together as the second argument of the MsgBox function sets the style of the dialog box to display the Information icon and to provide both OK and Cancel buttons. Other constants allow you to check return codes, as shown by the use of vbCancel in the If statement. The appropriate use of the Quit method is also demonstrated in the If statement:

```
Sub TwoButtonMessageBox()

    Dim intReturnValue



    intReturnValue =  MsgBox(strMsgBoxText,      _

                      vbOKCancel + vbInformation,       _

                      strMsgBoxTitle )

    If intReturnValue = vbCancel Then

        WScript.Quit

    End If

End Sub
```

Although I don't have the space to provide an exhaustive VBScript reference in this chapter, you do have some good, understandable lines of code that work to get you started. Check out the examples that Microsoft provides to gain additional insights, especially into how to handle errors when working with the Network object. Unfortunately, networks are chancy places, where things work most of the time but not all of the time. The file NETWORK.VBS shows you some good error-handling techniques. In addition, you should remember that all good Windows programmers steal working code wherever they can find it. Copying and pasting and then revising to suit your needs can prevent lots of bugs later on.

Scripting in Java

Scripting in Java works very much the same way as scripting in Visual Basic, except that Java requires C syntax (backwards from English or Basic syntax) and some different keywords. Once you have access to the shell object, you work in much the same way. Examine the following lines and compare them to the VBScript code that performs the task of creating a shortcut:

```
var WshShellObject = WScript.CreateObject("WScript.Shell");
var StrDesktopPath = WshShellObject.SpecialFolders("Desktop");

var ShctPMA = WshShellObject.CreateShortcut _
        (StrDesktopPath + "\\Shortcut to notepad.lnk");



ShctPMA.TargetPath = WshShellObject.ExpandEnvironmentStrings _
        ("%windir%\\notepad.exe");

ShctPMA.WorkingDirectory = WshShellObject.ExpandEnvironmentStrings _
        ("%windir%");

ShctPMA.WindowStyle = 4;

ShctPMA.IconLocation = WshShellObject.ExpandEnvironmentStrings _
        ("%windir%\\notepad.exe, 0");

ShctPMA.Save();



WScript.Echo("A shortcut to Notepad is on the Desktop.");
```

Note that you need to use var instead of dim to create a variable. Unlike in VBScript, all variables must be defined before they're used. All statements are supposed to end with a semicolon. Also, all methods use parentheses to surround parameters, whereas VB allows some statements to work without the parentheses. Comments begin with double slashes (//) instead of a single quote ('). Files for JavaScript scripts end in .JS. Those are the basic differences. Of course, as you move into using Java statements, you'll find additional differences. Consult a good JavaScript reference for the particulars of the JavaScript language. Of course, you can also consult a good VBScript reference for the particulars of that language, too.

On Your Own

Try running the sample scripts Microsoft provides (at `http://msdn.microsoft.com/ scripting/default.htm?/scripting/windowshost/default.htm`) using both `WSCRIPT.EXE` and `CSCRIPT.EXE`. Experiment with the command-line options for `CSCRIPT`. Try taking the `NETWORK.VBS` sample and modifying it so that it works with printers instead. Alter the questions to try and get the appropriate information to locate and connect to the proper printer. Use the various properties and methods to collect information about the user, network drives, and printers. Then store the information in an Excel spreadsheet or a Word document. This technique comes in handy when you're troubleshooting later and want to see what these settings and variables might have been before problems started.

Try building a script that manages the choices you have to make during a typical logon. Do you need to choose between two sets of startup options? Do you need to set up different printer connections depending on the work you'll be doing? Do you need to set up a different set of network drive mappings to reflect the project of the day? Do you need to set up a path environment variable that reflects your working context? Try working each of these into a script that you can use to control your own working environment.

Glossary

This glossary contains definitions of terms found throughout this book, including the acronyms that the computer community is so fond of and concepts that aren't blatantly obvious.

Access Control Entry   See *ACE*.

Access Control List   See *ACL*.

ACE (Access Control Entry)   Part of the Windows 2000 security API used by the system to define a user's or group's rights. It defines the object rights for a single user or group. Every ACE has a header that defines the type, size, and flags for the ACE. Next comes an access mask that defines the rights a user or group has to the object. Finally, there's an entry for the user's or group's security identifier (SID).

ACL (Access Control List)   Part of the Windows 2000 security API used to determine both access and monitoring properties for an object. Each ACL contains one or more ACEs (Access Control Entries) that define the security properties for an individual or group. There are two major ACL groups: SACL (Security Access Control List) and **DACL (Discretionary** Access Control List). The SACL controls the Windows 2000 auditing feature. The DACL controls actual access to the object.

Active Directory   A method of storing machine, server, and user configuration within Windows 2000 that supports full data replication so that every domain controller has a copy of the data. This is essentially a special purpose database that contains information formatted according to a specific schema. Active Directory is designed to make Windows 2000 more reliable and secure, while reducing the work required by both the developer and network administrator for application support and distribution. The user benefits as well since Active Directory fully supports roving users and maintains a full record of user information, which reduces the effects of local workstation down time.

active partition   A disk drive's bootable partition. Its boot sector tells the ROM BIOS at startup that this partition contains the operating system's bootstrap code. The active partition is usually the same as the primary partition.

ActiveX   Just as DDE evolved into OLE over the years, so, too, in its turn, has OLE now morphed into ActiveX. ActiveX is a very, very broad term. Microsoft is using the term *Active* in many ways. One concept underlying the idea of ActiveX is that previously inert, passive, or static objects can come alive (and contain their own capabilities, such as methods for self-modification, animation, and calculation). Objects are referred to as a combination of data with the capability to act on that data—this capability to act is now being distributed to locations that were previously static. For example, server HTML pages used to be simple page-description documents. Now they can contain scripts (behaviors) that execute on the server side (they're called *Active Server Pages*). And, of course, there's the Windows Active Desktop. However, ActiveX refers generally to a set of related phenomena: It's a technology, a set of operating system features (DLLS and API functions), a way of programming, and a collection of objects you can plug into your own programs or Web pages. *ActiveX* is therefore a generic term covering a variety of initiatives from Microsoft.

Address Resolution Protocol   See *ARP.*

Advanced Power Management   A specification developed by Microsoft and Intel that enables the operating system, applications, BIOS, and system hardware to work cooperatively to manage power and extend battery life.

allocation unit   See *cluster.*

American Standard Code for Information Interchange   See *ASCII.*

API (application programming interface)   A method of defining a standard set of function calls and other interface elements. It usually defines the interface between a high-level language and the lower-level elements used by a device driver or operating system. The ultimate goal is to provide some type of service to an application that requires access to the operating system or device feature set.

APM   See *Advanced Power Management.*

application independence   A method of writing applications so that they don't depend on the specific features of an operating system or hardware interface. This normally requires the use of a high-level language and an API. The programmer also needs to write the application in such a way as to avoid specific hardware or operating system references. All user and device interface elements must use the generic functions provided by the API.

application programming interface   See *API.*

ARP (Address Resolution Protocol)   When a machine wants to send a message to a particular IP address, the network driver needs to figure out which piece of hardware (which NIC or other device) the IP address is associated with. The network driver sends out a broadcast message asking which piece of hardware is associated with a particular IP address. If a piece of hardware responds with a combination of its IP address and hardware identification number, then the network driver makes the association and sends the message to that particular piece of hardware. This technique is normally used with devices like SCSI host adapters, where using the SCSI ID is much easier than using the 48-bit Ethernet hardware address.

ASCII (American Standard Code for Information Interchange)   A standard method of equating the numeric representations available in a computer to human-readable form. The number 32 represents a space, for example. The standard ASCII code contains 128 characters (seven bits). The extended ASCII code uses eight bits for 256 characters. Display adapters from the same machine type usually use the same upper 128 characters. Printers, however, might reserve these upper 128 characters for nonstandard characters. Many Epson printers use them for the italic representations of the lower 128 characters, for example.

baud rate   The number of signal changes (which might be variations in voltage or frequency, depending on the modulation standard being used) per second that can be exchanged between two modems. In most cases, this isn't the same as bits per second (bps).

Bayonet Nut Connector or British Naval Connector   See *BNC*.

bidirectional support   Defines a printer's capability to transfer information both ways on a printer cable. Input usually contains data or printer control codes. Output usually contains printer status information or error codes.

binary value   Refers to a base-2 data representation in the Windows Registry. Normally used to hold status flags or other information that lends itself to a binary (on/off) format.

bitmap   An array of bits (pixels) that contains data that describes the colors and shapes found in an image. It's effectively a one-to-one copy of the image it stores. (See *vector font*.)

BMP files   The Windows standard bitmap graphics data format (a format for storing a graphics image in a file). This is a raster graphics data format (as opposed to a vector format), and it doesn't include any form of compression.

BNC (Bayonet Nut Connector or British Naval Connector)   A standard connector normally used for coaxial cable connections like those found on 10Base-2 Ethernet systems. The center pin of the connector is used for data transmission, while the outer connection is for the signal return and cable shielding. A rotating ring locks the male connector onto the two nubs protruding from the female connector.

BootP (Bootstrap Protocol)   This protocol is used with diskless workstations. It allows the workstation to discover its IP address. This, in turn, allows the workstation to communicate with the server and download a special file containing the workstation's operating system. This file gets loaded into memory, which allows the workstation to boot without use of any type of disk drive.

Bootstrap Protocol   See *BootP*.

bps (bits per second)   The rate at which a modem or other communications device transmits data.

bridge   A network device that connects two LANs, provided that the two LANs are using the same NOS. The bridge can either be a standalone device or can be implemented in a server with the addition of a second network card.

CAD (Computer-Aided Drafting/Design) A graphics program that specializes in assisting you in the creation and editing of architectural, electrical, mechanical, or other forms of engineering drawings. CAD programs normally provide precise measuring capabilities and libraries of predefined objects, such as sinks, desks, resistors, and gears.

CardBus An advanced form of PCMCIA card that provides several enhancements over its predecessor, including 32-bit bus mastering support and burst-mode data transfers. CardBus also allows the use of 3.3 volt cards and the capability to place more than one device on a single card (for example, you could have a modem and a NIC on one card). The typical bus speed for CardBus is 33MHz, which is the same as the PCI bus. CardBus is backward compatible with PCMCIA, which means you can place a 16-bit PCMCIA card in a CardBus slot.

Carrier Sense Multiple Access/Collision Detection See *CSMA/CD*.

CAS (Communicating Applications Specification) An older facsimile (fax) communications standard originally defined by Intel and Digital Communications Associates (DCA). Many DBMS libraries still use this standard because it provides a consistent method for defining fax communications even if the host machine contains multiple boards. In addition, the API provides a simple method for interacting with the host machine's hardware. Problems with this standard include the need to define a special initialization file for each fax board in the system and the high cost of the hardware itself.

cascading style sheet See *CSS*.

CDFS (Compact Disc File System) The portion of the file subsystem specifically designed to interact with compact disc drives. It also provides the user interface elements required to tune this part of the subsystem. The CDFS takes the place of an FSD for CD-ROM drives.

client The recipient and requestor of data, services, or resources from a file, application, or server. The term *client* can refer to a workstation or to an application. The server can be another PC or another application.

Client Services for NetWare See *CSNW*.

client/server network A network model that splits the computing workload into two separate but related areas. On the one hand, you have users working at intelligent front-end systems called *clients*. In turn, these client machines interact with powerful back-end systems called *servers*. The basic idea is that the clients have enough processing power to perform tasks on their own, but they rely on the servers to provide them with specialized resources or services, or even access to information that would be impractical to implement on a client, such as a large database. (See also *peer-to-peer network*.)

CLSID (class ID) A method of assigning a unique identifier to each object in the Registry. Also refers to various high-level language constructs.

cluster The basic unit of storage on a hard disk or floppy disk.

cluster chain   The sequence of clusters that defines an entire file.

CMOS (complementary metal oxide semiconductor)   Normally refers to a construction method for low-power, battery-backed memory. When used in the context of a PC, this term usually refers to the memory used to store system configuration information and the real-time clock status. The configuration information normally includes the amount of system memory, the type and size of floppy disk drives, the hard drive parameters, and the video display type. Some vendors include other configuration information as part of this chip as well.

codec   A compressor/decompressor device driver. During playback of audio or video data, the codec decompresses the data before sending it to the appropriate multimedia device. During recording, the codec decompresses the raw data so that it takes up less disk space. Most codecs offer a variety of compression ratios.

COM   See *Component Object Model*.

Communicating Applications Specification   See *CAS*.

compact disc file system   See *CDFS*.

complementary metal oxide semiconductor   See *CMOS*.

Component Object Model (COM)   A Microsoft specification for an object-oriented code and data encapsulation method and transference technique. It's the basis for technologies such as OLE (object linking and embedding) and ActiveX (the name now used for, among many other technologies, *OCX file*—an object-oriented code library technology). COM is limited to local connections. DCOM (Distributed Component Object Model) is the technology used to allow data transfers and the use of OCXs within the Internet environment.

Compressed Serial Line Internet Protocol   See *CSLIP*.

Computer-Aided Design   See *CAD*.

container   Part of the object-oriented terminology that has become part of ActiveX. A *container* is a drive, file, or other resource used to hold objects. The container is normally referenced as an object itself.

context menu   A menu that appears when you right-click an object. The context menu gives you access to the properties and actions associated with that object.

cooperative multitasking   The multitasking mode used by Windows 3.*x* and 16-bit applications. It's up to the individual applications to decide when they will relinquish control of the system. (See also *preemptive multitasking*.)

cross-linked cluster   A cluster that has somehow been assigned to two different files or that has two FAT entries that refer to the same cluster.

CSLIP (Compressed Serial Line Internet Protocol)   A type of connection supported by older UNIX remote servers. CSLIP works much like a SLIP connection, except it also adds file compression. Windows 2000 provides support for remote network connections as a client. It doesn't provide this support as a server.

CSMA/CD(Carrier Sense Multiple Access/Collision Detection)   A method of detecting when two devices try to access the network at the same time (a collision). Normally, devices will listen to the network to see if there is activity. If no activity is taking place, then the device tries to transfer data. When a collision occurs, the device will wait a random amount of time, listen to the network for activity again, and then attempt to transfer the data again. This is the method that Ethernet uses to keep data moving smoothly.

CSNW (Client Services for NetWare)   A client service on Windows 2000 workstations that provides access to Novell NetWare servers and services. An applet is added to the Control Panel when you install CSNW. The applet enables you to configure the NetWare connection.

CSS (cascading style sheet)   A method for defining a Web page template. You can redefine the familiar HTML elements to suit your needs or the style you want enforced in your Internet site. For example, you can define H1 as using a red, 36-point Times New Roman typeface. Ordinarily, a browser would not translate the H1 (headline) HTML element into that size, color, or typeface. You can force it to happen, however, by creating a style sheet. You can redefine most HTML elements, including headings, backgrounds, and divider lines. Using a style sheet also makes it easier to enforce a common (coordinated) look across an entire Web site. The reasons for using CSSs include efficiency when creating a Web site (it takes less time if you don't have to repeatedly define the overall design for each page) and consistency. Making changes later to the overall appearance of a site also becomes as easy as changing the style sheet instead of changing each particular use of the redefined element everywhere in the site.

DACL   See *Discretionary Access Control List.*

DAT (digital audio tape)   A tape drive that uses a special tape cassette to store data. The cassette and drive use the same technology as the audio version of the DAT drive. The internal circuitry of the drive formats the tape for use with a computer system, however. The vendor must also design the interface circuitry with computer needs in mind. DAT tapes enable you to store large amounts of information in a relatively small amount of space. Typical drive capacities range from 1.2GB to 8GB. Although a serial format, DAT backup has become popular with graphics departments because data can be surprisingly quickly retrieved from a DAT tape; the tapes tend to be more robust than some kinds of high-density removable disks. What's more, the DAT tape storage medium is by far the least expensive of all high-density formats.

data bits   In modem data transfer, this is the number of bits used to represent a character.

Data Communication Exchange   See *DCE.*

Data Link Control   See *DLC.*

datacentric   See *docucentricity*.

DBMS (database management system)   A method for storing and retrieving data based on tables, records, and fields. Each field represents a specific piece of data, such as an employee's last name. Records are made up of one or more fields. Each record is one complete entry in a table. A table contains one type of data, such as the names and addresses of all the employees in a company. It's composed of records (rows) and fields (columns), just like the tables you see in books. A database may contain one or more related tables. It may include a list of employees in one table, for example, and the pay records for each of those employees in a second table.

DCE (Data Communication Exchange)   A specification created by the Open Software Foundation (OSF) that defines methods for data exchange between a client and server. The Remote Procedure Call (RPC) support built into Windows 2000 is compatible with the DCE specification.

DDE (Dynamic Data Exchange)   The capability to cut data from one application and paste it into another application. You can cut a graphics image created with a paint program, for example, and paste it into a word processing document. After it's pasted, the data doesn't reflect changes made to it by the originating application. DDE also provides a method for communicating with an application that supports it and requesting data. You can use an Excel macro to call Microsoft Word and request the contents of a document file, for example. Some applications also use DDE to implement file-association strategies. Microsoft Word, for example, uses DDE in place of command-line switches to gain added flexibility when a user needs to open or print a file.

Dependent client   A term that normally defines a client that relies on the server for resources. In other words, the client requires a network connection and server communication to complete specific tasks. This term is applied to Microsoft Management Queue and other technologies where clients can be either dependent or independent. Independent clients normally provide their own queues so that they can operate for some period of time without a network connection or server resources.

device-independent bitmap   See *DIB*.

DHCP (Dynamic Host Configuration Protocol)   A method for automatically configuring a system's TCP/IP parameters. This includes the IP address, gateway, subnet mask, and other parameters used with a TCP/IP connection. A server provides this address to the client as part of the setup communications. Using DHCP means that a server can use fewer addresses to communicate with clients and that clients do not need to provide a hard-coded address to the server. You must configure your server to provide these services.

DIB (device-independent bitmap)   A method of representing graphics information that doesn't reflect a particular device's requirements. This has the advantage of allowing the same graphic to appear on any device in precisely the same way, despite differences in resolution or other factors that normally change the graphic's appearance.

digital audio tape   See *DAT*.

DIP (Dual In-line Package)   A method of encasing computer chip circuitry that relies on two rows of parallel pins to make contact between the chip circuitry and the circuit board.

DIP switch   A set of configuration switches normally found within a computer system. These switches control everything from the port addresses and IRQ settings on expansion boards, to the number of supported floppy disk drives on the motherboard. Most vendors use software settings stored in CMOS rather than DIP switches now to reduce the number of times a user needs to open the computer case.

direct cable connection   A type of connection that relies on a serial or parallel cable rather than network cards or telephone communications. Direct cable connections have the advantage of being easy to implement and inexpensive. Negative features include low transmission rate and the inability to allow more than a single pair of PCs to talk with each other. Normally, direct cable connections are used for short-term data transfer between a desktop and laptop (or other portable) computer.

direct memory access   See *DMA*.

Discretionary Access Control List (DACL)   A Windows NT-specific security component. The DACL controls who can actually use the object. You can assign both groups and individual users to a specific object.

Disk Defragmenter   An application used to reorder the data on a long-term storage device, such as a hard or floppy disk drive. Reordering the data so that it appears in sequential order—file by file—reduces the time required to access and read it. The sequential order enables you to read an entire file without moving the disk head at all in some cases and only a little in others. This reduction in access time normally improves overall system throughput and therefore enhances system efficiency.

DLC (Data Link Control)   Normally, a protocol used to establish communications with a remote server. The Microsoft DLC provides connections to mainframes and network printers.

DLL (dynamic link library)   A file that contains programming code. DLLs are loaded into memory by request when their code is needed. A DLL is not executable by itself, like an EXE application. A DLL is a library that contains one or more discrete routines (procedures) that an application or the operating system can use to do certain jobs. There's a DLL, for example, that includes the classic File Save As dialog box as well as other file-related dialog boxes. Various applications can therefore call on this DLL rather than having to include file management–related dialog box programming themselves. More than one application can use the functions provided by a DLL, thereby reducing overall memory requirements when more than one application is running. (Each application doesn't contain duplicate code to handle that particular job.)

DMA (direct memory access)   A memory-addressing technique in which the processor doesn't perform the actual data transfer. This method of memory access is faster than any other technique.

DNS   See *Domain Name System*.

Domain   An area of control in a network. Members of a domain can share resources and are controlled by one or more member servers. One or two servers normally control the security of the network; these servers are normally called *domain controllers*.

Domain controller   One or more special servers that are used to store user, machine, server, and resource configurations. The domain controller maintains a database of information. It's also used to verify the identity of users or other entities that want to log onto the system and use resources under domain control. Windows installations normally have one Primary Domain Controller (PDC) that is in charge of the domain. Backup Domain Controllers (BDC) provide reliability in case the PDC becomes non-functional.

Domain Name System (DNS)   An Internet technology that allows a user to refer to a host computer by name rather than by its unique IP address.

DOS Protected-Mode Interface   See *DPMI*.

DPMI (DOS Protected-Mode Interface)   A method of accessing extended memory from a DOS application using the Windows extended Memory Manager.

drag and drop   A technique used in object-oriented operating systems to access data, without actually opening a file, using conventional (Explorer) methods. Drag and drop enables the user to pick up a document's icon or filename, drag it to the printer icon, and drop it, for example. The printer then prints the document using its default settings. No need for menus—it's just an intuitive kind of behavior.

dual boot   Putting more than one operating system on the hard drive so that, when you turn on the computer's power, you can select which OS you want to use. Common dual-boot configurations include DOS and Windows 2000 (so you can more easily recover from problems if Windows 2000 won't load) and Windows 95/98 and Windows 2000 so that you can play games in Windows 95/98 that won't work in Windows 2000.

Dual in-line package   See *DIP*.

dual-ported Video RAM   See *VRAM*.

Dvorak layout   An alternative keyboard layout that reduces stress on the typist and increases speed. Keys are arranged differently from the more familiar QWERTY layout used by most keyboards and typewriters.

Dynamic Data Exchange   See *DDE*.

Dynamic Host Configuration Protocol   See *DHCP*.

dynamic link library   See *DLL*.

EEMS (Enhanced Expanded Memory Specification)   This specification defines one method of extending the amount of memory a processor can address from the conventional memory area. It was a solution to an old DOS problem that was significant in 1986.

EMB (extended memory blocks)   Refers to the remaining extended memory (above the high memory area) available to an extended memory specification (XMS) driver. (Another DOS feature no longer of much significance.)

embedded systems   A combination of processor, operating system, and device-specific applications used with a special-purpose device. The control used to set the time and temperature on a microwave is an embedded system, for example. Another form of embedded system is the computer that controls engine efficiency in a car.

EMF (enhanced metafile)   A graphics file format that's not widely used. It's a vector graphics format, so it provides a certain level of device independence and scalability. It's also the default file type for Windows 2000 printing components.

EMM (Expanded Memory Manager)   A device driver such as EMM386.EXE that provides expanded memory services on an 80386 and above machine. Yet another no-longer-of-much-significance DOS memory fix.

emoticon   A set of characters used to express body language or an emotion of some sort. Normally, the characters form some visual representation of the person's face. For example, :^) when viewed sideways looks like a person smiling. Emoticons normally appear within electronic mail where the sender's meaning may be unclear. Tongue-in-cheek comments or jokes can cause problems when sent in written format because the receiver sometimes doesn't understand that the intent is ironic. "You're nuts!" can be either mild, friendly teasing (if you're smiling and patting someone on the back when you say it) or an insult if you're frowning. An emoticon clarifies your email message by indicating the body language or emotion you want to attach to the words you're sending. Get it?

EMS (Expanded Memory Specification)   This specification defines one method of extending the amount of memory a processor can address from the conventional memory area. It's yet another DOS memory fix.

Enhanced Expanded Memory Specification   See *EEMS*.

enhanced metafile   See *EMF*.

enhanced mode   A Windows operating mode that supports the capabilities of the 80386 and above processors. This means that Windows will use any extended memory found in the workstation by using the processor's protected mode. This mode also fully supports the virtual memory capabilities of the 80386, which means that the size of the hard disk's swap files plus the amount of physical RAM determines the amount of memory available for applications. You also receive the full multitasking capabilities of the 80386 using this mode.

Expanded Memory Manager   See *EMM*.

Expanded Memory Specification   See *EMS*.

extended memory blocks   See *EMB*.

extended partition   The hard disk space that isn't allocated to the primary partition. If you have a 1.2GB disk and you allocate 300MB to the primary partition, for example, the extended partition will be 900MB. You can then subdivide the extended partition into logical drives.

FAT (file allocation table)   The method of formatting a hard disk drive used by DOS and other operating systems. This technique is one of the oldest formatting methods available. There have been several different versions of FAT based on the number of bits used to store disk locations. The original form was 12-bits, which was quickly followed by the 16-bit version used by many computers today. A 32-bit version of FAT, also called FAT32, was introduced with the OSR2 version of Windows 98. This new version of FAT stores data more efficiently on the large hard drives available on today's computers.

file allocation table   See *FAT*.

file system driver   See *FSD*.

file transfer protocol   See *FTP*.

font   A unique set of design characteristics common to a group of letters, numbers, and symbols. Four qualities collectively define the font of any character: the typeface, the type size, the type style, and the character spacing.

frame buffer   A piece of system memory set aside to hold video. An application draws on the system memory rather than actual video card memory to prevent conflicts when multiple applications need to draw at the same time. When the draw on the buffer is complete, the entire buffer is sent to video memory at one time. Anything sent to video memory usually ends up on the display. This process is known as *virtualization*.

FSD (file system driver)   A file subsystem component responsible for defining the interface between Windows and long-term storage. The FSD also defines features such as long filenames and what types of interaction the device supports. The CD-ROM FSD, for example, won't support file writes unless you provide a device that can perform that sort of task.

FTP (file transfer protocol)   One of several common data transfer protocols for the Internet. This particular protocol specializes in data transfer in the form of a file download. The user is presented with a list of available files in a directory list format. An FTP site may choose DOS or UNIX formatting for the file listing, although the DOS format is extremely rare. Unlike HTTP sites, an FTP site provides a definite information hierarchy through the use of directories and subdirectories, much like the file directory structure used on most workstation hard drives.

gateway   A way to link two different kinds of networks. It can involve both hardware and software that allow the networks to communicate. The gateway translates the incoming and outgoing packets so that each system can work the data.

GDI (graphics device interface)   One of the main Windows root components. This is an API, a collection of functions (and a few subroutines) that provide standard, commonly needed services to the operating system and applications that want to tap into the GDI library. GDI displays common graphics elements (such as the mouse frames around windows) onscreen. Every application must use this component when it wants to draw something or perform other graphics-related tasks. The other two main APIs are named Kernel and User.

GDT (global descriptor table)   A memory construct that contains the information required to control all the extended memory in an 80386 or above processor. The GDT normally passes control of smaller memory segments to the LDTs used by an individual application.

general protection fault   See *GPF*.

global descriptor table   See *GDT*.

GPF (general protection fault)   A processor or memory error that occurs when an application makes a request the system can't honor. This type of error results in some type of severe action on the part of the operating system. Normally, the operating system terminates the offending application.

graphical device interface   See *GDI*.

graphical user interface   See *GUI*.

GUI (graphical user interface)   A set of icons and graphics elements that replace the character-mode (text-based) system used in operating systems such as DOS. The GUI can ride on top of another operating system (such as DOS or UNIX) or merely be part of the operating system itself (such as Windows 95/98 and Windows 2000). Advantages of a GUI are ease of use and high-resolution graphics. Disadvantages are greater hardware requirements and slower performance over a similar system using a character-mode interface. Of course, no one today seriously considers using the out-of-date character-mode interface any more than families still sit around the living room listening to radio dramas. A superior technology has all but killed its predecessor.

HAL (Hardware Abstraction Layer)   A conceptual element of the Windows NT architecture. Microsoft wrote the drivers and other software elements so that it could easily move Windows NT to other platforms. That's how it moved Windows NT to the MIPS and Alpha machines. The basic architecture of Windows NT is the same, but the low-level drivers—the ones that directly interface with the hardware—are different. The important thing to remember is that as far as your application is concerned, it's still running on an Intel machine. The only time you'll run into trouble is if your application bypasses the Windows API and goes directly to the hardware.

Hardware Abstraction Layer   See *HAL*.

hardware flow control   A system whereby the computer and modem use individual wires to send signals to each other that indicate whether they're ready to receive data. To stop outgoing data, the modem turns off its CTS (Clear To Send) line. To stop incoming data, the processor turns off its RTS (Request To Send) line.

high memory area   See *HMA*.

HMA (high memory area)   The 64KB area of memory beyond the 1MB boundary that the processor can access in real mode on an 80286 or above processor.

HTML (Hypertext Markup Language)   A page-description language that is now the default method of displaying text, graphics, and sound on the Internet. HTML provides commands (elements, or *tags*, as they're called) that specify where on a page, and how large, text and graphics will appear. An Internet browser then interprets the HTML source code and displays the result to the user. Depending on the browser's capabilities, some tags are translated into graphics elements, sounds, or text with special characteristics such as color, font, or other attributes. Most browsers discard any keywords they don't understand, allowing browsers of various capabilities to explore the same page without problem. Obviously, there's a loss of capability if a browser doesn't support a specific HTML element. HTML is constantly being revised and supplemented by such additional techniques, such as DHTML (Dynamic HTML), that enrich the Internet experience with animation, dramatic audio, and other multimedia effects.

hub   A central connection point for network cables. They range in size from small boxes with six or eight RJ-45 connectors to large cabinets with dozens of ports for various cable types.

hyperlink   A word or phrase that, when clicked, jumps you to another location in the current document, to another document altogether, or to a Web site on the Internet. Generally, a hyperlink is a different color (often blue) than surrounding text, and it's usually underlined as well.

Hypertext Markup Language   See *HTML*.

ICM (image color matcher)   A component of the graphics subsystem that allows Windows to match the colors produced by one device with those available on another device. The result is that the output of both devices doesn't show the normal variations in color that Windows applications currently produce.

icon   A symbol used to graphically represent the purpose and/or function of an application or file. The Recycle Bin's icon is a wastebasket; the Keyboard applet icon in Control Panel is a keyboard. Applications designed for the environment or operating system usually appear with a special icon depicting the purpose of the application or the vendor's logo.

IFS Manager (Installable File System Manager)   The API component of the file subsystem. It provides a consistent interface that applications can use to access a variety of devices, both local and remote. This component also provides a standard interface that device drivers can use to provide services, such as file opening and drive status.

image color matcher   See *ICM*.

independent client   A term that normally defines a client that doesn't need constant contact with the server for resources. In other words, the client doesn't require a network connection and server communication to complete specific tasks. However, the independent client will eventually require access to the server to perform updates and renew resources before breaking contact again. This term is applied to Microsoft Management Queue and other technologies where clients can be either dependent or independent. Independent clients normally provide their own queues so that they can operate for some period of time without a network connection or server resources.

INF file   A configuration file (for an application or device). It contains all the parameters Windows requires to install or configure the device or application. An application INF file might contain the location of data files and the interdependencies of DLLs, for example. Both application and device INF files contain the Registry and INI file entries required to make Windows recognize the application or device.

inherited rights mask   See *IRM*.

installable file system helper   A real-mode component of the IFS Manager used to allow access of Windows drive functions by DOS applications. It uses the same DOS interface as before, but all processing is performed by the Protected-Mode Manager.

Installable File System Manager   See *IFS Manager*.

Internet packet exchange   See *IPX*.

interrupt request   See *IRQ*.

intranet   The implementation of Internet technologies, such as TCP/IP and World Wide Web servers, for use within a corporate organization rather than for (or in addition to) connection to the public Internet.

IPX (Internet packet exchange)   A Novell-specific peer-to-peer communication protocol based on the internet protocol (IP) portion of the TCP/IP pair. It describes a set of rules that allows two nodes to talk to each other. Think of this as the language used on the network. If everyone speaks the same language, then all the nodes can understand each other. Messages are exchanged in the form of packets on a network. Think of a packet as one sheet of a letter. There is a letterhead saying who sent the letter, an introduction saying who the letter is for, and a message that tells the receiving party what the sending party wants to say.

IRM (inherited rights mask)   A NetWare term describing the set of rights a person inherits as part of his or her trustee, group, file, and directory rights.

IRQ (interrupt request)   The set of address lines that connect a peripheral to the processor. Think of an IRQ as an office telephone with multiple incoming lines. Every time a device calls, its entry lights up on the front of the telephone. The processor selects the desired line and picks up the receiver to find out what the device wants. Everything works fine as long as there's one line for each device that needs to call the processor. If more than one device were to try to call in on the same line, the processor wouldn't know who was at the other end. This is the source of IRQ conflicts that you hear about from various sources. Older PC-class machines provided eight interrupt lines. The newer AT-class machines provide 16 interrupt lines. Only 15 of those lines are usable, however, because one of them is used for internal purposes.

Kerberos   This is Microsoft's primary replacement for the Windows NT LAN Manager (NTLM) security currently used to ensure that your data remains safe when using Windows. Kerberos Version 5 is a relatively new industry-standard security protocol devised at MIT that offers superior security support through the use of a private-key architecture. This protocol supports mutual authentication of both client and server, reduces server load when establishing a connection, and allows the client to delegate authentication to the server through the use of proxy mechanisms. Kerberos connects to an online Key Distribution Center (KDC) and the Directory Service (DS) account to obtain session tickets used for authentication purposes.

kernel   A core Windows 2000 component (an API) that loads applications (including any DLLs needed by the program), handles all aspects of file I/O, allocates virtual memory and works with the Memory Pager, and schedules and runs threads started by applications.

LAN (local area network)   A combination of hardware and software used to connect a group of PCs to each other and/or a mini- or mainframe computer. Two main networking models are in use: peer-to-peer and client/server. The peer-to-peer model doesn't require a dedicated server. In addition, all the workstations in the group can share resources. The client/server model uses a central server for resource sharing, but some special methods are provided for using local resources in a limited fashion.

lazy writes   A method for writing data to disk that enables the operating system to use idle CPU time to its best advantage. Data is written to disk from a memory buffer when the CPU isn't performing other tasks. The advantage of this method is an overall improvement in system response time and efficiency. Disadvantages include potential data loss if the user shuts off the system without forcing a write first. Under Windows 2000 and Windows 95/98, the forced write occurs during the shutdown sequence.

LDT (local descriptor table)   A memory construct that controls access to the memory used by a single application or a group of applications that share the same memory. The LDT is subservient to the GDT that manages system memory overall.

Light Remote Procedure Call   See *LRPC*.

list box   A dialog box control that displays a list of items. Normally, the user selects one or more of these items to respond to an application or operating system query. When you use the File, Open option in most applications, you'll be shown a list box of filenames.

local area network   See *LAN*.

local descriptor table   See *LDT*.

locally unique identifier   See *LUID*.

LRPC (Light Remote Procedure Call)   Essentially, a method for calling a procedure not associated with the current application or local machine. OLE 2 enables you to create links to other documents, even if they aren't physically located on the local drive. It implements this using an LRPC mechanism. Unfortunately, this linking mechanism has limitations. You'll find that it works fine with some peer-to-peer networks, for example, but it works only marginally with other network types.

LUID (locally unique identifier)   Essentially, a pointer to a Windows 2000 security object. The object could include files, directories, or services. LUIDs provide an operating system reference to the object and work much like your Social Security number.

MAC (Media Access Control)   The unique address that identifies each node on a network. The MAC layer is at the data link control (DLC) layer of the OSI reference model for networks. It directly interacts with the network media, which means that each type of network will have a different MAC that identifies the nodes on that network. The MAC layer also referred to the DLC layer on some networks.

macros   A kind of programming that works within an application. It's used to automate the application's features (although macros can also reach outside their host application to make use of features in other applications or the operating system itself). For example, I wrote a macro that will go through an entire document and remove any double spaces (because publishers don't like double spaces). It saves me a lot of time. You can also record macros in most applications. Turn on the Macro Recorder and it'll remember keystrokes and menu selections you make. Then you turn off recording and the macro exists. You can run the macro any time in the future to cause the same steps, the same keystrokes, or whatever, to repeat automatically.

management information file   See *MIF*.

MAPI (Messaging API)   The set of functions and other resources Windows provides to communications programs. It allows the application to access a variety of communications channels using a single set of calls and without regard to media. This is the component of Microsoft operating systems that allows Exchange and Outlook to process information from email and online services using the same interface.

MCA (microchannel architecture)   A bus introduced by IBM. It's faster than the old ISA bus and gives the operating system information about the peripheral devices connected to the bus. It also provides the means for devices to become self-configuring.

Media Access Control   See *MAC*.

message queuing   The act of storing a message for later processing by the client or server. Microsoft Message Queue (MSMQ) uses message queuing technology to allow a developer to create disconnected applications on independent clients. A disconnected application stores messages for the server on the local hard drive until the client establishes a connection to the server. The messages are then transferred in the background to the server's queue to await further processing by the server.

Messaging API   See *MAPI*.

microchannel architecture   See *MCA*.

Microkernel   The Windows 2000 component primarily responsible for the scheduling of activities on processors and coordinating the rest of the Windows 2000 Kernel-mode components. The Microkernel contains the scheduler or dispatcher that controls when a thread may run on a processor.

Microm Networking Protocol   See *MNP*.

MIDI (Musical Instrument Digital Interface)   A computer language devoted to music. It describes all aspects of music (tone, note, loudness, timbre, duration, vibrato, accents, you name it). Then, a sound card, such as the Sound Blaster AWE, that contains a stored bank of digitally recorded instruments can reproduce a song or symphony with remarkable fidelity. You can also feed MIDI to various standalone electronic instruments, such as computerized keyboards by Yamaha and other manufacturers. MIDI can also be recorded. You could get a famous pianist to play a Bach fugue on an electronic piano, all the while recording most every nuance of the performance into a MIDI file on disk. Think of MIDI as the computer equivalent of a player piano roll, only much, much more subtle and detailed than holes punched into paper could ever be.

MIF (management information file)   A file used with Desktop Management Interface (DMI) support that contains all the particulars about a piece of equipment. When the System Management Server looks at a workstation and finds this file, it adds its contents to a SQL database that you can open with any number of products. Besides the hardware information, System Management Server adds the software-auditing information it finds to the database. The combined software and hardware information will give you the data required to know whether a particular workstation can run a piece of software without an upgrade.

miniport driver   A Windows component that provides access to a resource—normally, a peripheral device of some type. It's also used to access pseudo-devices and network resources.

MNP (Microm Networking Protocol)   A standard method of error correcting for modems. The precise differences between levels aren't important from a user prospective. A higher level is generally better. Essentially, MNP provides a method of sending data in larger blocks, thus eliminating some of the control characters that usually impede data transmission.

Moore's Law   Processing power doubles every 18 months (from Gordon Moore, cofounder of Intel).

Motion Picture Experts Group   See *MPEG*.

MPEG (Motion Picture Experts Group)   A standards group that provides file formats and other specifications in regard to full-motion video and other types of graphics displays.

MPR (multiple provider router)   A method of using more than one protocol with Windows. It allows you to mix and match protected-mode drivers on the same network. You can mix NetBEUI and IPX/SPX, for example, on the same network. In addition, some protocols automatically load when you request a specific service. The Microsoft Data Link Control (DLC) falls into this category. It provides connections to mainframes and network printers. All network protocols require a network provider. The whole function of the MPR is to accept network requests from the API and send them to the appropriate network provider (NP).

multiple provider router   See *MPR*.

multitasking   The capability of some processor and environment/system combinations to perform more than one task at a time. The tasks appear to be carried out simultaneously. You can download messages from an online service, print from a word processor, and recalculate a spreadsheet all at the same time, for example. Each application receives a slice of time before the processor moves to the next application. Because the timeslices are fairly small, it appears to the user that these actions are occurring simultaneously. Technically, multitasking requires two or more microprocessors (one CPU can't do two things simultaneously). But, in common parlance, a single-CPU system is often described as a *multitasking environment*.

Musical Instrument Digital Interface   See *MIDI*.

national language support   See *NLS*.

NDIS (Network Device Interface Specification)   A driver that translates each Windows-specific request into a call the NIC driver can understand. Using NDIS means that Windows can provide standardized requests regardless of NIC type, thus greatly enhancing flexibility and extensibility.

nested objects   Two or more objects that are coupled in some fashion. The objects normally appear within the confines of a container object. Object nesting allows multiple objects to define the properties of a higher-level object. It also allows the user to associate different types of objects with each other.

NetBEUI   The NetBIOS Extended User Interface protocol. (NetBIOS is an API that lets network applications such as redirectors communicate with networking protocols.) It's a combined Transport-layer protocol and Network-layer protocol developed by IBM and supported by all Microsoft networks. It's a simple, efficient protocol that works well in small LANs. However, it lacks the capability to route packets, so it isn't suitable for WANs.

NetBIOS   An application interface for allowing network applications access to resources and services on other system in the network. NetBIOS is not a network protocol. On Microsoft operating systems, NetBEUI, TCP/IP, and IPX/SPX (NWLink) are NetBIOS-supported protocols.

Network Device Interface Specification   See *NDIS*.

network interface card   See *NIC*.

network provider   See *NP*.

NIC (network interface card)   The device responsible for allowing a workstation to communicate with the file server and other workstations. It provides the physical means for creating the connection. The card plugs into an expansion slot in the computer. A cable that attaches to the back of the card completes the communications path.

NLS (national language support)   A method of reconfiguring the keyboard and other system components to support more than one language through the use of code pages. Each code page defines a different language configuration. Unfortunately, this technique doesn't change the language used for display purposes. In other words, NLS won't cause your English-language version of Windows to suddenly display prompts and other text in German.

NP (network provider)   Performs all the protocol-specific functions an application requires under Windows. It makes or breaks connections, returns network status information, and provides a consistent interface for the multiple provider router (MPR) to use.

NTFS (NT File System)   The method of formatting a hard disk drive offered by Windows 2000. Although it can provide significant speed advantages over other formatting techniques (notably FAT) on large partitions, only the Windows NT operating system can access a drive that's formatted using this technique.

object conversion   A method of changing the format and properties of an object created by one application to the format and properties used by another. Conversion moves the data from one application to another, usually without a loss of formatting but always without a loss of content.

object linking and embedding   See *OLE*.

ODBC (Open Database Connectivity)   One of several methods of exchanging data between DBMS. ODBC normally relies on SQL to translate DBMS-specific commands from the client into a generic language. The ODBC agents on the server translate these SQL requests into server-specific commands.

OLE (object linking and embedding)   The process of packaging a filename and any required parameters into an object and then pasting this object into the file created by another application. You can place a graphics object within a word processing document or spreadsheet, for example. When you look at the object, it appears as if you just pasted the data from the originating application into the current application (similar to DDE). When linked, the data provided by the object automatically changes if you change the data in the original object. When embedded, the data doesn't change unless you specifically edit it, but the data still retains its original format and you still use the original application to edit the data. Often, you can start the originating application and automatically load the required data by double-clicking the object. The OLE 2 specification allows in-place data editing as well as editing in a separate application window.

Open Database Connectivity   See *ODBC*.

Open System Interconnection (OSI) Reference Model   A theoretical seven layer protocol model of network connectivity commonly used to teach how network protocols interact. Data is passed from one layer to the next until it gets physically transmitted to another machine. The reverse process takes place when the data arrives at the receiving machine—unwrapping layer after layer of protocol information, until the data appears in its original form. The OSI reference model was originally supposed to unite all network models, but proprietary formats prevented full acceptance by vendors and the OSI reference model became a teaching tool instead. (The X.400 and X.500 standards are directly based on the OSI reference model.) The seven OSI reference model layers include application, presentation, session, transport, network, data link, and physical.

packet   The data transfer unit used in network and modem communications. Each packet contains not only data but also a *header,* which contains information about which machine sent the data, which machine is supposed to receive the data, and a few extra tidbits that let the receiving computer put all the original data together in the correct order and check for errors that might have cropped up during the transmission.

password caching   A method of saving the passwords for resources a user might need to access. The user still needs to enter the main password required to access Windows, but Windows remembers the passwords required to access other resources, such as a network or an online service that directly supports the Windows password-caching capability.

PCX file   A raster graphics data format originally used by the ZSoft Paintbrush application. This format has gone through many nonstandard transitions and occasionally presents problems when accessed by applications other than the original. It provides for various levels of color and includes data compression. The latest version is PCX 5.

PD (port driver)   Performs the task of communicating with the device through an adapter. It's the last stage before a message leaves Windows and the first stage when a message arrives from the device. The PD is usually adapter specific. You would have one VxD for each hard drive and one PD for each hard drive adapter, for example.

peer-to-peer network   A network in which no one computer is singled out to provide special services. Instead, all the computers attached to the network have equal status (at least as far as the network is concerned), and all the computers can act as both servers and clients. This is a simpler kind of networking (up to 10 workstations) than a client/server network.

Performance Monitor A software component that monitors resources and reports data regarding usage. The Performance Monitor is an integrated portion of the general Windows 2000 release. Microsoft has changed the name to System Monitor.

permissions The level of access granted to an individual user, machine, process, or a Windows object to access and use resources controlled by the host machine and/or the server.

PIF (program information file) A configuration file (see also *INF file* and *Registry value*) that Windows uses to define the environment for a DOS application. The PIF usually includes various memory settings, along with the application's command path and working directory.

Plug and Play The combination of BIOS, operating system, and peripheral device components that provides a self-configuring environment. This self-configuring feature allows the operating system to avoid potential hardware conflicts by polling the peripheral devices, assessing their requirements, and determining and implementing optimal settings for each device.

Point-to-Point Protocol See *PPP*.

port driver See *PD*.

POSIX A government-specified form of UNIX that's supposed to be portable across a variety of platforms. It appeared in 1988 as IEEE Standard 1003.1-1988.

POST (Power-On Self Test) The set of diagnostic and configuration routines the BIOS runs during system initialization. The memory counter you see during the boot sequence is part of this process, for example.

Power-On Self Test See *POST*.

PPP (Point-to-Point Protocol) A set of communications rules that provide a method for conducting online (from one point to another) communications. In most cases, you'll use PPP to connect to a UNIX host or the Internet or to enhance your Dial-Up Networking capability.

preemptive multitasking A multitasking model used by 32-bit applications in which the scheduler or dispatcher uses a sophisticated algorithm to monitor all running processes, assign each one a priority level, and allocate CPU resources according to the relative priority of each process. (See also *cooperative multitasking*.)

program information file See PIF.

protected mode The processor mode in which the processor can access all of extended memory. This mode also provides a better level of application error detection as part of the processing cycle.

protected-mode mapper   An application that converts real-mode device driver calls into those used by a protected-mode counterpart. It enables you to use your DOS drivers under Windows. Without the support of this VxD, Windows couldn't support legacy devices that lack Windows-specific drivers.

quoting   The practice of including all or part of an original email message within a response. Quoting enables the viewer to see what the original question was without looking up the original message.

RAID (redundant array of inexpensive disks)   One method of hard disk error recovery that relies on two or more hard drives working in unison. Each drive contains part of the data required to re-create the entire data set. The data is striped onto each drive and is followed by error-correcting bits. If one drive fails, the data can be reconstructed on a new drive using the contents of the other drives in the array.

raster font   A typeface technology that contains one-for-one copies of a character set. Think plug-in cartridges for laser printers. This technology is no longer in use for all practical purposes. (See *vector font*, the victor in the typeface competition.)

raw   Unprocessed data that is sent directly to an input/output device like a printer. Contrast this with cooked data, which is processed in some way before it is transferred. There are usually efficiency and quality trade-offs when considering raw versus cooked data. Raw data requires fewer host machine resources and is therefore more efficient for the host machine; cooked data is more efficient for the input/output device to work with. The quality of cooked versus raw data depends a great deal on the capabilities of the host machine versus the input/output device.

real mode   A Windows operating mode that supports the capabilities of the 8088/8086 processor. This essentially limits you to loading one application within the confines of conventional memory. Windows versions after 3.0 don't support this mode. You must use these versions with workstations containing an 80286 or higher processor.

redundant array of inexpensive disks   See *RAID*.

REG file   A file saved by the REGEDIT.EXE program that can be used to later restore Registry information. REG files hold a text version of the keys and values they contain in the Registry. Windows 2000 does not normally use this format for storing information in the Registry. However, REG files are useful to administrators as a way to update the Registry. Also, it's always a good idea to first save the entire Registry before you make changes to it. Some applications provide REG files you can use to incorporate their file associations and OLE (ActiveX) capabilities into Windows.

Registry key   This is a Registry heading (it's like a user-defined array in programming). It provides the structure required to hold values and other information required by Windows and the applications running within it.

Registry value   The same as a value in programming (data, such as the number 2 or the word *blue*). Registry values provide, among other things, configuration information. *Blue* might be a value of, for instance, your desktop color.

remote access   The capability to use a remote resource as you would a local resource. In some cases, this also means downloading the remote resource to use as a local resource.

Remote Procedure Call   See *RPC*.

repeater   A device that boosts a network cable's signal so that the length of the network can be extended. Repeaters are needed because copper-based cables suffer from *attenuation*, a phenomenon in which the degradation of the electrical signal carried over the cable is proportional to the distance the signal has to travel.

router   A device that makes decisions about where to send the network packets it receives. Unlike a bridge, which merely passes along any data that comes its way, a router examines the address information in each packet and then determines the most efficient route the packet must take to reach its eventual destination.

routing   The process whereby packets travel from host to host until they eventually reach their destination.

RPC (Remote Procedure Call)   The capability to use code or data on a remote machine as if it were local. This is an advanced capability that will eventually pave the way for decentralized applications.

SCSI Manager   Windows NT introduced something called the *miniport driver*. With Windows 95/98, you can use the Windows 2000 miniport binaries. Before you can actually do this, however, Windows 95/98 must translate its commands into a format the miniport driver will understand. The SCSI Manager performs this service.

SCSIzer   A file subsystem component that deals with the SCSI command language. Think of the command language as the method the computer uses to tell a SCSI device to perform a task. The command language isn't the data the SCSI device handles; instead, it's the act the SCSI device will perform. There's one SCSIzer for each SCSI device.

Secure Socket Layer (SSL)   A digital signature technology used for exchanging information between a client and a server. Essentially an SSL compliant server will request a digital certificate from the client machine. The client can likewise request a digital certificate from the server. These digital certificates are obtained from a third party vendor like VeriSign who can vouch for the identity of both parties.

security identifier   See *SID*.

Sequential Packet Exchange (SPX)   This is the part of the IPX/SPX protocol pair that guarantees delivery of a message sent from one node to another. Think of SPX as the postal clerk that delivers a certified letter from one place to another. In network terms each page of the letter is called a *packet*. SPX delivers the letter one page at a time to the intended party.

server   An application or workstation that provides services, resources, or data to a client application or workstation. The client usually makes requests in the form of OLE, DDE, or other command formats. (Also, when applications communicate with each other, one can be called the "server" if it supplies, say, spell-checking services to the other (client) application, which lacks a spell checker.)

shell extension   An application that gives some type of added value to the operating system interface. In most cases, the application must register itself with the Registry before the operating system will recognize it.

SID (security identifier)   The part of a user's access token used to identify the user throughout the network; it's like having an account number. The user token the SID identifies tells what groups the user belongs to and what privileges the user has. Each group also has a SID, so the user's SID contains references to the various group SIDs that he or she belongs to rather than a complete set of group access rights.

Simple Network Management Protocol (SNMP)   A network protocol (originally designed for the Internet) to manage devices from different vendors.

SPX   See *Sequential Packet Exchange*.

snap-ins   Component technologies allow one application to serve as a container for multiple sub-applications. A snap-in refers to a component that is designed to reside within another application. The snap-in performs one specific task, out of all of the tasks that the application as a whole can perform. The Microsoft Management Console (MMC) is an example of a host application. All Windows 2000 management tasks are performed through the use of snap-ins designed to work with MMC.

SNMP   See *Simple Network Management Protocol*.

SSL   See *Secure Socket Layer*.

stripe set   One disk within a redundant array of inexpensive disks (RAID) setup.

system resource   Data, peripheral devices, or other system components used to create, delete, or manipulate documents and produce output.

System VM (virtual machine)   The component of the Windows operating system tasked to create virtual machines and manage DOS applications.

TAPI (Telephony API)   An interface used by applications to interface with various types of communications equipment. This currently includes both modems and fax devices.

task switching   The capability of an operating system to support more than one application or thread of execution at a time. The foreground application or task is the only one that executes. All other threads of execution are suspended in the background. Contrast this with multitasking, in which all threads—background and foreground—execute.

TCP/IP   See *Transmission Control Protocol/Internet Protocol*.

TDI (Transport Driver Interface)   Virtualizes access to the network protocol under Windows. This is the reason more than one virtual machine running on a system can access the network drives at the same time.

Telephony API   See *TAPI*.

Terminate and Stay Resident   See *TSR*.

thread   One executable unit within a Windows application. Running an application creates a main thread. One of the things the main thread does is display a window with a menu. The main thread can also create other, secondary threads. Background printing may appear as a thread, for example. Only 32-bit applications support threads.

thunk   The programming interface that translates 32-bit data and system calls to their 16-bit counterparts. The opposite translation takes place going from a 16-bit application to its 32-bit counterpart.

Transmission Control Protocol/Internet Protocol (TCP/IP)   A standard communication line protocol developed by the United States Department of Defense. The protocol defines how two devices talk to each other. Think of the protocol as a type of language used by the two devices.

Transport Driver Interface   See *TDI*.

traps   A programming term used to denote special code designed to detect and usually react to specific system conditions. For example, an error trap will detect a program error condition and try to fix it. In some cases, the error can't be fixed internally, at which time the trap code will either notify the user of the problem, make some type of error log entry, or request that the user or an administrator fix the problem externally.

TrueType   A vector font technology originally provided with Windows but used with other operating systems now as well. TrueType provides hinting and other features that give it a smoother appearance onscreen.

TSD (type-specific driver)   Part of the file subsystem, this layer deals with logical device types rather than specific devices. One TSD handles all the hard drives on your system, for example, and another TSD handles all the floppy disk drives. A third TSD would handle all network drives.

TSR (Terminate and Stay Resident)   An application (usually relatively small) that loads itself into memory and stays there after you execute it. This was a DOS tech-nology. The program usually returns you directly to the DOS prompt after loading. Pressing a hotkey combination activates the application, enabling you to use the application. In most cases, TSRs provide some type of utility, print spooling, or other short-term function.

type-specific driver   See *TSD*.

UAE (unrecoverable application error)   A processor or memory error that occurs when an application makes a request the system can't honor. The operating system normally doesn't detect an error of this type. The result is that the system freezes or becomes unstable to the point of being unusable. (See also *GPF*.)

UART (universal asynchronous receiver transmission)   The chip that allows a serial port to communicate with the outside world. Serial-type devices such as internal modems also rely on this chip for communications purposes. Newer versions of this chip include special features such as a buffer that stores incoming and outgoing characters until the CPU can process them.

UMB (upper memory block)   The area of memory between 640KB and the 1MB boundary in DOS. UMB is no longer of much interest in the 32-bit Windows 2000 world. Various memory managers enabled you to load applications and device drivers in this area under DOS.

UNC (Uniform Naming Convention)   A method of addressing remote resources. The typical syntax appears as this:

```
\\[server name]\[share name]
```

Microsoft operating systems and many applications support this type of reference for a connection to a shared resource. Other applications may still require that a specific drive letter be mapped to the server and share name.

uniform resource locator (URL)   An Internet addressing scheme that spells out the exact location of a Web site or other Internet resource. Most URLs take the following form:

```
protocol://host.domain/directory/file.name
```

- `protocol`. The TCP/IP protocol to use for retrieving the resource (such as HTTP or FTP)

- `host.domain`. The domain name of the host computer where the resource resides

- `directory`. The host directory that contains the resource

- `file.name`. The filename of the resource

Universal Serial Bus (USB)   A form of serial bus that allows multiple external devices to share a single port. This technique reduces the number of interrupts and port addresses required to service the needs of devices such as mice and modems.

unrecoverable application error   See *UAE*.

upper memory block   See *UMB*.

USB   See *Universal Serial Bus*.

USB Host   A communication coordination device, usually powered, designed to provide connections for USB devices. The host computer normally provides a hub with two connectors, which can be further extended by dedicated hubs or hubs that appear as part of other devices like monitors. The hub will also automatically detect the addition or loss of device connections and inform the host machine. The host machine will reconfigure itself to work without the device.

User A core Windows 2000 component (an API) that handles all user-related I/O tasks. On the input side, User manages incoming data from the keyboard, mouse, joystick, and any other input devices that are attached to your computer. For output, User sends data to windows, icons, menus, and other components of the Windows 2000 user interface. User also handles the sound driver, the system timer, and the communications ports. (See also *graphical device interface* and *kernel*.)

VBA (Visual Basic for Applications) A macro language from Microsoft. It has replaced the individual macro languages (such as WordBasic) built into Microsoft's major applications. VBA is, essentially, Visual Basic embedded into applications, giving you great freedom to program the behaviors of the applications as well as to communicate between applications.

VCPI (Virtual Control Program Interface) A method of accessing extended memory from a DOS application using a third-party XMM. (See also *DPMI*.)

VDD (Virtual Display Driver) Windows 3.*x* uses this module as its sole source of communications with the display adapter. Windows 2000 and Windows 95/98 provide it for compatibility purposes and for DOS applications. It translates application requests into graphics commands and draws the result in video memory.

VDM (virtual DOS machine) Essentially, a single copy of a DOS machine created in memory. This machine provides all the access features of the real thing, but it doesn't physically exist. Windows 2000 places each DOS application in its own VDM. The reason is simple: To provide the higher level of system reliability users demand, Microsoft had to make sure that each application had its own environment—an environment completely separate from that used by every other application. It's also important to remember that 16-bit Windows applications share one VDM. You need to remember that Windows 2000 always starts a VDM and then runs a copy of 16-bit Windows in it to service the needs of 16-bit Windows applications. This effectively adds two layers to every interaction: one for the VDM and another for the WIN32 subsystem. As with everything else, this additional layering is transparent to the programmer. You still use the same interfaces as before.

vector font A type of font that uses mathematical expressions rather than a one-for-one bitmap to define its characteristics and how it should be drawn onscreen or on paper. TrueType is a vector font. Because they're calculated mathematically, rather than stored as images, vector fonts can be scaled (made larger or smaller) very easily.

VESA (Video Electronics Standards Association) A standards group responsible for creating display adapter and monitor specifications. This group has also worked on other standards, such as the VL bus used in some PCs.

VFAT (virtual file allocation table)   An enhanced method of disk formatting based on the FAT system. It allows for additional functionality, such as long filenames.

Video Electronics Standards Association   See *VESA*.

virtual anything driver   See *VxD*.

Virtual Control Program Interface   See *VCPI*.

Virtual Display Driver   See *VDD*.

virtual DOS machine   See *VDM*.

virtual file allocation table   See *VFAT*.

Virtual Memory Manager   See *VMM*.

Virtual Private Network (VPN)   A special setup that Windows 2000 and Windows 98 SE provide for allowing someone on the road to use the server at work. This is where the virtual part comes in—the connection isn't permanent, you're just using it for a short time. The reason that this connection has to be private is that you don't want anyone else to have access to your company's network. What you do is call into your ISP using Dial-Up Networking. Now that you have access to the Internet, you can use Dial-Up Networking to make a second connection to the server using Point-to-Point Tunneling Protocol (PPTP). The setup is very secure because it actually uses two levels of data encryption, digital signing of packets, and encrypted passwords.

Visual Basic for Applications   See *VBA*.

VMM (Virtual Memory Manager)   The part of the Windows Memory Manager responsible for creating and maintaining the swap file on disk. The swap file contains data that can no longer fit in the machine's internal RAM memory and stores it in "virtual" memory on the hard drive. The VMM also takes care of the actual task of swapping data between disk and physical memory as applications request specific data.

volume-tracking driver   See *VTD*.

VPN   See *virtual private network*.

VRAM (dual-ported Video RAM)   A type of memory that allows simultaneous reads and writes. It provides a serial-read interface and a parallel-write interface. The advantage of VRAM is that it's very fast and doesn't require as much detection code on the part of an application or device driver.

VTD (volume-tracking driver)   This file subsystem component handles any removable devices attached to your system.

VxD (virtual anything driver)   A special form of DLL that provides low-level system support.

waveform audio   A process that re-creates an audio waveform by using digital samples of the waveform. This is the standard Windows sound format.

wide area network (WAN)   A network that consists of two or more LANs (or internetworks) that are spaced out over a relatively large geographical area, such as a state, a country, or the entire world. The networks in a WAN typically are connected via high-speed fiber-optic phone lines, microwave dishes, or satellite links.

Windows Management Instrumentation (WMI)   A special set of Windows features that reduce total cost of operation (TCO) by allowing the network administrator to remotely monitor, control, and configure workstations. This particular technology falls into the agent category and is very common on many network operating systems. An agent (special files executing on the client machine) allows the server to gain access to client machine resources and configuration information. Obviously, only machines that have the agent installed will be accessible to the network administrator.

Windows Sockets Application Programming Interface (WinSock)   A set of functions and support tools that enables developers to add TCP/IP communication support to Windows applications.

WINMSD   Diagnostic program.

WinSock   See *Windows Sockets Application Programming Interface*.

wizard   A series of dialog boxes that step you through a task. The Windows 2000 Add Printer Wizard, for example, makes it easier to install a new printer. Microsoft Word has a Resume Wizard that helps you create a professional-looking resume. A wizard asks you questions and then, based on your answers, it can accomplish a job that you, working alone, might find complex or burdensome.

WMI   See *Windows Management Instrumentation*.

WYSIWYG   "What You See Is What You Get"

Index

D

E

V